THE BLUE GUIDES

*in preparation

St. Theresa in Ecstasy by Gian Lorenzo Bernini in
Santa Maria della Vittoria

BLUE GUIDE

ROME

AND ENVIRONS

Alta Macadam

Maps and plans by John Flower

A & C Black
London

W W Norton
New York

Fourth edition 1989

Published by A & C Black (Publishers) Limited
35 Bedford Row, London, WC1R 4JH

© A & C Black (Publishers) Limited 1989

Published in the United States of America by
W W Norton & Company, Inc.
500 Fifth Avenue, New York, NY 10110

Published simultaneously in Canada by
Penguin Books Canada Limited,
2801 John Street, Markham, Ontario L3R 1B4

ISBN   0–7136–3149–X

A CIP catalogue record for this book
is available from the British Library.

ISBN   0–393–30487–6   USA

Alta Macadam learnt the craft of writing Blue Guides when she
became assistant in 1970 to Stuart Rossiter, distinguished editor of
many Guides in the series. She has lived in Florence since 1973 and,
as author of the Blue Guides to *Northern Italy*, *Rome*, *Venice*, *Sicily*,
and *Florence*, she travels extensively in Italy every year in order to
revise new editions of the books. Combined with work on writing the
guides she also spent four years up-dating the well-known Italian
photo library of Alinari, and now works part time for Harvard
University at the Villa I Tatti in Florence.

Typeset by CRB Typesetting Services, Ely, Cambs
Printed and bound in Great Britain by
BPCC Hazell Books Ltd
Member of BPCC Ltd
Aylesbury, Bucks, England

PREFACE

Rome, like all the other big cities of Italy in the last few years, has had to begin to come to terms with the problems of traffic congestion. Much of the centre of Rome is now closed to cars for most of the day, although many vehicles have special permits to enter at any time. There is no doubt that this has greatly improved conditions and the visitor will find the city much more peaceful and also easier to see by public transport. A small electric bus is now in operation in the very centre of the city where other buses are no longer allowed. But there is still a lot to be done to cut down the volume of traffic in Rome, since the suburbs have now become more congested than ever and the air pollution has reached unacceptable levels. This also continues to cause damage to the great monuments of the city.

Since the last edition, the beautiful Circus of Maxentius on the Appian Way has been opened regularly to the public. It is now possible to follow the walkway along the Aurelian Walls from Porta San Sebastiano as far as Via Cristoforo Colombo. The Museo di Palazzo Venezia, the Galleria dell'Accademia di San Luca, and part of the Galleria Nazionale d'Arte Moderna have all been reopened. Excavations of the greatest interest continue in the Forum and on the Palatine, as well as in the area of the 'Cripta Balbi' and in the courtyard of the Palazzo della Cancelleria. Magnificent restoration work has been carried out on Trajan's Column, the Column of Marcus Aurelius, and the Arch of Constantine, the scaffolding on all of which was coming down during the author's visit to the city in November 1988. The church of Santa Maria della Pace is now open regularly after restoration. The cleaning of the Sistine ceiling is progressing while the chapel remains open to visitors who can immediately see the spectacular results. In 1988 the Comune of Rome declared they were interested in putting into operation the long discussed projects to re-excavate the Imperial Fora and to institute the archaeological park to protect the Appian Way.

On the negative side the Museo Nazionale Romano is still almsot totally closed (although work on the restoration of the nearby Palazzo Massimo, where the works are to be rehoused is in progress). Palazzo Braschi, the Museo Barracco, the top floor of the Galleria Borghese, the Tabularium, the Braccio Nuovo of the Palazzo dei Conservatori, the House of Cardinal Bessarion, the Antiquarium Comunale, all the Imperial Fora, the Curia in the Roman Forum, Santo Stefano Rotondo, the upper tiers of the Colosseum, and the Loggia of Raphael in the Vatican, were all closed in 1988. The Domus Aurea is no longer open regularly to the public in order to protect the decorations.

Since the last edition nearly every museum and monument in the city has changed its opening times. It is therefore inevitable that the hours of admission given in the Guide will not be entirely accurate by the time the book goes to press: visitors must allow for these variations when planning their day. However, more and more museums and monuments have longer opening hours, and, best of all, often remain open on Monday, which for years has been the standard closing day for nearly every State-owned museum. The opening times of many churches have been added to the text in this edition to facilitate planning a visit.

Any suggestions for the improvement of the Guide are always welcome.

A NOTE ON BLUE GUIDES

The Blue Guide series began in 1918 when Muirhead Guide-Books Limited published 'Blue Guide London and its Environs'. Finlay and James Muirhead already had extensive experience of guide-book publishing: before the First World War they had been the editors of the English editions of the German Baedekers, and by 1915 they had acquired the copyright of most of the famous 'Red' Handbooks from John Murray.

An agreement made with the French publishing house Hachette et Cie in 1917 led to the translation of Muirhead's London Guide, which became the first 'Guide Bleu'—Hachette had previously published the blue-covered 'Guides Joanne'. Subsequently, Hachette's 'Guide Bleu Paris et ses Environs' was adapted and published in London by Muirhead. The collaboration between the two publishing houses continued until 1933.

In 1931 Ernest Benn Limited took over the Blue Guides, appointing Russell Muirhead, Finlay Muirhead's son, editor in 1934. The Muirheads' connection with Blue Guides ended in 1963 when Stuart Rossiter, who had been working on the Guides since 1954, became house editor, revising and compiling several of the books himself.

The Blue Guides are now published by A & C Black, who acquired Ernest Benn in 1984, so continuing the tradition of guide-book publishing which began in 1826 with 'Black's Economical Tourist of Scotland'. The Blue Guide series continues to grow: there are now more than 35 titles in print with revised editions appearing regularly and many new Blue Guides in preparation.

'Blue Guides' is a registered trade mark.

CONTENTS

8 CONTENTS

MAPS AND PLANS

EXPLANATIONS

Type Smaller type is used for historical and preliminary paragraphs and (generally speaking) for descriptions of greater detail or minor importance.

Asterisks indicate points of special interest or excellence.

Distances in the environs of Rome are given cumulatively from the starting-point of the route or sub-route in kilometres. Heights are given in metres.

Populations are given in round figures according to the latest official figures (estimates based on the census of 1971).

Abbreviations. In addition to generally accepted and self-explanatory abbreviations, the following occur in the guide:

Abp	archbishop
Adm	admission
Bp	bishop
Card.	Cardinal
C	century
c	circa
C.I.T.	Compagnia Italiana Turismo
d	died
E.N.I.T.	Ente Nazionale Italiano per il Turismo
E.P.T.	Ente Provinciale per il Turismo
exc.	except
fest.	*festa*, or festival (i.e. holiday)
incl.	including
fl.	floruit (flourished)
hr	hour
km	kilometre(s)
m	metre(s)
p	page
Pal.	Palazzo
Pl.	atlas plan
R.	room(s)
Rte	route
SS.	Saints (in English); Santissimo, -a (in Italian)
T.C.I.	Touring Club Italiano

For abbreviations of Italian Christian names, see p 408; for glossary see p 32.

References in the text (Pl. 1; 1) are to the 15-page Atlas at the back of the book, the first figure referring to the page, the second to the square. Ground plan references are given as a bracketed single figure or letter.

HISTORICAL SKETCH OF ROME

Rome was founded—probably at least a century earlier than the traditional date of 753 BC—at the spot where the territories of the Latins, the Sabines, and the Etruscans met, and where the Isola Tiberina provided an easy crossing-place of the Tiber. The agricultural and pastoral community of the Palatine united with the inhabitants of the surrounding hills. In a central position in the Italian peninsula, and fairly close to the sea, Rome rapidly grew in importance. Under its seven more or less legendary kings (Romulus, Numa Pompilius, Tullus Hostilius, Ancus Marcius, Tarquinius Priscus, Servius Tullius, and Tarquinius Superbus) it waged war, almost always successfully, with the Latins and Etruscans.

Rome became a republic c 510 BC, and despite a long internal dispute between the Plebs and Patricians, it was strong enough to conquer the Etruscans of Veio and Tarquinii, the Latins, and the Volscians. The Etruscans were defeated at the famous Battle of Cuma in 474 BC. Although almost totally destroyed by the Gauls in 390 BC, Rome was able to defeat the Samnites in three campaigns. After a splendid victory over Pyrrhus (275 BC), Rome declared war on Magna Graecia and Sicily and challenged the naval power of Carthage (264 BC). Hannibal transferred the fight to Italy in the Second Punic War, and inflicted severe defeats on the Romans at the Ticinus, the Trebia, Lake Trasimene, and Cannae. However the Republic was able to conquer Spain, and return to battle in Africa where the famous victory of Zama took place in 202 BC. Its most dangerous rival was finally defeated in the Third Punic War (146 BC).

The defeat of Carthage seems to have stimulated the ambition of the Romans, who subsequently took over control not only of all Italy but also of Gallia Cisalpina, Illyria, Greece, and Macedonia, and finally proceeded to the conquest of the known world. The Teutons and Cimbri were defeated in 102–101 BC; the insurrection of the Italic peoples (the Social War) was put down in 89 BC; Asia Minor, Tauris, Syria, and Palestine were won over, and Julius Caesar conquered Gallia Transalpina and Britain. The civil war between Marius and Sulla and between Caesar and Pompey, and the brief coalitions of the two triumvirates (Pompey, Caesar and Crassus; Antony, Lepidus, and Octavian) resulted in the founding c 27 BC, of the Empire under Octavian (afterwards Augustus), marking the triumph of the democratic party over the old oligarchy, the centre of which was in the Senate. In spite of the incapacity and tyranny of many of the emperors, the dominion of Rome continued to extend and reached its maximum expansion under Trajan (98–117). The language and the laws of Rome were accepted as standards by the world and the solidity and strength of the Roman state were still unbroken in the 3C AD, although some of the farthest provinces had been lost.

The decline of Rome as capital of the world began under Diocletian (284), who divided the empire into a Western Empire and an Eastern Empire, and it was confirmed when Constantine transferred the seat of government to Byzantium (AD 330). The imperial city was sacked by Alaric the Goth in 410, by Genseric the Vandal in 455, and by Ricimer the Sueve in 472. Finally, in 476, Odoacer compelled Romulus Augustulus to abdicate and so put an end to the Western Empire.

The Roman Church was not recognized until the reign of Constantine

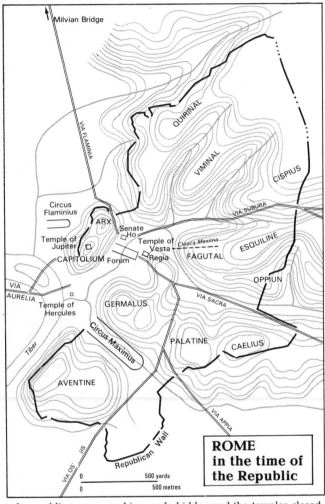

Milvian Bridge

VIA FLAMINIA

QUIRINAL

VIMINAL

CISPIUS

Circus
Flaminius

ARX

VIA SUBURA

Senate
Ho

Temple of
Jupiter

Temple of
Vesta

Cloaca Maxima

ESQUILINE

CAPITOLIUM   Forum

Regia

FAGUTAL

VIA
AURELIA

OPPIUN

VIA SACRA

Temple of
Hercules

GERMALUS

Circus Maximus

PALATINE

CAELIUS

Tiber

AVENTINE

VIA APPIA

VIA OS   IS

Republican Wall

**ROME
in the time of
the Republic**

| 0 | 500 yards |
| 0 | 500 metres |

when public pagan worship was forbidden and the temples closed.
The supremacy of the bishop of Rome was gradually recognized by a
Christianized world. Rome, the possession of which was disputed in
the 6C by Goths and Byzantines, passed at the beginning of the 7C
under the temporal protection of the Popes, a protection which was
transformed into sovereignty by the force of circumstances and as a
consequence of papal endowments. Pope Stephen III, threatened by
the Lombards, appealed to Pepin the Frank, who defeated the enemy
and bestowed upon the Pope a portion of Lombardy (AD 754). This
marked the beginning of the temporal power of the popes over the
States of the Church. On Christmas Day, 800, Charlemagne, son of
Pepin, was crowned by Leo III in St Peter's as Augustus and Emperor,

and so began the 'Holy Roman Empire' which survived until the abdication of Francis II of Austria in 1806.

The upheaval following the death of Charlemagne damaged the papacy. Gregory VII, however, reasserted the papal authority although he was unable to prevent Robert Guiscard, the Norman, from devastating the city in 1084. Paschal II and Calixtus II did much to restore the city. A brief Republican period which followed was terminated by Frederick Barbarossa, and Alexander III reassumed power. From the 11C to the 13C the city became a great administrative centre. During the splendid pontificate of Innocent III (d 1216) Rome became the capital of the Christian world.

Nearly a century later, in 1309, and a few years after the jubilee

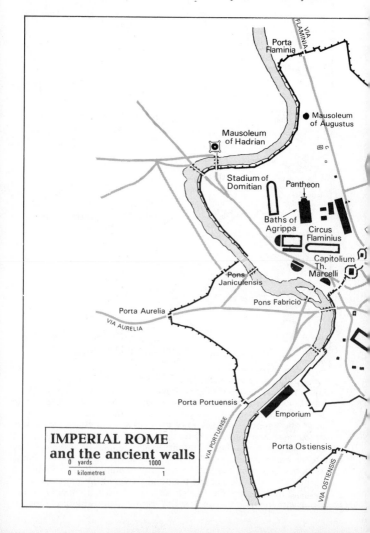

**IMPERIAL ROME
and the ancient walls**

0 yards 1000
0 kilometres 1

proclaimed by Boniface VIII, Pope Clement V fled from Rome to
Avignon, where he remained under the protection of France. Meanwhile Rome, and the surrounding countryside, was devastated by the
wars between the rival factions of the Colonna, Caetani, and Orsini
aristocratic families. In 1347 the tribune Cola di Rienzo failed in his
patriotic but utopian attempt to revive the ancient power and glory of
the Imperial City. In 1378 Gregory XI was persuaded by St Catherine
of Siena to retransfer the papal seat from Avignon to Rome, but the
western schism still engaged the attention of the popes, and it was
not until 1420 that Martin V began to restore the city, which had
suffered both physically and socially during the so called 'Babylonish
Captivity'.

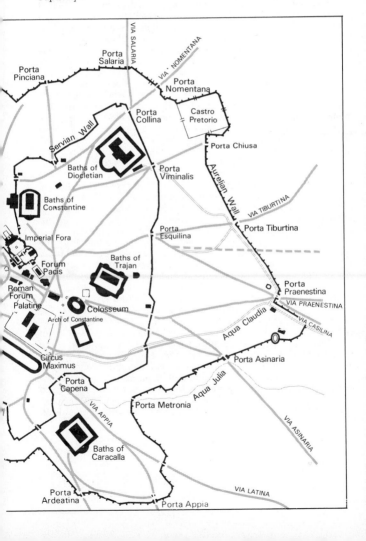

Under Julius II and Leo X Rome recovered brilliantly and became the centre of the Italian Renaissance in art; but in 1527, under Clement VII, the ally of Francis I against Charles V, it was captured and sacked by German mercenary troops. Many later popes restored and embellished the city. In February 1798, the French entered Rome and proclaimed a republic; Pius VI was taken as a prisoner to France, where he died in 1799. In 1809 Napoleon annexed the States of the Church, already diminished, to the French Empire; in 1810 the French Senate proclaimed Rome to be the second capital; and in 1811 Napoleon conferred the title of King of Rome on his new-born son. On the fall of Napoleon, Pius VII returned to Rome, to which were restored, also, almost all the works of art that had been removed by the emperor. The city took an active part in the agitated period of the 'Risorgimento', or political renaissance of Italy. Pius IX issued a political amnesty in 1846, and in 1848 granted a 'Statuto' or constitution. He supported the war against Austria and sent his troops to take part in it, but he soon withdrew from the enterprise, since he was afraid of being threatened by the liberals in his own country. He retired to Gaeta, and a republic was proclaimed at Rome, under the triumvirate of Mazzini, Saffi, and Armellini, who entrusted the defence of the city to Garibaldi. The army despatched by France to help the pope entered Rome on 3 July 1849, and Pius IX returned in the following April. In 1859 the Romagna joined Piedmont; in 1860, after the defeat of the papal forces at Castelfidardo, Cialdini occupied the Marches and Umbria; and on 20 September 1870, the Italian army, under Raffaello Cadorna, entered Rome by a breach in the walls beside the Porta Pia. Shortly afterwards Rome was proclaimed the capital of united Italy.

After the First World War (which had little direct effect on Rome), the movement known as *Fascismo*, organized by Benito Mussolini, rapidly developed. 28 October 1922, saw the 'March on Rome' of Mussolini and his myrmidons, after which the King, Victor Emmanuel III, invited Mussolini to form a government. Fascist rule prevailed until its overthrow on 25 July 1943, in the middle of the Second World War. In the period between the wars—on 11 February 1929—the Lateran Treaty (the 'Concordat') was signed. By its provisions the Vatican City became an independent sovereign state. Italy entered the Second World War on the Axis side on 10 June 1940. In 1943 the Allies landed in Sicily, and the Allied invasion of the mainland began. After the landings at Anzio and Nettuno in 1944 the American 5th Army entered the city of Rome by the Porta Maggiore and the Porta San Giovanni. On 28 April 1945 Mussolini was killed after his capture by Italian partisans while attempting to escape into Switzerland. On 9 May 1946, Victor Emmanuel III abdicated. Less than a month later a general election, with a referendum on the form of government, was held. The referendum approved the establishment of a republic. The royal family left the country on 13 June and on 28 June a provisional President was elected. On 22 December 1947, the Constituent Assembly passed the new republican constitution.

Growth of Rome

According to legend, supported by archaeological evidence, the first settlements were on the Palatine, where excavations have revealed the remains of a hut village of the Early Iron Age. The Sabines settled on the Quirinal, while the Romans built a citadel on the Capitoline Hill. In the valley between the Palatine, the Capitoline, and the Esquiline—later the site of the Roman Forum—was the necropolis of the original settlers. Here have been discovered a cemetery of the Early Iron Age (10C–8C BC) and the Lapis Niger, possibly the burial-place of Romulus. King Ancus Marcius is said to have built the Tulianum, or Mamertine Prison, and to have founded Ostia, the port of Rome. Tarquinius Priscus is credited with the building of the Temple of Jupiter Capitolinus and Servius Tullius with the building of the Servian Wall. Livy ascribes to Tarquinius Superbus, the last of the kings of Rome, the construction of the Cloaca Maxima, which still functions after 25 centuries.

The city grew in size and importance under the Republic. After the conquest of Greece in 146 BC Roman architects took inspiration from the developed forms of Greek art, although long before this they had produced some remarkable monuments. The Appian Way, dating from 312 BC, was lined with tombs, among them the Tomb of the Scipios and the Tomb of Cecilia Metella. Some of the most ancient buildings in the Roman Forum were rebuilt or restored centuries later; among them are the Temple of Saturn, founded in 497 BC and rebuilt in the 1C BC and again in the 4C AD; the Temple of Castor (or of the Dioscuri), built in 484 BC and several times rebuilt; and the Temple of Concord, built in 366 BC and restored in the 2C BC. On the ancient walls of the first citadel was erected the Tabularium in 78 BC. The elegant Temple of Fortuna Virilis dates from the 3C BC. On the left bank of the Tiber were built the great warehouses of the Emporia (193 BC). Julius Caesar added the Basilica Julia to the Roman Forum, and he built the forum named after himself, the first of the imperial fora.

Under the Empire the city expanded rapidly and many beautiful monuments were built. To Augustus are ascribed the Porticus of Octavia, the Temple of Julius Caesar, the Theatre of Marcellus, the Forum of Augustus, with its Temple of Mars Ultor, the emperor's house on the Palatine, his own Mausoleum, and the Ara Pacis Augustae. Augustus restored many buildings and he is said to have boasted that he found the city brick and left it marble. Rome, which he divided into 14 *Regiones*, had in his reign virtually attained the size that it preserved for centuries. M. Vipsanius Agrippa built a temple of Neptune in celebration of naval victories, and the first Baths in Rome (19 BC).

Tiberius restored the Temple of Castor (Dioscuri) and built the Temple of Augustus. Caligula is said to have united his palace on the Palatine with the Temple of Jupiter on the Capitol by means of a bridge, of which no traces survive. He also began in AD 38 the aqueduct which Claudius finished in 52. After the fire of AD 64, Nero began to rebuild the city on a regular plan and he erected his huge Domus Aurea, which he decorated with a colossal statue of himself as the Sun. Vespasian rebuilt the Temple of Claudius. He began in 72, and his son Titus completed in 80, the famous Colosseum. Titus built his Baths on the Oppian Hill and, with his brother Domitian, the Temple of Vespasian in the Forum. The Senate and Roman people commemorated his and Vespasian's victories in Judaea by erecting the Arch of Titus. Domitian built his elaborate palace on the Palatine, rebuilt the Curia in the Roman Forum and began the Forum completed by Nerva in 97. Under Trajan the architect Apollodorus designed the Forum of Trajan, with its famous column and the large Basilica Ulpia.

Hadrian ordered the execution of several important projects. These included the Pantheon, the masterpiece of Roman architecture, the Temple of Venus and Rome, overlooking the Colosseum and of vast dimensions, his Mausoleum, later the Castel Sant'Angelo, and the neighbouring Pons Aelius (Ponte Sant'Angelo). Perhaps his most remarkable undertaking was the planning of his famous Villa near Tibur (Tivoli). Under Antoninus Pius the Senate decreed the erection of the Temple of Faustina, one of the most beautiful in the Roman Forum, dedicated also to him after his death. The victories of Marcus Aurelius were commemorated by his famous column (in Piazza Colonna).

The Arch of Septimius Severus (AD 203), despite its rich ornamentation, is perhaps inferior to earlier monuments. In 217 Caracalla erected his famous Baths, which eclipsed in size and magnificence all previous construction of this type. From the 3rd century date also the Arch of Janus, the Amphitheatrum Castrense, the Septizonium of Septimius Severus (demolished by Sixtus V) the Arch of Gallienus, and the so-called Temple of Minerva Medica. Aurelian (AD 270–275) built a new city wall which enclosed all the seven hills and part of the Janiculum across the Tiber. It was several times restored; most of it survives as the greatest monument of the late Empire.

At the beginning of the 4C the Temple of Saturn (see above) was restored again. In 302 Diocletian began the erection of his Baths, the largest in Rome, which were completed by Constantine in 306. Maxentius built a temple and a circus in honour of his son Romulus Maxentius, and began the huge basilica in the Forum which Constantine completed. The Arch of Constantine, built close to the Colosseum in 315, is the last notable specimen of Roman architecture, but its statues and reliefs come from earlier works, and it is generally taken to mark the beginning of the decadence of Roman architecture. The contemporary mausoleum of Constantine's daughter, Constantia, later became the church of S. Costanza. The Portico of the Dii Consentes, erected in 367, is probably the last pagan monument of Rome.

Constantine granted liberty of worship to Christians in 313. A primitive aedicula had been built between AD 160 and 180 over the tomb of St Peter and the first basilica of St Peter was consecrated in November 326. Other early Christian places of worship were the church of Santa Pudenziana, the chapel of Santa Petronilla, and the churches of San Crisogono, Santi Giovanni e Paolo, and Sant' Anastasia. To Constantine is attributed the foundation of San Giovanni in Laterano and its Baptistery, San Pietro, Santa Croce in Gerusalemme, Sant' Agnese fuori le Mura, San Sebastiano, and San Lorenzo fuori le Mura. To the 4C are assigned San Paolo fuori le Mura, Santa Maria in Trastevere, Sant' Alessio, and Santa Prisca on the Aventine. Public pagan worship was forbidden in the city in 346 and ten years later temples were closed. Christianity became the State religion under Theodosius (d 395). The population of the city, in the 4C estimated at about 500,000, was gradually to diminish in succeeding centuries until the city began to expand again in the 11C.

The churches of the 5C include Santa Maria Maggiore, Santa Sabina, Santo Stefano Rotondo, San Vitale, and San Lorenzo in

Lucina. Santi Cosma e Damiano dates from the 6C. To the 7C belongs the oratory of San Venanzio, the apse-mosaics in which are the last expression of Roman art before it succumbed to Byzantine influence. Santa Maria Antiqua and the reconstructed church of Santi Nereo ed Achilleo, dating from the 8C; and the rebuilt church of Santa Maria in Domnica, the chapel of St Zeno, and the church of Santa Cecilia in Trastevere, dating from the 9C, are all remarkable for their mosaics. The walls of the Leonine City also date from the 9C.

The papacy of Gregory the Great marked the foundation of medieval Rome, although very little is known about the city in this period since little archaeological evidence has survived. The characteristic portal of San Cosimato is of the 10C; so also are the puteal in the cloisters of St John Lateran and probably the Casa di Crescenzio. Santa Maria in Cappella was built in the 11C. The 12C saw, after the devastation of Robert Guiscard, the restoration of San Clemente, Santi Quattro Coronati, Santi Giovanni e Paolo, San Lorenzo in Lucina, Santa Maria in Cosmedin, Santa Maria in Trastevere, and Santa Maria Nova. In the same century were built the cloisters of San Cosimato, the campanile of Santa Cecilia in Trastevere, and the cloister of San Lorenzo fuori le Mura.

In the early 13C San Saba and San Giorgio in Velabro were rebuilt, and the Torre dei Conti and Torre delle Milizie were erected, together with a large number of similar towers, afterwards pulled down; the senator Brancaleone is said to have demolished 140 of them in 1257. From this century date also the present basilica of San Lorenzo fuori le Mura, the charming cloisters of St John Lateran and San Paolo fuori le Mura, the rebuilding of Santi Vincenzo ed Anastasio, the reconstruction of Santa Maria in Aracoeli in the Franciscan Romanesque-Gothic style, the portal of Sant'Antonio, and the Cosmatesque chapel of the Sancta Sanctorum. Santa Maria sopra Minerva, built near the close of the century, is the only church in Rome with a Gothic interior.

There was very little building activity in the 14C with the popes in Avignon and the wars between the rival noble families in the city. To the Renaissance, which appeared late in Rome, belong Palazzo Capranica and Palazzo di Venezia, which still looks like a fortress despite its graceful 15C windows and portals. To the last part of the century belong also the House of Manlius, the Palazzi del Governo Vecchio, dei Penitenzieri, and Santacroce; the church of Sant'Agostino; the rebuilt Ponte Sisto; the hospital of Santo Spirito with its beautiful tower; the Sistine Chapel in the Vatican; the rebuilding of San Cosimato, Santa Maria del Popolo, and Santa Maria in Via Lata; and the façade of Santa Maria sopra Minerva. Palazzo della Cancelleria is the masterpiece of the 15C in Rome. In the latter half of the century Hadrian's Mausoleum began to be transformed into a fortress and Alexander VI commissioned the decoration of the Borgia Rooms in the Vatican.

Pope Julius II (1503–13), who laid the first stone of the new St Peter's and built Via Giulia, enlarged the Vatican Palace and employed Bramante, Michelangelo, and Raphael, the three greatest artists of the age, to carry out his plans. The golden age of Italian art lasted into the papacy of Leo X (1513–21). Among the monuments of the two reigns are the little temple of San Pietro in Montorio, Palazzo Cenci, Santa Maria dell'Anima, the cloister of Santa Maria della Pace, Palazzo Torlonia, Santa Maria di Loreto, San Giovanni dei Fiorentini (much altered), Villa Farnesina, Palazzo Baldassini, and Villa Madama.

Also from the 16C date Palazzo Massimo alle Colonne, Palazzo Farnese, perhaps the most dignified and impressive in Rome, the Porta Santo Spirito, the rearrangement of Piazza del Campidoglio by Michelangelo, Palazzo Spada, Villa Medici, Villa di Papa Giulio, the Casina of Pius IV, Michelangelo's transformation of the great hall of Diocletian's Baths into the church of Santa Maria degli Angeli and his building of the adjoining cloisters, Palazzo Regis, Santa Caterina dei Funari, the Gesù, Santa Maria in Vallicella, Palazzo del Collegio Romano, Palazzo del Quirinale (not completed until the reign of Clement XII), and many other public and private buildings.

Pope Sixtus V (1585–90) did more than any of his predecessors to improve and adorn the city. He not only built new long and straight streets (the Strada Felice was over 3km long), but he completed the dome of St Peter's, and enlarged the Vatican and Lateran palaces. He brought the water of the Acqua Felice to the centre of Rome. Palazzo Borghese and the church of Sant'Andrea della Valle date from the end of the 16C. Many obelisks were set up to close vistas at the end of straight streets or as focal points in piazze, so that they have become a feature of the city (13 obelisks exist in Rome, while only 5 survive in Egypt itself).

It is to the 17C that Rome owes its Baroque aspect of today. Paul V (1605–21) completed St Peter's (consecrated by Urban VIII in 1626), and erected the great fountain on the Janiculum for the Acqua Paola, which he had brought to Rome. Urban VIII (1623–44) was the patron of Bernini, one of whose most remarkable works was the colonnade in Piazza San Pietro. To this period belong also Palazzo Mattei, Palazzo Barberini, Sant'Ignazio, Villa Doria Pamphilj, Palazzo Pamphilj, now Palazzo Doria, the twin churches in Piazza del Popolo, Palazzo Altieri, Palazzo di Montecitorio, and the delightful fountains of Bernini, the most elaborate of which is in Piazza Navona. In the latter half of the 17C were built the façade of Santa Maria della Pace, and the church of Santa Maria in Campitelli. The chief exponent of the Baroque school was Borromini, who built the church and dome of Palazzo della Sapienza, the oratory of the Filippini, and the campanile and apse of Sant'Andrea delle Fratte. Palazzo Doria is a striking late Baroque building.

The flamboyant staircase and façade of the Trinità dei Monti date from the 18C, as do the façades of San Giovanni dei Fiorentini and San Giovanni in Laterano. To the 18C belong also the Fontana di Trevi, Villa Torlonia (ex-Albani), Palazzo Corsini, Palazzo della Consulta, the façade of Santa Maria Maggiore, and Palazzo Braschi. The present appearance of Piazza del Popolo dates from the pontificate of Pius VII (1800–23). Leo XII (1823–29) began the rebuilding of San Paolo fuori le Mura, and Pius IX erected the Column of the Immaculate Conception.

The obtrusive Victor Emmanuel monument (1911) prepared the way for the cold 'Imperial' style of the Mussolini era. The climax of replanning was reached in the thirties of this century. The Capitol was flanked by broad thoroughfares, both opened in 1933—Via dei Fori Imperiali on one side and Via del Teatro di Marcello on the other. Beyond the Tiber, the old district of the Borgo was transformed by the building of Via della Conciliazione (1937), which also altered the dramatic effect of Bernini's Piazza in front of St Peter's. Of the other developments one of the most significant was the construction of the district known as E.U.R., typical of the grandiose conception of Fascist Rome. Instead of five bridges spanning the Tiber there are now twenty-one, among the newest being the Ponte Flaminio (1951).

The vast complex of buildings of the University of Rome known as the Città Universitaria was completed in 1935. For the Olympic Games of 1960 the Foro Italico of 1931 was enlarged and modernized, and the Stadio Flaminio and the impressive Palazzo dello Sport were built. The main railway station, the Stazione di Termini, was opened in December 1950.

The city of Rome was hardly damaged in the Second World War, although the surrounding country suffered much devastation. The church of San Lorenzo fuori le Mura, however, was partly wrecked by bombing in 1943.

The Walls of Rome

Rome has from time immemorial been a walled city. The earliest settlements on the Palatine, united, according to tradition by Romulus, to form the city in 753 BC, were surrounded with a wall of tufa blocks. The area enclosed was more or less rectangular and became known as *Roma Quadrata*. Fragments of this wall, which had three gates, still exist. Little by little the inhabitants of Roma Quadrata obtained the mastery of the neighbouring hills and formed the city of the *Septimontium* by the union of the three summits of the Palatine (Palatium, Germalus, and Velia) with the four of the Esquiline (Oppius, Cispius, Fagutalis, and Subura).

After further acquisitions there arose the *City of the Four Regions*. The regions were the Palatine, the Subura (incl. the Celian), the Esquiline, and the Collina (incl. the Quirinal). This area was eventually surrounded by a formidable line of fortifications c 11km long, known as the **Servian Wall**. Its traditional creator was Servius Tullius, sixth king of Rome; it is now thought that the wall dates from about 378 BC. There were 12 gates, the sites of some of which are conjectural. The wall ran S from the Porta Collina (N of the Baths of Diocletian) past the Porta Viminale and the Porta Esquilina (W of the Stazione Termini) to the Porta Celimontana, near the present Porta San Giovanni. At this point the wall curved to the W round the base of the Celian to the Porta Capena, below the Palatine, the starting-point of the Appian Way. From there it took an irregular course round the Aventine (several gates) to the Tiber, which it bordered as far as the Pons Aemilius (Ponte Rotto). It then ran N and NE past the W side of the Capitol, and the W and N sides of the Quirinal to the Porta Salutare. From here, after a slight detour, it bore E to the Porta Collina.

After 87 BC, during a period of civil strife between Marius and Sulla, a part of Trastévere was fortified. A new wall ran from the Pons Aemilius to the Porta Aurelia (Porta San Pancrazio), on the Janiculum, and another back to the Tiber, opposite the Aventine.

To Aurelian (emperor 270–275) and Probus (emperor, 276–82) is due the building of the **Aurelian Wall**, most of which survives to this day. Although Aurelian had defeated the invading Alemanni in two decisive battles, he erected his wall immediately afterwards. The enceinte took in all the seven hills, the Campus Martius, and the previously fortified area of Trastevere. It was about 18km round and had 18 main gates and 381 towers. From the Porta Flaminia (now Porta del Popolo) it ran irregularly along the Pincio to the Porta Salaria. From there it turned SE, took in the Castro Pretorio and continued SE to the Porta Tiburtina (Porta San Lorenzo) and the Porta Prenestina (Porta Maggiore). Here describing an acute angle, it bent back past the Porta Asinaria (Porta San Giovanni; near the Porta

Caelimontana; see above) to the Porta Metronia. It next ran S past the Porta Latina to the Porta Appia (Porta San Sebastiano), thus enclosing part of the Appian Way within the city boundaries. From this point the wall turned W to the Tiber. It now followed the left bank of the river. By the Pons Sublicius (the present Ponte Aventino) it crossed the river. Passing the Porta Portuense (Porta Portese) it ran NW to the Porta Aurelia (see above). Returning NE to the Porta Settimiana, it recrossed the Tiber, and followed the left bank of that river, skirting the Campus Martius, until it turned E to reach the Porta Flaminia. Aurelian made a bridgehead of the Castel Sant'Angelo in his fortifications.

The walls were raised to almost twice their height by Maxentius (306–12), and then restored by Honorius and Arcadius in 403 AD. They continued to be the defence of Rome until 1870 when the army of the Kingdom of Italy breached them with modern artillery, NW of the Porta Pia.

The walls are mostly well preserved and many of the gates are still in use under their modern names. Although the city has spread far beyond Aurelian's wall, most of its famous monuments are within its confines. One important exception is the basilica of San Paolo fuori le Mura; others are San Lorenzo and Sant'Agnese fuori le Mura.

LIST OF ROMAN EMPERORS

27 BC–AD 14	Augustus
14–37	Tiberius
37–41	Caligula
41–54	Claudius
54–68	Nero
68–69	Galba
69	Otho
69	Vitellius
Flavians	
69–79	Vespasian
79–81	Titus
81–96	Domitian
96–98	Nerva
98–117	Trajan
Antonines	
117–38	Hadrian
138–61	Antoninus Pius
161–80	Marcus Aurelius
161–69	Lucius Verus
180–92	Commodus
193	Pertinax
193	Didius Julianus
Severians	
193–211	Septimius Severus
211–17	Caracalla
211–12	Geta
217–18	Macrinus
218–22	Heliogabalus
222–35	Alexander Severus
235–38	Maximinus
238	Gordian I
	Gordian II
238	Pupienus
	Balbinus
238–44	Gordian III
244–49	Philip I
247–49	Philip II
249–51	Decius
251–53	Trebonianus Gallus
253	Aemilian
253–60	Valerian

253–68	Gallienus
268–70	Claudius II
270	Quintillus
270–75	Aurelian
275–76	Tacitus
276	Florian
276–82	Probus
282–83	Carus
282–85	Carinus
283–84	Numerian
285–305	Diocletian
286–305	Maximian
305–06	Constantius Chlorus
305–10	Galerius
308–24	Licinius
306–07	Flavius Severus
306–12	Maxentius
308–14	Maximinus
306–37	Constantine the Great
337–40	Constantine II
337–50	Constans
337–61	Constantinus II
350–53	Magnentius
361–63	Julian
363–64	Jovian
364–75	Valentinian I
364–78	Valens
367–83	Gratian
375–92	Valentinian II
378–95	Theodosius I
WESTERN EMPIRE	
395–423	Honorius
425–55	Valentinian III
455	Petronius Maximus
455–56	Avitus
457–61	Majorian
461–65	Libius Severus
467–72	Anthemius
472	Olybrius
473	Glycerius
474–75	Julius Nepos
475–76	Romulus Augustulus

CHRONOLOGICAL LIST OF POPES

Various points in early papal history must be regarded as still uncertain: thus the evidence for Dioscuros as legitimate pope is perhaps stronger than the evidence for Boniface II (No. 55); Leo VIII (No. 132) is an antipope if the deposition of John XII (No. 131) was illegal, and if Leo VIII was a legitimate pope, Benedict V (No. 133) is an antipope; and if the triple deposition of Benedict IX (No. 146) was illegal, Sylvester III, Gregory VI, and Clement II (Nos. 147, 149, 150) must rank as antipopes. Among the popes named John there was never a John XX. The title 'pope' was first assumed by John VIII (d. 882); the triple tiara first appears on the sepulchral effigy of Benedict XII (d. 1342). Adrian IV (d. 1159) was the only English pope, Gregory XI (d. 1378) the last French pope and Adrian VI (d. 1523) the last non-Italian pope, before John Paul II. Anacletus II (d. 1138) was a converted Jew. 'Pope Joan' is placed between John V (d. 686) and Conon.

The names of antipopes and of illegal occupants of the papal chair and particulars as to papal tombs imperfectly identified or no longer in existence are enclosed in square brackets[]. Conjectural dates are followed by a query (?). The title of each pope is given, together with the date of his consecration (for the early popes) or of his election (from Gelasius II onward; No. 162), the date of his death, the duration of his pontificate, and, as far as possible, his birthplace, family name, and place of interment. Martyred popes are indicated by the letter M. Most of the early tombs in the old basilica of St Peter were scattered or lost on the demolition of the church by Julius II; but some of the remains of the popes were collected in two ossuaries in the Grotte Vaticane.

St Peter's remains are preserved beneath the altar of the Confession in St Peter's and the thirteen following popes are believed to be interred close by. Churches mentioned below are in Rome, unless otherwise indicated.

		Began to reign
1.	ST PETER; M.; 42–67	42
2.	ST LINUS of Tuscia (Volterra?); M.; 67–78	67
3.	ST ANACLETUS I, of Rome; M.; 78–90 (?)	78
4.	ST CLEMENT I, of the Roman Flavian gens; M.; 90–99 (?). D. at Cherson (Crimea), relics in San Clemente	90
5.	ST EVARISTUS of Greece (or of Bethlehem); M.; 99–105 (?)	99
6.	ST ALEXANDER I, of Rome; M.; 105–115 (?)	105
7.	ST SIXTUS I, of Rome, M.; 115–125 (?)	115
8.	ST TELESPHORUS, of Greece; M.; 125–136 (?)	125
9.	ST IGINUS, of Greece; M.; 136–140 (?)	136
10.	ST PIUS I, of Italy; M.; 140–155 (?)	140
11.	ST ANICETUS, of Syria; M.; 155–166 (?)	155
12.	ST SOTER, of Campania (Fundi?); M.; 166–175 (?)	166
13.	ST ELEUTHERUS, of Epirus (Nicopolis?); M.; 175–189	175
14.	ST VICTOR I, of Africa; M.; 189–199	189
15.	ST ZEPHYRINUS, of Rome; M.; 199–217. Int. near the Cimitero di San Callisto	199
16.	ST CALIXTUS I, of Rome; M.; 217–222. Int. in the Cimitero di Calepodio, on the Via Aurelia Vetus; relics in Santa Maria in Trastevere [HIPPOLYTUS, 217–235]	217
17.	ST URBAN I, of Rome; M.; 222–230. Int. in the Cimitero di San Callisto; relics in Santa Cecilia in Trastevere	222
18.	ST PONTIANUS, of Rome; M.; 21 July 230–28 Sept. 235. Int. in the Cimitero di San Callisto; relics in Santa Prassede	230
19.	ST ANTERUS, of Greece; M.; 21 Nov. 235–3 Jan. 236. Int. in the Cimitero di San Callisto; relics in San Silvestro in Capite	235
20.	ST FABIAN, of Rome; M.; 10 Jan. 236–20 Jan. 250. Int. in the Cimitero di San Callisto; relics in Santa Prassede (?)	236
21.	ST CORNELIUS, of Rome; M.; March 251–June 253. Int. near the Cimitero di San Callisto; relics in Santa Maria in Trastevere [NOVATIAN, 251–258]	251
22.	ST LUCIUS I, of Rome; M.; 25 June 253–5 March 254. Int. in the Cimitero di San Callisto; relics in Santa Cecilia in Trastevere	253
23.	ST STEPHEN I, of Rome; M.; 12 May 254–2 Aug. 257. Int. in the Cimitero di San Callisto; relics in San Silvestro in Capite	254
24.	ST SIXTUS II, of Greece (?); M.; 30 Aug. 257–6 Aug. 258. Int. in the Cimitero di San Callisto; relics in San Sisto Vecchio	257

56. JOHN II, of Rome; 2 Jan. 533–8 May 535. [Int. under the portico of
St Peter's]   533
57. ST AGAPITUS I, of Rome; 13 May 535–22 April 536. Died at
Constantinople. [Int. under the portico of St Peter's]   535
58. ST SILVERIUS, of Frosinone; M.; 8 June 536–deposed 11 March
537. Died in exile on the island of Ponza 538 (?). [Int. on the island
of Ponza]   536
59. VIGILIUS, of Rome; June 538 (?)–7 June 555 (but elected 29
March 537). Died at Syracuse. Int. at Rome [in the Cimitero di
Priscilla]   538
60. PELAGIUS I, of Rome; 16 April 556–4 March 561. [Int. under the
portico of St Peter's]   556
61. JOHN III, of Rome; 17 July 561–13 July 574. [Tomb in St Peter's]   561
62. BENEDICT I, of Rome; 2 June 575–30 July 579. [Tomb in St
Peter's]   575
63. PELAGIUS II, of Rome; 26 Nov. 579–7 Feb. 590. [Tomb in St
Peter's]   579
64. ST GREGORY I the Great, of Rome, of the Gens Anicia; 3 Sept.
590–13 March 604. Tomb and relics in St Peter's (Capp.
Clementina)   590
65. SABINIANUS, of Tusculum; 13 Sept. 604–22 Feb. 606. [Tomb in St
Peter's]   604
66. BONIFACE III, of Rome; 19 Feb. 607–12 Nov. 607. [Tomb in St
Peter's]   607
67. ST BONIFACE IV, of Valeria de' Marsi; 25 Aug. 608–8 May 615.
Tomb in St. Peter's; transferred to the new basilica, altar of St.
Thomas   608
68. ST DEUSDEDIT I, of Rome; 19 Oct. 615–8 Nov. 618. [Tomb in St
Peter's]   615
69. BONIFACE V, of Naples; 23 Dec. 619–25 Oct. 625.[Tomb in St
Peter's]   619
70. HONORIUS I, of Campania; 27 Oct. 625–12 Oct. 638. (Int. in
Sant'Agnese fuori le Mura)   625
71. SEVERINUS, of Rome; 28 May 640–2 Aug. 640. [Tomb in St
Peter's]   640
72. JOHN IV, of Dalmatia; 24 Dec. 640–12 Oct. 642. [Tomb in St
Peter's]   640
73. THEODORE I, of Jerusalem (? or Greece); 24 Nov. 642–14 May
649. [Tomb in St Peter's]   642
74. ST MARTIN I, of Todi; M.; 21 July 649–exiled 18 June 653–16
Sept. 655. Died at Sebastopol; relics in San Martino ai Monti   649
75. ST EUGENIUS I, of Rome, 16 Sept. 655–2 June 657; consecrated
10 Aug. 654. [Tomb in St Peter's]   655
76. ST VITALIAN, of Segni; 30 July 657–27 Jan. 672. [Tomb in St
Peter's]   657
77. DEUSDEDIT II, of Rome; 11 April 672–17 June 676. [Tomb in St
Peter's]   672
78. DONUS, of Rome; 2 Nov. 676–11 April 678. [Tomb in St Peter's]   676
79. ST AGATHO, of Sicily; 27 June 678–10 Jan. 681. [Tomb in St
Peter's]   678
80. ST LEO II, of Sicily; 17 Aug. 682–3 July 683. Tomb and relics in St
Peter's (Cappella della Colonna)   682
81. ST BENEDICT II, of Rome; 26 June 684–8 May 685. [Tomb in St
Peter's]   684
82. JOHN V, of Antioch; 23 July 685–2 Aug. 686. [Tomb in St Peter's]   685
83. CONON, of Thrace; 21 Oct. 686–21 Sept. 687. [Tomb in St Peter's]   686
[THEODORE, 22 Sept. 687–Oct. 687]
[PASCHAL, 687]
84. ST SERGIUS I, of Palermo; 15 Dec. 687–8 Sept. 701. [Tomb in St
Peter's]   687
85. JOHN VI, of Greece; 30 Oct. 701–11 Jan. 705. [Tomb in St
Peter's]   701
86. JOHN VII, of Greece; 1 March 705–18 Oct. 707. [Tomb in St
Peter's]   705
87. SISINNIUS, of Syria; 15 Jan. 708–4 Feb. 708   708
88. CONSTANTINE, of Syria; 25 March 708–9 April 715. [Tomb in St
Peter's]   708
89. ST GREGORY II, of Rome 19 May 715–11 Feb. 731. [Tomb in St
Peter's]   715

90. ST GREGORY III, of Syria; 18 March 731–10 Dec. 741. [Tomb in St Peter's]   731
91. ST ZACHARIAS, of Greece; 10 Dec. 741–22 March 752. [Tomb in St Peter's]   741
92. STEPHEN II, of Rome; 23 March 752–25 March 752. Burial place unknown   752
93. ST STEPHEN III, of Rome; 26 March 752–26 April 757. [Tomb in St Peter's]   752
94. ST PAUL I, of Rome; 29 May 757–28 June 767. [Tomb in St Peter's]   757
    [CONSTANTINE II, 5 July 767–murdered 769]
    [PHILIP, elected 31 July 768–abdicated 768]
95. STEPHEN IV, of Sicily; 7 Aug. 768–3 Feb. 772. [Tomb in St Peter's]   768
96. HADRIAN I, of Rome; 9 Feb. 772–26 Dec. 795 [Tomb in St Peter's]; epitaph, dictated by Charlemagne, under the portico of St Peter's   772
97. ST LEO III, of Rome; 27 Dec. 795–12 June 816. Tomb and relics in St Peter's (Cappella della Colonna)   795
98. ST STEPHEN V, of Rome; 22 June 816–14 Jan. 817. [Tomb in St Peter's]   816
99. ST PASCHAL I, of Rome; 25 Jan. 817–11 Feb. 824. [Tomb in St Peter's]   817
100. EUGENIUS II, of Rome; 21 Feb. 824–27 Aug. 827.   824
101. VALENTINE, of Rome; Aug. (?) 827–Sept. (?) 827. Burial place unknown.   827
102 GREGORY IV, of Rome; Oct. 827–25 Jan. 844. [Tomb in St Peter's]   827
103. SERGIUS II, of Rome; Jan. 844–27 Jan. 847. [Tomb in St Peter's]   844
    [JOHN, 844]
104. ST LEO IV, of Rome; 10 April 847–17 July 855. Tomb and relics in St Peter's (Cappella della Colonna)   847
105. ST BENEDICT III, of Rome; 6 Oct. 855–17 April 858. [Tomb in St Peter's]   855
    [ANASTASIUS, 29 Sept. 855–20 Oct. 855]   855
106. ST NICHOLAS I, the Great, of Rome; 24 April 858–13 Nov. 867. [Tomb in St Peter's]; epitaph in the Grotte Vaticane   858
107. HADRIAN II, of Rome; 14 Dec. 867–14 Dec. 872. [Tomb in St Peter's]; epitaph in the Grotte Vaticane   867
108. JOHN VIII, of Rome, 14 Dec. 872–16 Dec. 882. [Tomb in St Peter's]   872
109. MARINUS I (MARTIN II) of Gallesium; 16 Dec. 882–15 May 884. [Tomb in St Peter's]   882
110. ST HADRIAN III, of Rome; 17 May 884–17 Sept. 885. Tomb at Nonantola   884
111. STEPHEN VI, of Rome; Sept. 885–Sept. 891. [Tomb in St Peter's]   885
112. FORMOSUS, bishop of Porto; 6 Oct. 891–4 April 896. Thrown into the Tiber   891
113. BONIFACE VI, of Gallesium; April 896   896
114. STEPHEN VII, of Rome; May 896–Aug. 897. Strangled in prison   896
115. ROMANUS, of Gallesium; Aug. 897–end of Nov. 897   897
116. THEODORE II, of Rome; Dec. 897–Dec. 897   897
117. JOHN IX, of Tivoli; Jan. 898–Jan. 900. [Tomb in St Peter's]   898
118. BENEDICT IV, of Rome; Jan. 900–end July 903. [Tomb in St Peter's]   900
119. LEO V, of Ardea; end of July 903–Sept. 903. Deposed and imprisoned. [Int. in St John Lateran]   903
    [CHRISTOPHER, of Rome; 903, deposed in Jan. 904]
120. SERGIUS III, of Rome; 29 Jan. 904–14 April 911. [Tomb in St Peter's]   904
121. ANASTASIUS III, of Rome; April 911–June 913. [Tomb in St Peter's]   911
122. LANDO, of Sabina; end of July 913–Feb. 914   913
123. JOHN X, of Ravenna; March 914–May 928. Strangled in prison. [Int. in St John Lateran]   914
124. LEO VI, of Rome; May 928–Dec. 928. [Tomb in St Peter's]   928
125. STEPHEN VIII, of Rome; Jan. 929–Feb. 931   929
126. JOHN XI, of Rome; Son of Pope Sergius III and Marozia; March 931–Dec. 935. Died in prison   931
127. LEO VII; 3 (?) Jan. 936–13 (?) July 939   936
128. STEPHEN IX, of Germany (?); 14 (?) July 939–end of Oct. 942   939
129. MARINUS II (MARTIN III), of Rome; 30 (?) Oct. 942–May 946   942

130. AGAPITUS II, of Rome; 10 May 946–Dec. 955. [Int. in St John Lateran] — 946
131. JOHN XII, Ottaviano, of the family of the Counts of Tusculum, aged 19 yr; 16 (?) Dec. 955–deposed 14th May 964. [Int. in St John Lateran] — 955
132. LEO VIII, of Rome, 4 Nov. 963–1 March 965 — 963
133. BENEDICT V, Grammatico, of Rome; 22 (?) May 964–expelled from the pontifical see 23 June 964; died at Bremen 4 July 966. Int. first in Bremen, afterwards in Rome (church unknown) — 964
134. JOHN XIII, of Rome; 1 Oct. 965–5 Sept. 972. [Int. in St Paolo fuori le Mura] — 965
135. BENEDICT VI, of Rome; 19 Jan. 973–June 974. Strangled in prison [BONIFACE VII, Francone, of Rome; June–July 974 for the first time] — 973
136. BENEDICT VII, of the family of the Counts of Tusculum, of Rome; Oct. 974–10 July 983. Tomb in Santa Croce in Gerusalemme — 974
137. JOHN XIV, of Pavia; Dec. 983–20 Aug. 984; killed by Francone (Boniface VII). [Int. in St John Lateran] [BONIFACE VII, Francone; for the second time, Aug. 984– murdered July 985] — 983
138. JOHN XV, of Rome; Aug.. 985–March 996 — 985
139. GREGORY V, Bruno, of the family of the Counts of Carinthia; 3 May 996–18 Feb. 999. Tomb (an ancient Christian sarcophagus) now in the Grotte Vaticane [JOHN XVI, John Philagathus, of Greece; March 997–Feb. 998] — 996
140. SYLVESTER II, Gerbert of Aurillc, Auvergne; 2 April 999–12 May 1003. [Tomb in St John Lateran]; epitaph in the S. aisle — 999
141. JOHN XVII, Sicco, of Rome; June (?) 1003–6 Nov. 1003. [Tomb in St John Lateran] — 1003
142. JOHN XVIII, of Rapagnano; Jan. (?) 1004–July (?) 1009. [Tomb in San Paolo fuori le Mura]; epitaph in the convent — 1004
143. SERGIUS IV, of Rome; 31 July 1009–12 May 1012. [Tomb in St John Lateran]; epitaph in the S. aisle — 1009
144. BENEDICT VIII, John, of the family of the Counts of Tusculum, of Rome; 18 May 1012–9 April 1024 [Gregory, 1012] — 1012
145. JOHN XIX, of Rome, brother of Benedict VIII; April 1024–1032 — 1024
146. BENEDICT IX, Theophylact, of the family of the Counts of Tusculum; elected (at 15 yr of age) for the 1st time in 1032– deposed in Dec. 1044; elected for the 2nd time 10 March 1045– deposed 1 May 1045; elected for the 3rd time 8 Nov. 1047– deposed 17 July 1048. Tomb in the monastery of St Nilus at Grottaferrata — 1032
147. SYLVESTER III, John, bishop of Sabina; 20 Jan. 1045–deposed 10 March 1045 — 1045
148. GREGORY VI, Gratian, of Rome; 5 May 1045–banished 20 Dec. 1046; died 1047 — 1045
149. CLEMENT II, Suidger, bishop of Bamberg; 25 Dec. 1046–died at Pesaro 9 Oct. 1047. Tomb in Bamberg Cathedral — 1046
150. DAMASUS II, Poppo, bishop of Bressanone, of Bavaria; 17 July 1048–9 Aug. 1048. Died at Palestrina. [Tomb in St John Lateran] — 1048
151. ST LEO IX, Bruno, of Germany, bishop of Toul; 12 Feb. 1049–19 April 1054. Int. in St Peter's and transferred to the new basilica — 1049
152. VICTOR II, Gebhard, of Germany, bishop of Eichstätt; 16 April 1055–28 July 1057. Died at Arezzo; tomb at Florence — 1055
153. STEPHEN X, Frédéric, of the family of the Dukes of Lorraine; 3 Aug. 1057–29 March 1058. Died and int. in Florence [in the church of Santa Reparata, afterwards in the crypt of Santa Maria del Fiore] [Benedict X, of Rome; 5 April 1058–deposed 24 Jan. 1059. Tomb in Santa Maria Maggiore] — 1055
154. NICHOLAS II, Gérard de Bourgogne; 24 Jan. 1059–27 (?) July 1061 — 1059
155. ALEXANDER II, Anselmo of Milan; 30 Sept. 1061–21 April 1073. [Tomb in St John Lateran] [Honorius II, appointed by Imperial Diet of Basle 1061–1072] — 1061
156. ST GREGORY VII, Hildebrand, di Bonizio Aldobrandeschi, of Sovana; 22 April 1073–25 May 1085. Tomb in Salerno Cathedral [Clement III, Ghiberto; 25 Jan. 1080–Sept. 1100] — 1073

157. B. VICTOR III, Desiderio Epifani, of Benevento; elected 24 May 1086, consecrated 9 May 1087–16 Sept. 1087. Tomb at Monte Cassino   1086
158. B. URBAN II, of Reims; 12 March 1088–29 July 1099. [Tomb in St Peter's]   1088
159. PASCHAL II, Rainiero, of Breda; 14 Aug. 1099–21 Jan. 1118. [Tomb in St John Lateran]   1099
     [THEODORIC, Sept.–Dec. 1100; epigraph in the cemetery of La Cava]
     [ALBERT, Feb.–March 1102]
     [SYLVESTER IV, 18 Nov. 1105–12 April 1111]
160. GELASIUS II, Giov. Caetani, of Gaeta; 24 Jan. 1118–28 Jan. 1119 [Tomb at Cluny]   1118
     [GREGORY VIII, Maurice Bourdain, of Limoges, 8 March 1118– deposed April 1121]
161. CALIXTUS II, Gui de Bourgogne, of Quingey; 2 Feb. 1119–13 Dec. 1124. [Tomb in St John Lateran]   1119
162. HONORIUS II Lamberto Scannabecchi, of Fanano (Modena); 15 Dec. 1124–13 Feb. 1130. Died [and buried] in the monastery Sant'Andrea   1124
163. INNOCENT II, Gregorio Papareschi, of Trastevere; 14 Feb. 1130– 24 Sept. 1143. Int. in St John Lateran; transferred in 1617 to Santa Maria in Trastévere (monument of 1849) where the original epitaph is under the portico   1130
     [ANACLETUS II, Pierleone, a converted Jew; 14 Feb. 1130–25 Jan. 1138]
     [VICTOR IV, Gregorio da Monticelli, elected 15 March 1138, abdicated 29 May 1138]
164. CELESTINE II, Guido, of Città di Castello; 26 Sept. 1143–8 March 1144. [Tomb in St John Lateran]   1143
165. LUCIUS II, Gerardo Caccianemici dell'Orso, of Bologna; 12 March 1144–15 Feb. 1145. [Tomb in St John Lateran]   1144
166. B. EUGENIUS III, Bernardo Paganelli, of Montemagno (Pisa); 15 Feb. 1145–8 July 1153. [Tomb in St Peter's]   1145
167. ANASTASIUS IV, Corrado, of the Suburra, Rome; 12 July 1153–3 Dec. 1154. Int. in St John Lateran, in the porphyry sarcophagus of St Helena (now in the Vatican)   1153
168. HADRIAN IV, Nicholas Breakspeare, of Bedmond (Hertfordshire, England); 4 Dec. 1154–1 Sept. 1159. Died at Anagni; tomb in St Peter's; sarcophagus in the Grotte Vaticane (tablet, 1925)   1154
169. ALEXANDER III, Rolando Bandinelli, of Siena; 7 Sept. 1159–30 Aug. 1181. Died at Civita Castellana; tomb in St John Lateran; epitaph in the S. aisle, on a monument commissioned by Alexander VII   1159
     [VICTOR IV (V), Ottaviano; 7 Oct. 1159–20 April 1164]
     [PASCHAL III, Guido da Crema; 22 April 1164–20 Sept. 1168]
     [CALIXTUS III, John of Strumio, a Hungarian, Sept. 1168, abdicated 29 Aug. 1178]
     [INNOCENT III, Lando Frangipane of Sezze, elected 29 Sept. 1179, deposed in Jan. 1180]
170. LUCIUS III, Ubaldo Allucingoli, of Lucca; 1 Sept. 1181–25 Nov. 1185. Died in exile at Verona, int. in the cathedral of Verona (tomb of 1383)   1181
171. URBAN III, Uberto Crivelli, of Milan; 25 Nov. 1185–20 Oct. 1187. Died at Ferrara; int. in the cathedral of Ferrara (sarcophagus of 1305)   1185
172. GREGORY VIII, Alberto di Morra, of Benevento; 21 Oct. 1187–17 Dec. 1187. Int. in the cathedral of Pisa (sarcophagus destroyed in 1595)   1187
173. CLEMENT III, Paolino Scolare, of Rome; 19 Dec. 1187–Mar 1191 [Tomb in St John Lateran]   1187
174. CELESTINE III, Giacinto Bobone Orsini, of Rome; 30 March 1191– 8 Jan. 1198. [Tomb in St John Lateran]   1191
175. INNOCENT III, Lotario dei Conti di Segni, of Anagni; 8 Jan. 1198– 16 July 1216. Died at Perugia; remains transferred from Perugia Cathedral to St John Lateran in 1891 (tomb by Giuseppe Luchetti)   1198
176. HONORIUS III, Cencio Savelli, of Rome; elected in Perugia, 18 July 1216–died at Rome, 18 March 1227. Tomb in Santa Maria Maggiore   1216

177. GREGORY IX, Ugolino dei Conti di Segni, of Anagni; elected at the age of 86; 19 March 1227–22 Aug. 1241. [Tomb in St Peter's]   1227

178. CELESTINE IV, Castiglione, of Milan; 25 Oct. 1241–10 Nov. 1241. [Tomb in St Peter's]   1241

179. INNOCENT IV, Sinibaldo Fieschi, of Genoa; 25 June 1243–7 Dec. 1254. Died and int. at Naples (monument in San Gennaro, Naples)   1243

180. ALEXANDER IV, Orlando dei Conti di Segni, of Anagni; 12 Dec. 1254–25 May 1261. Died at Viterbo [and int. in Viterbo Cathedral]   1254

181. URBAN IV, Hyacinthe Pantaléon, of Troyes; elected at Viterbo 29 Aug. 1261; died at Perugia 2 Oct. 1264. Tomb in the cathedral of Perugia   1261

182. CLEMENT IV, Gui Foulques Le Gros, of St-Gilles; elected at Viterbo 5 Feb. 1265–died at Viterbo 29 Nov. 1268. Int. at Viterbo in Santa Maria in Gradi, afterwards in San Francesco (mon. by Pietro Oderisio)   1265

183. GREGORY X, Teobaldo Visconti of Piacenza; elected at Viterbo 1 Sept. 1271–died at Arezzo 10 Jan. 1276. Tomb in the cathedral of Arezzo (monument ascribed to Agost. di Giovanni and Angelo di Ventura)   1271

184. INNOCENT V, Pierre de Champagny, of the Tarentaise; 21 Jan. 1276–22 June 1276. [Tomb in St John Lateran]   1276

185. HADRIAN V, Ottobono de' Fieschi, of Genoa; elected at Rome 11 July 1276–18 Aug. 1276. Tomb at Viterbo in San Francesco (mon. by Arnolfo di Cambio)   1276

186. JOHN XXI, Pedro Julião, of Lisbon; elected at Viterbo 8 Sept. 1276–20 May 1277. Tomb in the cathedral of Viterbo (mon. of 1884)   1276

187. NICHOLAS III, Giov. Gaetano Orsini, of Rome; elected at Viterbo 25 Nov. 1277–died at Soriano nel Cimino 22 Aug. 1280. Tomb in St Peter's (sarcophagus in the Grotte Vaticane)   1277

188. MARTIN IV, Simon de Brion, of Montpincé in Brie; elected at Viterbo 22 Feb. 1281–died at Perugia 28 March 1285. Tomb in Perugia cathedral   1281

189. HONORIUS IV, Iacopo Savelli, of Rome; elected at Perugia 2 April 1285–3 April 1287. [Tomb in St Peter's]; sarcophagus with recumbent statue, in Santa Maria Aracoeli   1285

190. NICHOLAS IV, Girolamo Masci, of Lisciano di Ascoli; 15 Feb. 1288–4 April 1292. Tomb in Santa Maria Maggiore (mon. designed by Dom. Fontana)   1288

191. ST CELESTINE V, Pietro Angeleri da Morrone; of Isérnia, 5 July 1294–abdicated 13 Dec. 1294. Died in the Castello di Fumone near Alatri 19 May 1296. Int. at Sulmona, afterwards in Santa Maria Collemaggio, at Aquila (mon. by Girol. da Vicenza, 1571)   1294

192. BONIFACE VIII, Benedetto Gaetani, of Anagni; 24 Dec. 1294–11 or 12 Oct. 1303. [Tomb in St Peter's]; sarcophagus, with recumbent figure, in the Grotte Vaticane   1294

193. B. BENEDICT XI, Niccolò Boccasini, of Treviso; 22 Oct. 1303–died at Perugia 7 July 1304. Mon. in San Domenico, Perugia (mon. by Lorenzo Maitani or Nic. di Nuzzo)   1303

194. CLEMENT V, Bertrand de Got, of Villandraut, near Bordeaux; elected at Perugia 5 June 1305, died at Roquemaure 14 April 1314. Int. at Uzeste, Gascony (tomb of 1359)   1305

195. JOHN XXII, Jacques d'Euse, of Cahors; elected at Avignon 7 Aug. 1316–died at Avignon 4 Dec. 1334. Tomb in the cathedral of Avignon   1316

[NICHOLAS V, Pietro da Corvara, 12 May 1328–30 Aug. 1330]

196. BENEDICT XII, Jacques Fournier, of Saverdun, near Toulouse; 20 Dec. 1334–25 April 1342. Tomb in the cathedral of Avignon (mon. by Jean Lavenier; destroyed)   1334

197. CLEMENT VI, Pierre Roger de Beaufort, of Château Maumont, near Limoges; 7 May 1342–6 Dec. 1352. Tomb at La Chaise-Dieu, Auvergne (mon. destroyed, only the sarcophagus remains)   1342

198. INNOCENT VI, Etienne d'Aubert, of Mont, near Limoges; 18 Dec. 1352–12 Sept. 1362. Tomb in the Chartreuse of Villeneuve-lés-Avignon (mon. partly destroyed)   1352

199. URBAN V, Guillaume de Grimoard, of Grisac, near Mende in Languedoc; 16 Oct. 1362–19 Dec. 1370. Tomb in the Abbey of St Victor, Marseille (mon. partly destroyed; only the recumbent figure now remains)   1362

200. GREGORY XI, Pierre Roger de Beaufort, nephew of Clement VI, of Château Maumont, near Limoges; elected at Avignon 30 Dec. 1370–died at Rome 27 March 1378. Mon. in Santa Francesca Romana   1370
201. URBAN VI, Bart. Prigano, of Naples; 9 April 1378–15 Oct. 1389. Tomb in St Peter's (mon. transferred to the Grotte Vaticane)   1378
202. BONIFACE IX, Pietro Tomacelli, of Naples; 2 Nov. 1389–1 Oct. 1404. [Tomb in St Peter's]   1389
203. INNOCENT VII, Cosimo de' Migliorati, of Sulmona; 17 Oct. 1404–6 Nov. 1406. [Tomb in St Peter's]; sarcophagus in the Grotte Vaticane   1404
204. GREGORY XII, Angelo Correr, of Venice; 30 Nov. 1406–abdicated 4 June 1415–died at Recanati 17 Oct. 1417. Tomb in the cathedral at Recanati   1406

Popes at Avignon:
    [CLEMENT VII, Robert of Savoy, of Geneva; elected at Fondi 20 Sept. 1378–16 Sept. 1394]
    [BENEDICT XIII, Pedro de Luna, of Aragon; 28 Sept. 1394–23 May 1423]

Antipopes at Avignon:
    [CLEMENT VIII, Gil Sanchez Muñoz, of Barcelona; 10 June 1423–16 July 1429]
    [BENEDICT XIV, Bernard Garnier; 12 Nov. 1425–1430 (?)]

Popes at Pisa:
    [ALEXANDER V, Pietro Filargis, of Candia; 26 June 1409–3 May 1410. Tomb in San Francesco, Bologna; mon. by Sperandio]
    [JOHN XXIII, Baldassarre Cossa, of Naples; 17 May 1410, deposed 29 May 1415–died at Florence 23 Dec. 1419. Tomb in the Baptistery, Florence; mon. by Donatello and Michelozzo]

205. MARTIN V, Oddone Colonna, of Genazzano; elected (aged 50) at Constance, 11 Nov. 1417–20 Feb. 1431. Tomb in St John Lateran (by Simone Ghini)   1417
206. EUGENIUS IV, Gabriele Condulmero of Venice; elected (aged 48) 3 March 1431–23 Feb. 1447. Int. in St Peter's; whence the mon. (by Isaia de Pisa) has been transferred to the refectory of the Congregation of San Giorgio in Alga, an ancient convent adjoining San Salvatore in Lauro   1431
    [FELIX V, Amadeus, duke of Savoy; 5 Nov. 1439–7 April 1449; died 1451 at the Château de Ripaille on the Lake of Geneva]   1447
207. NICHOLAS V, Tommaso Parentucelli, of Sarzana; elected (aged 49) 6 March 1447–24 March 1455. Tomb tin St Peter's (sarcophagus with recumbent figure and fragments of the monument in the Grotte Vaticane)   1447
208. CALIXTUS III, Alfonso Borgia, of Xativa, in Spain; elected (aged 78) 8 April 1455–6 Aug. 1458. Int. in Sant'Andrea near St Peter's (destroyed). The body was removed to Santa Maria di Monserrato (mon. by F. Moratilla, 1881); cenotaph in the Grotte Vaticane   1455
209. PIUS II, Aeneas Silvius Piccolomini, of Corsignano (Pienza); elected (aged 53) 19 Aug. 1458–15 Aug. 1464. Int. in St Peter's, in 1623 the mon. (by Niccolò della Guardia and Pietro da Todi) was reconstructed in Sant'Andrea della Valle   1458
210. PAUL II, Pietro Barbo, of Venice; elected (aged 48) 30 Aug 1464–26 July 1471. Tomb in St Peter's; the mon. by Mino da Fiesole has been reconstructed in the Grotte Vaticane   1464
211. SIXTUS IV, Fr. della Rovere, of Savona; elected (aged 57) 9 Aug 1471–12 Aug 1484. Int. in St Peter's. The tomb was violated during the sack of Rome, 1527; the bronze sarcophagus by Ant. Pollaiolo now in the Museo Storico Artistico in St Peter's   1471
212. INNOCENT VIII, G. B. Cibo, of Genoa; elected (aged 52) 29 Aug 1484–25 July 1492. Int. in St Peter's; the monument, by Ant. and Pietro del Pollaiolo, is in the present basilica   1484
213. ALEXANDER VI, Roderigo Lenzuoli-Borgia, Valencia, Spain; elected (aged 62) 11 Aug 1492–18 Aug 1503. Int. in St Peter's, afterwards removed to the chapel of San Diego in Santa Maria di Monserrato (mon. by F. Moratilla, 1881)   1492
214. PIUS III, Fr. Todeschini-Piccolomini, of Siena; elected (aged 64) 22 Sept. 1503–18 Oct 1503. Tomb in St Peter's; mon. by Pasquino da Montepulciano, reconstructed in Sant'Andrea della Valle   1503

215. JULIUS II, Giuliano della Rovere, of Savona; elected (aged 60) 31
Oct 1503–21 Feb 1513. Int. in St Peter's, afterwards in the
sarcophagus of Sixtus IV (?); his remains were scattered in 1527.
Parts of a projected mausoleum by Michelangelo are now in San
Pietro in Vincoli 1503
216. LEO X, Giov. de' Medici, of Florence; elected (aged 38) 9 March
1513–1 Dec 1521. Tomb in Santa Maria sopra Minerva 1513
217. ADRIAN VI, Adrian Florisz Dedel, of Utrecht; elected (aged 63) 9
Jan 1522–14 Sept 1523. Tomb in Santa Maria dell'Anima 1522
218. CLEMENT VII. Giulio de' Medici, of Florence; elected (aged 45)
19 Nov 1523–25 Sept 1534. Tomb in Santa Maria sopra Minerva,
by Ant. da Sangallo. 1523
219. PAUL III, Aless. Farnese, of Camino (Rome) or of Viterbo (?),
elected (aged 66) 13 Oct 1534–10 Nov 1549. Tomb in St Peter's
(mon. by Gugl. della Porta) 1534
220. JULIUS III, Giov. Maria Ciocchi del Monte, of Monte San Savino,
near Arezzo; elected (aged 63) 7 Feb 1550–23 March 1555. Tomb
in the Grotte Vaticane (sarcophagus) 1550
221. MARCELLUS II, Marcello Cervini, of Montefano (Macerata);
elected (aged 54) 9 April 1555–30 April 1555. Tomb in the Grotte
Vaticane (sarcophagus) 1555
222. PAUL IV, Giov. Pietro Caraffa, of Capriglio, Avellino; elected
(aged 79) 23 May 1555–18 Aug 1559. Tomb in Santa Maria sopra
Minerva (mon. by Tom. da Cerignola from designs by Pirro
Ligorio) 1555
223. PIUS IV, Giov. Angelo de' Medici, of Milan; elected (aged 60) 26
Dec 1559–9 Dec 1565. Int. in Santa Maria degli Angeli 1559
224. ST PIUS V, Ant. Ghislieri, of Bosco Marengo, near Tortona;
elected (aged 62) 7 Jan 1566–1 May 1572. Tomb in Santa Maria
Maggiore 1566
225. GREGORY XIII, Ugo Boncompagni, of Bologna; elected (aged 70)
13 May 1572–10 April 1585. Tomb in St Peter's by Camillo Rusconi 1572
226. SIXTUS V, Felice Peretti, of Grottammare; elected (aged 64) 24
April 1585–27 Aug 1590. Tomb in Santa Maria Maggiore 1585
227. URBAN VII, G. B. Castagna, of Rome; elected (aged 69) 15 Sept
1590–27 Sept 1590. Tomb in Santa Maria sopra Minerva 1590
228. GREGORY XIV, Niccolò Sfondrati, of Cremona; elected (aged 55)
5 Dec 1590–15 Oct 1591. Tomb in St Peter's (sarcophagus without
mon.) 1590
229. INNOCENT IX, Giov. Ant. Facchinetti, of Bologna; elected (aged
72) 29 Oct 1591–30 Dec 1591. Tomb in the Grotte Vaticane
(sarcophagus) 1591
230. CLEMENT VIII, Ippolito Aldobrandini, of Fano; elected (aged 56)
30 Jan 1592–3 March 1605. Tomb in Santa Maria Maggiore 1592
231. LEO XI, Aless. de' Medici, of Florence; elected (aged 70) 1 April
1605–27 April 1605. Tomb in St Peter's 1605
232. PAUL V, Camillo Borghese, of Rome; elected (aged 53) 16 May
1605–28 Jan 1621. Tomb in Santa Maria Maggiore 1605
233. GREGORY XV, Aless. Ludovisi, of Bologna; elected (aged 67) 9
Feb 1621–8 July 1623. Tomb in Sant'Ignazio (mon. by Pierre Le
Gros) 1621
234. URBAN VIII, Maffeo Barberini, of Florence; elected (aged 55) 6
Aug 1623–29 July 1644. Tomb in St Peter's (mon. by Bernini) 1623
235. INNOCENT X, G. B. Pamphilj, of Rome; elected (aged 72) 15 Sept
1644–7 Jan 1655. Tomb in Sant'Agnese in Agone (mon. by Maini) 1644
236. ALEXANDER VII, Fabio Chigi, of Siena; elected (aged 56) 7 April
1655–22 May 1667. Tomb in St Peter's (mon. by Bernini) 1655
237. CLEMENT IX, Giulio Rospigliosi, of Pistoia; elected (aged 67) 20
June 1667–9 Dec 1669. Tomb in Santa Maria Maggiore, under the
pavement (mon. in the nave by Guidi, Fancelli and Ercole Ferrata
from designs by Carlo Rainaldi) 1667
238. CLEMENT X, Emilio Altieri, of Rome; elected (aged 80) 29 April
1670–22 July 1676. Tomb and mon. in St Peter's 1670
239. INNOCENT XI, Bened. Odescalchi, of Como; elected (aged 65) 21
Sept. 1676–11 Aug 1689. Tomb in St Peter's (by Etienne Monnot
from designs by Carlo Maratta) 1676
240. ALEXANDER VIII, Pietro Ottoboni, of Venice; elected (aged 79) 6
Oct 1689–1 Feb 1691. Tomb in St Peter's (mon. by Arrigo di San
Martino from designs by Angelo de Rossi) 1689

241. INNOCENT XII, Ant. Pignatelli, of Spinazzola (Bari); elected (aged 76) 12 July 1691–27 Sept 1700. Tomb and mon. in St Peter's   1691
242. CLEMENT XI, Giov. Fr. Albani, of Urbino; elected (aged 51) 23 Nov 1700–19 March 1721. Tomb in St Peter's (beneath the pavement of the choir)   1700
243. INNOCENT XIII, Michelangelo Conti, of Rome; elected (aged 66) 8 May 1721–7 March 1724. Tomb in the Grotte Vaticane (no monument)   1721
244. BENEDICT XIII, Vinc. Maria Orsini, of Gravina (Bari); elected (aged 75) 29 May 1724–21 Feb 1730. Tomb in Santa Maria sopra Minerva   1724
245. CLEMENT XII, Lor. Corsini, of Florence; elected (aged 79) 12 July 1730–6 Feb 1740. Tomb in St John Lateran   1730
246. BENEDICT XIV, Prospero Lambertini, of Bologna; elected (aged 65) 17 Aug 1740–3 May 1758. Tomb in St Peter's (mon. by Pietro Bracci)   1740
247. CLEMENT XIII, Carlo Rezzonico, of Venice; elected (aged 65) 6 July 1758–2 Feb 1769. Tomb in St Peter's (mon. by Canova)   1758
248. CLEMENT XIV, Giov. Vincenzo Ganganelli, of Sant'Arcangelo di Romagna (Forlì); elected (aged 64) 19 May 1769–22 Sept 1774. Tomb in Santi Apostoli   1769
249. PIUS VI, Angelo Braschi, of Cesena; elected (aged 58) 15 Feb 1775–29 Aug 1799. Died at Valence, France; int. in the Grotte Vaticane; mon. by Ant. Canova in the Confessio, St Peter's; the heart of Pius VI is preserved at Valence   1775
250. PIUS VII, Giorgio Barnaba Chiaramonti, of Cesena; elected (aged 58) at Venice; 14 March 1800–died at Rome, 20 Aug 1823. Tomb in St Peter's   1800
251. LEO XII, Annibale della Genga, born at La Genga, near Foligno; elected (aged 63) 28 Sept 1823–10 Feb 1829. Tomb in St Peter's, beneath the pavement of the chapel of St Leo the Great; mon. by Gius. Fabris, in the nave   1823
252. PIUS VIII, Francesco Saverio Castiglioni, of Cingoli; elected (aged 69) 31 March 1829–30 Nov 1830. Tomb in St Peter's (mon. by Pietro Tenerani)   1829
253. GREGORY XVI, Bart. Cappellari, of Belluno, elected (aged 66) 2 Feb 1831–1 June 1846. Tomb in St Peter's (mon. by Amici)   1831
254. PIUS IX, Giov. Maria Mastai Ferretti, of Senigallia; elected (aged 54) 16 June 1846–7 Feb 1878. Tomb in the crypt of San Lorenzo. Fuori le Mura   1846
255. LEO XIII, Gioacchino Pecci, of Carpineto Romano, elected (aged 68) 20 Feb 1878–20 July 1903. Int. in St John Lateran (mon. by Giulio Tadolini)   1878
256. ST PIUS X, Giuseppe Sarto, of Riese (Treviso); elected (aged 68) 4 Aug 1903–20 Aug 1914. Tomb in the Cappella della Presentazione (St Peter's); mon. in St Peter's by Pietro Astorri and Florestano di Fausto   1903
257. BENEDICT XV, Giacomo della Chiesa, of Genoa; elected (aged 60) 3 Sept 1914–22 Jan 1922. Tomb in the Grotte Vaticane; sarcophagus with recumbent effigy by Giul. Barberi (1924). Mon. in St Peter's by Pietro Canonica   1914
258. PIUS XI, Achille Ratti, of Desio (Milan); elected (aged 65) 6 Feb 1922–10 Feb 1939. Tomb in the Grotte Vaticane; mon. in St Peter's by Fr. Nagni   1922
259. PIUS XII, Eugenio Pacelli, of Rome; elected (aged 63) 2 March 1939–9 Oct 1958. Tomb in the Grotte Vaticane; mon. in St Peter's by Fr. Messina   1939
260. JOHN XXIII, Angelo Roncalli, of Sotto il Monte, Bergamo; elected (aged 77) 28 Oct 1958–3 June 1963. Tomb in the Grotte Vaticane; mon. by Emilio Greco in St Peter's   1958
261. PAUL VI, Giov. Battista Montini, of Brescia; elected (aged 65) 21 June 1963–6 August 1978. Tomb in the Grotte Vaticane   1963
262. JOHN PAUL I, Albino Luciani, of Forno di Canale, Belluno; elected (aged 65) 26 August 1978–29 September 1978. Tomb in the Grotte Vaticane   1978
263. JOHN PAUL II, Karol Wojtyla, of Wadowice (Krakow), Poland; elected (aged 58) 16 October 1978   1978

GLOSSARY

AEDICULE, small opening framed by two columns and a pediment originally used in classical architecture

AMBO (pl. *ambones*), pulpit in a Christian basilica; two pulpits on opposite sides of a church from which the gospel and epistle were read

AMPHORA, antique vase, usually of large dimensions, for oil and other liquids

ANTEFIX, ornament placed at the lower corners of the tiled roof of a temple to conceal the space between the tiles and the cornice

ANTIPHONAL, choir-book containing a collection of *antiphonae*—verses sung in response by two choirs

ANTIS, *in antis* describes the portico of a temple when the side-walls are prolonged to end in a pilaster flush with the columns of the portico

APODYTERIUM, dressing-room in a Roman bath

ARCA, wooden chest with a lid, for sacred or secular use. Also, monumental sarcophagus in stone, used by Christians and pagans

ARCHITRAVE, the lowest part of an entablature, the horizontal frame above a door

ARCHIVOLT, moulded architrave carried round an arch

ATLANTES (or *Telamones*), male figures used as supporting columns

ATRIUM, forecourt, usually of a Byzantine church or a classical Roman house

ATTIC, topmost story of a classical building, hiding the spring of the roof

BADIA, *abbazia*; abbey

BALDACCHINO, canopy supported by columns, usually over an altar

BASILICA, originally a Roman hall used for public administration; in Christian architecture, an aisled church with a clerestory and apse, and no transepts

BORGO, a suburb; a street leading away from the centre of a town

BOTTEGA, the studio of an artist: the pupils who worked under his direction

BOZZETTO, sketch, often used to describe a small model for a piece of sculpture

BUCCHERO, Etruscan black terracotta ware

BUCRANIA, a form of classical decoration—heads of oxen garlanded with flowers

CALDARIUM or CALIDARIUM, room for hot or vapour baths in a Roman bath

CAMPANILE, bell-tower, often detached from the building to which it belongs

CAMPOSANTO, cemetery

CANEPHORA, figure bearing a basket, often used as a caryatid

CANOPIC VASE, Egyptian or Etruscan vase enclosing the entrails of the dead

CARCERES, openings in the barriers through which the competing chariots entered the circus

CARDO, the main street of a Roman town, at right angles to the Decumanus

CARTOON, from *cartone*, meaning large sheet of paper. A full-size preparatory drawing for a painting or fresco

CARYATID, female figure used as a supporting column

CAVEA, the part of a theatre or amphitheatre occupied by the row of seats

CELLA, sanctuary of a temple, usually in the centre of the building

CHIAROSCURO, distribution of light and shade, apart from colour in a painting

CIBORIUM, casket or tabernacle containing the Host

CIPOLLINO, a greyish marble with streaks of white or green

CIPPUS, sepulchral monument in the form of an altar

CISTA, casket, usually of bronze and cylindrical in shape, to hold jewels, toilet articles, etc., and decorated with mythological subjects

COLUMBARIUM, a building (usually subterranean) with niches to hold urns containing the ashes of the dead

CONFESSIO, crypt beneath the high altar and raised choir of a church, usually containing the relics of a saint

CORBEL, a projecting block, usually of stone

CRYPTOPORTICUS, vaulted subterranean corridor

CUNEUS, wedge-shaped block of seats in an antique theatre

CYCLOPEAN, the term applied to walls of unmortared masonry, older than the Etruscan civilization, and attributed by the ancients to the giant Cyclopes

DECUMANUS, the main street of a Roman town running parallel to its longer axis

DIACONIA, early Christian welfare centre

DIPTERAL, temple surrounded by a double peristyle

DIPTYCH, painting or ivory tablet in two sections

EXEDRA, semicircular recess

EX-VOTO, tablet or small painting expressing gratitude to a saint

FORUM, open space in a town serving as a market or meeting-place

FRESCO, (in Italian, *affresco*), painting executed on wet plaster. On the wall beneath is sketched the *sinopia*, and the *cartone* is transferred onto the fresh plaster (*intonaco*) before the fresco is begun either by pricking the outline with small holes over which a powder is dusted, or by means of a stylus which leaves an incised line on the wet plaster. In recent years many frescoes have been detached from the walls on which they were executed

FRIGIDARIUM, room for cold baths in a Roman bath

GIALLO ANTICO, red-veined yellow marble from Numidia

GONFALONE, banner of a medieval guild or commune

GRAFFITI, design on a wall made with an iron tool on a prepared surface, the design showing in white. Also used loosely to describe scratched designs or words on walls

GREEK-CROSS, cross with the arms of equal length

GRISAILLE, painting in various tones of grey

GROTESQUE, painting or stucco decoration in the style of the ancient Romans (found during the Renaissance in the Domus Aurea in Rome, then underground, hence the name, from 'grotto'). The delicate ornamental decoration usually includes patterns of flowers, sphinxes, birds, human figures, etc. against a light ground

HERM (pl. *hermae*), quadrangular pillar decreasing in girth towards the ground, surmounted by a bust

HEXASTYLE, temple with a portico of six columns at the end

HYPOGEUM, subterranean excavation for the interment of the dead (usually Etruscan)

IMPASTO, early Etruscan ware made of inferior clay

INSULA (pl. *insulae*), tenement house

INTARSIA (or *Tarsia*), inlay of wood, marble or metal

KRATER, antique mixing-bowl, conical in shape with rounded base

KYLIX, wide shallow vase with two handles and short stem

LACONICUM, room for vapour baths in a Roman bath

LATIN-CROSS, cross with a long vertical arm

LOGGIA, covered gallery or balcony, usually preceding a larger building

LUNETTE, semicircular space in a vault or ceiling often decorated with a painting or relief

MATRONEUM, gallery reserved for women in early Christian churches

METOPE, panel between two triglyphs on the frieze of a Doric temple

MITHRAEUM, temple of the god Mithras

MONOLITH, single stone (usually a column)

NARTHEX, vestibule of a Christian basilica

NAUMACHIA, mock naval combat for which the arena of an amphitheatre was flooded

NIELLO, black substance used in an engraved design

NIMBUS, luminous ring surrounding the heads of saints in paintings; a square nimbus denoted that the person was living at that time

NYMPHAEUM, a sort of summer-house in the gardens of baths, palaces, etc., originally a temple of the Nymphs, and decorated with statues of those goddesses

OCTASTYLE, a portico with 8 columns

OINOCHOE, wine-jug usually of elongated shape for dipping wine out of a krater

OPUS ALEXANDRINUM, mosaic design of black and red geometric figures on a white ground

OPUS INCERTUM, masonry of small irregular stones set in mortar (a type of concrete)

OPUS QUADRATUM, masonry of large rectangular blocks without mortar; in *Opus Etruscum* the blocks are placed alternately lengthwise and endwise

OPUS RETICULATUM, masonry arranged in squares or diamonds so that the mortar joints make a network pattern

OPUS SECTILE, mosaic or paving of thin slabs of coloured marble cut in geometrical shapes

OPUS SPICATUM, masonry or paving of small bricks arranged in a herring-bone pattern

OPUS TESSELLATUM, mosaic formed entirely of square tesserae

OPUS VERMICULATUM, mosaic with tesserae arranged in lines following the design contours

PALAZZO, any dignified and important building

PALOMBINO, fine-grained white marble

PAVONAZZETTO, yellow marble blotched with blue

PAX, sacred object used by a priest for the blessing of peace, and offered for the kiss of the faithful, usually circular, engraved, enamelled or painted in a rich gold or silver frame

PENDENTIVE, concave spandrel beneath a dome

PEPERINO, earthy granulated tufa, much used in Rome

PERIPTERAL, temple surrounded by a colonnade

PERISTYLE, court or garden surrounded by a columned portico

PIETÀ, group of the Virgin mourning the dead Christ

PISCINA, Roman tank; a basin for an officiating priest to wash his hands before mass

PLUTEUS, (pl. *plutei*), marble panel, usually decorated; a series of them used to form a parapet to precede the altar of a church

PODIUM, a continuous base or plinth supporting columns, and the lowest row of seats in the cavea of a theatre or amphitheatre

POLYPTYCH, painting or tablet in more than three sections

POZZOLANA, reddish volcanic earth (mostly from Pozzuoli, near Naples) largely used for cement

PREDELLA, small painting or panel, usually in sections, attached below a large altarpiece

PRESEPIO, literally, crib or manger. A group of statuary of which the central subject is the Infant Jesus in the manger

PRONAOS, porch in front of the cella of a temple

PROPYLAEA, columned vestibule approaching a temple

PROSTYLE, temple with columns on the front only

PULVIN, cushion stone between the capital and the impost block

PULVINAR, Imperial couch and balcony on the podium of a theatre

PULVINATED, convex in profile; a term usually applied to a freize

PUTTO, (pl. *putti*) figure sculpted or painted usually nude, of a child

ROSSO ANTICO red marble from the Peloponnese

RHYTON, drinking-horn usually ending in an animal's head

SCHOLA CANTORUM, enclosure for the choristers in the nave of an early Christian church, adjoining the sanctuary

SINOPIA, large sketch for a fresco made on the rough wall in a red earth pigment called *sinopia* (because it originally came from Sinope, a town on the Black Sea). By detaching a fresco it is now possible to see the sinopia beneath and detach it also

SITULA, water-bucket

SOLOMONIC COLUMN, barley-sugar or twisted column, so called from its supposed use in the Temple of Solomon

SPANDREL, surface between two arches in an arcade or the triangular space on either side of an arch

SPINA, low stone wall connecting the turning-posts (*metoe*) at either end of a circus

STAMNOS, big-bellied vase with two small handles at the sides, closed by a lid

STELE, upright stone bearing a monumental inscription

STEREOBATE, basement of a temple or other building

STOA, a porch or portico not attached to a larger building

STRIGIL, bronze scraper used by the Romans to remove the oil with which they had anointed themselves

STYLOBATE, basement of a columned temple or other building

TELAMONES, see *Atlantes*

TEMENOS, a sacred enclosure

TEPIDARIUM, room for warm baths in a Roman bath

TESSERA, a small cube of marble, glass, etc., used in mosaic work

TETRASTYLE, having four columns at the end

THERMAE, originally simply baths, later elaborate buildings fitted with libraries, assembly rooms, gymnasia, circuses, etc.

THOLOS, a circular building (Greek)

TONDO, round painting or bas-relief

TRANSENNA, open grille or screen, usually of marble, in an early Christian church

TRAVERTINE, tufa quarried near Tivoli; the commonest of Roman building materials

TRICLINIUM, dining-room and reception-room of a Roman house

TRIGLYPH, small panel of a Doric frieze raised slightly and carved with three vertical channels

TRIPTYCH, painting or tablet in three sections

TROMPE L'OEIL, literally a deception of the eye. Used to describe illusionist decoration, painted architectural perspectives, etc.

TROPAEUM, (or Trophy), victory monument

TUMULUS, a burial mound

VELARIUM, canvas sheet supported by masts to protect the spectators in an open theatre from the sun

VERDE ANTICO, green marble from Tessaglia

ZOÖPHORUS, frieze of a Doric temple, so-called because the metopes were often decorated with figures of animals

PRACTICAL INFORMATION

Approaches to Rome

The Approaches from the North are described in 'Blue Guide Northern Italy'.

Information Offices. General information may be obtained in London from the *Italian State Tourist Office (E.N.I.T., Ente Nazionale Italiano per il Turismo)*, 1 Princes Street, W1R 8AY, who distribute free an invaluable 'Traveller's Handbook' (revised c every year), an annual list of hotels in Rome, a practical Guide and map to the city, etc. Their office in Rome is at No. 2 Via Marghera. The headquarters of the *Ente Provinciale per il Turismo di Roma* (E.P.T.) is at No. 11 Via Parigi; E.P.T. information offices at No. 5 Via Parigi, the main station (Termini; with hotel booking service), and Fiumicino airport.

Travel Agents (most of whom belong to the Association of British Travel Agents) sell travel tickets and book accommodation, and also organize inclusive tours and charter trips to Rome. These include: *C.I.T.*, 50 Conduit St., W.1. (agents for the Italian State Railways), *Thomas Cook & Son*, 45 Berkeley St., W.1., and other branches, *American Express*, 6 Haymarket, W.1., etc.

Passports or **Visitors Cards** are necessary for all British travellers entering Italy and must bear the photograph of the holder. American travellers must carry passports. Travellers are strongly advised to carry some means of identity with them at all times while in Italy.

Currency Regulations. Exchange controls have been suspended by the British Government since 1979. There are now no restrictions on the amount of sterling travellers may take out of Great Britain. There are frequent variations in the amount of Italian notes which may be taken in or out of Italy. Since there are normally strict limitations, the latest regulations should be checked before departure.

Money. In Italy the monetary unit is the Italian lira (pl. lire). Notes are issued for 1000, 2000, 5000, 10,000, 50,000 and 100,000 lire. Coins are of 5, 10, 20, 50, 100, 200 and 500 lire. The rate of exchange in 1988 is approximately 2,300 lire to the £ and 1,300 lire to the U.S. dollar. Travellers' cheques are the safest way of carrying money while travelling. Certain credit cards are generally accepted. For banking hours, see below. Money can also be changed at exchange offices ('cambio') at Fiumicino Airport and Termini Station (open all day, and sometimes until late at night). Hotels, restaurants, etc. normally give a lower rate of exchange.

Police Registration. Police Registration is required within three days of entering Italy. For travellers staying at a hotel the management will attend to the formality. The permit lasts three months, but can be extended on application.

Airports. Fiumicino (*Leonardo da Vinci*), 26km SW of Rome, served by an autostrada, is the airport for both international and internal air services. The *Town Air Terminal* is in Via Giolitti, at the side of Termini Station (airport buses depart every 15 minutes).—**Ciampino**, 13km SE of Rome, a subsidiary (used mainly for internal flights and international charter flights) of Fiumicino, is reached by underground (line A) from Termini station to 'Anagnina' station; then from

Osteria del Curato, the airport bus (A.CO.TRA.L.) leaves every hour, at half past the hour.

Railway Stations. Stazione Termini (Pl. 5; 4), Piazza dei Cinque-cento, the main station for all services of the State Railways and for the Underground Railway. **Stazione Roma Tiburtina** is used by some fast trains which do not stop at Stazione Termini. Less central than the main station, it is well served by buses.—Suburban stations (of little interest to the tourist) include *Roma Tuscolana, Ostiense, Trastevere, San Pietro,* and *Prenestina.*

European Bus Service. A bus service now operates in two days between London (Victoria Coach Station), and Rome (Piazza della Repubblica) via Florence. Information in London from the National Express Office at Victoria Coach Station, and in Rome from SITA office.

Driving in Rome. Most of the centre of the city is closed to private cars (without special permits) from 7–11, 15–19. Access to hotels is allowed. Many hotels have garages. Car parking is extremely dif-ficult anywhere in the city. It is never advisable to leave luggage etc. in parked cars. Visitors are strongly advised not to use a car in Rome; public transport has become much more efficient since the partial closure of the centre of the city to cars.

Hotels

Rome has numerous hotels all over the city. These are all listed with charges in the annual (free) publication of the E.P.T. of Rome: *'Alberghi di Roma e provincia'* (available from their offices). It is essential to book well in advance at Easter and in summer; to confirm the booking a deposit should be sent. Information about hotels in Rome may be obtained in London from the E.N.I.T. office, and on arrival at the tourist office at the railway station (which also has booking facilities), or at the information offices of the E.P.T.

Every hotel has its fixed charges agreed with the Provincial Tourist Board. In all hotels the service charges are included in the rates. V.A.T. is added at a rate of 9 per cent (14 per cent in 5-star hotels). However the total charge is exhibited on the back of the door of the hotel room. Breakfast should by law be a separate charge, but is now often included in the price of the room. Hotels are obliged by law (for tax purposes) to issue an official receipt to customers, who should not leave the premises without this document (*'ricevuta fiscale'*).

In 1986 a new classification of hotels in Italy was introduced by 'stars' as in the rest of Europe. At the same time, the official categories of 'pensione' and 'locanda' were abolished. There are now five official categories of hotels from the luxury 5-star hotels, to the most simple 1-star hotels. In the following list, the category of the hotel has been given. Hotels with more than 100 rooms (100 R) have been indicated. Rome has over 600 hotels and pensions and it has been thought necessary to give only a small selection; omission does not imply any derogatory judgement.

Accommodation in Rome and Environs

Near Termini Station. 5-STAR: **Grand Hotel et de Rome** (a; Pl. 4; 4), 3 Via V. E. Orlando, 180 R.—4-STAR: **Mediterraneo** (c; Pl. 4; 4), 15 Via Cavour, 280 R; **Mondial** (ii; Pl. 4; 4), 127 Via Torino; **Atlantico** (e; Pl. 4; 4), 23 Via Cavour (no restaurant); **Massimo d'Azeglio** (f; Pl. 5; 6), 18 Via Cavour, 210 R; **San Giorgio** (g; Pl. 5; 6), Via G. Améndola, 190 R; **Quirinale** (b; Pl. 4; 4), 7 Via Nazionale, 200 R; **Genova** (aa; Pl. 5; 6), 33 Via Cavour, 110 R.—3-STAR: **Esperia** (bb; Pl. 4; 4),

22 Via Nazionale, 100 R; **Nord-Nuova Roma** (cc; Pl. 4; 4), 3 Via G. Amendola, 160 R; **Diana** (dd; Pl. 4; 4), 4 Via Principe Amadeo, 180 R; **Impero** (ee; Pl. 4; 4), 19 Via Viminale; **San Remo** (ff; Pl. 4; 4) 36 Via M. d'Azeglio; **Tirreno** (gg; Pl. 4; 6), 17 Via San Martino ai Monti; **Rex** (hh; Pl. 4; 4), 149 Via Torino; **Ariston** (uu; Pl. 5; 6), Via Fil. Turati.—2-STAR: **Igea** (vv; Pl. 5; 6), 97 Via Principe Amadeo.

In the Ludovisi district and near Piazza Barberini. 5-STAR:**Ambasciatori Palace** (i; Pl. 4; 1), 70 Via Veneto, 140 R; **Excelsior** (j; Pl. 4; 1), 125 Via Veneto, 380 R; **Bernini-Bristol** (l; Pl. 4; 3), 23 Piazza Barberini, 130 R.—4-STAR: **Imperiale** (d; Pl. 4; 3), 24 Via Veneto; **Flora** (k; Pl. 4; 1), 191 Via Veneto, 180 R; **Regina Carlton** (n; Pl. 4; 1), 72 Via Veneto, 140 R; **Eliseo** (o; Pl. 4; 1), 30 Via di Porta Pinciana; **Savoia** (p; Pl. 4; 1), 15 Via Ludovisi, 110 R; **Victoria** (q; Pl. 4; 1), 41 Via Campania, 110 R; **Boston** (r; Pl. 4; 1), 47 Via Lombardia, 120 R; **Parco dei Principi**, 5 Via Frescobaldi.—3-STAR: **Alexandra** (jj; Pl. 4; 3), 18 Via Veneto.— 2-STAR: **Dinesen** (kk; Pl. 4; 1) 18 Via di Porta Pinciana.

Near Piazza di Spagna. 5-STAR: **Hassler-Villa Medici** (s; Pl. 4; 1), 6 Piazza Trinità dei Monti, 110 R.—4-STAR: **De La Ville** (t; Pl. 4; 3), 69 Via Sistina, 200 R; **Plaza** (n; Pl. 3; 4), 126 Via del Corso, 210 R; **Marini Strand** (v; Pl. 3; 4), 17 Via del Tritone, 120 R.—3-STAR: **Internazionale** (nn; Pl. 4; 3), 79 Via Sistina.

Near Piazza Colonna and the Pantheon. 4-STAR: **Nazionale** (x; Pl. 3; 4), 131 Piazza Montecitorio; **Raphael** (y; Pl. 2; 6), 2 Largo Febo.—3-STAR: **Tiziano** (qq; Pl. 3; 6), 110 Corso Vitt. Emanuele.

Near the Vatican. 4-STAR: **Michelangelo** (z; Pl. 1; 6), 14 Via Stazione di San Pietro 150 R.—3-STAR: **Columbus** (ss; Pl. 1; 6), 33 Via della Conciliazione, 100 R.

Monte Mario. 5-STAR: **Cavalieri Hilton** (tt; Pl. 15; 7), Via Cadlolo, 400 R.— 3-STAR: **Clodio** (rr; Pl. 15; 8), 10 Via Santa Lucia.

Hotels without restaurants. Near Termini Station. 3-STAR: *Columbia*, 15 Via Viminale; *Nizza*, 16 Via Massimo d'Azeglio; *Torino*, 8 Via Principe Amadeo, 100 R; *Touring*, 34 Via Principe Amadeo; *Patria*, 36 Via Torino.—2-STAR: *Alba*, 12 Via Leonina; *Doria*, 4 Via Merulana; *Capitol*, 77 Via Giov. Amendola; *Adria*, 58 Via Venti Settembre; *Hanover*, 4 Via Venti Settembre; *Aberdeen*, 48 Via Firenze (with restaurant); *Quisisana*, 107 Via Torino; *Magenta*, 39 Via Magenta; *Abadan*, 122 Via Torino; *Augustea*, 251 Via Nazionale; *Bel Soggiorno*, 117 Via Torino.

In and near Piazza di Spagna. 4-STAR: *d'Inghilterra*, 14 Via Bocca di Leone, 100 R.—3-STAR: *Lugano*, 132 Via del Tritone; *Concordia*, 15 Via Capo le Case. 2-STAR: *Homs*, 71 Via della Vite; *Ausonia*, 35 Piazza di Spagna; *Suisse*, 56 Via Gregoriana; *City*, 97 Via due Macelli; *Elite*, 49 Via F. Crispi.

Near Piazza Colonna and the Pantheon. 3-STAR: *Santa Chiara*, 21 Via Santa Chiara; *Cesari*, 89a Via di Pietra; *del Senato*, 73 Piazza della Rotonda; *Genio*, 28 Via G. Zanardelli; *Sole al Pantheon*, 63 Piazza della Rotonda.—2-STAR: *Abruzzi*, 69 Piazza della Rotonda; *Portoghesi*, 1 Via dei Portoghesi.

In the Ludovisi district and near Piazza Barberini. 2-STAR: *Merano*, 155 Via Veneto; *Amati*, 155 Via Veneto.

In the Parioli district. 2-STAR: *Paisiello Parioli*, 47 Via Paisiello.

To the N, NE and E of Porta Pia. 3-STAR: *Villa del Parco*, 110 Via Nomentana (with restaurant).—2-STAR: *Laura*, 109 Viale Ventuno Aprile; *Pilla*, 4 Viale Ventuno Aprile.

Aventine. 3-STAR: *Sant'Anselmo*, Piazza Sant'Anselmo.

Alberghi Diurni ('day hotels'), with bathrooms, hairdressers, cleaning services and other amenities but no sleeping accommodation: *Stazione Termini*; *Cobianchi*, 136 Via Cola di Rienzo (in Trastevere); *Damiani*, 32 Via Castelfidardo; *Allegrini*, 32 Via La Spezia.

Youth Hostels and Students' Hostels. *Italian Youth Hostels Association* (Associazione Italiana Alberghi per la Gioventù), 44 Via Cavour (Regional office, 2 Via Carlo Poma). The Rome Youth Hostel is the *Ostello del Foro Italico*, 61 Viale delle Olimpiadi. Enrolled university students can sometimes find accommodation at the 'Civis' International Students' House, 5 Viale Ministero degli Affari Esteri, *Y.W.C.A.*, 4 Via Balbo, and the *Ostello Marello*, 50 Via Urbana.

Religious organizations run some hostels for students and visitors (list available from the E.P.T.).

Camping. A list and location map of camping sites in Rome and environs can be obtained free from the *Federazione Italiana del Campeggio* at their headquarters, Caselle Postale 23, 50141 Calenzano, Firenze. Among the sites on the outskirts of Rome are: *Roma Camping*, Via Aurelia; *Capitol*, 45 Via Castelfusano, Ostia Antica; *Flaminio*, Via Flaminia; and *Nomentano*, Via della

Cesarina (corner of Via Nomentana). In the environs there are sites at Anzio, Nettuno, Bracciano, and Subiaco.

HOTELS IN THE ENVIRONS OF ROME.
Fregene. 3-STAR: *Golden Beach*; *La Conchiglia*.—**Lido di Ostia**. 3-STAR: *Sirenetta*; 2-STAR: *Belvedere, La Scaletta, Lido*.—**Albano Laziale**. 3-STAR: *Villa Maria*.—**Anzio**. 3-STAR: *Golfo*; 2-STAR: *La Bussola, La Tavernetta, Riviera*.—**Ariccia**. 2-STAR: *Paradiso*.—**Bracciano**. 2-STAR: *Casina del Lago*.—**Castel Gandolfo**. 2-STAR: *Lucia*.—**Frascati**. 3-STAR: *Flora*; 2-STAR: *Bellavista*.—**Genzano**. 2-STAR: *Villa Robinia*.—**Marino**. 2-STAR: *Villa Svizzera*.—**Nemi**. 2-STAR: *Al Bosco*.—**Nettuno**. 3-STAR: *Astura*.—**Palestrina**. 3-STAR: *Stella*.—**Rocca di Papa**. 3-STAR: *Europa, Angeletto*.—**Subiaco**. 2-STAR: *Belvedere*.—**Tivoli**. 4-STAR: Torre Sant'Angelo.

Restaurants and Cafés

Restaurants (*Ristoranti, Trattorie*) of all kinds and categories abound in Rome. The least pretentious restaurant usually provides the best value. Prices on the menu generally do not include a cover charge (*coperto*, shown separately on the menu) which is added to the bill. The service charge is now almost always automatically added at the end of the bill. Tipping is therefore not strictly necessary, but a few thousand lire are appreciated. The menu displayed outside the restaurant indicates the kind of charges the customer should expect. However, many simpler establishments do not offer a menu, and here, although the choice is usually limited the standard of the cuisine is often very high. Lunch is normally around 1 o'clock, and is the main meal of the day, while dinner is around 8 or 9 o'clock. Restaurants are now obliged by law (for tax purposes) to issue an official receipt to customers, who should not leave the premises without this document ('ricevuta fiscale').

It has become extremely difficult to recommend restaurants in Rome since they change hands frequently and the standard often deteriorates once they become well known. In the simplest trattorie the food is usually good, and considerably cheaper than in the well-known restaurants. However they are less comfortable, and do not often have tables outside. A selection of the most famous restaurants in the city (none of them inexpensive) is given below.

Near Piazza di Spagna. *Dal Bolognese*, 1–2 Piazza del Popolo; *Ranieri*, 26 Via Mario dei Fiori; *Al Moro*, 13 Vicolo delle Bollette.

Near the Pantheon. *l'Eau Vive*, 85 Via Monterone; *Alfredo alla Scrofa*, 104 Via della Scrofa; *Hostaria dell'Orso*, 93 Via Monte Brianzo; *El Toulá*, 29 Via della Lupa; *Il Passetto*, 14 Via G. Zanardelli; *Il Buco*, 8 Via Sant'Ignazio; *Hosteria 'La Maiella'*, Piazza Sant'Apollinare; *Carmelo alla Rosetta*, 9 Via della Rosetta.

Near the Corso Vittorio Emanuele. *Angelino a Tormargana*, 37 Piazza Margana; *Pierluigi*, 144 Piazza de' Ricci; *Vecchia Roma*, 18 Piazza Campitelli; *Piperno*, 9 Via Monte dei Cenci; *Taverna Giulia*, 23 Vicolo del'Oro; *Da Pancrazio*, Piazza Biscione.

In Trastevere. *Tentativo*, 5 Via della Luce; *Romolo*, 8 Via di Porta Settiminiana; *Pastarellaro*, 33 Via San Crisogono; *Corsetti*, Piazza San Cosimato; *Checco e carettiere*, 13 Via Benedetta; and many trattorie.

Near the Vatican, *Pierdonati*, 39 Via della Conciliazione.

Via Veneto area. *Le Jardin*, 5 Via De Notaris; *Piccolo Mondo*, 39 Via Aurora; *Girarrosto Toscano*, 29 Via Campania.

Parioli district. *Ambasciata d'Abruzzo*, 26 Via Pietro Tacchini.—Ponte Milvio. *La Vigna dei Cardinali*, 34 Piazzale Ponte Milvio.—Porta Pia. *Da Vincenzo*, 4 Via Castelfidardo.

There are a number of self-service restaurants in the centre of the city (including *Il Delfino*, 67 Corso Vittorio Emanuele, Largo Argentina), and pizzas and other good hot snacks are served in a *Pizzeria*, *Rosticceria*, and *Tavola Calda*. Some of these have no seating accommodation and sell food to take away or eat on the spot. Sandwiches ('panini') are made up on request at *Pizzicherie* and *Alimentari* (grocery shops), and *Fornai* (bakeries) often sell individual pizze, cakes, etc.

   Cafés (*Bar*) are open all day. The numerous excellent refreshments they serve are usually eaten standing up. The cashier should be paid first, and the receipt given to the barman in order to get served. If the customer sits at a table the charge is considerably higher (at least double) and he will be given waiter service (and should not pay first). Black coffee (*caffè* or *espresso*) can be ordered diluted (*lungo* or *alto*), with a dash of milk (*macchiato*), with a liquor (*corretto*), or with hot milk (*cappuccino* or *caffè-latte*). In summer cold coffee (*caffè freddo*) and cold coffee and milk (*caffè-latte freddo*) are served.

The best well-known cafés in the city which serve good snacks and all of which have tables (some outside) include *Caffè Greco*, 86 Via Condotti (a famous café, see Rte 8); *Babington* (English tea rooms), Piazza di Spagna; *Rosati*, 4 Piazza del Popolo; *Tre Scalini*, 31 Piazza Navona, noted for its *tartufi* (truffles) and ices; *Giolitti*, 40 Uffici dei Vicario (famous for its ice-creams); *Camilloni a Sant'Eustachio*, Piazza Sant'Eustachio; and *Doney* and *Caffè de Paris*, 90 and 145 Via Veneto.—*Pascucci*, Via di Torre Argentina, is justly famous for its fresh fruit milk-shakes. *La Casa del Caffè*, Via degli Orfani (near the Pantheon) serves particularly good coffee.

Picnic Places. Excellent food for picnics may be purchased from grocery shops, bakeries, cafés, *rosticcerie*, etc. Some of the most pleasant spots in the city to have a picnic include: the Palatine hill, the Parco Savelli on the Aventine, the Borghese gardens, the Pincio, the Belvedere di Monte Tarpeo on the Capitol Hill, the Circus Maximus, the Villa Doria Pamphilj, the public gardens off Via del Quirinale, the Parco Oppio, the Villa Celimontana on the Celian hill, the Janiculum hill, the Parco dei Scipioni (between Via di Porta Latina and Via di Porta San Sebastiano), and on the Appian Way (in the Circus Maxentius or beyond the tomb of Cecilia Metella).

Food and Wine. The chief speciality of Italian cookery is the *pasta asciutta*, served in various forms with different sauces and sprinkled with cheese. Rome has its specialities and some of its restaurants are famous for them. *Fettuccine* are ribbon noodles, often served with butter and cheese, or 'alla Matriciana', with a salt pork and tomato sauce. *Gnocchi alla Romana* is a heavy dish made from potato, flour and eggs. Young artichokes are served in many different ways; among them are *cariciofi alla giudia*, that is cooked in oil. An unexpected dish is *fichi col prosciutto*, green figs with Parma ham. Among the main dishes are *Abbacchio*, roast suckling lamb and *Saltimbocca alla Romana*, veal escalope with ham and sage. *Trippa al sugo* is stewed tripe, served with a sauce and tomatoes. Another traditional dish is *Coda alla vaccinara*, oxtail cooked with herbs and wine. *Zuppa di pesce* is a rich fish stew, usually made with a wide variety of fish. Cheese specialities include *ricotta*, made from ewe milk; *pecorino*, a stronger hard cheese made from ewe milk; *mozzarella*, made from buffalo milk, the cheese used in pizzas (also 'affumicato', smoked). Roman confectionery, cakes, pastries, and ices are renowned.

   Wines. The most famous wines of Lazio are the Vini dei Castelli; pre-eminent among these are the white wines of *Frascati*, *Grottaferrata*,

Albano, and *Genzano,* with their clear amber tint, their characteristic bouquet, and their occasionally piquant flavour. The red Castelli wines, of which *Marino* and *Velletri* are the most liked, are stronger. It is often advisable to accept the 'house wine' (white and red usually available) which is suggested at a restaurant. This varies a great deal, but is normally a 'vin ordinaire' of average standard and reasonable price.

The MENU which follows includes many dishes that are likely to be available in Roman restaurants:

Antipasti, Hors d'oeuvre

Prosciutto crudo o cotto, ham, raw or cooked
Prosciutto e melone, ham (usually raw) and melon
Salame, salami
Salame con funghi e carciofini sott'olio, salami with mushrooms and artichokes in oil
Salsicce, dry sausage
Tonno, tunny fish
Frittata, omelette
Verdura cruda, raw vegetables
Carciofi o finocchio in pinzimonio, raw artichokes or fennel with a dressing
Antipasto misto, mixed cold hors d'oeuvre
Antipasto di mare, seafood hors d'oeuvre

Minestre e Pasta, Soups and Pasta

Minestra, zuppa, thick soup
Brodo, clear soup
Stracciatella, broth with beaten egg
Minestrone alla toscana, Tuscan vegetable soup
Spaghetti al sugo or *al ragù,* spaghetti with a meat sauce
Spaghetti al pomodoro, spaghetti with a tomato sauce
Penne all'arrabbiata, short pasta with a rich spicy sauce
Timbalo, a rich pasta dish cooked in the oven
Tagliatelle, flat spaghetti-like pasta, almost always made with egg
Lasagne, layers of pasta with meat filling and cheese and tomato sauce
Cannelloni, rolled pasta 'pancakes' with meat filling and cheese and tomato sauce
Ravioli, filled with spinach and ricotta cheese
Tortellini, small coils of pasta, filled with a rich stuffing served either in broth or with a sauce
Agnolotti, ravioli filled with meat
Fettuccine, ribbon noodles
Spaghetti alla carbonara, spaghetti with bacon, beaten egg, and black pepper sauce
Spaghetti alla matriciana, spaghetti with salt pork and tomato sauce
Spaghetti alle vongole, spaghetti with clams
Cappelletti, form of ravioli often served in broth
Gnocchi, a heavy pasta made from potato, flour and eggs
Risotto, rice dish
Risi e bisi, risotto with peas and ham
Polenta, yellow maize flour, usually served with a meat or tomato sauce

Pesce, Fish

Zuppa di pesce, mixed fish usually in a sauce (or soup)
Fritto misto di mare, mixed fried fish
Fritto di pesce, fried fish
Pesce arrosto, Pesce alla griglia, roast, grilled fish
Pescespada, sword-fish
Aragosta, lobster (an expensive delicacy)
Calamari, squid
Sarde, sardines
Coda di Rospo, angler fish
Dentice, dentex
Orata, bream
Triglie, red mullet
Sgombro, mackerel
Baccalà, salt cod

Anguilla (con piselli in umido), eel (stewed with peas)
Sogliola sole
Tonno, tunny fish
Trota, trout
Cozze, mussels
Gamberi, prawns
Polipi, octopus
Seppie, cuttlefish
Sampiero, John Dory

Pietanze, Entrées

Vitello, veal
Manzo, beef
Agnello, lamb
Maiale (arrosto), pork (roast)
Pollo (bollito), chicken (boiled)
Petto di Pollo, chicken breasts
Pollo alla Cacciatora, chicken with herbs, and (usually) tomato and pimento sauce
Bistecca alla Fiorentina, rib steak (grilled over charcoal)
Costoletta alla Bolognese, veal cutlet with ham, covered with melted cheese
Abbacchio, roast sucking lamb
Costolette Milanese, veal cutlets, fried in breadcrumbs
Saltimbocca, rolled veal with ham
Scaloppine al marsala, veal escalope cooked in wine
Bocconcini, as above, with cheese
Ossobuco, stewed shin of veal
Coda alla vaccinara, oxtail cooked with herbs and wine
Porchetta, roast suckling pig, with herbs, fennel, etc.
Arista, pork chop
Stufato, stewed meat served in slices in a sauce
Polpette, meat balls (often served in a sauce)
Involtini, thin rolled slices of meat in a sauce
Coratella d'abbacchio, stew of young lamb's liver, heart, etc.
Spezzatino, veal stew, usually with pimento, tomato, onion, peas, and wine
Cotechino e Zampone, pig's trotter stuffed with pork and sausages
Stracotto, beef cooked in a sauce, or in red wine
Trippa, tripe
Fegato, liver
Tacchino arrosto, roast turkey
Cervello, brains
Rognoncini trifolati, sliced kidneys in a sauce
Animelle, sweetbreads
Bollito, stew of various boiled meats
Fagiano, pheasant
Coniglio, rabbit
Lepre, hare
Cinghiale, wild boar
Piccione, pigeon

Contorni, vegetables

Insalata verde, green salad
Insalata mista, mixed salad
Pomodori, tomatoes
Pomodori ripieni, stuffed tomatoes
Funghi, mushrooms
Spinaci, spinach
Broccoletti, tender broccoli
Piselli, peas
Fagiolini, beans (French)
Carciofi, artichokes
Asparagi, asparagus
Zucchine, courgettes
Melanzane, aubergine
Melanzane alla parmigiana, aubergine in cheese sauce
Peperoni, pimentoes
Finocchi, fennel
Patatine fritte, fried potatoes
Insalata di Puntarelle, a typical Roman salad served with garlic and anchovies

Dolci, Sweets

Torta, tart
Monte Bianco, mont blanc (with chestnut flavouring)
Saint Honore, meringue
Gelato, ice cream
Zuppa inglese, trifle
Crostata, fruit flan

Frutta, Fruit

Macedonia di frutta, fruit salad
Fragole con panna, strawberries and cream
Fragole al limone, ... with lemon
Fragole al vino, ... with wine
Fragoline di bosco, wild strawberries (in May and June)
Mele, apples
Pere, pears
Arance, oranges
Ciliege, cherries
Pesche, peaches
Albicocche, apricots
Uva, grapes
Fichi, figs
Melone, melon
Popone, watermelon (*Anguria* and *Cocomero* are also common names for
watermelon)

Transport

Buses provide a good means of transport in Rome where most of the
centre of the city has been closed to private traffic. The service is run
by A.T.A.C. (Information offices, Piazza dei Cinquecento, outside the
station, and 65 Via Volturno; Tel. 46951). Tickets are obtained from
tobacconists, bars, and newspaper kiosks, as well as the A.T.A.C.
information offices. There are also daily tickets valid for 24 hours on
any line; half-day tickets; and monthly season tickets. A weekly
tourist ticket may be purchased at the Information Office, Piazza dei
Cinquecento. Tickets are stamped at an automatic machine on
board. Because of one-way streets, return journeys do not always
follow the same route as the outward journey. A selection of the more
important routes is given below. A map may usually be purchased at
the Information office, Piazza dei Cinquecento.

Buses

119 An electric mini-bus which serves the centre of the city on a circular route.
Piazza Augusto Imperatore—Via della Ripetta—Via Monte Brianzo—Via della
Dogana Vecchia—Pantheon—Via dei Pastini—Piazza Colonna—Via del
Tritone—Via Due Macelli—Piazza di Spagna—Via del Babuino—Piazza del
Popolo—Via della Ripetta—Piazza Augusto Imperatore

53 (weekdays only) Piazza San Silvestro—Largo Tritone—Piazza Barberini—
Via Po (for Galleria Borghese)

56 Largo Argentina—Piazza Venezia—Via del Corso—Largo Tritone—Piazza
Barberino—Via Veneto—Via Po (for Galleria Borghese)

60 Piazza Sonnino—Ponte Garibaldi—Largo Argentina—Piazza Venezia—Via
del Corso—Largo del Tritone —Piazza Barberini—Via XX Settembre—Porta
Pia—Via Nomentana—Piazza Sempione

64 Stazione Termini—Via Nazionale—Piazza Venezia—Corso Vittorio
Emanuele—San Pietro.

70 Via Giolitti—Santa Maria Maggiore—Via Nazionale—Piazza Venezia—
Largo Argentina—Corso Rinascimento—Ponte Cavour—Piazza Cavour—Viale
Giulio Cesare—Piazzale Clodio

71 Via Giolitti—Traforo Umberto I—Piazza San Silvestro

85 Piazza San Silvestro—Piazza Venezia—Colosseum—San Giovanni in Laterano

87 Corso Rinascimento—Largo Argentina—Piazza Venezia—Via dei Fori Imperiali—Colosseum—San Giovanni in Laterano

90 Piazza Venezia—Via del Teatro di Marcello—Terme di Caracalla—Porta Metronia—Piazza Zama

93 Stazione Termini—Santa Maria Maggiore—San Giovanni in Laterano—Porta Metronia—Terme di Caracalla—Via Cristoforo Colombo—Stazione E.U.R.

94 Largo Argentina—Piazza Venezia—The Aventine—Via G. A. Sartorio

95 Piazzale Ostiense—Lungotevere Aventino—Piazza Bocca della Verità—Via del Teatro di Marcello—Piazza Venezia —Via del Corso—Via del Tritone—Via Vittorio Veneto—Villa Borghese—Piazzale Flaminio

97 Viale della Tecnica (E.U.R.)—Viale Marconi—Viale Trastevere—Piazza Sonnino

118 (less frequent service) San Giovanni in Laterano—Colosseum—Terme di Caracalla—Porta San Sebastiano (return by Via di Porta Latina)—Via Appia Antica—Catacombs of San Calisto—Catacombs of San Sebastiano—Tomb of Cecilia Metella—Via Appia Pignatelli—Largo dei Claudiani (Via Appia Nuova)

218 San Giovanni in Laterano—Piazza Epiro—Piazza Galeria—Via di Porta Latina—Via Appia Antica—Fosse Ardeatine

223 Basilica San Paolo—Abbazia Tre Fontane

Trams

30 Monteverde—Viale Trastevere—Ponte Sublicio—Porta San Paolo—Colosseum—Porta San Giovanni—Porta Maggiore—Piazzale Verano—Viale Regina Margherita—Piazza Ungheria—Viale Belle Arti—Ponte Matteotti—Viale delle Milizie—Piazza Risorgimento

19 Centocelle—Via Prenestina—Porta Maggiore—Piazzale Verano—Viale Regina Margherita—Piazza Ungheria—Viale Belle Arti

13 Porta Maggiore—Piazza Santa Croce—San Giovanni in Laterano—Colosseum—Piazza di Porta Capena—Piazzale Ostiense—Ponte Sublicio—Viale di Trastevere

Night Service

Tram **30** operates throughout the night on a slightly modified route

60 Piazza Sonnino—Piazza Venezia—Piazza Barberini—Via Nomentana—Tufello

75 (barred). Largo Argentina—Viale Trastevere—Monteverde

78 Piazzale Clodio—Piazzale Flaminio—Piazza Cavour—Corso Rinascimento—Piazza Venezia—Stazione Termini

Underground Railway. *Line A*, opened in 1980, runs from near the Vatican (Via Ottaviano) via Piazzale Flaminio, Piazza di Spagna, and Piazza Barberini, to Termini Station. From there it continues to San Giovanni and the S suburbs of Rome along the Via Appia Nuovo and Via Tuscolana to beyond Cincecittà. It runs underground for the whole of its length (14km) except for the bridge across the Tiber. The intermediate stops are: *Ottaviano, Lepanto, Flaminio, Spagna, Barberini, Repubblica, Termini, Vittorio, Manzoni, San Giovanni, Re di Roma, Ponte Lungo, Furio Camillo, Colli Albani, Arco di Travertino, Porta Furba, Numidio Quadrato, Lucio Sestio, Guilio Agricola, Subaugusta, Cinecittà,* and *Anagnina.*

Line B, opened in 1952, runs SW from Stazione Termini to *Porta San Paolo*, in Piazzale Ostiense, where it comes to the surface just beyond the station of that name, running from there alongside the Rome-Lido railway as far as *Magliana*, beyond the Basilica of San Paolo fuori le Mura. It then runs underground (NE) to terminate at *Tre Fontane (Laurentina)*. There are intermediate stations at *Via Cavour, Colosseo, Circo Massimo, Piramide (Porta San Paolo), Garbatella, San Paolo, Magliana,* and *E.U.R.* There are plans to extend this line from the station to the Policlinico, Tiburtina, as far as Rebibbia.—A service also runs from Termini via San Paolo to *Ostia Antica* and *Ostia Lido.*

Taxis (yellow in colour) are provided with taximeters; it is advisable to make sure these are operational before hiring a taxi. They are hired from ranks; there are no cruising taxis. For Radio taxis dial 3570, 3875, 4994, or 8433. Additional night charge (22–7); and for each piece of luggage. Modest tipping is expected. Horse Cabs are now used exclusively by tourists. The fare must be established before starting the journey.

Bicycle Hire. Stands in Piazza del Popolo, Via dei Pellegrini, etc.

Car Hire. The principle car-hire firms have offices at Fiumicino airport and at Termini station as well as in the centre of Rome. The main car-hire firms include: *Hertz*, 28 Via Sallustiana; *Maggiore*, 8 Via Po, 57 Piazza della Repubblica; *Avis*, 1 Piazza Esquilino, 38 Via Sardegna.

Sight-seeing Tours of Rome and environs. Tours of Rome are run by A.T.A.C. (see above). Bus No. 110 departs from Piazza dei Cinquecento daily in summer at 15.30, and in winter on Saturday, Sunday, and fest. at 14.30. The tour lasts c 3hrs. CIT and American Express also organize tours of the city and environs, and provide long-distance excursions.

Boat trips on the Tiber from Porto di Ripa Grande (Porta Portese) to Ostia Antica (return trip: 9.30–17.30). Information from the E.P.T., 5 Via Parigi.

Coach and train services in the environs. There is no central coach station in Rome; the coaches start from and return to various squares or streets. In some instances there is a booking office; in others, tickets are bought on board. The services are run by A.CO.TRA.L. (Azienda Consortile Trasporti Lazio), 25 Via Portonaccio (Tel. 57531). For further details about transport in the environs, see the beginning of Rtes 28–35. *Castro Pretorio* for buses to Tivoli; *Piazza dei Cinquecento* for Palestrina; *Viale Castro Pretorio* for Subiaco; *Via Lepanto* for Cerveteri; *E.U.R.* underground station ('Fermi') for Anzio and Nettuno; *'Anagnina'* underground station for the Alban Hills.

TRAIN SERVICES *Stazione Termini* for Anzio and Nettuno, Cerveteri, and Velletri.—*Porta San Paolo* (Pl. 8; 7), Piazzale Ostiense, for trains (of the Ferrovia Roma-Lido) to *Ostia Antica* and *Lido di Ostia.*

Useful Addresses

Information Offices and Tourist Agents. *E.N.I.T. (Ente Nazionale Italiano per il Turismo)*, 2 Via Marghera (Tel. 49711); *E.P.T. (Ente Provinciale per il Turismo)*, 11 Via Parigi (Tel. 461851), and 5 Via Parigi (Tel. 463748).—*C.I.T. (Compagnia Italiana Turismo)*, 64 Piazza della Repubblica, Stazione Termini, etc; *American Express Co.*, 38–40 Piazza di Spagna; *Italturist*, 114 Via Quattro Novembre; *Agriturist*, 101 Corso Vittorio Emanuele.—STUDENT TRAVEL OFFICES: *A.T.G.*, 47 Via di Torre Argentina; C.T.G., 49 Via Piave; *C.T.S.*, 16 Via Genova; *European Student Travel Centre*, 55 Largo Brancaccio.

Head Post Office (Pl. 3; 4), Piazza San Silvestro, open weekdays 8.30–21; Sat 8.30–12 (open until 21 for the issue of mail addressed 'fermo posta' and for the acceptance of special delivery registered mail only). *Telegraph* and *Telephone Offices*, open always.

Public Offices. For emergencies, Tel. 113. *Questura* (Central Police Station), 15 Via San Vitale (Tel. 4686). Office for Foreigners, 2 Via Genova (Tel. 4686/2987). City Police (emergencies: Tel. 67691).—AIRPORTS: *Fiumicino* (Tel. 60121); *Ciampino* (Tel. 4694).—MAIN RAILWAY STATION (*Termini*), Information (Tel. 4775); Lost Property

Office (Tel. 4730).—CITY TRANSPORT: *A.T.A.C.*, 65 Via Volturno, & Piazza dei Cinquecento (Tel. 46951).

Motoring Organizations. *Automobile Club d'Italia (A.C.I)*, 8 Via Marsala (for breakdowns, Tel. 116); *Touring Club Italiano*, 7 Via Ovidio; *Rome Automobile Club*, 261 Via C. Colombo.

Airline Offices. *Alitalia*, 13 Via Bissolati; *British Airways*, 48–54 Via Bissolati; *T.W.A.*, 67 Via Barberini; *Pan American*, 46 Via Bissolati; *Air France*, 93 Via Veneto; *K.L.M.*, 76 Via Bissolati; *Air Canada*, 63 Via Barberini.

Medical Services. 24-hour service run by the Municipality of Rome, 20 Via del Colosseo (Tel. 4756741). For emergencies, Tel 113. *San Giovanni*, Accident Hospital ('Pronto Soccorso'), for road accidents and other emergencies (Tel. 77051). *Policlinico* (Tel. 49971). Some chemists remain open all night and on holidays (listed in the daily newspapers).

Banks are usually open Monday–Friday, 8.30–13.30, and for one hour in the afternoon (usually 14.45–15.45). They are closed on Saturday and holidays. *Banca Commerciale Italiana*, 226 Via del Corso; *Banca d'Italia*, 91 Via Nazionale; *Banco di Roma*, 307 Via del Corso; *Credito Italiano*, 374 Via del Corso; *Banca d'America e d'Italia*, 161 Largo del Tritone; *Banco di Santo Spirito*, 18 Piazza del Parlamento; *First National City Bank*, 26 Via Boncompagni.

Embassies. British Embassy (and Consulate) to Italy, 80 Via XX Settembre; British Embassy to the Holy See, 91 Via Condotti.—American Embassy (and Consulate) to Italy, 119 Via Veneto.

Learned Institutions and Cultural Societies. *British School at Rome*, 61 Via Antonio Gramsci (Valle Giulia); *British Council*, Palazzo del Drago, 20 Via delle Quattro Fontane; *American Academy*, 5 Via Angelo Masina; *French Academy*, Villa Medici, 1 Viale Trinità dei Monti; *Goethe Institut*, 267 Via del Corso; *German Archaeological Institute*, 79 Via Sardegna.—*Università degli Studi*, Viale dell'Università (Città Universitaria); *Istituto Nazionale di Archeologia e Storia dell'Arte*, 3 Piazza Venezia; *Accademia dei Lincei*, 10 Via della Lungara; *Società Italiana Dante Alighieri* (with Italian language courses), 27 Piazza Firenze; *Istituto Centrale del Restauro*, Istituto di San Michele, Ripa Grande, and 9 Piazza San Francesco di Paola; *Società Geografica Italiana*, 12 Via della Navecella (Villa Celimontana); *Accademia Filarmonica Romana*, 116 Via Flaminia; *Accademia Nazionale di Santa Cecilia*, 6 Via Vittoria.—*Associazione Italia Nostra*, 287 Corso Vittorio Emanuele; *Amici dei Musei di Roma*, Palazzo Braschi (Piazza San Pantaleo).

Libraries. *Biblioteca Nazionale Centrale*, Viale Castro Pretorio; *Istituto Nazionale di Archeologia e Storia dell'Arte*, 3 Piazza Venezia; *Archivio di Stato*, 40 Corso Rinascimento; *Biblioteca Alessandrina Universitaria*, Città Universitaria; *Biblioteca Hertziana*, 28 Via Gregoriana; *Biblioteca Angelica*, 8 Piazza Sant' Agostino; *Gabinetto Fotographico Nazionale*, 1 Piazza di Porta Portese; *English Library*, 20 Via delle Quattro Fontane; *American Library*, 62 Via Veneto.

Churches and Church Ceremonies

St Peter's and the other three great basilicas are open all day (7–19). Other churches are usually closed between 12 and 15.30, 16 or 17, but almost all of them open at 7 a.m. Some churches, including several of importance, are open only for a short time in the morning and evening, but admission at other times may sometimes be obtained on application to the sacristan, who generally lives nearby. The sacristan will also show closed chapels, crypts, etc. and a small tip should be given. Many pictures and frescoes are difficult to see without lights which are often coin operated (100 lire coins). A torch and a pair of binoculars are especially useful to study fresco cycles, etc. During Passion Week and for part of Holy Week many works of art in churches are veiled and are not shown. Some churches now ask that sightseers do not enter during a service, but normally visitors may do so, provided they are silent and do not approach the altar in use. Churches in Rome are very often not orientated. In the text the terms N and S refer to the liturgical N (left) and S (right), taking the high altar as at the E end.

The four great or PATRIARCHAL BASILICAS are *San Giovanni in Laterano* (St John Lateran; the cathedral and mother church of the world), *San Pietro in Vaticano* (St Peter's), *San Paolo fuori le Mura*, and *Santa Maria Maggiore*. These, with the three basilicas of *San Lorenzo fuori le Mura*, *Santa Croce in Gerusalemme*, and *San Sebastiano*, comprise the 'Seven Churches of Rome'. Among minor basilicas rank *Sant'Agnese fuori le Mura*, *Santi Apostoli*, *Santa Cecilia*, *San Clemente*, and *Santa Maria in Trastevere*.

Ave Maria or **Angelus**. The ringing of the evening Ave Maria bell at sunset is an important event in Rome, where it signifies the end of the day and the beginning of night. The hour varies according to the season.

Roman Catholic Services. On Sunday and, in the principal churches, often on weekdays, Mass is celebrated up to 13 and from 17 until 20. High Mass, with music, is celebrated in the basilicas (see above) on Sunday at 9.30 or 10.30 (10.30 in St Peter's). Confessions are heard in English in the four main basilicas and in the Gesù, Santa Maria sopra Minerva, Sant'Anselmo, Sant'Ignazio, and Santa Sabina.

ROMAN CATHOLIC SERVICES IN ENGLISH take place in San Silvestro in Capite, St Thomas of Canterbury, and Santa Susanna; in Irish at St Patrick's, Sant'Isidoro, San Clemente and Sant' Agata dei Goti.

Church Festivals. On saints' day mass and vespers with music are celebrated in the churches dedicated to the saints concerned.— Octave of the Epiphany at Sant'Andrea della Valle.—Blessing the lambs at Sant'Agnese Fuori le Mura, 21 January c 10.30.—Procession with the Santo Bambino at Santa Maria in Aracoeli, 6 January in the evening.—Holy Week liturgy on Wednesday, Thursday, and Friday in Holy Week, at St Peter's, St John Lateran, Santa Croce, and other churches.

Audience of the Pope, see Rte 27.

British and American Churches. *All Saints* (Anglican), 153 Via del Babuino; *St Paul's* (American Episcopal), Via Nazionale; *St Andrew's*

(Scottish Presbyterian), 7 Via Venti Settembre; *Methodist*, 38 Via Firenze; *Christian Science Society*, 42 Via dei Giardini.

Jewish Synagogue. Lungotevere dei Cenci.

Theatres, Annual Festivals, etc.

Theatres. *Argentina*, Largo di Torre Argentina; *Valle* (Pl. 3; 6), Via del Teatro Valle; *Eliseo*, 183 Via Nazionale; *Delle Arti*, 59 Via Sicilia; *Delle Muse*, 43 Via Forlì; *Parioli*, 20 Via G. Borsi; *Quirino*, 1 Via Marco Minghetti; *Goldoni*, 3 Vicolo di Soldati, and many others.

Concert Halls. *Accademia Nazionale di Santa Cecilia*, 7 Via dei Greci (chamber music; in summer at the Basilica of Constantine); *Auditorium del Foro Italico*, 26 Lungotevere Diaz; *Oratorio del Gonfalone*, 32 Via del Gonfalone; *San Leone Magno*, 38 Via Bolzano; *Teatro Olimpico*, 17 Piazza Gentile da Fabriano.—**Opera**: *Teatro dell'Opera* (Pl. 4; 4), Via del Viminale (December to May); in summer at Terme di Caracalla.

Annual Festivals. *Epiphany (Befana)*, on the night of 5–6 January, celebrated in Piazza Navona; *Carnival* is celebrated in the streets and piazze on Shrove Tuesday; *Festa di San Giovanni*, on the night of 23–24 June, near the Porta San Giovanni; *Festa di San Giuseppe*, 19 March, celebrated in the Trionfale district; *Festa della Repubblica*, first Sunday in June, military parade in the Via dei Fori Imperiali; *Anniversary of the Birth of Rome*, 21 April celebrated on the Campidoglio; *Festa di Noantri*, celebrations in Trastevere for several weeks in July.

Sport. Horse Racing under the auspices of the *Federazione Italiana Sport Equestri (F.I.S.E.)*, Foro Italico. At the racecourses of *Le Capanelle*, Via Appia Nuova, *Tor di Valle*, Via del Mare, *Tor di Quinto*, Viale Tor di Quinto, and *Piazza di Siena*, Villa Borghese (international horse-show in April–May).—Polo. *Campo del Roma Polo Club*, Viale dell'Acqua Acetosa.—Football. *Federazione Italiana Gioco Calcio*, 70 Viale Tiziano; ground in the Stadio Flaminio.—Golf. *Federazione Italiana Golf*, 70 Viale Tiziano; *Circolo del Golf di Roma*, Via Appia Nuova, near Acqua Santa.—Lawn Tennis. *Nuovo Circolo Tennis Club Parioli*, Via di Ponte Salario, Forte Antenne; *Federazione Italiana Tennis*, 70 Viale Tiziano. Tennis courts in the grounds of the Foro Italico, and in the *Centro Tre Fontane* at E.U.R.—Swimming Baths (covered and open-air) in the *Foro Italico*, and *E.U.R.* (open-air).

Museums, Collections, and Monuments

The table below gives the hours of admission to the various museums, galleries, and monuments in Rome, in force in 1988. *Opening times vary and often change without warning*; those given below should therefore be accepted with reserve. All museums, etc. are usually closed on the main public holidays: 1 January, Easter Day, 25 April, 1 May, 15 August, and Christmas Day. On other holidays (see below) they open only in the morning (9–13). More and more museums are introducing longer opening hours, and staying open also on Mondays (which used to be the standard closing day for all State-owned musuems). Admission charges are normally between

Lire 2000 and Lire 5000. British citizens under the age of 18 and over the age of 60 are entitled to free admission to State-owned museums and monuments.

Lecture tours of museums, villas etc. (sometimes otherwise closed to the public) are organized by the '*Amici dei Musei di Roma*'. These are advertised in the local press and on a duplicated sheet obtainable at most museums. Museum Week (*Settimana dei Musei Italiani*) has now become established as an annual event (usually in April or May). Entrance to most museums is free during the week, and some have longer opening hours, and private collections may be specially opened.

The museums owned by the Comune of Rome have been marked 'C' in the Museum table below.

Hours of Admission to the Museums, Collections and Monuments in Rome

Name	Open (see Note x)	Page
Accademia di San Luca	Monday, Wednesday, Friday, and last Sunday of the month, 10–13	154
Alto Medio Evo, Museo dell'	9–14; Sunday 9–13	286
Antiquarium Comunale	closed indefinitely	68
Antiquarium of the Forum	partially closed; adm as for the Forum	89
Ara Pacis Augustae	(C) 9–13.30; Sunday 9–13; closed Monday (in summer usually also 16–19 on Tuesday, Thursday, and Saturday)	147
Arti e Tradizioni Popolari, Museo delle	9–14; Sunday 9–13 (sometimes 9–17 on weekdays)	285
Auditorium of Maecenas	(C) see note b	193
Barberini Gallery	daily 9–14	177
Barracco, Museo	(C) closed in 1988	128
Bessarion, House of Cardinal	(C) closed in 1988	221
Borghese Gallery	upper floor only open in 1988: 9–19; Monday 9–14; Sunday 9–13	162
Burcardo, Raccolta Teatrale del	closed in 1988	119
Calcografia Nazionale	9–13 except Sunday	154
Canonica, Museo	(C) usually open 9–13 except Monday	160
Capitoline Museums	(C) daily except Monday 9–13.30; Tuesday & Saturday also 17–20 in winter, and 20–23 in summer	55
Caracalla, Baths of	9–two hours before sunset; Sunday and Monday, 9–14	218
Casino Pallavicini	1st of every month 10–12, 15–17	175
Castel Sant'Angelo	winter: 9–14, Sunday 9–13; Monday 14–19; summer: 9–19, Sunday 9–13; Monday closed	269
Catacombs (see note e)	normally 8.30–12 and 14.30 (or 15) to dusk	237
Priscilla	closed Monday	253
Sant'Agnese	9–12, 16–18; Sunday 16–18	249
San Callisto	closed Wednesday	237
Santa Domitilla	closed Tuesday	242
San Sebastiano	closed Thursday	241
Circus of Maxentius and Tomb of Romulus	(C) 9–13.30; Sunday 9–12.30; closed Monday	242
Civiltà Romana, Museo della	(C) weekdays except Monday 9–13.30, Sunday 9–13; Thursday also 16–19	286
Colonna Galleria	Saturday only 9–13	151
Colosseum	9–two hours before sunset; Sunday & Wednesday 9–13	110
Corsini Gallery	9–19; Sunday 9–13; Monday 9–14	260
Diocletian, Baths of	see Museo Nazionale Romano	
Domus Aurea of Nero	see note f	

Doria Pamphilj Gallery	Sunday, Tuesday, Friday, Saturday 10–13; private apartments shown at 10.30 and 12	140
Ethnographic and Prehistoric Museum (Luigi Pigorini)	daily 9–14; Sunday 9–13	285
Farnese, Palazzo	adm by previous written appointment	134
Folklore Museum	9–13.30; Sunday 9–12.30; closed Monday; Tuesday and Thursday also 17–19.30	259
Forum, Roman, and Palatine	9–one hr before sunset; Sunday & Tuesday 9–13	73
Forum of Augustus, Forum of Nerva, and Antiquarium	(C) closed in 1988	106
Forum of Caesar	(C) closed	105
Forum of Trajan	see Markets of Trajan	
Galleria Comunale d'Arte Moderna	closed in 1988	174
Galleria Nazionale d'Arte Antica	see Barberini Gallery, and Corsini Gallery	
Galleria Nazionale d'Arte Moderna	(partially closed) 9–14; Sunday 9–13; closed Monday	165
Genio, Museo del	by appointment	276
Geologico, Museo	adm with written permission	181
Goethe Museum	closed in 1988	148
Jewish Museum	Monday–Thursday 9.30–14, 15–17; Friday 9.30–13.30; Sunday 9.30–12; closed Saturday	226
Keats' House	9–13, 14.30–17 (summer 9–12, 15.30–18), closed Saturday & Sunday	157
Maltese Villa, church and garden	permission from the Cancelleria, 68 Via Condotti	234
Mamertine Prison	daily, 9–12.30, 14–17.30	105
Markets and Forum of Trajan	(C) Forum closed in 1988; Markets: 9–13.30; April– September 9–13.30, 16–19; Sunday 9–13; closed Monday	103
Mausoleum of Augustus	(C) closed (see note b)	146
Medicine, National Museum of	by appointment, weekdays, 9–13	277
Museo delle Mura (Porta San Sebastiano)	9–13.30; Tuesday, Thursday & Saturday also 16–dusk; closed Monday	223
Museo Nazionale Romano, Baths of Diocletian	almost totally closed in 1988; 9–14; 9–18 in summer; closed Monday	183
Musical Instruments, Museum of	9–13.30; Sunday 9–12.30; closed Monday	205
Napoleonic Museum	(C) 9–13.30; Sunday 9–13; Thursday also 17–20; closed Monday	139
Numismatico, Museo della Zecca	weekdays 9–11	181
Oriental Museum	9–14; Sunday 9–13; Thursday also 15.30–19	193
Palatine	see Roman Forum	
Palatine Antiquarium	closed in 1988	99
Pallavicini Gallery	adm only with special permission	175
Pantheon	mid-October–June, 9–14; July–September 9–18	113
Porta Maggiore, Basilica di	closed in 1988, but see note f	206
Poste e Telecomunicazioni, Museo Storico delle	daily except Monday & Sunday 9–13	276
Risorgimento, Museo Centrale del	closed in 1988	70
Roma, Museo di	(C) closed in 1988	121
Sepolcreto Ostiense	closed (see note b)	281
Spada Gallery	Wednesday–Saturday 9–14, 15–19; Sunday 9–13; Monday & Tuesday 9–14	133
Tasso Museum	apply to the Cavalieri del Santo Sepolcro, 33 Via della Conciliazione	267
Tomb of Cecilia Metella	9–13.30, 14–one hour before sunset; November– April 9–13.30; Sunday & Monday 9–13	243

Tomb of the Scipios	(C) 9–13.30; closed Monday; April– September, Tuesday, Thursday, and Saturday also 16–19	221
Torlonia Museum	closed indefinitely	260
Vatican Museums	*see* page 303	
Venezia, Museo del Palazzo	9–14, Sunday 9–13	70
Via Ostiense, Museo della	closed in 1988	280
Villa Albani	*see* Villa Torlonia	
Villa Farnesina	weekdays 9–13; closed Sunday	262
Villa Giulia	9–19; Sunday 9–13; closed Monday	168
Villa Medici	garden only: usually Saturday & Sunday 10–13	158
Villa Torlonia (ex-Albani)	by special permission	251
Walls, Museum of	*see* Museo delle Mura	
Waxworks Museum	9–20	151
Zoological Gardens	8.30–sunset	165
Zoological Museum	Wednesday 9.30–12.30	165

Notes

b Special permission sometimes given by the Ripartizione Antichità, Belle Arti, e problemi della Cultura (Comune di Roma), 3 Piazza Caffarelli (on the Capitol Hill).

e The other catacombs may be visited by special permission only. Apply Pontificia Commissione di Archeologia Sacra, 1 Via Napoleone III

f Special permission required from the Soprintendenza Archeologica di Roma, 1 Piazza delle Finanze

x The opening hours for Sundays apply also to holidays (*giorni festivi*).

General Information

Plan of Visit. The itineraries in the Guide can be accomplished on foot in a day (with the help of public transport only for those routes outside the historical centre of the city). For visitors with only a short time at their disposal, the following areas and monuments should not be missed:

1. The Capitol Hill (Rte 1)
2. The Forum and Palatine (Rtes 2 and 3)
3. The Pantheon and Piazza Navona (Rtes 5 and 6)
4. The Corso (and Galleria Doria Pamphilj), Piazza del Popolo, and Piazza di Spagna (Rtes 7 and 8)
5. The Colosseum and Esquiline Hill (Rtes 4 and 11)
6. The Baths of Caracalla and the Appian Way (Rtes 14 and 17)
7. St Peter's and the Vatican Museums (Rte 27)
8. Trastevere (Rte 21)
9. Villa Borghese (Rte 9)
10. The Quirinal hill and the Museo Nazionale Romano (Rte 10)

In the environs, at least Hadrian's Villa at Tivoli (Rte 32B) and the excavations at Ostia (Rte 28A) should be visited.

Season. the climate of Rome is exceptionally good except in the height of summer and periodically in the winter. For tourists the best months are April, May, June, September, and October. In January and February it can be unexpectedly cold and at times very wet.

Public Holidays. The main holidays in Rome, when offices, shops and schools are closed are as follows: New Year's Day, 25 April (Liberation Day), Easter Monday, 1 May (Labour Day), 15 August

(Assumption), 1 November (All Saints' Day), 8 December (Conception), Christmas Day, and 26 December (St Stephen). In addition, the festival of the patron Saints of Rome, Peter and Paul, is celebrated on 29 June as a local holiday in the city.

Telephones and Postal Information. Stamps are sold at tobacconists (displaying a blue 'T' sign) and post offices. There are numerous public telephones all over Rome in kiosks, bars, restaurants, etc. These are operated by 100 lire coins, or by a metal disk known as a 'gettone', which are bought (200 lire each) from tobacconists, bars, some newspaper stands, and post offices (and are considered valid currency). Most cities in Europe can now be dialled direct from Rome (prefix for London, 00441).

Shopping. The smartest shops are in Via Frattina and Via Condotti (the Bond Street of Rome), leading from Piazza di Spagna. A good shopping area (less expensive) is near the Pantheon. Department Stores: *La Rinascente*, Piazza Colonna; *Standa*, Piazza Santa Maria Maggiore, Viale Trastevere: *Upim*, Via del Corso. Book Shops; *Rizzoli*, Largo Chigi, Galleria Colonna, 76 Via Veneto; *Einaudi*, 56a and 58 Via Veneto; *Lion Bookshop*, 181 Via del Babuino (for English books). Antique shops in Via del Babuino and Via dei Coronari. Open air markets: *Porta Portese* (general 'flea market'; open Sunday morning only); *Via Sannio* (Porta San Giovanni), new and second-hand clothes; *Campo dei Fiori*, *Piazza Vittorio Emanuele II*, and *Via Andrea Doria*, all for food.

Newspapers. The most widely read Italian newspapers in Rome are *La Repubblica*, *Corriere della Sera*, *Paese Sera*, *Messaggero*, and *Il Tempo*. Foreign newspapers and weekly publications in English giving news of events in Rome are obtainable at most kiosks.

Working Hours. Government offices usually work weekdays from 8–13.30 or 14. Shops are normally open from 8 or 9–13 and 16.30 or 17–19.30 or 20, although in 1988 some shops stayed open all day and on Sundays as an experiment (which may not last). For banking hours, see above.

ROME

ROME (2,781,000 inhab.), in Italian **Roma**, is the capital of Italy and the metropolis of the Roman Catholic Church. The Eternal City, the 'Urbs' par excellence, to which all roads lead, was the Alma Mater of Mediterranean civilisation, and the Caput Mundi, from which law and the liberal arts and sciences radiated to the confines of its vast empire, which covered the whole of the known Western World. Its superb ancient monuments survive all over the centre of the modern city, and blend with the great Renaissance and Baroque buildings. The yellow Tiber, here some 35km from its mouth, divides the city into two unequal parts; but the Rome of the Republic and the early Empire was confined to the left bank, with the famous seven hills; the Palatine and Capitoline in the centre, the Aventine, Celian, Esquiline, Viminal, and Quirinal (from S to N) in an arc to the E.

Detail from a fresco by Benozzo Gozzoli (in San Agostino, San Gimignano) showing Rome in 1465 (with Castel Sant' Angelo, the Pantheon, the Capitol and Santa Maria in Aracoeli, etc.)

1   The Capitol and Piazza Venezia

Piazza Venezia (Pl. 4; 5), a huge and busy square, is the focus of the
main traffic arteries of the city. Towards it converge Via del Corso
from the N, Via del Plebiscito (the continuation of the Corso Vittorio
Emanuele) from the W (and St Peter's), Via Battisti (the continuation
of Via Quattro Novembre) from the E (and the Station), and, from the
SE and SW respectively, Via dei Fori Imperiali and Via del Teatro di
Marcello. The piazza was transformed at the end of the 19C when
parts of the Renaissance city were demolished and the Capitol Hill
itself encroached upon to make way for the colossal Victor
Emmanuel Monument (see p 70) which is an unforgivable intrusion
into the centre of the city. A policeman regulates the traffic at the
head of the Corso which from the N side of the piazza runs straight
for over a mile to Piazza del Popolo with its obelisk. From here can be
seen (left) the Palazzo delle Assicurazioni Generali di Venezia
(1907), with a fine winged lion from Padua, and (right) Palazzo di
Venezia (see p 70). Dwarfed by the Monument, and to the right of
it is the Capitol Hill. It is separated from Piazza d'Aracoeli
(with a fountain of 1589 designed by Jacopo della Porta) by a wide,
modern, traffic-ridden road (Via del Teatro di Marcello), one of
the most difficult in the city to cross on foot, which runs S to the
Tiber past the foot of the hill. Beside the Victor Emmanuel
Monument here are the interesting ruins discovered this century of
a Roman tenement house or 'insulae' built in the 2C AD and over four
stories high.

The **Capitoline Hill** (in Italian, *Campidoglio*; 50m) is the smallest
but most famous of the Seven Hills of Rome. It was the political and
religious centre of Ancient Rome, and since the end of the 11C has
been the seat of the civic government of the city.

Recent archaeological finds have confirmed that the hill was already inhabited
in the Bronze Age. Its two summits are separated by a depression, occupied by
the Piazza del Campidoglio. On the S summit (*Capitolium*) stood the Capitol
proper, with the *Temple of Jupiter Optimus Maximus Capitolinus*, the most
venerated in Rome, as Jupiter was regarded as the city's special protector. The
investiture of consuls took place here, and the triumphant procession awarded
to victorious generals ended at the temple (see p 76). It was founded, according
to tradition, by Tarquinius Priscus, completed by Tarquinius Superbus, dedicated in 509 BC, and is the largest temple known of this period. It was destroyed
by fire in 83 BC during the civil wars, rebuilt by Sulla, destroyed again in AD 69,
rebuilt by Vespasian and again by Domitian, and was still standing in the 6C.
Remains of the earliest temple still exist (see pp 65 & 68). The N summit (altered
by the construction of the Victor Emmanuel Monument) was occupied by the
Arx, or citadel of Rome. During a siege by the Gauls in 390 BC the Capitol was
saved from a night attack by the honking of the sacred geese of Juno kept
here, who alerted the Romans to the danger. In 343 BC a temple was erected to
Juno Moneta; the name came to be connected with the Mint later established
here. The site of the temple is now covered by the church of Santa Maria in
Aracoeli.

Formerly the Capitoline Hill was accessible only from the Forum but since the
16C the main buildings have been made to face the north, in conformity with
the direction of the modern development of the city.

There are three approaches to the hill from Piazza d'Aracoeli. On the
left a long flight of 124 steps (dating from 1348) mounts to the church
of Santa Maria in Aracoeli, more easily reached from Piazza del
Campidoglio (see p 68). On the right, Via delle Tre Pile (a carriage
road of 1873 now used by cars), winds up to the Capitol, passing

fragments of temples and a stretch of archaic wall. In the middle, a stepped ramp known as 'La Cordonata' designed by Michelangelo (modified c 1578 by Giac. della Porta) provides the easiest ascent. It is guarded by two Egyptian lions in black granite (veined with red) of the Ptolemaic period, from the Isaeum. In the garden on the left (traversed by another flight of steps shaded by a pergola) a 19C statue of Cola di Rienzo marks the spot where he was killed in 1354. Higher up is a cage which, until recently, contained a she-wolf, a symbol of Rome.

At the top is *Piazza del Campidoglio (Pl. 4; 7), beautifully designed by Michelangelo to give grandeur to the historical centre of Rome (it was completed to his design in the 17C). It is surrounded on three sides by stately palaces and a balustrade defines its open end. At the back is Palazzo Senatorio; on the left is Palazzo del Museo Capitolino; facing it, on the right Palazzo dei Conservatori. The latter has a very unusual design with Ionic columns supporting a flat open loggia below, and handsome windows with coupled columns on the piano nobile, below a prominent entablature with a balcony. The two stories are united by the use of the giant order, the first time this solution was used in secular architecture. The similar palace opposite, also designed by Michelangelo, was not built until the mid 17C.

The handsome pavement with an oval star design gives prominence to the famous gilded bronze *Statue of Marcus Aurelius, dating from the emperor's reign (AD 161–80), and the only Roman equestrian statue of this period to survive. It has been removed since 1981, and is still undergoing a lengthy and complicated restoration (see p 257). It may have to be replaced here by a copy, and the original displayed under cover.

This popular statue appears time and again in medieval representations of the city. As early as the 10C it was believed to represent the Christian emperor Constantine the Great. It was set up outside the Lateran palace in the 12C or 13C and brought from there by order of Paul III in 1538 when Michelangelo, having just been made a citizen of Rome, provided its small and elegant base, and its theatrical setting. In 1873 Henry James commented 'I doubt if any statue of king or captain in the public places of the world has more to commend it to the general heart'.

On the balustrade are colossal figures of the Dioscuri (much restored), late Roman works, found in the Ghetto in the 16C, two trophies of barbarian arms (Flavian period), known as the 'Trophies of Marius', statues of Constantine and his son Constans (from the Baths of Constantine), and two milestones, the first and seventh of the Appian Way.

Palazzo Senatorio (Pl. 4; 7) is the official seat of the Mayor of Rome. An 11C fortress was built by the Corsi on the remains of the ancient Tabularium (see below), and the Senate was probably installed here c 1150. The medieval castle with four towers was renewed in the 13C and redesigned by Michelangelo in the 16C. The present façade (1592), by Giac. della Porta and Girol. Rainaldi, is a modification of Michelangelo's design. In front of the double stair-case, with converging flights, is a fountain with two colossal statues (2C AD) of the Tiber (right) and the Nile (left); in the recess is a porphyry statue of Minerva, found at Cori and transformed into the Dea Roma. The palace is crowned by a bell-tower (1582), with a clock, a statue of Minerva, and a gilded cross; two bells (1803–4) replace the famous *Patarina*, which had been installed in 1200 to summon the people to 'Parlamento'.

The INTERIOR may only be visited by special permission and previous appointment. The entrance is in Via San Pietro in Carcere. On the left of the entrance hall is a room with sculptural fragments, models, and inscriptions. On the first floor in the COUNCIL CHAMBER is a colossal marble statue of Julius Caesar (the only statue of him which survives), of the period of Trajan, and in the antechamber, L'Aurora by *Pietro da Cortona*. The ROOM OF THE FLAG contains a fragment of the 14C flag of St George, from the church of San Giorgio in Velabro.—In the PROTOMOTECA is a large collection of busts of the famous, mostly dating from the 18C and 19C. The GREAT HALL also has a Canova monument, and from here there is access to a terrace with a remarkable view of the Forum.

The **Tabularium** or depository of the State archives lies under Palazzo Senatorio, and its great blocks of porous tufa built into the unhewn rock dominate the view of the hill from the Forum. It was erected in 78 BC by Q. Lutatius Catulus: the inscription stone can still be seen by one entrance on the left flank of Palazzo Senatorio. Beyond this, in Via San Pietro in Carcere, is the arcaded gallery of the Tabularium (no adm in 1988) with a splendid view of the Forum. Here, also, is part of the frieze from the Temple of Concord (p 82), and in the adjoining gallery (seen through a closed iron gate) is a cast of part of the frieze from the Temple of Vespasian, another section of which can be seen through the arch, still in position above three columns at the foot of the Capitol.

For adm to the Tabularium special permission is required (apply at Palazzo Caffarelli). There are several entrances, as a gallery was constructed in 1938 under the Piazza and Palazzo Senatorio, connecting this with Palazzo dei Conservatori and Palazzo del Museo Capitolino. Numerous inscriptions, some in Greek, have been arranged along the gallery.

The Tabularium had a rectangular plan, with a central court and two stories. The first story is the most interesting; the lower floor was used as a medieval prison and is now a store. Here are considerable remains of the *Temple of Veiovis*, erected first in 196 BC, and rebuilt after fire in the 1C BC. The pronaos is orientated towards Via del Campidoglio, and the podium and cella are well preserved. The external wall of the Tabularium may be seen on two sides; a small gap was left between it and the Temple. Behind the Temple is a colossal marble statue of Veiovis (1C AD, after a 5C BC type), found in the cella.—To the right is a perfectly preserved staircase of the Republican period, leading steeply down to the Forum. It was blocked at the bottom by a tufa wall (still in place) when the Temple of Vespasian was built.

The collections housed in the Palazzi del Museo Capitolino, dei Conservatori, and Caffarelli are grouped under the comprehensive title of *Capitoline Museums*. The title is somewhat confusing, as one of the museums is called the Capitoline Museum (see below). They are above all famous for their magnificent Roman sculptures.

The nucleus of the exhibits is the oldest collection in the world, and dates from 1471, when Sixtus IV made over to the people of Rome a valuable group of bronzes, which were deposited in Palazzo dei Conservatori. Later, up to the foundation of the Pius-Clementine Sculpture gallery in the Vatican, this nucleus was enriched with discoveries in Rome and various acquisitions, notably the collection of Cardinal Alessandro Albani. New discoveries led to the opening of a second Museum in 1876. Adm, see p 48.

CAPITOLINE MUSEUM

PALAZZO DEL MUSEO CAPITOLINO (Pl. 4; 5), built in the reign of Innocent X (1644–55), contains the *Capitoline Museum, an extremely interesting collection of ancient sculpture, begun by Clement XII and added to by later popes. It was opened to the public in 1734, during the pontificate of Clement XII.

GROUND FLOOR. INNER COURT (R. II). Fountain, by *Giac. della Porta*, with a colossal figure of a river-god, known as 'Marforio', probably of the 2C AD found at the foot of the Capitol (one of Rome's 'talking' statues; see p 123). In the side niches are two figures of Pan (telamones), from the Theatre of Pompey.—PORTICO (III): Egyptian sculptures from the Isaeum Campense, including two apes from the tomb of Nectanebes II (358–341 BC).—Corridor (I). 2. Colossal statue of Minerva, from a 5C original.—At the left end is the entrance to three rooms (often closed; apply at entrance gate), containing monuments of Oriental cults. R. IV. Three representations of Mithras; Base dedicated to the Magna Mater, with reliefs representing the Miracle of the Vestal Claudia, who with her girdle drew the ship bearing the image of the goddess to Rome (205 BC). In the centre is an altar to Sol Sanctissimus, the God of the Sun. Statue of a Gaul (early 3C AD), formerly at Wilton House near Salisbury.—R. V. 12. Bust of a young boy, follower of the cult of Isis (3C AD); 14. Bust of Serapis.—R. VI. Sculptures relating to the cult of Zeus Dolichenos.

At the right end of the corridor: (17, 14.) Two statues of women, after Kalamides' Aphrodite Sosandra, with portrait heads of the 2–3C AD; colossal statue of Mars, dating from the Domitian period. Here is the entrance to three more rooms (if closed apply at entrance gate): R. VII. Heads, busts, and fragments of calendars from the Palatine and Ostia, including a finely preserved Order of Precedence of the

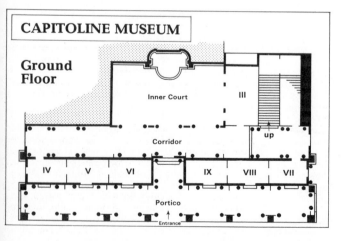

citizens of Ostia (from the time of the Emperor Pertinax).—R. VIII. 1. Roman head from the period of Trajan; *4. Celebrated Amendola Sarcophagus, with reliefs representing a battle between Gauls and Romans, showing a remarkable affinity with the Pergamene school; 10. Cippus of the master-mason Titus Statilius Aper, with his tools.— R. IX. Colossal double *Sarcophagus, formerly supposed to be that of Alexander Severus, a splendid work of the 3C AD, with portraits of the deceased and reliefs representing the story of Achilles; Cippus of Vettius Agorius Praetextatus, pro-consul of Achaia.—Opposite the colossal statue of Mars is the staircase.

FIRST FLOOR. Beyond the gallery (see below) is ROOM I. *DYING GAUL, an exquisitely modelled figure of a Celtic warrior who lies mortally wounded on the ground. It was discovered in the gardens of Sallust and is a copy of the Roman period of one of the bronze statues dedicated at Pergamon by Attalos I in commemoration of his victories over the Gauls (239 BC). The statue was formerly called the 'Dying Gladiator', 'butcher'd to make a Roman holiday', in Byron's phrase. It was beautifully restored in 1986 when the position of the right arm was changed, having been altered in a 17C restoration. Nearly all the other statues in this room were found at Hadrian's Villa, near Tivoli. Round the room: 1. Amazon, a Roman work after an original attributed to Pheidias (wrongly restored); 2. Colossal head of Alexander the Great; 3. Hermes, Hadrianic version of a 4C original; 4. Lycian Apollo, copy of a work by Praxiteles; 6. Head of a youth; *7. Satyr Resting, a good replica of an original by Praxiteles (the 'Marble Faun' of Hawthorne's romance; other replicas in the Vatican); *8. Head of Dionysos; 9. Greek cynic philosopher, Roman copy in marble of a bronze original; 10. Head of a general, a Pheidian type; 11. Priestess of Isis, period of Hadrian; 12. Eros and Psyche, Hellenistic work.

R. II. In the centre, *1. Laughing Silenus, in red marble, of the Imperial period from a Hellenistic bronze; 2. Alabaster bust of an unknown Roman, period of Gallienus; 5. Sarcophagus depicting the Hunt of the Calydonian Boar; 8. Child with mask, a Hellenistic work;

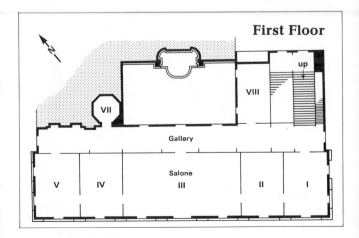

11. Sarcophagus with figures of Endymion and Selene (early 3C AD);
16. Herm of Hercules (2C AD); 17. Boy with a goose, copy of a bronze
by Boethos of Chalcedon (2C BC); Sarcophagus (2C AD) with the life
of Dionysos including his birth, a graceful work.

On the wall is a bronze plaque on which is inscribed the *Lex Regia* ofVespasian,
the historic decree conferring sovereign power on that emperor; it was first
brought to notice by Rienzo, whom it served as a text for demonstrating the
greatness and the rights of Rome.

R. III. (SALONE). In the centre 1, 5. Statues of Zeus and Asklepios, both
from originals of the 4C BC; 2, 4. Young or laughing centaur, Old or
weeping centaur, two vigorous works from Hadrian's Villa, signed
by his contemporaries Aristeas and Papias of Aphrodisias in Caria;
3. Infant Hercules, a colossal ugly figure in green basalt, of the
late Imperial epoch, on a base decorated with scenes from the myth of
Zeus.

Round the room (left to right): 7. Colossal statue of Apollo (the head
does not belong); 11. Hera, from an original attributed to Agorakritos
(5C BC), badly restored with a portrait head; 13. Hadrian as Mars; 20.
Archaic statue of Apollo, copy of the so-called Omphalos Apollo in
Athens; 21. Statue of a young Roman of the time of Hadrian as
Hermes; *22. Old woman in terror, a striking example of the
Hellenistic period; 23. Muse, once probably representing Hera, from
a 4C original; 24. Colossal statue of Demeter, restored as Hera, from
an Attic original of the 4C BC; 27. Huntsman, head of the period of
Gallienus on a body of the late-Archaic type; 28. Statue of Harpo-
crates, period of Hadrian; *30. Apollo, from a work of the first half of
the 5C; 31. Pothos, from an original by Skopas; 33. Wounded
Amazon, signed by the copyist Sosicles, from a 5C original; 34.
Roman couple as Mars and Venus, period of Septimius Severus; 36.
Athena Promachos, a 4C type from the Villa d'Este.

R. IV. The identifications of the busts of philosophers, poets, and
others in this room are not all certain (they are being cleaned one by
one). Those whose identity is most probable are Socrates (various
types), Theon (17), Sophocles (22–23), Chrysippos (27), Euripides
(30–31), Homer (39–41), Demosthenes (43), Aeschines (50), Metrodorus (51), *Double portrait of Epicuros and Metrodorus (52), Epicuros (53), Antisthenes (55), Cicero (56), Theophrastus (74). In the
centre, 75. Seated figure ('Marcellus') from an original of the 4C BC
(head modern). On the walls are fragments of a frieze, perhaps from
the Porticus of Octavia, with sacrificial instruments and parts of ships,
and Greek votive reliefs.

R. V contains a rich collection of Roman imperial busts, interesting
as portraits and also in some cases because of the precious materials
used. (On columns): *Augustus, wearing a wreath of myrtle; *15.
Woman of the late Flavian period; 20. Domitia; 21. Plotina, wife of
Trajan, considered her best portrait; 24. Matidia; 32. Faustina the
Younger; 39. Julia Domna; *55. Heliogabalus. On the walls are
reliefs, two of which are works of great delicacy, executed in the first
centuries of the Empire and following Hellenistic types: F. Perseus
rescuing Andromeda; H. Sleeping Endymion. In the centre: 59.
Helena, mother of Constantine, a beautiful seated figure inspired by
the Aphrodite of Pheidias.

GALLERY 35. Colossal head of an Emperor, 4C AD; 36. Portrait of
Marcus Aurelius as a boy; 53. Colossal head of Aphrodite, perhaps
an original of the Hellenistic period; 57. Sarcophagus of the 3C AD
with reliefs of the rape of Persephone; 61. Roman matron of the

Flavian period in the guise of Venus; 65. Torso of the Discobolos of Myron, badly restored by Monnot as a fighting gladiator; 67. Cupid as archer, a good copy of the celebrated work by Lysippos; 68. Hercules slaying the Hydra (so restored by Algardi: and the antique model he used can be seen beside it. It was more probably intended to represent Hercules capturing the hind). 4a. Relief of a man and wife, probably reading a will; 7. Leda and the Swan, replica of a work attributed to Timotheos (4C BC); 8. Head of Marsyas, probably a Hellenistic original; 10. Drunken old woman, perhaps after Myron the Younger, a Pergamene sculptor of the end of the 3C BC; 22. Psyche winged, from a Hellenistic original; 24. Head of Dionysos, a good copy from a 4C BC original; 31. Minerva, copy of a bronze of c 400 BC; 34. Decorative vase (krater) of the 1C AD, resting on a *Well-Head from Hadrian's Villa, with archaistic decoration representing the procession of the twelve gods (Dii Consentes).

R. VII (CABINET OF VENUS), contains the celebrated *Capitoline Venus, found in the 17C in a house near San Vitale, a superbly modelled statue of Parian marble. It is a Roman replica of a Hellenistic original, derived from the Cnidian Aphrodite of Praxiteles.

R. VIII (HALL OF THE DOVES) is named from a delicate *Mosaic (9) from Hadrian's Villa, after a work by Sosias of Pergamon; 8. Sarcophagus with the story of Prometheus (3C AD); 23. Herm of Hermes Propylaios; 37. Diana of Ephesus; 52. Front face of a sarcophagus, with the Triumph of Bacchus. In glass cases: 53. Tabula Iliaca or Trojan Tablet, a plaque with small reliefs representing the Trojan cycle, by Theodorus (1C AD); 76. Piece of a shield of Achilles by the same sculptor. In the centre of the room is a charming little statue of a child protecting a dove, a Roman copy of a Greek work of the 2C BC (wrongly restored with a snake).

PALAZZO DEI CONSERVATORI

The **Palazzo dei Conservatori** (Pl. 4; 7) was rebuilt by Nicholas V about 1450 and remodelled after 1564 by *Giacomo della Porta* and *Guidetto Guidetti* from a design by Michelangelo. It contains the **Sale dei Conservatori**, the **Museo del Palazzo dei Conservatori**, and the **Pinacoteca**, or picture gallery. The first two are situated on the first floor, and the Pinacoteca on the second floor. Adjoining the building, and reached from the Museo del Palazzo dei Conservatori, is the **Museo Nuovo**, which is at ground level.

From the piazza is the entrance to the interior COURT. On the right are fragments of a colossal statue (c 12m high) of Constantine the Great, including the head, hand, and foot, which were brought from the Basilica of Constantine in 1486. Near the head is an inscription from the time of Boniface VIII. On the left are bases and transennae with sculptured representations of provinces and nations subject to Rome, which once decorated the Temple of Hadrian in the Piazza di Pietra. Above is an inscription from the arch erected in AD 51 on Via Lata to celebrate the conquest of Britain by Claudius. Beneath the portico at the farther end, a figure of Roma from the time of Trajan or Hadrian, and statues of Barbarians. 1st LANDING: Four reliefs from triumphal arches, three being from one erected to Marcus Aurelius; to the right, Sacrifice before the Temple of Jupiter Capitolinus. 2nd LANDING: Hadrian, relief from the demolished Arco di Portogallo (all of these reliefs were restored in 1986); statue of Charles of Anjou, by the workshop of Arnolfo di Cambio (made for Santa Maria in Aracoeli c 1270). From this landing at the top of the stairs, open the Sale dei Conservatori.

SALE DEI CONSERVATORI

ROOM I, SALA DEGLI ORAZI E CURIAZI. Frescoes (restored in 1983) by *Cavalier d'Arpino*, representing episodes from the reigns of the early kings. *Urban VIII, marble statue, a studio work begun by *Bernini*; *Innocent X, bronze by *Algardi*. Here in 1957 the Treaty of Rome, the foundation of the European Economic Community, was signed by Italy, Belgium, France, West Germany, Luxembourg, and Holland.   ·

R. II, SALA DEI CAPITANI. Handsome doors in carved wood (17C); further frescoes from Roman history, by *Tom. Laureti*, and 16–17C statues, including one of Alessandro Farnese and of Marcantonio Colonna.

R. III, SALA DEI TRIONFI DI MARIO (being restored in 1988). Frieze by *Mich. Alberti* and *Giac. Rocchetti* representing the triumph of Emilius Paulus over Perseus of Macedon. The most famous of the bronzes presented to the Conservatori by Sixtus IV are exhibited here. In the middle is the celebrated *SPINARIO, or Boy plucking a thorn from his foot.

This was formerly known as the 'Fedele Capitolino', because it was thought to be the portrait of Marcius, a Roman messenger who would not delay the execution of his mission though tortured by a thorn in his foot. It is a delicate Hellenistic composition in the eclectic style of the 1C BC.

Bronze *Head, known as L. Junius Brutus, of Etruscan or Italic workmanship of the 3C BC; Camillus, or acolyte (1C AD); Bronze krater with an inscription, the gift of King Mithridates to a gymnastic association, part of the booty from a Mithridatic war, found at Anzio; fine sarcophagus front (3C AD).

R. IV, SALA DELLA LUPA, with more frescoes from Roman history. On the wall opposite the windows are fragments of the Fasti Consulares et Triumphales, from the inner walls of the Arch of Augustus in the Forum, in a frame designed by *Michelangelo*. These are records of Roman magistrates and of triumphs of the great captains of Rome in 13 BC–AD 12. The famous *SHE-WOLF of Rome is thought to be an Etruscan bronze of the late 6C or early 5C BC, probably belonging to the school of Vulca, an Etruscan sculptor of Veio. It originally stood on the Capitol and may be the wolf which was struck by lightning in 65 BC, when the hind feet are said to have been damaged. It was taken to the Lateran palace sometime in the Middle Ages. The twins were added by Antonio Pollauolo c 1509.

R. V, SALA DELLE OCHE, an interesting example of a 17C apartment, contains various works of art, among which a figure of Isis and two 'Geese', more likely ducks (antique bronzes), a bronze bust of Michelangelo, and a marble Head of Medusa, by *Bernini*; in the centre: Mastiff in rare green marble.

R. VI, SALA DELLE AQUILE. Sleeping Eros, after a Hellenistic type; Head of a charioteer (1C AD).

R. VII, SALA DEGLI ARAZZI. Tapestries executed for the municipality; one shows the goddess Roma, the others represent the Birth of Romulus and Remus (from the painting by Rubens in the Capitoline Gallery), the Vestal Tutia, and the 'defeatist' schoolmaster of Falerii punished by Camillus.

R. VIII, CAPPELLA NUOVA (closed for restoration). On the altar, Madonna in glory with Saints Peter and Paul, by *Avanzino Nucci*.

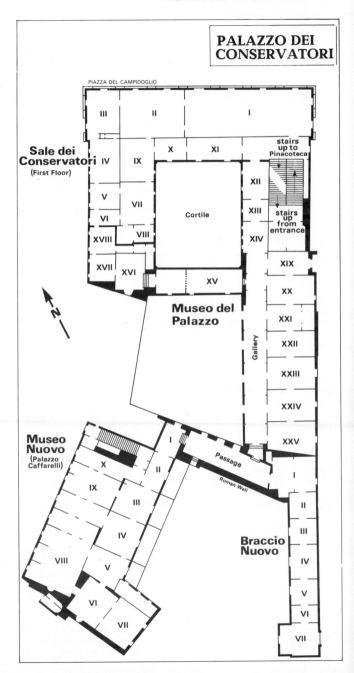

R. IX, SALA DELLE GUERRE PUNICHE, is decorated with frescoes by *Giac. Ripanda*. In the middle, Two girls playing, Hellenistic work (removed for restoration).

R. X, CAPPELLA VECCHIA. On the ceiling, Frescoes and stuccoes, by *Alberti* and *Rocchetti*; on the walls, Madonna and angels, by *Ant. da Viterbo*.

R. XI, CORRIDOR. 16C Flemish tapestry; Roman scenes by *Gasp. Vanvitelli.*—The Corridor leads back to the landing, where, to the right, is the entrance to the—

MUSEO DEL PALAZZO DEI CONSERVATORI

RR. XII, XIII, XIV, SALE DEI FASTI MODERNI. These rooms contain lists of the chief magistrates of Rome since 1640, and a collection of busts and herms. R. XII. 8. Fragment of a group of a giant fighting with two satyrs, deriving from the Gigantomachia of Pergamon.—R. XIII. 2. Cow, Roman copy, thought to be derived from the Cow of Myron; 4. Bust of Faustina, wife of Antoninus Pius; 5. Sarcophagus, depicting a Dionysiac ceremony; 6. Bust of Sabina, wife of Hadrian.—R. XIV. 4. Panther and wild boar in combat; Roman imperial busts.—From the gallery (see below) is the entrance (right) into—

R. XV, SALA DEGLI ORTI LAMIANI, containing sculptures found in the Lamiani Gardens, on the Esquiline. 3. Old fisherman; 5. Old woman with a lamb, two Hellenistic statues of great realism; 4. *Seated girl, a remarkably graceful figure, recently restored. It is probably a Roman copy of a Greek original of the 3C BC. 7. Centaur's head, probably an original of Pergamene art; (in the second part of the gallery) 12. Bust of Commodus as Hercules, a work of considerable refinement; 13, 14. Tritons, perhaps its supporters; 15. Female statue, after an original of the 4C BC.—In the centre, *29. Esquiline Venus, a young girl probably connected with the cult of Isis, an eclectic work of the school of Pasiteles, 1C BC. The pavement in marble and alabaster is from the Esquiline.

R. XVI SALA DEI MAGISTRATI. 2, 5. Roman umpires starting a race in the time of Constantine; column of rare green breccia from Egypt; inscriptions recording the conferment of Roman citizenship on Petrarch, Michelangelo, Titian, and Bernini; 4. Artemis, from a 4C original, restored to represent Christian Rome; 6. The emperor Decius as Mars. There is also a temporary display of Imperial Roman glass in this room.

The *SALE DEI MONUMENTI ARCAICI (RR. XVII–XVIII). R. XVII. In the centre, *10. Torso of an Amazon (late 6C BC), designed for the angle of the temple pediment of Apollo Daphnephoros at Eretria. 2. Headless female statue from a bronze original c 460 BC; 4. Fragment of a stele (5 or 4C BC); 5. Latona, from a 5C original; 7, 9. Two young initiates of the Eleusinian mysteries.—Room XVIII. 6, 7. Korai in the Archaizing style of the early Imperial era; 8. Nike, probably from a 5C original; 10. Fragment of a stele of Attic workmanship; 11 Head of a lion (5C); 12. Stele representing a girl with a dove (late 6C).

GALLERY 14. Colossal foot, probably of the Rhodian school; 35. Copy of the 'Grande Ercolanese' (original formerly at Dresden); 41. Relief of a 'Scaenae frons' (1–2C AD); 44. Aedicula, or shrine, dedicated to the Earth Mother; 53, 54. Athletes, from 4C types; 56. Fragment of a relief from the Auditorium of Maecenas; 58. Claudia Justa as Fortune (2C AD); 68. Youth, perhaps from an original of the

Polykleitan school. The GARDEN (reached from the gallery) contains decorative sculpture. From the beginning of the gallery is the entrance to RR. XIX, XX, the SALE CRISTIANE. Sarcophagi with the Good Shepherd; inscriptions; 13. Head of a Roman matron (5–6C AD).

R. XXI, SALA DEL CAMINO, with remains of a chimneypiece (camino) of the Conservatori. 1. Sarcophagus, with the Calydonian boar hunt. In glass cases: Greek red- and black-figure vases, and antefixes from Capua (6–5C); in a case towards the gallery, Tragliatella oinochoe (7C BC) with paintings and graffiti, and below, Attic kylix of 470 BC from Cerveteri.

R. XXII, PRIMA SALA CASTELLANI, contains part of the collection presented by Augusto Castellani, the fruit of excavations between 1860–66 in S Etruria and Latium. In glass cases along the walls: Etruscan, Italic and Faliscan vases. In the centre of the room: *Capitoline Tensa, reconstruction of a triumphal chariot overlaid with bronze, which carried the images of the gods at the opening of the Circensian games; Etruscan statuette in terracotta from Cerveteri (end of 7C BC).

R. XXIII, SECONDA SALA CASTELLANI. In glass cases along the walls: Corinthian and Attic vases, with red and black figures (6C BC) including (No. 64) the Amphora of Nikosthenes. In the middle of the room: *Krater of Aristonothos, with Odysseus and the Cyclops (7C); (No. 132) hydria from Ceretani; three sides of an Etruscan funerary bed, with animal reliefs.

R. XXIV, SALA DEI BRONZI. 2, 3, 8. Head, hand, and globe from a colossal statue of Constans II; 5. Rear half of a colossal bull, of finest workmanship; 6. Globe which originally adorned the Vatican Obelisk, damaged by a musket shot during the Sack of Rome in 1527; *10. Horse, since its restoration thought to be a Greek original dating from the early 4C BC. In 1988 it had not yet been returned after its restoration. *11. Bed with exquisite decoration, of the 1C AD; *12. Litter, composed of bronze, found on the Esquiline by Castellani. In a glass case, to the right of the door to R. XXV, statuette of a Lar, with rhyton and patera; statuette of Hecate.

R. XXV. SALA DEGLI ORTI MECENAZIANI, containing sculptures found in the Gardens of Maecenas on the Esquiline. In the centre, *13. So-called 'Auriga', or charioteer mounting (copy of a 5C original). Since its recent restoration this statue is now thought to represent a hero, possibly Theseus, driving his chariot (it was formerly attached to a horse, also displayed here). 2. Statue of Hercules, from an original by Lysippos; 3. Eros (?), from an early 4C BC original; 6. Punishment of Marsyas, in Phrygian marble, probably of the Rhodian school; 7. Head of Augustus; 8. Hygieia, Roman copy of a Hellenistic original; *9. Dancing Maenad, in relief, from an original by Kallimachos; 10. Headless statue of Aphrodite, a fine copy of an Ionic Greek original; *11. Head of an Amazon, from an original by Polykleitos; 18. Rhyton, part of the decoration of a fountain, by Pontios of Athens, in the neo-Attic style of the 1C AD.

BRACCIO NUOVO

At the end of the gallery is (left) the PASSAGE OF THE ROMAN WALL (contents, see below), a tufa wall belonging to the Temple of Jupiter Capitolinus (6C BC; see p 53). Here is the entrance to the New Wing, arranged between 1950 and 1952 and devoted to finds from more recent excavations. This has been closed since 1984, and when it is reopened the arrangement described below may be altered. On the floor and walls of the first three rooms may be seen remains of the foundations of the Temple of Jupiter Capitolinus (clarified by a plan in R. II).

R. I. 1. Portrait of a man (1C BC); 2. Base dedicated to Hercules by the dictator Minucius, colleague of Q. Fabius Maximus, in 217 BC; *35. Fragment of a fresco from a tomb of the early 3C BC. The subject is possibly Q. Fabius Rullianus, consul in 322, and this example is the earliest known of Roman painting; 36. (in front of the window), Relief of Marcus Curtius riding into the abyss (1C BC); 37. Sarcophagus cover of the Etruscan type (4C BC).

R. II. Further works of the Republican period. 1, 12. Two fragments of a frieze of a triumphal procession; 2, 3, and 4. Pediment with frieze from a Republican tomb; 13–19. Terracotta group of statues for the pediment of a temple; 5, 6. Two funerary statues; 7–10. Fragments of a sepulchral monument, finely executed; 11. Fragment of a frieze with a ritual dance.

R. III. Roman portraits. 7. Statue of a man, holding two busts of his forebears, 1C AD; 9. Agrippa; 10. Claudius; 11. Domitian, one of the few portraits of him extant; 15. Trajan; 25. Lucilla, daughter of Marcus Aurelius; 32. Fresco (2–3C AD), found during the construction of the underground railway; in the centre, 31. Round base with Bacchic dance, neo-Attic.

R. IV. *3. Apollo shooting an arrow, a Greek statue of the first half of the 5C BC, perhaps by Pythagoras of Rhegion; brought to Rome and altered, it was placed in the Temple of Apollo Sosianus. 2. Head of Hercules, after an original by Polykleitos; 4. Head of an Amazon, from an original by Kresilas, with a subtle expression of pain; 5, 6. Two replicas of Pothos, from an original by Skopas (No. 5 is particularly fine); *8. Aristogeiton, the best replica of one of the two statues of the tyrannicides by Kritios and Nesiotes (477–476 BC) which stood in the Agora at Athens.

R. V. 1, 4, 7, and 8. Four fragments of a richly decorated frieze (1C BC); Head of a youth, after the Kyniskos of Polykleitos; 2. Head of a girl, Archaic style, found on the Appia Antica; 14. Warriors in combat, metope of the 4C BC, probably from the Temple of Poseidon at Isthmia; 17. Headless statue of Aphrodite, from an original of the Rhodian school; 18. Archaic base of a candelabrum with the divinities of Delos; on the floor, polychrome mosaic (1C BC).

R. VI. 2. Sarcophagus with winged victories, and a frieze of animals (3C AD); 9. Sarcophagus with the myth of Apollo and Marsyas of 2C AD; 13. Neo-Attic relief of the contest between Apollo and Marsyas.

R. VII. On the floor, coloured Mosaic of the Rape of Proserpina, with personifications of the seasons (late 2C AD); 4, 7, 8, and 10. Colossal female head, arm, and two feet of a cult statue from the Area Sacra of the Largo Argentina; 3, 5. Two altars, with bucrania; 1, 2, 6, 12, and 13. *Frieze from the pediment of the Temple of Apollo Sosianus (or Apollo Medico), three columns of which remain in front of the Theatre of Marcellus. This has recently been restored and reconstructed; it represents a battle between Greeks and Amazons, with Athena in the centre. The fragments are now thought to be Greek works of the 5C BC. 9. Frieze of cupids with the arms of Mars, from the Temple of Venus Genetrix (c AD 113); Statue (fountain) of a reclining river-god, with a beautiful head. Dating from the late 2C or early 3C AD, the statue was found in this century in the centre of Rome.

MUSEO NUOVO

The collection of sculptures comprising the Museo Nuovo is exhibited in the **Palazzo Caffarelli**, which rises at the SW end of the Palazzo dei Conservatori, on the other side of the garden. This palazzo was built for Giovanni Pietro Caffarelli in 1580 by *Gregorio Canonico*. Formerly the German Embassy, it was taken over by the Italian Government in 1918, and, after restoration, was opened as a museum in 1925. For some time it was known as the Museo Mussolini. Some of the rooms were closed in 1988 while being used as a restoration laboratory.

To reach the museum, it is necessary to return to the PASSAGE of the Roman Wall. 11. Inscribed base of a statue of Cornelia, mother of the Gracchi, from the Porticus of Octavia; 12. Inscription from the beaked column erected in honour of the Consul C. Duilius after his naval victory off Mylae over the Carthaginians; 9. Cinerary stele of Agrippina the Elder.

ROOM I. 1. Funerary relief from the Baker's tomb at Porta Maggiore, depicting the baker and his wife; 2-6. Fragments of a pediment, with pastoral subjects (1C AD); Cinerary urns.—R. II. 1. Sarcophagus with tritons and nereids (4C AD); behind glass, Busts and statuettes, among which, (12.) Head of a young boy, a Greek original of the early 5C.—R. III. Archaizing and neo-Attic sculpture. 2. Headless statue of a youth, showing traces of colour; 18. Priapus.

R. IV. Hellenistic art. In the centre, *24. The Muse Polyhymnia; 1. Head of Isis-Nechbet-Aphrodite, perhaps an Alexandrian original of the 2C BC; 4. Head of a youth; 7. Isis (?), an Antonine copy of a 4C BC original; 11. Torso of Hercules, from an original attributed to Skopas; *17–21. Groups of satyrs, maenads, and hermaphrodites, after a work at Pergamon by Kephisodotos the Younger.

R. V. In the centre, 18. Praying woman in grey basalt, from a bronze of the early 4C; 6. Votive relief to Asklepios and Hygieia (?), 4C original; 10. Aphrodite, from the same original as the Arles Aphrodite in the Louvre (? Praxiteles), the only copy preserving an arm; 15. Icarus, reworking of a Polykleitan original in the 2C AD; 16. Herm of Hercules replica of a work by Skopas; 17. Athena from the Castro Pretorio, copy of a work by Kephisodoros, once in Piraeus.

GARDEN. Fragments of fluted columns from the Temple of Jupiter, dating from a rebuilding in the time of Domitian. In the centre, *Group of a lion attacking a horse.

RR. VI, VII. Roman art. 1. Funerary altar from the Porta Salaria, of Q. Sulpicius Maximus, an infant prodigy who won a poetic contest at the age of 11 in the reign of Domitian (AD 94); 8. Stele of the shoemaker, Julius Aelius, with an expressive portrait-bust (Flavian period); 11. Sarcophagus, with relief of a battle between the Romans and Barbarians, and a fine relief above, of hunting scenes (end of 2C AD).—R. VII (left). 5. Lower part of a marble neo-Attic bowl, beautifully decorated; 10. Corbulo, the celebrated general, father-in-law of Domitian, and conqueror of the Germans and Parthians (died AD 67); 12. Portrait of a girl, a charming work of the early Empire; 21. Fragment of a relief with an Ionic temple (this and Nos. 17 and 23 were found together with the reliefs incorporated into the façade of the Villa Medici, and were probably all part of the Ara Pietatis); 24. Domitian, the best portrait bust of this emperor; 26. Bust of a man, a vivid study from the end of the 3C AD; 27. Fragment of a marble fountain adorned with a ship's prow (1C AD).

R. VIII. Reproductions of Greek sculpture of the 5C BC. This room was formerly the chapel of the German Embassy; it was partly built over the cella of the Temple of Jupiter. In the pavement, fragments of the original building. *18. Colossal statue of Athena, fine reproduction of an original by Kresilas; 1. Torso of Perseus (?) of mid-5C BC type; 2. Statue of Demeter, from a mid-5C original; 3. Discobolos resting, perhaps by Naukydes, son of Polykleitos (much restored); 5, 6. Athena Parthenos, fragmentary reduced reproductions of the statue by Pheidias: No. 6 is particularly interesting, with part of the shield decorated with reliefs still intact; 7. Head of Ares, after an original attrib. to Alkamenes; 8. Head of Diomedes (c 420 BC); 9. Head of the type of the Tyrannicides (c 475 BC); 11. Poseidon, of the early 5C type; 15. Herm of Anacreon, perhaps taken from a bronze statue by Pheidias (c 450 BC); 16. Head of Perseus, from a mid-5C BC original (perhaps belonging to the torso No. 1); 17. Statue of a woman, from an original attrib. to Kalamides; 19. Asklepios, Attic original of the late 5C BC.—R. IX. 9. Torso of Apollo Kitharoidos (from a 5C original); the head of Apollo to the left (No. 11) is probably from the same original; 8. Head of a young athlete, from an original by Polykleitos.—R. X. 17–18. Fragments of a sarcophagus of Asiatic type; portraits of the Imperial period.

PINACOTECA CAPITOLINA

The **Capitoline Picture Gallery**, founded in 1749 by Benedict XIV, was based on the Pio and Sacchetti collections, formed respectively by Prince Gilberto Pio of Savoy and Card. Sacchetti. In the 19C it lost some of its treasures to the Vatican Picture Gallery and to the Accademia di San Luca. More recently it was enriched by the Cini bequest, which included some interesting 14–15C paintings from the Sterbini collection, as well as the ceramics of that collection. The Pinacoteca has good works, native and foreign, of artists of the 16C, 17C, and 18C.

The gallery is on the second floor. On the LANDING: Apotheosis of Sabina, relief from the Arco di Portogallo (see p 145); Head of a priest of Isis (?); Bull attacked by a tigress, two examples of marble intarsia work from the basilica of Junius Bassus on the Esquiline (4C AD).

ROOM I. 4. *School of Ferrara*, Portrait of a girl; 5. *Dosso Dossi*, Holy Family; 7. *Mazzolino*, Christ and the Doctors; *10. *Emilian School* (1513), Madonna and Child with Saints; *Garófalo*, *14. Annunciation, 21. Madonna in Glory (restored in 1978), 22. Holy Family; 17. *Fr. Francia*(?), Presentation in the Temple; 23. *Scarsellino*, Adoration of the Magi.

R. II. *Paolo Veronese*, 1. Strength, 3. Temperance, 6. Rape of Europa; *2. *Girol. Savoldo*, Portrait of a Lady with a Dragon Fur, also identified as St Margaret, 4. *Gentile Bellini* (attrib.), Portrait of a man; *5. *Giov. Bellini*, Portrait of a young man; *8. *Palma Vecchio*, *9. *Titian*, Baptism of Christ; 10. *Lor. Lotto*, Man with crossbow; *Domenico Tintoretto*, 11–13. Scourging of Christ, Crown of Thorns, Baptism of Christ, *17. St Mary Magdalene.

R. III. *Bart. Passarotti*, 1, 7. Two portraits of unknown men; 5. Portrait of a man with dog; *Van Dyck*, 2. The engravers Pieter de

Jode, father and son, 10. The painters Luke and Cornelius de Wael; 3. *Anon.* (taken from a painting by Jacopino del Conte), Portrait of Michelangelo; 4. *Guido Reni*, Self-portrait; 6. *Rubens*, Romulus and Remus fed by the wolf (finished by pupils); 8. *Federico Zuccari*, Self-portrait; *11. *Velazquez*, Portrai. of a man (? Bernini); *Salvator Rosa*, 13. Soldier, 15. The witch; *17. *Jean Leclerc*, Christ with the doctors; 18. *Carlo Maratta*, Holy Family; 19, 21. *Il Borgognone*, Two battle scenes; 20. *Simon Vouet*, Allegory; 23. *Luca Cambiaso*, Madonna and Child; 22. *Metsù*, Crucifixion; 25. *Guercino*, Holy Family; 26. *Denis Calvaert*, Marriage of St Catherine.

R. IV. Mainly 14C and 15C. *1. *Cola dell'Amatrice*, Death and Assumption of the Virgin; *5. *Macrino d'Alba*, Madonna and saints; *8. *Barnaba da Modena*, Ascension; 11. *G. A. Sogliani*, Madonna and Child; 12–16. *Central Italian master* (1376), Annunciation, Nativity, Presentation in the Temple, Flight into Egypt, Massacre of the Innocents; 17, 19. *Follower of P. Lorenzetti*, St Mary Magdalene and St Bartholomew; 18. *Nic. di Pietro Gerini*, Trinity.

To the right is R. V (the CINI GALLERY), containing part of the bequest of Count Giuseppe Cini (1881), and including a noteworthy collection of bronzes and ceramics. In glass cases: *Ceramics from various sources, including excellent Saxon porcelain, clocks, and tobacco boxes. 17. *Caravaggio*, St John the Baptist, a replica of one in the Galleria Doria.—At the end of the gallery is the *Medagliere* (adm by special permission), containing a rich collection of Roman, medieval, and modern coins and medals.

R. VI. *Pier Fr. Mola*, 1. Diana and Endymion, 7. Esther and Ahasuerus; *Pietro da Cortona*, 3. Rape of the Sabines, 12. Sacrifice of Polyxena, 14. Triumph of Bacchus; 6. *Pietro Testa*, Joseph sold into bondage; 9. *G. M. Bottalla*, Meeting of Esau and Jacob; 10, 11. *Crescenzio Onofri*, Landscapes.—(Above window), Bust of Benedict XIV; inlaid 17C cabinets. Hercules in gilt bronze, found in the time of Sixtus IV in the demolition of the Ara Maxima, near the Forum Boarium.

R. VII. (to right of R. IV.). 1. *Domenichino*, Sibyl; 2. *Guercino*, St John Baptist; 3. *Giov. Lanfranco*, Herminia among the shepherds; *Guido Reni*, 5. Magdalen, 6. Anima Beata; *Guercino*, 12. St Petronilla, a vast canvas, formerly in St Peter's, 14. Antony and Cleopatra, 16. St Matthew and the angel, 22. Persian Sibyl; 10. *Elisabetta Sirani*, Ulysses and Circe; 17. *Fr. Albani*, Nativity of the Virgin; *19. *Caravaggio*, Gipsy fortune-teller (recently restored).

R. VIII (left). 3. *Pietro da Cortona*, Madonna and Child; 9. *Veronese*, Mary Magdalene; 10. *School of Tintoretto*, Pentecost; 15. *Guido Reni*, Christ Child and St John; 16, 18. *Agostino Tassi* (?), two landscapes; 17. *Poussin*, Triumph of Flora (replica of a painting in the Louvre).

R. IX. *Garofalo*, 3. Holy Family, 5. Marriage of Catherine; 7. *Guido Reni*, Madonna and Child with SS. Albert and Cecilia; 8. *Fr. Albani*, Madonna and Child; 9. *Ann. Carracci*, Madonna and Child; 11. *Lod. Carracci*, Head of a boy, a very fine early work; 18. *Ann. Carracci*, St Francis adoring the Crucifix.

From Piazza del Campidoglio the short Via del Campidoglio skirting the right side of Palazzo Senatorio runs downhill, past a stretch of Roman road, to a terrace with an excellent *View of the Forum backed by the Colosseum. The rest of the Capitol hill can be seen by taking Via di Monte Tarpeo and then Via del Tempio di Giove back uphill from the terrace (or by the staircase which ascends from Piazza del Campidoglio to a portico named after Vignola, the arches of which have been closed in with glass). At the top of Via del Tempio di Giove, enclosed by a modern wall and very much below the level of the road, are the remains of the E angle of the façade of the Temple of Jupiter (see p 53). From the peaceful gardens on the terrace known as the BELVEDERE DI MONTE TARPEO there is another extensive *View of Rome to the S and SE, taking in the Forum, the Palatine, the Baths of Caracalla, the Aventine, and the Tiber. The precipice below is thought to be the notorious Tarpeian Rock from which condemned criminals were flung in ancient Rome, although it has also been connected with the N side of the hill. The road continues past a little 19C temple to the edge of the hill (where steps lead down to Via di Teatro di Marcello), and then turns right under an arch to skirt the side of the hill above gardens and paths which descend to its foot.

In front of the 16C *Palazzo Caffarelli*, built on the site of the Temple of Jupiter, there is another splendid panorama of Rome, this time towards St Peter's. The palace houses the offices of the Capitoline museums and a selection of exhibits from the **Antiquarium Comunale** (admission only with special permission).

The Antiquarium was founded in 1885 for objects found during excavations in Rome and illustrates the everyday life of the city from earliest times to the end of the Empire (including material from the Esquiline necropolis, and excavations near Sant'Omobono and on the Capitol). This extremely important archaeological collection has been closed to the public for decades: part of it is in store in Palazzo dell'Esposizione, and part has remained on the Celian hill, where it was formerly exhibited.

*Santa Maria in Aracoeli** (Pl. 4; 5), an austere brick-built church, dating from before the 7C, when it was already considered ancient, stands on the highest point of the Capitoline Hill. It is approached by a monumental flight of steps, but from the top of the hill it is more easily reached by steps to the E of the Capitoline Museum. The church occupies the site of the Roman citadel, where, according to medieval tradition, the Tiburtine Sibyl foretold to Augustus the imminent coming of Christ in the words, 'Ecce ara primogeniti Dei': hence the name Aracoeli, Church of the Altar of Heaven. In the 10C the church belonged to the Benedictines; in 1250 Innocent IV handed it over to the Franciscans, who rebuilt it in the Romanesque style. The façade, overlooking the great staircase from Piazza d'Aracoeli, was never completed. The staircase was built in 1348 as a thank-offering for deliverance from a plague.

In the Middle Ages the church was the meeting-place of the Roman Council. Here Rienzo addressed the assembly after the events of Whitsun 1347; Charles of Anjou held his parliament of the Romans; and Marcantonio Colonna celebrated his triumph after the battle of Lepanto. It was also in this church, as Gibbon 'sat musing amidst the ruins of the Capitol, while the friars were singing vespers, that the idea of writing the Decline and Fall of the City first started to his mind' (5 October 1764).

In the tympanum of the S door is a mosaic of the Madonna and two angels by the school of *Pietro Cavallini*.

The INTERIOR (closed 12–15.30), hung with chandeliers, has been freely restored but has retained its grandeur and severity. The ceiling of the NAVE, with naval emblems and much gold ornamentation, dates from 1575 and commemorates the victory of Lepanto (1571).

The 22 antique columns in the nave, of varying sizes and styles, were taken from pagan buildings; the 3rd on the left bears the inscription 'a cubiculo Augustorum'. Many tombs are set in the Cosmatesque pavement. To the right of the central door is the *Tomb of Cardinal d'Albret, by *And. Bregno* (1465), and the *Tomb slab of the archdeacon Giovanni Crivelli (1432; very worn), signed by *Donatello*; on the left is the tomb of the astronomer Lodovico Grato Margani (1531), of the school of *And. Sansovino*, who himself executed the figure of Christ.

There are notices on each chapel describing their contents. SOUTH AISLE. 1st chapel (Bufalini): *Frescoes from the life of St Bernardino, considered among the finest works of *Pinturicchio* (c 1486; restored by Camuccini); between the 2nd and 3rd chapels, colossal statue of Gregory XIII, by *Pier Paolo Olivieri*. 5th chap., 16C paintings by *Girol. Muziano*; the 6th chapel is a pretty 17C work designed by Giovanni Battista Contini. By the S door (right), Monument of Pietro da Vicenza by *And. Sansovino*, and (left) tomb of Cecchino Bracci (d 1545) by *P. Urbano* on a design of Michelangelo. In the last chapel are two Caravaggesque paintings by *Dan. Seiter.*—In the crossing, on the pilasters facing the high altar, are two *Ambones, by *Lorenzo* and *Giacomo di Cosma* (c 1200).—SOUTH TRANSEPT. The Savelli Chapel contains two fine *Tombs: on the left is that of Luca Savelli attrib. to *Arnolfo di Cambio*, with a 3C Roman sarcophagus beneath, and on the right, the 14C tomb of Vana Aldobrandi, wife of Luca, with a statue of her son Honorius III. The Cappella di Santa Rosa (seen through the Cappella del SS. Sacramento, to the right) has a fine mosaic of the Madonna enthroned between SS. John the Baptist and Francis dating from the 13C.

CHOIR. Over the high altar is a small *Madonna, known as the 'Madonna d'Aracoeli', usually attrib. to a 10C̆ master. Here from 1512 to 1565 was hung Raphael's 'Madonna of Foligno' (p 335), commissioned by Sigismondo Conti, whose tomb is in the pavement near the stalls on the S side. In the APSE, on the left, is the fine monument of Giov. Battista Savelli (school of *And. Bregno*, 1498).— In the centre of the NORTH TRANSEPT is the little Temple of St Helena, or Santa Cappella, a 17C shrine (reconstructed in the 19C) with eight columns. Beneath it (light) remains of an altar (12C or 13C) showing the apparition of the Virgin to Augustus. Excavations also revealed remains of a Roman wall here. At the end of the transept is the beautiful Cosmati *Tomb of Cardinal Matteo di Acquasparta (d 1302), mentioned by Dante ('Paradiso', xii, 124), with a fresco by Pietro Cavallini. To the right is the entrance to the Cappella del Santissimo Bambino, which contains a figure of the Infant Christ, reputed to have been carved from the wood of an olive tree in the Garden of Gethsemane and an object of immense veneration (see below).—NORTH AISLE, 5th chapel, St Paul, by *Girol. Muziano*, and the fine tomb of Filippo Della Valle (1494; l.), by *Michele Marini* or the school of *And. Riccio*; 3rd chapel, St Antony, by *Benozzo Gozzoli*, and the Renaissance tomb of Antonio Albertoni (1509; right); between the 3rd and 2nd chapels, a statue of Paul III. The 2nd chapel (Cappella del Presepio) is open only during the Christmas festival, when the Christ Child is exhibited (from the Cappella del Santissimo Bambino; see above). Every afternoon, children of from 5 to 10 years of age recite little poems and speeches before its crib.

The overwhelming **Monument of Victor Emmanuel II** (Pl. 4; 5) was inaugurated in 1911 to symbolize the achievement of Italian unity. Some 80 metres high, it changed irrevocably the aspect of the city, throwing out of scale the Capitol hill itself, and causing indiscriminate demolition in the area. Familiarly known as 'the wedding cake' or 'Mussolini's typewriter', it can only be described as a colossal monstrosity. It was begun in 1885 by *Giuseppe Sacconi*, winner of an international competition in which there were 98 entries. He used an incongruous dazzling white 'botticino' marble from Brescia to further alienate it from its surroundings.It has been closed to the public for many years, although there are now plans to reopen it and use it for exhibitions and conferences.

At the sides of the monument are fountains representing the Tyrrhenian Sea, by *Pietro Canonica*, and the Adriatic, as well as the remains of the tomb of Gaius Publicius Bibulus, dating from the early 1C BC. Above the stylobate are sculptures by *Ettore Ximenes, Leon. Bistolfi, Lud. Poliaghi*, and *Augusto Rivalta*. The grave of Italy's Unknown Soldier from the First World War, guarded by two sentinels, lies at the foot of the Altare della Patria by *Angelo Zanelli*. The equestrian statue of Victor Emmanuel II is by *Enrico Chiaradia*. The two Quadrigae are by *Paolo Bartolini* and *Carlo Fontana*.

The **Museo Centrale del Risorgimento** (closed in 1988) is entered on the right of the monument, or in Via di San Pietro in Carcere. It contains exhibits illustrating the story of Italy's struggle for independence. It has a section devoted to the First World War. The *Archives* contain a collection of documents and autographs of the period of the Risorgimento. Also in the building is the *Museo Sacrario delle Bandiere della Marina Militare* with material relating to naval history.

Across Piazza Venezia (left) is the battlemented ***Palazzo di Venezia**, the first great Renaissance palace in Rome. *Giul. da Maiano, Bern. Rossellino*, and *Leon Batt. Alberti* have all been suggested as its architect, but it has recently been attributed to *Francesco del Borgo*. It was begun in 1455, enlarged in 1464, and finally finished in the 16C. It was built, partly of stone from the Colosseum, for the Venetian Cardinal Pietro Barbo, afterwards Paul II (1464–71), the first of the great Renaissance popes. Barbo is said to have built the palace in order to view the horse-races in the Corso. It later became a papal residence, and was often occupied as such even after it had been given by Pius IV (1559–65) to the Venetian Republic for its embassy. Charles VIII of France stayed here after entering Rome with 20,000 soldiers in 1494. From the Treaty of Campoformio in 1797 until 1915 it was the seat of the Austrian ambassador to the Vatican. In 1917 Italy resumed possession and the palace was restored. During the Fascist régime it was occupied by Mussolini, who had his office in the Sala del Mappamondo. Some of his most famous speeches were made from the balcony overlooking Piazza di Venezia. The door in the piazza is finely carved and attrib. to Giul. da Maiano. The picturesque inner court (reached from No. 49, Piazza di San Marco), with its tall palm trees, has a large unfinished 15C loggia on two sides, of beautiful proportions. In the centre is a fountain by Carlo Monaldi (1730).

Adjoining the palace and facing the Via and Piazza di San Marco, to the S and E, is the **Palazzetto di Venezia**. This was originally (c 1467) in Piazza di Venezia, but was moved to its present position in 1911 because it obstructed the view of the Victor Emmanuel Monument. To see the beautiful court and garden, special permission is needed (apply at No. 49, Piazza di San Marco).

The ***Museo del Palazzo di Venezia** (admission see p 50) occupies several of the papal apartments and many rooms in the Palazzetto di Venezia. The entrance is in Via del Plebiscito. The museum was finally reopened in 1988 after years of closure and the collections are now displayed in modern show-cases designed by Franco Minissi. In addition to interesting paintings, there is a good collection of wood sculptures, bronzes, Romanesque and 14C ivories, majolica, church silver, and terracottas. It is the only museum of the decorative arts in the city. Up to now the State rooms have been open only for temporary exhibitions, but it now seems these will be integrated into the Museum and no longer used for exhibitions. These include the Sala Regia, the Sala del Concistoro, the Sala del Mappamondo (so called from a large map mentioned in 1534), and the Sala delle Fatiche d'Ercole ('Labours of Hercules'), named from a painted frieze by the school of Mantegna. In 1988 the important collection of arms and armour (some of them left to the city by the Odescalchi in 1976) and the 15–17C tapestries (German, Flemish and Italian), formerly exhibited in these rooms, were not on display.

From Via del Plebiscito a monumental staircase by Luigi Marangoni (1930) leads up to the first floor and the ticket office. To the right is the Appartamento Cibo, the appartments of the Cardinals of San Marco, with some good ceilings and colourful floors, where the first part of the collection is arranged. The rooms are un-numbered but the works are all labelled. ROOM 1. Architectural fragments (early 8C–end of 9C) including a well-head; bronzes, ivories, including a 10C *Triptych of the 'Deësis' and Saints.—ROOM 2. Sculptural fragments; seated statue of a Pope, sometimes identified as Nicholas IV or as Boniface VIII, a Roman work of the late 13C. The marble transenna with donars is attributed to *Giovanni di Stefano* (fl. 1366–91).—ROOM 3 (to the left). The *Madonna of Acuto, an early 13C wood polychrome seated statue, the earliest known work of its kind; *Crucifix, probably painted by a follower of Giotto in the last decade of the 13C. It comes from the church of San Tommaso dei Cenci (and was originally in Santa Maria in Aracoeli).—ROOM 4 (beyond R. 2). *Head of a woman by *Nicola Pisano*; 13C relief of an Angel in gilded bronze and cloisonnè enamel; 13C Byzantine *Crosses, and a *Relief of the Crucifixion; Christ Pantocrator, an unusual work in metal and enamel (13C, Byzantine); gilded bronze incised *Lunette from Palestrina (thought to be an early 13C German work). It may have been the back of an episcopal seat.—To the left, ROOM 5 has a ceiling with signs of the zodiac. Here are 14C ceramics from Orvieto, and early medieval ceramics from Rome and Lazio, and a valuable series of cassoni.

In ROOM 6 (beyond R. 4) is exhibited the Sterbini collection of paintings, mostly Tuscan 'fondi oro', all of them in good condition. Three exquisite small works: *Florentine, early 15C*, *Triptych; *Master of Santa Chiara di Montefalco*, *Reliquary with the Madonna and Child and Saints; *Sienese, early 14C*, *Diptych; *Bicci di Lorenzo*, Imprisonment and Martyrdom of St Catherine of Alexandria; *Nanni di Jacopo*, Triptych with the Madonna and Child and angel musicians, and four Saints; *Cristoforo da Bologna*, Madonna of Humility; *15C Spanish School*, *Madonna enthroned.—In the little chapel: *Francesco Zaganelli da Cotignola*, Christ carrying the Cross; *Sassoferrato*, *St Francis; *Girolamo da Santacroce*, Rape of Europa, Head of St Michael Archangel; *Bachiacca*, Vision of St Bernardino.—ROOM 7 (Salone Altoviti) has grotteschi on the ceiling attributed to *Vasari*. Here are two *Crosses made in Abruzzi in the 14C and 15C, the latter from Alba Fucens; reliquary by *Jacopo Tondi*; and a 14C Venetian *Triptych in wood, silver, and enamel with minatures of the Madonna and Child, Evangelists, Prophets, and stories from the Life of Christ.—ROOM 8. Fine wood statues, including two of the *Magi (14C works from the Marches); *'Cassa di Terracina', an 11C cedar wood chest with reliefs, a rare example of wood intaglio. To the left is ROOM 9 with materials found in Tivoli (coptic fragments of the 5C and 6C as well as 14C works). The little room beyond (10) displays 12–13C seals.—ROOM 11 (beyond R. 8) has a view of the E end of the church of the Gesù.

The long corridor (12) which connects these apartments to the Palazzetto di Venezia has a splendid view of the delightful courtyard, with palms and a fountain. Here is displayed a representative collection of Italian ceramics with examples from all the main workshops (Faenza, Urbino, Montelupo, Deruta, Pesaro, Casteldurante, etc.). The second half of the corridor displays porcelain (Meissen, Sèvres, Staffordshire, etc.).—The first rooms (13–15) of the Palazzetto contains some furniture. ROOM 16 contains a 15C marble bust of the Venetian Cardinal Pietro Barbo (afterwards Paul II) who built Palazzo Venezia.—In ROOM

17 begins the splendid display of small *Bronzes, continued in ROOM 18. Here are works by Il Riccio, Nicolò Roccatagliata, Girolamo Campagna, Giovanni Francesco Susini, Pietro Tacca, Pietro Bracci, Il Moderno, Tiziano Aspetti, Giambologna, Francesco Duquesnoy, Alessandro Algardi, Antonio Susini, and Gian Lorenzo Bernini.—ROOM 19. Sculptures by Baccio da Montelupo (Head of the Redeemer), and Francesco Segala, and two *Reliefs of the Miracle of St Mark by Jacopo Sansovino (models for the bronze reliefs in the chancel of the basilica of San Marco in Venice).—Beyond ROOM 20, ROOM 21 has small sculptures, including two models for sculptures on the Trevi fountain.—ROOM 22 displays numerous busts, statuettes and terracotta *Bozzetti by Bernini (model for an angel on Ponte Sant'Angelo and for details of his Roman fountains), and Alessandro Algardi (bust of Giacinta Sanvitali Conti, and St Agnes appearing to St Constance).—ROOM 23. Relief of the deposition by Ignazio Marabitti; two 18C portraits by Vincenzo Pacetti.—ROOM 24 contains bozzetti by Antonio Canova.—ROOM 25. Bozzetti by Francesco Mochi and others.—Beyond the little room (26) with a pretty barrel vault is the last room (27) of sculpture, with a head ('Seneca') attributed to Guido Reni, and a bust of Benedict XIII by Pietro Bracci (1724).

The rooms of paintings, beyond, were closed in 1988. These include: Giov. Bellini, *Portrait of a young man; Giorgione (?), Double Portrait; Nicolò de' Barberi, Woman taken in adultery; Giov. Cariani, Lovers in a landscape, Portrait of a devotee; Rocco Marconi, Woman taken in adultery; Lelio Orsi, Pietà; Bachiacca, Lady as St Mary Magdalene; Fed. Zuccari, Scenes in the life of Taddeo Zuccari; Benozzo Gozzoli, The Redeemer (part of a fresco); Dom. Puligo, Madonna; Gius. Maria Crespi, David and Abigail, Finding of the infant Moses; Donato Creti, Nymphs dancing; Girol. da Cremona, Nativity and Annunciation (triptych); School of Giovanni Bellini, Moses rescued from the water, Meeting of the Madonna and St Anne; Giov. da Modena, Crucifixion; Ottaviano Nelli, Madonna; Segna di Tura, Madonna and Child; Paolo Veneziano, Angelic choir; Bened. Diana, Redeemer; Garófalo, St Jerome; Guercino, St Peter; Cornelius Johnson, Child with a puppy; Jacob Cuyp, Portraits of a woman and of a man; Ciro Ferri, Marriage of St Catherine; Sim. Canterini, Madonna; Fr. Solimena, Marriage at Cana; Carlo Maratta, Cleopatra.

The palace is also the seat of the Istituto Nazionale di Archeologia e Storia dell'Arte (entered at No. 49, Piazza San Marco), founded in 1922. The library, the most important of its kind in Italy, with c 350,000 vols, is partially closed and in urgent need of new premises (hopefully it will be · moved to the Collegio Romano).

At the corner of Piazza San Marco is a colossal mutilated bust of Isis, known as 'Madama Lucrezia'. It has been here since the 15C and was once used for the display of satirical comments and epigrams like those of Pasquino and Marforio. In the garden in front (right) is a fountain (1927) with a pine-cone, the emblem of this district, the Rione della Pigna.

In Piazza San Marco is the church of **San Marco** (Pl. 3; 6), which forms part of Palazzo di Venezia. It was founded in 336 by St Mark the Pope, restored in 833, rebuilt in the 15C by Paul II, and again restored in the 17C and 1744. The campanile is Romanesque, and the façade an elegant Renaissance work with a portico and a loggia which was once used by the pope in the benediction ceremony. Under the portico are sculptural fragments and inscriptions, and over the central door, a relief of St Mark enthroned attrib. to Isaia da Pisa (1464).

Steps lead down to the fine INTERIOR which retains its ancient basilican form with a raised sanctuary. There is a good Renaissance ceiling and remains of a Cosmatesque pavement (E end). The bright columns of Sicilian jasper and the stucco reliefs in the nave (between 17C frescoes) date from the Baroque restoration in the 18C. South side: 1st chapel, Palma Giovane, Resurrection; 3rd chapel, Carlo Maratta, Adoration of the Magi. Beyond a niche with a monument to Card. Vidman (died 1660) by Cosimo Fancelli, the 4th chapel contains 17C works by Bernardino Gagliardi. By the steps up to the presbytery is the funerary monument of Leonardo Pesaro by Ant. Canova. The chapel to the right of the high altar, by Pietro da Cortona, contains a painting of St Mark the Pope by

Melozzo da Forlì and frescoes (very ruined) by *Borgognone*. In the apse (coin-
operated light) a *Mosaic (c 829–30; recently restored) represents Christ with
saints and Gregory IV offering a model of the church. In the sacristy (if closed,
ring on the left in the church porch), is a recomposed tabernacle by *Mino da
Fiesole* and *Giov. Dalmata*, and St Mark the Evangelist (much darkened) by
Melozzo.—The niches on the North side contain notable Baroque monuments,
and here the 4th chapel has works by *Fr. Mola* and *Borgognone*. The 2nd chapel
was decorated by Emidio Sintes (1764).—Remains of the earlier churches have
been found beneath the pavement (apply to the sacristan).

2   The Roman Forum

Admission, see p 49. The admission ticket includes the Palatine (Rte 3). The
main entrance is in Via dei Fori Imperiali, opposite the end of Via Cavour. There
is another entrance at the Arch of Titus near the Colosseum: this however is
reserved for the handicapped, the elderly, and for school children. In the
following description the exit is here. The entrance to the Palatine on Via San
Gregorio (see Rte 3) can also be used. There is another exit onto Via del Foro
Romano, above the Basilica Julia. A full exploration of the Forum and the
Palatine requires more than a single day.

The *** *Roman Forum** is the heart of ancient Rome. Here is reflected
almost every event of importance in the city's development from the
time of the kings through the Republican and Imperial eras to the
Middle Ages. The ruins stand in the centre of modern Rome as a
romantic testament to her past greatness. The plants and shrubs
which now surround them add to their charm. However, the visible
remains are difficult to understand in detail without preparatory
study and constant reference to the plans (pp 78–9). Important
excavations are being carried out at the foot of the Capitol hill, where
a road which formerly cut off the monuments at the extreme W end of
the Forum has been eliminated. There are plans to connect the
Forum with the Capitol again via the Clivus Capitolinus. Meanwhile some of the monuments in this area are covered for restoration,
and access has been temporarily suspended while excavations
continue.

The best comprehensive view of the Forum is from the Capitol hill, from the
terrace at the bottom of Via del Campidoglio or from the Belvedere di Monte
Tarpeo (see Rte 1). The Palatine also provides a good view.
    The Forum runs WNW and ESE, following the direction of the Capitoline end
of the Sacra Via and that of the Nova Via. In the following description it is taken
as running W and E, the left side, looking towards the Colosseum, being N and
the right side S. The plans are thus orientated.

History. The site of the Forum was originally a marshy valley lying between the
Capitoline and Palatine Hills. It was bounded on the N and E by the foothills of
the Quirinal and Esquiline and by the low ridge of the Velia, which connected
the Palatine with the Esquiline. In the Iron Age it was used as a necropolis.
Buildings appeared here after the union of the Latin villages of the Palatine with
the Sabines of the Quirinal, which is traditionally said to have followed the
battle of Romans and Sabines on the Palatine slopes. To the period of the kings
are ascribed the first monuments of the Forum, such as the Lapis Niger, the
Vulcanal, the Temple of Janus, the Regia, the Temple of Vesta, and the Curia.
The Tarquins made the area habitable by canalizing its stagnant waters into the
Cloaca Maxima and it became the market-place (Forum) of Rome.
    The original Forum was a rectangle bounded at the W by the Lapis Niger and
the Rostra, on the E by a line through the site of the Temple of Julius Caesar,
and on the N and S by two rows of shops (*Tabernae*) approximately on the line
of the Basilica Aemilia (N) and the Basilica Julia (S). This area was about 115m
by 57m. Adjacent, on the NW, was a second rectangle including the Comitium,

reserved for political assemblies, or *Comitia Curiata*. Here also were the Curia, or senate-house, and the Rostra, or orators' tribune. Beyond the limits of this second square, to the E, were the Regia, seat of the Pontifex Maximus, the Temple of Vesta, and the House of the Vestals. In this direction ran the *Sacra Via*. Other streets were the *Argiletum* to the N, the *Vicus Jugarius* and the *Vicus Tuscus* to the Velabrum, the *Clivus Argentarius*, which ran between the Capitol and the Quirinal to the Via Flaminia and the Campus Martius, and the *Nova Via*, on the S side, dividing the Forum from the Palatine.

Three distinct areas of the Forum thus became defined—the Comitium, or political centre, the religious centre of the Regia, and the Forum proper. This last gradually lost its character of market-place and became a centre of civic importance and the scene of public functions and ceremonies. The greengrocers and other shopkeepers were banished to the Velabrum and replaced by money-changers (argentarii).

In the 2C BC a new type of building, the basilica, was introduced. This large covered space was used for judicial hearings and public meetings when these could not be held outside. The new construction involved the demolition of private houses behind the tabernae. The first basilica was the Basilica Porcia, built by the censor Cato in 185 BC and destroyed in 52 BC. Others were the Basilica Aemilia (179 BC), and the Basilica Sempronia (170 BC), built by T. Sempronius Gracchus, father of the tribunes, and later replaced by the Basilica Julia. The last to be built is the Basilica of Constantine (4C AD).

In 133 Tiberius Gracchus was killed in the Forum. After Julius Caesar's assassination on the Ides of March, 44 BC, his body was cremated in the Forum. He had begun the enlargement of the Forum which Sulla had planned some years before. It was left to Augustus to complete the work. Between 44 and 27 BC the Basilica Julia, Curia, and Rostra were completed, the Temple of Saturn and the Regia restored, the Temple of Julius Caesar dedicated, and the Arch of Augustus erected. According to Suetonius, Augustus found the city brick and left it marble.

By this time the area of the Forum had become inadequate for the growing population and the emperors were obliged to build their own Fora (see Rte 4). A fire in the old Forum in the 3C AD caused much damage, which was repaired by Diocletian, but the area shared in the general decay of the city. Temples and sanctuaries were neglected under Christian rule and robbed of most of their treasures. The few that remained were finally despoiled in the barbarian invasions and the abandoned buildings were further damaged by earthquakes.

The medieval Roman barons, notably the Frangipani family, used the tallest of the ruined buildings as foundations for their fortress-towers, and a few churches were constructed. But most of the Forum became the *Campo Vaccino*, or cattle-pasture. Its monuments were used as quarries and its precious marbles were burned in lime-kilns.

The Forum inspired the artists of the Renaissance and suggested the plans of their great constructions of the 15–18C, to which only too often portions of ancient buildings were sacrificed. A new archaeological movement at the end of the 18C brought about the systematic excavation of the site, continued with little interruption through the 19C, especially after 1870. The distinguished archaeologist, Giacomo Boni, after 1898, conducted the excavations and found archaic monuments of supreme interest, a discovery which threw much light upon the primitive history of Rome. After his death in 1925 the work was continued by Alfonso Bartoli. Excavations now being carried out are at the W end at the foot of the Capitol Hill, in the area of the Temple of Castor and the Lacus Juturnae, by the Basilica Aemilia, and between the Arch of Titus and the House of Vestals.

From the main entrance on Via dei Fori Imperiali (Pl. 4; 7) a broad path descends between the Temple of Antoninus and Faustina (left; see p 87) and the Basilica Aemilia on the level of the ancient Forum. The **Basilica Aemilia** was built by the censors M. Aemilius Lepidus and M. Fulvius Nobilior in 179 BC, restored by members of the Aemilia gens in 78 BC and rebuilt in the time of Julius Caesar. It was rebuilt in AD 22 after a fire and nearly destroyed by another fire during Alaric's sack of Rome in 410. On the side towards the Forum it faces the Sacra Via; on its W side is the *Argiletum*, once one of the Forum's busiest streets, which led N to the quarter of the Subura through the Forum of Nerva.

This ancient building was for the most part demolished during the Renaissance for the sake of its marble. It comprised a vast rectangular hall 70m by 29m, divided by columns into a central nave and aisles, single on the S side and double on the N. In the fine pavement of the hall, in coloured marble, are embedded some coins that fused with the bronze roof-decorations during the fire of 410. Casts of fragments of a frieze of the Republican era have been assembled below the terrace at the NE corner. On the S side, facing the Forum, was a two-storied portico covering a row of shops, the *Tabernae Novae*, still well preserved. The portico was restored during the late empire; evidence of this restoration is claimed in the three granite columns that have been set up in front of the Basilica. On the W side are remains (covered) of the earliest basilica.

The open space in front of the Basilica Aemilia is the original **Forum**; through it runs the Ima Sacra Via (see below). As the meeting-place of the whole population, and a market-place, the Forum was kept

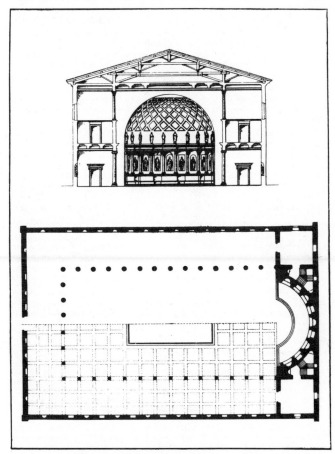

The Roman Basilica, after Vitruvius, architect and surveyor to Augustus ('De architectura', before AD 27), published by Carlo Amati in 1829

free of obstructions in Republican days. Here took place all important ceremonies and public meetings. Orators spoke from the Rostra, where magistrates' edicts, legal decisions, and official communications were published. All the main religious festivals took place here; political offenders were executed; the funeral ceremonies of illustrious personages were held; it was in the Forum that the body of Julius Caesar was cremated. Under the Empire the Forum lost its original character. New buildings encroached upon the area, which became merely an official centre, while the crowds migrated to the Imperial Fora.

The **Sacra Via**, the oldest street in Rome, traverses the length of the Forum and extends beyond it on either side. It received its name, according to tradition, from the fact that it was the scene of the peace treaty between Romulus and the Sabine king Titus Tatius. A more likely explanation is that it was lined with important sanctuaries. Its oldest section is that between the Temple of Castor and the Velia. The section through the original Forum as far as the Temple of Julius Caesar was called the *Ima Sacra Via*; from there to the point where it begins to climb to the Arch of Titus it was called the *Media Sacra Via*; the actual rise to the Arch was the *Clivus Sacer* or *Summa Sacra Via*. On the W side it was continued as the *Clivus Capitolinus*, which climbed round the Portico of the Dii Consentes to the Temple of Jupiter on the Capitol. On the E side the road was continued in late Imperial times beyond the Arch of Titus to the Arch of Constantine, near the Colosseum.—It was along the Sacra Via that a victorious general awarded a triumph passed in procession to the Capitol to offer sacrifice in the Temple of Jupiter. He rode in a chariot drawn by four horses, preceded by his captives and spoils of war, and followed by his soldiers.—Roughly parallel with the Sacra Via, on the S, runs the *Nova Via*, which separates the Forum from the Palatine (see p 87).

In the Sacra Via, by the SE corner of the Basilica Aemilia, is a dedicatory inscription to Lucius Caesar, grandson and adopted son of Augustus, set up in 2 BC; there was probably an arch here dedicated to him and his brother Gaius.

On the S side of the Sacra Via is the **Temple of Julius Caesar**, the site of which marks the E limit of the original Forum. The body of Julius Caesar was brought to the Forum after the Ides of March in 44 BC, and here his body was probably cremated. The temple was dedicated by Augustus in 29 BC in honour of the Divine Julius Caesar ('Divus Julius'). Here his will was read by Mark Antony, and Tiberius gave a funeral oration over the body of Augustus before it was buried in his mausoleum in AD 14.

This temple (probably Corinthian prostyle hexastyle) was preceded by a terrace which was an extension of the podium. This was called the *Rostra ad Divi Julii*, from the beaks of the Egyptian ships of Antony and Cleopatra captured at Actium with which it was decorated. Nothing remains except for the central block of the podium and the round altar (under cover), probably marking the spot where Caesar was cremated. Fragments, thought to belong to the frieze, are in the Antiquarium of the Forum. Remains of foundations on the N and S sides of the temple are thought to be those of the arcaded *Porticus Julia*, which surrounded the temple on three sides.

About 50m farther W, near the steps of the Basilica Aemilia, are the foundations of the circular *Shrine of Venus Cloacina*, which stood on the point where the Cloaca Maxima entered the Forum. This great drain crossed the Forum from N to S on its way to the Tiber (see p 280). It was beside the shrine that Virginia is said to have been killed by her father to save her from the advances of the decemvir Appius Claudius Crassinus.—At the W end of the Basilica Aemilia is the presumed site of the *Shrine of Janus*, whose bronze doors were closed only in peace-time. This is said to have occurred only three times in the history of Rome.

To the W, in front of the Curia building lies the area of the COMITIUM, the place where the *Comitia Curiata*, representing the 30 Curiae into which the city was politically divided, met to record their votes. The earliest political activity of the Republic took place here and this was the original site of the Rostra. During the Empire the Comitium was restricted to the space between the Curia, and the Lapis Niger; under the Republic the area was much more extensive. Here is the **Lapis Niger** with the oldest relics of the Forum. The Lapis Niger was a pavement of black marble laid to indicate a sacred spot. Tradition placed here the tomb of Romulus or of the shepherd Faustulus or of Hostus Hostilius, father of the third king of Rome. The pavement was discovered in 1899 and, with it, the monuments below it. These are now reached by a flight of iron steps (no adm in 1988). They comprise the base of a truncated column (possibly the base for a statue), an altar, and a square stele with inscriptions on all four sides. These provide the most ancient example of the Latin language (6C or early 5C BC) and, though not fully deciphered, are generally understood to refer to a lex sacra, i.e. a warning against profaning a holy place. In the space between the pavement and the monuments were found, mixed with profuse ashes (indicating a great sacrifice), bronze and terracotta statuettes, fragments of 6C vases and later material; these relics are now in the Antiquarium of the Forum.—Excavations to the E of the Lapis Niger have revealed some remains of the Republican *Rostra*, dating partly from 338 BC, and partly (the curved front and steps) from Sulla's time.

At the N end of the Comitium rises the ***Curia Senatus**, or *Senate House*. For several years this has been open only for exhibitions, for three or four months of the year. In 1988 it was closed for repairs to the roof, and it is hoped that when it reopens it will no longer be used for exhibitions, but only for the display of the two Plutei of Trajan (described below) and for the column base commemorating the decennial games which has recently been restored (see below). The existing building, known as the *Curia Julia*, was begun by Sulla in 80 BC, and rebuilt after a fire by Julius Caesar in 44 BC. It replaced the original *Curia Hostilia* said to have been built by Tullus Hostilius and several times rebuilt. Fifteen years after Caesar's death the Curia Julia was completed by Augustus, who dedicated a statue of Victory in the interior. The Senate House was restored by Domitian and rebuilt by Diocletian after a fire in 283. In 638 it was converted into the church of *Sant' Adriano*. In 1935–38 Alfonso Bartoli restored to it the form it had under Diocletian. The brick façade was originally covered with marble in the lower and with stucco in the upper courses; it was preceded by a portico. The existing doors are copies of the originals, removed by Alexander VII to St John Lateran. A simple pediment with travertine corbels crowns the building.

The remarkable interior, 27m long, 18m wide and 21m high, has a beautiful pavement in opus sectile, revealed by the removal of the floor of the church. On either side is a series of three marble-faced steps, extending along the whole length; here were seats for c 300 senators. At the end, by the president's tribune, is a brick base which may have supported the golden statue of Victory presented by Augustus. The side walls were partly faced with marble and were and still are adorned with niches. Two doors at the rear end opened into a columned portico of the Forum of Caesar. Here was found a

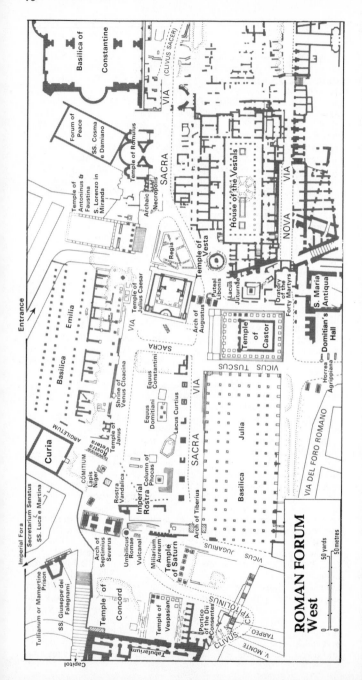

ROMAN FORUM
West

50 yards
50 metres

Basilica of Constantine

Forum of Peace

SS. Cosma e Damiano

Temple of Romulus

VIA (CLIVUS SACER)

VIA SACRA

Temple of Antoninus & Faustina
S. Lorenzo in Miranda

Archaic Necropolis

House of the Vestals

VIA NOVA

Temple of Vesta

Regia

Temple of Julius Caesar

Puteal Libonis

Lacus Juturnae

Oratory of the Forty Martyrs

S. Maria Antiqua

Arch of Augustus

Temple of Castor

Domitian's Hall

Horrea Agrippiana

Entrance

Basilica Emilia

VIA SACRA

Shrine of Venus Cloacina

Temple of Janus

Rostra Vetera

Equus Constantini

VICUS TUSCUS

VIA DEL FORO ROMANO

Curia

ARGILETUM

COMITIUM

Lapis Niger

Rostra Vandalica

Equus Domitiani

Lacus Curtius

VIA SACRA

Basilica Julia

Secretarium Senatus
SS. Lucia e Martina

Imperial Fora

Imperial Rostra

Column of Phocas

Arch of Tiberius

Arch of Septimius Severus

Umbilicus Romae

Vulcanal

Miliarium Aureum

Temple of Saturn

VICUS JUGARIUS

Tullianum or Mamertine Prison

SS. Giuseppe dei Falegnami

Temple of Concord

Temple of Vespasian

Portico of the Dii Consentes

Tabularium

Capitol

V MONTE TARPEO

CLIVUS CAPITOLINUS

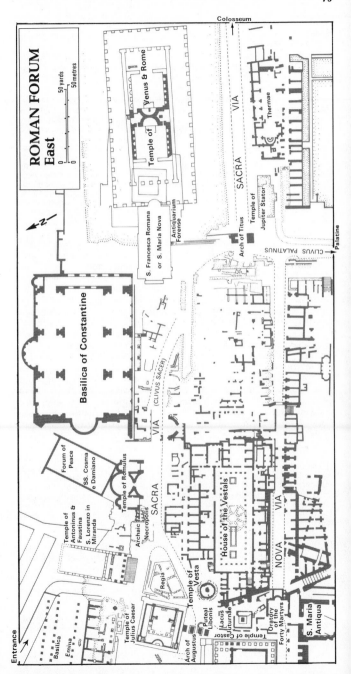

ROMAN FORUM
East

0 50 yards
0 50 metres

Colosseum

Temple of Venus & Rome

S. Francesca Romana or S. Maria Nova

Antiquarium Forense

Arch of Titus

VIA SACRA

Therme

Temple of Jupiter Stator

Palatine

CLIVUS PALATINUS

Basilica of Constantine

VIA (CLIVUS SACER)

VIA SACRA

Forum of Peace

SS. Cosma e Damiano

Temple of Romulus

Temple of Antoninus & Faustina

S. Lorenzo in Miranda

Archaic Necropolis

SACRA VIA

House of the Vestals

NOVA VIA

Regia

Basilica Emilia

Temple of Julius Caesar

Temple of Vesta

Puteal Libonis

Lacus Iuturnae

Temple of Castor

Oratory of the Forty Martyrs

Arch of Augustus

S. Maria Antiqua

Entrance

headless porphyry statue, possibly of Hadrian. Connected to the Senate House was the *Secretarium Senatus* used by a tribunal set up in the late Empire to judge senators.

The Curia houses the *PLUTEI OF TRAJAN, or *Anaglypha Trajani*, two finely sculptured balustrades or parapets, found in the Forum between the Comitium and the Column of Phocas.

On the inner faces are depicted the animals offered up at public sacrifices (suovetaurilia), a pig, a sheep, and a bull; on the outer faces are famous deeds of the emperor. The first represents the emperor burning the registers of outstanding death duties, an event which took place in 118, during Hadrian's reign; in the second an emperor standing on a Rostra with a statue of Trajan, is receiving the thanks of a mother for the founding of an orphanage. The architectural backgrounds show the buildings on the W, S, and E sides of the Forum systematically depicted. From the right of the 1st panel to the left of the 2nd: Temple of Vespasian, an arch without decoration, Temple of Saturn, the Vicus Iugarius, and the arcades of the Basilica Julia. The arches are continued on the 2nd panel, followed by an interval for the Vicus Tuscus (?), Temple of Castor, Rostra of the Temple of Julius Caesar (on which the emperor is standing); his attendants mount the ramp of the Rostra through the Arch of Augustus. On both sides is shown the statue of Marsyas beside the sacred fig-tree (see p 82).

Between the Lapis Niger and the Imperial Rostra (see below) is a large marble *Column Base* bearing an inscription of Diocletian to commemorate the decennial games of AD 303; the reliefs on the other sides depict scenes of sacrifice. This has recently been restored, and it may be taken in under cover and in future exhibited in the Curia (see above). Close by is the marble base of an equestrian statue with a dedicatory inscription celebrating the victory of Arcadius and Honorius over the Goths in 403.

The remaining part of the NW side of the Forum has been fenced off since 1980 while excavations are in progress and the monuments are being restored. The huge building of the Tabularium on the edge of the Capitol Hill which dominates this area has recently been restored. The triple **Arch of Septimius Severus**, nearly 21m high and over 23m wide, entirely faced with marble, was erected in AD 203 in honour of the tenth anniversary of the emperor's accession, and dedicated by the senate and the people to Severus and his sons Caracalla and Geta in memory of their victories over the Parthians, Arabs, and Adiabenians of Assyria. In 1988 half of its scaffolding had been taken down after restoration.

The name of Geta, elder son of Severus, who was murdered by Caracalla in 212, was replaced by an inscription in praise of Caracalla and his father, but the holes made for the original letters are still visible. On the well-proportioned arch the four large reliefs depict scenes from the two Parthian campaigns; in the small friezes are figures symbolic of the homage paid by the Orient to Rome; and at the bases of the columns are captive barbarians. There is a small interior staircase (no adm) which leads up to the four chambers of the attic.

To the S of the Arch of Severus are the ruins of the **Imperial Rostra**, or orator's tribune brought from its original site in front of the Curia during Caesar's restoration. It is 3m high, 24m long and 12m deep.

The original structure (see above), of very early date, was adorned with the 'rostra' or iron beaks of the ships captured at the battle of Antium (338 BC). On the platform rose columns surmounted by commemorative statues, and its parapet was probably decorated with the sculptured plutei of Trajan. In front, on the right, are the *Rostra Vandalica*, an extension of the 5C AD; the modern name is taken from an inscription commemorating a naval victory over the Vandals in 470.

At the back of the Rostra is a semicircular wall (*Hemicyclium*), formed by alterations during the building of the Arch of Septimius Severus. At its N end, by the Arch, is a cylindrical construction, the *Umbilicus Urbis* (? 2C BC), supposed to mark the centre of the city. Opposite the other end of the wall is the site of the *Milliarium Aureum*, the 'golden milestone', a bronze-covered column set up by Augustus as the symbolic starting-point of all the roads of the Empire, with the distance from Rome to the chief cities engraved in gold letters on its base.

Immediately behind the Umbilicus, protected by a roof, is a quadrangular area identified as the *Volcanal*, or Altar of Vulcan, part of a larger area dedicated to the god, dating from before the 6C BC. By it grew, in Republican times, two trees—a lotus and a cypress—said to be older than the city itself.

From the SW corner of the original Forum, the *Vicus Jugarius* runs S to the Velabrum between the Basilica Julia on the left (see below) and the Temple of Saturn on the right. The ***Temple of Saturn**, one of the most ancient sanctuaries in the Forum, may have been inaugurated in 498 BC in honour of the mythical god-king of Italy, whose reign was the fabled Golden Age. The temple was rebuilt, after several previous reconstructions, by L. Munatius Plancus in the year of his consulship, 42 BC. It was again restored after fires in 283 and c 400 AD. The high podium and eight columns of the pronaos with part of the entablature survive, all dating from Plancus. The pavement and podium are to be entirely reconstructed after excavations have been completed. The columns are nearly 11m high. Six of them, in grey granite, are in front; the other two, in red granite, are at the sides. The Ionic capitals were added in the 5C restoration. The temple was the State treasury, where gold and silver ingots and coined metal were kept. The room (*Aerarium*) E of the narrow stairway of the temple could be locked (the holes for the lock can still be seen). The 'Saturnalia' was held here every year on 17 December.

Near the Temple of Saturn stood the *Arch of Tiberius*, erected in AD 16 in honour of the emperor and of his nephew Germanicus, who avenged the defeat of Varus in the Teutoburg Forest (AD 9) by his victory over the German tribes at Idisiavisus (on the Weser). Behind the temple excavations are in progress in an area formerly covered by houses; it is possible another temple may be found beneath the medieval constructions.

The last monuments on the W side of the Forum at the foot of the Capitol Hill lie beyond the *Clivus Capitolinus*, the whole of which has been uncovered since 1980 beneath the modern Via del Foro Romano (which has been eliminated). This is the ancient road with a flint pavement built in 2C BC which was the W continuation of the Sacra Via (p 76) in the Forum, and the only way up to the Capitol in ancient times. It was used for triumphal and other processions to the Temple of Jupiter. There are long-term plans to reopen it to pedestrians when excavations and restorations in this area have been completed. The **Portico of the Dei Consentes** preserves twelve white columns forming an angle; the original seven columns are in marble, the restorations in limestone. Rebuilt by the prefect Vettius Praetextatus in AD 367, on the pattern of a Flavian structure, and dedicated to twelve Roman deities whose statues were here, it is the last monument of the pagan religion. The portico was reconstructed in 1858 and is being restored.

Beyond are three high columns, all that remains of the hexastyle pronaos of the rich and elegant **Temple of Vespasian** erected in honour of that emperor at the foot of the Tabularium staircase by his sons Titus and Domitian after his death in AD 79. The front part of the basement has recently been excavated. To the N are the remains of the **Temple of Concord**. This was a reconstruction by Tiberius (7 BC–AD 10) of a sanctuary which traditionally was thought to have been built by Camillus in 366 BC to commemorate the concordat between the patricians and the plebeians. The temple may instead have been built for the first time in 218 BC and then rebuilt in 121 BC by the consent of Opimius after the murder of Gracchus. It became a museum and gallery of paintings and sculptures by famous Greek artists. Only the pavement remains in situ; part of the frieze is in the Tabularium. Excavations are also in progress here.

On the other side of the Temple of Saturn (see above) are the scanty but extensive ruins of the **Basilica Julia**, which occupies the area between the Vicus Jugarius and Vicus Tuscus. The basilica, built on the site of the Basilica Sempronia (170 BC), was begun by Julius Caesar in 54 BC, and finished by Augustus. After fire, it had to be reconstructed and re-dedicated by Augustus in AD 12. It was again damaged by fire in AD 283 and reconstructed by Diocletian in 305. It was damaged yet again in Alaric's sack of 410 and was restored for the last time by Gabinius Vettius Probianus six years later. The Basilica Julia was the meeting-place of the four tribunals of the *Centumviri*, who dealt with civil cases. In the Middle Ages the church of *Santa Maria in Cannapara* was built on its W side. The surviving remains mostly date from 305; the brick piers of the central hall are 19C reconstructions.

The basilica, even larger than the Basilica Aemilia, measured 101m by 49m. It had a central hall 82m long and 18m wide, bordered all round by a double row of columns which formed aisles. On the long side, facing W, was a colonnade of arches and piers with engaged columns; this contained a row of shops. On the steps here can be seen graffiti in the marble used as 'gaming boards'.

The *Vicus Tuscus* was so called either from its Etruscan shopkeepers or from a colony of workmen from Veio who built the Temple of Jupiter Capitolinus.

In front of the Basilica Julia is a row of seven brick bases, dating from the 4C. These mark the S limit of the original FORUM which was first paved in the Etruscan period. The surviving pavement was laid by L. Surdinus in the Augustan period (as the restored inscription records). On the bases stood columns bearing statues of illustrious citizens. Two of the columns have been re-erected. In front, towards the W rises the **Column of Phocas** (recently restored), not only a conspicuous feature of the Forum but the last of its monuments. It was set up in 608 by Smaragdus, exarch of Italy, in honour of the centurion Phocas who had seized the throne of Byzantium; its erection may have been a mark of gratitude for the emperor's gift of the Pantheon to Boniface IV. The fluted Corinthian column, probably taken from some building of the best Imperial era, is 13·5m high. It stands on a high base, formerly faced with marble and surrounded by steps. On the top was originally a statue of the usurper.

To the N of the column of Phocas were placed the Plutei of Trajan (now in the Curia; see above). In the intervening pavement is a small square unpaved space, where once stood the statue of Marsyas next to the sacred fig-tree, the olive, and the vine (all recently re-planted here), mentioned by the Elder Pliny. In one of the pavement slabs is incised the name of L. Naevius Surdinus, praetor peregrinus in the time of Augustus, who may have had his tribunal here. This legal dignitary had to deal with cases involving *peregrini*, i.e. individuals who were not Roman citizens.

To the E is the paved area of the *Lacus Curtius*, with the substructure of a puteal (covered), surrounded by a twelve-sided structure of peperino blocks. The lake must have been a relic of the marsh drained by the Cloaca Maxima. According to one tradition a great chasm opened here in 362 BC which the soothsayers said could be closed only by throwing into it Rome's greatest treasure. Marcus Curtius, announcing that Rome possessed no greater treasure than a brave citizen, rode his horse into the abyss which promptly closed (the relief found here illustrating this legend is now in the Palazzo dei Conservatori, p 64; a cast is shown in situ). Livy, instead, suggests the name comes from the consul C. Curtius who fenced off this area in 445 after it had been struck by lightning.

In the SE corner of the Forum (surrounded by iron railings, and below ground level) are three travertine blocks formerly taken to be the base of the *Equus Domitiani* (AD 91) but now considered by some scholars to be the base of the equestrian statue of Constantine (*Equus Constantini*), probably dedicated in AD 334 (Domitian's statue is now thought to have been in the centre of the Forum).

Wall-painting of the Crucifixion c 741 in Santa Maria Antiqua

At the E end of the original Forum is the Temple of Julius Caesar, described above. To the S are the foundations of the *Arch of Augustus*, erected in 29 BC to commemorate the victory over Antony and Cleopatra at Actium two years earlier. A second triple arch was erected in 19 BC, after the standards captured by the Parthians had been returned. The structure was of unusual design. Only the central portion had an arch, properly so called; the side-passages, which were lower and narrower, were surmounted by pediments. The consular and triumphal registers (*Fasti*) were placed inside these lateral passageways; fragments of the records are now in the Sale dei Conservatori (p 60).

Near the S pier foundation of the arch a rectangular monument in the shape of a well-head was found in 1950. This is a remnant of the *Puteal Libonis*, a monument which stood beside the tribunal of the Praetor Urbanus, who dealt with cases involving Roman citizens.

The monuments to the S of the Arch, including the Temple of Castor and the Lacus Juturnae are all fenced off in 1988 during excavations and restoration work. Beyond the Arch and facing the E end of the Basilica Julia across the Vicus Tuscus is the ***Temple of Castor**, or *Temple of the Dioscuri*. It was almost certainly built in 484 BC by the dictator Aulus Postumius in honour of the twin heroes Castor and Pollux, whose miraculous appearance at the battle of Lake Regillus (496 BC) resulted in victory for the Romans over the Tarquins and their Latin allies. The temple was several times rebuilt; the most important reconstructions were by L. Caecilius Metellus in 117 BC (when a tribune for orators was installed) and by Tiberius during the reign of Augustus (AD 6). Peripteral in plan, and c 26 × 40 metres in area, it had eight Corinthian columns at either end and eleven at the sides. The wide pronaos, excavated in 1982–85, was approached by a flight of steps. Three of the columns, which are 12·5m high, survive from the last temple, with their beautifully proportioned entablature. The Roman knights regarded the Dioscuri as their patrons; every year, on 15 July, they staged an impressive parade before the temple. Fragments of statues of the Dioscuri found here, are now in the Antiquarium. Excavations and restoration work were carried out on the Temple in 1982–85.

On the E side of the temple is the *Lacus Juturnae*, or Basin of Juturna, inextricably connected with the story of the Dioscuri. It was here, immediately after they had turned the tide of battle at Lake Regillus, that they were seen watering their horses. Juturna, the nymph of healing waters, was venerated in connection with the springs that rise at this spot. The fountain has a square basin of opus reticulatum lined with marble; at its centre is a rectangular base, probably of a statue. On the parapet is a small marble altar (replaced by a copy; the original is in the Antiquarium), with reliefs of the Dioscuri and their sister Helena on two of its sides, and of their parents Jupiter and Leda, on the other two. In the 4C the Lacus Juturnae was the seat of the city's water administration. In the late Empire a series of rooms was built presumably to accommodate invalids who came to take the waters. These rooms contain fragments of statues of gods and other sculptures. To the S is the shrine proper, an aedicula, restored in 1953–55, with the front built into the brick walls, and with two columns. Before the front of the aedicula is a marble puteal, with a dedicatory inscription to Juturna by the curule aedile M. Barbatius Pollio. In front again is a marble altar, with a relief of Juturna and her brother Turnus. Excavations are in progress here.

Adjoining the shrine, on the S, is an apsidal building of the late Empire, converted into the *Oratory of the Forty Martyrs* and preserving remains of 8–9C frescoes (seen through the locked gate). The forty were soldiers martyred at Sebaste, in Armenia, by being frozen to death in an icy pool. The building closes the W end of the Nova Via.

To the S of the Oratory are the considerable remains of the church of ***Santa Maria Antiqua** (closed indefinitely; but adm sometimes granted with special permission from the Forum Antiquarium), the oldest and most important Christian building in the Forum. The 7–8C wall-paintings here are of the highest importance in the history of early Christian art. The buildings include an adjacent rectangular hall, once thought to be connected with the Temple of Augustus (which is now placed elsewhere, in the area S of the Basilica Giulia). This large brick hall (which was originally vaulted) was instead probably a monumental vestibule erected by Domitian in connection with his palace on the Palatine. It was part of the general reconstruction of the Palatine begun by Domitian and completed by his successors; this included an ambitious bridge, probably of wood, built by Caligula, whereby the emperor was able to go from his palace to the Capitol without having to descend into the Forum.

By the 6C the hall is thought to have been used as a guardroom at the foot of the covered ramp which led up to the Palatine where the Byzantine governors were living. The first murals may date from this time during its gradual transformation into a church. Pope John VII (705–7) restored the church, repainted the presbytery, and installed the stone pulpit. The paintings were renovated under Zacharias (741–52) and Paul I (757–67). Following a series of disasters to the building, caused by earthquakes and landslides and perhaps also by the Saracens, Leo IV (847–55) transferred the diaconate to Santa Maria Nova and rebuilt the church completely. In the 12C a further rebuilding was found necessary, perhaps because of more earthquakes, and the church was renamed *Santa Maria Liberatrice*. In 1702 a restoration brought to light the remains of the original church, and in 1901–2 Santa Maria Liberatrice, by that time entirely modernized, was pulled down.

The church comprises a quadrangular atrium, a quadriporticus, nearly square, and a presbytery, with three chapels, the central chapel being apsidal. On the right is the monumental vestibule; on the left a ramp leading up to the Palatine. The ATRIUM, the oldest part, is perhaps the atrium of Caligula's palace, but dates more probably from the time of Domitian. It was used as the vestibule of the church and preserves its impluvium. It has (on the walls) frescoes painted at the time of Hadrian I (772–95), and fragments of ancient and medieval sculptures. Beyond the narthex is the central hall converted into a church. Four Corinthian columns with traces of painting divide it into a nave and two aisles. In the nave are the low brick walls of the 8C schola cantorum. The 7–8C *Wall-paintings are of the highest interest, although they are very ruined. On the walls dividing the hall from the presbytery: left, Annunciation (period of Martin I; 649–53); right, *Salome and her seven sons, the Maccabean martyrs (period of John VII; 705–7). Left aisle: paintings in four bands: second band, Christ enthroned with the doctors of the Church (Byzantine influence; Paul I; 757–67); above, two series of panels with Latin inscriptions depicting scenes from the Old Testament. Right aisle: detached fresco from the atrium, showing the Virgin enthroned between saints and a pope with a square nimbus (indicating that he was alive at the time of the painting). Some of the sarcophagi in the hall are of pagan origin. Doors on the right lead into Domitian's vast hall.

PRESBYTERY. To the right, on the continuation of the schola cantorum, two panels showing Isaiah at the death-bed of Hezekiah and David with the vanquished Goliath. On the side walls are heads of the Apostles; above, in two bands, scenes from the New Testament. In the *Apse* and on the wall to the right are the remarkable *Palimpsests, superimposed layers of painting from the 6C to the 8C; especially noteworthy are a Madonna enthroned (lowest layer; 6C), an Annunciation (second layer; c 580), with a beautiful angel head, known as the 'Fair Angel', and (third layer; period of John VII), Fathers of the Church (Greek lettering).—*Right Chapel* (of Saints

Cosmas and Damian): figures of saints, in a poor state of preservation.—*Left Chapel* (of Saints Cyriac and Julitta), with murals of c 741: in niche above rear wall, *Crucifixion, with Christ on the Cross, the Virgin and St John, St Longinus and the soldier holding the sponge dipped in vinegar. The painting below, with the Virgin between Saints Peter and Paul, Saints Cyriac and Julitta, Pope Zacharias and the dean Theodotus, has been detached, and is now in the Antiquarium. On the other walls are eight paintings with scenes from the life of Saints Cyriac and Julitta, the Virgin adored by a family, possibly that of Theodotus (note the square nimbi of the two children), Theodotus kneeling, and the pathetic representation of four unknown saints, with the inscription *quorum nomina Deus scit.*

Behind Santa Maria Antiqua, on the Vicus Tuscus, is a vast brick building known as the *Horrea Agrippiana*. This was a grain warehouse of three courtyards, each provided with three stories of rooms, built by Agrippa. The church of San Teodoro (see p 231) stands on the second courtyard.

Vicus Tuscus returns N between the Basilica Julia and the Temple of Castor, and then E, past the Arch of Augustus (see above), to reach the religious centre of the Forum. Here are the Temple of Vesta, the House of the Vestals, and the Regia.

The *Temple of Vesta, where the vestals guarded the sacred fire, is a circular edifice of 20 Corinthian columns. It was partially reconstructed in 1930 by Alfonso Bartoli. The circular form recalls the Latin hut and the first temple on this site was possibly made, like the hut, of straw, and wood. Vesta goddess of the hearth, protected the fire, which symbolized the perpetuity of the State. The task of the vestals was to keep the fire for ever burning. Its extinction was the most fearful of all prodigies, as it implied the end of Rome. The origin of the cult is supposed to go back to Numa Pompilius, second king of Rome, or even to Aeneas, who brought from Troy the eternal fire of Vesta with the images of the penates.

The temple was burned down several times, notably during Nero's fire of AD 64 and in 191. It was rebuilt as often, the last time by Septimius Severus and his wife Julia Domna. It was closed by Theodosius and was in ruins in the 8C. For centuries until 1930 all that remained was the circular basement surmounted by tufa blocks and architectonic fragments. In the interior was an adytum, or secret place containing the unknown pledges of the duration of Rome (*pignora imperii*). These included the *Palladium*, or statue of Pallas Athena, supposedly taken from Troy by Aeneas. No one was allowed inside the adytum except the vestals and the Pontifex Maximus and its contents were never shown. The Palladium was an object of the highest veneration, as on its preservation depended the safety of the city. The emperor Heliogabalus tried to steal it but the vestals are supposed to have substituted it by another statue, (see p 100). The cult statue of Vesta was kept, not in the temple, but in a small shrine near the entrance to the House of the Vestals.

Immediately E of the Temple of Vesta is the *House of the Vestals, or *Atrium Vestae*. This is a large rectangular structure arranged round a spacious courtyard. It dates from Republican times, but was rebuilt after the fire of Nero in AD 64, and was last restored by Septimius Severus; remains of both structures can still be seen.

The **Vestals**, or virgin priestesses of Vesta, numbered only six. At first they were chosen by the king; during the Republic and Empire by the Pontifex Maximus. Candidates had to be between six and ten years old, from a Patrician family. After election the vestal lived in the Atrium Vestae for thirty years; ten learning her duties, ten performing them, and ten teaching novices. During this period she was bound by the vow of chastity. At the end of the 30 years she was free to return to the world and even to marry. The senior among them was called *Vestalis Maxima* or *Virgo Maxima*. If a vestal let out the sacred fire, she was scourged by the Pontifex Maximus, and he rekindled the fire by the friction of two pieces of wood from a *felix arbor*. The vestals' other duties included periodic offerings to Vesta, sprinkling her shrine daily with water from the Egerian fount, assisting at the consecration of temples and other public ceremonies, and guarding the Palladium. Maintained at the public expense, they had many privileges, such as an exalted order of precedence, and the right of intercession. Wills—even the emperor's will—and treaties were entrusted to their keeping. If a vestal broke her vow of chastity she was immured alive in the Campus Sceleratus and the man was publicly flogged to death in the Forum.

The building is seemingly too large for the accommodation of six vestals, and part of it may have been reserved for the Pontifex Maximus, whose official seat was in the Regia (see below). The House of the Vestals is remarkable for its courtyard, which is 61m long and 20m wide. In the middle are three ponds irregularly spaced and unequal in size. The central pond is the largest; at one time it was partly covered by an octagonal structure of unknown purpose. A charming rose-garden has been planted among the ruins. Along the sides of the courtyard are statues and statue-bases of vestals; they date from the 3C AD onwards. Near the entrance is a base from which the name of the vestal has been removed, possibly because she became a Christian.

The portico surrounding the courtyard was of two stories. In the middle of the short E side is a large hall paved with coloured marbles and flanked on either side by three small rooms, thought to be the sacristy of the priestesses. Behind this hall, towards the Palatine, are an open courtyard with a fountain, and other rooms. Along the S side, which abuts on the Nova Via, is another series of rooms (no adm) opening out of a corridor. In the first of these are the remains of a mill; the second is probably a bakery. On this side staircases lead to the upper floor and to the Nova Via. Near the last staircase is a small shrine. In the middle of the W side is a large room, perhaps the dining-room, leading to the kitchen and other rooms. The N side of the building is less well preserved. It certainly had more than two stories, as stairways are found on the second floor.

The *Nova Via* (not accessible; excavations in progress) runs parallel with the Sacra Via along the S side of the Forum. It was built to provide a means of communication with the buildings on the slopes of the Palatine.

To the N of the Temple of Vesta and E of the Temple of Julius Caesar are the remains of the **Regia**, the traditional palace of Numa Pompilius, the second king of Rome, and the official headquarters of the Pontifex Maximus. Primitive huts, similar to those on the Palatine (see p 93) have been found here, and the earliest permanent construction excavated dates from the 7C BC. The edifice, rebuilt by Domitius Calvinus after a fire in 36 BC retains its 6C form. Scattered fragments of his building may be recognized by the elegance of their architectural style. Other portions date from a reconstruction of the time of Septimius Severus.

The Regia may have been the depository of State archives and of the *Annales Maximi*, written by the Pontifex Maximus. It also included the Sacrarium of Mars, with the *ancilia*, or sacred shields, and the chapel of Ops, goddess of plenty.

At the SE corner of the Regia have been discovered the foundations of the arch, erected in 121 BC by Q. Fabius Maximus Allobrogicus to span the Sacra Via.

To the N of the Regia rises the **Temple of Antoninus and Faustina** (no adm), near the main entrance to the Forum. One of the most notable buildings of Imperial Rome, it was dedicated by the Senate in AD 141 to the memory of the Empress Faustina and, after his death in 161, to Antoninus Pius also. The temple was converted into the church of *San Lorenzo in Miranda* before the 12C, and given a Baroque façade in 1602. There survive, reached by a reconstructed flight of steps, the pronaos, of Corinthian cipollino monolithic columns (17m high), six in front and two on either side, the architrave and frieze of vases and candelabra between griffins, and the side walls of the cella, of peperino blocks, originally faced with marble. Sculptures placed in the pronaos include a female torso. The dedication of the church commemorates the trial of St Laurence, which may have taken place in this temple.

To the E of the temple is the **Archaic Necropolis**, discovered in 1902. This was the cemetery of the ancient inhabitants of the Esquiline or of the original settlement on the Palatine, and dates back to the Early Iron Age, before the date of the traditional foundation of Rome. Tombs were found for both cremated and buried bodies. The cremated ashes were discovered, in their urns and with their tomb-furniture, in small circular pits. The buried bodies had been placed in tufa sarcophagi, hollowed-out tree-trunks, or trenches lined with tufa slabs. The yields are in the Antiquarium.

Here the Sacra Via, known as the *Clivus Sacer*, begins to ascend the Velia to the Arch of Titus. On either side of the road are the ruins of private houses and shops (some under cover), including one dating from the Republican era, once wrongly called the Carcer, or prison.

On the left is the so-called **Temple of Romulus** (no adm), a well-preserved 4C structure formerly thought to have been dedicated to Romulus, son of Maxentius who died in AD 309. It has recently been suggested that it could have been the audience hall of the city prefect, or identified with a Temple of Jupiter. It is a circular building built of brick and covered by a cupola flanked by two rectangular rooms with apses, each originally preceded by two cipollino columns (only those on the right survive). The curved pronaos has two porphyry columns and an architrave taken from some other building; the splendid antique bronze *Doors are a remarkable survival. Behind is a rectangular hall, probably the library of the *Forum of Peace* built by Vespasian in AD 70 (see pp 106–7; previous ascriptions are considered erroneous). This hall was converted in the 6C into the church of Saints Cosmas and Damian (described on p 108), the temple serving as a vestibule. In the Forum of Peace were probably kept the city plans, cadastral registers, and other documents. On the wall towards Via dei Fori Imperiali was affixed the plan of Rome, or *Forma Urbis*, fragments of which are in the Antiquarium Comunale.

Beyond tower the remains of the *Basilica of Constantine, or **Basilica of Maxentius**, also called the *'Basilica Nova'*, the largest monument in the Forum and one of the most impressive examples of Roman architecture in existence. The skill and audacity of its design inspired many Renaissance builders: it is said that Michelangelo closely studied it when he was coping with the problems of the dome of St Peter's. The three huge barrel-vaulted niches on the N side still dominate the Forum. It was begun by Maxentius (306–10) and completed by Constantine, who considerably modified the original plan. In summer concerts are given in the Basilica by the Accademia di Santa Cecilia (entrance on Via dei Fori Imperiali).

The huge building is a rectangle 100m long and 65m wide, divided into a nave and two aisles by massive piers supported by buttresses. As first planned, it has a single apse, on the W side. Against the central piers were eight Corinthian

The Basilica of Constantine

columns 14·5m high; the only survivor was moved by Paul V (1605–21) to Piazza Santa Maria Maggiore. The original entrance was from a side road on the E; Constantine added on the S side a portico opening on the Sacra Via. The portico had four porphyry columns, partly surviving. In the middle of the N wall Constantine formed a second apse, which was shut off from the rest of the building by a colonnaded balustrade; here the tribunal probably held its sittings. The interior walls, decorated with niches, were faced with marble below and with stucco above. The three arches of the N aisle are 20·5m wide, 17·5m deep, and 24·5m high: the arches of the groin-vaulted nave, whose huge blocks have fallen to the ground, were 35m high and had a radius of nearly 20m. Parts of a spiral staircase leading to the roof can be seen on the ground, having collapsed in an earthquake. A tunnel was built under the NW corner of the basilica, for a thoroughfare which had been blocked by its construction. The entrance to the tunnel (walled up since 1566) can still be seen.

In the W apse was found in 1487 a colossal statue of Constantine, fragments of which are now in the courtyard of the Palazzo dei Conservatori. The bronze plates of the roof were removed in 626 by Pope Honorius I to cover Old St Peter's.

On the opposite side of the Sacra Via is a mass of ruins, among which is a large *Portico*, the vestibule to the Domus Aurea of Nero. Domitian used this to build the *Horrea Piperataria*, a bazaar for Eastern goods, pepper and spices, to the N of the Sacra Via. Later, the S part became commercialized. Domitian's building was finally destroyed in 284. A small circular base with a relief of a Maenad and an inscription recording restoration by Antoninus Pius (originals in the Antiquarium) in front, on the Sacra Via, may be the remains of a *Sanctuary of Bacchus*.

On the ascent to the Arch of Titus is the church of Santa Francesca Romana, or Santa Maria Nova (entered from Via dei Fori Imperiali and described on p 108). The former convent of this church is now the seat of the Forum and Palatine excavation offices and contains the **Antiquarium of the Forum** (or *Antiquarium Forense*). Most of it has been closed for a number of years; in 1988 only the first three rooms were open (adm as for the Forum). The collection occupies several rooms on two floors of the cloister and between the cloister and the cella of the Temple of Venus and Rome.

In the first room is tomb-furniture from the Archaic Necropolis, and a model. RR. II & III: objects found near the House of the Vestals; yields from wells, Italo-geometric and Etrusco-Campanian vases, votive objects, glass ware, bones, and lamps. R. IV (beyond R. II) has a good view of the cella of the Temple of Venus and Rome (see p 109). Here are displayed objects from the area of the Lapis Niger, Comitium, Cloaca Maxima, Regia,, and Basilica Aemilia. R. V. Contents of various wells and a model of the Arch of Augustus area of the forum.

UPPER FLOOR. R. VI. Fragment of a statuette of Aphrodite (in the case on the right). R. VII. Portrait of young M. Aurelius; large capital from the Temple of Concord.—PORTICO: inscriptions and architectonic fragments; red porphyry statue (headless) of the 2C AD. R. VIII. Large marble basin reconstructed from original fragments found near the Lacus Juturnae; fragments of the frieze of the Basilica Aemilia. R. IX (the ancient refectory of the convent): sculptures from the Lacus Juturnae, including a headless statue of Apollo from a Greek original of the 5C BC; fragments of a group of the Dioscuri with their horses; marble heads and architectural decoration from the Basilica Aemilia, including two fragments of low relief, beautifully executed: Apollo and Nike (Hadrianic), and a Neo-Attic relief of dancers (Augustan). On the right wall is part of the *Fresco removed from the chapel of Saints Cyriac and Julitta in Santa Maria Antiqua: it shows the Virgin enthroned and Child between Saints Peter and Paul and Saints Cyriac and Julitta. At the sides, wearing square nimbi are Pope Zacharias and the ecclesiastic Theodotus.

Dominating the summit of the Clivus Sacer is the *Arch of Titus, erected under Domitian (AD 81) in honour of the victories of Titus and Vespasian in the Judaean War, which ended with the sack of Jerusalem (AD 70). In the Middle Ages the Frangipani incorporated the arch in one of their strongholds, but the encroaching buildings were partly removed by Sixtus IV (1471–84) and finally demolished in 1821. Restoration of the arch was then undertaken by Gius. Valadier, travertine being used instead of marble to repair the damaged portions.

The beautiful single archway, in perfect proportion, is covered with Pentelic marble; its columns are of the Composite order. The two splendid reliefs within the arch are very worn. On one side is Rome guiding the imperial quadriga in which are seen Titus and Victory; opposite is the triumphal procession bringing the spoils from Jerusalem, including the altar of Solomon's temple decorated with trumpets, and the seven-branched golden candlestick. In the centre of the panelled vault is the Apotheosis of Titus, who is mounted on an eagle. On the exterior frieze is another procession in which the symbolic figure of the vanquished Jordan is carried on a stretcher.

The large area to the W of the Arch of Titus as far as the House of the Vestels (between the Via Nova and the Via Sacra) is fenced off during excavation work. Remains of a wall thought to date from the 8C BC have been found here. The Forum can be left by the gate beyond the Arch of Titus. The path descends the last extension of the Sacra Via with the Temple of Venus and Rome (p 109) on the left to the Colosseum.

3   The Palatine

Admission, see p 49, and Rte 2. The Palatine can be reached from the Roman Forum near the Arch of Titus (see above; and see the Plan on pp 94–5), where the Clivus Capitolinus begins, or by a separate entrance on Via San Gregorio (through a portal by Vignola and Rainaldi). Other ways up from the Forum (by the ramp on the side of the church of Santa Maria Antiqua and from a stairway at the SW corner of the House of the Vestals) have been closed indefinitely.

The topography of the Palatine is intricate, one level after another of multi-story buildings having been erected on and through the previous levels. Several of the more interesting sites are apt to be fenced off, because of fresh excavations or damage of some kind. Visitors may, therefore, have to make their own adjustments to the description given below. The custodians are informed and helpful. The House of Livia is open regularly to the public; other enclosed monuments, including the House of Augustus, the House of the Griffins, and the Aula of Isis can usually only be visited with permission from the excavations office in the Forum (see p 89). The Palatine Antiquarium, closed for restoration in 1988, is normally open only in the morning.

The ****Palatine** (Pl. 4; 7) is a four-sided plateau S of the Forum rising to a height of 40m above it and 51m above sea-level. It is about 1750m in circumference. It was here that the primitive city was founded, and splendid imperial palaces were later built over its slopes, so that the word Palatine came to be synonomous with the 'palace of the emperor' (hence 'Palace'). A park, with a profusion of wild flowers and fine trees, and birds, and beautifully kept, now surrounds the ruins. It is one of the most romantic and charming spots in the centre of the city, remarkably isolated from the traffic-ridden streets at the foot of the hill.

History and Topography. The Palatine now has the appearance of a plateau, the intervening hollows having been filled in by successive constructions in the imperial era. In ancient times the central summit was called the *Palatium*. It sloped down towards the Forum Boarium and the Tiber, with a declivity called the *Germalus* on the W and N (now occupied by the Farnese gardens) looking towards the Capitol. The *Velia*, a second lower summit, was connected by a saddle through the Roman Forum with the Esquiline. The name of Palatium is said to be derived from Pales, the divinity of flocks and shepherds, whose festival was celebrated on 21 April, the day on which (in 754 or 753 BC) the city of Rome is supposed to have been founded. Long before that date, however, the hill was settled, according to legend, from Greece. Sixty years before the Trojan War (traditional date 1184 BC), Evander, son of Hermes by an Arcadian nymph, led a colony from Pallantion, in Arcadia, and built at the foot of the Palatine Hill near the Tiber a town which he named after his native village. At all events, traces of occupation going back to the 9C BC have certainly been discovered.

When the twins Romulus and Remus decided to found a new city, the honour of naming it was accorded to Romulus by the omen of twelve vultures which he saw on the Palatine. Some time after its foundation on the hill, the city was surrounded by a strong wall forming an approximate rectangle: hence the name *Roma Quadrata*. Three gates were provided in the walls—the Porta Mugonia on NE, the Porta Romanula on the NW, and the Scalae Caci at the SW corner overlooking the valley of the Circus Maximus.

Under the Republic many prominent citizens lived on the Palatine. They included Q. Lutatius Catulus, the orator Crassus, Cicero, the demagogue Publius Clodius, the orator Hortensius, and the triumvir Antony. Augustus was born on the Palatine; he acquired the house of Hortensius and enlarged it. His new buildings included the renowned Temple of Apollo, with Greek and Latin libraries attached. Part of his palace has recently been excavated. The example of Augustus was followed by later emperors, whose residences became more and more magnificent, and the Palatine tended to become an imperial reserve.

Tiberius built a new palace, the Domus Tiberiana, in the NW of the Germalus, destroying all the private houses on the site. Caligula extended it towards the Forum, adapted a hall near it, the Aula of Isis, and built a bridge over the tops of the buildings in the Forum to connect the palace with the Capitol. Nero (or possibly Claudius) began a palace—the Domus Transitoria—which was destroyed in the fire of AD 64. Over the ruins Nero built the outworks of his immense Domus Aurea, and added the Cryptoporticus. The whole of the Palatium was reserved for the constructions of the Palace of Domitian, which comprised the official palace, the emperor's residence, and the Stadium. Additions to this complex included a Temple of Augustus, which became a shrine of the deified emperors, or Aedes Caesarum, and a monumental entrance to the palace from the Forum (see p 85). To provide a water supply, Domitian extended the Aqua Claudia from the Caelian to the Palatine. Hadrian preferred to live on his estate near Tivoli, but he extended the Domus Tiberiana and carried out other works on the Palatine. A new spate of building was begun by Septimius Severus (193–211). He increased the area of the hill to the S by means of a series of arcades. Other remarkable edifices were the emperor's box overlooking the Circus Maximus and the monumental Septizonium. Heliogabalus built a new temple by the Aedes Caesarum, in which he placed the most venerated treasures of Rome.

Odoacer, first king of Italy after the extinction in 476 of the Western Empire, lived on the Palatine; so for a time did Theodoric, king of the Ostrogoths, who ruled Italy from 493 to 526. The hill later became a residence of the representatives of the Eastern Empire. From time to time it was favoured by the popes. Christian churches made their appearance; a Greek monastery flourished here in the 12C.

In the course of time, after a period of devastation, the Frangipani and other noble families erected their castles over the ruins. In the 16C most of the Germalus was laid out as a villa for the Farnese (the Orti Farnesiani). Systematic excavations were begun about 1724 by Francesco Bianchini, shortly after Duke Francis I of Bourbon Parma had inherited the Farnese Gardens. They were mainly concentrated in the area of the Domus Flavia. Little more was done till 1860; in that year the gardens were bought by Napoleon III, who entrusted the direction of the excavations to Pietro Rosa. After 1870, when the Palatine was acquired by the Italian Government, Rosa continued with the work. In 1907 D. Vaglieri began to explore the Germalus; he was succeeded by Giac. Boni, who worked on the buildings below the Domus Flavia. Alfonso Bartoli later carried out research under the Domus Augustana and elsewhere and brought to light much information about the earliest inhabitants. Excavations are at present being carried out on the SW corner of the hill in the area of the Temple of Cybele, the Lupercal, and the House of Augustus.

The Clivus Palatinus ascends from the Forum passing the Nova Via on the right. Hereabouts was the *Porta Mugonia,* one of the three gates of Roma Quadrata, but its exact location is unknown. On the right paths and steps lead up to the *Farnese Gardens, laid out by Vignola in the middle of the 16C for Cardinal Alessandro Farnese, grandson of Paul III. They extended from the level of the Forum, then much higher, to the Germalus; the various terraced levels were united by flights of steps. Vignola's work was completed by Girol. Rainaldi at the beginning of 17C. The modern stairs lead up to the first terrace (formerly approached by a monumental ramp from the Nova Via in the Forum) with a Nymphaeum. Above another terrace with a fountain stand the twin pavilions of the Aviary on the highest level of the gardens, overlooking the Forum. The classical *Viridarium* instituted by Alessandro Farnese was replanted here by the archaeologist Giac. Boni (1859–1925). The gardens are still very beautiful. Boni's tomb stands beneath a palm-tree in the part of the gardens overlooking the Forum. Delightful paths continue through the gardens to the W side of the hill. To the S is an ancient palm-tree beneath which is a box-hedge maze reproducing that in the peristyle of the Domus Flavia.

The gardens cover the site of the **Domus Tiberiana**, or *Palace of Tiberius*, very little of which has been excavated. An atrium was traced in the course of excavations in the 18C and 19C, but it has been covered up again. The only visible remains are an oval fishpond in the SE corner near the stairs leading down to the Cryptoporticus and a series of rooms with brick vaults on the S slope overlooking the Temple of Cybele. These rooms (no adm) are of much later date than the rest of the palace, as they were built by the Antonines for the accommodation of the Praetorian Guard; graffiti in them indicate their occupation by soldiers. The W side of the Domus Tiberiana faced the Clivus Victoriae; here the façade was altered by Domitian. Trajan and Hadrian made further additions on the N side, so that it reached the Nova Via.

The *Clivus Victoriae*, leading from the Velabrum (p 230), was originally the principal means of access to the Palatine. It derived its name from a Temple of Victory founded (it is said) by Evander, the site of which is undetermined. The road skirted the W side of the Germalus and led past the Horrea Agrippiana to the Forum (Santa Maria Antiqua), joining the top of the ramp on the W side of the church. Near here was the *Porta Romanula*. Stairs (no adm) lead down to the Clivus Victoriae from the W side of the Farnese Gardens.

Excavations have been in progress since 1978 in the SW part of the hill around the Temple of Cybele, the so-called Auguratorium, and the top of the Scalae Caci, so that some of the ruins may be temporarily fenced off. From the S side of the gardens a modern flight of steps descends past (left) considerble remains of the Domus Tiberiana (see above). On the right are the remains of the **Temple of Cybele** (*Magna Mater*) covered by a thicket of ilex. The temple was built in 204 BC, and consecrated in 191 BC in obedience to a prophecy of the Sibylline books. Thirteen years earlier, during a critical period of the second Punic War, the oracular books had stated that the tide of battle would be turned only if the Romans obtained from Phrygia the black stone, attribute of the goddess. After this was done, matters improved immediately and a temple was built to accommodate the statue. The temple, raised on a high podium, had six Corinthian columns in antis. It was burned in 111 BC and rebuilt by Q. Caecilius Metellus, consul in 109. It was restored again in the reign of Augustus (AD 3). It is depicted on a relief in the garden façade of the Villa Medici—one of those belonging to the Ara Pietatis Augustae. The podium and the walls of the cella survive: the statue of Cybele and fragments of a marble lion found here have been placed under an arch of the Domus Tiberiana.

Cybele, the Magna Mater, mother of the gods, was the great Asiatic goddess of fertility. The town of Pessinus, in Phrygia (Asia Minor), was regarded as the principal seat of her worship, and it was from this town that the statue was brought to Rome. The goddess was the beloved—some say the mother—of Attis, and she was served by priests who, following the example of Attis, mutilated themselves on entering her service. The festival of Cybele and Attis was celebrated annually (22–24 March) with primitive orgies.

To the E of the temple is a smaller building dating from the time of Hadrian. Formerly identified as the *Auguratorium*, it was probably a Sanctuary of Juno Sospita. Further E are two *Archaic Cisterns* (under cover) dating from the 6C BC, one of which is particularly well preserved. It is circular in form, with a beehive vault of cappellaccio blocks laid in gradually diminishing courses until the top could be closed with a single slab. The construction recalls the Mycenean *tholos*.

The area to the S is the most ancient part of the hill. Here are traces of a wall of tufa and the site of the *Scalae Caci*, one of the three gates of Roma Quadrata. Cacus was the giant who stole the oxen from Hercules, and according to legend, had his den in the Forum Boarium, at the foot of the hill, and was killed there by Hercules. A tradition which survived till the 4C AD placed in the vicinity the *House of Romulus*, or rather the hut of Faustulus where the twins were brought up after their discovery by the shepherd. Excavations begun here in 1907, and resumed in 1948–49, revealed the traces of a HUT VILLAGE of the Early Iron Age (9C BC). On the rocky level of the hill are numerous holes and channels indicating the plan of three

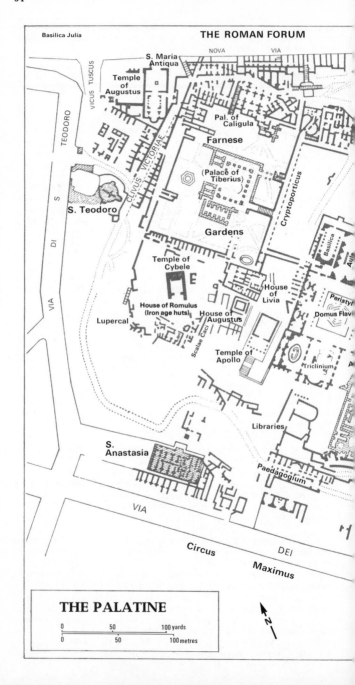

Basilica Julia

THE ROMAN FORUM

NOVA VIA

S. Maria Antiqua

Temple of Augustus

VICUS TUSCUS

S TEODORO

Pal. of Caligula

Farnese

(Palace of Tiberius)

S. Teodoro

CLIVUS VICTORIAE

Cryptoporticus

VIA DI S

Gardens

Basilica

Aula

Temple of Cybele

House of Livia

Peristyl

Domus Flav

House of Romulus (Iron age huts)

House of Augustus

Lupercal

Scalae Caci

Temple of Apollo

Triclinium

Libraries

S. Anastasia

Paedagogium

VIA

Circus Maximus

DEI

THE PALATINE

0   50   100 yards
0   50   100 metres

N

SACRA VIA

Arch of Titus

Arch of Constantine

Entrance

Thermae

CLIVUS PALATINUS

VIA DI S. GREGORIO

S. Sebastiano

Aedes Cæsarum

Lararium

S. Bonaventura

Entrance

Domus Augustana

arium

Aqueduct

Stadium

Baths of Septimius Severus

CERCHI

huts. In the holes were placed poles supporting the roofs. The channels were used to carry away the rain-water from the roofs.

In this part of the hill was the **Lupercal**, although traces of it have not yet been found. This was the cave sanctuary of the she-wolf, an animal sacred to Rome. It contained an altar and was surrounded by a grove sacred to the god Lupercus. Here was held the annual festival of the *Lupercalia* on 15 February, when the priests of the god, the *Luperci*, dressed in goatskins, went in procession around the hill, whipping whoever they met, especially women since the castigation symbolized fertility. The name February means purification and expiation. These rites were later connected with the mythical legend of Romulus and Remus suckled by the she-wolf.

The part of the hill between the Temple of Cybele and the Temple of Apollo (see below) has been fenced off while excavations (begun in 1961) of the **House of Augustus** (not to be confused with the Domus Augustana, see below) have been carried out. It is hoped this will soon be open to the public, but meanwhile admission is only granted with special permission from the excavation office in the Forum Antiquarium.

In the W wing of the house, thought to be the private quarters of the Emperor, have been found rooms with paintings of the highest interest: one has a charming frieze of pine cones, and another architectural and theatrical motifs. A series of larger rooms were probably used for public ceremonies and included two libraries, and a little nymphaeum decorated with shells. The wall-paintings, dating from 25 BC–AD 25, are remarkable for their vivid colour and intricate design (and refined figure studies). Considerable fragments of the stuccoed vaults and pavements of marble inlay have also come to light.

To the SE of the House of Augustus are the meagre remains once thought to belong to the *Temple of Jupiter Victor*, built by Q. Fabius Rullianus in 295 BC after his victory over the Samnites at Sentinum. This identification is now thought to be erroneous, as a building of the late Republican era was discovered underneath. The remains are, instead, considered to be those of the famous **Temple of Apollo** vowed by Augustus in 36 BC and dedicated eight years later. A corridor which is thought to have connected the Temple to the House of Augustus has been excavated here, and more wall paintings have recently been discovered near the podium of the temple. Fragments of a colossal statue of Apollo were found near the site of the temple, although they do not belong to the renowned statue of Apollo by Skopas known to have been placed here. All that survives is the basement of the temple 44m by 24m reached on the S side by a long flight of steps (no adm; the existing flight is a modern reproduction). The Temple of Apollo was surrounded by the *Portico of the Danaids*, on which were statues of the fifty daughters of Danaus. Some magnificent painted terracotta panels (now in the Palatine Antiquarium) were found here. Near by were the renowned Greek and Latin libraries, rebuilt by Domitian.

To the N of the House of Augustus is the so-called ***House of Livia**, famous for its wall-paintings. When it was discovered by Pietro Rosa in 1869, the finding of some lead pipes bearing the inscription *Iulia Augusta* suggested its identification as the house of Livia, wife of Augustus. It is now considered to be part of the house of Augustus himself (see above). The masonry dates from the 1C BC; the mural paintings are Augustan. The house is open to the public.

An original staircase descends into the rectangular *Courtyard*, in which there are two pillar bases and architectural paintings. The most important rooms open onto it. In front are the three rooms of the *Tablinum*, or reception suite; on the right is the *Triclinium*, or dining-room. (Some authorities hold these ascriptions to be arbitrary.) The decorations of the tablinum are in the second Pompeian style (1C BC), which imitates in painting the marble of Greek and Roman domestic architecture and introduces figures. The paintings have been detached but are exhibited in situ. The paintings in the central room are the best preserved, especially that on the right wall of this room. It has panels separated by columns of fantastic design in a free interpretation of the Corinthian style. In the central panel Hermes is seen coming to the rescue of Io, the beloved of Zeus, who is guarded by Argus of the hundred eyes; in the left panel is a street scene; the right panel is lost. In the intercolumniations are small panels with scenes of mysterious rites. The central painting on the rear wall of this room, now almost obliterated, shows Polyphemus pursuing Galatea into the sea; on the left wall, which lost its paintings in ancient times, are fixed the lead pipes which gave the house its name (see above).

In the room on the left the decoration, which is in a poor state, is architectural, with panels of griffins and other fantastic creatures. The room on the right is also architectural in its decorative scheme. The delicate yellow frieze depicts small landscapes and genre scenes. Below is the representation of a Corinthian portico; between the columns are rich festoons of fruit and foliage. In the *Triclinium* (no adm) the decorations are also mainly architectural. On the wall opposite the entrance is a portico with an exedra; in front is a trophy with spoils of the chase, and below is a pond with ducks. Above are branches of trees.

To the N of the House of Livia is one of the most interesting features of the Palatine. This is the *Cryptoporticus, a vaulted passage 128m long, skirting the Farnese Gardens and the Domus Tiberiana. Decorated in the vault with fine stuccoes (replaced by casts; originals in the Antiquarium) for part of its length, it receives light and air from windows set high on the E side. It is thought to have been built by Nero to connect the Domus Aurea with the palaces of Augustus, Tiberius, and Caligula; or it may have belonged to the Palace of Tiberius. A branch corridor was later added to link it with the Domus Flavia. The Cryptoporticus may be reached also by stairs leading down from the Farnese Gardens.

To the E extends the vast area of the **Palace of Domitian**, which occupies nearly the whole of the Palatium and the former depression between it and the Germalus. This vast collection of buildings was brilliantly planned for Domitian by the architect C. Rabirius, who levelled the central part of the hill to fill up the depression on the W. In the process he demolished or buried numerous earlier constructions, from private houses to imperial palaces; some of these have been revealed by excavations. The complex includes the Domus Flavia, or official palace, the Domus Augustana, or imperial residence, and the Stadium. Originally it was reached from the N by a monumental staircase of three flights.

The splendour of the *Domus Flavia, northernmost of the constructions, was praised with excruciating flattery by the Roman poets. On the N side it has a portico of cipollino columns which may have served as a loggia. In the centre of the palace is the spacious *Peristyle* with an impluvium in the form of an octagonal maze surrounding a fountain. A box-hedge reproduction of this maze is in the Farnese Gardens. In Domitian's constant dread of assassination he is supposed to have had the walls covered with slabs of Cappadocian marble whose mirror-like surface enabled him to see anyone approaching. On the W side is a series of small rooms with apses, statue-bases, and baths; on the E side are traces of three more rooms.

To the N of the peristyle are three large halls (fenced off) facing N onto an open space identified with the Area Palatina. The central hall is the so-called *Aula Regia*, or throne room, originally decorated with 16 columns of pavonazzetto and with 12 black basalt statues: two of the statues were found in 1724 and are now in Parma Museum. In the apse was placed the imperial throne where the emperor sat when he presided over meetings of his council and received foreign ambassadors. To the E is the so-called *Lararium* (under cover), in fact thought to be another room used for public ceremonies, or as a guardroom to protect the main entrance to the palace. To the W is the *Basilica Jovis*, divided by two rows of columns of giallo antico; it has an apse at the further end, closed by a marble screen. This may have been used as an Auditorium. A flight of steps leads down from the Basilica to the Cryptoporticus.

To the S of the peristyle is the *Triclinium*, or banqueting hall. This is almost certainly the well-known *Coenatio Jovis*. It has an apse reached by a high step; in this was placed the table where the emperor took his meals apart. The hall was paved with coloured marbles, which are well preserved in the apse. Leading out of the hall on either side was a court with an oval fountain. Around the fountain on the W side, which is well preserved, is a magnificent pavement in opus sectile belonging to the Domus Transitoria of Nero. Here, too, is a pavilion constructed by the Farnese as part of their gardens with a double loggia looking NW and decorations attrib. to the Zuccari.

Behind the triclinium is a row of columns (partly restored) belonging to the Domus Flavia. Further S are two rooms with apses, which are supposed to be Domitian's reconstruction of the *Greek and Latin Libraries* of the Temple of Apollo. It is now thought that Augustus used the libraries as reception rooms for legates.

The Domus Flavia covers several earlier constructions of considerable interest. Various underground areas are sometimes shown by custodians; for permission to visit them, apply at the Forum Antiquarium (9–13). Beneath the Lararium is the *House of the Griffins*, named from two griffins in stucco which decorate a lunette in one of the rooms. It is the oldest Republican building preserved on the Palatine (2C or 1C BC). Its wall-paintings, like those in the House of Livia, are in the second Pompeian style. The house is on two levels; the decorations are on the lower level. Of the several rooms reached by the staircase, the large hall is the best preserved. The pavement is in opus sectile. The mural paintings simulate three planes of different depth; the columns imitate various marbles. Round the top of the room runs a cornice and the ceiling is stuccoed. Paintings from two of the rooms have been detached and are now in the Palatine Antiquarium. Beneath the Basilica is the **Aula of Isis**, a large rectangular hall, with an apse at one end. The mural paintings have been detached and are now exhibited in a room of the Domus Augustana (see below).

Steps lead down from the triclinium to part of the *Domus Transitoria of Nero* (formerly called the Baths of Tiberius). At the foot of the steps is a court with a partly restored nymphaeum, decorated with rare marbles. Other rooms have traces of pavements with fine marble inlay. Small paintings of Homeric subjects found in a room leading off the court have ben removed to the Antiquarium. Beneath the Peristyle is the so-called *Palatine Mundus* (no adm; a grate now covers the entrance to the stairs), a pit with a well at one end. This was thought by Boni, when it was discovered, to be the Mundus of Roma Quadrata, but it was more probably a silo. In 1952, on the wall of a building—one of the many destroyed when the Domus Flavia was built—was found a Christian inscription, believed to refer to the celebration of the Eucharist in AD 78 and, if so, the earliest yet discovered.

Overlapping the Domus Flavia on the E are the vast remains of the **Domus Augustana**. This was the private residence of the emperor, 'the Augustus', not that of the Emperor Augustus. It was built on two levels. There are two peristyles on the upper and one on the lower level. Only the bases of the columns survive. The first peristyle, towards Via di San Bonaventura, was open. In the middle of the second peristyle is a large basin with a quadrangular shrine, possibly dedicated to Vesta. Around the court are remains of rooms, one of which has been identified with the 4C *Oratory of St Caesarius*. Close by is the Palatine Antiquarium (see below). In another of the rooms is a graceful 16C loggia decorated with grotesques, formerly part of the Villa Mattei. Here are exhibited the *Paintings detached from the Aula of Isis (see above).

Dating from the Republican period these were painted before the edict of 21 BC banning Isis-worship. The fantastic architectural paintings have panels with scenes of the cult of Isis and the fragments of the ceiling decoration are especially interesting. When the hall, with the House of the Griffins, was discovered in 1720–22, the paintings, which were in much better condition than they are now, were copied by Gaetano Piccini and by Fr. Bartoli. Bartoli's water-colours are now in the Topham Collection at Eton.

Another peristyle of the Domus Augustana is on a much lower level (no adm but well seen from above). In the middle is the basin of a fountain. Beyond are rooms with pavements of coloured marbles. A doorway in the bottom wall leads to the exedra of the palace overlooking the Circus Maximus; this was originally embellished with a colonnade.

The **Palatine Antiquarium** occupies the former Convent of the Visitation betwen the Domus Flavia and the Domus Augustana. It was formed with the material collected in 1860–70 from the excavations instituted by Napoleon III in the Farnese Gardens and amplified by Pietro Rosa. It lost its most important sculptures on the opening of the Museo Nazionale Romano. It is closed for restoration in 1988, and when it reopens the arrangement described below may have changed, and new material will be on exhibition. It may only be open in the mornings.

In the room to the left are wall decorations from a Republican house, near the House of Livia, and from the Domus Transitoria; a fresco of Apollo, found near the Scalae Caci; paintings, including a charming frieze from a house dated 130 BC found beneath the Baths of Caracalla; paintings from the Schola of the Praecones, dating from the 3C AD, and graffiti from the Paedagogium, including the notorious *Graffito of Alexamenos*, discovered in 1855. This is a caricature of the Crucifixion and shows a youth standing before a cross on which hangs a figure with the head of an ass; the legend says in Greek 'Alexamenos worships his god'. In the small room opposite are fragments of the stuccoed vault of the Cryptoporticus. In the vestibule, two fragments of marble intarsia from the pavement of the Domus Tiberiana (early 1C AD) and an archaic altar of an unknown god. The second room on the left contains torsoes of Mercury (copy of a Greek 5C original) and Diana (Roman copy of a Greek original), and two heads of Attis. Also, *Painted terracotta panels from near the Temple of Apollo. The rooms to the right (usually closed) contain objects found beneath the Domus Flavia, and from the Temple of Cybele, and finds (with a model) from the area of the Hut Village.

To the E of the Domus Augustana lies the *Stadium. This is an enclosure 146m long, with a series of rooms at the N end and a curved wall at the S. The interior had a two-storied portico with engaged columns covering a wide ambulatory or cloister. The arena has a semicircular construction at either end, presumably once supporting a turning-post (*meta*). In the centre are two rows of piers of a portico of the late Empire. Towards the S end are the remains of an oval enclosure of the early Middle Ages which blocked the curved end of the Stadium. On the surface of the arena lie columns of granite and cipollino, Tuscan, Corinthian, and Composite capitals, and fragments of a marble altar with figures of divinities. In the middle of the E wall is a wide exedra shaped like an apse, of two stories, and approached from the outside by a curved corridor. This structure is usually called the *Imperial Box*. Its existence strengthens the view that the Stadium was, as its name implies, used for races and athletic contests commanded by the emperor, though it has also been suggested that it was a garden, used occasionally as a hippodrome.

Behind the Stadium was the so-called **Domus Severiana**, which was built over a foundation formed by enlarging the S corner of the hill by means of enormous substructures that extended almost as far as the Circus Maximus. The scant remains include part of the *Baths*. To the N is the *Aqueduct* built by Domitian to provide water for his palace; it was an extension of the Aqua Claudia which ran from the Celian to the Palatine. The aqueduct was restored by Septimius Severus.

To the S is the site of the imperial box built by Septimius Severus, from which he watched the contests in the Circus Maximus. In the SE corner of the Palatine is the probable site of the *Septizonium* or *Septizodium*, built by Septimius Severus in AD 203 to impress visitors to Rome arriving by the Appian Way. Here in 1241 cardinals, imprisoned by Matteo Orsini, were forced to elect Celestine IV, who, with three of the cardinals, died as a result of the conditions. It was demolished by Sixtus V at the end of the 16C. Renaissance drawings of this building show that it had three floors, each adorned with columns; the façade was divided vertically into seven zones, the number corresponding either to that of the planets or to the days of the week; hence the uncertainty about the name. The columns and other material from this ornate structure were used for various purposes in different churches in Rome; the blocks of marble and travertine and the columns all found new homes.

Beyond the Severian arches, the S end of the Stadium, and the exedra of the Domus Augustana, lies the **Paedagogium** (no adm), halfway down the hill and facing the Circus. The Paedagogium is so called because it is supposed to have been a training school for the court pages. The name keeps on recurring in the numerous graffiti scratched on the walls; the best-known one is the graffito of Alexamenos, now in the Antiquarium. The building dates from the 1C or 2C AD; the graffiti are later.

Other rooms (inaccessible) are situated on the edge of the hill above Via dei Cerchi, including the so-called *Schola of the Praecones*; the paintings and mosaics are in the Antiquarium.

The Palatine can be left either by descending the hillside to the E of the Domus Augustana to the exit on Via San Gregorio or by returning across the Domus Augustana and descending the Clivus Palatinus (see the Plan) to the exit at the Arch of Titus in the Forum.

Outside the arch (and not included in the Palatine enclosure) Via di San Bonaventura ascends between remains thought to be those of the *Temple of Jupiter Stator* (founded in 294 BC on the site of an ancient sanctuary), to the NE summit of the Palatine. Here, approached by a 17C portal in the wall of the former Barberini vineyard, is the small medieval church of *San Sebastiano al Palatino*; its apse has interesting murals (c 970). Excavations in the churchyard have unearthed the probable site of the **Aedes Caesarum**, the temple erected by Tiberius to the deified Augustus and later consecrated to all emperors who were accorded deification. Heliogabalus added a *Temple of the Sun*, in which he placed the treasures rifled from various shrines in Rome, including (as he imagined) the Palladium (see p 86); hence the medieval name of this area. *Palladii* or *in Pallara*, which was given also to the church of St Sebastian. The last section of Via di San Bonaventura (which ends at the church) is flanked by 18C terracotta Stations of the Cross.

4   The Imperial Fora and the Colosseum

The five **Imperial Fora**, of Caesar, of Augustus, of Vespasian, of Nerva, and of Trajan, occupy the huge area between the Roman Forum and the lower slopes of the Quirinal and Viminal. They are traversed by the wide **Via dei Fori Imperiali** (Pl. 4; 5, 7) lined with gardens and opened in 1933 by Mussolini as the Via dell'Impero. From Piazza Venezia it runs in a straight line to the Colosseum past the Fora of Trajan and Augustus on the left and the Forum of Caesar on the right. It then crosses over the Fora of Nerva and of Vespasian. During the construction of this thoroughfare, built to add dignity to Fascist military parades, numerous 16C buildings were demolished, the Velia hill levelled, and the Imperial Fora hastily and inconclusively excavated. In 1980 a project was mooted to eliminate the stretch of road between Piazza Venezia and Via Cavour and to carry out systematic excavations of the Fora at a considerably lower level. After much discussion the Minister declared in 1983 that funds were insufficient at present to put such a scheme into operation. However in 1988 the local government decided to fence off a large area of gardens beside the Forum of Nerva and excavations were begun here, seen as a positive step towards the eventual closure of the road. Meanwhile only one fifth of the Fora are visible and the motor traffic along this unfortunate road continues to damage the ancient monuments. The Imperial Fora are all visible from outside (with the exception of the Forum of Vespasian) but in 1988 only the Markets of Trajan were open to the public.

With the ever-increasing population of the city, the Roman Forum had become, in the last days of the Republic, too small for its purpose, congested as it was with buildings and overcrowded by citizens and by visitors from abroad. There was no alternative to expansion and the only direction in which expansion was possible was to the N. As this area also was encumbered with buildings, their demolition was inevitable. The purpose of any new forum was to be the same as that of the Roman Forum, namely to serve, with its basilicas, temples and porticoes, as a judicial, religious, and commercial centre.

The first step was taken by Julius Caesar, who built his Forum during the decade before his death in 44 BC. In it he placed the Temple of Venus Genetrix in commemoration of the victory of Pharsalus (48 BC). His example was followed by his successors, most of whom erected temples in memory of some outstanding event in Roman history for which they took the credit. The Forum of Augustus, with the Temple of Mars Ultor, commemorated the battle of Philippi (42 BC); the Forum of Vespasian had its Temple of Peace erected with the spoils of the campaign in Judaea (AD 70); and the Forum of Trajan, completed by Hadrian, had a temple to the deified Trajan in honour of his conquest of Dacia (AD 106). The Forum of Nerva had a Temple of Minerva. All the fora were connected and the whole area was arranged in conformity with a definite plan.

During the Middle Ages and the Renaissance the Fora were pillaged for their building material and robbed of their marbles and bronzes, and the area was later built over. Until the 20C only parts of the Fora of Trajan and Augustus and the so-called 'Colonnacce' were visible; the clearance of the area was begun in 1924 to make way for Via dei Fori Imperiali.

At the W end of Via dei Fori Imperiali, opposite the corner of the Victor Emmanuel Monument stands Trajan's Column (see below) beside two domed churches of similar design (usually closed). The first, *Santa Maria di Loreto*, by Antonio da Sangallo the Younger, with a lantern by Giac. del Duca (1582), is a fine 16C building. It contains an altarpiece attrib. to Marco Palmezzano, and a statue of St

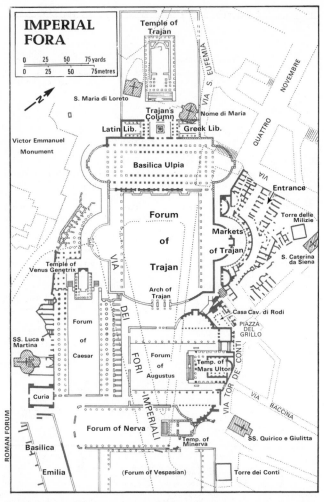

IMPERIAL FORA

0   25   50   75 yards
0   25   50   75 metres

S. Maria di Loreto

Victor Emmanuel Monument

Temple of Trajan

Trajan's Column

Latin Lib.   Greek Lib.

Nome di Maria

Basilica Ulpia

Forum
of
Trajan

Temple of Venus Genetrix

Forum
of
Caesar

SS. Luca e Martina

Curia

ROMAN FORUM

Basilica

Emilia

Arch of Trajan

Markets of Trajan

Entrance

Torre delle Milizie

S. Caterina da Siena

Casa Cav. di Rodi

PIAZZA DEL GRILLO

Forum
of
Augustus

Temp. of Mars Ultor

Forum of Nerva

Temp. of Minerva

(Forum of Vespasian)

SS. Quirico e Giulitta

Torre dei Conti

VIA S. EUFEMIA
NOVEMBRE
QUATTRO
VIA
VIA DEI FORI IMPERIALI
VIA TOR DE' CONTI
VIA BACCINA

Susanna by Fr. Duquesnoy (1630). The second church, dedicated to the *Nome di Maria* is by Ant. Dérizet (1738).

In front of the churches extends the ***Forum of Trajan** (normally entered through the Markets of Trajan, see below, but closed in 1988), built between 107 and 113 and the last and most splendid of the imperial fora. It was designed by Apollodorus of Damascus in a site excavated in the saddle between the Capitol and Quirinal hills. The Forum itself is in the form of a rectangle 118m by 89m, with a portico and exedra on each of the long sides. In the centre was an equestrian statue of Trajan. At the W end, occupying the whole of its width, was the Basilica Ulpia. Adjoining, on the W, were the Greek and Latin libraries, with Trajan's Column between them, and, still farther W, beneath the area of the two churches, the Temple of

Trajan. The entrance was from the E, adjoining the Forum of Augustus, through a monumental arch. To the N of the forum and virtually adjoining it is the semicircle of the Markets of Trajan. In the opinion of ancient writers these constructions made up a monumental group unequalled in the world. Further excavations are to be carried out here.

*Trajan's Column is generally considered to be the masterpiece of Roman sculptural art, still almost intact, and carefully restored in 1980–88. It was dedicated to Trajan in 113 in memory of his conquest of the Dacians, the inhabitants of what is now Romania. Around the column shaft winds a spiral frieze 200m long and between 0·89m and 1·25m high, with some 2500 figures in relief illustrating in detail the various phases of the Dacian campaigns (101–102 and 105–106). The carving was carried out in less than four years by an unknown Roman master and his workshop. It is known that the column could originally be seen from buildings which surrounded it on various levels in the Forum of Trajan: it is now more difficult to appreciate the beautiful details of the carving with the naked eye.

The column is 100 Roman feet (29·7m) high, or with the statue, 39·8m; it is constructed of a series of marble drums. The details of the carving may be studied in the casts (made before restoration) in the Museo della Civiltà Romana.

A spiral stair of 185 steps (no adm) carved in the marble ascends to the top of the Doric capital on which once stood the statue of Trajan (replaced by the statue of St Peter in 1588). The ashes of the emperor, who died in Cilicia in 117, and of his wife Plotina, were enclosed in a golden urn and placed in a vault below the column. An inscription at the base has been interpreted to indicate that the top of the column reached to the original ground-level, thus giving an idea of the colossal excavations necessary for the construction of the forum.

Steps by the column descend to the level of the forum (when this entrance is closed, it is necessary to use the main entrance in Via Quattro Novembre, reached up the steps of Via Magnanapoli; see the Plan on p 102, although this was also closed in 1988). On the left of the column is the *Latin Library* and on the right the *Greek Library*, both of them rectangular, with wall niches surmounted by marble cornices to hold the manuscripts. These can be seen (usually illuminated) through railings; the area to the left is particularly interesting with many architectural fragments from the forum. Behind the column is a fragment of a colossal granite column (with its marble capital), virtually all that remains of the huge *Temple of Trajan* erected after his death in 117 by Hadrian.

The area in front of the column has extensive remains of the **Basilica Ulpia**, dedicated to the administration of justice; it was the largest in Rome. Though not so spacious as the Basilica of Constantine, it was longer (120m; not counting the apses at either end); its width was 60m. It was divided by rows of columns into a nave and four aisles. On each short side was an extensive apse; the N apse was found under Palazzo Roccagiovine beside Via Magnanapoli. The front of the basilica, towards the interior of the forum, had three doors; at the back, towards Trajan's Column, there were two doors. Part of the pavement in coloured marbles has survived; also a fragment of the entablature, with reliefs depicting scenes of sacrifice and candelabra.

An underground passage leads into the main area of the Forum, where excavations revealed the site of the *North Portico*. This, made up of precious marbles, was stripped in the Middle Ages. There survive the remains of three steps of giallo antico, a column base, traces of the polychrome marble pavement, and a column of the apse. Behind the apse was the wall of the enceinte; part of this is visible on the left. The site of the *South Portico* is under Via dei Fori Imperiali. On the E side of the forum little has been discovered.

Behind the N portico and conforming to its semicircular shape is the conspicuous agglomeration of the *Markets of Trajan (admission see p 49; entrance on Via Quattro Novembre, reached by the steps of Via Magnanapoli), built before the Forum of Trajan, at the beginning

Detail of Trajan's Column (AD 113)

of the 2C AD. The markets consisted of 150 individual shops, used for general trading.

They form a large semicircle of three superimposed rows of shops with arcaded fronts, built on the slopes of the Quirinal. The semicircle ends on either side in a well-preserved apsidal hall (only the one on the left can be visited). The portico of the fourth shop on the left of the bottom row has been reconstructed. Staircases lead to the top of the building; from the roof (usually closed) of the apse on the right there is an excellent view of the imperial fora. The apsidal buildings on the second floor are particularly well preserved. At the back of the semicircle an ancient road, the Via Biberatica, leads from the 13C Torre del Grillo under an arch through the markets, and is now blocked by Via Quattro Novembre. The exit from the markets is through a rectangular *Hall* of two stories, with six shops on each floor; on the upper story is a large covered hall which may have served as a bazaar.

The medieval *Torre delle Milizie* (reached from the right of the Hall) rising behind the Markets of Trajan was probably built on Byzantine fortifications. The present massive brick-built leaning tower, only two-thirds of its original height, probably dates from the 13C. It was for long known as Nero's Tower, from the tradition that from its top Nero watched Rome burning. The view from the top is excellent, but it has been closed indefinitely.

At the beginning of Via dei Fori Imperiali, beyond the Victor Emmanuel Monument, the steep Via di San Pietro in Carcere (open only to cars with special permits) diverges right to climb above the Mamertine Prison (see below) to the Capitol. Here, well beneath the level of the road, are the remains of the **Forum of Caesar** (no adm), first of the imperial fora, and said by Dio Cassius to have been more beautiful than the Roman Forum. It contained the Temple of Venus Genetrix, from whom Julius Caesar claimed descent. In the temple, dedicated in 46 BC, two years after the battle of Pharsalus, were exhibited a statue of the goddess by Arcesilaus, a statue of Julius Caesar, a gilded bronze statue of Cleopatra, and two pictures by Timomachus of Byzantium (1C BC) of Ajax and of Medea. In front of the temple stood an equestrian statue of Caesar. Trajan rebuilt the temple and forum and added the Basilica Argentaria, or Exchange, and five large shops over which was an extensive (heated) public lavatory (Forica).

The entrance to the ruins (which has been locked for many years) is by a staircase near the church of Santi Luca e Martina (see below). Beyond (right) the remains of the *Forica*, the level of the Forum is reached. On the left are the shops; at the end is the *Basilica Argentaria*. In the middle is the high base of the **Temple of Venus Genetrix**, which has lost its marble facing; three of its Corinthian columns have been re-erected. In front of the basilica are the remains of a large arch which may have been used in a later restoration to reinforce the temple.

From Via San Pietro in Carcere (see above) the *Clivus Argentarium*, a well preserved Roman road (usually open to pedestrians, but closed in 1988), with remains of shops and a nymphaeum dating from the time of Trajan, descends to the little church of *San Giuseppe dei Falegnami* (often closed). This was built in 1598 perhaps by G.B. Montano, above the *Tullianum*, called the **Mamertine Prison** (adm see p 49) in the Middle Ages, and later consecrated as *San Pietro in Carcere*.

This is thought originally to have been a cistern, like those at Tusculum and other Etruscan cities. On the lower level, the form can be seen of a round building which may have had a tholos (which could date it as early as the 6C BC). A spring still exists in the floor. The building was used as a dungeon in Roman times for criminals and captives awaiting execution. Jugurtha, Vercingetorix, the accomplices of Catiline, and, according to Christian tradition, St Peter and St Paul were imprisoned here.

Beside the church steps lead up to the Capitol. There is a good view from here of the monuments at the W end of the Roman Forum (see p 81).

Opposite is the handsome church of *Santi Luca e Martina (Pl. 8; 2; often closed), probably founded in the 7C by Honorius I on the site of the Secretarium Senatus (p 80). It was rebuilt in 1640 by *Pietro da Cortona*, and is considered one of his masterpieces. The two stories, the upper dedicated to St Luke and the lower to St Martina, have an original and complex design. The façade, built of travertine, and the dome are particularly fine. The church of St Luke has a centralized Greek cross plan. The lower church of Santa Martina is reached by a staircase to the left of the High Altar.

In a well-designed chapel (left) are the tombs of Saints Martina, Epifanio, and Concordio, and a tabernacle by *Pietro da Cortona*. The side chapel with a pretty scallop motif has a fine terracotta group of the three saints by *Aless. Algardi*. In the corridor is the tomb of Pietro da Cortona, and in the vestibule, statuettes by *Cosimo Fancelli*, and a bas-relief of the Deposition by *Algardi*.

On the other side of Via dei Fori Imperiali, in front of their respective fora, are modern bronze statues of Trajan, Augustus, and Nerva. Adjoining the Forum of Trajan is the *Forum of Augustus** (closed since 1984), built to commemorate the victory of Philippi (42 BC) and dedicated to Mars Ultor (the Avenger). It is seen from the railings along Via dei Fori Imperiali (which, however, covers half its area), but the entrance (when it reopens) is at the back, in Piazza del Grillo. This can sometimes be reached by the raised walk-way (Via di Campo Carleo) which leads out of Via dei Fori Imperiali, and passes between the Markets of Trajan and the Forum of Augustus; if this is closed it must be approached by Via Tor de' Conti (see the Plan).

From Piazza del Grillo a modern stairway descends to an arcaded entrance to the Forum, beside a huge wall built to isolate the forum from the Subura district. From there a wide antique staircase leads on to the podium of the Temple of Mars Ultor.

The octastyle *Temple of Mars Ultor**, dedicated in 2 BC, had columns on three sides. It had a large pronaos and an apsidal cella. A centre of solemn ceremonies and the Imperial sanctuary, it became a museum of art and miscellaneous relics; among these were the sword of Julius Caesar and the Roman standards surrendered by the Parthians in 20 BC. Three columns at the end of the right flank are still standing. Of the eight Corinthian columns in front four (the two middle and the two end ones) have been partly reconstructed from antique fragments. A broad flight of steps ascends to the capacious pronaos. In the cella, where the effect of undue width is lessened by a colonnade on either side, are the stepped bases of the statues of Mars, Venus, and perhaps Divus Julius. Behind is the curve of the large apse. A stairway (usually closed) on the left descends to an underground chamber once thought to be the temple treasury.

On either side of the temple, marble steps lead up to the site of a *Basilica*. These twin basilicas were almost completely destroyed during the Renaissance for their marble; each had a great apse, which Augustus decorated with statues of famous Romans, from Aeneas onwards (some of the niches can still be seen). On the ground between the surviving columns of the temple and the right-hand basilica are architectural fragments of great interest. Behind these is the *Arch of Pantanus*, formerly an entrance to the forum. The left-hand basilica had an extension at the N end known as the *Hall of the Colossus*, a square room which held a colossal statue of Augustus or of Mars, the base of which remains. Two ancient columns have been re-erected at the entrance.

At the E end of the Forum of Augustus is the **Forum of Nerva**, or *Forum Transitorium* (excavations in progress), so called because it led into the Forum of Vespasian. Nerva's Forum, which was begun by Domitian and completed in AD 97, was, in effect, a development of the *Argiletum*, the street that led from the Roman Forum to the Subura. In the middle rose the *Temple of Minerva*, the ponderous basement of which remains in place. The temple was still standing at the beginning of the 17C, when it was pulled down by Paul V to provide marble for the Fontana Paolina on the Janiculum. Beyond the temple and close to the enceinte wall are two enormous Corinthian columns (covered for restoration), the so-called *Colonnacce*. In the attic between the columns is a high-relief of Minerva, after an original of the school of Skopas. In the rich frieze of the entablature Minerva (Athena) is seen teaching the arts of sewing and weaving and punishing Arachne, the Lydian girl who excelled in the art of weaving and had dared to challenge the goddess. In front of the Colonnacce is a section of the Argiletum.

To the E of the Forum of Nerva extended the **Forum of Vespasian** or *Forum of Peace*, built in AD 70 with the spoils of the Jewish War. Excavations revealed and identified a shrine under the Torre dei

Conti, some prone columns, and remains of a pavement in opus sectile; a large hall was converted in the 6C into the church of Santi Cosma e Damiano (see below).

From Piazza del Grillo (see above) is the entrance to the **Casa dei Cavalieri di Rodi**, ancient seat of the Roman priorate of the Order of the Knights of St John of Jerusalem (Hospitallers, Knights of Rhodes, or Knights of Malta). The house was built over a Roman edifice at the end of the 12C, and restored in 1467–70 by Card. Marco Balbo, nephew of Paul II. It has a well-preserved colonnaded Atrium, dating from the time of Augustus; the roof is a Renaissance addition. It is now used as a chapel by the Knights of St John. The atrium leads into the *Antiquarium of the Forum of Augustus* (closed indefinitely), arranged in three Roman shops. The exhibits include: ROOM 1. Fragments of sculpture: *Head of Jupiter from the frieze of one of the

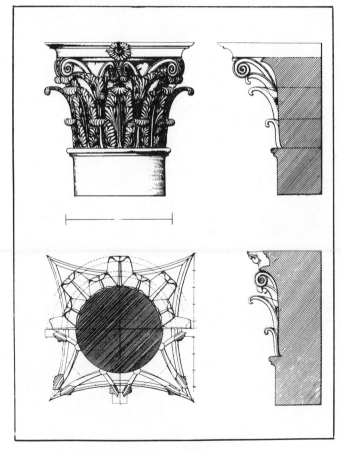

The Corinthian capital, after Vitruvius, architect and surveyor to Augustus ('De architectura', before AD 27), published by Carlo Amati in 1829

basilicas; R. 2. Medieval fragments from the churches in the area; R. 3. Model of the Forum; capitals and other architectural fragments; foot of a bronze statue.

To the left, at the top of a flight of Roman stairs (restored) is a fine Renaissance hall (adm sometimes on request), off which are several contemporary rooms; one of these, the Sala del Balconcino contains part of the attic story of the portico of the Forum of Augustus, with caryatids. Stairs lead up to a loggia with restored frescoes and fine views over the fora.

Via di Campo Carleo or Via Tor de' Conti lead back to Via dei Fori Imperiali which continues towards the Colosseum, passing the entrance to the Roman Forum. Here a large area of gardens has been fenced off adjoining the Forum of Nerva and excavations were begun in 1988. A stairway on the left of the entrance to the Roman Forum leads to the church of San Lorenzo in Miranda (p 88). Farther on is the church of **Santi Cosma e Damiano**, dedicated to two brothers who were miraculous healers from Cilicia. This church occupies a large rectangular hall (probably a library) of the Forum of Vespasian, which St Felix IV adapted in 527, adding mosaics to the apse. The so-called Temple of Romulus in the Roman Forum served as a vestibule to the church. It was rebuilt in 1632, when the pavement was added to make it a two-storied building. The church is reached through the early 17C cloisters of the adjoining convent with contemporary frescoes by *Fr. Allegrini*.

The INTERIOR (lights in each chapel) is celebrated for its 6C *Mosaics, copied in several Roman churches (especially in the 9C). On the triumphal arch is the Lamb enthroned, surrounded by seven candlesticks, four angels, and the symbols of the Evangelists. In the apse (covered for restoration in 1988), Saints Cosmas and Damian presented to Christ at his Second Coming by St Peter and St Paul; on the right, St Theodore; on the left St Felix IV (restored) presenting a model of the church; also, palms and the phoenix, the symbol of resurrection. Below the Lamb on a mount from which four rivers (the Gospels) flow, and twelve other lambs (the Apostles) issuing from Bethlehem and Jerusalem (coin-operated light near the entrance).

The ceiling of 1632 has a fresco by *Marco Montagna*, who also painted frescoes in the nave. The Baroque altar by *Dom. Castelli* (1637) is adorned with a 13C Madonna and Child. In the 1st chapel in the right aisle, is a striking fresco of Christ encrowned on the Cross, derived from the Volto Santo in Lucca. It dates perhaps from the 13C, but more probably from a repainting in the 17C by an unknown Lucchese artist. In the vault are frescoes by *G.B. Speranza*. In the 2nd chapel paintings by *Giov. Baglione*. In the 3rd chapel part of the 18C Neapolitan presepio (the rest is preserved in a domed Roman vestibule off the cloister) was stolen in 1988. The models and figures in wood, terracotta, and porcelain are of exceptionally fine workmanship. The 3rd chapel also has an altarpiece of St Anthony of Padua by *Spadarino*, and frescoes by *Allegrini* (who also painted the frescoes in the 1st and 2nd chapels in the left aisle).

Via dei Fori Imperiali next passes on the right the colossal ruins of the Basilica of Constantine (see p 88). Here, on a brick wall facing the street, were set up in 1932 an interesting series of four relief *Maps* of the Roman dominion at various stages in history: in the 8C BC; in 146 BC, after the Punic Wars; in AD 14, after the death of Augustus; and in the time of Trajan, AD 98–117.

Adjoining the Basilica of Constantine (and reached by a flight of steps from Via dei Fori Imperiali, or by a short road from Piazzale del Colosseo) is the church of **Santa Francesca Romana** (Pl. 8; 2; open 9.30–12.30, 15.30–dusk), formerly **Santa Maria Nova**. It is on the summit of the Velia and encroaches on the Temple of Venus and

Rome (see below); a fine stretch of ancient Roman road is conspicuous on the approach to the W door.

The church incorporates an Oratory of Saints Peter and Paul formed by Paul I
(757–67) in the W portico of the Temple of Venus and Rome. In 847, after grave
structural damage to the church of Santa Maria Antiqua in the Forum, that
church was abandoned and the diaconate was transferred to the oratory, which
became *Santa Maria Nova*. The church was enlarged, and the apse mosaic and
*Campanile added before it was consecrated anew in 1161. The façade,
designed by Carlo Lombardi, was added during his reconstruction in 1615.
   Santa Francesca Romana (Francesca Buzzi; 1384–1440), wife of Lorenzo
Ponziani, founded here in 1421 the Congregation of Oblates, which she herself
joined after her husband's death in 1436. Canonized in 1608, she is the patron
saint of motorists and on her festival (9 March) the street between the church
and the Colosseum is congested with cars. The painter Gentile da Fabriano was
buried in the church in 1428. The former conventual buildings now contain the
excavation offices and Antiquarium of the Roman Forum (see p 112).

INTERIOR. The Cosmatesque pavement in the raised E end was
restored in 1952. In the vestibule of the side entrance (right), Tombs
of Cardinal Marino Bulcani (died 1394) and of Ant. da Rio (or Rido),
castellan of Castel Sant' Angelo (c 1450). S transept, Tomb of
Gregory XI, by *Olivieri*, set up in 1585 by the Roman people in
honour of the pope who restored the seat of the papacy from Avignon
to Rome (1377). Let into the S wall (behind grilles) are two flagstones
of the Sacra Via on which are shown the imprint of the knees of St
Peter, made as the saint knelt to pray for the punishment of Simon
Magus, who was demonstrating his wizardry by flying. The legendary site of Simon's consequent fall is in the neighbourhood.—From
here stairs lead down to the crypt with a bas-relief of St Francesca
Romana and an angel (17C). The confessio, an early work by *Bernini*
has a marble group of the same subject, by G. *Meli* (1866).
   In the apse, *Mosaics, the Madonna and saints (probably completed in 1161), and on either side, statues of angels of the school of
Bernini. Above the altar, a 12C Madonna and Child, revealed in 1950
and detached from another painting found beneath it. The earlier
painting, a colossal *Virgin and Child, which may have come from
Santa Maria Antiqua, is now kept in the SACRISTY. Probably dating
from the end of the 6C, it is one of the most ancient Christian
paintings in existence. Also in the sacristy, Paul III and Cardinal
Reginald Pole (left wall) attrib. to *Perino del Vaga*; fragments of
medieval frescoes; Miracle of St Benedict, by *Subleyras*. On the
entrance wall, Madonna enthroned between St Benedict and Santa
Francesca Romana, by *Girol. da Cremona*, and Madonna enthroned
with Saints, by *Sinibaldo Ibi* of Perugia (1545).
   Beyond the church is the summit of the Velia, transformed into a
terrace (closed in 1988), the area of which (145m by 100m) virtually
coincides with that of the enormous ***Temple of Venus and Rome**.
The temple was built by Hadrian, who chose to place it on the site of
the vestibule of the Domus Aurea, where Nero had placed a colossal
bronze statue of himself as the Sun. The statue had therefore to be
moved (see p 112). The temple was built in honour of Venus, the
mother of Aeneas and the ancestor of the gens Julia, and of Roma
Aeterna, whose cult appears to have been localized on the Velia. It
was dedicated in 135, damaged by fire in 283, and restored by
Maxentius (307). It is said to have been the last pagan temple which
remained in use in Rome, as it was not closed till 391 (by Theodosius).
It remained virtually entire till 625, when Honorius I stole the bronze
tiles of its roof for Old St Peter's.

To counteract the unevenness of the ground, it was necessary to build a high basement; this was of rubble, with slabs of peperino and marble-faced travertine. The temple was amphiprostyle peripteral, with ten granite Corinthian columns at the front and back and twenty on each of the sides. It had two cellae placed back to back; that facing the Forum was the shrine of Rome and the other that of Venus. The two cellae (the apses and diamond-shaped coffers were added by Maxentius) are still standing. That facing the Forum has been partly restored. The brick walls were formerly faced with marble and provided with niches framed with small porphyry columns. The apse contains the base of the statue of the goddess. The floor is of coloured marbles. In 1935 the surviving columns and column-fragments were re-erected; the line of the missing columns is indicated by the arrangement of the terrace, which is laid out as a garden.

Piazzale del Colosseo (closed to traffic on its W and S sides), lies in a valley between the Velia on the W, the Esquiline on the N and the Celian on the S. The ****Colosseum** (Pl. 5; 7) is the most famous monument of ancient Rome and the emblem of her eternity. The original designation, *Flavian Amphitheatre*, commemorates the family name of Vespasian, who began the building, and of his son Titus, who completed it. The popular name of the amphitheatre first occurs in the writings of the Venerable Bede (c 673–735), who quotes a prophecy of Anglo-Saxon pilgrims: 'While the Coliseum stands, Rome shall stand; when the Coliseum falls, Rome shall fall; when Rome falls, the world shall fall.' This name is thought to be derived from the proximity of Nero's colossal statue (p 109), rather than from the size of the building itself. There is free access to the ground floor from the S, W, and N sides (adm times, see p 48). The first floor (adm from the main entrance on the side facing the Roman Forum; fee) is also open, although the upper stories are still closed while restoration work on the top gallery, begun in 1973, continues. An Antiquarium recently arranged in underground rooms has been closed indefinitely because of humidity.

History. The amphitheatre, begun by Vespasian between AD 70 and 76 on the site of the lake in the gardens of Nero's Domus Aurea, was completed by Titus in 80. The inaugural festival lasted 100 days, during which many gladiators and 5000 wild beasts were killed. The amphitheatre was restored c 230 under Alexander Severus and in 248 the thousandth anniversary of the foundation of Rome was celebrated here. There is no historical basis for the tradition that Christians were martyred in the arena. Gladiatorial combats were suppressed in 407 and fights with wild beasts in 523. The damage from the earthquake of 422 was probably repaired by Theodosius II and Valentinian III. The building was again shaken by earthquakes in 1231 and 1349. It was later converted into a castle by the Frangipani, and the Annibaldi.

In 1312 the Colosseum was presented to the senate and people of Rome by the Emperor Henry VII. By the 15C it had become a recognized quarry for building material. The Palazzi di Venezia, and della Cancelleria, and the Quay of Ripetta were built of its travertine. Other parts of the building were reused in St Peter's and Palazzo Barberini. In 1749, however, Benedict XIV dedicated the Colosseum to the Passion of Jesus and pronounced it sanctified by the blood of the martyrs. Pius VII, Leo XII, Gregory XVI, and Pius IX carried out restorations, erecting buttresses and other supports. In 1893–96 it was freed from obstructive buildings by Guido Baccelli, and the interior structures revealed. Further clearances were carried out after the construction in 1933 of Via dei Fori Imperiali. Restoration work was resumed in 1973.

It was particularly admired by 19C travellers to Rome because of its romantic ruined state. Dickens in 1846 declared: 'It is the most impressive, the most stately, the most solemn, grand, majestic, mournful sight, conceivable. Never, in its bloodiest prime, can the sight of the gigantic Coliseum, full and running over with the lustiest life, have moved one heart, as it must move all who look upon it now, a ruin. God be thanked: a ruin!'

Exterior. The elliptical amphitheatre is built of travertine outside and of brick and tufa in the interior. The travertine blocks were originally

fastened together with iron tenons; these were torn out in the Middle
Ages and their sockets are conspicuous. Despite being pillaged
for centuries, the Colosseum preserves its remarkable grandeur
and the NE side appears almost undamaged. The mighty
exterior wall, which supports the complicated interior, has four
stories. The lower three have rows of arches decorated with
engaged columns of the three orders superimposed: Doric on the
lowest story, Ionic on the middle, and Corinthian on the top. The
fourth story, dating from the restoration of Alexander Severus, has no
arches but is articulated by slender Corinthian pilasters. Statues
origin ally occupied the arches of the second and third stories.
The exterior dimensions are: length 188m, breadth 15m, circumference
527m, height 50m.

There were 80 entrance arches. All were numbered except the four
main entrances at the ends of the diameters of the ellipse, situated
NE, SE, SW and NW. That on the NE (between arches XXXVIII and
XXXIX), which was without a cornice and was wider than the others,
opened into a hall ornamented with stuccoes; it was reserved for the
emperor. The numbered arches led to the concentric vaulted corridors giving access to the staircases. Each spectator entered by the
arch corresponding to the number of his ticket, ascended the appropriate staircase and found his seat in the cavea by means of one of the
numerous passages.

Interior. This was divided into three parts—the Arena, the Podium,
and the Cavea. Though more than two-thirds of the original building
has been removed, and the rows of the seats in the cavea are missing,
the magnificence of the amphitheatre, which could probably hold
some 50,000 spectators, can still be appreciated (although the best
view is from the top story, at present closed). The effect of the scene is
reduced by the fact that the underground passages of the arena are
exposed: they were formerly covered by a wood floor. The *Arena*
measures 76m by 46m. It was so called from the sand with which it
was covered to prevent combatants from slipping and to absorb the
blood. It could be flooded for mock sea-battles (or 'naumachiae'). The
subterranean passages which can now be seen were used for the
arrangement of the spectacles, the dens of the wild beasts, and
provided space for the mechanism by which scenery and other
apparatus were hoisted into the arena. The *Cross* replaces an earlier
one which was supposed to commemorate the martyrs of the Colosseum. The Chapel of Santa Maria della Pietà was reopened here in
1982. The arena was surrounded by a wall c 5m high to render the
spectators safe from the attacks of wild beasts. At the top of this wall
was the *Podium*. This was a broad parapeted terrace in front of the
tiers of seats, and on it was placed the imperial couch, or pulvinar.
The rest of the terrace was reserved for senators, pontiffs, vestals,
foreign ambassadors, and other very important persons. The *Cavea*
was divided into three tiers, or *Moeniana*. The lowest tier was
reserved for the knights, the middle one for the wealthier citizens,
and the top one for the populace. The tiers were separated by
landings (*Proecinctiones*), reached by several staircases. Each tier
was intersected at intervals by *Vomitoria*, 160 in all, passages left
between the seats, and a section between any two such passages was
called a *Cuneus*, or wedge, from its shape. Above the topmost tier
was a colonnade, to which women were admitted. At the very top
was the narrow platform for the men who had to attend to the
Velarium, or awning, which kept off the sun; the holes for the
supporting poles may still be seen.

Access to the **First Story** (for adm, see above) is from the second arch on the left of the main entrance via a modern staircase. The view of the interior is spectacular. A model of the Colosseum and a few architectural fragments can be seen in a hall (behind glass). Above the entrance on the side towards the Palatine another staircase (closed since 1973) leads up to the second and (left) the third floors. From the latter a flight of steps continues to a gallery with a magnificent *View of the Amphitheatre, and of the city, in which the salient features are the Forum backed by the green slopes of the Palatine.

The **Antiquarium** (arranged in 1984 but since closed indefinitely because of humidity), is reached by a steep flight of stairs. It is arranged in part of the interesting sub-vaults built by Vespasian and used for all the trappings necessary for the spectacles in the arena above. Here are exhibited architectural elements (notably capitals) from the highest part of the building, the upper portico, of which hardly anything survives, and sculptural fragments from the terminals of the balustrades of the cavea.

Between the Colosseum and the end of Via dei Fori Imperiali is the site (marked by a raised lawn) of the huge brick base, 7m square, of the *Colossus of Nero*, the remains of which were demolished in 1936. This huge gilt bronze statue of Nero as god of the Sun, by Zenodorus, was 35m high and the largest bronze statue ever made, even larger than its model, the Colossus of Rhodes. The statue was provided with a new base and moved here from the vestibule of the Domus Aurea by Hadrian when he built the Temple of Venus and Rome. Decrianus, the architect assigned to the task of removal, used 24 elephants to shift the statue.—Next to it a stretch of Roman road has been uncovered, and, beyond, surrounded by a fence, is the base, re-excavated in 1982 of the *Meta Sudans*, a marble-faced fountain erected by Domitian in front of the Via Sacra and restored by Constantine. It received its name from its resemblance to the conical

Detail of the Arch of Constantine

turning-post (meta) for chariot races in circuses, and from the fact that it 'sweated' water through numerous small orifices. It was surrounded by a circular basin. Its remains were demolished in 1936 by order of Mussolini.

The triple ***Arch of Constantine** (Pl. 4; 7, 8) was erected in AD 315 in honour of Constantine's victory over Maxentius at Saxa Rubra (p 398). This triumphal arch was decorated with sculptural fragments from older Roman monuments, a sad testimony to the decline of the arts in the late Empire. However, the proportions of the arch are good, and many of the individual reliefs are of the highest quality. These have been severely damaged by the polluted air, and they are being restored. Restoration of the top half of the arch was completed in 1988 and the scaffolding was dismantled.

The splendid large *Reliefs on the inside of the central archway and the two above on the sides of the arch come from the frieze of a monument commemorating Trajan's victories over the Dacians and are probably by the sculptor who carved Trajan's Column. The eight medallions on the two façades, depicting hunting-scenes and pastoral sacrifices, belonged to a monument of Hadrian. The eight high reliefs let into the attic have been taken (like the three in the Palazzo dei Conservatori) from a monument to Marcus Aurelius, and represent a sacrifice, orations to the army and to the people, and a triumphal entry into Rome. The small bas-reliefs of the frieze and the victories and captives at the base of the columns are of the period of Constantine.

5 The Pantheon and Piazza Navona

The **Pantheon** (Pl. 2; 6), the best-preserved monument of ancient Rome, remains the most magnificent symbol of the Empire. As the Pantheon, dedicated to all the gods, it was conceived as much as a secular imperial monument as a shrine. In 609 it was converted into a church, the first temple in Rome to be Christianized. A pedimented pronaos precedes a gigantic domed rotunda, and a rectangular feature as wide as the pronaos and as high as the cylindrical wall is inserted between the two. This combination of a pronaos and rotunda gives it a special place in the history of architecture. Originally the pronaos was raised by several steps and preceded by a much larger piazza. Admission see p 49.

The original temple was built apparently of travertine, during the third consulate of Agrippa (27 BC), son-in-law of Augustus, to commemorate the victory of Actium over Antony and Cleopatra. It was injured by fire in AD 80 and was restored by Domitian. In spite of the dedicatory inscription on the pediment of the pronaos (*M. Agrippa, L.F. Cos. tertium fecit*), it has been conclusively proved (by examination of the brick stamps) that the existing temple (including the pronaos) is not that of Agrippa, but a new one built and probably also designed by Hadrian of brick, on a larger scale and on different lines. This second building, begun in AD 118 or 119 and finished between AD 125 and 128, received and retained the name of Pantheon.

It was restored by Septimius Severus and Caracalla. Closed and abandoned under the first Christian emperors and pillaged by the barbarians, the Pantheon was given to Boniface IV by the Byzantine emperor Phocas (whose column is in the Forum). Boniface IV consecrated it as a Christian church in 609. It was dedicated to Santa Maria ad Martyres; there was a legend that some twenty-eight wagon-loads of martyrs' bones had been transferred here from the catacombs. In 667 Constans II, emperor of Byzantium, on a twelve-day visit to Rome, robbed the temple of what the Goths had left, and, in particular, stripped off the gilded roof-tiles (probably of bronze). Benedict II (684) restored it, Gregory III (735) roofed it with lead; in 1153 Anastasius IV built a palace at the side. During the residence of the popes at Avignon the Pantheon served as a fortress in the struggles between the Colonna and the Orsini. In 1435 Eugenius IV isolated the building, and from that time it was the object of such veneration that the Roman Senator on taking office swore to preserve 'Maria Rotonda' intact for the pontiff, together with the relics and sacred treasures of the City. The monument was greatly admired during the Renaissance; Pius IV repaired the bronze door, and had it practically re-cast (1563). Urban VIII (Barberini), however, employed Bernini to add two clumsy turrets in front, which became popularly known as the 'ass-ears of Bernini'. Urban VIII also melted down the bronze ceiling of the portico to make the baldacchino at St Peter's and 80 cannon for the Castel Sant' Angelo, an act of vandalism that prompted Pasquino's stinging gibe, 'Quod non fecerunt barbari fecerunt Barberini'. Alexander VII had the portico restored by Giuseppe Paglia (1662) and the level of the piazza lowered, so that the façade of the building could be seen to better advantage; Clement IX surrounded the portico with an iron railing (1668); Benedict XIV employed Paolo Posi (1747) to restore the interior and the atrium. The first two Kings and the first Queen of Italy are buried here. The incongruous turrets added by Bernini were removed in 1883.

The PORTICO (which has been partially in restoration for many years) is nearly 34m wide and 15·5m deep, and has 16 monolithic Corinthian columns of red or grey granite, without flutings, each 12·5m high and 4·5m in circumference. The superb capitals and the bases are of white marble. The three columns on the E side are replacements, one by Urban VIII (1625), the others by Alexander VII (1655–67); the armorial bearings of these popes may be seen in the decoration of the capitals. Eight of the columns stand in front, and the others are disposed in four rows, so as to form three aisles, the central one leading to the bronze door, which dates from Pius IV, and the others to the two great niches which may formerly have contained colossal statues of Augustus and Agrippa.

The visual impact of the *INTERIOR is unforgettable. The use of light from the opening in the dome displays the genius of the architect. The height and diameter of the interior are the same—43·3m. The great dome has five rows of coffers diminishing in size towards the circular opening in the centre, which measures almost 9m across. The intricate design of the coffers is mainly responsible for the effect of space and light in the interior. They were probably ornamented with gilded bronze rosettes. The diameter of the dome, the largest of its kind ever built, exceeds by more than 1m that of the dome of St Peter's. Its span, which contains no brick arches or vaults, begins at the level of the highest cornice seen on the outside of the building, rather than, as it appears in the interior, at the top of the attic stage.

The cylindrical wall is 6m thick; it contains seven great niches, or recesses, each, except the central apse preceded by two Corinthian columns of giallo antico, and flanked by pilasters. The apse instead has two free-standing columns. Between the recesses, which originally contained statues, are eight shrines (aediculae), those flanking the apse and entrance with triangular pediments, and the others with segmented pediments. They are supported by two Corinthian columns in giallo antico, porphyry, or granite. Above the recesses is the entablature with a beautiful cornice, and still higher is an attic, unfortunately restored in 1747, making this stage more pronounced than was intended. Part of the original decoration can be seen over the recess to the right of the apse: between the rectangular openings (fitted with grilles) were shallow pilasters of reddish marble alternating with three marble panels. More than half of the original coloured marble sheets on the walls are still in place. The floor, though restored, retains its original design.

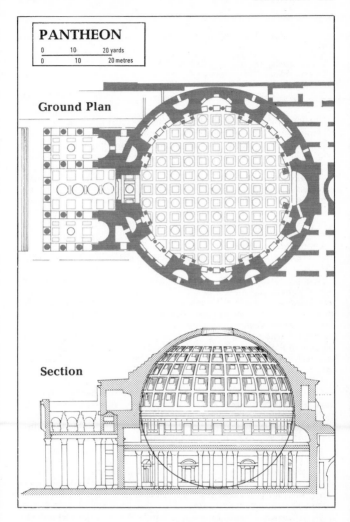

PANTHEON

| 0 | 10 | 20 yards |
| 0 | 10 | 20 metres |

Ground Plan

Section

In the 1st chapel on the right, *Annunciation, a fresco attrib. to *Melozzo da Forlì* or *Antoniazzo Romano*, and two 17C marble angels. In the aedicule, 14C fresco of the Coronation of the Virgin. 2nd chapel on the right, tomb of Victor Emmanuel II, first king of Italy (died 9 January 1878), designed by *Manfredo Manfredi*; 3rd chapel, 15C Madonna and Saints. In the main apse, above the high altar, 7C icon of the Virgin and Child. In the 3rd chapel on the left, 16C Crucifix and (right) a monument by *Thorvaldsen* to Card. Consalvi (died 1824), secretary of Pius VII, who represented the Holy See at the Congress of Vienna. 3rd aedicule, TOMB OF RAPHAEL, inscribed with the famous distich of Bembo, translated by Pope in his Epitaph on Sir Godfrey Kneller ('Living, great Nature feared he might outvie Her works, and dying, fears herself may die'). On the altar is the statue of the Madonna del Sasso, by *Lorenzetto*, probably with the help of *Raff. da Montelupo*, from Raphael's original design. The bronze bust is by *De Fabris*. Below the empty niche on the right is the short epitaph of Maria

Bibbiena, niece of Cardinal Dovizi da Bibbiena, who was betrothed to Raphael and died before him. 2nd chapel: tomb of Humbert I (who was assassinated at Monza on 29 July 1900), designed by *Gius. Sacconi*. Below Humbert's tomb is that of Margherita di Savoia, first queen of Italy (died 5 January 1926). Among other artists buried in the Pantheon are Giov. da Udine, Perino del Vaga, Taddeo Zuccari, Ann. Carracci, and Bald. Peruzzi.

A door on the left of the pronaos leads to a staircase to the cupola (extensive views; adm only with special permission).

In PIAZZA DELLA ROTONDA is a fountain (1575), on a model of Giacomo della Porta, surmounted by an obelisk of Rameses the Great, formerly belonging to the Isaeum and erected here in 1711. In Via della Palombella, at the back of the Pantheon, are remains of Agrippa's *Basilica of Neptune*, reconstructed by Hadrian. In Piazza Minerva is a bizarre but delightful work by Bernini (1667), a marble elephant supporting a small obelisk which belonged to the *Isaeum Campense*, or *Temple of Isis*, that formerly stood nearby. Other relics from the temple are in the Capitoline Museum, in Piazza dei Cinquecento, and in the Egyptian Museum in the Vatican. The hieroglyphic inscription on the obelisk relates to Apries, the last of the independent Pharaohs of Egypt (the Hophrah of the Bible), who was the ally of Zedekiah, king of Judah, against Nebuchadnezzar (6C BC).

*Santa Maria Sopra Minerva (Pl. 2; 6; closed 12–16) stands on the site of a small oratory probably built here before AD 800 on the ruins of a Temple of Minerva. It was rebuilt in 1280 by the Dominicans who modelled it on their church (Santa Maria Novella) in Florence (according to Vasari it was by the same architects, Fra Sisto and Ristoro). It was altered and over-restored in the Gothic style in 1848–55. On the right side of the simple façade (1453) small marble plaques register the heights reached by floods on the Tiber before it was canalized.

In the INTERIOR (coin-operated lights in every chapel) the vault, the rose-windows, and the excessively colourful decorations date from the 19C restoration. On the right of the central door is the tomb of Nerone Diotisalvi, a Florentine exile (died 1482), and, on the right of the S door, that of Virginia Pucci Ridolfi (1567), the latter with a fine bust by an unknown Florentine.

SOUTH AISLE. By the 1st chapel, tomb of the archivist Castalio, with a fine portrait.—5th chapel (Chapel of the Annunciation, by *Carlo Maderno*). *Antoniazzo Romano*, Annunciation, (removed for restoration), with Card. Juan de Torquemada (uncle of Tomás de Torquemada, the inquisitor) presenting three poor girls to the Virgin, commemorating the Confraternity of the Annunziata, founded in 1460 to provide dowries for penniless girls (removed for restoration); on the left, tomb of Urban VII, by *Ambr. Buonvicino*.—6th chapel. Frescoed ceiling by *Cherubino Alberti*; altarpiece of the Institution of the Eucharist, by *Barocci*; at the sides, tombs of the parents of Clement VIII, by *Giac. della Porta*, and (in a niche to the left) a statue of Clement VIII. A statue of St Sebastian has recently been removed from a niche and placed in the centre of the chapel since its attribution to *Michelangelo*. Probably made as a model for his Christ (see below), it may have been finished by *N. Cordier*.—7th chapel. On the right, tomb of Bp. Juan Diaz de Coca (1477), by *And. Bregno*, with a fresco attrib. to *Melozzo da Forlì*; on the left, tomb of Bened. Sopranzi, Bp. of Nicosia (died 1495), by the school of A. Bregno.

SOUTH TRANSEPT. 1st chapel, wooden crucifix (early 15C); *2nd chapel, at the end (Cappella Carafa or di San Tommaso; being restored), with a fine marble arch (attrib. to *Mino da Fiesole, Verrocchio*, and *Giul. da Maiano*) and a beautiful balustrade, contains celebrated *Frescoes by *Filippino Lippi* (1489): over the altar, Annunciation and St Thomas Aquinas presenting Card. Olivieri Carafa to the Virgin; altar wall, Assumption; right wall, below, St Thomas confounding the heretics, the central figures being Arius and Sabellius (the two youths in the right-hand group are probably the future Medici popes, Leo X and Clement VII, both buried in this church). On the left wall, monument of Paul IV (died 1559) by *Giac.* and *Tom. Cassignola*, from a design by Pirro Ligorio. In the vault, Four sibyls, by *Raffaellino del Garbo*.—To the left of this chapel, *Tomb of Guillaume Durand (died 1296), bishop of Mende, by *Giov. di Cosma*, with a beautiful 13C mosaic of the Madonna and Child.— 3rd chapel, *Carlo Maratta*, Madonna and saints.—4th chapel, Frescoed ceiling by *Marcello Venusti*; on the right, tomb of Card. Capranica (1458).

CHOIR. At the foot of the steps, on the left, is *Christ bearing the Cross by *Michelangelo* (1514–21), commissioned at a cost of 200 ducats by Metello Vari and P. Castellani. The bronze drapery is a later addition. Under the 19C high altar lies the body of St Catherine of Siena (see below). In the apse are the tombs of Leo X (left) and Clement VII, designed by Ant. Sangallo the Younger, with statues by *Raff. da Montelupo* and *Nanni di Baccio Bigio* respectively. In the pavement is the slab-tomb of Card. Pietro Bembo (1547), secretary to Pope Leo X from 1512–20, and friend of Michelangelo, Raphael, and Ariosto.

NORTH TRANSEPT. To the left of the choir, in a passageway which serves as an exit, are several large monuments, including those of Card. Michele Bonelli (Alexandrinus), by *Giac. della Porta*, and of Card. Dom. Pimentel, designed by *Bernini*. Surrounded by a bronze fence (1975) is the *Tomb-slab of Fra Angelico, with some charming lines composed by Pope Nicholas V.—2nd chapel to the left of the choir, Tomb of Giov. Arberini (died c 1470) by a Tuscan sculptor (*Agost. di Duccio?*), who has introduced a Roman copy of a Greek *Bas-relief of the 5C BC, representing Hercules and the lion. To the left is the entrance to the sacristy, behind which is the room in which St Catherine of Siena died in 1380; it was brought from Via di Santa Chiara by Card. Barberini. The frescoes, poorly preserved, are by *Antoniazzo Romano* and his school (1482).—At the end of this transept is the Cappella di San Domenico, with the Baroque monument of Benedict XIII (died 1730). At the corner of the nave and transept is the charming small tomb of And. Bregno (1421–1506). On the 2nd pillar is the tomb of Maria Raggi, a colourful early work by *Bernini*.

NORTH AISLE. Between the 4th and 3rd chapels, tomb of Giov. Vigevano (died 1630) with a bust by *Bernini* (c 1617). 3rd chapel. Tiny altarpiece (the Redeemer), attrib. to *Perugino* or to *Pinturicchio*; on the right, statue of St Sebastian, attrib. to *Mich. Marini*; on the left, St John the Baptist, by *Ambr. Buonvicino*; against the side-walls, tombs of Benedetto and Agostino Maffei, attrib. to *L. Capponi* (15C). 2nd chapel. The tomb of Gregorio Naro, showing the cardinal kneeling at a prieu-dieu, has recently been attrib. to *Bernini*. 1st chapel. Bust of Girol. Bottigella, perhaps by *Iac. Sansovino*.—Near the door is the tomb of Francesco Tornabuoni (1480), by *Mino da Fiesole*, and above is that of Card. Tebaldi (1466), by *And. Bregno* and *Giov. Dalmata*.

The monastery was once the headquarters of the Dominicans, in which Fra Angelico died (1455) and Galileo was tried (1633). It now serves as offices for the Chamber of Deputies. A small *Museum* (usually kept locked) contains icons from Jugoslavia (17–19C), ecclesiastical vestments, a detached fresco of the Madonna and Child (late 13C or early 14C), etc.

From the piazza the narrow Via dei Cestari (with a number of shops selling liturgical articles) runs S towards the busy Corso Vittorio Emanuele. On the right in Via dell'Arco della Ciambella, part of the circular wall of the central hall of the *Baths of Agrippa* is charmingly incorporated into the street architecture. These were the first public baths in the city, begun by Agrippa in 25 BC. Opposite, Via della Pigna leads past the 16C Palazzo Maffei Marescotti to a little piazza in front of the Baroque church of *San Giovanni della Pigna* (usually closed; with interesting tomb slabs inside the entrance wall). At a house here (No. 6) Mussolini met Card. Gasparri in 1923 to initiate discussions on the Concordat. Via del Gesù (with a beautiful Renaissance doorway at No. 85) leads down to Palazzo Altieri (1650–60; interesting courtyards) on the traffic-ridden Piazza del Gesù.

Here rises the ***Gesù** (Pl. 3; 6; closed 12.30–16.30), properly the church of the *SS. Nome di Gesù*, the principal Jesuit church in Rome and the outstanding type of the sumptuous style to which the Order has given its name. It was built between 1568 and 1575 at the expense of Alessandro Farnese. Both the façade (by *Giacomo della Porta*) and the interior (by *Vignola*) are important to the development of the design of Baroque churches in Rome. The cupola designed by Vignola was completed by Della Porta.

The heavily decorated INTERIOR has a longitudinal plan, with an aisleless nave and lateral chapels (coin-oprated lights in each chapel, and at the W end, for the vault). On the vault is a *Fresco of the Triumph of the Name of Jesus, a bold and original work, with marvellous effects of foreshortening, by *Baciccia*. The frescoes of the cupola and the tribune are by the same artist. He also designed the stucco decoration, executed by *Ant. Raggi* and *Leon. Retti*. The marble decoration of the nave dates from 1858–61. SOUTH SIDE. The 3rd chapel has an altarpiece by *Fed. Zuccari* who also painted the vault and walls. The lunettes and pendentives are by *Ventura Salimbeni*. The four marble festoons incorporated in the decoration are supposed to have come from the Baths of Titus. The elegant SACRISTY is by *Girol. Rainaldi.*—SOUTH TRANSEPT. Altarpiece from a sketch by Pietro da Cortona with the Death of St Francis Xavier, by *Carlo Maratta.*—MAIN APSE. Over the High Altar, gorgeous with coloured marbles, is the Circumcision, by *Aless. Capalti* (1842). On the left, a bust of Card. Roberto Bellarmine, by *G.L. Bernini*, was placed in a neo-classical setting after the tomb was destroyed during rebuilding in 1843. The two pretty little circular domed chapels on either side of the main apse were designed by *Gius. Valeriani* (1584–88).—NORTH TRANSEPT (light on left). *Altar-tomb of St Ignatius, by *And. del Pozzo* and others (1695–1700), resplendent with marble and bronze; the columns are encrusted with lapis lazuli and their bronze decorations are by *And. Bertoni*. The statue of St Ignatius is a copy by *Tadolini* of the original by *Legros* (melted down during the French Revolution). Above is a group of the Trinity by *Leon. Retti* with a terrestrial globe formed of a splendid block of lapis lazuli, the largest known. In front of the altar is a magnificent balustrade, and at the sides are marble groups: Religion triumphing over Heresy, by *P. Legros* (right), and Barbarians adoring the Faith, by *J. Théodon* (left).—NORTH SIDE. 3rd chapel, altarpiece of the Holy Trinity by *Fr. Bassano*, and Baptism of Christ (right wall) by *Ventura Salimbeni*. The 2nd chapel has vault frescoes by *Pomarancio*, 17C paintings by *Giovanni Francesco Romanelli* and interesting sculptures. The 1st chapel also has its vault frescoed by *Pomarancio* and two paintings by *Fr. Mola.*—The singing of a Te Deum in this church annually on 31 December is a magnificent traditional ceremony.

Via d'Aracoeli leads from Piazza del Gesù (with the headquarters of the Christian Democrat Party) to Piazza d'Aracoeli and the Capitol. On the right, in Via delle Botteghe Oscure (with the headquarters of the Italian Communist Party) are the remains of a temple (seen from the railings), probably a *Temple of*

Nymphs, dating from the 1C BC. On the S side of this road Palazzo Paganica is covered for restoration. It was purchased in 1983 by the Italian State and excavations are in progress beneath it and the adjoining site (entrance at No. 6C Via Caetani). Remains of the small *Theatre of Balbus* inaugurated in 13 BC have been uncovered, adjoined to the W by a cryptoporticus known as the *Crypta Balbi*. Later buildings also excavated here include the medieval church of Santa Maria, and a Renaissance monastery. The interesting remains may be opened to the public. In Via Caetani a plaque marks the place where the body of the statesman Aldo Moro was abandoned by his murderers in 1978.

CORSO VITTORIO EMANUELE (Pl. 3; 5, 6), now one of the main traffic arteries of Rome running from Piazza Venezia to the Tiber, dates from 1876. It leads from Piazza Gesù to the LARGO ARGENTINA, a traffic-ridden square with an impressive group of **Four Republican Temples**, known as the *Area Sacra di Largo Argentina*. The site was demolished in 1926–29 for a new building which, after the temples had been discovered and excavated, was never built. The ruins, now inhabited by cats, are well seen from the railings outside (the entrance on Via di San Nicola dei Cesarini is kept locked).

All the temples face a courtyard to the E paved with travertine. It is not yet known with certainty to whom they were dedicated. The first temple ('A') is peripteral and hexastyle; the tufa columns and stylobate are largely preserved. In the Middle Ages the church of St Nicholas was built over it; the apses of the church (otherwise demolished) may still be seen.—The second temple ('B'), the most recent, is circular, and six columns survive, as well as the original flight of steps and the altar. A podium behind this temple near Via di Torre Argentina, almost certainly belongs to the Curia Pompei where Caesar was murdered.—The third temple ('C'), oldest of the four, was built at a lower level; it dates from the end of the 4C or the beginning of the 3C BC. In the Imperial era the cella was rebuilt and the columns and podium covered with stucco. In 1935 the altar, with an inscription relating to c 180 BC, was discovered; even this was a replacement of an older altar.—The fourth temple ('D'), in travertine, is the largest; it has not been completely excavated as part of it is under Via Florida, to the S.—During the excavations the medieval *Torre del Papito* here was restored and isolated.

To the N of the square, on Via dei Cestari, is the church of the *Stimmate*, rebuilt at the beginning of the 18C by G.B. Contini. It contains paintings by Fr. Trevisani, including the high altarpiece of St Francis receiving the Stigmata (1714). On the W side of Largo Argentina is the *Teatro Argentina* dating from 1730, and the most important theatre in Rome during the 18C. The façade is by Pietro Holl (1826). Here in 1816 was held the first performance of Rossini's 'Barber of Seville', and in 1851 that of Verdi's 'Rigoletto'. It is now noted for prose productions and the 'Teatro di Roma' is the resident company. On the right of the theatre, Via del Sudario leads out of the square past the handsome S façade of *Palazzo Caffarelli Vidoni*, attributed to Lor. Lotti (c 1515). The *Chiesa del Sudario* (1604), opposite, was the court church of the House of Savoy from 1871 to 1946. The façade is by Carlo Rainaldi, and inside are late 19C works by Cesare Maccari. Adjoining is the delightful *Casa del Burcardo*, built in 1503 for Bishop Hans Burchard or Burckhardt.

He was author of a remarkable account of the papal court under Innocent VIII and Alexander VI, and called the house the Torre Argentina, which in turn became the name of the piazza. The back doors of the Teatro Argentina (see above) open on to the court. It now houses a theatrical museum and library. Temporarily closed in 1988, but for adm when it reopens, see p 48.

Via del Sudario ends in the little Piazza Vidoni where a Roman statue (recently decapitated) called 'Abate Luigi' (one of Rome's 'talking' statues, see p 122) has been placed against the side wall of the

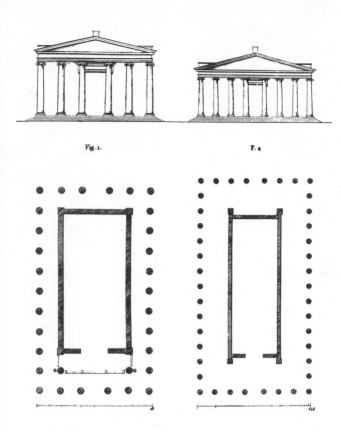

Fig.1.   F. 2

*Peripteral (fig.1) and pseudoperipteral (fig.2) temples,
after Vitruvius, architect and surveyor to Augustus
('De architectura', before AD 27), published by
Carlo Amati in 1829*

church of *Sant'Andrea della Valle (Pl. 3; 6; entrance to right). It was
begun in 1591 by *Fra Fr. Grimaldi*, and continued by *Carlo Maderno*
who crowned it with a fine dome, the largest in Rome after that of St
Peter's. The façade (1665; to be restructured) is by *Carlo Rainaldi*.

The aisleless INTERIOR has a high barrel-vault and spacious apse. Inspired by
the Gesù, it gives the impression of a sumptuous reception hall rather than a
house of prayer.
    SOUTH SIDE. The 1st chapel, by *Carlo Fontana*, has colourful marble columns
and sculptures by *Ercole Ant. Raggi*. The design of the 2nd chapel (Cappella
Strozzi) shows the influence of *Michelangelo* and contains reproductions in
bronze of his Pietà and of his statues of Leah and Rachel from the tomb of Julius
II. At the end of the nave, high up, are similar monuments of two popes of the
Piccolomini family: on the right, Pius III (died 1503) attrib. to *Fr. Ferrucci*

and his son *Sebastiano*; on the left Pius II (died 1464) attrib. to *Paolo Taccone* and a follower of *And. Bregno*. In the dome is the Glory of Paradise, by *Lanfranco*; in the pendentives, the Evangelists by *Domenichino* (1623). He also designed the splendid presbytery and apse and painted the Six Virtues and the Scenes from the life of St Andrew; the gigantic frescoes in the tribune are by *Mattia Preti*. In the S transept, Sant'Andrea Avellino, by *Lanfranco*.

Opposite the church façade, at the beginning of Corso del Rinascimento, is a fountain by Carlo Maderno decorated with an eagle and a dragon. Corso Vittorio Emanuele continues past *Palazzo Massimo alle Colonne*, skilfully set in a narrow, irregular site, by Baldassarre Peruzzi (1532–36). The convex façade, much blackened by the polluted air (but being restored), follows the line of the cavea of the Odeon of Domitian which stood here. The beautiful portico is decorated with stuccoes.

The palace has two courtyards: one a charming Renaissance work with a frescoed loggia, and a Baroque fountain, and the second (in very poor repair) with 17C decorations. In Piazza dei Massimi, behind the palace (reached from Corso Rinascimento) is the so-called 'Palazzo Istoriato', or *Palazzetto Massimi* with remains of its painted façade (1523; by the school of Daniele da Volterra). Here Pannartz and Sweynheim transferred their press (from Subiaco; see p 396) in 1467 and issued the first books printed in Rome. The marble cipollino column set up in the piazza belonged to the Odeon of Domitian (see above).

The Corso widens at a little piazza in front of the church of *San Pantaleo* (usually closed) dating from 1216. It was rebuilt in 1681 by Ant. De Rossi and preserves its 17C interior with a vault fresco by Fil. Gherardi. The façade was added by Gius. Valadier in 1806. The huge **Palazzo Braschi** by Cosimo Morelli (after 1792) now houses the **Museo di Roma** (Pl. 2; 8; closed for restoration in 1988, but for adm when it reopens, see p 49). Important exhibitions are mounted here.

The museum was founded in 1930 to illustrate the history and life of Rome from the Middle Ages to the present day. Many of the works of art come from demolished buildings. The collection has been undergoing rearrangement for many years, and the order of the contents described below may have changed when it reopens.

Off the Courtyard is the train built in Paris in 1858 for Pius IX, and the carriage of Leo XIII. To the left is the Vestibule at the foot of the stairs with a colossal statue of Christ and St John by *Fr. Mochi*. Here are four rooms (opened on request) which house part of the Pinacoteca of the Accademia dell' Arcadia (see p 264) which contains portraits of illustrious members including Vittorio Alfieri and Isaac Newton. The magnificent staircase ascribed to Valadier (1802–04) and decorated by Luigi Acquisti leads to the first floor.

ROOM I. *Fr. Mochi*, Bust of Carlo Barberini; ceiling fresco of the Annunciation of the school of *Zuccari*.—R. II. *Baciccia*, Portrait of Card. Ginnetti.—(right) R. III. Three large 16C paintings of tournaments in Rome.—R. IV. Ceiling *Frescoes of the fable of Psyche by *Cigoli*. These were detached from a room, since demolished, in Palazzo Rospigliosi. In the cases, wooden corbels from 12–17C.—R. V. The oval ceiling is painted in the form of a pavilion. In the centre, tabernacle by *Girolamo da Carpi*. Bust of Clement XII by *Filippo Valle*.—R. VI. Fragments of frescoes, those on the large wall from a house belonging to Card. da Carpi. The others are by *Polidoro da Caravaggio* and *Maturino da Firenze*.—R. VII. Detached *Frescoes from the Papal hunting lodge at Magliana; attributed to *Lo Spagna* (early 16C), they represent Apollo and the Nine Muses.—R. VIII. Tournament in Piazza Navona, and the Visit of Urban VIII to the Gesù, both by *Andrea Sacchi*. Investiture of Taddeo Barberini by *Agostino Tassi*. Urban VIII, portrait by *Pietro da Cortona*. The three adjacent rooms are to exhibit Medieval frescoes.—R. IX (with a fine view of Piazza Navona). 17C cabinet with a series of miniature scenes of Rome, and on the walls, paintings of Piazza S. Pietro and Piazza del Popolo.—In the large GALLERY are Gobelins tapestries. The room is designed by *Valadier*, who also designed the adjoining CHAPEL (opened on request), with a fine stucco vault. It contains a St Francis, attrib. to *Guido Reni*, and on the altar an 18C ivory crucifix. Beyond R. XI, R. XII has a pretty majolica floor and fine *Paintings by *Pompeo Batoni* (portraits of Pio VI, and John Staples, Self-portrait, and Woman at her toilet) and *Giov. Paolo Pannini* (Portrait of Benedict XIV and a Cardinal).—R. XIII. *And. Sacchi*, Portrait of Card. Dom. Ginnasi. Works by *Canova* are exhibited in R. XIV, including the original plaster model for his Self-portrait, two bozzetti, and a painted Self-portrait. Beyond R. XV with church furniture, R. XVI exhibits weights and measures. A corridor leads back to R. I and the staircase.

SECOND FLOOR. Many of the rooms have ceilings decorated by *Liborio Coccetti* (early 19C). In the Vestibule are three huge paintings illustrating the story of Helen and Paris, by *Gavin Hamilton*. Beyond R. I with works by *Fr. Gai*, R. II contains fresco fragments from Palazzo Caffarelli. R. III: collection of water-colours of old Rome by *Ettore R. Franz* (1845–1907; continued in R. VI). Beyond an oval room, R. V. contains fresco fragments (end of 13C) and *Mosaics from the old façade of St Peter's. An interesting series of views of Rome in the nineteenth century, by *Ippolito Caffi*, and a portrait of Piranesi are to be exhibited on this floor.

The Third Floor is still in the course of arrangement. The exhibits will include a collection of drawings and water-colours of Roman costumes by *Bart. Pinelli*, scenes of Rome by *Dom. Morelli* and *De Sanctis*, and other 19C works from the GALLERIA COMUNALE D'ARTE MODERNA. Also on this floor is the *Archivio Fotografico Comunale*.—Sculptures by *Pietro Tenerani* are to be arranged on the Fourth Floor.

Via di San Pantaleo, which skirts the left side of Palazzo Braschi, ends in Piazza Pasquino. Here is a fragment of a marble group representing Menaleus with the body of Patroclus, the copy of a Hellenistic work of the Pergamene school which may once have decorated the Stadium of Domitian (see below). This famous statue has been known as PASQUINO since it was placed here in 1501.

It became the custom to attach witty or caustic comments on topical subjects to the pedestal of the statue. The credit for originating this method of public satire was ascribed to a certain Pasquino, a tailor in the vicinity, hence the origin of the term 'pasquinade'. There were other 'talking statues' in the city (see pp 56, 72, 142); as Stendhal noted on his visit to the city in 1816 'what the

18C engraving of Piazza Navona by Piranesi

people of Rome desire above all else is a chance to show their strong contempt for the powers that control their destiny, and to laugh at their expense: hence the dialogues between 'Pasquino' and 'Marforio''. Many printing houses and bookshops were established in the vicinity of the piazza.

From Piazza Pasquino the narrow VIA DEL GOVERNO VECCHIO, an ancient papal thoroughfare with many traces of the early Renaissance, leads W. On the right (No. 39) is *Palazzo Nardini* (or Palazzo del Governo Vecchio), built in 1473 by Card. Stefano Nardini, created Governor of Rome by Paul II. It has a splendid Renaissance portal. Opposite is the remarkable *Palazzo Turci* (1500), once attrib. to Bramante.

Via di Pasquino leads into ***Piazza Navona** (Pl. 2; 6) which occupies the site of the Stadium of Domitian. Its form, preserving the dimensions of the Roman building which could probably hold some 30,000 spectators, represents a remarkable survival within the modern city. The name, too, is derived from the athletic games, the 'Agoni Capitolini' held here after the stadium was inaugurated in AD 86. In the Middle Ages the piazza was called the 'Campus Agonis'; hence 'agone', 'n'agona', and 'navona'. Historic festivals, jousts, and open-air sports took place here, and it was also used as a market place from 1477 until 1869. From the 17C to the late 19C the piazza was flooded every week-end in August, for the entertainment of the Romans (the nobles enjoyed the spectacle from their carriages). During the Christmas festival, statuettes for the Christmas crib are sold here, and the fair and toy-market of the Befana, or Epiphany is held. In the total absence of wheeled traffic it remains the most animated piazza in Rome. It has several famous cafés.

Three splendid fountains decorate the piazza. At the S end, the *Fontana del Moro* was begun in the 16C (the sculptures were substituted by copies in 1874). It was altered by Bernini in 1653 when he designed the central figure, known as 'Il Moro' (executed by Ant. Mari).—The central **Fontana dei Quattro Fiumi* is one of the most famous works by Bernini. In the mass of rockwork and grottoes are colossal allegorical figures of the rivers Danube, Ganges, Nile, and Plate, representing Europe, Asia, Africa, and America, carved by Bernini's pupils, Ant. Raggi, Giac. Ant. Fancelli, Claude Poussin, and Fr. Baratta. The tall obelisk was cut in Egypt and brought to Rome by order of Domitian. It was moved here by Innocent X from the Circus of Maxentius and bears the names of Vespasian, Titus, and Domitian in hieroglyphics. The popular story told to illustrate the rivalry between Bernini and Borromini that the Nile is holding up an arm to block out the sight of Sant'Agnese is apocryphal since the fountain was finished in 1651 before Borromini started work on the church.—The fountain at the N end, representing Neptune struggling with a marine monster, Nereids, and sea-horses, is by Ant. della Bitta and Gregorio Zappalà (1878).

Remains of the N curve of the stadium, with the entrance gate, may be seen beneath the modern buildings N of the piazza, in Piazza di Tor Sanguigna.

On the W side of the piazza is **Sant'Agnese in Agone** (open only 17–19; and fest. 10–13), an ancient church built on the ruins of the stadium which Christian tradition marks as the spot where St Agnes was exposed (see p 248). It was reconstructed by *Girol.* and *Carlo Rainaldi* in 1652. The splendid concave *Façade which adds emphasis to the dome was begun by *Borromini* (1653–57). The lantern of the dome is by *Carlo Rainaldi*, and the twin bell-towers are by *Giov. Baratta* and *Ant. del Grande*.

The small Baroque *INTERIOR has an intricate Greek-cross plan in which a remarkable effect of spaciousness is provided by the cupola. The fresco on the dome is by *Ciro Ferri* and *Seb. Corbellini*; the pendentives are by *Baciccia*. Above the seven altars 17C bas-reliefs or statues (including an antique statue of St Sebastian altered by *Paolo Campi*) take the place of paintings. The high altarpiece is a Holy Family by *Dom. Guidi*. Above the entrance is the monument by *G.B. Maini* of Innocent X, who is buried here.—Beneath the church the Oratory of St Agnes (usually closed), built before AD 800, survives (although

poorly restored) in a vault of the Stadium of Domitian. It contains badly
damaged 13C frescoes, and the last work of *Aless. Algardi*, a bas relief of the
miracle of St Agnes.

To the S of the church is **Palazzo Pamphilj** (sometimes called *Palazzo*
Doria) started by *Girol. Rainaldi*, and completed by *Borromini* for
Innocent X, in the mid-17C. It was later occupied by the sister-in-law
of Innocent, the notorious Olimpia Maidalchini. It is now the Brazilian Embassy (adm only by written permission).

INTERIOR. At the top of the stairs is the SALA PALESTRINA. This is a magnificent
example of *Borromini*'s secular architecture, using the minimum of surface
decoration. The busts are by *Aless. Algardi*. It has had an interesting history as a
music room, since the first performance of the Concerti Grossi of Corelli took
place here in the 17C.—To the right are the State rooms overlooking Piazza
Navona, decorated with delightful friezes, all painted between 1634 and 1671.
In the first room, Bacchic scenes, by *Andrea Camassei*. R. II (to the right),
Agostino Tassi, seascapes. R. III. *Gaspard Dughet*, landscapes. R. IV. *Giacinto
Gemignani*, scenes from Roman history. R. V. *Giacinto Brandi*, episodes in
Ovid's Metamorphoses.—The long *GALLERY (designed by *Borromini*), has a
magnificent fresco of the story of Aeneas by *Pietro da Cortona*. His organization
of the long vault is masterly. The charming papal bedroom also has a ceiling
fresco by *Cortona*.

On the opposite side of the piazza, is the church of the MADONNA
DEL SACRO CUORE, formerly *San Giacomo degli Spagnoli*, which was
rebuilt in 1450 and restored in 1879. The entrance from the piazza is
by a side door at the E end. On the S side the choir-gallery is almost
certainly by *Pietro Torrigiani*; the *Chapel off the N side is by *Ant. da
Sangallo the Younger*.

Just out of the NW corner of the piazza, in the street of the same
name, is the German church of **Santa Maria dell'Anima** (Pl. 2; 6),
rebuilt in 1500–23. The façade was possibly designed by *Giul. da
Sangallo*. Above the door the Virgin (removed for restoration; it will
probably be replaced here by a copy and the original displayed in the
sacristy of the church) attrib. to *And. Sansovino* is a copy of a highly
venerated Madonna between two souls in Purgatory, which was
formerly in the church and was the origin of its name.

The INTERIOR (if closed ring at the door of the Hospice behind the church, No.
20 Vicolo della Pace) has an unusual plan, derived from late-Gothic German
churches. The painting of the vault and walls is by *L. Seitz* (1875–82), who also
designed the window over the central door. S side. 1st chapel, San Benno by
Carlo Saraceni; 2nd chapel, Holy Family, by *Giacinto Gimignani*; 4th chapel,
Pietà, by *Lorenzetto* and *Nanni di Baccio Bigio*, in imitation of Michelangelo. In
the sanctuary, Holy Family with saints, by *Giulio Romano*, over the high altar;
on the right, the magnificent tomb of Hadrian VI (died 1523; of Utrecht),
designed by *Bald. Peruzzi*, with sculptures by *Michelangelo Senese* and *Nic.
Tribolo*; on the left, Tomb of Karl Friedrich of Clèves (died 1575), by *Gilles de
Rivière* and *Nicolas d'Arras* (a bas-relief from this tomb is in the corridor leading
to the sacristy).—N side. 4th chapel, Descent from the Cross and frescoes, by *Fr.
Salviati*; 3rd chapel, Life of St Barbara, frescoes by *Michiel Coxcie*; 1st chapel,
Martyrdom of St Lambert, by *Carlo Saraceni*.

Vicolo della Pace, on the right, leads to the beautiful church of
*Santa Maria della Pace** (Pl. 2; 6; recently restored; open 8–13, 15–
18). The entrance is usually through the cloister (see below) entered
beyond the arch to the left of the facade, at No. 5 Via Arco della Pace.
It was rebuilt by Sixtus IV (1480–84) to celebrate the successful
outcome of the Pazzi conspiracy and victory over the Turks. There
was also a popular legend that a miraculous image of the Virgin in
the portico of the old church bled on being struck by a stone. The

architect is believed to have been *Baccio Pontelli*. The church was
partly rebuilt in 1611 and again by Alexander VII, under whose
auspices the façade and beautiful semicircular porch with Tuscan
columns were erected by *Pietro da Cortona*; his design of the
delightful little piazza and the surrounding area was never
completed.

The INTERIOR consists of a domed octagon preceded by a simple
rectangular nave. Above the arch of the 1st chapel on the S side are
the *SIBYLS of *Raphael* (c 1514), executed for Agostino Chigi,
founder of the chapel. They represent (beginning on the left) the
Cumaean, Persian, Phrygian, and Tiburtine Sibyls, to whom the
future is being revealed by angels, and their varying shades of awe
and wonder are beautifully conveyed in look and gesture. The
paintings were restored in 1816 by Palmaroli. Above them are four
Prophets, by *Timoteo Viti* (Raphael's pupil): on the right, Daniel and
David, on the left, Jonah and Hosea. On the altar, Deposition, a fine
bronze by *Cosimo Fancelli*.—The 2nd chapel (Cesi) was designed by
Ant. da Sangallo the Younger, and has remarkable marble decoration by *Simone Mosca* (1540–42). The ruined frescoes in the window
lunette are by *Rosso Fiorentino*. The Cesi tombs and sculptures are
by *Vinc. de'Rossi*.—N side: 1st chapel. In the niche is a *Fresco of
the Virgin, Saints Bridget and Catherine, and the donor Ferdinando
Ponzetti, by *Baldass. Peruzzi*, who also painted the small frescoes of
Old Testament subjects on the vaulting of the niche. At the sides of
the chapel are the delightful little *Tombs of the Ponzetti family
(1505 and 1509), with delicately carved decoration and four busts.
2nd chapel. Altarpiece (much darkened), Madonna and saints, by
Marcello Venusti, perhaps from a design by Michelangelo.
OCTAGON. Above the high altar, by *Carlo Maderno*, is the highly
venerated 15C image of the Madonna della Pace. The beautiful
marble tabernacle in the chapel of the Crucifix (left) is attrib. to
Pasquale da Caravaggio. On the octagon, to the right of the high
altar, *Baldass. Peruzzi*, Presentation in the Temple.

The *Cloisters (well restored in 1971), are among *Bramante's* finest works in
Rome (1504). They have two rows of arcades one above the other; columns of
the upper row rise from the centres of the arches in the lower row. The tomb of
Bp. Bocciaccio (1497) on the right is of the school of *Luigi Capponi*.

Off the other side of Piazza Navona (see above) Via di Sant'Agostino
leads to the church of **Sant'Agostino** (Pl. 2; 6), which was built for
Cardinal d'Estouteville by *Giac. da Pietrasanta* (1479–83). It is
dedicated to St Augustine, author of the Confessions. The severely
plain façade is one of the earliest of the Renaissance.

The INTERIOR, renovated by *L. Vanvitelli* (1750) contains good frescoes on the
vault and nave by *Pietro Gagliardi* (1855), including five prophets on the nave
pilasters which accompany the *PROPHET ISAIAH frescoed on the 3rd pillar on
the N side by *Raphael*. This was commissioned by the Humanist scholar Giov.
Goritz in 1512 for his funerary monument, and shows how greatly the painter
was influenced by Michelangelo's frescoes in the Sistine Chapel. It was restored
by Daniele da Volterra. In 1982 the *Madonna and Child with St Anne, sculpted
from a single block of marble by *And. Sansovino* was replaced beneath the
fresco (it had been moved to a side chapel) since it also formed part of the Goritz
monument on this pillar. At the W end is the so-called *Madonna del Parto, by
Iac. Sansovino (1521), a greatly venerated statue and the object of innumerable
votive offerings.—Right Aisle. 2nd chapel, Madonna della Rosa, a copy by
Avanzino Nucci of the original painting by *Raphael* which was stolen from
Loreto and subsequently disappeared.—4th chapel, Christ giving the keys to St
Peter, sculpted by *G.B. Cotignola*.—Right Transept. Chapel of Sant'Agostino,
altarpiece by *Guercino* and side panels by his school; Baroque tomb

of Cardinal Renato Imperiali, by *Paolo Posi*. On the high altar, by *Bernini*, is a Byzantine Madonna brought from Constantinople. In the chapel to the left of the choir is the tomb of St Monica (mother of St Augustine), by *Isaia da Pisa*.— Left Aisle, 4th chapel, St Apollonia, by *Girol. Muziano*; 1st chapel, *Our Lady of Loreto, by *Caravaggio* (light on left).—In the little vestibule at the N door are Four Doctors by *Isaia da Pisa*, statues belonging to the tomb of St Monica, and a crucifix by *L. Capponi* (15C).

In Via delle Coppelle, to the right off Via della Scrofa, is (No. 35) *Palazzo Baldassini*, a smaller version of Palazzo Farnese, by *Ant. Sangallo the Younger* (1514–23), with a handsome courtyard and loggia. Garibaldi lived here in 1875.

Via dei Pianellari skirts the left side of Sant'Agostino as far as Via dei Portoghesi. Here are a delightful 15C doorway and tower and, behind a pretty balustrade, the ornate façade of the 17C church of **Sant'Antonio dei Portoghesi**. The good Baroque interior (usually closed) has a painting (1st left altar) of the Madonna and Child with Saints Anthony and Francis by Antoniazzo Romano. Across Via della Scrofa Via della Stelletta continues E to the piazza and church of **Santa Maria in Campo Marzio** (Pl. 2; 6; recently restored). The church, of ancient foundation, was rebuilt in 1685 by G. Ant. De Rossi on a Greek cross plan, with a good portico and court. Over the high altar is a Madonna, part of a triptych probably of the 12–13C. Since 1920 the church has belonged to the Roman Catholic Patriarchate of Antioch of the Syrians (services on fest.).

To the S, reached by a street of the same name is the little church of *Santa Maria Maddalena* with a Rococo façade (1735; covered for restoration in 1988) by *G. Sardi*. The pretty INTERIOR (1695–99), on an original plan, was designed by *Giovanni Antonio de' Rossi* and *Giulio Carlo Quadrio*. The statues of Virtues in the nave are attributed to *Paolo Morelli*, except for the 1st and 3rd on the left which are by *Carlo Monaldi*, and by *Giuseppe Raffaelli*. The vault is frescoed by *Michelangelo Cerruti* (1732) and the cupola by *Stefano Parrocel* (1739). The confessionals are by *Giuseppe Palma* (1762). Right Side: 2nd chapel, 16C painting of the Madonna and Child; 3rd chapel, elaborate marble altar with a vault fresco by *Sebastiano Conca*. By the side door is a fine wood statue of Mary Magdalene (15C). Over the high altar, Mary Magdalene in Prayer by *Michele Rocca*, and, above, a fresco by *Aureliano Milani*. North Side: 3rd chapel, St Nicholas of Bari by *Baciccio*; 2nd chapel, St Lawrence Giustiniani in adoration of the Child by *Luca Giordano* (1704). The elaborate cantoria and organ date from the early 18C. The Sacristy (1741) of unique design is entered from the left aisle.

Via delle Colonnelle (which passes the right side of the church dating from the late 17C) leads to Piazza Capranica, which is dominated by the *Palazzo Capranica*, partly Gothic and partly Renaissance in style. The tower has a delightful loggia.—From the Maddalena Via del Pantheon (with a hotel at No. 63 on the left where Ariosto stayed in 1513; plaque) returns to the Pantheon (p 113).

From Sant'Agostino Via della Scrofa continues S past the church of **San Luigi dei Francesi** (Pl. 2; 6; closed 12.30–16 and Thursday afternoon), the French national church (1518–89). The façade, attrib. to *Giac. della Porta*, with two superimposed orders of equal height, was over-restored in 1977.

The INTERIOR was heavily encrusted with marble and decorated with white and gilded stucco on a design by *Ant. Dérizet* (1756–64). South Aisle. By the 1st pillar is the monument to the French who fell in the siege of Rome in 1849.—2nd chapel, *Frescoes (recently damaged by restoration) by *Domenichino*; to the right, St Cecilia distributing garments to the poor, and St Cecilia and her betrothed crowned by angels; to the left, St Cecilia refusing to sacrifice to idols, and her martyrdom; on the ceiling, St Cecilia in Paradise. The altarpiece is a copy by *Guido Reni* of Raphael's St Cecilia at Bologna.—4th chapel, Altarpiece by *Iacopino del Conte*, Oath of Clovis; to the right, Army of Clovis, by *Pellegrino Tibaldi*; to the left, Baptism of Clovis, by *Girol. Sermoneta*. The high altarpiece is an Assumption of the Virgin by *F. Bassano*.—North Aisle. The 5th chapel (coin-operated light on right) contains three famous and very well preserved *Paintings by *Caravaggio* (1597–1602): (left) Calling of St Matthew, (right) his Martyrdom, and (altarpiece) St Matthew and the Angel. On the 1st pillar is a monument to Claude Lorrain (1600–82) by *Lemoyne*.

Nearly opposite the church is *Palazzo Giustiniani*, by G. Fontana; the main doorway is by Borromini. The huge **Palazzo Madama** (Pl. 2; 6; no adm) has its main façade on the modern Corso del Rinascimento. It has been the seat of the Italian Senate since 1871.

Originally this was a house belonging to the Crescenzi, which passed to the Medici in the 16C as part of the dowry of Alfonsina Orsini. In the 17C the building was enlarged and decorated by Lod. Cardi and Paolo Marucelli, who are responsible for the interesting Baroque façade. It owes its name to the residence there of 'Madama' Margaret of Parma, illegitimate daughter of Charles V, who married first Alessandro de' Medici and afterwards Ottavio Farnese, and was Regent of the Netherlands from 1559 to 1567. Benedict XIV bought the palace in 1740, and it became successively the residence of the Governor of Rome and the seat of the Ministry of Finance (1852–70), before it became the Palazzo del Senato. The right wing was added in 1931.

Across Via degli Staderari (with a tiny wall fountain) is **Palazzo della Sapienza** (Pl. 2; 6) with a fine Renaissance façade, also on Corso del Rinascimento, by Giac. della Porta. It was the seat until 1935 of the University of Rome, founded by Boniface VIII in 1303. It now houses the *Archivio di Stato*, and exhibitions are held in a library designed by Borromini. Through the door can be seen the beautiful *COURT by Borromini, which has porticoes on three sides, and the church of *St Ivo at the far end. Begun for the Barberini pope, Urban VIII, both the courtyard and the church incorporate his device (the bee) into their design, as well as the Chigi 'monti' of Alexander VII. The church (open on Sunday at 10; or shown by the porter) is a masterpiece of Baroque architecture, with a remarkable light interior. The dome is crowned by an ingenious spiral campanile (copied many times, especially in Germany).

In Piazza Sant'Eustachio (with two well-known cafés) there is a good view of the campanile of St Ivo, and a charming palace with fine windows, a pretty cornice, and remains of its painted façade. Here also is a house (No. 83) built by Giulio Romano for the Maccarani. The church of *Sant'Eustachio*, of ancient foundation, preserves its campanile of 1196. The pretty interior (usually closed) was designed by Ant. Canevari after 1724 (the two large 18C altarpieces in the transepts are by Giac. Zoboli). Via della Palombella returns to the Pantheon.

6 Piazza Navona and Campo dei Fiori to the Tiber bend

This route covers part of the ancient **Campus Martius**, or Plain of Mars, which at first included the whole area between the Capitol Hill, the Tiber, and the Quirinal and Pincio hills, but more precisely came to refer to the low-lying ground enclosed in the Tiber bend. It was said originally to have been the property of the Tarquins, and to have become public land on the expulsion of the kings. It took its name from an ancient Altar of Mars here, which gave a predominently military nature to the area. After the 2C BC many temples and edifices for public entertainments were built, and on other parts of the land military exercises and athletic competitions were held. The S part of the Campus Martius was the Prata Flaminia, with the Circus of Flaminius. The area was not included in the walls of Rome until Aurelian built his famous wall round the city (272–79).

Between Piazza Navona (described on p 123) and Campo dei Fiori, opposite Palazzo Braschi (see p 121), on the noisy Corso Vittorio

Emanuele, is the elegant ***Piccola Farnesina** (Pl. 2; 8), which now houses the Museo Barracco. This fine Renaissance palace was built in 1523 to the order of the French prelate Thomas Le Roy; the architect was almost certainly *Ant. da Sangallo the Younger*. The palace is also called the *Farnesina ai Baullari* and *Palazzo Le Roy* or *Regis*.

Le Roy, who held important posts at the pontifical court, played an important part in the concordat of 1516 between Leo X and Francis I of France. For his services he was ennobled and permitted to augment his coat of arms with the lilies of France. This heraldic privilege is recorded in the architectural details of the palace: the three floors are divided horizontally by projecting bands displaying the Le Roy ermines and the Farnese lilies, which were substituted for the lilies of France and gave the palace the name of Piccola Farnesina by which it is best known. It has no connection with the Villa Farnesina in Trastevere.

The Piccola Farnesina was built to face Vicolo dell'Aquila, to the S. The construction of the Corso Vittorio Emanuele left exposed the N side of the palace, which backed on houses that had to be pulled down to make room for the new street. A new façade on the Corso was accordingly built in 1898–1901; the architect was Enrico Guj, who also modified the side of the palace facing Via dei Baullari.

Since 1948 the palace has contained the ***Museo Barracco**, a museum of ancient sculpture. The collection, not large but choice and well arranged, was formed by Senator Giovanni Barracco (1829–1914), and by him presented to the city of Rome in 1902. The entrance to the museum is on Corso Vittorio Emanuele; it was closed for restoration in 1988. For admission times when it reopens, see p 48.

COURTYARD. Bust of Giovanni Barracco, by *Giuseppe Mangionello* (1914). Below, the foundation inscription of the palace (found during rebuilding). Headless Egyptian sphinxes.—ATRIUM. 245. Christian sarcophagus (4C). Stairs lead up to the first floor. ROOM I (straight ahead). Egyptian sculpture from the beginning of the 3rd millennium to the end of the Roman era. 2. Bas-relief of 5th Dynasty, with a cow being milked and other scenes; *21. Head of a youth (?Rameses II), with a blue chaplet (1299–1233 BC); 1. Fragment of a relief of Nofer, a court official (3rd Dyn., 2778–2723 BC); 33. Painted stucco head of a mummy (Roman era); 30. Head of a Greek; 15. Head of a prince (18th Dyn., 1580–1320 BC); *31. Head of a priest wearing a diadem, once thought to be a portrait of Julius Caesar, an interesting example from Roman Egypt; 13. Sphinx of a queen, perhaps Hatshepsut, with the seal of Thutmosis III (1504–1450 BC).—R. II. Assyrian and Phoenician Art. 58. Relief of Assyrian huntsmen with a horse; 59. Alabaster lion mask, Phoenician, found in Sardinia; 60. Statue of the Phoenician god Bes, from a villa in the Alban Hills; 48. Assyrian relief of five women prisoners in a palm grove (period of Sennacherib, 705–681, or Assurbanipal, 669–626 BC); 47. Assyrian relief of a winged deity, from the NW palace of Assurnasirpal (884–860 BC); 57. Relief of an Assyrian archer.

Off the loggia, at the top of the stairs, is R. III (sometimes closed). Greek art to the middle of the 5C BC; sculptures from Cyprus and elsewhere. *97. Head of Marsyas, replica of the head of the famous statue by Myron; 64. Head of a bearded priest wearing a chaplet, showing traces of colour (Cyprus, end of 5C); 115, 116. Statuettes in rosso antico of hydrophorai (girls carrying water-vessels); 101. Head of a girl (5C); 83. Upper part of a statue of Hermes Kriophoros, possibly derived from the statue of Kalamis at Tanagra (c 480 BC); 76. Statuette of a woman wearing a chiton (early 5C); 77. Statuette of a woman in a peplos (c 470 BC); 88. Attic head (early 5C); 66.

Colossal head of a priest (Cyprus, 6–5C); 79. Head of a general (Attica; 490–480 BC); 81. Head of Athena, 5C original from Greece or Southern Italy; 80. Archaic head of a youth (Aeginetan, early 5C); 73. Fragment of an Attic sepulchral stele (early 5C; original found in Rome).—FIRST-FLOOR LANDING. 205. Head of a woman, part of a tomb-decoration found near Bolsena; 204. Head of a woman, from a tomb found near Orvieto; both Etruscan, 3C BC; 78. Archaic statue of Minerva.

SECOND FLOOR. R. IV (straight ahead at the top of stairs). Greek 5C art at its zenith. *102. Upper part of a statue of the Amazon of Polykleitos, after the original in the Temple of Diana at Ephesos; 103. (in the window corner), Part of a leg of this statue; 130. Sepulchral relief (Attica, 4C); *92. Head of Apollo, after an original by Pheidias, possibly the bronze statue seen by Pausanias near the Parthenon (Athens, before 450 BC); *109. Statuette of Hercules, after a work of Polykleitos; 113. Head of a girl (Argive-Sikyonian school); 127, 128. Attic funeral lekythoi (4C BC); 108. Head of the Doryphoros of Polykleitos, good copy of the original bronze; 135. Fragment of an Attic sepulchral relief; 96. Herm of Pericles, replica of that in the Vatican; 110. Head of an athlete in the style of Polykleitos; 134. Fragment of a relief of a horseman stroking the mane of his horse, from a representation of the Dioscuri (4C, Greco-Italian); 107. Head of the Diadumenos of Polykleitos, after the original bronze. In the middle of the room; *99. Replica of the Westmacott athlete in the British Museum, after an original by Polykleitos, possibly a portrait of Kyniskos, victor at Mantinea.

R. V. Greek art of the 4C BC. *131. Head of Apollo Kitharoidos, the best existing replica of the statue by Praxiteles; 143. Head of an old man, possibly Demosthenes; 160. Bust of Hermes (replica of a 4C original). GLASS CASE A. Upper Shelf. 44, 45. Sumerian bronze statuettes (3rd millennium BC). 155. Bust of Epicurus, after an Ionian original, 270 BC; *129. Votive relief to Apollo (early 4C). GLASS CASE B. Greek and Italiot vases from the 8th to the 3C BC. 132. Head of a veiled woman, part of an Attic sepulchral relief; *139. Bitch licking her wounds, perhaps a replica of the masterpiece by Lysippos, formerly in the Temple of Jupiter on the Capitol.

R. VI. Hellenistic sculpture. 176. Archaistic relief, depicting the cave of Pan; *151. Statuette of Neptune, from a 4C Greek original; 157. Head of Alexander the Great or Mithras, in the style of Leochares (330–300 BC).—R. VII. Roman art. 190. Bust of a young Roman (probably period of Tiberius); 195. Head of Mars (period of Trajan); *194. Head of a Roman boy, perhaps C. Caesar, nephew of Augustus.—SECOND-FLOOR LANDING. 206, 249, 250. Sepulchral reliefs (Palmyra, 3C BC); 140. Head of Demosthenes, from an original attributed to Polieuctes.

In the basement of the Piccola Farnesina (no adm) are remains of a late-Roman building, with columns, which is now under water. The 4C frescoes, discovered in 1899 during the reconstruction of the palace, have been detached.

On the right of the Museo Barracco, opening onto Corso Vittorio Emanuele, is Piazza della Cancelleria, along one whole side of which is the pure and simple façade of the *Palazzo della Cancelleria (Pl. 3; 5), a masterpiece of the Renaissance. It was built for Cardinal Raff. Riario by an unknown architect. It is thought that *Bramante* may have helped at a late stage, possibly designing the beautiful court; it is also probable that *And. Bregno* was involved in the building. It is

The 15C courtyard of Palazzo della Cancelleria

now the seat of the three Tribunals of the Vatican, including the
Sacra Rota, and of the Pontificia Accademia Romana di Archeologia.

The building was probably begun in 1486, and the long main façade shows
Florentine influence, with a double order of pilasters. The magnificent *COURT
has double loggie with antique columns. At the back of the courtyard excavations (now under cover) in 1988 revealed 4C and 15C remains of the huge
palaeochristian basilica of San Lorenzo in Damaso (see below). Inside the
palace (special permit required) the Sala Grande, decorated under Clement XI
in 1718, has twelve paintings by *Marcantonio Franceschini* and frescoes by
Gius. Nicola Nasini and *Baciccia*. The adjoining Salone was decorated by

Vasari and his pupils (including *Raffaellino dal Colle*) in a hundred days in 1546. The chapel was decorated by Fr. Salviati (restored in 1985).—The interesting old Via del Pellegrino skirts the side of the Cancelleria, with shops set into the façade on the street level.

Incorporated into the palace is the church of **San Lorenzo in Damaso** (entered by a doorway in the main façade, right). The ancient basilica (see above) founded in the 4C was finally demolished in the 15C when the present church (built on part of the site), contemporary with the palace, had been completed. It was entirely restored in 1868–82, and again in this century after fire. It has a double atrium, and over the fine doorway in the right aisle is a lunette fresco of angel musicians by *Cav. d'Arpino* (detached; formerly in the nave). The adjoining chapel has a 14C crucifix in wood. In the main apse, Coronation of the Virgin, with Saints, by *Fed. Zuccari*. At the end of the left aisle is the tomb of Cardinal Ludovico Trevisan, called Mezzarota Scarampi (1505), and in the chapel of the Sacrament, a 12C icon of the Virgin brought here from Santa Maria di Grottapinto in 1465.

The S end of Piazza della Cancelleria opens into **Campo dei Fiori** (Pl. 3; 5), once a meadow, which became one of the most important piazze in Rome in the 15C. Executions were occasionally held here; the fine monument (by Ettore Ferrari; 1889) to Giordano Bruno, in the centre, stands on the spot where he was burned alive in 1600. It has been a market place since 1869, with attractive old stalls and canvas shades. It is the centre of a distinctive district of the city, with numerous artisans' workshops. The beautiful old Via dei Cappellari which leads out of the NW side of the piazza, and the parallel Via del Pellegrino are worth exploring. The huge 15C *Palazzo Pio* (*Righetti*), at the E end of the piazza, was built over the ruins of Pompey's Theatre (see below), which was surmounted, on the highest part of the cavea, by a Temple of Venus. The late–16C façade of the palace by Camillo Arcucci faces Piazza del Biscione, where at No. 89 is a small house with a painted façade. From here a frescoed archway leads into a dark passageway by the old (deconsecrated) chapel of Santa Maria di Grottapinta to Via di Grotta Pinta. If this is closed it is necessary to reach Via di Grotta Pinta via Via del Biscione (where the Albergo Sole is thought to be the oldest hotel in the city), Piazza del Paradiso and Via dei Chiavari (with a good view of the dome of Sant'Andrea della Valle). The semi-circular Via di Grotta Pinta follows the line of the auditorium of the *Theatre of Pompey* (55 BC; Rome's first stonebuilt theatre); to the E of it formerly stood the great rectangular Porticus of Pompey, off which opened the 'Curia' (see p 119) where Julius Caesar was murdered (15 March, 44 BC) at the foot of a statue of Pompey (see p 134). The modern Teatro dei Satiri is here.

The animated Via de' Giubbonari, a busy local shopping street (closed to cars), leads out of the Campo dei Fiori, skirting the side of Palazzo Pio. It ends at Piazza Cairoli, with the domed church of **San Carlo ai Catinari** (Pl. 3; 6), by *Rosato Rosati* (1612–20), many times restored. The façade was erected in 1636 by *G.B. Soria*.

The INTERIOR is interesting for its 17C works. On the right side (1st chapel), decorations by *Simone Costanzi*, and an Annunciation by *Giov. Lanfranco*. The 3rd chapel the *°**Cappella di Santa Cecilia** is splendidly decorated by *Ant. Gherardi*. In the pendentives of the cupola are the Cardinal Virtues, by *Domenichino*, and over the high altar San Carlo carrying the sacred Nail to the plague-stricken, a good late work by *Pietro da Cortona*. In the apse is San Carlo received in heaven, by *Giov. Lanfranco*.—Opposite the church is the Palazzo Santacroce, by Carlo Maderno (1602).

On the other side of Via de' Giubbonari several short streets lead into the piazza in front of the *Monte di Pietà* (now a bank), with a long

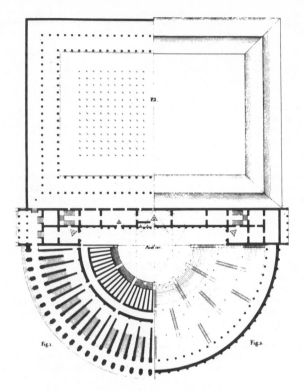

*The Roman Theatre, after Vitruvius, architect and surveyor
to Augustus ('De architectura', before AD 27): (fig.1: lower
tiers; fig. 2: upper tiers; fig. 3: portico behind the scena in
case of bad weather), published by Carlo Amati in 1829*

history as a pawn-shop. The façade by Ottaviano Nonni (Il Mascherino) was enlarged by Carlo Maderno, with the clock tower attrib.
to Borromini. The fine domed Chapel (admission on request) by
Carlo Maderno (1641; restored 1725) contains high reliefs by Dom.
Guidi, Pierre Legros, and Giov. Théodon. Via dell'Arco del Monte di
Pietà skirts the right flank of the building into the little piazza in front
of the church of *Santissima Trinità dei Pellegrini* (open 7.30–8.30
only, and fest. 11.30–13), by Paolo Maggi (1603–16). The façade was
added in 1723 by Fr. De Sanctis. The interior contains 17C works by
Guido Reni (the Trinity), Borgognone, and Cav. d'Arpino. In the
neighbouring *Hospice* (1625) the poet Goffredo Mameli, author of
the national hymn which bears his name, died in 1849 at the age of
22 from wounds received fighting for the Roman Republic.

From the piazza Via dei Pettinari leads to the Tiber, here crossed by Ponte Sisto
(described on p 260). The little church of *San Salvatore in Onda* (usually closed)
was built at the end of the 11C but transformed in the 17C. The interesting crypt
was built over a Roman building of the 2C AD.
   Via San Paolo alla Regola leads out of Piazza dei Pellegrini beyond the church

of San Paolo alla Regola to the *Case di San Paolo*, a group of over-restored 13C houses now used as offices. Other medieval buildings were demolished to make way for the huge *Ministry of Justice* built here in 1920 by Pio Piacentini. To the left is the ancient church of *Santa Maria in Monticelli* (closed indefinitely), with a 12C campanile, radically restored in 1860. In the apse is a mosaic head of Christ, and fragments of mosaic decoration dating from the 12C. In the 2nd chapel to the right is a Flagellation (detached fresco) by Ant. Carracci; opposite is a 14C wooden Crucifix.

The narrow Via Capodiferro (where an ancient house has columns set in to the façade) leads out of Piazza dei Pellegrini into Piazza Capodiferro with the huge *•Palazzo Spada* (Pl. 3; 5), built for Cardinal Girolomo Capodiferro in 1540, probably by *Giulio Mazzoni*. The palace was acquired in the 17C by Cardinal Bernardino Spada, and has been the seat of the Council of State since 1889. The court and façade are by *Giulio Mazzoni* or *Girol. da Carpi* and are outstanding examples of stucco decoration. *Borromini* restored the palace for his friend Cardinal Spada, and added an ingenious trompe l'oeil perspective on the S side (reached through a door into the garden, right of the stairs leading up to the gallery; ask at the ticket office). This makes use of the waste space between the Spada garden and the adjoining Palazzo Massari. The dimension of the tunnel is perspectively multiplied more than four times through the use of light and spacing of the columns.

Reached by a staircase from a corridor at the back of the palace is the *•Galleria Spada* (adm, see p 49), a collection of paintings formed by Cardinal Spada and augmented by successive generations of his family. Arranged in four rooms which preserve their 17C decoration and furnishings, the important collection of 17C and 18C paintings (and 2C and 3C Roman sculpture) is a very interesting example of a 17C Roman Patrician family's private collection, which survives almost intact. It was acquired by the State in 1926. Handlists are available in each room.

Room 1. *Guido Reni*, 37. Lucretia (a copy), *32. Cardinal Bernardino Spada; 34. *Guercino*, Cardinal Bernardino Spada.
Room II. 60. *School of Titian*, Musician (unfinished); *56. *Andrea del Sarto*, Visitation; 94. *15C Umbrian School*, Madonna and Child; 92. *16C Florentine School*, Madonna and St John the Baptist; 90. *Lavinia Fontana*, Cleopatra; 89. *Parmigianino* (attributed), Three heads (a fresco); 86. *Titian*, Paul III (a copy); 81. *Giovanni Battista Bertucci*, Madonna and Child with St John; 80. *Marco Palmezzano*, Way to Calvary, Eternal Father; 76. *Fiorenzo di Lorenzo*, St Sebastian; *77. *Jan van Scorel*, Young Man; 78. *Hans Dürer*, Young Man. 16C Tabernacle in carved and gilded walnut, with a bas-relief of the Annunciation. On the two long walls, fragments of a larger painted frieze by *Perino del Vaga*, originally intended for the wall below Michelangelo's 'Last Judgment' in the Sistine Chapel.
Room III. 100. *Nicolò dell'Abate*, Landscape; 101. *Ciro Ferri*, Vestals; 146. *David Teniers the Younger*, Winter Scene; *Pietro Testa*, 145. Iphigenia, 144. Massacre of the Innocents; 141. *Annibale Carracci*, Young Man; 139. *Francesco Trevisani*, Antony and Cleopatra; 136. *Sofonisba Anguissola*, Young Girl (in restoration); 133. *Baciccia*, *Sketch for the vaulting of the Gesù; 132. *Guercino*, Death of Dido; 126. *Baciccia*, Christ and the woman of Samaria; 123. *Francesco Furini*, St Lucy; *120. *Rubens*, Portrait of a Cardinal; 117. *Annibale Carracci*, Portrait of a young boy; *J. F. Voet*, 119. Gentlewoman, 110, 105. Portrait of Urbano and Pompeo Rocci; 113. *Nicolò Tornioli*, Cain and Abel; 103. *P. Snayers*, Sack of a village; 102. *Jan ('Velvet') Breughel*, Landscape with windmills.— Among the Roman sculpture are a Seated Philosopher, and a bust of a woman of the 2C AD.
Room IV. 148. *School of Gherardo delle Notti*, Betrayal of Christ; 149. *Artemisia Gentileschi*, St Cecilia (removed); 150. *Mattia Preti*, Christ tempted; 152. *Michelangelo Cerquozzi*, At the water trough; 155. *Orazio Gentileschi*, David; 158. *Cerquozzi*, Death of the donkey; 159. *Anon 17C*, Boy with a plumed

Palazzo Spada: trompe l'oeil perspective by Borromini

hat; *161. *Cerquozzi*, Market-place at Naples; 165. *Willem Reuter* (formerly attributed to Sweerts), Market; 168. *A. Bauguin*, Still-life; 171. *Bartolomeo Cavarozzi*, Madonna (removed); 172. *Orazio Borgianni*, Pietà; 175. *School of Caravaggio*, Madonna and St Anne; 176. *Nicolò Renieri* (also attributed to Bartolomeo Manfredi), David; 178. *School of Carlo Saraceni* (also attributed to Francesco Albani), Christ scourged; 182. *Cerquozzi*, Traveller and shepherds; 184. *Il Valentin*, Holy Family.—Sculptures: Bust of a boy, of the Julio-Claudian era; two Roman statuettes of a boy, one dressed in the lion-skin of Hercules, and another in the philosophic pallium.

The *State Rooms on the first floor can be seen either with special permission, when not in use, or sometimes on Sunday morning if the porter is available. The GENERAL COUNCIL CHAMBER has magnificent trompe l'oeil frescoes by the 17C Bolognese artists, *Agostino Mitelli* and *Michelangelo Colonna*, with birds and figures peering into the room from around columns and window ledges. The colossal statue of Pompey is traditionally thought to be the one at the foot of which Caesar was murdered. The decoration in the next room is extremely fine, with frescoes and stucco in high relief. The last room on this side of the palazzo has another fine ceiling. From here is the entrance to the CORRIDOR OF STUCCOES, a delightful work by *Giulio Mazzoni* (1559), complemented by his ornamentation of the façade of the court seen through the windows. Further rooms lead to the MERIDIANA, a corridor decorated by *G.B. Ruggeri*, mapping the times at various places in the world. The eight Hellenistic reliefs of mythological subjects of 2C AD are very fine, and in a good state of preservation.

Vicolo de' Venti continues to PIAZZA FARNESE, created by the Farnese in front of their splendid palace. Here are two huge baths of Egyptian granite brought from the Baths of Caracalla in the 16C and used by the Farnese as a type of 'royal box' for spectacles which were held in the square. They were adapted as fountains (using the Farnese Lilies) in 1626. *Palazzo Farnese (Pl. 3; 5) is the most magnificent Renaissance palace in Rome. It is now the French Embassy; it was first used as such in 1635. It was begun by *Ant. Sangallo the Younger* for Cardinal Alessandro Farnese, afterwards Paul III. He began the piazza façade and the two sides, and after his death in 1546, *Michelangelo* continued the upper stories and added the superb entablature. The work on the back of the palace was continued by *Vignola* and *Giac. della Porta*. In the 18C the palace became the property of the Bourbons of Naples.

The palace is entered through *Sangallo*'s *VESTIBULE, with a beautiful colonnade and stuccoed ceiling, which leads into the *COURTYARD. This was also designed by Sangallo on the first two stories; the upper story is by *Michelangelo*.
    INTERIOR (adm only by previous written appointment). At the top of the stairs, to the right, is the huge SALON d'HERCULE, named after the gigantic statue (copy to right of the entrance to the room) of the Farnese Hercules. On his visit to Rome in 1787 Goethe records the loss of the statue together with the magnificent Farnese collection of sculpture to Naples (transferred there by the Bourbons), lamenting 'If they could detach the Gallery with the Carracci from Palazzo Farnese and transport it, they would.' The Salon has a fine wood ceiling by Sangallo. The two statues on either side of the fireplace of Piety and Abundance, by *Gugl. della Porta*, were designed (but never used) for the tomb of Paul III in St Peter's.—At the end of the loggia is the GALLERIA, with *Frescoes of mythological scenes, the masterpiece of *Annibale Carracci* (1597–1603). The ingenious treatment of the angles, and the magnificent over-all scheme centring on the Triumph of Bacchus, demonstrate the great imagination of the artist, who here created the model for subsequent Baroque ceiling paintings. Carracci was assisted by his brother *Agostino*, and (in the frescoes above the doors and niches) by *Domenichino*.

Just out of the square, on Via di Monserrato, is the *English College* and the

Palazzo Farnese courtyard: the first two stories by Antonio Sangallo the Younger; upper story by Michelangelo

church of **St Thomas of Canterbury**, rebuilt by *Poletti* and *Vespignani* in 1888 (entrance at No. 45). The ground on which they stand has been the property of English Catholics since 1362, when it started as a hospice for pilgrims, and the record of visitors shows the names of Thomas Cromwell (1514), Thomas Hobbes (1635), Harvey (1636), Milton (1638), Evelyn, and Manning. The church contains the simple and beautiful tomb of Cardinal Bainbridge (1514), and in the gallery are paintings of English martyrdoms, and in the college, of which Cardinal Howard and Cardinal Wiseman were rectors, are portraits of English cardinals.—In Piazza Santa Caterina della Rota is the church of **San Girolamo della Carità** (open 8–11 only; when closed ring at No. 63 Via San Girolamo), rebuilt in the 17C by Dom. Castelli, with a façade by Carlo Rainaldi. The 1st chapel on the right has long been attributed to *Borromini* but recently discovered documents now suggest *Cosimo Fanzago* as its author. The architect's adaptation of a cramped space into a beautiful funerary house for the Spada is masterly. The next chapel has a wood crucifix of 15C. To the left of the high altar is a decorative chapel (1710) dedicated to San Filippo Neri, by Fil. Juvarra (light to left).—The church of *Santa Caterina della Rota* has a fine ceiling from a demolished church and 18C works.

Via dei Farnese (with a charming small palace at No. 83) skirts the right flank of Palazzo Farnese, whose rear façade, adapted from Michelangelo's designs by Giac. della Porta, can be glimpsed above the wall. The design of Michelangelo to connect the palace with the Villa Farnesina by a bridge across the Tiber was never carried out, but a single arch (hung with vines) of the viaduct to the bridge spans Via Giulia at this point. The fountain in the wall on the left, the 'Mascherone', was erected by the Farnese; both the colossal mask and the porphyry basin are Roman.

The straight ***Via Giulia** (Pl. 3; 5) runs parallel to the Tiber for over one kilometre. It was laid out by Julius II (1503–13) and was for long the most beautiful of the 16C streets of the city. The church opposite the end of Via dei Farnese, *Santa Maria dell'Orazione e Morte* (open only on Sunday and fest. at 18) was rebuilt in 1733–37 by Ferd. Fuga. *Palazzo Falconieri*, enlarged by Borromini, is distinguished by the giant falcons' heads at either end of its façade (it has been the seat of the Hungarian Academy since 1928). Several rooms inside have fine ceilings (restored in 1979) decorated in stucco by Borromini. Further on, the church of *Santa Caterina da Siena* (closed for restoration), rebuilt by Paolo Posi in 1766, stands opposite *Palazzo Varese* by Carlo Maderno (c 1617). A street on the left leads to *SANT'ELIGIO DEGLI OREFICI (open 10–13 except fest., Saturday, and Wednesday; ring at No. 9 Via di Sant'Eligio). This beautiful small 16C church surmounted by a cupola, and Greek-cross in plan, is by Raphael (clearly influenced by Bramante). After his death Baldassarre Peruzzi continued the building and added the cupola. The façade, following Raphael's designs, was rebuilt by Flaminio Ponzio.

From the Lungotevere here there is a fine view of the Janiculum, the dome of St Peter's, and the Villa Farnesina. Via della Barchetta, on the other side of Via Giulia, leads to Via di Monserrato on which (right) is the church of **Santa Maria di Monserrato** (Pl. 2; 7; closed for restoration in 1988; for adm apply at No. 151 Via Giulia), the Spanish national church. It was begun by Ant. da Sangallo the Younger (1518) but altered later, with a façade by *Fr. da Volterra*.

INTERIOR. The 1st chapel on the right contains a San Diego, by *Ann. Carracci*, and the 19C tombs of the two Borgia popes, Calixtus III (died 1458) and Alexander VI (died 1503), and of Alfonso XIII (died 1941). In the 3rd chapel left is a statue of St James, by *Iac. Sansovino*, and two fine wall tombs attrib. to *And. Bregno*; in the 1st chapel a group of the Madonna and Child with St Anne, by *Tom. Boscoli* (1544), and a ciborium (behind wooden doors) attrib. to *Luigi Capponi*.—In the court, reached through the Sacristy at the end of the nave on the right (or at No. 151 Via Giulia), are several fine tombs, notably that attrib. to

And. Bregno of Cardinal Giov. de Mella. In a room off the courtyard is the monument to Pedro de Foix Montoya; this incorporates a remarkable portrait bust, an early work (c 1621) by *Gian Lorenzo Bernini*.

Via Giulia continues past (left) the church of the *Spirito Santo dei Napoletani*, begun by Ottaviano Mascherino in 1619, and restored by Carlo Fontana, and again in the 19C, when the façade was built by Ant. Cipolla. It contains paintings by Pietro Gagliardi and a martyrdom of San Gennaro by Luca Giordano. The street opposite leads to the 16C *Palazzo Ricci* with a painted façade by Polidoro da Caravaggio, heavily restored, and now badly faded. Via Giulia next traverses an area demolished before 1940 for a new road, never built; the 18C façade by Fil. Raguzzini of San Filippo Neri survives here. It is now necessary to make a detour from Via dei Banchi Vecchi (right; see Pl. 3; 5). Opposite the church of Santa Lucia del Gonfalone, Vicolo Cellini (the sculptor had his workshop in the area) leads back to Corso Vittorio Emanuele across which is the **Chiesa Nuova** or *Santa Maria in Vallicella* (Pl. 3; 5), built under the inspiration of St Philip Neri and the patronage of Cardinal Angelo Cesi. Among the architects were *Matteo Bartolini da Città di Castello* and *Martino Longhi the Elder* (1575–1605), but the façade is by *Fausto Rughesi*.

Born in Florence in 1515 St Philip Neri came to Rome c 1530. He was an outstanding figure of the Counter Reformation and founded an 'Oratorio' here. In recognition of his Order Gregory XIII gave him Santa Maria in Vallicella in 1575 which he proceeded to rebuild.

The vault, apse, and dome were decorated by *Pietro da Cortona* (1664), and the whole interior is brilliantly gilded. In the sanctuary are three *Paintings by *Rubens* (1608), of superb colouring: over the high altar, Madonna and angels; to the right, Saints Domitilla, Nereus, and Achilleus; to the left, Saints Gregory, Maurus, and Papias. On the right of the apse, under the organ, is the Cappella Spada, designed by *Carlo Rainaldi*, with an altarpiece by *Carlo Maratta* (Madonna between SS. Charles and Ignatius). St Philip Neri is buried beneath the altar of the sumptuous chapel of St Philip, on the left of the apse; his portrait in mosaic is copied from a painting by Guido Reni. In the N transept, Presentation, by *Barocci*.—In the fine sacristy, with a fresco by *Pietro da Cortona*, is a statue of St Philip Neri and an angel, by *Algardi*. From here there is access to another chapel and the Rooms of St Philip Neri (works by *Guercino*, *Pietro da Cortona*, *Guido Reni*, *Garofalo*, etc.) with mementoes of the saint.

In the neighbouring **Oratorio dei Filippini**, rebuilt largely by Borromini (1637–52), St Philip instituted the musical gatherings which became known as oratorios, and have given their name to a form of musical composition. The *Façade, between that of a church and a palace, has a remarkably subtle design. The delightful clock-tower can be seen from Via dei Banchi Nuovi, on the right. The extensive convent buildings, also by Borromini, are now occupied by the Vallicelliana Library (history of Rome), the Municipal Archives, and various learned societies.

On Corso Vittorio Emanuele at No. 217 (left) is the 16C *Palazzo Sora*, and (right), in a little piazza, *Palazzo Sforza Cesarini* (with a 15C courtyard).

Vicolo Cellini (see above) and Via delle Carceri return to Via Giulia. The *Carceri Nuove* here, built in 1655 by Ant. Del Grande were long considered a model prison. The *Museo Criminale* (closed for restoration) is arranged in an adjacent prison building designed in 1827 by Gius. Valadier (entrance on Via del Gonfalone). The 16C *Oratorio di Santa Lucia del Gonfalone* (entrance on Vicolo della Scimmia) has a façade by Dom. Castelli. Concerts are given here regularly by the Coro Polifonico Romano, and it has a fine pavement, and carved and gilded ceiling by Ambr. Bonazzini. But it is above all interesting for its frescoes by the Tuscan-Emilian school of the late-16C including Jacopo Bertoia, Raffaellino da Reggio, Fed. Zuccari, Livio Agresti, Cesare Nebbia, and Marco Pino. On Via del Gonfalone and beyond the church of *Santa Maria del Suffragio* (by Carlo Rainaldi), several large rough blocks of masonry protruding into the street are all that remains of a great court of justice designed for Julius II by Bramante but never finished. Here is yet another church, the small San Biagio della Pagnotta. At No. 66 rises *Palazzo Sacchetti*, by Ant. Sangallo the Younger (1543). At the end of Via Giulia is **San Giovanni dei Fiorentini** (Pl. 2; 5), the church of the Florentines. Leo X ordered a competition for its erection. Raphael and Peruzzi were among the contestants; but *Iac. Sansovino* was successful and began the work. It was continued by *Ant. da Sangallo the Younger* and completed by *Giac. della Porta*; *Carlo Maderno* added the transept and cupola. The façade is by *Aless. Galilei* (1734).

INTERIOR. In the S aisle, above the door into the Sacristy, is a 16C Tuscan statuette of St John the Baptist. On either side of the arch here is a portrait bust; that on the left by *Pietro Bernini* (1614), and that on the right by his son *Gian Lorenzo* (1622). 3rd chapel: *Santi di Tito*, *St Jerome; (right wall) *Ludovico Cigoli*, St Jerome, and (left wall) *Passignano*, Construction of the church. In the S transept, Saints Cosmas and Damian at the stake, by *Salvator Rosa*. N aisle. 1st chapel, altarpiece by *Giovanni Battista Vanni*; 4th chapel, putti on the wall tombs of the Bacelli, carved by *Francois Duquesnoy*. Behind the high altar (opened by the sacristan) is a crypt sepulchre of the Falconieri family, a fine late work by *Borromini*.

It is now necessary to return across Corso Vittorio Emanuele and take Via Banco Santo Spirito out of Largo Tassoni. From here Vicolo del Curato leads to the piazza at the beginning of *VIA DEI CORONARI (Pl. 2; 5), a beautiful Renaissance street on the line of the Roman Via Recta. It is now famous for its antique shops.

From Piazza dei Coronari Via di Panico leads right into Via di Monte Giordano. Here the 18C *Palazzo Taverna* (Pl. 2; 5), formerly *Gabrielli*, has a beautiful fountain by Ant. Casoni (1618) in the court. The palace stands on **Monte Giordano**, a small, apparently artificial, hill already inhabited in the 12C. It takes its name from Giordano Orsini (13C) whose legendary fortress stood here. Dante mentions the 'Monte' ('Inferno', XXVIII, 12) in the description of the pilgrims crossing the Ponte Sant'Angelo on the occasion of the jubilee of 1300. The Orsini continued to own the castle until 1688, and the buildings, here still crowded together, betray their medieval origins.

At the beginning of Via dei Coronari, on the right (Nos 122–3) stands the so-called House of Raphael. In the piazza on the left is *San Salvatore in Lauro* a church with a Palladian interior by Mascherino (1594). To the left of the church (No. 15) is the entrance to the fine Renaissance cloister (in poor repair). A small courtyard beyond has two Renaissance portals. The refectory contains the *Tomb of Eugenius IV (died 1447) by *Isaia da Pisa*, one of the earliest sepulchral monuments to exhibit the characteristic forms of the Renaissance.—Farther on in Via dei Coronari is the Piazzetta di San Simeone with *Palazzo Lancellotti* (no adm), begun by Fr. da Volterra and finished by Carlo Maderno. From the piazzetta the interesting Via della Maschera d'Oro leads to *Palazzo Sacripante Ruiz* (a fine building attrib. to Bart. Ammannati), while to the S, also parallel to Via dei Coronari, is the medieval Vicolo dei Tre Archi. Via dei Coronari ends in Piazza di Tor Sanguigna at the N end of Piazza Navona (see p 123).

The busy Via Giuseppe Zanardelli leads N from here to Ponte Umberto I past (right) PALAZZO ALTEMPS, begun c 1480 for Girolamo Riario and completed by Martino Longhi the Elder, with a charming belvedere in the form of a turret. The palace has recently been acquired by the State, and is being restored for use as a museum (it is possible the Museo Torlonia, see p 260, may be housed here). The *Teatro Goldoni*, which adjoins the palace, preserves its 17C decoration.

In Piazza Ponte Umberto I is *Palazzo Primoli*, seat of the Fondazione Primoli. On the ground floor is the **Napoleonic Museum** (adm see p 49), presented to the city of Rome in 1927 by Count Joseph Primoli. The collection belonged to Count Joseph and his brother Louis, who were sons of Carlotta Bonaparte. In the fourteen period rooms of the museum are paintings, statues, and relics of the Bonaparte family, with special reference to the Roman branch. The more important works include paintings by *David* of Zenaide and Carlotta, daughters of Joseph, king of Naples, by *Gerard* of Elisa Baciocchi, by *Wicar* of Louis, king of Holland, by *Winterhalter* of Napoleon III and the Empress Eugénie; sculptures by *Canova, Bartolini, Carpeaux* and *Thorvaldsen*; miniatures by *Isabey*; prints illustrating the contest between Napoleon and Pius VII; State robes; autographs, including the marriage contract of Napoleon and Marie Louise.

The top floor of Palazzo Primoli was the residence of the art historian and man of letters Mario Praz from the late 1960s until his death in 1981. His remarkable collection of the decorative arts, paintings, sculpture, furniture, etc., particularly representative of the Neo-classical period, has been acquired by the State. It is hoped that it will be exhibited in his apartment here and opened to the public.

Nearby, on the corner of Via di Monte Brianzo, is the *Osteria dell' Orso*. The medieval building was altered c 1460, and it first became a hotel in the 16C. Rabelais, Montaigne, and Goethe were among its patrons. It is now a celebrated restaurant.

7   The Corso and Piazza del Popolo

Via del Corso (Pl. 3; 6, 4, 2), now called simply *Il Corso*, has been one of the most important thoroughfares in the city since Roman times. It is a straight and fairly narrow street nearly a mile long connecting Piazza Venezia with Piazza del Popolo. It has recently been closed to private traffic and yet remains one of the busiest streets in Rome, with many fashionable shops, particularly between Piazza Venezia and Via Condotti. The pavements are hardly wide enough to accommodate the almost incessant stream of pedestrians in either direction during working hours.

The Corso represents the urban section of the Via Flaminia (221 BC), the main road to northern Italy. It was called the *Via Lata* because of its width, exceptional in ancient Rome. Its present name is derived from the celebrated races inaugurated here by Paul II in 1466. Many palaces were built along the street from the 16C to 18C, and the straightness of its line between Piazza Venezia and Piazza Colonna was perfected by Alexander VII, when he demolished two triumphal arches that formerly spanned it. The Carnival celebrations here from the 17C onwards became famous spectacles; John Evelyn, Goethe, Dickens, and Henry James have left vivid descriptions of the festivities. The street has given its name to the principal street in numerous other Italian cities.

The Corso runs N from Piazza Venezia. At its left corner is *Palazzo d'Aste Rinuccini Bonaparte* by Giov. Ant. dei Rossi (17C), where Letizia Ramolino, mother of Napoleon I, died in 1836. On the right beyond Vicolo del Piombo, are *Palazzo Salviati*, by Carlo Rainaldi (1662), and *Palazzo Odescalchi*, of the 17–18C, but with a façade (1887–88) in the Florentine 15C style.

On the opposite side of the Corso is the huge **Palazzo Doria Pamphilj** (Pl. 3; 6), which dates from 1435, but has suffered many vicissitudes. It has been the residence of this important Roman noble family since the 17C. The façade towards the Corso, by Gabriele Valvassori (1731–34), is perhaps the finest and most balanced Rococo work in Rome. The S façade is by Paolo Ameli (1743); that on the N in

Piazza del Collegio Romano is by Ant. Del Grande (1659–63), with two very fine wings. At No. 1A in the piazza is the entrance to the Gallery (admission, see p 49).

The *Galleria Doria Pamphilj, the most important of the Roman patrician art collections which survive in the city, dates from the period of splendour in the house of Pamphilj. The collection was initiated by Olimpia Maidalchini, the acquisitive sister-in-law of Innocent X, in her palace on Piazza Navona; it was increased by the Aldobrandini and Doria bequests and has been entailed by the State since 1816. Visitors enter on the first floor. The period rooms, richly decorated in white and gold, and beautifully maintained, provide a sumptuous setting for the collection. The paintings are identified by their number.

1ST GALLERY (right). 10. *Titian*, Spain succouring Religion; 15. *Tintoretto*, Portrait of a Man; 17. *Bern. Licinio* (?), Portrait of a Man; *20. *Correggio*, Triumph of Virtue (unfinished sketch for the painting now in the Louvre); *23. *Raphael* (attrib.), Navagero and Beazzano (?), Venetian savants; 26. *Lor. Lotto*, St Jerome; 28. *Paris Bordone*, Venus, Mars, and Cupid; *29. *Titian*, Salome with the head of St John the Baptist; and, to the left of the door, 38. *Carlo Saraceni*, St Roch and the angel; *Caravaggio*, *40. Mary Magdalene, *42. Rest on the flight into Egypt (one of his best works), 44. Young St John the Baptist; 46. *Lo Spagnoletto*, St Jerome; 48. *Mattia Preti*, The Tribute money; I. *Aless. Algardi*, Bust of Olimpia Maidalchini; and, to the right of the door, 53. *Sassoferrato*, Virgin.—SALONE ALDOBRANDINI. Antique sculptures, and four Brussels tapestries of the battle of Lepanto. The paintings include: 77. *Guercino*, Herminia and Tancred; and 103. *Mattia Preti*, Concert. The two marble reliefs (VII and VIII) of Sacred and Profane Love, and Bacchanalia of Putti are by *Franc. Duquesnoy*.—2ND GALLERY. 120. *Ann. Carracci* (attrib.), St Jerome; 122. *Sassoferrato*, Holy Family; and on the wall behind, 131. *Dom. Fetti*, Mary Magdalene; behind, IV. *Algardi*, Bust of Innocent X; 135. *Lod. Carracci*, St Sebastian; 136. *Guido Reni*, Madonna; 137. *Ann. Carracci* (copy from), Pietà.

ROOM II. 172. *Giov. Bellini* (possibly with the help of his workshop), Madonna and Child with St John; *Giov. di Paolo*, 174. Marriage of the Virgin, *176. Birth of the Virgin; *Nic. Rondinelli*, 178, 182. Madonnas; 180. *Ortolano*, Nativity; 183. *Bicci di Lorenzo*, St Christopher and St John the Baptist; 185. *Vinc. Catena* (attrib.; a copy from Giov. Bellini), Circumcision; *186. *Boccaccino*, Madonna and Child; 187. *Marco Basaiti*, St Sebastian; 191. *Nic. Frangipani*, Christ and St Veronica; 194. *Iac. Bassano*, Adam and Eve in Earthly Paradise.—R. III. 195. *School of And. del Sarto*, Madonna and Child with St John; 207. *Parmigianino*, Madonna and Child; *Garofalo*, 208. Visitation, *Dosso Dossi*, 209. Portrait of Girolamo Beltramoto, 211. Dido; 212. *And. del Sarto* (follower of), Holy Family with St John; *Mazzolino*, 216. Jesus in the Temple, 217. Massacre of the Innocents, 219. Pietà; 231. *Garofalo*, Holy Family adored by saints.—In the next two rooms, Dutch and Flemish schools. R. IV. *237. *Thos. de Keyser*, (attrib.), Portrait of a lady; 252. *Wijbrand de Geest* (attrib.), Portrait of a man; 244. *Jan Lievens*, Sacrifice of Abraham; 258. *Adriano Isenbrandt*, Mary Magdalene; 266. *David Ryckaert III*, Rural feast; 277. *David Teniers the Younger*, Fête Champêtre; 278. *P. Brill*, Creation of Man; 279. *Jan Scorel*, Agatha van Schoenhoven; 280. *P. Brueghel the Younger*, Vision of St John in Patmos.—R. V. *J.F. van Bloemen*, Seven Landscapes; *Paul Brill*, 287, Landscape with huntsmen;

Nicolas Juvenel, 288, 294. Portraits; 290. *Q. Massys*, Usurers; *291. *Rubens* (or his School), Franciscan; 295. *Jan Brueghel the Elder*, Earthly Paradise; 306. *Herri met de Bles*, Ascent to Calvary; 316. *P. Brueghel the Younger*, Snow scene; 317. *P. Brueghel the Elder*, Battle in the Bay of Naples.—1ST CABINET. 17C Dutch and Flemish schools.

The Galleria degli Specchi (3rd Gallery) was created in the 18C by Valvassori (the vault is decorated by Aureliano Milani). 337. *School of Raphael*, Joan of Aragon, princess Colonna.—2ND CABINET. *339. *Velazquez*, Innocent X (1650), the gem of the collection.—VII. *Bernini*, Bust of Innocent X.—4TH GALLERY. *Claude Lorraine*, *343. The Mill, 346. Rest on the flight into Egypt, 348. Sacrifice at Delphi, 351. Meeting with Diana, 352. Mercury runs away with the oxen of Apollo; 357. *Fr. Albani* and *Ann. Carracci*, Assumption; *Ann. Carracci*, *359. Flight into Egypt, 362. Christ carried to the sepulchre; 365. *Jan Joust van Cossiau*, River estuary; 381. *Aless. Allori*, Christ on the road to Golgotha; *Gasp. Vanvitelli*, 384, 385. Two views of Venice.

In the ***Private Apartments** red dominates the decorations (guided visits of groups of not more than ten people are arranged at 10.30 and 12 o'clock). The Winter Garden is decorated with antique busts, a 16C Brussels tapestry, and an 18C sedan chair. Next is the FUMOIR, containing a large polyptych, with gold background, of the early 15C Tuscan school (Virgin and Child with saints and angels); a triptych of the Madonna between St John Baptist and St Bernardine by *Sano di Pietro*; and a 16C Brussels tapestry depicting the month of February. Off this is a room furnished in 19C style. In the ROOM OF ANDREA DORIA a glass case contains some of his possessions, while two Brussels tapestries show further scenes of Lepanto. The SMALL DINING ROOM contains a bust of Princess Emily Doria by *Canonica*, a collection of Trapani corals, ambers, and ivories, and a 19C frieze showing the fiefs of the Doria-Pamphilj family. Next is the GREEN SALON, containing a Madonna, by *Beccafumi*; Deposition, by *Hans Memling*; large mid-15C Tournai tapestry with the medieval legend of Alexander the Great; bronze bust of Innocent X, by *Algardi*; *Portrait (perhaps of himself), by *Lor. Lotto*. In the centre, rare 18C cradle in carved and gilded wood.—In the recess to the left: Portraits of And. Doria, by *Seb. del Piombo*, and of Gianetto Doria, attrib. to *Bronzino*; tender *Annunciation, by *Filippo Lippi*.—From the Gallery, the APPARTAMENTO DI RAPPRESENTANZA is reached, the ceiling of which is decorated with an 18C fresco of Venus and Aeneas by *Ant. Nessi*, and containing a 17C Florentine marble table with a carved and gilded wooden base in the shape of four dolphins. In the charming BALL ROOM is a Gobelins tapestry woven for Louis XIV from a 16C Flemish design, representing the month of May. The altar of rare marbles in the CHAPEL is 17C work. Tapestries of the signs of the Zodiac by *Claude Audran* in the YELLOW ROOM were executed to Louis XV's order, and two exquisite Ming vases are displayed here. The ceiling fresco is by *Tom. Maria Conca*. The SMALL GREEN DRAWING ROOM is in the elegant 18C Venetian style, with three Venetian scenes attrib. to Longhi. Lastly, in the SMALL RED DRAWING ROOM are a 17C Gobelins tapestry, four allegorical paintings of the Elements and Seasons by *Jan Brueghel the Elder*, and a portrait of James Stuart, the Old Pretender, by *A.S. Belle*.

On the N side of Piazza del Collegio Romano (Pl. 3; 6) is the **Collegio Romano**, a large building erected in 1585 by order of Gregory XIII for the Jesuits. The architect was thought to have been Bartolomeo Ammannati, but was more probably, the Jesuit Giuseppe Valeriani. It is now partly used by the Ministry of 'Beni Culturali'.

The founder of the Jesuit College was St Francis Borgia, duke of Gandia, third in succession after Ignatius Loyola as General of the Jesuits. Its pupils included eight popes: Urban VIII, Innocent X, Clement IX, Clement X, Innocent XII, Clement XI, Innocent XIII, and Clement XII. The building used to house the *Museo Preistorico Etnografico Luigi Pigorini* which was moved to E.U.R. The Jesuit library founded here formed the nucleus of the *Biblioteca Nazionale Centrale Vittorio Emanuele* which was moved to new premises near the Castro Pretorio in 1975. The Salone della Crociera, with its original bookcases, may be used to house part of the library from Palazzo di Venezia (see p72).

On the S side of the piazza is the former church of *Santa Marta* (restored in 1966 as an exhibition centre), by Carlo Fontana, with a good doorway. Inside (closed when not in use) is a good vault decoration designed by Baciccia, with paintings by him and Paolo Albertoni.—Just beyond, on the left of Via del Piè di Marmo, in Via di Santo Stefano del Cacco, is a colossal marble foot (perhaps from an ancient Roman statue of Isis).

In the Corso, beyond Palazzo Doria, rises **Santa Maria in Via Lata**, a small church of ancient foundation, rebuilt in the 15C. The graceful *Façade (much blackened by the polluted air) and vestibule are by Pietro da Cortona (1660).

The pretty little INTERIOR is usually open only in the evening. At the end of the left aisle is the tomb (1776) of the poet Ant. Tebaldeo (1463–1537), tutor of Isabella d'Este, secretary of Lucrezia Borgia, courtier of Leo X, and friend of Raphael (who painted his portrait in the Vatican, a copy of which is placed here). The church also contains tombs of the families of Joseph and Lucien Bonaparte. The high altar and apse, decorated with coloured marbles, have been attrib. as an early work to Bernini, but they are now instead thought to be by Santi Ghetti.

The lower level (ring on left of the façade at No. 306; but usually closed) has remains of a large Roman building which probably served as a warehouse (and which extended along the Via Lata also beneath Palazzo Doria). In the 3C AD the portion beneath the church was divided into six storerooms and two of these in the 5C were converted into a Christian chapel and welfare centre, rebuilt and enlarged as a church in the 7C and 11C. Interesting murals (7–9C) discovered here have been detached because of the humidity and removed for restoration. A tradition that St Paul was guarded here on his second visit to Rome, led to excavations as early as the 17C. The high relief over the main altar of the saints Peter, Paul, Luke, and Matthew by *Cosimo Fancelli* dates from this period. Also to be seen: an ancient well (still in use) and a column inscribed with words of St Paul, and an altar (derived from a pagan cult altar) in a chapel to the right.

Here the Corso was spanned by the *Arcus Novus* erected by Diocletian in 303–4, and demolished in 1491 when the church was rebuilt. Nearby was the *Ara Pietatis* erected by Claudius in AD 43.

In the Corso, beyond Via Lata, the Banco di Roma now occupies *Palazzo Simonetti* (No. 307), once the property of the Boncompagni-Ludovisi and for years the residence of Card. de Bernis, ambassador of Louis XV at the papal court.

Low down on the corner of this Palazzo in Via Lata is the *Fontanella del Facchino* with a sturdy porter holding a barrel; water issues from the bung-hole. Water-sellers are supposed to have resold Tiber or Trevi water from their barrels. 'Il Facchino' was one of Rome's 'talking' statues (see p 122); and, with his flat beret, was once thought to be a caricature portrait of Martin Luther, though it is more likely Abbondio Rizio, a heavy drinker. In 1751, Vanvitelli attributed the sculpture to Michelangelo.

Opposite Palazzo Simonetti is **San Marcello** (Pl. 3; 6), a very old church, rebuilt on a design by Iac. Sansovino after a fire in 1519, with a façade by Carlo Fontana (1683).

The INTERIOR was frescoed in the 17C by *G.B. Ricci da Novara*. To the left of the entrance, Tomb of Card. Michiel (died 1503) and his nephew Bishop Orso (died 1511), by *Iac. Sansovino*. RIGHT SIDE. 3rd chapel, 15C fresco of the Madonna and Child in a marble frame, and frescoes by *Fr. Salviati*. On the ceiling of the 4th chapel are frescoes begun by *Perino del Vaga* (Creation of Eve, St Mark, and St John the Evangelist), completed after the sack of Rome by *Daniele da Volterra* and *Pellegrino Tibaldi*. Beneath the altar is an interesting Roman cippus. The 5th chapel has paintings by *Aureliano Milani* (c 1725). The 4th chapel on the left side has frescoes by *Taddeo Zuccari* and busts of three members of the Frangipane family by *Aless. Algardi*.

Via del Caravita diverges to the left for the delightful rococo *Piazza di Sant'Ignazio, a 'theatrical' masterpiece by Fil. Raguzzini (1728). The Jesuit church of **Sant'Ignazio** (Pl. 3; 6) rivals the Gesù in magnificence. It was begun in 1626 by Card. Ludovisi as the church of the Collegio Romano (see p 141), to celebrate the Canonization of St Ignatius de Loyola by the cardinal's uncle Gregory XV. The design by *Carlo Maderno* and others was carried out by a Jesuit mathematician from the College called *Orazio Grassi* who is also responsible for the fine façade.

The spacious aisled INTERIOR is sumptuously decorated. In the vaulting of the nave and apse are remarkable *Paintings representing the missionary activity of the Jesuits and the Triumph of St Ignatius, the masterpiece of *Andrea dal Pozzo*. The amazing trompe l'oeil perspective projects the walls of the church beyond their architectural limits, and Pozzo even provided a cupola, never built because of lack of funds, in a canvas 17 metres in diameter (restored in 1963). The vaulting and 'dome' are best seen from a small yellow disc let into the pavement about the middle of the nave (coin-operated light in the nave). In the lavishly decorated 2nd right chapel, Death of St Joseph, by *Fr. Trevisani*. In

The ceiling of Sant' Ignazio painted in 1685 by Andrea Pozzo

the ornate chapels of the transepts, designed by *And. dal Pozzo*, with marble
solomonic columns, are large marble high reliefs: on the S side, the Glory of St
Louis Gonzaga, by *Pierre Legros*, with a lapis-lazuli urn containing the remains
of the saint, and two angels, 18C works by *Bern. Ludovisi*; on the N the
Annunciation by *Filippo Della Valle*, and another lapis-lazuli urn with the relics
of St John Berchmans (died 1621), and two 18C angels by *P. Bracci*. In the
chapel to the right of the High Altar, funerary monument to Gregory XV and his
nephew Card. Ludovisi, the founders of the church, by *Pierre Legros*. From the
sacristy there is a lift to a chapel frescoed by *Borgognone*.

Farther on in the Corso is (No. 239, on the right) *Palazzo Sciarra-
Colonna*, built in the late 16C by Flaminio Ponzio, under which, in
1887, was found part of the Aqua Virgo. Opposite is the *Savings
Bank*, by Cipolla (1874). The street here was once spanned by the
triumphal *Arch of Claudius* (fragments in Palazzo dei Conservatori).
Via delle Muratte diverges (right) for the Fontana di Trevi (see
p 154).

In Piazza di Pietra, a few metres to the left of the Corso by Via di
Pietra, are the remains of the **Temple of Hadrian**, built by Antoninus
Pius in 145 and dedicated to his father. The wall of the cella and the
peristyle of the right side with eleven fluted Corinthian *Columns
(15m high) remain (the disengaged columns have recently been
cleaned). They are incorporated in the façade of the *Borsa*.

The Corso next reaches **Piazza Colonna** (Pl. 3; 4), which for
centuries was the centre of the city, and is still one of its busiest
squares. On the N side rises the great flank of PALAZZO CHIGI, begun
in the 16C by Matteo di Castello (and also possibly Giac. Della Porta
and Carlo Maderno) and finished in the 17C by Felice Della Greca. It
is now the official residence of the Prime Minister (no adm; but the
interesting 17C courtyard can be seen through the entrance). The
famous Chigi library founded by Alexander VII, was presented by
the State to the Vatican in 1923. The main façade of the palace faces
the Corso and *Largo Chigi* from which the busy Via del Tritone leads
towards Piazza Barberini.—The E side of the piazza is closed across
the Corso, by the *Galleria Colonna* (1914), with shops and cafés in an
interior arcade in the form of a Y. On the opposite side of the piazza is
the façade of *Palazzo Wedekind* (1838), incorporating on the ground
floor a handsome portico, with 12 Ionic marble columns, brought
from a Roman building at Veio.

The little church on the S side is *San Bartolomeo dei Bergamaschi* (1561). At the
beginning of Via del Tritone (see above) is *Santa Maria in Via* rebuilt in 1594,
with a good Baroque front, completed in 1670.

In the centre of the piazza, beside a graceful fountain, designed by
Giac. della Porta (the dolphins, etc., are a 19C addition by Achille
Stocchi), rises the monument from which it derives its name, the
majestic *Column of Marcus Aurelius* (*Colonna Antonina*; restored
in 1984–88). It was erected in honour of his victories over the
Germans and Sarmatians (AD 169–76), and dedicated to the Emperor
and his wife, Faustina.

Like Trajan's Column, by which this was inspired, if not in the middle of a true
Forum, it was at all events in the centre of an important group of monuments of
the Antonine period. In the vicinity were the *Ustrina Antinorum* (that of Marcus
Aurelius under Palazzo del Parlamento, and that of Antoninus Pius S of the
column of Antoninus Pius), the *Temple of Hadrian* in Piazza di Pietra (see
above), and the *Porticus Vipsanioe* (on the other side of the Corso, in the area of
Palazzo della Rinascente). The column, which was erected between 180 and
196, is made entirely of marble from Luni, and is formed of 27 blocks. The
ancient level of the ground was nearly 4m lower than at present. The shaft

measures 100 Roman feet (29·6m), and the total height of the column, including the base and the statue, is nearly 42 metres. The ancient base was decorated with Victories, festoons, and reliefs. In 1589 Dom. Fontana restored it, and a statue of St Paul was placed on the summit, where there were originally figures of Marcus Aurelius and Faustina. Around the shaft a bas-relief ascends in a spiral of 20 turns, interrupted half-way by a Victory; the lower part of the relief commemorates the war against the Germanic tribes (169–173), the upper that against the Sarmatians (174–176). In these heroic struggles, which delayed the barbaric invasion for several centuries, the philosopher-emperor was always to be found at the head of his troops. On the third spiral (E side) the Roman soldiers are represented as being saved by a rain storm, which in the 4C was regarded as a miracle brought about by the prayers of the Christians in their ranks. Casts of the reliefs are in the Museo della Civiltà Romana. The summit is reached by 203 steps (no adm) lit by 56 tiny windows, in the interior of the column.

A little farther W is Piazza di Montecitorio, with the old façade of **Palazzo di Montecitorio**, which, since 1871, has been the seat of the Italian *Chamber of Deputies*. The original palace was begun for the Ludovisi family in 1650 by *Bernini*, who was responsible for the general plan of the building and for the idea of enhancing the effect of the façade by giving it a convex, slightly polygonal form. The N façade of the palazzo is in Piazza del Parlamento.

In 1918 it was enlarged and given its new façade by Ernesto Basile; the principal entrance is now on this side. The Art Nouveau red-brick front is in contrast to the prevailing style of architecture. The Chamber, also of this period, is panelled in oak and brightly illuminated from above by a row of windows pierced in the cornice. Below the cornice is an encaustic frieze by Aristide Sartorio, representing the development of Italian civilization. The fine bas-relief in bronze in honour of the House of Savoy is by Davide Calandra.

The **Obelisk** (22m high) in the centre of the piazza was originally erected at Heliopolis by Psammetichus II (c 590 BC). It was brought to Rome by Augustus to celebrate his victory over Cleopatra, and set up in the Campus Martius, where it served as the gnomon of an immense sundial. In 1748 it was discovered underground in the Largo dell' Impresa (an open space N of the palazzo) and in 1792 it was placed on its present site; it was restored in 1966.

In the Corso, beyond Largo Chigi, stands *Palazzo della Rinascente*, and *Pal. Marignoli* (1889), and (left) *Palazzo Verospi* where Shelley lived in 1819 (plaque). Via delle Convertite leads (right) to Piazza San Silvestro, an important bus terminus, with the **Central Post Office** (Pl. 3; 4). The church of SAN SILVESTRO IN CAPITE was originally erected here by Pope Stephen III (752–7) on the site of a Roman building, possibly Aurelian's Temple of the Sun. It was bestowed on the English Roman Catholics by Leo XIII in 1890. The 12–13C Campanile is surmounted by a 12C bronze cock. It contains interesting 17C works, including the organ, and paintings by Giacinto Brandi, Orazio Gentileschi, Fr. Trevisani, Lod. Gimignani, and Pomarancio.

Farther along the Corso (now less busy), beyond Piazza del Parlamento (see above), is *Palazzo Fiano* (left), built over the remains of the *Ara Pacis* (p 147). Here once stood the Roman Arco di Portogallo, demolished in 1662 by order of Alexander VII. A small square opens out just beyond, opposite the pretty Via Frattina, the first of several long straight pedestrian streets which open off this side of the Corso and end in Piazza di Spagna (see p 157). In the square, on the left, is **San Lorenzo in Lucina** (Pl. 3; 4), a church probably dating from the time of Sixtus III (432–440), or even earlier, rebuilt in the 12C, and again in 1650. Of the 12C church there remain the campanile (restored) which has several rows of small loggie with colonnettes, the portico with six Ionic columns, and the doorway.

INTERIOR. South side: by the 2nd pillar, tomb of Nicolas Poussin (1594–1665) by
Lemoyne, erected by Chateaubriand in 1830; in the 1st chapel is preserved a
portion of the gridiron on which St Lawrence was martyred; and the 4th chapel,
designed by *Bernini* for Innocent X's doctor Gabriele Fonseca, has a fine
portrait bust by him. The Crucifixion on the High Altar is by *Guido ·Reni*.
Pompilia (in Browning's 'The Ring and the Book') was married in this church.
Excavations have revealed interesting remains of the palaeochristian basilica,
and Roman material, including a black-and-white mosaic.

Beyond *Palazzo Ruspoli* (No. 418A; left), by Ammannati, with a great
marble staircase by Martino Longhi the Younger, Largo Carlo
Goldoni is reached. Here three streets converge on the Corso: Via
Condotti, with its fine shops, leading past *SS. Trinità dei Spagnoli*,
with an eliptical interior of the 18C, to Piazza di Spagna (p 157), Via
Fontanella di Borghese, ending in Piazza Borghese (see below), and
Via Tomacelli, which leads to *Ponte Cavour*, an important bridge
over the Tiber leading to the Prati district. Farther on, where the
street widens, stands **Santi Ambrogio e Carlo al Corso** (Pl. 3; 4;
closed for restoration) built in 1612 by Onorio Longhi, completed by
his son Martino. The fine cupola is by Pietro da Cortona. The façade
is by G.B. Menicucci and Fra Mario da Canepina (1690). The
altarpiece (poorly lit; the Madonna presenting San Carlo to Christ) is
one of *Carlo Maratta*'s best works, and on an altar behind it is a rich
urn containing the heart of St Charles Borromeo.

In the neighbouring *Oratory of Sant'Ambrogio* (at No. 437, to the left of the
church; ring for the porter), on the site of the old church built by the Lombards
in 1513 on a piece of land granted them by Sixtus IV, is a marble group of the
Deposition, by Tom. della Porta (1618).

Behind the apse of San Carlo is the ugly Piazza Augusto Imperatore
(Pl. 3; 2; now used by tourist buses) laid out by the Facist regime in
1936–38 around the *Mausoleum of Augustus (Pl. 3; 2), or *Tumulus
Caesarum* (no adm; part of the interior can be seen through the main
S entrance). This was the tomb of Augustus and of the principal
members of his family, the gens Julia-Claudia, and was one of the
most sacred monuments of Ancient Rome. The last Roman emperor
to be buried here was Nerva in AD 98. Erected in 28 BC, it is a
circular structure 87m in diameter. It was originally surmounted by a
tumulus of earth some 44m high, planted with cypresses and probably crowned with a statue of the emperor.

Excavations carried out in 1926–30 freed the crypt of the mausoleum from the
debris that surrounded and partly buried it, and restored as far as possible its
original appearance. The circular base, of opus reticulatum, has a series of large
niches on the outside. From the entrance a passageway leads into the interior
past a series of 12 compartments arranged in a circle to an outer ring-passage,
at the entrance to which are fragments of statues; beyond is an inner ring and
finally the sepulchral cella, with walls of travertine blocks, a central pillar, and
three niches. In the central niche were found the cinerary urns of Augustus and
of his wife Livia; on either side were those of his nephews Gaius and Lucius
Caesar and of his sister Octavia, with an inscription to his beloved nephew
Marcellus. On either side of the entrance were two obelisks, one of which is
now in Piazza del Quirinale, and the other in Piazza dell'Esquilino, as well as
bronze inscriptions with the official will of Augustus, a copy of which was found
at Ankara (it is reproduced on the outside wall of the pavilion protecting the Ara
Pacis, see below).
In the Middle Ages the tomb became a fortress of the Colonna. Later it was
despoiled to provide travertine for other buildings and after further vicissitudes
a wooden amphitheatre was built into it. Goethe watched beast-baiting here in
1787. Later still it was converted into a concert hall and was used as such until
1936.

To the W of the Mausoleum, between Via di Ripetta and the Tiber, is a platform approached by a flight of steps at either end. Here a building with glass walls was built in 1938 to protect the *Ara Pacis, reconstructed in 1937–38 from scattered fragments and from reproductions of other fragments not available. This monumental altar is a splendid example of Roman sculpture, influenced by Greek Classical and Hellenistic art. Adm, see p 48.

The Ara Pacis Augustae was consecrated in the Campus Martius on 4 July 13 BC, and dedicated four years later after the victorious return of Augustus from Spain and Gaul, in celebration of the peace that he had established within the Empire. This much is known from the document (*Res gestae Divi Augusti*) which the emperor had engraved on bronze tablets (see above) in Rome a year before his death in AD 14. A copy of this has been engraved on the wall of the modern pavilion.

In 1568, during excavations for the foundations of Palazzo Fiano (on the Corso), nine blocks belonging to the frieze of the altar were found and bought by Card. Ricci da Montepulciano for the Grand Duke of Tuscany. To facilitate transport, each block was sawn into three. These went to the Uffizi Gallery in Florence. The cardinal overlooked two other blocks unearthed at the same time. One of these eventually passed to the Louvre in Paris; the other to the Vatican Museum.

In 1859, during a reconstruction of Palazzo Fiano, the contractors found the base of the altar, with the left half of the relief panel of the sacrifice of Aeneas and other architectural and decorative elements. These were acquired in 1898 by the Italian Government for the Museo Nazionale Romano. In 1903 excavations brought to light further fragments: these included most of the basement of marble cubes supporting the altar, portions of the acanthus frieze (see below) and the right half of the relief of the sacrifice of Aeneas, in which Augustus himself appeared. There was also found a panel with two *Flamines* (priests), but this could not then be dislodged.

Finally, in 1937, the Italian Government decided on further excavations with a view to complete reconstruction. The work involved digging down to a depth of 10·5m and freezing the subsoil water. Outlying fragments were recovered from the Museo Nazionale and the Uffizi Gallery; those in the Louvre, the Vatican, and the Villa Medici were copied. Thus the monument has recovered, so far as possible, its original form and appearance. Restoration of the E side was carried out in 1983; and the work may be continued on the N side.

The monument, built throughout of Luni marble, has a simple base with two horizontal bands. On the base is an almost square-walled enclosure, with two open and two closed sides. The open sides are 11·5m and the closed sides 10·5m long. The two openings are each 3·5m square; one of them is approached by a flight of steps. The external decoration of the enclosure is in two zones divided by a horizontal Greek key-pattern border. The lower zone is covered with an intricate and beautiful composition of acanthus leaves on which are swans with outstretched wings. In the upper zone is the frieze of reliefs, with a decorated cornice above it. Between the jambs of the main or W entrance are scenes illustrating the origins of Rome. The left panel (almost entirely lost) represented the *Lupercalia*; the right panel shows *Aeneas sacrificing the white sow. The panels of the E entrance depict *Tellus, the earth goddess, possibly an allegory of Peace (left), and Rome (right), much damaged. These were beautifully restored in 1983. Mythology and allegory give way to realism in the subjects of the side panels, which represent the ceremony of the consecration of the altar. In procession are seen Augustus, members of his family including children, State officials, and priests. The interior of the enclosure is also in two zones; in view of the nature of the operations here, the lower part has no decoration other than simple fluting. The upper zone, however, is decorated with beautifully carved bucrania.

The altar is an exact reconstruction of all recovered fragments. Approached by a flight of steps, it has a back and two side walls; a further flight of narrow steps, leads up past the walls to the altar proper. The cornice and the anta of the left side wall have been the best preserved; the reliefs indicate the *Suovetaurilia*, or sacrifice of a pig, a sheep, and an ox. Little else of the decoration survives.

To the S, on Via di Ripetta, in a district once inhabited by the Serbs (Schiavoni) who came here as refugees after the battle of Kossovo (15 June 1389) are two churches, *San Girolamo degli Schiavoni*, rebuilt in 1587, and *San Rocco* with a neo-classical façade by Valadier (1834), and an early altarpiece by Baciccia in the sacristy. Farther S, Via Borghese diverges left from Via di Ripetta (the name of which is a reminder of the old river bank and port) to **Palazzo Borghese** (Pl. 2; 6, 4; no adm), called from its shape the 'harpsichord of Rome'. It was begun perhaps by Vignola (c 1560) and completed by Flaminio Ponzio, who designed the beautiful terrace on the Tiber front. The palace was acquired by Cardinal Camillo Borghese, who became Pope Paul V in 1605, and was renowned for its splendour. For nearly two centuries it contained the paintings from the Galleria Borghese; they were restored to their former residence in 1891. It is now the seat of the 'Circolo della Caccia', an exclusive club founded in 1869. The pretty Court has long lines of twin columns in two stories, and colossal statues representing Ceres and the empresses Sabina and Julia; a garden beyond contains fountains and Roman sculpture.

It is now necessary to return across Piazza Augusto to the Corso. In Via Vittoria (right) is the renowned Accademia Musicale di Santa Cecilia. Farther N the Corso passes (left) the church of *San Giacomo in Augusta* (so called from its proximity to the Mausoleum), with a façade by Maderno; it is known also as *San Giacomo degli Incurabili* from the adjoining hospital. Opposite is the small church of *Gesù e Maria*, with a façade by G. Rainaldi who was also responsible for the interior decoration completed c 1675. On the left (Nos 518–19) is the former *Palazzo Sanseverino*, now *Rondanini* with an imposing double porch. It is now a bank and is being restored.

Opposite (No. 18; plaque) is the house where Goethe lived in 1786–88. The *Goethe Museum* here, which contains interesting material relating to the poet's travels in Italy, has been closed for many years, but it is to be restored by the German government who acquired the museum in 1987.

*****Piazza del Popolo** (Pl. 3; 2), at the end of the Corso, provides a scenographic entrance to the city from Via Flaminia and the north. Numerous famous travellers in the 19C recorded their first arrival in Rome through the Porta del Popolo. It was created by Latino Giovenale Manetti in 1538 for Paul III in strict relationship to the three long straight roads which here penetrate the city as a trident, between the two twin-domed churches added in the 17C. The piazza was given its present symmetry by Gius. Valadier after the return of Pius VII from France in 1814. Between four fountains with lions by Valadier (1823; to a 16C design by Dom. Fontana) rises an *Obelisk* (24m; restored in 1984), the hieroglyphs on which celebrate the glories of the pharaohs Rameses II and Merenptah (13–12C BC); Augustus brought it from Heliopolis, after the conquest of Egypt, and it was dedicated to the sun in the Circus Maximus. Domenico Fontana removed it to its present site in 1589, as part of the urban plan of Sixtus V.

The three streets which converge on the piazza from the S are Via di Ripetta (see above) on the left, the Corso in the middle, and Via del Babuino (from Piazza di Spagna; see p 157) on the right. The ends of the streets are separated by a pair of decorative Baroque churches (not always open), **Santa Maria dei Miracoli** (left) and **Santa Maria in Montesanto** (right); the façades were modified by Bernini and Carlo Fontana (1671–78), after Carlo Rainaldi. In the centre of each hemicycle is a fountain with marble groups (on the left, Neptune with two Tritons, on the right, Rome between the Tiber and the Anio, both by Giov. Ceccarini; 1824) and at the ends are more neo-classical statues of the Four Seasons. On the W Via Ferdinando di Savoia comes in from Ponte, Margherita, and on the E a winding road designed by Valadier, Viale Gabriele d'Annunzio, descends from the Pincio (p 159). In the piazza is a fashionable café.

Across the piazza (to the right of the gate) rises the flank of *Santa Maria del Popolo (Pl. 3; 2; closed 12.30–16), on the site of a chapel erected by Paschal II in 1099 over the tombs of the Domitia family, which were believed to be the haunt of demons, because Nero was buried there. The Pope solemnly cut down a walnut tree that was supposed to shelter them. The church was rebuilt in 1227 and again under Sixtus IV (1472–77). The early Renaissance façade is attributed to And. Bregno.

The **Interior** (lights in each chapel and the apse) was renovated by *Bernini* and has many important works of art. SOUTH AISLE. 1st chapel (Della Rovere), *Frescoes by *Pinturicchio* (1485–89); over the altar, the Adoration of the Child; in the lunettes (very worn and restored), scenes from the life of St Jerome; on the right, tomb of Card. De Castro (1506), perhaps by *Ant. da Sangallo the Younger*; on the left, the tomb of Cardinals Crist. and Dom. Della Rovere (1477) by *Mino da Fiesole* and *And. Bregno*.—The 2nd chapel (Cybo) is well designed; the architecture is by *Carlo Fontana* and its marbles are especially rich and varied. The altarpiece (Assumption and Four Doctors of the Church) is by *Carlo Maratta*; at the sides are the tombs of the Cybo family, and of Bishop Girol. Foscari (died 1463).—The 3rd chapel, with a worn majolica pavement, was frescoed by the school of *Pinturicchio* (1504–7); over the altar, the Virgin, four saints, and the Eternal Father; in the lunettes, scenes from the life of the Virgin; on the left, the Assumption. To the right is the tomb of Giovanni Della Rovere (1483; school of And. Bregno).—4th chapel (Costa), altarpiece, Saints Catherine, Vincent, and Anthony of Padua (1489), by the school of *And. Bregno*. On the right, tomb of Marcantonio Albertoni (1485); on the left, tomb of the founder, Cardinal Giorgio Costa (1508). In the lunettes, frescoes by the school of *Pinturicchio*, the Fathers of the Church (1489).

SOUTH TRANSEPT. On the right, tomb of Cardinal Lodovico Podocataro of Cyprus (1508). A corridor, passing an altar from the studio of *And. Bregno*, leads to the Sacristy which contains a *Tabernacle by *Bregno*, with a painted Madonna of the early Sienese school, and the monuments of Bishop Rocca (died 1482) and Archbishop Ortega Gomiel of Burgos (died 1514).

The APSE of the church, with a shell design, is one of *Bramante*'s earliest works in Rome, commissioned by Julius II. It provides the setting for the two splendid *Tombs of Cardinal Girol. Basso della Rovere (1507) and Cardinal Ascanio Sforza (1505), signed by *And. Sansovino*. The *Frescoes high up in the vault, of the Coronation of the Virgin, Evangelists, Sibyls, and Four Fathers of the Church, are by *Pinturicchio* (1508–9). The stained glass, commissioned by Julius II, is by *Giullaume de Marcillat*. Over the high altar is a notable 13C Madonna.—NORTH TRANSEPT. In the 1st chapel to the left of the choir (right wall) are two dramatic paintings by *Caravaggio*: *Crucifixion of St Peter, and (left wall) *Conversion of St Paul. The altarpiece of the Assumption is by *Annibale Carracci*. In the chapel at the end of the transept, Tomb of Cardinal Bernardo Lonati (late 15C).

NORTH AISLE. 3rd chapel, to the right of the altar, tomb of Cardinal

Pietro Mellini (1483, a small but gracious work). The octagonal well-lit ***Chigi Chapel**, founded by the great banker Agostino Chigi (1465–1520) was designed in a fusion of architecture, sculpture, and painting by *Raphael* (1513–16). Work on the chapel was interrupted in 1520 with the death of Agostino and Raphael, and it was only completed after 1652 for Cardinal Fabio Chigi (Alexander VII) by *Bernini*. *Raphael* prepared the cartoons for the *Mosaics in the dome, executed by *Luigi De Pace*, a Venetian, in 1516. These represent God the Father as creator of the firmament, surrounded by symbols of the seven planets, each of which is guided by an angel as in Dante's conception. The frescoes depicting the Creation and the Fall, between the windows, and the medallions of the Seasons, are by *Fr. Salviati* (1552–54). The altarpiece (Nativity of the Virgin) is by *Seb. del Piombo* (1530–34); the bas-relief in front of Christ and the Woman of Samaria, by *Lorenzetto*, was intended for the base of the pyramidal tomb of Agostino, but was removed here by Bernini. Statues of Prophets: by the altar, *Jonah (left), designed by *Raphael*, executed by *Lorenzetto*, and Habakkuk (right) by *Bernini*; by the entrance, Daniel and the lion, by *Bernini* and Elijah, by *Lorenzetto*. The remarkable pyramidal form of the tombs of Agostino Chigi and of his brother Sigismondo (died 1526), executed by *Lorenzetto*, were dictated by *Raphael*'s architectural scheme and derived from ancient Roman models. They were altered by Bernini. An unfinished burial crypt has recently been discovered below the chapel with another pyramid, which in Raphael's original design would have been visible and illuminated from the chapel above. The lunettes above the tombs were painted by *Raff. Vanni* in 1653. The marble intarsia figure of Death, with the Chigi stemma, in the centre of the pavement was added by *Bernini* (removed in 1988).—On the left of the chapel is a colourful funerary monument, erected in 1771 in memory of Princess Odescalchi. In the baptistery are two ciboria by *A. Bregno*, and the tombs of Cardinals Fr. Castiglione (right; 1568) and Ant. Pallavicini (1507). Here has been placed the bronze effigy of Bishop Girolomo Foscari (buried in the 2nd S chapel), attributed to *Vecchietta*.—The former Augustinian convent adjoining the church was the residence in Rome of Martin Luther during his mission there in 1511.

Beside the church stands the monumental and historic **Porta del Popolo** (Pl. 3; 2; restored in 1984), which occupies almost the same site as the ancient *Porta Flaminia*. The inner face of the gate was executed by Bernini in 1655, on the occasion of the entry into Rome of Queen Christina of Sweden; the outer face (1561) is by Nanni di Baccio Bigio, who followed a design by Michelangelo. The two colossal statues of Saints Peter and Paul in the outer niches, late works by Francesco Mochi, have been removed for restoration since 1979. The two side arches were opened in 1879.—Outside the gate, in the busy *Piazzale Flaminio*, is an entrance to the huge park of the Villa Borghese (see Rte 9).

8 Piazza Venezia to Piazza di Spagna and the Pincio

From Piazza Venezia Via Cesare Battisti leads past (right) Pal. delle Assicurazioni Generali, and Pal. Valentini (1585), now the seat of the Prefecture, to (left) the long thin Piazza dei Santi Apostoli (left), the scene in recent years of political demonstrations. On the W side of the piazza is *Palazzo Odescalchi*, which extends to the Corso; the façade on the piazza is by Bernini, with additions by Nic. Salvi and L. Vanvitelli (1750). At No. 67 is a Museum of Waxworks (adm see p 50), opened in 1953. On the E side is the huge complex of the **Palazzo Colonna** (Pl. 4; 5) which is bounded S by Via Quattro Novembre, E by Via della Pilotta, and N by Via del Vaccaro and Piazza della Pilotta. On the side facing Piazza dei Santi Apostoli the palace embraces the church of the Santi Apostoli.

The palace was built by Martin V (Oddone Colonna), who lived here as pope from 1424 until his death in 1431, and rebuilt in 1730. Here, on 4 June 1802, after the cession of Piedmont to France, Charles Emmanuel IV of Savoy, king of Sardinia, became a Jesuit and abdicated in favour of his brother Victor Emmanuel I. Four arches spanning Via della Pilotta connect the palace with the Villa Colonna (no adm) which has a beautiful garden with tall cypresses (part of which can be seen from the Galleria Colonna; see below). In the garden are the remains of the huge Temple of Serapis, built in the time of Caracalla.

The palace contains the magnificent ***Galleria Colonna**, begun in 1654 by Cardinal Girolamo I Colonna, who employed the architect Antonio Del Grande, but it was not completed till nearly fifty years later. On Del Grande's death in 1671, Girol. Fontana took over direction. In 1703 the gallery was opened by Filippo II Colonna. One of the most important of the patrician collections in Rome, it is arranged in magnificent Baroque galleries, and is beautifully maintained. The entrance is at No. 17 Via della Pilotta (open to the public only on Saturday; see p 48). The paintings, most of them not labelled, are all numbered according to the description given below. The collection was recatalogued (and some of the attributions revised) in 1981.

From the entrance stairs mount to the VESTIBULE, in which is displayed a painting of St Julian, attributed to *Perino del Vaga*.—HALL OF THE COLONNA BELLICA. A 16C column of rosso antico, surmounted by a statue of Pallas Athena, gives the room its name. Ceiling frescoes by *Gius. Chiari*, Reception into heaven of Marcantonio II Colonna. 132. *Pietro Novelli*, Isabella Colonna with her son Lorenzo Onofrio; 139. *Palma Vecchio*, Madonna and Child, with St Peter and donor; 66. *Van Dyck* (attrib.), Lucrezia Tomacelli Colonna; *25. *Bonifacio Veronese*, Holy Family, with Saints Jerome and Lucy; 28. *After Hieronymus Bosch*, Temptation of St Anthony; *32. *Bronzino*, Venus with Cupid and a satyr; 156. *16C Roman School* (formerly attributed to Agostino Carracci), Cardinal Pompeo Colonna; 134. *Gian Paolo Olmo* (attributed; also attributed to Moretto), Portrait of a man with a dog; 186. *Domenico Tintoretto*, Adoration of the Sacrament; *147.*Scipione Pulzone*, Pius V; 53. *School of Dosso Dossi*, Giacomo Sciarra Colonna (?); *106. *Lor. Lotto* (attributed), Cardinal Pompeo Colonna; 37. *Bartolomeo Cancellieri* (attributed), so-called portrait of Vittoria Colonna; 189. *Iac. Tintoretto*, Narcissus; *Michele di Ridolfo del Ghirlandaio*, 117, 115, 116. Venus and Cupid, Dawn, and Night.—Sculpture: Hercules, Bacchus, and Head of Antinous. On the steps leading down to the Great Hall is preserved a cannon ball which fell here on 24 June 1849, during the siege of Rome.

The GREAT HALL is superbly decorated. The ceiling paintings, by *Giov. Coli* and *Fil. Gherardi*, depict incidents in the life of Marcantonio II Colonna, who commanded the papal contingent at Lepanto (1571); the central panel illustrates the battle. On the walls are four Venetian mirrors with flower paintings by *Mario de' Fiori* and *Giov. Stanchi*, and putti painted by *Carlo Maratta.—Salvator Rosa*, *162. St John the Baptist, once thought to be a self-portrait, 163. Preaching of St John the Baptist; 14. *Francesco Bassano the Younger*, Christ in the house of the Levite; 46. *Giovanni Domenico Cerrini*, St Irene taking the arrows from St Sebastian; 192. *Follower of Jacopo Tintoretto*, Portrait of a man with his secretary; *Pier Fr. Mola*, 123. Hagar and Ishmael, 124. Rebecca at the well; 104. *Lombard School* (formerly attributed to Scipione Pulzone), Family portrait of Alfonso III Gonzaga, Count of Novellara; 165. Copy from *Rubens* (formerly attributed to Van Dyck), Equestrian portrait of Carlo Colonna, duke of Marsi.—*Giov. Lanfranco*, 98. Magdalen in glory, 99. St Peter delivered from prison by the angel (perhaps a copy); 7. *Nicolò Alunno*, Madonna del Soccorso (the Virgin rescuing a child from a demon); 164. *Matteo Rosselli* (attributed), Allegory of The Fine Arts; 151. *Guido Reni*, St Francis of Assisi with two angels; 168. *Enea Salmeggia*, Martyrdom of St Catherine; 82. *Guercino*, St Paul the Hermit; 6. *Aless. Allori*, Descent into hell; 180. *Sustermans* (attrib.), Federico Colonna, viceroy of Valencia; 40. *17C Roman School* (formerly attributed to Ribera), St Jerome; 141. *Bart. Passarotti*, Family of Lodovico Peracchini; 167. *Rubens* (follower of), Assumption of the Virgin.—The Roman sculpture includes: Dancing faun; Marcus Aurelius; Gladiator. Fine bas-reliefs and sarcophagi fragments are set into the walls beneath the windows, and into statue pedestals.

The ROOM OF THE DESKS (or 'of the Landscapes') derives its name from two valuable *Desks displayed here. The first, in ebony, has 28 ivory bas-reliefs by Francis and Dominic Steinhard after drawings by Carlo Fontana; the central relief is a copy of Michelangelo's Last Judgment, the other 27 are copies of works by Raphael. The second desk, in sandalwood, is adorned with lapis lazuli, amethysts, and other semi-precious stones; in front are 12 small amethyst columns and at the top gilt bronze statuettes representing the Muses and Apollo seated under a laurel tree.—The ceiling frescoes, by *Seb. Ricci*, are of the battle of Lepanto. In this room is a noteworthy series of *Landscapes by *Gaspard Dughet* (54–65), and a further series by *J.F. van Bloemen*, with figures probably by *Placido Costanzi* (21–24).—*Borgognone*, 49. Stag hunt, 50. Battle scene; 182. *Herman van Swanevelt* (formerly attributed to Claude Lorraine), Landscape with ruins of the Palatine Hill; 146. *Nic. Poussin* (follower of), Apollo and Daphne; 126. *Jan Brueghel the Elder* (and *Josse de Momper*?), Landscape with figures; 31. *Paul Brill* (attrib.), Antigone recovering the bodies of her brothers; 121. *16C Flemish School*, Landscape with Noli me tangere; 89. *Jacob de Heusch* (formerly attributed to Salvator Rosa), Seascape; 181. *Herman van Swanevelt*, Landscape with the Good Samaritan; 113. *Circle of Michele Marieschi* (formerly attributed to Canaletto), View of the Campo and Scuola di San Rocco in Venice.—Sculpture, *Susini*, copy in bronze of the Farnese bull; two Roman fire irons in polished bronze; bronze group of a centaur and a female figure.

ROOM OF THE APOTHEOSIS OF MARTIN V. This room takes its name from the subject of the ceiling painting by *Benedetto Luti*. Above the windows, *Pietro Bianchi*, Fame crowning victory. Above the end wall, *Pompeo Batoni*, Time discovering truth.—159. *Roman School* (?), Cain and Abel; *Domenico Tintoretto*, 187, 188. Portraits; 152. *Workshop of Guido Reni*, St Agnese; *Guercino*, 85, 86. Annunciation; 183. *German School, 1524* (formerly attributed to Mabuse), Man with clasped hands; 33. *Bronzino*, Madonna and Child with Saints John and Elizabeth; 190. *Jacopo Tintoretto* (formerly attributed to Titian), Onofrio Panvinio, the Augustinian; *Fr. Salviati*, *170. Portrait of a Man, 169. Raising of Lazarus; 1. *Fr. Albani*, Rape of Europa; 83. *Guercino*, Guardian Angel; 178. *Giovanni di Pietro Spagna*, St Jerome; 191. *Follower of Iac. Tintoretto*, Spinet player; 8. *Andrea del Sarto* (formerly attributed to Puligo), Madonna and Child; 43. *Annibale Carracci* (also attributed to Bartolomeo Passarotti), Peasant eating beans; 26. *Paris Bordone*, Holy Family with Saints Jerome, Sebastian, and Mary Magdalene; *197. *Paolo Veronese*, Man in Venetian costume.—Sculpture, *Orfeo Buselli*, Bust of Cardinal Jerome I Colonna; two Roman marble busts.

The THRONE ROOM is reserved, as in other princely houses, for the Pope; the chair is turned to the wall so that no one else shall sit in it. 144. *Pisanello* (copy from), Portrait of Martin V, Oddone Colonna; *Scipione Pulzone*, 149. Portrait of Marcantonio II Colonna; 150. (attributed), Portrait of Felice Colonna Orsini. In this room are (198.) a nautical chart presented by the Roman people to Marcantonio II and a parchment diploma given him by the Roman senate after the battle of Lepanto. French clock by I. Godet of Paris.—Statuettes in bronze of a Satyr and Aphrodite; and marble busts of Zeus and a Woman.

ROOM OF MARIA MANCINI, or 'of the Primitives'. 51. *Fr. Cozza*, Birth of the Virgin; 143. *Pietro da Cortona*, Resurrection of Christ, with members of the

Colonna family; 92. *Jacob van Amsterdam*, Christ appearing to the Madonna and St John after the Resurrection; *198. *Bart. Vivarini*, Madonna enthroned; 105. *Luca Longhi*, Madonna with the young St John and a monk; *Fr. Albani*, 3, 4. Herminia among the shepherds; *35. *Giul. Bugiardini*, Madonna; *154. *Rocco Zoppo* (attributed; formerly attributed to Melozzo da Forlì), Portrait of a young man in profile, traditionally identified as Guidobaldo della Rovere, duke of Urbino; 10. *Iac. degli Avanzi*, Crucifixion; 102. *Copy from Leonardo da Vinci*, Madonna and Child; 175. *Girolamo Sicciolante da Sermoneta*, Madonna with the infant St John; *179. *Stef. da Zevio*, Madonna and Child enthroned with angels; 30. *School of Botticelli*, Madonna and Child; 130. *Gaspar Netscher* (attributed), Maria Colonna Mancini, the niece of Cardinal Mazarin; 38. *Simone Cantarini*, Holy Family; 166. *Rubens* (copy from), Reconciliation of Esau and Jacob; 29. *Workshop of Botticelli* (formerly attributed to Jacopo del Sellaio), Apostle St James; 137, 138. *Bernart van Orley*, The seven joys and seven sorrows of Mary; 90. *Inn. da Imola*, Holy Family with St Francis; 84. *Guercino*, Moses with the tables of law.

The church of the **Santi Apostoli** (Pl. 4; 5) was built by Pelagius I c 560 to commemorate the defeat and expulsion of the Goths by the Byzantine viceroy Narses, and dedicated to the Apostles James and Philip. It was restored and enlarged in the 15C and 16C and almost completely rebuilt by Carlo and Fr. Fontana in 1702–14. It was given a neo-classical façade by Valadier in 1827. The 15C apse was covered with frescoes by Melozzo da Forlì; fragments are preserved in the Quirinal and in the Pinacoteca of the Vatican. From the piazza only the upper part of the church is visible, as the stately portico of nine arches, closed by a grille, is surmounted by a Baroque story giving it the appearance of a palace.

THE PORTICO, the oldest part of the church, was erected by Baccio Pontelli at the cost of Cardinal della Rovere, afterwards Pope Julius II. On the left, tomb of the engraver Giov. Volpato, by *Canova* (1807). On right, *Bas-relief of the 2C AD, representing an eagle holding an oak-wreath in his claws; lion, signed by *Bassallectus*. Two Byzantine lions flank the entrance.

The Baroque INTERIOR is on a vast scale, with a nave 18m broad. The effect of immensity is enhanced by the manner in which the lines of the vaulting continue those of the massive pillars, and the lines of the apse those of the nave. From the end near the entrance can be seen the surprising effect of relief attained by *Giov. Odazzi* in his contorted group of Fallen Angels, on the vault above the high altar. On the ceiling are the Triumph of the Order of St Francis, by *Baciccia*, and the Evangelists, by *Luigi Fontana*.—SOUTH AISLE. The 1st chapel contains a Greek 15C Madonna donated to the church by Cardinal Bessarion (see below). Against the 2nd pillar is a monument to Clementina Sobieska, queen of James III (see below), by *Fil. Valle*. In the Baroque 3rd chapel remains of 15C frescoes were discovered behind the apse (difficult to see) in 1959. The chapel at the end of the aisle has eight columns from the 6C church. The high altarpiece, the largest in Rome, of the Martyrdom of Saints Philip and James, is by *Dom. Muratori*. On the right, tombs of Count Giraud de Caprières (1505) and Cardinal Raffaele Riario, perhaps to a design of Michelangelo; on the left, the beautiful monument of Cardinal Pietro Riario, of the *School of And. Bregno*, with a Madonna by *Mino da Fiesole*.

In the CRYPT (in the chapel ahead to the left), is the fine tomb by the school of And. Bregno, of Raffaele della Rovere (died 1477), brother of Sixtus IV and father of Julius II. Foundations of the earlier church can be seen here.—North Aisle. At the E end, *Mausoleum of Clement XIV, by *Canova*, and on the 2nd pillar is the tomb of Cardinal Bessarion (1389–1472), the illustrious Greek scholar; 2nd chapel St Joseph of Copertino (the 'flying monk'), by *Gius Cades* (1777), between two columns of verde antico, which are the largest known.— The two Renaissance CLOISTERS, approached from the left of the façade (at No. 51 in the Piazza) are entered. Here is a bas-relief of the Nativity by the school of Arnolfo di Cambio, and a palaeochristian sarcophagus.

The little Baroque *Palazzo Balestra* (formerly *Muti*), at the end of the piazza, was presented by Clement XI to James Stuart, the Old Pretender, on his marriage in 1719. Here were born his sons Charles, the Young Pretender (1720), and Henry, Cardinal York (1725); and here died James, in 1766, and Charles, in 1788.

At the N end of Piazza dei Santi Apostoli Via del Vaccaro leads right
into Piazza della Pilotta. At the E end of the square is the large
Università Gregoriana Pontificia (1930). From here Via dei Lucchesi
runs N past (right) Via della Dataria, leading up to Piazza del
Quirinale, and (left) Via dell' Umiltà, leading to the Corso. Beyond
the cross-roads the street, now called Via di San Vincenzo, continues
to the huge *Fontana di Trevi (Pl. 4; 3), one of the most famous sights
of Rome, and one of the city's most exuberant and successful 18C
monuments. The abundant water, which forms an essential part of
the design of the monumental fountain, fills the little piazza with its
sound although it is being restored in 1989. There is still a rooted
tradition that travellers who throw a coin into the fountain before
leaving the city will return to Rome.

Its waters are those of the 'Acqua Vergine', which Agrippa brought to Rome for
his baths in 19 BC, and which feed also the fountains of Piazza di Spagna,
Piazza Navona, and Piazza Farnese. The aqueduct, which is nearly 20km long,
runs through the Villa Giulia. The original fountain was a simple and beautiful
basin by L.B. Alberti; it was restored by Urban VIII, who is said to have obtained
the necessary funds by a tax on wine. Many famous architects, including
Bernini, Ferdinando Fuga, and Gaspare Vanvitelli presented projects for a new
fountain. In 1732 Clement XII held a competition and *Nicola Salvi* was given
the commission. His theatrical design incorporates, as a background, the entire
façade of Palazzo Poli, which had been completed in 1730. Two giant Tritons,
one blowing a conch, conduct the winged chariot of Neptune. In the side niches
are figures of Health (right) and Abundance (left); the bas-reliefs above
represent the Maiden of the legend from which the water took its name pointing
out the spring to the Roman soldiers, and Agrippa approving the plans for the
aqueduct. The four statues above these represent the Seasons with their gifts.
At the summit are the arms of the Corsini family, with two allegorical figures.
The fountain was completed in 1762, after Salvi's death.
    Opposite is the church of **Santi Vincenzo ed Anastasio**, rebuilt in 1630, with a
Baroque façade by Martino Longhi the Younger. In the crypt of this church, the
parish church of the neighbouring pontifical palace of the Quirinal, are
preserved the hearts and lungs of almost all the popes from Sixtus V (1590) to
Leo XIII (1903).

From Piazza di Trevi Via delle Muratte leads W to the Corso. In Via
della Stamperia, which runs N to the right of the fountain, is the
garden of the Accademia di San Luca (see below), opposite the
Calcografia Nazionale or *Calcografia di Roma*, the most important
collection of copper-plate engravings in the world. Adm, see p 48.

The collection was formed in 1738 by Clement XII and moved in 1837 to its
present site; the building is by Valadier. It contains almost all the engravings of
G.B. Piranesi (1432 plates) and examples of the work of Marcantonio Raimondi,
Rossini, Pinelli, and many others. It has a total of more than 19,600 plates.
Exhibitions are often held, and any items not on display can be seen on request,
and copies purchased.

The street opens out into Piazza dell'Accademia di San Luca. Here is
Palazzo Carpegna, seat of the **Accademia di San Luca**, moved from
the neighbourhood of the Roman Forum when Via dei Fori Imperiali
was built. The academy, founded in 1577 by the painter Girol.
Muziano of Brescia, incorporated the 15C Università dei Pittori
whose members used to forgather in the little church of San Luca.
Muziano's successor, Fed. Zuccari, gave the academy its first stat-
utes, and it soon became famous for its teaching and for its prize
competitions. The eclectic *Galleria dell' Accademia di San Luca is
formed of gifts and bequests from its members, together with
donations from other sources. Adm, see p 48.

The collection is arranged on the third floor (lift).

ROOM I (ahead, beyond the gallery). *Baciccia*, *Portrait of Clement IX; Girolamo* and *Giov. Battista Bassano*, Shepherds and sheep; *Pier. Fr. Mola,* Spinster; *Titian* (attrib.), St Jerome; *Raphael*, *Putto, fragment of a fresco (1512); Iac. Bassano*, Annunciation to the shepherds; *Marcello Venusti*, Deposition; Presumed mask of Michelangelo; *Carletto Caliari*, Venus with a mirror; *Seb. Conca*, La Vigilanza; *Carlo Maratta*, Death of Sisera; *Poussin* (copy of Titian), Triumph of Bacchus; *Titian* (attrib.), Portrait of Marino Cornaro.

R. II. Donation of Baron Michele Lazzaroni. *Paris Bordone*, Seduction; *Titian* (attrib.), *Portrait of Ippolito Rimanaldo; *G.B. Piazzetta*, Judith and Holofernes; *Cavalier d'Arpino*, Perseus and Andromeda, Taking of Christ; *Francesco di Giorgio Martini*, Madonna and Child; *Fed. Barocci*, Rest during the flight into Egypt; *School of Lorenzo di Credi*, Annunciation; *Baciccia*, Madonna and Child; *Florentine school of 15C*, Madonna and Child; *Flemish school of 17C*, Portrait of a woman; *Fed. Zuccari*, *Self-portrait; *Alessandro Allori*, Portrait of a woman.

R. III. Works of the 18C and 19C. *Dom. Pellegrini*, Augustus Frederick, duke of Sussex, Self-portrait, Hebe; *Gius. Grassi*, Portraits of the architect Henry Wood and of Vinc. Camuccini; *Mme. Brossard de Beaulieu*, Niobe; *Angelica Kauffmann*, Hope; *Anton Wiertz*, Portrait of the architect Angelo Uggeri; *Mme Vigée le Brun*, *Self-portrait; *Alessandro d'Este* (?), Bust of Canova; *Joseph Nollekens*, Bust of Piranesi.

R. IV. *Aniello Falcone*, Jacob's Dream; *Nicholas Berchem*, Cattle and shepherds in the Roman Campagna; *P. van Bloemen*, Cattle scene, Horses; *Sweerts*, Genre scene; *Giov. van Bloemen*, Pastoral scene; *Sweerts*, Interior scene, Drinker, Genre scene, Woman combing her hair; *Giov. van Bloemen*, Pastoral scene; *Master of the St Lucy Legend*, Virgin; *16C German School*, Deposition.

R. V. *Giovanni Bilivert*, Tarquin and Lucretia; *Canaletto*, Architectural perspective; *Giov. Paolo Pannini*, Landscapes with Roman ruins; *Van Dyck*, *Madonna and Child with angels; *Rubens*, Nymphs crowning Abundance; *John Parker*, Landscape; *Jan Asselijn*, Roman Campagna; *Palma Giovane*, Susanna; *Philip Wouwermans*, White horse; *Jan van Mytens*, Admiral Neewszom Kostenaer; *Salvator Rosa* (?), Study of cats' heads; *Philip Peter Roos (Rosa da Tivoli)*, Shepherd and animals; *Van Dyck*, Madonna and Angels (drawing for the painting above).

R. VI. (GALLERY). *Fr. Trevisani*, Scourging of Christ, St Francis; *Bened. Luti*, Mary Magdalene at the feet of Christ, *Self-portrait; *Anton von Maron*, Portraits of academicians Raphael Mengs, Teresa Mengs von Maron, Vincenzo Pacetti, Caterina Cherubini Preciado, Thomas Jenkins; *G.B. Canevari*, James II as a child, partial copy of Van Dyck's portrait of the children of Charles I in the Galleria Sabauda in Turin; *And. Locatelli*, Two genre scenes, Two landscapes; *Guercino*, Venus and Cupid (detached fresco); *Claude Joseph Vernet*, *Seascape; *Gasp. Vanvitelli*, View of Tivoli, Porto di Ripa Grande.—Sculpture. *Clodion* (?; formerly attrib. to Bernini), *Bust of a young girl; *Tribolo*, Allegorical figure of a river (terracotta).

R. VII. *Seb. Conca*, Marriage of St Catherine; *Baciccia*, Sketch for the Birth of St John Baptist in Santa Maria in Campitelli; *Sassoferrato*, Madonna and Child; *Michele Rocca*, St Cecilia; *Angelo Massarotti*, Madonna and sleeping Child; *Henrick van Somer*, *St Jerome and the Sadducees; *J.F. de Troy*, Faustulus finding Romulus and Remus; *Guido Reni*, L'Addolorata; *Ciro Ferri*, Martyrdom of St Luke.

R. VIII. Terracotta reliefs from prize competitions held in the 18C. *Pierre Legros the Younger*, The arts paying homage to Clement XI; *Michele Slodtz*, St Theresa transfixed by an angel; *Alessandro Algardi*, Leo XI and Henry IV.

STAIRCASE. *Aristide Sartorio*, Monte Circeo; *Fr. Hayez*, Il Vincitore; *Canova*, Self-portrait and Bust of Napoleon; *Pietro da Cortona*, Copy of Raphael's Galatea; *Guido Reni*, Fortune, Bacchus and Ariadne; *Pietro Bracci*, Sketch in terracotta.

Paintings and sculpture by 20C academicians, donated by the artist or his family, including works by Giorgio Morandi, Fausto, Pirandello, Felice Casorati, and Emilio Greco, are no longer on view.

The SALE ACCADEMICHE have also been closed to the public, except on St Luke's Day (18 October). They contain more important works from 15C to the present day.

Just N of the Accademia is the busy VIA DEL TRITONE. This street ascends gradually from Largo Chigi in the Corso, to Piazza Barberini. Half-way is *Largo del Tritone*, entered from the N by Via Francesco

Crispi and Via Due Macelli. On the S side Via del Traforo leads to the *Traforo Umberto I* (Pl. 4; 3), a road tunnel under the Quirinal Gardens, 347m long, built in 1902–5.

On the N side of Largo del Tritone, is Via Due Macelli, which runs NW. In the first street to the left, Via Capo le Case, is the church of SANT' ANDREA DELLE FRATTE, which belonged to the Scots before the Reformation. Here in 1678 Aless. Scarlatti was married.

The tower (unfinished), and refined fantastical campanile, both by *Borromini*, were designed to make their greatest impression when seen from Via Capo le Case.

INTERIOR. In the 2nd chapel on the right is the tomb of Miss Falconet (1856), with a recumbent figure by the American artist *Harriet Hossmer.* In the vestibule of the side door is the tomb of Angelica Kauffmann (1741–1807). The cupola and apse were decorated in the 17C by *Pasquale Marini*, and the three huge paintings of the Crucifixion, Death and Burial of St Andrew are by *G.B. Lenardi, Lazzaro Baldi*, and *Fr. Trevisani*. By the high altar are two beautiful

Angel sculpted by Bernini for Ponte Sant' Angelo now in Sant' Andrea delle Fratte

*Angels by *Bernini*, sculpted for Ponte Sant'Angelo but replaced on the bridge by copies.—The Cloister has four cypresses.

Via Due Macelli leads into the long and irregular ***Piazza di Spagna*** (Pl. 4; 1), for centuries the centre of the artistic and literary life of the city. Foreign travellers usually chose their lodgings in the pensions and hotels in the vicinity of the square, and here the English colony congregated. John Evelyn, on his first visit to Rome in 1644 stayed near the piazza. Keats died in a house on the square, the British Consul formerly had his office here, and there is still a well-known English tea-room. In the neighbouring Via del Babuino is the English church. The piazza retains a cosmopolitan atmosphere, always crowded with Romans and visitors. The elegant streets leading out of the W side of the piazza to the Corso are famous for their fashionable shops: Via Condotti, Via Frattina, and Via Borgognone are also now pedestrian precincts. At the S end of the piazza, between Via Due Macelli and Via di Propaganda is the *Collegio di Propaganda Fide*, with a façade (on Via di Propaganda) by Borromini (1622). The detailed friezes are particularly fine. The college, which has the privilege of extraterritoriality, was founded for the training of missionaries (including young foreigners) by Urban VIII as an annex to the Congregazione di Propaganda Fide established by Gregory XV in 1622. The Column of the Immaculate Conception (1857; being restored), commemorates the establishment by Pius IX in 1854 of the dogma of the Immaculate Conception of the Virgin Mary. On the W side, opposite the small Piazzetta Mignanelli, is *Palazzo di Spagna*, which gave the piazza its name, the residence since 1622 of the Spanish ambassador to the Vatican. It is a good building with a fine courtyard by Ant. Del Grande (1647).

In the narrow centre of the piazza is the *Fontana della Barcaccia*, the masterpiece of Pietro Bernini, father of a more famous son. The design (a leaking boat) is well adapted to the low water pressure of the fountain. The scenographic ***Scalinata*** or **Spanish Steps** were built in 1721–25 by Fr. De Sanctis to connect the piazza with the church of the Trinità dei Monti and the Pincio. The famous monumental flight of 137 steps, which rises between picturesque houses, some with garden terraces, has alway been well loved by Romans and foreigners. It is a masterpiece of 18C town planning. Every day there is a gorgeous display of flowers for sale at the foot, and the steps are covered with magnificent tubs of azaleas at the beginning of May. The elegant 18C house, on the right looking up, is the **House of John Keats** (tablet; entered from No. 26 in the Piazza), in which the poet died on 23 February 1821. He is buried in the Protestant Cemetery. The house is now a Keats-Shelley memorial and museum (adm see p 49) with a library, and relics of Keats, Shelley, Byron, and Leigh Hunt. In the house opposite, built by De Sanctis to form a pair with this one at the foot of the steps, 'Babington's English tea-rooms' survive. The piazza is particularly attractive at its N end with a row of 18C houses and four tall palm trees.

In the fashionable VIA CONDOTTI, named after the conduits of the Acqua Vergine, is the renowned *Caffè Greco* founded in 1760, and a national monument since 1953. Its famous patrons included Goethe, Gogol, Berlioz, Stendhal, Taine, Baudelaire, and Wagner, and it is decorated with personal mementoes, self-portraits, etc. Farther down is the 17C palace of the Grand Master of the order of the Knights of St John of Jerusalem.—At the NW end of the piazza Via della Croce leads to Via Bocca di Leone in which (right) at the corner of Vicolo del Lupo, was the Brownings' Roman residence.—VIA DEL

BABUINO, opened in 1525, connects Piazza di Spagna with Piazza del Popolo. Rubens lived here in 1606–08, and Poussin in 1624. In the neighbouring streets many artists still have their studios and it is the centre of the Bohemian artistic life of the city. It is also famous for its antique shops. It takes its name from a 16C fountain statue which has been placed beside the church of *Sant'Atanasio dei Greci* (by Giac. della Porta). The neo-Gothic English church of *All Saints* (Pl. 3; 2) was built in 1882 by G.E. Street. The apse mosaics were designed by Burne-Jones and the ceramic tiles by William Morris. On the right, near Vicolo Alibert, was the studio in which Thorvaldsen succeeded Flaxman as occupant; and parallel on this side is the 16C VIA MARGUTTA, the residence of Dutch and Flemish painters in the 17C. It is still a street of artists with art galleries and studios (with interesting courtyards and gardens towards the Pincio), and in Spring and Autumn a street fair is held with paintings for sale. More recently Via Margutta has also become Rome's 'Carnaby Street'.

On the terrace at the top of the Spanish Steps is *Piazza della Trinità dei Monti* with its church. From the balustrade there is a view of Rome and of the Villa Medici (see below). The Obelisk, probably brought to Rome in the 2C or 3C AD, when the hieroglyphs were incised (copied from those on the obelisk in Piazza del Popolo) formerly stood in the Gardens of Sallust. It was set up here in 1788 by Pius VI. The church of the **Trinità dei Monti** (Pl. 4; 1), attached to the French Convent of the Minims, was begun in 1493 by Louis XII. It was restored after damage caused by Napoleon's occupation by F. Mazois in 1816 at the expense of Louis XVIII. The unusual 16C façade has a double staircase (by Dom. Fontana).

The INTERIOR (when closed, ring at the door of the small side staircase on the left, but usually only open 10–12, 16–18) is divided by a grille into two parts, only one of which may ordinarily be visited. South side. 3rd chapel, *Assumption, by *Daniele da Volterra*, the best pupil of Michelangelo, whose likeness is seen in the last figure on the right of the picture, which has a remarkable design, but is in very poor condition. The whole chapel is decorated to his design by pupils; 2nd chapel, North side, *Descent from the Cross, an especially fine work (although very damaged) by the same painter, possibly executed from a design by his master.—The other part of the church contains *Frescoes by *Perino del Vaga, Giulio Romano* and others, in finely decorated chapels. The 4th chapel on left (N transept) has the Assumption and Death of the Virgin by *Taddeo Zuccari*, finished by his brother Federico. The vault is painted by *Perino del Vaga*.

From the Piazza the long and straight *Via Sistina* descends to Piazza Barberini and then ascends the Quirinal hill as Via delle Quattro Fontane. This handsome thoroughfare was laid out by Sixtus V as the 'Strada Felice' which ran for some 3km via Santa Maria Maggiore all the way to Santa Croce in Gerusalemme. In this street most of the illustrious visitors to Rome between the days of Napoleon and 1870 seem to have lodged. Nikolai Gogol (1809–52), lived at No. 126; No. 48 housed in succession G.B. Piranesi (1720–78), Bertel Thorvaldsen (1770–1844), and Luigi Canina, the architect and archaeologist (1795–1856). At the top end it still has some well known hotels and elegant shops. Between Via Sistina and Via Gregoriana is the charming and bizarre *Palazzo Zuccari*, built by the artist as his residence and studio. Reynolds lived here in 1752–3 and Wincklemann in 1755–68. In 1900 it was bought by Enrichetta Hertz who left her library, with the palace, to the German government. The *Biblioteca Hertziana* is now one of the most famous art history libraries in the country.

Viale della Trinità dei Monti leads along the edge of the hill to the **Villa Medici** (Pl. 4; 1), the seat of the French Academy since 1803. Here students who win the Prix de Rome at the École des Beaux-Arts in Paris for painting, sculpture, architecture, engraving, or music are sent to study for three years at the expense of the French Government. The grounds are normally open to the public on one or two days of the week (admission, see p 50). Important exhibitions are held in the Villa.

The palace built by Annibale Lippi for Cardinal Ricci da Montepulciano, c 1540, was bought by Ferdinando dei Medici, later Grand Duke of Tuscany in 1576. Here also lived Cardinal Alessandro (later Leo XI). The villa was modified by Bart. Ammannati for the Medici, who here housed their famous collection of ancient Roman sculpture, the masterpieces of which were later transferred to the Uffizi in Florence. In 1801 it was bought by Napoleon and the French Academy, founded in 1666 by Louis XIV, was transferred here. In the 17C Velazquez was a tenant, and Galileo was confined here by the Inquisition from 1630–33.

The villa is famous for its inner *Façade on the garden front decorated with numerous ancient Roman statues, medallions, columns, and bas reliefs (including four beautifully carved panels from the Ara Pietatis, 43 AD; see p 142). The beautiful 16C *Garden has long vistas through hedged walks, and fine views over Rome. The formal garden has several fountains and fragments of ancient sculpture, including the head of Meleager which might even be an original by Skopas.

The *Fountain, with an ancient Roman red granite vase, among the ilexes in front of the Villa Medici dates from 1589 (and is also the work of Ann. Lippi). The cannon ball is said to have been shot from Castel Sant'Angelo by Queen Christina of Sweden, when late for an appointment with the painter Charles Errard who was staying at the French Academy. The view is familiar from many paintings, although it is now somewhat impaired by trees in the foreground. The gently sloping Viale della Trinità dei Monti ends at a Monument by Ercole Rosa (1883) to the Brothers Cairoli, who died at Villa Glori in October 1867 in Garibaldi's attempt to rouse the Romans against the papal government. From this point Viale D'Annunzio descends to Piazza del Popolo while Viale Mickiewicz ascends to the Pincio.

The *Pincio (46m; Pl. 3; 2) was laid out as a Romantic park by Giuseppe Valadier in 1809–14 on the Pincian Hill. Adjoining the Villa Borghese, it forms the largest public garden in the centre of Rome and it is especially crowded on holidays. It was the most fashionable Roman 'passeggiata' in the last century when the aristocracy and foreign visitors came here in their carriages to hear the band play and admire the sunset. The *View from the terrace of the Piazzale Napoleone is dominated by the great cupola of St Peter's.

The Pincio was known as the *Collis Hortulorum* of ancient Rome since it used to be covered with the monumental gardens of the Roman aristocracy and Emperors. On part of the hill was the villa of L. Licinius Lucullus, built after 63 BC. Here, in the same villa, later the property of Valerius Asiaticus, Messalina, the third wife of the Emperor Claudius, murdered its owner. In the 4C it was owned by the Pinci, from whom the name of the hill is derived.

Piazzale Napoleone may be reached also by a fairly steep broad path which rises from the right-hand (NE) side of Viale della Trinità dei Monti near the Cairoli monument. At the top of the path is a terrace on which is the *Casina Valadier* (1813–17), still a fashionable restaurant and open-air café. Among the habitués of its most sumptuous period have been Richard Strauss, Mussolini, Farouk, Gandhi, and Chaing Kai-Shek. The view from its terrace is even better than that from Piazzale Napoleone, into which the pathway leads.

The park is intersected by broad avenues passing between magnificent trees, many of them remarkable specimens of their kind. One of these avenues, Viale dell'Obelisco, runs E to join Viale delle Magnolie in the Villa Borghese (see p 160). The obelisk which gives the avenue its name was placed there in 1822; it was originally erected by Hadrian on the tomb of his favourite Antinous, which was probably near Santa Croce in Gerusalemme. Throughout the park are busts of celebrated Italians from the days of ancient Rome to the present time. Of the fountains, the most notable are the Water Clock, in Viale dell'Orologio, and the Fountain of Moses, reached from there by a subsidiary walk.

The Pincio is bounded on the N and E by massive walls, which define its limits by a right angle. Part of these walls is the *Muro Torto*, or *Murus Ruptus*, the only portion of Aurelian's wall that was not fortified by Belisarius against the Goths. The wall has for centuries seemed on the point of collapsing. When Belisarius proposed to fortify it, the Romans prevented him, saying that it would be

defended by St Peter. Viale del Muro Torto, at the foot of the Pincio, is a busy
road running outside the wall from Piazzale Flaminio to Porta Pinciana.

9   The Villa Borghese and the Villa Giulia

Immediately N of the Aurelian wall is the magnificent *Villa
Borghese (Pl. 11; 5, 6, 7, 8), Rome's most famous public park, with a
circumference of 6km, in which is the suburban villa which houses
the celebrated Galleria Borghese (see below). The main entrance to
the park is on the WSW, from Piazzale Flaminio, just outside Porta
del Popolo.

There are four other entrances: S, from Piazzale Brasile, outside Porta Pinciana;
SE, from Via Pinciana; NE, from Via Mercadante; and N from Viale delle Belle
Arti (see below). Traffic is excluded from the main area of the park.
   The Villa owes its origin, in the 17C, to Cardinal Scipione Borghese, Paul V's
nephew, (see below). In the 18C Prince Marcantonio Borghese (father of Prince
Camillo Borghese who married Pauline Bonaparte) employed Jacob More from
Edinburgh to design the gardens. Early in the 19C the property was enlarged by
the addition of the Giustiniani Gardens and in 1902 it was bought by the State
and handed over to the city of Rome, and opened to the public. The Villa (c 688
hectares) is now connected with the Pincio and the Villa Guilia, so that the three
form one great park, intersected in every direction by avenues and paths, with
fine oaks, giant ilexes, umbrella pines and other trees, as well as statues,
fountains, and terraces.

From the classical main gateway, by Canina (1835), Viale Wash-
ington ascends to the Fountain of Aesculapius with a Roman statue.
From here a road leads (right) to the *Portico Egiziano*, another
imposing entrance, in the form of pylons. Straight on is a monument
to Victor Hugo (1905), presented by the Franco-Italian League. On
the left of the avenue is the *Giardino del Lago*, with hedged walks
and arbours. Here are several fountains, and statues of four Tritons
(1575) by Giacomo della Porta moved here from his fountain in
Piazza Navona in 1874 where they have been replaced by copies. On
an island in the little lake is a Temple of Aesculapius. From Piazza
delle Canestre, farther on, the broad Viale delle Magnolie, connecting the Villa with the Pincio, runs SW, and Viale San Paolo del
Brasile runs SE past a monument to Goethe (by Eberlein) to Piazzale
Brasile. Here is a monument, in Carrara marble, to Byron after
Thorvaldsen (1959). Beyond is Porta Pinciana.—From Piazza delle
Canestre an avenue leads NE to the attractive *Piazza di Siena*, a
rustic amphitheatre with tall pine trees (where equestrian events are
held), beside it is a monument to Humbert I, by Calandra. At the end
of the avenue is a reproduction of the Temple of Faustina.
   On the left 'La Fortezzuola' dates from the 16C. The crenellations
were added in the 19C. In 1926 it became the studio of the sculptor
and musician Pietro Canonica (born 1869) who lived here until his
death in 1959. He left the house and a large collection of his sculpture
to the Commune of Rome as the MUSEO CANONICA (admission, see
p 48).

The first room contains portraits of Donna Franca Florio (1903) and Princess
Emily Doria Pamphili; (1901), and 'Dopo il Voto', a statue of a young nun
exhibited in Paris in 1893. Room II has the model for a monument to Alexander II

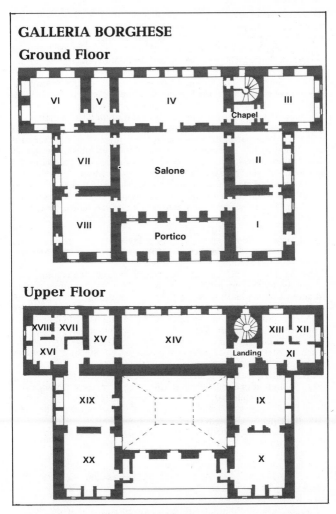

GALLERIA BORGHESE
Ground Floor

Upper Floor

of Russia (destroyed in the Revolution of 1917), and various funerary monuments. Room III. Equestrian statue of Simon Bolivar (1954), and the King of Irak (1933), and several war memorials. The gallery at the right of the entrance contains original models of portraits, notably Lyda Borelli (1920), Alexander II of Russia (1913), Luigi Einaudi (1948), the Duke of Portland (1896), Margaret of Savoy (1903), and casts of portraits of the English royal family made in 1902–22. The house and small studio are also shown, with some fine works of art collected by Canonica (some from Palazzo Reale in Turin).

A road leads right past the 18C *Fontana dei Cavalli Marini*, by Christopher Unterberger, a marble basin supported by four seahorses. A road to the left leads to the Galleria Borghese.

The direct approach to the Palazzina from Porta Pinciana, follows Viale del Museo Borghese. The *Palazzina Borghese* was begun for the Borghese in 1608 by Flaminio Ponzio, Paul V's architect, and continued after his death in 1613 by Jan van Santen (Giov. Vesanzio). It was altered for Marcantonio IV Borghese by Ant. Asprucci and Crist. Unterberger in 1775–90 when the splendid interior decoration was carried out. The villa houses the *Museo and Galleria Borghese* (Pl. 12; 5, 7), a collection of sculpture and paintings, founded by Cardinal Scipione Borghese. He acquired numerous works of art through the good offices of his uncle Paul V, including Raphael's Deposition which he carried off from the church of San Francesco in Perugia. The collection was added to by later members of the family, but much of the sculpture was sold in 1807 to Napoleon I by Camillo Borghese, husband of Paolina Bonaparte, and is now in the Louvre. The number and importance of the surviving paintings, which include examples of almost every school, make this one of the chief Roman galleries, and it was bought by the State in 1902. For nearly two centuries the paintings were housed in Palazzo Borghese; they were brought here in 1891. The Museum of Sculpture is on the ground floor, the Picture Gallery on the first floor. The beautiful formal garden behind the Palazzina can be seen from the first-floor windows. The building has been fenced off since 1984 and is undergoing lengthy structural repairs. Meanwhile only the ground floor is open (adm see p 48), and the entrance is at the rear, reached from Via Raimondo and Parco dei Daini (Viale Giovanni Vasanzio; see Pl. 12; 5).

Ground Floor. The present (temporary) entrance leads into Room IV (see the Plan). Roman numerals are used for the sculptures, arabic numerals for the paintings exhibited here. A fragment found in Rome in 1980 thought to be Michelangelo's first version of the head of Christ for the Rondanini Pietà (now in Milan) is probably to be exhibited in the gallery. PORTICO. XXV. Fragments of a triumphal frieze of Trajan (not from the arch of Claudius).—SALONE. Ceiling fresco by *Mariano Rossi* (1774), representing M. Furius Camillus at the Capitol breaking off peace negotiations with Brennus; on the pavement, five fragments of a Roman mosaic (early 4C) depicting fights of gladiators and bestiarii (found in 1834 at Torre Nuova, near Rome); XXXVI. Colossal figure of a satyr; XXXVII. Colossal head, possibly of Juno; XLI. Augustus; XLVIII. Colossal head of Hadrian; XLIX. Bacchus; L. Colossal head of Antoninus Pius.

Most of the ceilings on this floor were decorated by *G.B. Marchetti*, with numerous assistants, under Marcantonio Borghese (c 1750–60).

R. I (SALA DELLA PAOLINA). *LIV. Pauline Borghese, sister of Napoleon, as Venus Victrix, by *Canova* (1805), justly one of his best known works; *CCLXXI. St John the Baptist, plaster sketch by *J.A. Houdon* for a colossal marble statue, never executed, which was to have been a pendant to his St Bruno in Santa Maria degli Angeli; CCLXXII. Bust of Clement XII, by *Pietro Bracci*.—R. II (SALA DEL DAVIDE). LXXIX, XCV. Panels of a sarcophagus representing the Labours of Hercules and the Birth of Apollo and Diana; LXXX. Frieze depicting the arrival of the Amazons at Troy; *LXXVII. David, by *Bernini* at the age of 25 (1623–24); the face is a self-portrait.— Paintings. 23. *Ann. Carracci*, Samson in prison; 6. *Nicolò dell' Abate*, Landscape with deer hunt; 8. *Girol. da Carpi*, Landscape with procession of magicians; 180. *Guido Reni*, Moses; 192. *Pier Fr. Mola*, Liberation of St Peter.—R. III (SALA DI APOLLO E DAFNE). *CV. Apollo and Daphne, by *Bernini*, executed in 1624; the dramatic moment of capture is well portrayed.—14. *Cigoli*, Joseph and Portiphar's wife; 15. *Giov. Baglioni*, Judith and Holofernes; and, over the doors, two landscapes by *P. Brill*.—In the CHAPEL, frescoed by *Deruet* (d 1660):

16. *Giov. Lanfranco,* Norandino and Lucilla surprised by the ogre (removed for restoration).

R. IV (SALA DEGLI IMPERATORI). Busts of Roman emperors, in porphyry and alabaster, carved in the 17C. The decoration of the room is a notable example of 18C skill and taste in the ornamental arrangement of a great variety of precious marbles, and the incorporation of bas-reliefs and paintings into the design. CXLVII, CL, CLIII, CLVI. Vases in marble from Luni (Carrara), with the Seasons, by *Maximilien Laboureur; Bernini,* CCLXVIII. Rape of Proserpine, another early masterpiece (formerly in the Villa Ludovisi), 7386. Neptune, bozzetto in bronze for a fountain group now in the Victoria and Albert Museum, London; CXXXI. Two alabaster columns; CCXLIX. Farnese Bull, bronze by *Ant. Susini,* after the group now in the Museo Nazionale at Naples.

R. V. (SALA DELL' ERMAFRODITO). CLXXII. Hermaphrodite, a replica of the famous Hellenistic prototype; in niche above, alabaster vase on red porphyry base; CLXXI. Bust of Titus; CLXXIV. Sappho, after a 5C Greek original. On the floor: Roman mosaic of a fishing scene, and above the doors, landscapes by *P. Brill.*—R. VI (SALA DELL' ENEA ED ANCHISE). *CLXXXI. Bernini,* Aeneas and Anchises, carved at the age of 15 (1613) jointly with his father (Pietro Bernini); Colossal figure of Truth (on loan from the Bernini estate), sculpted by *Bernini* for the vestibule of his palace in Via del Corso, but left unfinished.—22. *Dosso Dossi,* Saints Cosmas and Damian; 347. *Garofalo,* Conversion of St Paul.—R. VII (SALA EGIZIANA). Paintings by *Tom.* Conca representing the gods and religions of ancient Egypt. CC. Youth riding on a dolphin, intended for a fountain (period of Hadrian); *CCXVI. Young girl, archaic Greek statue (head restored).—R. VIII (SALA DEL FAUNO DANZANTE). *CCXXV. Dancing faun, discovered in 1824 at Monte Calvo (Sabina) and restored under the superintendence of Thorvaldsen.—G. Honthorst,* 27. Susanna and the Elders; 31. Concert; 271. *Giorgio Vasari,* Nativity; 398. *Taddeo Zuccari,* Deposition; 464. *Perino del Vaga,* Holy Family.

From R. IV, a spiral staircase leads to the **Upper Floor** (closed in 1988). Here too arabic numerals are used for the paintings and Roman numerals for the sculptures. LANDING. Above the door, 346. *Sassoferrato,* Copy of Titian's Three Ages of Man; 123. *Luca Cambiaso,* Venus and Cupid.—R. IX. Ceiling decoration by *Antonio von Maron,* Story of Aeneas. *433. *Lor. di Credi,* Madonna and Child; 348. *Botticelli,* Madonna and Child with the infant St John and angels (studio piece); 375. *And. del Sarto,* Pietà with saints, an early predella; 439. *Fra Bartolomeo,* Holy Family; 369. *Deposition (or Christ carried to the Sepulchre) by *Raphael,* signed and dated 1507 and restored in 1972. Many preparatory sketches exist for this unusual painting, atypical of Raphael's work, which was executed for Atalanta Baglioni of Perugia in memory of her dead son. It shows the influence of Michelangelo. It was taken from the church of San Francesco in Perugia by Paul V and Cardinal Scipione Borghese. The *Lady with a unicorn (371.), possibly the portrait of Maddalena Strozzi, is another fine work by *Raphael.* The *Portrait of a man (397.) is also now generally attrib. to *Raphael.* 401. *Perugino,* Madonna; 343. *Piero di Cosimo,* Madonna and Child with St John and angel musicians; *377. *Pinturicchio,* Christ on the Cross, with Saints Jerome and Christopher.—R. X. Ceiling panels by *Crist. Unterberger,* Scenes in the life of Hercules.—*461. *Andrea Salario,* Christ carrying the Cross; *Sodoma,* 459. Holy Family, 462. Pietà; 335. *Alonso Berruguete,* Madonna and Child and Saints; 88. *And. del*

Brescianino, Portrait of a woman; *334. Andrea del Sarto*, Madonna and Child with St John; 399. *Ridolfo del Ghirlandaio*, Portrait of a young man; 435. *Marco d'Oggiono*, Christ blessing; 514. *Master of the Pala Sforzesca* (16C Lombard), Head of a woman; 287. *School of Dürer*, Portrait of a man; 326. *Lucas Cranach*, Venus and Cupid (harshly restored); 328. *Puligo*, Mary Magdalene; *444. Bronzino*, Youthful St John the Baptist; 332. *Rosso Fiorentino*, Holy Family.

From R. IX is the entrance to R. XI. *Lor. Lotto*, *185. Portrait of a man (possibly a self-portrait), *193. Madonna and Child with saints; *Savoldo*, 139. Portrait of a boy; *547. Tobias and the angel; 163. *Palma Vecchio*, Madonna and Child, with saints.—R. XII. 364. *Pietro da Cortona*, Portrait of Marcello Sacchetti; 542. *Pompeo Batoni*, Madonna and Child; 515. *Ann. Carracci*, Jupiter and Juno; 549. *Sim. Cantarini*, Holy Family; 318. *Carlo Dolci*, Madonna and Child; 231. *Cavalier d' Arpino*, Flight into Egypt; *55. Domenichino*, Music (formerly known as the Cumaean Sibyl); 81. *Lavinia Fontana*, Portrait of a young boy; 382. *Sassoferrato*, Madonna and Child; 83. *Ann. Carracci*, Head of a young boy laughing.—R. XIII. *Guglielmo della Porta*, Bas-relief of the Crucifixion, in wax; *Scipione Pulzone*, 313. Holy Family, 80. Portrait of a woman; 432. *Dom. Puligo*, Holy Family; 458. *Franciabigio*, Madonna and Child with St John; 320. *Giulio Romano* (?), Madonna and Child.

R. XIV. This large room was formerly a loggia (until 1786). Ceiling frescoes by *Giov. Lanfranco* of the gods on Olympos, restored by Dom. Corvi (who was responsible for the lunettes).—Opposite the windows, *Fr. Albani*, 35, 40, 44, 49. Mythological scenes (Venus, Adonis, Vulcan, Diana); above the door, 42. *Guercino*, Return of the prodigal son; 110. *Caravaggio*, *Madonna of the Serpent, painted for the Palafrenieri (the Papal Grooms), who placed it in St Peter's, from where it was later removed for what was considered its excessive realism; 41. *Lionello Spada*, Concert; *Caravaggio*, *455. David with the head of Goliath, 136. Boy with basket of fruit, 534. Boy crowned with ivy, 56. St Jerome; 53. *Domenichino*, Diana the huntress; 43. *Ant. Carracci*, Burial of Christ; *Caravaggio*, 267. St John the Baptist.—Sculpture. *Bernini*, *CXVIII. Young Jupiter with the goat Amalthea; CCLXV, CCLXVI. Portraits of Cardinal Scipione Borghese; *CCLXIX. Terracotta sketch for the equestrian statue of Louis XIV; the statue, which is less fine than the sketch, was altered to represent Q. Curtius Rufus and is in the park at Versailles; *CLX. Aless. Algardi*, Sleep, an admirably carved figure of a boy, in nero antico, asleep, with a dormouse by his side.

R. XV. On the ceiling, *Gaetano Lapis*, Allegory of Aurora. *411. Rubens*, Descent from the Cross (formerly attributed to Van Dyck); *Bernini*, 554, 545. Two self-portraits, 555. Portrait of a boy; *376. Andrea Sacchi*, Clemente Merlini; 403. *Fed. Barocci*, St Jerome.—R. XVI. On the ceiling, *G.B. Marchetti*, Flora; *Iac. Bassano*, *26. Nativity, 144. Last Supper, 120. Ewe and lamb, 565. Adoration of the Magi, 127. Holy Trinity; 30. *Girol. da Treviso*, Sleeping Venus.—R. XVII. On the ceiling, *Gius. Cades*, Story of Walter of Angers, returning unrecognized to his daughter's house. *Garofalo*, 240. Madonna and Child; *Lod. Mazzolino*, 247. Nativity, 451. Magi, 223. Christ appearing to Thomas; *Fr. Francia*, 57. St Francis; 390. *Ortolano*, Descent from the Cross; *Fr. Francia*, 65. St Stephen, 61. Madonna and Child; *Lod. Mazzolino*, 218. Adoration of the Magi; and above, *Scarsellino*, 222. Madonna and Child, 169. Christ in the house of the Pharisee, 226. On the road to Emmaus, 219. Venus bathing.—R. XVIII. Dutch and Flemish Schools. Ceiling decoration by *Benigne Gagneraux*, Antiope and Jupiter. *253. *Frans Francken*, Picture dealers; 272. *Pieter Codde*, Guardroom; 291. *David Teniers the Younger*, Topers; 284. *Gillis van Tilborgh*, Inn interior; 277. *Rubens*, Susanna and the Elders; 279. *Abraham Cuylenborch*, Bath of Diana; 354. *Paul Brill*, Harbour scene.

R. XIX. The ceiling of this room was decorated by the Scots painter *Gavin Hamilton* (1723–98), Story of Paris. *Dosso Dossi*, *217. Circe, 1. Apollo, 220. Adoration of the Shepherds, *304. Diana and Callisto; *125. *Correggio*, Danaê; *Marco Basaiti*, 129. Adam, 131. Eve; 85. *Parmigianino*, Portrait of a man.—Sculpture. *Aless. Algardi* (?), *CCLXX. Bust of Cardinal Domenico Ginnasi, CCLXVII. Vincenza Danesi.—R. XX. Ceiling paintings by *P. Ant. Novelli*, Mythological subjects. *Titian*, *147. Sacred and Profane Love, the masterpiece of the painter's youthful period. The subject is somewhat ambiguous, as both women have identical portraits. 188. *Titian*, St Vincent Ferrer (previously regarded as the portrait of St Dominic), *396. *Antonello da Messina*, Portrait of a man; 450. *Vitt. Carpaccio*, Portrait of a woman; 445. *Palma Vecchio*, Portrait of a man; 170. *Titian*, Venus blindfolding Cupid; *Paolo Veronese*, *137. Preaching of the Baptist; 101. St Anthony preaching to the fishes; 194. *Titian*, Scourging of Christ; 157. *Palma Vecchio*, Virgin and Saints; 132. *Giorgione* (?), The Passionate shepherd; *176. *Giov. Bellini*, Madonna and Child.

Behind the Palazzina is the Garden of Venus, with the picturesque Venus Fountain. A short road leads SE to Via Pinciana, with one of the subsidiary entrances to the park. Viale dell'Uccelliera runs NW to Viale del Giardino Zoologico, in which is the entrance to the **Zoological Gardens** (Pl. 11; 6), established in 1911 and enlarged in 1935. The gardens (with a restaurant) cover an area of about 12 hectares. The collection is strong in bears and large cats. Admission, see p 50.

In Via Ulisse Aldovrandi, on the N side of the Zoological Gardens, and accessible from there also are the *Zoological Museum* (1932) and the *African Museum* with an interesting *Shell Museum* in an annexe (sometimes open on Saturday).

Viale del Giardino Zoologico continues to the exit of Villa Borghese on Viale delle Belle Arti. In this Avenue, on the right, is the **Palazzo delle Belle Arti** (Pl. 11; 5), by Cesare Bazzani (1911; enlarged 1933). It contains the ***Galleria Nazionale d'Arte Moderna** (*National Gallery of Modern Art*; admission see p 49), the most important collection extant of 19–20C Italian art, founded in 1883. Important exhibitions are frequently held. The Gallery has been undergoing a lengthy structural restoration and rearrangement for years: in 1988 only twelve rooms of early 20C works were open, having been modernized and rearranged, and five rooms of 19C works. These five rooms may soon be closed and others opened as the 19C galleries are gradually repaired and rearranged. The rooms with works from 1945–72 have been modernized but are not yet open to the public. All the other room numbers will probably change when other sections of the gallery are reopened.

On the right of the entrance hall are the group of rooms recently reopened to display early 20C art. The works are displayed chronologically, and are well labelled, and excellent handsheets are available in each room. In the CORRIDOR: four large paintings of *Spring by *Galileo Chini* (1914; representative of Italian Art Nouveau); sculptures by *Duilio Cambellotti*, and two landscapes by

Giulio Aristide Sartorio.—In the small room to the right, portraits by *Armando Spadini*, including *The Painter and his wife.

Room I. The first decade of the century. *Giacomo Balla*, Portrait in the open, 1902, Villa Borghese: Il Parco degli Daini, 1910; *Umberto Boccioni*, Landscape, 1910; *Giorgio de Chirico*, Battle of the Centaurs, 1909; *Amedeo Modigliani*, Portrait of a lady with a collar, 1917; *Paul Cézanne*, Le Cabanon de Jourdan, 1906; *Giorgio Morandi*, Still life with silver plate, 1914; *Gustav Klimt*, *The Three Ages of Man, 1905; *Modigliani*, Nude.—Room II. Futurism. *Giacomo Balla*, Line of Velocity + Form + Noise, 1915, Bridge of Velocity, 1913/14; *Umberto Boccioni*, Ungracious Portrait, Horse + Rider + house; *Georges Braque*, Still Life, 1911; *Gino Severini*, Girl + Road + Atmosphere, 1913; *Boccioni*, Portrait of Maestro Busoni, Silvia; *Enrico Prampolini*, Figure + Window, 1914; and works by *Alberto Magnelli*.—Room III. The Twenties. *Piet Mondrian*, Large Composition A, 1919; *Laszlo Moholy-Nagy*, Yellow Cross Q.7; *Marcel Duchamp*, La Boîte-en-valise; *Giorgio de Chirico*, Hector and Andromaca; *Roberto Melli*, Study of a head, 1919; *Carlo Carrà*, Oval of the apparitions, 1918; *Giorgio Morandi*, Still Life, 1918 (a good work of the Metaphysical period).

The VERANDA exhibits sculpture (1920–30). *Libero Andreotti*, The Pardon; *Arturo Martini*, Relief of Orpheus; *Francesco Messina*, Boy at the sea; *Adolfo Wildt*, Bust of Arturo Toscanini. Numerous busts by *Bruno Innocenti, Francesco Messina, Arturo Martini*, and others. *Libero Andreotti*, Affrico and Mensola; works by *Giacomo Manzù*.—The SALONE is divided into sections. A. *Ardengo Soffici*, Washing the Boy; *Gino Severini*, Group of Things, 1930, Still Life, 1929; *Giorgio de Chirico*, Self-portrait, 1925, Battle of Gladiators, 1933–34, Horseman with red hat, Still Life, 1929; *Alberto Savinio*, Autumn, 1935.—B. *Carlo Carrá*, Horses, 1927, Boy on a horse, 1936; *Mario Sironi*, Solitude, 1925.—C. *Felice Carena*, Bathers, 1925; *Virgilio Guidi*, Head of a girl; *Ubaldo Oppi*, *Fishermen of Santo Spirito; *Virgilio Guidi*, *In the Tram; *Antonio Donghi*, *Hunter, 1929; *Francesco Trombadori*, *Still life with basket of fruit.—D. *Felice Casorati*, *Portraits, *Apples; *Massimo Campigli*, *Sailors' wives, 1934.—E. Works by *Giorgio Morandi*, and *Ottone Rosai*, and *Arturo Tosi*.—F. *Giacomo Balla*, Pessimism and Optimism, 1923; and works by *Fortunato Depero, Gerardo Dottori*, and *Enrico Prampolini*.—G. Works by *Mario Mafai* (including a self-portrait of 1942); *Scipione*, Portrait of his mother, 1930, Portrait of the poet Ungaretti.—H. Works by *Fausto Pirandello*; *Emanuele Cavalli*, *The Bride, 1934; *Giuseppe Capogrossi*, Female Portrait, *The Storm.—The sculpture in the Salone includes The Sisters (or The Stars) by *Arturo Martini*.

Room IV. Works by *Riccardo Francalancia, Antonio Donghi, Mario Broglio, Roberto Melli* (The Checked Dress), *Filippo De Pisis* (*Still Lives, A road in Paris, etc.).—Room V, *Amerigo Bartoli*, Friends at the café, 1929; *Gregorio Sciltian*, Bacchus at the Hostelry; *Gino Severini*, The Married couple, 1939; *Afro*, Self-portrait, 1935; and works by *Alberto Zivieri*.—Room VI. The 'Sei' of Turin (Enrico Paulucci, Carlo Levi, Gigi Chessa, Francesco Menzio, Nicola Galante, and Jessie Boswell). *Walter Richard Sickert*, Portrait of Baron Aloisi; *Wassily Kandinksky*, Angular Line, 1930, Joan; *Mirò*, Seated woman, 1935; *Carlo Levi*, Portrait of a friend, 1930; works by *Pio Semeghini*; *Maurice Utrillo*, Quai d'Anjou, 1925.—Beyond is a small room with two paintings by *Giacomo Balla*: The Stream of Borghetto, 1938, and the Queue in the street for lamb, 1942.—To the right is a room of early 20C engravings.—In the VERANDA are sculptures (*Pericle Fazzini*, Bust of Giuseppe Ungaretti, 1936; *Mirko*, David, 1937).

In 1988 the 20C rooms ended here. The other group of rooms, also on the right of the central halls of the building will exhibit art from 1945–72. Artists represented include: *Renato Guttuso, Lucio Fontana, Alberto Burri, Ettore Colla,* and *Umberto Mastroianni*. Also here will be exhibited: *Claude Monet*, Lilies; *Vincent Van Gogh*, L'arlesienne; *Edgar Degas*, After the Bath; *Paul Cézanne*, Track between rocks, Landscape with rocks (double water-colour); and works by *Kandinsky, Klee, Max Ernst*, and *Alberto Giacometti*.

The central halls of the building are used for exhibitions. A flight of stairs to the left leads up to the 19C rooms (in the process of being repaired and rearranged). The room numbers will probably change when all the rooms have been reopened. At present the first rooms still bear the old numbering. (Rooms XXII and XXXIV). *Frank Brangwyn*, Boys bathing; *Dante Gabriele Rossetti*, *Mrs William Morris; *Rodin*, Bust of the sculptor Dalou; *Bronze Age, Bozzetto for a ballerina.—R. XXIII displays large historical paintings. *Giovanni Fattori*, Battle of Custoza, 1880; *Aristide Sartorio*, Heroes, Diana of the Ephesians and Slaves; *Michele Cammarano*, Battle of Dorgali.—Sculpture: *Ettore Ximenes*, Rinascita; *Ercole Rosa*, Diana; *Vincenzo Vela*, 'Victims of Work' (bronze relief);

Adolfo Wildt, Bust of Atte; *Achille d'Orso*, *Proximus Tuus (weary tiller).—R. XXIV. Italian artists in Paris. *Marco Calderini*, Winter sadness; *Fed. Zandomeneghi*, House at Montmartre; *Giov. Boldini*, Two portraits of women, *Portrait of Giuseppe Verdi; *Gius. de Nittis*, *Bois de Boulogne; *Eduardo Gordigiani*, Portrait of a woman; *Urbano Nono*, 'Il Turbine' (statue); and three terracottas by *Giovanni Battista Amendola*.—R. XXVI. Works by *Antonio Mancini* and *Edoardo Dal Bono*.—R. XXVII. Paintings by *Ettore Tito* and *Gaetano Previati*, and sculptures by *Leon. Bistolfi* (Resurrection). In 1988 the 19C collection ended here.

To the left of the entrance hall will be displayed the rest of the 19C collection, including the following works. *Teodoro Matteini*, Portrait of two gentlemen; *And. Appiani*, Portrait of Vincenzo Monti; *Fil. Agricola*, Portrait of Costanza Monti Perticari; *Vinc. Podesti*, Still Life; *Natale Schiavoni*, Portraits; *Henry Raeburn*, Portrait; *George Romney*, The Tempest.—Sculpture. *Pietro Tenerani*, Self-portrait; *Ant. Canova*, Sketch for the monument to Vittorio Alfieri.—*Emile J.H. Vernet*, Portrait of Bariatinsky; *Tom. Minardi*, Blind Homer and the shepherd.—Sculpture by *Pietro Tenerani* and *Lor. Bartolini*.—Neapolitan school. *Dom. Induno*, Two Portraits, News of the Peace of Villafranca, Genre scene; *Giacinto Gigante*, Sea scene, Landscapes, and Views of Naples; *Ipp. Caffi*, View of Rome from Monte Mario; *Massimo d'Azeglio*, Landscape, Azalea; *Fr. Hayez*, The Bather; *Giov. Carnovali (Il Piccio)*, three *Portraits; *Gius. Molteni*, Portrait of a girl.—Works by *Fil. Palizzi*.—*Gioacchino Toma*, In the convent, Luisa Sanfelice in prison, Portrait, Sea scene, Villa Garzoni; *Mich. Cammarano*, Portrait, Landscapes, Roman Scene, Piazza San Marco; *Dom. Morelli*, Portrait of David Wonviller, Half-length study of a woman, Head of an angel, *Portraits, Self-portrait, Embalming of Christ, Christ walking on the waves.

The collection dedicated to the group of Tuscan artists known as the *Macchiaioli* includes works by *Ant. Puccinelli*, Portrait of Nerina Badioli; *Giov. Fattori*, Battle of Magenta; *Gius. Abbati*, Oxen by the sea; *Giov. Fattori*, *Portrait of his first wife; *Silvestro Lega*, *The visit; *Odoardo Borrani*, Two landscapes; *Fattori*, Portrait of Patrizio Senese; *Vinc. Cabianca*, Village scenes, Study of a woman; *Cristiano Banti*, Tuscan country girl; *Adriano Cecioni*, Two interior scenes; *Telemaco Signorini*, Florence ghetto, Rain in summer, Interior scene, A street in Ravenna; *Fattori*, Battle scenes; *Giov. Boldini*, Interior with figure; *Gius. Abbati*, Tuscan road; *Vito d'Ancona*, Signora with umbrella; *Cabianca*, Two landscapes; *Odoardo Borrani*, Ponte alle Grazie, Florence.—Sculpture. *Adriano Cecioni*, Bust of Giosué Carducci, Mother; *Valmone Gemignani*, Giovanni Fattori.

Historical paintings, including works by *Gius. Camino, Dom. Morelli, Napoleone Nani, Fed. Faruffini, Ipp. Caffi*, and *Massimo d'Azeglio.—Tranquillo Cremona*, Marco Polo; *Fr. Hayez*, Sicilian vespers.—Sculpture. *Giov. Dupré*, Sappho; *Ant. Allegretti*, Fallen Eve.—Works from the studio of *Dom. Morelli*.—Sculpture. *Giulio Monteverde*, Edward Jenner experimenting on a young boy; *Alf. Balzico*, Cleopatra.—Works by *Ces. Mariani, Enrico Gamba* and others.—*Fil. Palizzi*, Battle scenes, Forest of Fontainebleau; *Girol. Induno*, Portrait of Garibaldi.—Sculpture. *Ercole Rosa*, Bust and head of Garibaldi.—Lombard school. *Ant. Fontanesi*, Bath of Diana, The Po, Landscapes and country scenes; *Giac. Favretto*, After the bath, Waiting for the bride; *Tranquillo Cremona*, Two cousins; *Luigi Conconi*, Midnight variations, Sick child.—Sculpture. *Paolo Troubetzkoy*, Indian, My wife, *Mother and child.—*Sculpture by *Medardo Rosso*.—Landscapes by *Eugenio Gignous, Giov. Segantini, Gius. Pellizza* and others.—*Mosè Bianchi*, Chioggia Canal; *Fil. Carcano*, Sea scene; *Ces. Tallone*, Portrait of a child; *Emilio Gola, Pietro Fragiacomo*, Various paintings.—Sculpture, *Giov. Focardi*, Sweet Rest; *Ernesto Bazzaro*, The widow; *Giov. Mayer*, The Convalescent; *Giov. Prini*, Bust of a woman.—*Alberto Bonomi*, Val d'Adige; *Adriano Baracchini*, Sunset; *Ces. Maggi*, Nevaio 1908.—Northern Italian school. *Emma Ciardi*, Swallows and butterflies.

Fr. Paulo Michetti, Il voto, Studies, *Head of a child.—Sculpture. *Costantino Barbella*, April.—*Luigi Galli*, *Portraits, Galatea, Holy Family; *Norberto Pazzini*, Landscapes; *Luigi Serra*, St Bonaventura and St Francis, Entering Prague 1880; *Gius. Ferrari*, Two portraits; *Nino Costa*, Landscapes; *Luigi Serra*, Venetian scenes.—Sculpture. *Dan. de Strobel*, Boy and Death; *Fil. Cifariello*, Arnold Böcklin.—Artists of the Roman Campagna. Works by *Achille Vertunni, Gius. Raggio, Alf. Ricci* and others, and *Sculptures by *Vincenzo Gemito*.

European 19C prints and drawings from the collection of Luigi Sprovieri, include works by: Hogarth, Gillray, Cruickshank, Rowlandson, Blake, *Goya, Flaxman, Richter and German artists; Japanese artists: Hiroshige, Utamaro, and Hokusai.—Other 19C European prints and drawings include works by: Prud'hon,

Géricault, Delacroix, Ingres, Corot, Millet, Courbet, Fantin-Latour, Rodin, Manet, Degas, Sisley, Renoir, Pissarro, Toulouse-Lautrec, Gauguin, Edward Münch, Egon Schiele, Whistler, Beardsley, Burne-Jones, William Morris, Fattori, and Signorini.

Outside the Gallery Viale delle Belle Arti widens into Piazza Thorvaldsen, in which, on the right, is a copy of Thorvaldsen's Jason, the gift of the city of Copenhagen. Above the steps is a statue of Simon Bolivar (1934).

On the hill above, in Via Antonio Gramsci, is the *British School at Rome* (Pl. 11; 5), established in 1901 as a School of Archaeology. After the 1911 International Exhibition of Fine Arts in Rome, the site where the British Pavilion had stood was offered to the School by the Commune of Rome. The pavilion designed by Sir Edwin Lutyens, with a façade based on the west front of St Paul's Cathedral, was to be reproduced in permanent materials. In 1912, the School widened its scope to the study of the Fine Arts, Literature, and History of Italy. Scholarships are awarded, and an annual exhibition is held in June of the artists' work. The researches of the School are published annually in 'The Papers of the British School'. This district, known as the VALLE GIULIA, was laid out at the beginning of the century after Viale delle Belle Arti had been opened. Numerous foreign academies and cultural institutions have been established here: on the left of the Viale are the Belgian, Dutch, Swedish, and Rumanian Academies; on the right, in Via Gramsci, beyond the British School, is the Faculty of Architecture of Rome University, and the Austrian Academy.

Farther along Viale delle Belle Arti stands **Villa Giulia*, or correctly *Villa di Papa Giulio* (Pl. 11; 5), built in 1550–55 for pope Julius III by *Vignola*, *Vasari*, and *Bart. Ammannati*, with some help from *Michelangelo*. In the 17C the villa was used to house guests of the Vatican, including Queen Cristina of Sweden in 1665. Since 1889 it has been the home of the **Museo Nazionale di Villa Giulia* (admission, see p 50), devoted mainly to pre-Roman antiquities from Lazio, Umbria, and Southern Etruria. In 1908 the Barberini collection was donated to the museum, and later acquisitions include the Castellani and Pesciotti collections (in 1919 and 1972). Material from excavations in progress at the Etruscan sites of Northern Lazio is also exhibited here. Villa Poniatowsky (1870) in a park to the right of the Villa has recently been acquired by the State, and there are long-term plans to use it to enlarge the museum.

This charming suburban villa has lost much of its 16C decoration, including many pieces of ancient sculpture (which were taken to the Vatican). The façade is of two orders, Tuscan on the ground floor and Composite above. The porch, in rusticated masonry, leads to an ATRIUM, with Corinthian columns and niches for statues. This opens into a semicircular PORTICO, with Ionic columns and arches. The charming vaulted ceiling is painted with vine trellises, birds and putti, and the wall panels are painted in the Pompeian style (attrib. to *Paolo Venale*). Beyond lies the COURTYARD, enclosed by walls with Ionic columns, niches, and reliefs. Some of the delicate stucco decorations by *Ammannati* on the LOGGIA survive. The **NYMPHAEUM, shorn of much of its original ornamentation and in poor repair, was frequently copied in later 16C Italian villas. Two curved staircases lead down from the loggia to the first level, with fountains adorned with statues symbolizing the Tiber and the Arno. On the lower level are a ceiling relief of the miraculous finding of the Acqua Vergine and four marble caryatids. Behind the portico is an aedicula or shrine, with a statue of Hygieia, a Roman copy of a 5C Greek original. The garden extends on either side of the courtyard. On the right is a reconstruction of the Temple of Aletrium (Alatri) by Count Adolfo Cozza (1891), according to the account of Vitruvius and the evidence of the remains (see below). There is a café open at the back of the gardens.

On the left of the Atrium is a Room (A), with frescoes attrib. to Taddeo Zuccari and Prospero Fontana, which is usually closed. The temple relief illustrating the Seven against Thebes from Pyrgi (460

BC) was formerly exhibited here. It has been restored but is not yet on exhibition. The museum is arranged in modern galleries flanking the garden: the entrance is on the left of the semicircular portico. ROOMS 1–5 contain finds from the necropolis of VULCI, where some 15,000 tombs have been found, mostly dating from the 9C–5C BC. R. 1. Two stone sculptures of a Man astride a sea-horse and a Centaur showing Greek influence, found at the tomb entrances.—R. 2 contains fine bronze objects, including ossuaries, buckles, and razors, a statuette of a warrior in prayer with a pointed helmet, large shield, and long plaits (9C from Sardinia), bronze armour dating from the end of the 6C BC, and an *Urn in the shape of a hut (mid-7C BC).— RR. 3 and 4. Attic red and black figure vases imported from Greece or Iona, and local Etruscan-Corinthian ware, including a large amphora by the 'Painter of the Bearded Sphinx', and a black-figure hydra showing women at a fountain.—R.5. Three terracotta models of a

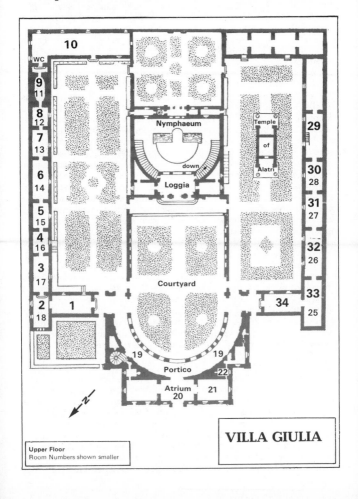

VILLA GIULIA

Upper Floor
Room Numbers shown smaller

temple, a stoa, and a tower, terracotta heads and figurines from Hellenistic Vulci, forming part of a *Stipe* (trench for a votive offering). Recent finds include seated figures of children.—Stairs lead down to the reconstruction of a *Tomb from the necropolis at Cerveteri, with two chambers, containing beds and the belongings of the dead.

ROOM 6. Tomb furniture from the Villanovian and archaic necropolis of BISENZIO-VESENTIUM, including 8C geometric pottery, and a small bronze rustic chariot decorated with figurines which was used as an incense burner (late 8C).—R. 7. Finds from the sanctuary of Portonaccio at VEIO (see p 400) discovered in 1916 and 1939, including the celebrated group of *Apollo and Herakles. These colossal statues in polychrome terracotta (restored) formed part of a votive group representing the contest between Apollo and Herakles for the sacred Hind in the presence of Hermes and Artemis, and are a splendid example of Etruscan sculpture of the late 6C or early 5C BC. They were probably the work of Vulca, a celebrated sculptor of Veio, who is said to have been summoned to Rome by Tarquinius Superbus to execute the statue and decorations for the Temple of Jupiter Capitolinus. Of the other figures in the group there remain only the Hind and the *Head of Hermes. From the same temple is the statue of Latoma holding Apollo as a child, and the antefixes with the head of a gorgon and the head of a Maenad.

RR. 8–10 house finds from the necropolis at CERVETERI (the ancient Caere; 7–1C; see p 404).—R. 8. Terracotta votive heads, sarcophagus 'of the Lions'. Here have been temporarily displayed the three famous gold-leaf plaques from Pyrgi, the Etruscan port of Cerveteri (see p 404), with inscriptions in Etruscan and Phoenician referring to the dedication of the sanctuary to the phoenician 'Astarte' and the Etruscan 'Uni'.—R. 9. Terracotta *Sarcophagus (6C), representing a husband and wife feasting upon a couch; this remarkable and rare specimen bears witness to the skill of the Etruscan artists, evident in the expressive rendering of the features, especially the hands and feet.—R. 10. The glass cases contain a collection of skyphoi (drinking cups), kylixes (cups on stems), vases for perfume and wine, and amphorae (7C–2C). *Glass Case 2*. Protocorinthian skyphoi, with geometric decoration, and a Corinthian krater, with warriors on horseback and chariots. *Case 3*. Bronze work. *Case 6*. Collection of small aryballoi (vases for perfume). *Cases 7–10*. Rare Attic kylix, with lively figures of satyrs dancing, Story of Polyphemus, Vine motif, etc. *Cases 14–17*. Small red-figured kylix, showing two exploits of Theseus and a young cithara player. *Case 19*. Attic red-figured psykter (global vase with cylindrical support), showing Zeus enthroned on one side, and Theseus fighting the Minotaur on the other. *Case 20*. Attic red-figured krater, with hoplite running, and, on the neck, athletes, and Herakles struggling with Kyknos. *Cases 21–24*. Etruscan and Faliscan vases; silver-painted vases from Bolsena.

UPPER FLOOR. ROOMS 11–18 display the ANTIQUARIAN collection; many of the objects here are of unknown provenance. R. 11. Bronze plates from a triumphal chariot, with hoplites and horsemen fighting (6C); buckles.—R. 12. Ploughman at work, found at Arezzo; bronze statuettes, including elongated votive figurines.—RR. 13 and 14 contain bronze domestic objects including mirrors, candelabra, cistae (see below), horse-bits, strigils and small containers for unguents in leather and metal used by athletes. R. 15. Statuette of Veiovis, 1C AD, found in 1955 at Monterazzone, near Viterbo. *Glass Case 4*. *CHIGI VASE found at Formello (Veio), of exquisite workmanship and

the finest extant example of the Protocorinthian style (first half of the
7C BC); among the subjects depicted are a lion-hunt, a hare-hunt, a
troop of soldiers, and the Judgment of Paris.—R. 16. Vases.—R. 17.
Fragment of a krater of Assteas, depicting a comic scene: Ajax,
fleeing from Kassandra, clings to the statue of Pallas Athena.—R. 18.
Etruscan Biga from Castro. Dating from the 6C BC this two-wheeled
chariot was found in 1967 in a tomb beside the skeletons of two
horses (also exhibited here). The chariot, with bronze decorations, is
particularly well preserved.

The CASTELLANI COLLECTION of ceramics (many of them from
Cervéteri) is housed in the hemicycle (19). This was amassed in the
19C by Augusto Castellani, a member of a firm of goldsmiths. The
rooms have a good view of the courtyard and garden of the villa.
Glass Case I. Alabaster vases imported from Greece and Cyprus,
Etruscan vases showing Oriental influence.—*Case 2.* Black- and red-
figure vases, many decorated with animals.—*Case 3.* Two pitchers,
one with the rape of Persephone, the other with Herakles and the
dog Cerberus before Eurystheus.—*Case 4.* Black-figured Attic vases;
Laconian krater decorated with lotus-flowers.—*Case 5.* Two
amphorae signed by Nikosthenes (540–510 BC).—*Case 6.* Group of
miniature kylixes.—*Case 7.* Amphora with large handles, red and
black figured.—*Case 8.* Red-figured Attic vases; pitcher with two
young men and leveret.—*Case 10.* Red-figured Attic vases, and
pelike showing Dionysus, Satyrs, and Maenads.—*Case 11.* Examples
of Faliscan, Campanian, and Apulian ware.—*Case 12.* Ceramics from
Egnatia in Apulia, white- and yellow-figured. Part of the hemicycle is
also used for exhibitions.—On the right are two rooms (20 and 21;
closed for restoration in 1988) which display more vases and bronzes
from the Castellani collection, as well as the PESCIOTTO collection (R.
20) with vases from the Villanovian and archaic periods (8–6C BC),
including incised bucchero ware and bronzes. From R. 21 there is
access to the two small rooms (22) which contain the Castellani
*Jewellery collection (opened on request; a document must be left
with the custodian), beautifully arranged. This is one of the finest
collections of antique jewellery in existence, dating from the Minoan
period, with splendid examples of Hellenistic and Roman, as well as
oriental, works. The exhibits are complemented by a remarkable
series of copies or reworkings made by the renowned Castellani
jewellers in the 19C.

ROOMS 25–33 are being slowly rearranged and restored. Rooms
25–29 exhibit material from the AGER FALISCUS, the area between
Lake Bracciano and the Tiber. The Falisci were an Italic people akin
to the Latins but much influenced by their Etruscan neighbours. R. 25
contains finds from Capena, including an Etrusco-Campanian *Dish
with a war elephant and her baby, evidence of the impression made
in Italy by the elephants of Pyrrhus. Three huge bronze shields,
decorated with quadrupeds and floral motives, from Narce. Vases,
mirrors and other relics from Corchiano and Monte Sant'Angelo. RR.
26–29 are devoted to the necropolis of Falerii Veteres (Civita Castellana). R. 26. Cinerary urn in the form of a small house. Psykter
(wine-cooler) showing the fight of the Centaurs and the Lapiths.
Krater with scenes of the devastation of Troy. Oinochoe, with a battle
of Amazons, and Actaeon being devoured by his hounds; two similar
bowls, with Dionysos and Ariadne and a Faliscan inscription (resembling Latin): 'Today I drink wine, tomorrow I shall have none'.
*Amphora with volutes, showing Eos and Kephalos and Boreas and
Orithyia. Large stamnos (two-handled jar) with two men feasting, a

girl fluteplayer, and two young men, drunk, in the background (c 440 BC); twin stamnoi with Dionysos carrying the Thyrsos, and Eros, with a nude girl seated on a panther skin.—R. 27. Black-figured kylix with Dionysos and Maenads on the outside; red-figured kylix, with men and boys conversing, signed by Hieron. *Rhytons (drinking horns) shaped respectively like a knuckle-bone and a dog's head, masterpieces of Greek ceramic art of the first half of the 5C BC; the first is signed by Syriskos and the second attributed to Brygos. Large *Krater (mid-5C) with girls dancing; krater from S Italy with Belerophon and the Chimaera.—R. 28. Amphorae and stamnoi from Volsinium (Bolsena), painted and with floral decoration. Stamnos, with a scene from the worship of Dionysos Perikonios at Athens. Red-figured *Krater with Herakles and the Nemean lion; *Krater of the end of the 5C, with Herakles being received into Olympos.

In R. 29, on two levels, are sculptures and architectonic terracottas from temples near Falerii Veteres. To the right: part of the decoration from the *Temple of Apollo* at Lo Scasato (4C–2C), with notable antefixes of Persian Artemis and a winged genius. To the left: Decoration of the pediment and entablature from one or both temples in the neighbourhood of Sassi Caduti, and decorative cover-slab from the temple which replaced them, including a representation of fluteplayers.

Below are large figured terracottas which decorated the pediments of each temple. They offer striking examples of the influence of Greek sculpture, and especially good are: *Apollo; fine head of Mercury; female head. In glass cases are excellent examples of temple decoration and cult statues: antefixes with heads of Maenads, of Silenus, and part of an acroterion with two warriors, from Sassi Caduti (early 5C); portraits from the *Stipes* of the Temple at Vignale, the acropolis of Falerii Veteres; female head in peperino, crowned in bronze-leaf, from Celle; head of Zeus from Scasato.

R. 30 contains material from the *Temple of Diana at Nemi* (4C–2C BC), the famous sanctuary of the Golden Bough in the sacred wood beside the lake: lower portion of a cover-slab in gilded bronze, votive objects, terracotta pediment of the temple. Male head from Antemnae (late 4C).—R. 31. Coffin formed from the trunk of an oak-tree (from Gabii); Antefix with maenad's head, from Lanuvium; terracotta model, perhaps of a temple, from Velletri.—R. 32. Collection from the Tomba delle Ambre, at Satricum in the territory of the Volsci, including sculptures from the temple of Mater Matuta (6C BC), and a votive stipe of the 7C BC.—R. 33. ANTIQUITIES FROM PRAENESTE, comprising the *Barberini* and *Bernardini Tombs*, two important examples of the Oriental period (7C BC). The *BARBERINI COLLECTION was formed of objects unearthed between 1855 and 1866 from tombs in the locality of Colombella, just S of the town of Palestrina (p 380), which was built on the site of the ancient Praeneste. Praeneste was a flourishing centre of Latin and Volscian civilization and, as the trade and industry of Etruria and Latium were derived from the same sources, the culture here naturally had much in common with the Etruscan. The Barberini Collection, acquired by the State in 1908, may be regarded (apart from certain additions) as divided into two main groups; the contents of a large tomb covered with marble slabs of the Oriental period (7C BC) and the contents of deep-laid tombs of the 4C–2C BC. THE *BERNARDINI TOMB, discovered in 1876, a trench-tomb lined with tufa and covered by a tumulus, exactly corresponds with the style of the Barberini tombs and with that of the Regolini-Galassi tomb in the Vatican.

The tombs of the Oriental period yielded gold and silver articles, bronzes and ivories, in which Egyptian, Assyrian, and Greek art are mingled. Notable among the goldsmith's work: two *Pectorals, or large buckles, of gold granulated work, decorated with cats' heads, chimaeras, and sphinxes; Patera in silver-gilt with Pharaoh in triumph, horses, and an Assyrian king's hunt; Caldaia, for heating or cooling water, in silver-gilt, with six serpents on the brim, and decorated with horsemen, foot-soldiers, farmers and sheep attacked by lions. Ivories: cups; lion with dead man on his back; mirror-handles (?) shaped like arms. Bronzes: conical vase-stand with fantastic animals in repoussé; throne in sheet-bronze, with ornamental bands and figures of men and animals.

The contents of the 4C–2C tombs include a full collection of bronze mirrors and CISTAE, which contained the mirrors, strigils, spatulae and other implements for the care of the body. The cistae are usually cylindrical, with engraved decoration in repoussé or pierced work, lids adorned with small figures, and feet and handles of cast metal. These toilet boxes were virtually unique to Praeneste (see p 380). Among them is the *CISTAE FICORONI, the largest and most beautiful yet discovered. It is named after Francesco Ficoroni who bought it and gave it to the Kircher collection (now incorporated in the Prehistoric and Ethnographic Museum). On the body of the cista is a representation of the boxing match between Pollux and Amykos, king of the Bebryces, an elaborate design pure in its lines and evidently inspired by some large Greek composition, possibly a wall-painting contemporary with those by Mikon in the Stoa Poikile at Athens. The names of both the maker and the buyer of the cista are recorded in an archaic Latin inscription: *Novios Plautios med Romai fecid, Dindia Macolnia fileai dedit*; and it was no doubt a wedding present.

R. 34. Goldsmith's work; bronze helmet inlaid with silver, from Todi; Attic *Bowl signed by Pampheios, showing Odysseus evading Polyphemos; head from Cagli.

Beyond the Villa Giulia Viale delle Belle Arti goes on past the red-brick church of *Sant'Eugenio* (1951), built to celebrate the 25th anniversary of the episcopal consecration of Pius XII in 1942, to the Via Flaminia, on which is the elegant *Palazzina of Pius IV*, attributed to Pirro Ligorio, who designed the Casina of Pius IV in the Vatican gardens. Via Flaminia leads back to Piazza del Popolo.

10   The Quirinal Hill and Museo Nazionale Romano

To the E of the Victor Emmanuel Monument, beside the two small churches in front of Trajan's Column (p 103), steps lead up to Via 4 Novembre (with the entrance to the Markets of Trajan, p 101). Beyond is the LARGO MAGNANAPOLI (Pl. 4; 5), at the beginning of the busy Via Nazionale. In the centre of the square is a little group of palm trees, with some remains of the *Servian Wall*; in the ancient *Palazzo Antonelli* (No. 158; restored) are other remains in several rooms off the courtyard, including an arch for a catapult. On the right, behind the church of *Santa Caterina da Siena* (not always open), with a good Baroque interior, rises the conspicuous Torre delle Milizie. At the beginning of Via Panisperna, high up on the right, is the tall façade of **Santi Domenico e Sisto** (often closed), reached by a fine

staircase (1654) by *Vincenzo della Greca*. Inside is a huge scenographic fresco (1674–75) by the Bolognese, *Domenico Canuti*, and
in the 1st chapel on the right a sculpture group (Noli me tangere) by
Ant. Raggi.

Via Nazionale (Pl. 4; 5, 4) leads from the largo to Piazza della Repubblica and
the Station. On the right it skirts the extensive garden of the *Villa Aldobrandini*,
built in the 16C for the Duke of Urbino, acquired by Clement VIII (Ippolito
Aldobrandini), and given by him to his nephews. The social centre of
Napoleonic Rome, the villa is now Government property, and contains an
international law library. It gave its name to the famous Roman painting of a
marriage scene found on the Esquiline in 1605 and kept in one of the garden
pavilions until 1838, when it was moved to the Vatican.—Via Nazionale skirts
the villa wall as far as Via Mazzarino, in which (right) is an open gate and steps
which lead up past impressive 2C ruins to the garden. Farther on in Via
Mazzarino, to the left, is the church of *Sant'Agata dei Goti* (if closed, ring at No.
16), built by an Arian community in 462–70, but much restored. The Byzantine
plan remains despite the disappointing 20C restorations, with antique columns
and decorative capitals with pulvins. In the apse is a well-preserved 12–13C
Cosmatesque tabernacle. The picturesque 17C court is hung with ivy. The
original fabric of the church can be seen on leaving the church by the door in
the right aisle.

Farther along Via Nazionale, on the right, is the huge neo-classical head
office of the *Banca d'Italia* by Gaetano Koch (1886–1904), behind a row of palm
trees and colossal lamps. On the left is the *Teatro Eliseo*. Just beyond Via
Milano, (with a road tunnel on the left; see p 156), rises the monumental
Palazzo dell'Esposizione (Pl. 5; 5), erected in 1878–82 to a design by Pio
Piacentini. As an important exhibition centre, it has been undergoing a radical
restoration since 1984 and a new system of illumination has been installed.

The **Galleria Comunale d'Arte Moderna** (entered from Via Milano, but
closed since 1984), will probably be moved to new premises. The works by
Italian and foreign artists from the beginning of the 20C to the present day,
include: *Rodin*, Head of a man, Bust of a woman; *Guglielmo de Sanctis*, Portrait
of Adele Castellani; *Mich. Cammarano*, Landscapes; *Vannutelli Scipione*, Sant'
Onoforio; *Vinc. Cabianca*, Palestrina; *Norberto Pazzini*, Self-portrait. 1924; *G.
Aristide Sartorio*, Terracina; *G. Balla*, Portrait of Nathan, Doubt; *Arturo Noci*,
Oranges; *Sartorio*, The Wise and Foolish Virgins; *Amer. Bertoli*, Circus, Portrait
of Longhi; *Ant. Donghi*, Landscapes; *Fausto Pirandello*, Roman landscape,
Frightened figure, The bathers; *Roberto Melli*, Various works; *Renato Guttuso*,
Self-portrait. Sculpture by *Tom. Bertolino*, Langour, Female nude (half-length).
A. Marasco, Night at Sea; *Renato Guttuso*, Roman roofs; *Carlo Levi*, Carrubo;
Giacomo Manzù, Female head, 1941; *Giorgio Morandi*, Two engravings (still-
lifes); *Pietro Annigoni*, Girl; *Renato Guttuso*, Head of a woman; and sculptures
by *Attilio Torresini, Michele Guerrisi, Giovanni Prini, Achille Stocchi, Amerigo
Bertoli*, and *Tommaso Bertolini*.

Part of the ANTIQUARIUM COMUNALE (see p 68) has also been housed here for
many years, but it is not on display. It includes finds from the Forma Urbis,
frescoes, mosaics, bronzes, and objects relating to the every-day life of the
Romans.

Beyond the palace, on a much lower level, is the little church of **San Vitale**,
dedicated in 416 and several times restored. It has a fine portico with old
columns and carved 17C doors (restored in 1984). In the interior is a carved
wood ceiling, and the walls are decorated with effective 17C trompe l'oeil
frescoes with landscapes by Cav. d'Arpino, Gasp. Dughet, And. Pozzo and
others.

From Largo Magnanapoli Via Ventiquattro Maggio climbs the Quirinal hill. This street was named to commemorate the day on which in
1915 Italy declared war on Austria. Near the beginning, on the left, is
the church of SAN SILVESTRO AL QUIRINALE (rebuilt 1524; not always
open), from which the cardinals used to march in procession to shut
themselves in the Quirinal when a conclave was held in summer. In
one of the neighbouring houses the poetess Vittoria Colonna met
with Michelangelo and others.

INTERIOR (reached by stairs through a door to the left of the façade). The plan is
a Latin cross; the entrance is in the left transept. In the nave, the 1st chapel on
the left has Della Robbian pavement tiles, and two fine landscapes by *Maturino*

and *Polidoro da Caravaggio*, who also painted the St Catherine and Mary Magdalene flanking the altar. In the vault, frescoes by *Cavalier d'Arpino*.—2nd chapel on the left, *Marcello Venusti*, Nativity.—In the chapel opposite, *Giacinto Gemignani*, Pius V and Card. Alessandrino, with, in the centre, a 13C Madonna and Child by a Roman artist.—The domed Bandini chapel at the end of the left transept contains tondi by *Domenichino*, and statues of Mary Magdalene and St John the Evangelist by *Aless. Algardi* (1628; probably his first Roman commission). The altarpiece of the Ascension is by *Scipione Pulzone*.

The street ascends between two of the most attractive of Rome's princely residences. On the left is the entrance to *Villa Colonna*, the garden dependency of Palazzo Colonna (p 151); on the right (behind a high wall), on the site of the *Baths of Constantine*, is **Palazzo Pallavicini-Rospigliosi** (Pl. 4; 5; admission only to the garden Casino, see p 48), built in 1613–16 probably by Carlo Maderno. It later passed to Cardinal Mazarin who enlarged it. In 1704 it was purchased by the Rospigliosi-Pallavicini family who still live here. In the 19C the beautiful gardens was greatly altered and diminished. The *Galleria Pallavicini* (not open to the public) on the first floor contains some important paintings of Italian and foreign schools (15C–18C).

In the charming little hanging garden is the *Casino Pallavicini (adm see p 48) designed by *Giovanni Vesanzio*. The fine façade (recently restored) is decorated with numerous good reliefs of mythological subjects from Roman sarcophagi (2C–3C AD). The pavilion contains *Guido Reni*'s celebrated *Fresco (1613–14) of Aurora scattering flowers before the chariot of the Sun, which is escorted by the Hours. It was greatly admired by travellers to Rome in the 19C. On the walls are four frescoes of the Seasons by *Paul Brill*, and two 'Triumphs' by *Antonio Tempesta*. The ceiling frescoes in the two side rooms are by (left) *Giovanni Baglione*, and (right) *Passignano*. Here are hung a number of 17C paintings and the sinopia of a fresco of the Allegory of Night by *Giovanni da San Giovanni*, from the ballroom of the palace.

At the top is the spacious and dignified PIAZZA DEL QUIRINALE (beware of fast traffic), with its two palaces: the Quirinal in front, and Palazzo della Consulta, to the right. The balustrade on the W side, overlooking Via della Dataria, provides a view across roof-tops to the dome of St Peter's in the distance.

The piazza occupies the summit of the **Quirinal** (61m), the highest of the Seven Hills. It received its name from a Temple of Quirinus, or from *Cures*, an ancient Sabine town NE of Rome from which, according to legend, the Sabines under their king Tatius settled on the hill. The name of Quirinus was a title of Romulus, after he had been deified; the festival in his honour was called *Quirinalia*.

In the middle of the square, on a high pedestal, flanking an obelisk (see below), are two famous colossal groups of the **Dioscuri** (Castor and Pollux), standing by their horses. Their height is over 5·5m. They are Roman copies, dating from the Imperial era, of Greek originals of the 5C BC.

The two groups were found nearby in the Baths of Constantine and placed here by Dom. Fontana under Sixtus V (1585–90), who was responsible for the recutting of the false inscriptions on the bases, 'Opus Phidiae' and 'Opus Praxitelis', which probably date from c AD 450. The statues appear in numerous representations of the city from medieval times. They were formerly called the horse-tamers, and the square was known as Monte Cavallo. The *Obelisk* (shaft 14·5m; restored in 1984), originally in front of the Mausoleum of Augustus, was brought here by Pius VI in 1786; Pius VII added the great basin (now a fountain) of dark grey granite, till then used as a cattle-trough in the Roman Forum.

At the corner of Via Ventiquattro Maggio, where Via della Dataria begins, is a part of the *Scuderie Pontificie*, or Papal Stables, built in

1722. The **Palazzo della Consulta**, the seat of the supreme court of the Papal States (Santa Consulta) and later of the Italian Ministry of Foreign Affairs, is now the seat of the Corte Costituzionale, a supreme court for matters concerning the constitution. The façade is by Ferd. Fuga (1739).

The stately front of the **Palazzo del Quirinale** (Pl. 4; 5, 3), the official residence of the President of the Republic since 1947, projects into the piazza, while its flank, known as the 'manica lunga' ('long sleeve'), is in Via del Quirinale. The palace was begun in 1574 by Flaminio Ponzio and Ottavio Mascherino, under Gregory XIII, on the site of a villa belonging to Cardinal d'Este, and was continued by Dom. Fontana, Carlo Maderno, Bernini (who worked on the 'manica lunga'), and Fuga, being completed in the time of Clement XII (1730–40). The principal entrance is by Maderno; the tower on the left of it was added in the time of Urban VIII.

The Quirinal was the habitual summer palace of the popes. Sixtus V died here in 1590; many official ceremonies have taken place and occasional conclaves have been held in it. From this palace Pius VII issued as the prisoner of Napoleon, and from its balcony Pius IX blessed Italy at the beginning of his pontificate. From 1870 to 1947 it was the royal residence. Victor Emmanuel II died here on 9 January 1878.

The INTERIOR has been closed to the public since 1979; admission is sometimes granted by appointment after written application. On the grand staircase is *Melozzo da Forlì*'s magnificent *Fresco (being restored) of Christ in Glory, with angels, formerly in the church of the Santi Apostoli. At the top of the stairs is the SALA REGIA, decorated in 1616–17, with a frieze designed by Agostino Tassi and executed by *Lanfranco* and *Saraceni*. This and the adjoining CAPPELLA PAOLINA are by *Carlo Maderno*. The chapel has fine stucco decoration by *Martino Ferrabosco*. The CAPPELLA DELL' ANNUNCIATA was decorated between 1609–12, under the direction of *Guido Reni* (who executed the scenes of the life of the Madonna and the prophets, in the pendentives), by *Lanfranco, Francesco Albani*, and *Antonio Carracci*.—The GALLERY OF ALEXANDER VII has frescoes carried out under the direction of *Pietro da Cortona* (1656–57) by *Grimaldi, Lazzaro Baldi, Ciro Ferri, Mola* (Joseph and his brothers, which is considered his most successful fresco), *Maratta, Gaspard Dughet, Ant. Carracci* and others.—The extensive garden was designed by Mascherino.

Via del Quirinale skirts the 'manica lunga' (see above) of the palace. On the right, beyond a public garden with an equestrian statue of Charles Albert by Romanelli (1900) rises the church of *Sant'Andrea al Quirinale* (closed 12–16 and on Tuesday), a masterpiece by *Bernini* (1658–70). The simple façade of a single order balances the fine domed elliptical interior, decorated with gilding and stucco. Cherubim look down from the lantern.

The high altarpiece of the Crucifixion of St Andrew is by *Borgognone* and is surmounted by a splendid group of angels and cherubim sculpted by *Raggi*. The fine 17C altarpieces include works by *Baciccia, Giacinto Brandi*, and *Carlo Maratta*. The Sacristy has a pretty frescoed ceiling by *Giovanni De La Borde* (approved by Bernini). The lavabo here is attrib. to *Bernini*.

Beyond, on the right, is another small oval church, *San Carlo alle Quattro Fontane (San Carlino)*, a masterpiece by *Borromini* offering an interesting contrast to the former church by Bernini. The tall curved façade (1665–68) is well adapted to the cramped site on the corner of a narrow street.

The INTERIOR (1638; if closed ring at door of the convent, right) has convex and concave surfaces in a complicated design using triangles in a unifying scheme. The symbolism throughout is of the Holy Trinity. In the chapel to the left of the altar: Rest on the flight into Egypt, attrib. to *Ann. Carracci* or *G.F. Romanelli*.
The small *CLOISTER which can be entered from the church is also designed

by Borromini. From here is the entrance to the *CRYPT, (temporarily closed because of problems of illumination), designed in a fantastical play of curves linked by a heavy continuous cornice. It is thought Borromini intended this as the place of his own burial.

At this point Via del Quirinale ends at the carfax known as the **Quattro Fontane** (Pl. 4; 4), with its four vistas ending in Porta Pia and the obelisks of the Quirinal, Pincio, and Esquiline, typical of the Rome of Sixtus V. The four small fountains (which give the busy cross-roads its name), dating from 1593, personify Fidelity, Strength, the Aniene, and the Tiber. Via delle Quattro Fontane leads right to Via Nazionale and left to Piazza Barberini.

Via Venti Settembre leads straight on, beyond the cross-roads, past *Palazzo del Drago*, by Domenico Fontana (1600), and the large *Ministry of Defence*, to Piazza San Bernardo (p 181), where this route is rejoined after a detour to the NW. At No. 7 in this street, on the left, is the Scottish presbyterian church of *St Andrew*, with a war memorial (1949) to the London Scottish.

To the left Via delle Quattro Fontane descends all the way to Piazza Barberini. Half-way down, on the right, is *Palazzo Barberini* (Pl. 4; 3), one of the grandest palaces in Rome. It was begun by Carlo Maderno for Urban VIII in 1624. The windows of the top story, the stairs, and some doorways were executed from a design by *Borromini*. The central block is attributed to *Bernini*. The garden flanks one side of the street where the huge stone pilasters and iron grille were added in the 19C by Fr. Azzurri. In 1949 the palace became the property of the State, and one wing now houses part of the *Galleria Nazionale d'Arte Antica*, a national gallery of paintings divided in two parts; the other section is in Palazzo Corsini (p 260). The right wing of the palace, at present occupied by offices of the armed forces, may eventually also be used by the gallery. Adm, see p 48.

After the State had purchased Palazzo Corsini with the picture-gallery of Card. Neri-Corsini, it was presented with the collections of Prince Tommaso Corsini and later acquired the Torlonia and other collections. The combined collections, opened to the public in 1895, are pre-eminent in Italian Baroque painting; there are also some good examples of the 15–16C, and a large selection of foreign works.

Across the garden, planted with palm trees, a door on the left beneath the portico leads into the palace. A monumental flight of stairs probably designed by Bernini lead up to the Gallery on the FIRST FLOOR (and the ticket office). The gallery has been undergoing re-arrangement for years. In the rooms with 17C works, the paintings are over-crowded and poorly hung. The rooms have not yet been numbered, but the pictures are all labelled.

From the ticket office a door on the right leads through a vestibule into the Hall (partly closed). Here are displayed: *Simone and Machilone*, Crucifix; *13C Tuscan School*, Crucifix; *12C Roman School*, 'Madonna Avvocata' (acquired in 1987, and removed for restoration). Room I. *Giovanni Baronzio*, Scenes from the life of Christ; *Bonaventura Berlinghieri*, Crucifixion; *Nicolò di Pietro*, Apostles, Coronation of Mary; *'Maestro dell'Incoronazione dell'Urbino'*, Birth of St John the Baptist.—R. II. *Filippo Lippi*, Madonna and Child, *Annunciation and donors.—Room III. *Piero di Cosimo*, *Mary Magdalene; *Francesco di Giorgio Martini*, Pietà, a terracotta group restored in 1985 (and formerly attributed to Giacomo Cozzarelli); *Circle of Filippino Lippi*, Madonna enthroned between Saints Peter and Paul.—Room IV. *Maestro di Tivoli* (formerly attributed to Antoniazzo Romano), St Sebastian; *Lorenzo di Viterbo*, Madonna

and Saints Peter and Michael; *L'Alunno*, Madonna and Child with
Saints; *Perugino*, St Nicholas of Tolentino.—Room V. *Michele Giam-
bono*, Madonna and Child; *Maestro di San Sebastiano*, Pilgrims at a
Sanctuary (a very unusual work); *15C Provencal School*, Addolorata;
Francesco Pagano (attributed), Saints Sebastian and Catherine;
Lorenzo Costa, Annunciation; *Marco Palmezzano*, St Jerome;
Giacomo Francia, La Pietà; *Andrea del Sarto*, *Holy Family;
Domenico Puligo, Madonna and Child with an angel; *Beccafumi*,
Madonna and Child with the young St John; *Brescianino*, Lady with
a turban.—Room VI. The Creation of the Angels in the vault is by
Andrea Camassei. Here is hung the famous portrait of a lady by
Raphael known as *'La Fornarina'. The sitter may be Raphael's
mistress, the daughter of a Sienese bakerwoman, although the
painting has also been attributed to the master's pupil, *Giulio
Romano*. Also here: *Baldassare Peruzzi*, *Ceres; *Sodoma*, Rape of the
Sabines, Three Fates (removed for restoration), Mystical marriage of
St Catherine; *Bronzino*, Stefano Colonna; *Girolamo Genga*, Marriage
of St Catherine; *Vincenzo Tamagni*, Marriage of the Virgin.—Room
VII. On the ceiling, *Divine Providence by *Andrea Sacchi* (1630–33).
Andrea Solario, Lute player; *Piazza Callisto da Lodi*, St Catherine of
Alexandria; *Nicolò dell'Abate*, Portrait of a boy; *Bartolomeo Veneto*,
*Portrait of a man (recently restored); *Lorenzo Lotto*, Mystical mar-
riage of St Catherine; *Gerolamo da Carpi*, Portrait of a man; *Il
Cariani*, *Madonna and Child, with Saints Anne and John; *Titian*,
Venus and Adonis (replica of a painting in the Prado); *Tintoretto*,
Christ and the Adulteress; *El Greco*, Nativity, Baptism of Christ.—
The CHAPEL contains frescoes of New Testament scenes by *Pietro da
Cortona* and *Giovanni Francesco Romanelli*.—Room VIII. *Master of
the Madonna of Manchester*, Pietà (being restored); *Marcello Ven-
usti*, Prayer in the Garden; *Sicciolante da Sermoneta*, Francesco II
Colonna; *Luis Morales* (attributed), Ecce Homo; *Marcello Venusti*, St
Lawrence; portraits by *Scipione Pulzone* and *Federico Zuccari*, and
works by *Scarsellino*.—Room IX has a ceiling painting of the Chariot
of the Sun by *Giuseppe Chiari*. *Jacopino dal Conte*, Deposition;
Jacques De Backer, Dead Christ supported by an angel.—Room X
has ceiling frescoes by *Pietro da Cortona* and his pupils (including
Francesco Romanelli). Here are displayed works by *Bartolomeo
Passarotti*.—Beyond Room XI, Room XII has landscapes by *Paul Brill*.
   Room XIII. *Luca Cambiaso*, Venus and Adonis; *Domenico Fetti*,
Jacob's Dream; *Cigoli*, St Francis in Prayer.—Room XIV. Works by
Carlo Saraceni, *Orazio Gentileschi*, and *Bartolomeo Manfredi*. Also
here: *Caravaggio*, *Narcissus, Judith killing Holofernes.—Room XV.
Works by *Valentin de Boulogne*.—Room XVI. Works by *Trophime
Bigot*; *Garrit van Honthorst* (attributed), Artist at work.—Room XVII.
Neapolitan 17C works. *Luca Giordano*, Self-portrait; *Salvatore Rosa*,
Allegories of Poetry and Music; *Mattia Preti*, Resurrection of Lazarus;
works by *Poussin*. Portrait bust of Nano del Duca di Créqui sculpted
by *Francesco Duquesnoy*.—Room XVIII. *Guido Reni*, Fresco of a
sleeping putto, *Portrait of a lady, supposed to be Beatrice Cenci,
Mary Magdalene; *Guercino*, Flagellation; *Alessandro Algardi*, Bust
of St Philip Neri; *Guercino*, Et in Arcadia Ego.—Room XIX. *Baciccia*,
Pietà, Clement IX, Portrait of Gian Lorenzo Bernini; two paintings by
Gian Lorenzo Bernini: David, and Urban VIII; *Sassoferrato*, Monsignor Ottaviano Prati; *Pietro da Cortona*, Guardian Angel.—Room XX
(right). *Jan Metsys*, Judith; works by *Frans Francken*; four interesting
illusionist paintings by *Jean Francois Niceron* (c 1635); *Holbein*,
Henry VIII (possibly a replica); *Quentin Metsys*, Erasmus.—The

SALONE has a magnificent ceiling fresco of *THE TRIUMPH OF DIVINE PROVIDENCE, by *Pietro da Cortona*, his main work, painted between 1633 and 1639 to celebrate the glory of the Papacy of Urban VIII and the Barberini family. It is a *tour de force*, particularly in the organization of the space, and the reduction of the composition into the angles. On the walls are hung seven cartoons by the school of *Pietro da Cortona* showing scenes from the life of Urban VIII, executed for tapestries manufactured in the Barberini workshops active in Rome from 1627–83 (and now in the Vatican, p 320). Also four cartoons for mosaics in the Cappella Colonna in St Peter's by *And. Sacchi, Bernini* and *Carlo Pellegrini*, and *Giov. Lanfranco*.

On the **Second Floor** are the impressive **18C collection** of paintings and the delightful 18C Barberini apartments, arranged with period furniture. In 1988 the 18C collection was closed for structural repairs.—In the entrance corridor are Roman paintings by *Placido Costanzi, Seb. Conca, Pietro Bianchi*, and others. ROOM 1 (right), bozzetti by *Seb. Conca*, and small works by *Carlo Maratta*.—R. 2. *Pierre Subleyras*, Madonna reading, Female nude; works by *Fr. Trevisani*; larger works by *Marco Benefial* (Pyramus and Thisbe) and *Fr. Mancini*.—R. 3 contains bozzetti for frescoes in Roman churches by *Baciccia*, and *And. Pozzo* (the dome and vault of Sant'Ignazio, see p 143).—R. 4. Portraits by *Ignazio Stern, Pompeo Batoni*, and *Angelica Kauffmann*.—R. 5. Works by *Fr. Solimena, Gaspare Traversi, Gius. Bonito* (a Neapolitan artist), and *Seb. Conca* (Adoration of the Magi).—R. 6 contains works by *Gius. Maria Crespi, Donato Creti, Aless. Magnasco*, and portraits by *Vittore Ghislandi* and *Pietro Ant. Rotari*.—R. 7. *G.B. Piazzetta*, Judith; *G.B. Tiepolo*, Old Faun and young satyr.— R. 8, frescoed with chiaroscuri in 1780–90 contains the Cervinara collection of charming small 18C French paintings, including: *Nicolas Lancret*, Le Faucon, Family Group; *Jean Baptiste Greuze*, Portrait of a girl; *Jean-Honorè Fragonard*, *Annette et Lubin; Hubert Robert*, Landscapes; *François Boucher*, Le Matin, Le Soir, La petite jardinière; and *Louis-Leopold Boilly*, La Fête du Grand-Père.—R. 9 contains interesting views of Rome by *Gaspar van Wittel*, and R. 10 views of ancient ruins by *Giov. Paolo Pannini*.—In R. 11 are more works from the Cervinara collection, by *Fr. Guardi* (the Giudecca Canal), and *Hubert Robert* (Bridge with washer-women).—R. 12. Views of Venice by *Luca Carlevarijs*, and *Canaletto; Bern. Bellotto*, The Schlosshof in Vienna.—The last room, with a pretty ceiling, is reserved for recently restored works.

Other rooms (usually closed) contain the exceptionally valuable *Numismatic Collection*, made by Victor Emmanuel III.

Also on this floor (but closed) are five rooms containing the DUSMET COLLECTION which was left to the State in 1949.—R. I. 16C majolica from Asia Minor.— R. II. 17–18C Chinese porcelain, and a Tien Lungli vase; 16C Flemish tapestries. R. III. *Neri di Bicci* (attrib.), Death of the Virgin, Madonna and Child (tabernacle); *14C Sienese school*, Diptych of San Vescovo and San Monaco; *14C artist from the Marches*, Bishop Saint.—R. IV. Terracotta works: *Leone Leoni*, Deposition; *Francavilla*, statuettes of Moses and Aaron; *16C Florentine school*, Pietà; *Susini*, Christ in the Garden.—R. V. 16C Flemish tapestries. *Guercino* (attrib.), Visitation of St Julian; *Ann. Carracci*, Self-portrait; *Lor. Costa*, Annunciation.

The 18C **Barberini Apartments**, with rococo decorations, contain furniture, porcelain, costumes, etc.

Opposite the palace was the *Scots College* from 1604 until 1962 when it moved to Via Cassia (p 400). The buildings dating from 1869, and the church of St Andrew (1645–76), deconsecrated in 1962, are now incorporated in a bank.

Via delle Quattro Fontane ends in **Piazza Barberini**, which was transformed between the Wars into one of the busiest traffic centres in the city. Here converge Via del Tritone (from the Corso), Via Sistina (from the Pincio), Via Vittorio Veneto, Via San Niccolò da Tolentino, and Via Barberini. Isolated in the centre of the square in this unpleasant setting is Bernini's masterpiece, the recently restored *Fontana del Tritone (1642–3), with four dolphins supporting a shell on which is seated a triton who blows water through a shell held up in his hands. On the N side, at the beginning of Via Veneto, is the little reconstructed *Fontana delle Api*, designed by Bernini a year later, bearing the Barberini device of the bee and with an inscription stating that the water is for the use of the public and their animals.— Here begins the broad and tree-lined **Via Vittorio Veneto** (Pl. 4; 3, 1), which climbs in two sweeping curves to Porta Pinciana. It was opened in 1886 on part of the site of the beautiful park of the *Villa Ludovisi* which was obliterated, and which gave its name to this aristocratic district of the city, laid out at the turn of the century. The street with its luxury hotels, great mansions, and famous cafés was especially fashionable for its ambiance of 'la dolce vita' in the sixties.

On the right is the church of the **Cappuccini** or **Santa Maria della Concezione** (Pl. 4; 3), architecturally simple and unpretending in accordance with Franciscan ideals and in strong contrast to the Baroque works of the time (1626). Its founder was Cardinal Ant. Barberini.

In the very dark INTERIOR all the pictures are labelled. South side, 1st chapel, *Guido Reni*, *St Michael*; to the left, *Honthorst*, Mocking of Christ; 3rd chapel, *Domenichino*, St Francis in Ecstasy, and Death of St Francis; 5th chapel, *And. Sacchi*, St Anthony raising a dead man. An inscription on the pavement (hic jacet pulvis, cinis et nihil) marks the grave of Cardinal Barberini in front of the high altar. North side, 5th chapel, *Andrea Sacchi*, The Virgin and St Bonaventura; 1st chapel, *Pietro da Cortona*, St Paul having his sight restored.—A CEMETERY (entered down the stairs to the right of the church) has five subterranean chapels lined with the bones and skeletons of over 4000 Capuchins, arranged in patterns. On the floor of two of these chapels is earth brought from Palestine. On All Souls' Day (2 November) this gruesome scene is illuminated.

Opposite, a street with steps ascends to **Sant'Isidoro** with a pink façade by *Carlo Bizzaccheri* (1704). The church (1620, by *Ant. Casoni*) was attached to a college for Irish students, founded by Luke Wadding (1588–1657), the distinguished Irish Franciscan, who instigated the Irish rebellion of 1641 against the confiscation of Ulster. His tomb is in the church, which contains several works by *Carlo Maratta*, and a chapel in the right transept designed by *Gian Lor. Bernini* with sculptures attrib. to his son *Paolo*.

Farther up Via Veneto, by its second curve (right) is PALAZZO PIOMBINO, or PALAZZO MARGHERITA, a huge building by Gaetano Koch (1886–90) standing in a garden, now the *United States Embassy*. Queen Margherita lived here after the death of Umberto I in 1900. At No. 2 Via Boncompagni is the *United States Information Service Bureau*. Farther on, Via Lombardia leads left from Via Veneto to the **Casino dell'Aurora** (No. 46; no admission), a relic of the famous Villa Ludovisi which belonged to Cardinal Ludovisi, nephew of Gregory XV. The first Roman scene in Henry James' 'Roderick Hudson' takes place in the gardens here. The garden-house contains a fine ceiling painting of Aurora and Fame by Guercino (Giov. Fr. Barbieri) (1621). Via Veneto ends at **Porta Pinciana**, a handsome fortified gateway erected by Honorius c 403 and since enlarged. Opposite is one of the entrances to the Villa Borghese (Rte 9).

On the city side of Porta Pinciana, Via di Porta Pinciana branches left from Via Vittorio Veneto and, passing the grounds of the Villa Medici, runs into Via Francesco Crispi, which ends in Largo del Tritone. Beyond the gate, the broad Corso d'Italia skirts a long stretch of the Aurelian wall (272–279) with some eighteen turrets as far as Piazza Fiume on the site of the demolished Porta Salaria, and continues to Porta Pia.

Via Barberini, opened in 1926, ascends from Piazza Barberini. On the left, in a side street called after it, is the church of SAN NICOLÒ DA TOLENTINO (ring at the Armenian College at No. 17), rebuilt in 1620 by Carlo Buti, and finished by Martino Longhi the Younger and Giovan Maria Baratta, who built the façade in 1670. The high altar was designed by Aless. Algardi. The 2nd chapel on the left is thought to be the last work of Pietro da Cortona (1668) and contains sculptures by Ercole Ferrata, Cosimo Fancelli, and Ant. Raggi.—Via Barberini ends at Largo Santa Susanna, another traffic centre, where it is joined on the left by Via Leonida Bissolati, with numerous tourist agencies. The square is dominated by the building of the *Ufficio Geologico* (1873, by Raffaele Canevari), containing the *Geological Museum* (admission by appointment after written application), with a collection of minerals, marbles (archaeological and modern), and fossils.

Adjoining Largo Santa Susanna on the SE is the busy *Piazza San Bernardo*, with its fountain and three churches. It is, in effect, a widening of Via Venti Settembre. On its NW side is the church of SANTA SUSANNA (Pl. 4; 4), a Paulist church, probably dating from the 4C restored in 795, and remodelled in the 15C and 16C. It is now the American National church. The façade is by Maderno (1603), and is by many considered his masterpiece; in the good late-Mannerist interior (1595) are large frescoes by Baldass. Croce. Opposite, at the beginning of Via Torino, is the round church of *San Bernardo alle Terme* built into one of the two circular halls flanking the exedra of the Baths of Diocletian (see p 182) in the 16C (in an unattractive colour). The domed interior contains eight colossal stucco statues of saints by Camillo Mariani (c 1600–5), and a neoclassical monument to the sculptor Carlo Finelli (died 1853) by Rinaldo Rinaldi.

The **Fontana dell'Acqua Felice** (covered for restoration) is fed by an aqueduct (1585–87) from Colonna in the Alban Hills. The fountain dates from the time of Sixtus V and is by Dom. Fontana; the unsuccessful figure of Moses is attrib. to Prospero Antichi or Leonardo Sormani. The bas-relief of Aaron is by G.B. della Porta, and that of Gideon by Flaminio Vacca and P.P. Olivieri; the four lions are copies of Egyptian antiques removed by Gregory XVI to the Egyptian Museum founded by him in the Vatican.

The church of ***Santa Maria della Vittoria** (Pl. 4; 4), is a fine edifice by Maderno (1620), with a façade by G.B. Soria. Originally dedicated to St Paul, it was renamed from an image (burned in 1833) of the Virgin that gave victory to the Catholic army over the Protestants at the battle of the White Mountain, near Prague, on 8 November 1620 (Thirty Years War).

The INTERIOR is considered one of the most complete examples of Baroque decoration in Rome, rich in colour and glowing with marbles. It has good stucco work and a fine organ and cantoria by a pupil of Bernini, *Mattia De Rossi*. The frescoes are by *Giov. Dom. Cerrini*. The 2nd S chapel has an altarpiece of the Madonna and St Francis by *Domenichino*. The *CORNARO CHAPEL (4th chapel on the N side; push-button light), by *Bernini*, is a splendid architectural achievement, using the shallow space to great effect. Over the altar is his famous sculptured group representing the Ecstasy of St Theresa, and below is a gilt bronze relief of the Last Supper. At the sides are expressive portraits of the Venetian family of Cornaro, by pupils and followers of Bernini. The last half-hidden figure on the left is said to be a portrait of Bernini.—The fresco, by *L. Serra* (1885), in the apse of the church, commemorates the triumphal entry into Prague of the Catholic army.

Via Venti Settembre continues to Porta Pia (see Rte 19), passing on the left the *Ministry of Agriculture and Forests* (1902); and on the right, the colossal *Ministry of Finance* by Raff. Canevari (1870), containing a *Numismatic Museum* (adm see p 49; document required). Interesting is a collection of wax seals by Benedetto Pistrucci, who designed the St George and dragon on the English sovereign. The short Via Servio Tullio, opposite, leads N to *Piazza Sallustio*, where, behind Villa Maccari (right), is a considerable fragment of a Villa which used to stand in the *Gardens of Sallust*, laid out in 40 BC, on which the historian C. Sallustius Crispus lavished the wealth he had accumulated during his African governorship. Here also are the foundations of the Trinità dei Monti obelisk, showing where it stood in the Middle Ages.

The Cornaro chapel by Bernini in Santa Maria della Vittoria

The short Via Orlando runs from Piazza San Bernardo past the Grand Hotel opened in 1894, (the first hotel in Italy with electric light), to the large circular PIAZZA DELLA REPUBBLICA (Pl. 5; 3), formerly *dell' Esedra* (from the exedra of the Baths of Diocletian, the buildings of which may be seen on the opposite side). The semicircular porticoed fronts of the palazzi on either side of the entrance to the piazza (by Koch; 1896–1902), follow the line of the exedra. The abundant *Fountain of the Naiads* (1870) is supplied by the Acqua Marcia. Four groups of reclining nymphs and the central Glaucus were sculpted by Mario Rutelli (1901–11). The *Baths of Diocletian, or Thermae of Diocletian were built in 298–306 by Diocletian and Maximian. The largest of all the ancient Roman baths, they could accommodate over 3000 people at once. They covered a rectangular area, c 380m by 370m, corresponding to that now bounded SE by Piazza dei Cinquecento, SW by Via Torino, NW by Via Venti Settembre, and NE by Via Volturno.

The main buildings included the Calidarium, the Tepidarium, and the Frigidarium. The Calidarium, which survived into the late 17C, occupied part of the present piazza. The Tepidarium and the huge central hall of the baths are now occupied by the church of Santa Maria degli Angeli (see below). The Frigidarium was an open-air bath behind this hall. Numerous large and small halls, nymphaea, and exedrae were located within the precincts. The only entrance to the baths was on the NE side, near the present Via Volturno. On the SW side the closed exedra was flanked by two circular halls: one of these is now the church of San Bernardo alle Terme; the other is at the corner of Via Viminale and Via delle Terme. A third (octagonal) hall survives on the corner of Via Parigi at the NW angle of the main complex. In the 16C a Carthusian convent was built in the ruins (see below). Much damage was done to the baths in the 16–19C by architects and builders who used the materials for other purposes. After the opening in 1889 of the Museo Nazionale Romano, numerous encroaching buildings were removed.

Along the modern Via Parigi stand conspicuous remains of buildings demolished to make way for the Baths. At the beginning of the street is a Roman column, surmounted by a caravel, a gift from Paris (1961).

Santa Maria degli Angeli (Pl. 5; 3) occupies the great central hall of the baths, converted into the church of the Carthusian convent. The work of adaptation was carried out in 1563–66 for Pius IV by *Michelangelo*, who may also have designed the cloisters and other conventual buildings. Michelangelo placed the entrance of· the church at the short SE side of the rectangle and thus had at his disposal a nave of vast proportions. The effect was spoiled by *Vanvitelli* who, instructed by the Carthusian fathers in 1749, altered the orientation. He made the entrance in the long SW side and so converted the nave into a transept. To compensate for the loss of length, he built out on the NE side an apsidal choir, which broke into the monumental SW wall of the Frigidarium. The façade on Piazza della Repubblica, with Vanvitelli's doorway, incorporates an apsidal wall—all that is left of the Calidarium. Excavations during the restoration of the floor in 1970 revealed further remains of the baths.

In the disappointing INTERIOR, the circular VESTIBULE stands on the site of the Tepidarium. Here are the tombs of Carlo Maratta (died 1713; right) and Salvator Rosa (died 1673; left). By the entrance into the transept is (right) a fine colossal statue of St Bruno, by *Houdon* (1766). The vast TRANSEPT is nearly 100m long, 27m wide and 28m high. The eight monolithic columns of red granite, nearly 14m high and 1·5m in diameter, are original; the others, in brick, were added when the building was remodelled.—Right transept: in the pavement, a meridian dating from 1703; tomb by *Ant. Muñoz*, of Marshal Armando Diaz (died 1928), Italian commander-in-chief in the First World War.—The huge paintings include (left transept): Mass of St Basil, by *Subleyras*; Fall of Simon Magus, by *Pompeo Batoni*.—In the Choir, on the right, *Romanelli*, Presentation in the Temple; *Domenichino*, Martyrdom of St Sebastian; left, *Pomarancio*, Death of Ananias and Sapphira (painted on slate); *Carlo Maratta*, Baptism of Christ. In the apse, on the left, Monument of Pius IV, from Michelangelo's design, which inspired also the monument of Cardinal Serbelloni opposite.—The door to the Sacristy in the left transept leads to impressive remains of the frigidarium (see above).

The ***Museo Nazionale Romano** (Pl. 5; 4; admission see p 49) is one of the great museums of the world. Founded in 1889, it contains sculptures and other antiquities found in Rome since 1870, part of the Kircherian collection formerly in the Collegio Romano, and the treasures of the Ludovisi collection (formerly in Villa Ludovisi). The collections occupy part of the Baths of Diocletian (see above), as well as the Carthusian convent. The Museum has been almost totally closed for many years, and the collection is to be partly rehoused in Palazzo Massimo in Piazza dei Cinquecento, recently acquired by the State, and being restored. The main entrance is from Viale delle Terme but the secondary entrance through the garden (see the Plan on p 185) is at present in use. In 1988 only two rooms were open. The following description will be out of date when the whole museum is eventually reopened.

THE BATHS

Seven of the rooms of the baths, with high and massive walls and remarkable vaults, surround the SE or right transept of the church of Santa Maria degli Angeli. Four more are located in and near the Frigidarium.

ROOM I. On the floor, Mosaic with volutes and animals; three sarcophagi depicting respectively the Three Graces, a Bacchic procession, and the story of Phaedra.—R. II. Against the wall, Plaster reconstruction of the base of the Temple of Hadrian. In front, Sarcophagus with figures of Muses and two other sarcophagi; funerary altars; architectural fragments.—R. III. Polychrome mosaics; Christian sarcophagi, among them that of Marcus Claudianus, with scenes from the Old and New Testaments.

R. IV. On the wall, in which was Michelangelo's entrance to the church of Santa Maria degli Angeli, is a dedicatory inscription of the Baths of Diocletian (reconstituted). Nilotic mosaic with a landscape with pygmies, hippopotami, and crocodiles (from Collemancio, near Assisi); colossal statue, Artemis of Ariccia, copy of an original attrib. to Alkamenes; reconstruction of a small tetrastyle temple from Torrenova on the Via Casilina (2C AD); sarcophagi, including one to the right of the temple, with a magnificent battle scene.—R. V. So-called group of Mars and Venus, said to represent the emperor Commodus and his wife Crispina; to left, Shaft of an oriental alabaster column, on a white marble base, found, with other architectural fragments, during the building of the extension to the Chamber of Deputies; sarcophagi.—R. VI. On left of entrance, against the wall of the church, Plaster reproduction of the door of the Temple of Augustus and Rome at Ancyra (Ankara); on this temple was engraved the *Monumentum Ancyranum*; (on a pedestal) statue of Jupiter, after a Hellenistic original; polychrome mosaic of Charioteers (found in 1939); *Dancers of the Via Prenestina, a cylindrical drum of 9 marble slabs (two missing); Sarcophagi, one with a Bacchic procession.—R. VII. Mosaics, inscriptions, etc.

Beyond the cluster of rooms round the church lies the FRIGIDARIUM (R. VIII). This was the swimming pool of the Baths, open to the sky and, with an area of 2500 sq.m, it was as large as a small lake. It was bounded on the long NE side by a garden and had porticoes on both short sides. The SW side was bounded by a monumental wall with five pedimented niches, alternately rectangular and curved, and adorned with statues. Most of the adornment had disappeared when Vanvitelli broke through the centre of the wall to build his apsidal choir out into the middle of the area. It had already been diminished by the construction of the small cloister of the Carthusian convent (this now houses the Ludovisi collection; see below), and the combination of these intrusions has naturally robbed the Frigidarium of its character. The architectural fragments along the walls of the baths, and in front of the modern wall of the small cloister, were found during the extension of the Chamber of Deputies.

To the right is R. IX, with a double exedra; here is a sarcophagus of Egyptian style.—R. X. Reconstructed tomb of G. Sulpicius Platorinus and of his family; inside are niches for cinerary urns; chamber tomb of the 2C AD, with pictorial decoration on the walls and ceiling, found in 1951 at the foot of the hill of Monteverde.—R. XI. Roman mosaics: Hercules wrestling with Achelous (from Anzio); Nereids riding on sea-monsters (from Casalotto, on the Via Cornelia); Rampant panthers (from the Termini Station).—From R. X is the entrance to the *Garden* looking on Piazza dei Cinquecento. In it is a colossal marble fountain-basin shaped like a flower calyx. On the NE side the garden is bounded by the ancient perimeter wall of the Baths. A modern flight of steps leads down through an arch cut in the wall to the *Forica*, with niches for statues and a floor mosaic. Along the curved wall were ranged some thirty lavatory seats separated by marble slabs.—In the left (W) corner of the garden is the entrance to the Museum.

THE MUSEUM

PORCH. On the left, Telamon in the form of a young satyr, Roman copy of a Hellenistic original; polychrome mosaics.—ENTRANCE HALL. On column shafts, twelve busts of Roman personages of

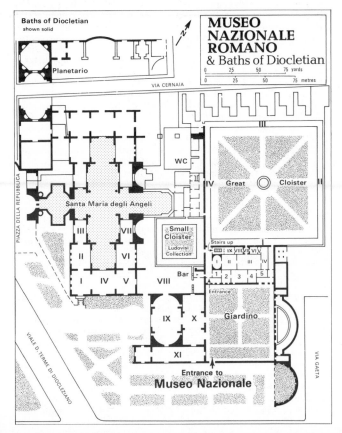

doubtful authenticity; herm of Mercury; mosaics, including one of a *Skeleton with inscription in Greek, 'Know thyself'.

On the left a door leads to the **Ludovisi Collection**. The famous Ludovisi throne has been removed, and is now exhibited in Room 2 (see below). The collection was formed by Card. Ludovico Ludovisi, nephew of Gregory XV (Alessandro Ludovisi; pope 1621–23). It was originally housed in Villa Ludovisi and was moved to the new palace in Via Vittorio Veneto on its completion in 1890. In 1901, after the palace had become the residence of Queen Margherita, the State bought the collection from the Prince of Piombino, Rodolfo Boncompagni-Ludovisi, and it was placed in the Museo Nazionale. It occupies the small cloister mentioned above. Notable are the Hermes Ludovisi, the god as orator, copy of a 5C original, and the Ludovisi Hera, a colossal head, copy of a 4C original. Many of the sculptures have been poorly restored.

Opposite the entrance to the cloister is the first of a series of eight rooms, containing an important collection of Greek and Hellenistic sculptures.

ROOM I. Floor mosaic depicting the head of Pan and four satyrs; (left) fragments of a large neo-Attic rhyton, (right) marble neo-Attic fountain cover. Cinerary urns from the tomb of C. Sulpicius Platorinus (p 184).—R. II. In an impluvium, Polychrome mosaic with head of Oceanus and sea-monsters. 106164. Statue, from a Herakles after Polykleitos, from the baths of Caracalla; *608. Apollo of the Tiber, school of Pheidias, or perhaps by Kalamis, found in the Tiber; *124697. Aura of the Palatine, believed to have been the central acroterion of the Temple of Apollo Epikourios at Bassae (430 BC); 1085. Head of Hygieia, in the style of the 4C BC; *124696. Dancer of the Palatine, wearing a chiton (5C BC); 124667. Peplophoros, probably a Greek original of the first half of the 5C BC, found in Piazza Barberini; *51. Juno of the Palatine, possibly the portrait of an empress as the goddess; 55051. Colossal head of Athena, an acrolith; 124665. Torso of Minotaur, copy of a 5C bronze original.

R. III contains the most outstanding examples. *56039. DIS-COBOLOS OF CASTEL PORZIANO, copy of a bronze statue by Myron; *72274. DAUGHTER OF NIOBE, from the Gardens of Sallust, a Greek original of the 5C BC of the School of Kresilas; **72115. VENUS OF CYRENE, an original Greek work of the 4C BC, possibly by a predecessor of Praxiteles, representing the goddess just risen from the sea; near her right leg is her cloak, supported by a dolphin; the head and arms are missing. The statue was found in the Baths at Cyrene; *1075. EPHEBUS OF SUBIACO, Roman copy of an original of the 4C BC, probably one of the Niobids, found in Nero's villa at Subiaco; *Torso Valentini (no number) a hero or athlete, a remarkable work of the early 5C BC, formerly in the court of Palazzo Valentini (p 151); 124680. Head of Hypnos, attrib. to Praxiteles, from Hadrian's Villa; 1049. Bronze statue of a young man leaning on a lance, perhaps Pollus or one of the Seleucids, in the identical pose as the Alexander the Great of Lysippos; *1055. Boxer resting, a magnificent work signed by Apollonius; his coarse face is scarred and his body is relaxed as if he were every tired after his fight; 121302. Apollo of Anzio, by an unknown Attic predecessor of Praxiteles; **50170. MAIDEN OF ANZIO, a masterpiece of Greek art dating from the end of the 4C or beginning of the 3C BC by a sculptor of the school of Lysippos who had come under the influence of Praxiteles. It represents a young girl approaching an altar and carrying implements for a sacrifice. It was discovered in the imperial villa at Anzio in 1878; *126371. DISCOBOLOS EX-LANCELOTTI, the finest and best-preserved replica of the statue of Myron. In defiance of Italian law it was sold to Hitler in 1938, but was restored to Italy ten years later; 124679. Head of the goddess of Butrinto, discovered in 1929 at Butrinto in Albania (the arrangement of the hair somewhat resembles that of the Apollo of Anzio). Of the polychrome floor mosaics the best is that of a whirling wheel with 14 carved spokes (from Settecamini, on the Via Tiburtina).

R. IV. 607. Charis, or Grace, from a type by Kallimachos, similar in style to the Venus Genetrix by Arcesilaus; *108596. Dancer of Tivoli, Roman copy of a Hellenistic original; 124678. Riding Amazon charging a barbarian, of the school of Pergamon; *499. Young satyr turning round to look at his tail, Hellenistic; 121315. Young satyr laughing, Roman copy of a Hellenistic original; 60750, 108597. Crouching Venus, two replicas of the work by the Bithynian sculptor Doidalsas; on the wall, *Mosaic with volutes and a shield adorned with the head of Medusa; *12. Seated Muse, found in the Palatine Stadium; *121987. Goddess personifying a seaport, accompanied by a child merman (1C BC; recalling 4C); 124722. Muse or Nymph, found in the Palatine Stadium, possibly along with No. 12 (above). It was part of a group of the Muses, Apollo, and Marsyas by Philiscos of Rhodes (3C BC).

R. V. ROMAN DECORATIVE ART. To the right, marble *Altar (1C AD) found near Ponte Sant'Angelo, the front and sides with plane-branch decoration surmounted by a bull's head. To the left, *Sepulchral altar, comprising an ossuary and a cippus; on the front of the cippus is a relief depicting a nuptial scene; on the other sides are figures of maenads dancing and of youths carrying implements for a sacrifice.—RR. VI and VII. ROMAN PORTRAITS. *56230. Augustus as Pontifex Maximus, one of the finest portraits of the emperor, found in the Via Labicana; 618. Head of Nero, the best of his portraits; 124493. Head of an old woman of the early Empire; *639. Half-length figure of a chief Vestal, from the House of the Vestals in the Roman Forum.—R. VII. In the middle of the room, *Altar from Ostia, with reliefs of the origins of Rome (Mars and Rhea Silvia, Romulus and Remus suckled by the she-wolf, etc.); the altar is dated 1 October AD 124; 1043. Head of a maiden, with hair in tight curls, from the tomb of Sulpicius Platorinus; 124129. Head of a princess of the Julio-Claudian gens wearing a diadem, possibly Agrippina, mother of Nero; 1219. Antoninus Pius as a young man; 124489. Commodus as a youth; 629. Head of Sabina, wife of Hadrian (with traces of colour still visible); 124491. Head of Hadrian, from the Stazione Termini; *330. Head of Vespasian, from Ostia, one of the best surviving Roman portraits; 106538. Head of Nerva (emperor 96–98).

R. VIII. 126732. Sarcophagus of Acilia, badly damaged, with figures in high relief on front and sides (3C AD); 125802. Sarcophagus with pastoral scenes; 58561. Bearded head of Lucius Verus (emperor 161–69); *1119. Head of a young girl, an exquisite work of great tenderness and refinement, from the Palatine; 644. Bearded head of Gallienus (emperor 253–68), found in the House of the Vestals; 124486. Bust of a bearded personage (3C AD), from the Piazza della Chiesa Nuova; 56199. Bust of Constantius II (emperor 337–61).—R. IX. Mosaics, including a polychrome mosaic from a Republican villa on the Via Nomentana; 15826. Herakles, a colossal torso of the 2C AD; 168186. Sarcophagus of a child from Grottarossa.

From the corridor (see above) five more rooms are reached, containing less important works.

R. 1. 108518. Maiden as Diana, from Ostia; 30067. Archaic Kore, Roman replica of one of the series on the Acropolis at Athens.—R. 2. ***Ludovisi Throne** (exhibited here, while the rest of the Ludovisi collection is closed to the public, see above). This is a large throne thought to have been intended for the statue of a divinity, and usually considered to be an original work of the 5C BC found in the Villa Ludovisi. The back and sides are adorned with reliefs. The central subject is apparently the birth of Aphrodite, who rises from the sea supported by two Seasons; on the right side is the representation of a young woman sitting clothed on a folded cushion; she is taking grains from a box and burning them in a brazier; on the left side is a naked flute girl, also sitting on a folded cushion, playing a double pipe. Doubts about the authenticity of the three fine reliefs were raised in 1988 by a well known art critic.

1059. Statuette of young athlete, in green basalt, probably Autolykos, winner of the pankration in 422 BC (copy of a 5C original); 108604. Peplophoros, resembling the caryatids of the Erechtheion in Athens; further examples of peplophori; 52575. Head of a carytid from Via del Cardello in Rome. R. 3. Attic torso from the Via della Spinola; *622. Dionysos, from Hadrian's Villa, Hadrianic copy of a 4C Greek original; 108595. Athena, also from Hadrian's Villa; 75675. Apollo or Eros, after a bronze original, from Palazzo Chigi.

R. 4. 125375. Maenad holding a goat by the horn, Hadrianic relief; 1087. Sleeping hermaphrodite, copy of a Hellenistic work; 1194. Young girl or nymph sleeping, from Nero's villa at Subiaco; *603. Head of a dying Persian, of the school of Pergamon, one of a series of sculptures set up at Pergamon to commemorate the victory of Attalos I over the Gauls.—R. 5. Against the wall, polychrome mosaic, with figures of the seasons, and, in the centre, Apollo punishing Marsyas (5C AD); 124495. Colossal statue of a seated veiled goddess, possibly Roma; 124482. Colossal statue of a Dacian; 115164. Marble and alabaster equestrian statue of a boy.

*GREAT CLOISTER. Built in 1565 (date on a pilaster near the entrance), this cloister is ascribed to Michelangelo, who died the year before. It has a perimeter of 320m, and the arcades, having alternate square and oval windows, are supported by 100 travertine columns. The fountain in the cloister garden dates from 1695; it is shaded by four cypresses, one of which is the original. Seven colossal heads of animals (probably from the Forum of Trajan) surround the fountain. In the cloister and garden are sculptures and inscriptions of relatively minor importance.

WING I. Four statues of Roman generals, three with breastplates; group of seated man and woman; nude youth, possibly the emperor Heliogabalus; altar with six girls dancing; three female statues.—WING II. Near the angle with Wing I, Granite slab with relief of Egyptian deities.—At the corner of WING III, *Pilasters with inscriptions relating to the Ludi Saeculares, celebrated in the reigns of Augustus (17 BC) and of Septimius Severus (AD 204). The earlier inscription records the festival ordained by Augustus, during which the Carmen Saeculare of Horace was sung at the Capitol. Between the pilasters, Nilotic mosaic.—WING IV. Statue of Jupiter standing with chlamys over his left arm; headless Herakles with club and lion-skin, after Lysippos; athlete, after Polykleitos.—In the garden, along the cloister wings, Inscriptions; Base from the Temple of Hercules at Tivoli; landmarks delimiting the land bordering the Tiber, with records of the consuls, censors, and *curatores alvei et riparum Tiberis*; other landmarks.

From the corridor a staircase leads to the **First Floor**. At the top are exquisite mosaic fragments of animals and fish, most found in Rome.—On the left, off the Sala degli Stucchi (see below) is the *SALA DEGLI AFFRESCHI DELLA VILLA DI LIVIA A PRIMA PORTA. This is a reconstruction of a rectangular room from the Imperial Villa of Livia, wife of Augustus, the walls of which are decorated with frescoes of a fruit and flower garden. It constitutes the masterpiece of naturalist decoration of the second style of Roman painting. Restored in 1952–53 and moved to the museum from Prima Porta, the painting was saved just in time from complete decay.

In the Sala degli Stucchi and the Sale dei Dipinti Murali are displayed the stucco and painted decoration of a building of the Augustan age discovered in the grounds of the Villa Farnesina near the banks of the Tiber. These are works of high artistic value, and the paintings are second in importance only to those from Pompeii and

Herculaneum, now in the Museo Nazionale at Naples. In the SALA DEGLI STUCCHI are *Ceilings decorated in stucco, masterpieces of their kind, from three of the rooms (Cubicula B, D, and E). The friezes are decorated with festoons and cupids, interspersed with land-scapes and mythological scenes.

At the end of the hall a door (left) leads into the SALE DEI DIPINTI MURALI containing the painted decoration, arranged according to the rooms of the Augustan house, known as Cubicula B, C, D, and E. The paintings are in the second and third Pompeian styles: the former (1C BC) imitating marble decoration and introducing figures, the latter (early 1C AD), the best period, introducing more figures.—R. I. Paintings detached from Cubiculum E, with aediculae surmounted by fantastic cornices and paintings in which love-scenes and winged genii recur.

The next three sections contain the finest paintings found in the Roman house.—R. II. In Cubiculum B the prevailing colour is cin-nabar red. The decorations include aediculae and caryatids. The paintings are of mythical subjects, including one of Aphrodite seated on a throne, attended by one of the Graces and by young Eros.—R. III. Room C has the largest painting of the series, a frieze 8·5m by 2m, with scenes from the legend of the Egyptian king Bocchoris, the wise and noble judge. The walls have a black background.—R. IV. Cubiculum D, like its twin B, has walls mainly of red. Here is a representation of a seated female figure to whom a girl on tiptoe is offering a gift. Paintings of male and female figures issuing from flower petals show Egyptian influence. In the frieze are charming pictures of seated nymphs. On a column is inscribed the name (in Greek) of the artist, Seleukos.—R. V (closed indefinitely) contains paintings from two corridors (F and G).

Off the landing, opposite the staircase, are two rooms (usually closed) contain-ing mosaics from Rufinello, near Tusculum, from Genazzano, and from the Villa of Septimius Severus at Baccano.

Beyond the garden to the right of the Museo Nazionale Romano lies the vast Piazza dei Cinquecento. In the garden is the Monument to the Fallen at Dogali, by Azzurri, erected in memory of 548 Italian soldiers ambushed at Dogali, Eritrea, in 1887. It incorporates an Egyptian obelisk found in the Isaeum Campense (its companion is in Florence) inscribed with hieroglyphs recording the glories of Rameses the Great or Sesostris, the Pharaoh of the time of Moses. (The monument, first erected in front of the old railway station was moved here in 1924; in 1936–44 it was decorated with the Lion of Judah plundered from Addis Ababa.)—The **Piazza dei Cinquecento**, by far the largest square in Rome, is the terminus or junction of many urban bus and tram services and the starting-point of numerous bus and coach services to the environs.

The **Stazione di Termini** (Pl. 5; 4; called after the Baths of Diocletian), on the SE side of the square, with its 12 main and numerous subsidiary platforms, is one of the largest and most modern railway stations in Europe. Its reconstruction, begun in 1938 and delayed by war, was completed 12 years later, and it was formally opened on 20 December 1950. Strictly functional in design, the station extends from Via Giovanni Giolitti on the SW to Via Marsala on the NE. The façade is a plain white rectangular block, pierced horizontally by nine continuous lines of windows. In front is a gigantic quasi-cantilever construction sweeping upwards and out-wards and serving as a portico for vehicles. The older and more conventional wings had been partly completed when the war stopped building operations in 1942. A covered way through the station connects the streets on either side. The Stazione di Termini is also the starting-point of the Underground railway.

In front of the station (left), is the best preserved fragment of the so-called *Servian Wall*, formed of massive blocks of tufa. This wall was actually built after the invasion of the Gauls in 390 BC and was restored in the last days of the Republic (for a note on the walls of Rome, see p 19). Further fragments of the wall were unearthed during the reconstruction of the station. Beneath the station have been found also remains of a private house and of some baths, with good mosaics, dating from the 2C AD.

11   The Esquiline Hill and Santa Maria Maggiore

The **Esquiline** (65m), the highest and most extensive of the Seven Hills of Rome, was formerly a region of vineyards and gardens, and had few inhabitants. Even today, it is not wholly built over. Of its four summits, the *Oppius* or *Oppian Hill* is largely taken up by a park, the Parco Oppio, on which were built the Baths of Titus and of Trajan and Nero's Domus Aurea. The *Cispius*, extending to the NE, is crowned by the basilica of Santa Maria Maggiore. The other two summits— the *Subura*, above the low-lying district of that name, and the *Fagutalis*—are insignificant. According to the erudite Varro, the name of Esquiline was derived from the word *excultus*, in reference to the ornamental groves planted on the hill by Servius Tullius—such as the Querquetulanus (oak grove) and Fagutalis (beech grove), the latter giving its name to one of the four summits.

Although the hill was generally unhealthy, part of it was a fashionable residential district. This was called the *Carinoe* and stretched from the site of the Tor de' Conti to the slopes of the Oppian Hill. Pompey lived here, in a small but famous house, occupied after his death by Antony. The villa of Maecenas was situated on the ground afterwards occupied by the Baths of Titus. The villa was eventually acquired by Nero, who incorporated it in his famous Domus Aurea. Virgil had a house near the gardens of Maecenas. Propertius lived in the vicinity and Horace may have done so: he was certainly a constant visitor at the villa of his patron.

Via Cavour (Pl. 8; 2), opened in 1890 and now an important traffic artery of the city, runs direct from Via dei Fori Imperiali (p 101) to Piazza dei Cinquecento and the railway station. At the beginning on the left is the base of the massive *Torre dei Conti*, all that remains of a great tower erected after 1198 by Riccardo dei Conti, brother of Innocent III. It was damaged by an earthquake in 1348 and reduced to its present state by Urban VIII in the 17C. Via Cavour now passes through the ancient *Subura*, the scarcely noticeable hill of which was one of the four summits of the Esquiline included in the Septimontium, the city that succeeded Roma Quadrata. The district was connected to the Roman Forum by the Argiletum. At the first important cross-roads Via degli Annibaldi (right) provides an interesting glimpse of the Colosseum, and Via dei Serpenti (left) leads to the MADONNA DEI MONTI, a fine church by Giac. della Porta (who also designed the fountain nearby).

The 17C INTERIOR contains stuccoes by *Ambr. Buonvicino* and frescoes by *Crist. Casolani*. S side: 1st chapel, frescoes by *Giov. da San Giovanni*; 3rd chapel, *Paris Nogari*, Christ carrying the Cross. The cupola was decorated in 1599–1600 by *Cesare Nebbia*, *Orazio Gentileschi*, and others. N side: 2nd chapel, Adoration of the Shepherds by *Girol. Muziano* and two paintings by *Cesare Nebbia*; 1st chapel, *Durante Alberti*, Annunciation.

On Via Cavour, at the end of a high wall, a flight of steps ascends to the right, called Via San Francesco di Paola, on the site of the ancient Via Scelerata, so called from the impious act of Tullia, who drove her chariot over the dead body of her royal father Servius Tullius. On the right is the base with bands of black and white stone, of a medieval tower.

To the right is Piazza San Francesco di Paola, with a large 17C palazzo which houses the administrative offices of the *Istituto Centrale del Restauro*, which now has its main laboratories in San Michele (see p 257).

The steps pass beneath an archway above which is an attractive Doric loggia, once part of the house of Vannozza Catanei, mother of Lucrezia Borgia. At the top is a square in front of the church of **San Pietro in Vincoli** (Pl. 5; 7; open 7–12.30, 15.30–18), or *Basilica Eudoxiana*, traditionally founded in 442 by the Empress Eudoxia, wife of Valentinian III, as a shrine for the chains of St Peter. The church was restored in 1475 under Sixtus IV by *Meo del Caprina*, who was responsible for the façade, with its beautiful colonnaded portico. During 1956–59 remains of previous buildings, some going back to Republican times, were discovered beneath the church.

The two chains with which St Peter was supposed to have been fettered in the Tullianum are said to have been taken to Constantinople. In 439 Juvenal, Bishop of Jerusalem, gave them to the Empress Eudoxia, wife of Theodosius the Younger. She placed one of them in the basilica of the Apostles at Constantinople, and sent the other to Rome for her daughter Eudoxia, wife of Valentinian III. The younger Eudoxia gave the chain to St Leo I (pope 440–61) and built the church of San Pietro in Vincoli for its reception. Later the second chain was sent to Rome. On being brought together, the two chains miraculously united.

The basilican INTERIOR, much affected by restoration, preserves its twenty ancient columns with Doric capitals (the Ionic bases were added in the 17C). The NAVE (covered with scaffolding in 1988 during repairs to the roof), almost four times as wide as the aisles, has a ceiling-painting by *G.B. Parodi*, representing the cure of a demoniac by the touch of the holy chains. SOUTH AISLE. 1st Altar, *Guercino*, St Augustine; 2nd altar, *Domenichino* designed the tomb on the left and painted the portraits above both tombs; the altarpiece is a copy of his Deliverance of St Peter, now in the sacristy. At the end of the aisle is the TOMB OF JULIUS II, the famous unfinished master-piece of *Michelangelo*, who was so harassed while working on the monument that he called it 'tragedy of a sepulchre'. Hindered by his quarrels with Julius and by the jealousy of that pope's successors, the artist left his task unfinished, and the great pontiff, who had con-templated for himself the most splendid monument in the world, lies uncommemorated in St Peter's. Some forty statues were to have decorated the tomb, including the two slaves now in the Louvre, and the four unfinished slaves in the Accademia gallery in Florence. No idea of the original design of the monument (for which many drawings survive) can be gained from this very unsatisfactory group-ing of statues and niches. Only a few magnificent fragments remain, notably the powerful figure of *Moses, Michelangelo's most strongly individualized work, in whose majestic glance is seen the prophet that spoke with God. The satyr-like horns represent the traditional beams of light, an attribute of the prophet in medieval iconography. The beautiful flanking figures of *Leah and *Rachel, symbols of the active and contemplative life (Dante, 'Purgatorio', xxvii, 108), are also by *Michelangelo*. The rest is his pupils' work: an ineffectual effigy of the Pope, by *Maso del Bosco*; a Madonna, by *Aless. Scherano*; a Prophet and Sibyl, by *Raff. da Montelupo*.

In the last chapel of this aisle, *St Margaret, by *Guercino*.—The bishop's throne in the APSE, which is frescoed by *Giac. Coppi*, is a marble chair brought from a Roman bath. The baldacchino over the high altar is by *Virginio Vespignani* (19C). In the confessio below are the Chains of St Peter, displayed in a tabernacle with beautiful bronze *Doors attributed to *Caradosso* (1477). Stairs lead down to a tiny crypt (usually closed), in which is a fine late 4C Roman sarcophagus with figures representing scenes from the New Testament, containing the relics of the seven Maccabee brothers.—NORTH AISLE. 2nd altar, 7C mosaic *Icon of the bearded St Sebastian, well preserved (coin-operated light, on right); 1st altar, *Pomarancio*, Descent from the Cross; (near the W wall) *And. Bregno*, Tomb of Cardinal De Cusa, with a good coloured relief (1465). On the end wall (covered with scaffolding in 1988) to the right of the entrance door, is the little Tomb of the brothers Pollaiuolo with two expressive portrait busts by *Capponi*. Above is a very worn fresco of the Plague of 1476 by an unknown 15C artist, and to the left, an early fresco of the Head of Christ (behind glass).—The CLOISTER (entrance at No. 16 Via Eudossiana, on the right, now the University Faculty of Engineering), is attributed to *Giul. da Sangallo*. The arches have sadly been enclosed, but the lovely well-head by *Simone Mosca* remains.

The narrow and pretty Via delle Sette Sale leads out of the piazza on the left of San Pietro in Vincoli. This unexpectedly rural street passes between two of the summits of the Esquiline, the Cispius (left) and the Oppius (right). The park which now covers the Oppian hill contains scattered remains of the huge *Baths of Trajan*, built after a fire in 104 by Apollodorus of Damascus and inaugurated in 109. The conspicuous ruins include an exedra which was decorated as a nymphaeum, and a hall with two apses. Between Via Terme di Traiano and Viale del Colle Oppio is a nymphaeum (well below ground level) on a basilican plan, probably part of Nero's Domus Aurea, restored by Trajan. At No. 2 Via Terme di Traiano is the entrance to the so-called SETTE SALE, in fact a remarkable large vaulted building with nine rooms, the reservoir of the Baths of Trajan. Recent excavations have shown that a house was built above the reservoir in the 4C. The rest of the park is occupied by Nero's Domus Aurea, described on p 207).

At the end of Via delle Sette Sale, by its junction with Viale del Monte Oppio, is the church of **San Martino ai Monti** (Pl. 5; 5, 6), the church of the Carmelites, built c 500 by St Symmachus and dedicated to Saints Sylvester and Martin. It replaced an older church founded in the 4C by Pope St Sylvester I, who came from Mount Soracte to cure Constantine of an illness. It was rebuilt in the 9C and given its present appearance c 1650 by *Fil. Gagliardi*. It stands on remains of the old church and incorporates part of a Roman edifice.

In this church were proclaimed, in the presence of Constantine, the decisions of the Council of Nicaea, and the heretical books of Arius, Sabellius, and Victorinus burnt. In the INTERIOR the broad nave is divided from the aisles by 24 ancient Corinthian columns which support an architrave, and the presbytery is raised above the crypt. The fine 17C decoration, with statues, stucco medallions, and frescoes, is by *Paolo Naldini* and *Fil. Gagliardi*. In the lower side aisles are frescoes of the life of Elijah and landscapes of the Roman Campagna by *Gaspard Dughet*, and (left aisle) interesting views of the interiors of St John Lateran and St Peter's before reconstruction, by *Fil. Gagliardi*. The Council of Pope Sylvester is by *Galeazzo Leoncino*. The tribune, with a double staircase, leading to the high altar, and the tabernacle are by *Gagliardi*, who also designed the elaborate stucco decoration of the CRYPT. Here on the left a door (key in the Sacristy) leads to stairs which descend to a private chapel of the 3C, with traces of frescoes and mosaics, incorporated in eight large halls of a Roman building.—In the left aisle, 2nd altar, St Albert by *Girol. Muziano*, and (1st altar), Vision of St Angelo by *Pietro Testa*.

A door on the right of the apse leads out to a busy cross-roads with two heavily restored medieval towers, from which the church of Santa Prassede may be reached (see p 197).

Viale del Monte Oppio ends at the Largo Brancaccio, on the busy 19C Via Merulana. Here (right) is *Palazzo Brancaccio* (1896, on a design by Luca Carimini) which houses the *Istituto Italiano per il Medio ed Estremo Oriente*. On the second floor is the **Museo Nazionale di Arte Orientale** (adm see p 49), with a fine collection of Oriental art in sixteen superbly arranged rooms (handsheets are provided in each room).

ROOM I. Pre-Mohammedan Iran. Prehistoric ceramics, decorated with animal and geometric motifs, terracotta vases. Luristan bronzes, weapons, and horsebits.—RR. II and III. Mohammedan Iran.—R. III. 9–15C glazed pottery, finely coloured. On the wall, a 16C gold-embroidered cope, with hunting motif; 9–10C Oriental-type vases (Tang), 12–18C Mohammedan ceramics, including exquisite tiles. Indian and Siamese stelae and images, 8C BC sculpture from Afghanistan, of the god Durga killing the demon buffalo.—RR. IV and V (G. Auriti donation). Chinese, Japanese, and Korean bronzes, ceramics, and Buddhas.—R. VI contains Japanese screen paintings.—R. VII. Sculpture, and 18C paintings on decorated vellum from Tibet.—RR. VIII and IX. Architectural fragments and sculpture from Swat, in NE Pakistan; RR. X–XII are used as offices and for exhibitions. The last rooms (XIII–XVI) complete the collections from Swat, including material from recent Italian excavations of necropoli (14C–4C BC).

To the S in Largo Leopardi is the so-called **Auditorium of Maecenas** (usually closed; adm see p 48). An Augustan apsidal building, this was in the gardens of Maecenas, and may have been a nymphaeum. The unusual apse has tiered seats in a semicircle. Traces of red landscape paintings can be seen in the apse and wall niches.— Adjoining is a portion of the Servian Wall.

Via Leopardi leads NE to the large 19C **Piazza Vittorio Emanuele** (Pl. 5; 6) surrounded by porticoes and planted with plane trees, cedars of Lebanon, and oleanders. It is now the scene of Rome's most important food market, particularly noted for fish. In the garden of the square are the ruins of a fountain of the time of Alexander Severus, where the marble panoplies known as the 'Trophies of Marius', now on the balustrade of Piazza del Campidoglio, remained until the 16C. Near the fountain is the curious *Porta Magica*, with an alchemist's prescription for making gold. In the N corner of the square is the church of SANT'EUSEBIO, founded in the 4C and rebuilt in 1711 and 1750. The ceiling painting, the Triumph of St Eusebius, is by *Raphael Mengs*; in the apse are fine, elaborately carved 16C stalls. In the Sacristy, in the right aisle, is the carved top of the tomb of St Eusebius (15C) from the earlier church.

Via Carlo Alberto leads NE from the square to Santa Maria Maggiore, passing the *Arch of Gallienus* (restored in 1986), the middle arch of a triple gate erected in the time of Augustus and dedicated in AD 262 in honour of Gallienus and his consort Salonina by the city prefect M. Aurelius Victor; it occupies the site of the Porta Esquilina of the Servian Wall. On the left is the church of **Santi Vito e Modesto** (4C; restored in 1900 and again in 1977). It contains frescoes by Antoniazzo Romano, and excavations have revealed traces of the Servian wall and a Roman acqueduct. Farther on, on the right, is **Sant'Antonio Abate**, the church of the Russo-Byzantine rite, with a doorway attrib. to the Vassalletto (1262–66).

At the end of Via Merulana is *Piazza Santa Maria Maggiore*, occupying the highest point (55m) of the Cispian summit of the Esquiline. In the square rises a fluted cipollino column 14·5m high, a relic of the basilica of Constantine. It was set up here in 1613 for Paul V by Carlo Maderno (who designed the fountain), and crowned with a statue of the Virgin. Dominating the square is the ornate porticoed façade of *Santa Maria Maggiore** (Pl. 5; 6; open 7–20; 7–19 in winter), once also called the *Basilica Liberiana*, which, more completely than any other of the four patriarchal basilicas, retains its

original interior magnificence. Santa Maria Maggiore has the privilege of extraterritoriality.

According to a 13C legend, the Virgin Mary appeared on the night of 4–5
August 352, to Pope Liberius and to John, a patrician of Rome, telling them to
build a church on the Esquiline on the spot where they would find in the
morning a patch of snow covering the exact area to be built over. The prediction
fulfilled, Liberius drew up the plans and John built the church at his own
expense. The original title was therefore Santa Maria della Neve. The church
was afterwards called *Santa Maria del Presepe*, after a precious relic of the Crib
of the Infant Jesus. The church in fact almost certainly dates from the 5C (c 420),
and it was completed by Sixtus III (432–40). Nicholas IV (1288–92) added the
polygonal apse and transepts, Clement X (1670–76) rebuilt the apse, and
Benedict XIV ordered Ferd. Fuga to carry out further alterations and add the
main façade.
  Two important ceremonies are held here annually. On 5 August the legend of
the miraculous fall of snow is commemorated in a pontifical Mass in the
Borghese Chapel (see below). On Christmas morning occurs the procession in
honour of the Santa Culla, or Holy Crib, which culminates in the exposure of the
relic on the high altar.
  In 366 supporters of the antipope Ursinus barricaded themselves in the
church and surrendered only when the partisans of Pope Damasus I took off the
roof and pelted them with tiles. In 1075 Gregory VII (Hildebrand) was carried
off from Mass by the rebel Cencio, but was rescued next day by the people. In
1347 Rienzo was crowned here as Tribune of Rome.
  Exterior. The MAIN FAÇADE, masking one of the 12C, was designed by *Fuga*
(1743); it is approached by steps and is flanked by two grandiose wings. The
portico is surmounted by a loggia of three arches, above which are statues. In
the loggia are the mosaics (difficult to see; admission only with special
permission) of the earlier façade, dating from the time of Nicholas IV, which
depict the Legend of the Snow (see above) and saints by *Filippo Rusuti* (c 1293–
97); the lower part was probably completed by assistants. Five openings admit
to the portico with a statue of Philip IV of Spain, after Bernini. The fine
*CAMPANILE, the highest in Rome, was given its present form in 1377 by
Gregory XI, and the polychrome decoration has recently been restored. The
APSIDAL FAÇADE, completed c 1673, is approached by an imposing flight of
steps from Piazza dell'Esquilino. The right-hand section, with its dome, is by
Flaminio Ponzio; the central and left sections by *Carlo Rainaldi*; the left-hand
dome by *Dom. Fontana*.

The vast but well-proportioned **Interior** (86m long), which still
preserves the basilican form, is divided into nave and aisles by 36
columns of shining Hymettian marble and 4 of granite, all with Ionic
capitals supporting an architrave, the whole discreetly rearranged
and regularized by *Fuga*. Over the triumphal arch and in the nave
are *MOSAICS, set up by Sixtus III (432–440), the most important
mosaic cycle in Rome of this period, of exquisite workmanship, in the
classical tradition. The small biblical scenes high up above the
architrave in the nave are difficult to see with the naked eye. On the
left, scenes from the life of Abraham, Jacob, and Isaac; right, scenes
from the life of Moses and Joshua (restored; in part painted); over the
triumphal arch, scenes from the early life of Christ. The coffered
*Ceiling, attrib. to *Giul. da Sangallo*, is said to have been gilded with
the first gold brought from America by Columbus, presented to
Alexander VI by Ferdinand and Isabella. The fine Cosmatesque
pavement dates from c 1150. At the W end (A) are the monuments of
Clement IX (1670), by *C. Rainaldi*, and others, and (B) that of
Nicholas IV (1574), by *Dom. Fontana* and others.
  RIGHT AISLE. From the Baptistery (C), with a high relief by *Pietro
Bernini*, is the entrance to the Sacristy (D), designed, like the
Baptistery, by *Flaminio Ponzio* (early 17C), with a tomb by *Aless.
Algardi*. In the Cappella San Michele (E) are traces of 15C frescoes
(restored in 1981) including two evangelists by the circle of Piero

Mosaic panel dating from 432–440 in the nave of Santa Maria Maggiore

della Francesca and a Pietà attrib. to Benozzo Gozzoli. A column in the adjoining courtyard celebrates the conversion of Henry IV of France. The Cappella delle Reliquie (F) has ten porphyry columns. The *SISTINE CHAPEL (G), or Chapel of the Holy Sacrament, on a domed Greek-cross plan, is a work of extraordinary magnificence by *Dom. Fontana* (1585). It is a veritable church in itself decorated with statues, stuccoes (by *Ambr. Buonvicino*), and late-16C Mannerist frescoes by *Cesare Nebbia, G.B. Pozzo, Paris Nogari, Lattanzio Mainardi,* and *Giac. Stella.* The marble decoration was brought from the Septizodium (demolished by Sixtus V) and set up here by Carlo Maderno. Here are the sumptuous tombs of Sixtus V, with a statue by *Valsoldo,* and of Pius V with a statue by *Leon. Sormani.* The temple-like baldacchino covers the original little Cosmatesque Chapel of the relics, redesigned by *Arnolfo di Cambio* (late 13C), with figures of the crèche by his assistants.—Outside the chapel is the simple tomb slab in the pavement of the Bernini family, including Gian Lorenzo. The beautiful *Tomb of Cardinal Consalvo Rodriguez (died 1299; H) is a

masterpiece by *Giov. Cosmati*, showing the influence of Arnolfo di
Cambio. The mosaic of the Madonna enthroned, with saints, fits well
with the architectonic lines of the tomb, which was completed by the
beginning of the 14C.

The Confessio (J), reconstructed in the 19C by *Vespignani*, contains a kneeling statue of Pius IX by *Ignazio Iacometti*. The baldacchino over the high altar, with four porphyry columns, is by *Fuga*; a
porphyry urn which contains the relics of St Matthew and other
martyrs serves as the high altar; the fragment of the Crib of the Infant
Jesus is kept below in the Confessio in a reliquary adorned with
reliefs and silver statuettes.—The mosaic of the APSE (K) dating from
the time of Nicholas IV (1288–94), is signed by *Iac. Torriti* (1290–95).
It represents the *Coronation of the Virgin, with angels, saints,
Nicholas IV, Cardinal Iac. Colonna, etc. It is the culminating point of
all the mosaics in the church, which commemorate the declaration at
the Council of Ephesus (5C) that the Virgin was the Mother of God
(Theotókos). The Virgin is seated on the same throne as Christ, a
composition probably derived from the 12C mosaic in the apse of
Santa Maria in Trastevere. Below, between the windows, are more
mosaics by Torriti of the life of the Virgin, notably, in the centre, the
Dormition of the Virgin. The four reliefs, below the windows, are
from the old ciborium by *Mino del Reame*.

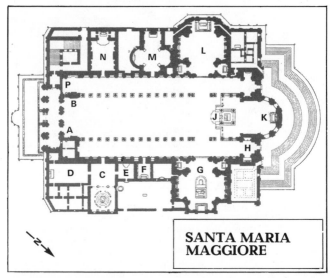

SANTA MARIA
MAGGIORE

LEFT AISLE. Balancing the Sistine Chapel is the even more sumptuous BORGHESE CHAPEL, or *Cappella Paolina* (L). This chapel, built
by Paul V on the plans of *Flaminio Ponzio* (1611), is frescoed by
Cigoli, Cav. d'Arpino, Guido Reni, and *Lanfranco*. On the altar,
decorated with lapis lazuli and agate, is a Madonna and Child with
crossed hands, now thought to date from the 12–13C, although it has
also been attrib. to a Byzantine artist working before the 10C. The
tombs of Clement VIII and Paul V, with statues by *Silla Longhi*, are
on either side.—The SFORZA CHAPEL (M), erected by Giac. della
Porta to a design by Michelangelo, contains an Assumption, by

Girol. da Sermoneta. In the CESI CHAPEL (N), by *Guidetto Guidetti* (c 1550), are two tombs, by *Gugl. della Porta* and a St Catherine, by *Sermoneta.*—The tomb of Cardinal Philippe de Levis de Quelus and his younger brother Archbishop Eustache (1489), above the Porta Santa (P) is in the style of *Giov. Dalmata.*

Just out of Piazza Santa Maria Maggiore Via Santa Prassede leads to the inconspicuous side entrance of the church of *Santa Prassede (Pl. 5; 6; open 7–12, 16–18.30), built by St Paschal I in 822 and still enveloped on all sides by medieval and later buildings.

An oratory is said to have been erected here about AD 150 by St Pius I, and a church is known to have been in existence here at the end of the 5C. Paschal's 9C church was restored in 1450, 1564, 1832, and 1869. The building is dedicated to Praxedes, sister of Pudentiana (p 199) and daughter of Pudens, in whose house St Peter is traditionally supposed to have first found hospitality at Rome. Here in 1118 the Frangipani attacked Pope Gelasius II with arrows and stones, driving him to exile in France, where he died.

　　The main W entrance, on the old Via San Martino ai Monti, is kept locked: it is preceded by a medieval porch with two reversed Doric capitals. The only part of the exterior visible is the Zeno Chapel, beside the S entrance.

The NAVE has 16 granite columns and six piers supporting an architrave made up from ancient Roman fragments. The effective trompe l'oeil frescoes date from the late 16C (by *Paris Nogari, Baldass. Croce, Ciampelli*, and others). In the nave a large porphyry disk with an inscription indicates the well where St Praxedes is supposed to have hidden the bones of Christian martyrs. The CHOIR is approached by steps of rosso antico. The fine Baroque baldacchino by *Fr. Ferrari* (1730) partially hides the splendid 9C *Mosaics (coin-operated light on right): on the entrance-arch (outer face) the New Jerusalem, whose doors are guarded by angels, (inner face) Christ and saints; on the apse-arch, the Agnus Dei with the seven golden candlesticks, the symbols of the Evangelists,' and 24 Elders; in the semi-dome, Christ between (right) Saints Peter, Pudentiana, and Zeno, and (left) Saints Paul, Praxedes, and Paschal; below, the Lamb, the flock of the Faithful and a dedicatory inscription; above, the monogram of Paschal I.—On the left and right of the sanctuary are six Roman *Columns of very unusual design incorporating the form of acanthus and laurel leaves.—In the Confessio beneath are sarcophagi, including one with the remains of Saints Praxedes and Pudentiana, and a 13C Cosmatesque altar, with a damaged fresco above.

　　In the S aisle is the *CHAPEL OF ST ZENO (coin-operated light on left), a remarkable Byzantine structure, built in 817–824 by St Paschal as a mausoleum for his mother, Theodora. The entrance is flanked by two ancient porphyry columns with 9C Ionic capitals which support a rich 1C architrave from some pagan temple, elaborately sculptured; on this rests a Roman marble urn (3C). Above is a double row of 9C mosaic busts; in the inner row, the Virgin and Child, Saints Praxedes and Pudentiana, and other saints, in the outer, Christ and the Apostles, and four saints (the lowest two perhaps added in the 13C). The vaulted interior, the solitary instance in Rome of a chapel entirely lined with mosaics, was known as the 'Garden of Paradise'. The pavement is perhaps the oldest known example of opus sectile. Over the door, Saints Peter and Paul uphold the throne of God; on the right, Saints John the Evangelist, Andrew, and James, and Christ between St Paschal and Valentine (?); inside the altar-niche, Madonna between Saints Praxedes and Pudentiana; on the

*The 9C vault mosaic in the Chapel of St Zeno
(Santa Prassede)*

left, Saints Praxedes, Pudentiana, and Agnes, and four female half-
lengths including Theodora (with the square nimbus). In the vault,
Christ and four angels. The bases of the four supporting columns
date from the 9C, except for the one on the right of the altar which is
a fine 5C Roman work. In a niche on the right are fragments of a
column brought from Jerusalem after the 6th Crusade (1228), and
said to be that at which Christ was scourged.—In the adjoining
funerary chapel is the *Tomb of Cardinal Alain Coëtivy (1474) by
And. Bregno. Outside, on a nave pillar, is the tomb of G.B. Santoni
(died 1592), one of the earliest works of *Bernini*. At the E end of the
aisle a chapel contains the Cosmatesque tomb of Cardinal Pantaleon
of Troyes (died 1286) and architectural fragments.—NORTH AISLE. At
the W end, marble slab on which St Praxedes is said to have slept;
3rd chapel, frescoes by *Cav. d'Arpino*; Christ bearing the Cross, by
Fed. Zuccari; 2nd chapel, chair and table of St Charles Borromeo. In
the Sacristy, Flagellation, attrib. to *Giulio Romano*.—To the right a
spiral staircase (no admission) leads up to the campanile with 9C wall
paintings.

Behind the apse of Santa Maria Maggiore is *Piazza dell'Esquilino*
with an obelisk, nearly 15m high, set up by Sixtus V in 1587. Like its
twin in Piazza del Quirinale it once stood outside the entrance to the
Mausoleum of Augustus. Via Cavour (see p 190) cuts across the
piazza. Opposite Santa Maria Maggiore Via Agostino Depretis runs

metres to **Santa Pudenziana** (Pl. 5; 5), one of the oldest churches in Rome, thought to have been built c 390 above a Roman thermal hall of the 2C. It was rebuilt several times later, notably in 1589.

The church is dedicated to Pudentiana, sister of Praxedes (see p 197), and daughter of the Roman senator Pudens, a legendary figure who is supposed to have given hospitality to St Peter in his house on this site.

The church is now well below the level of the modern street. The façade was rebuilt and decorated in the 19C; the fine campanile probably dates from the late 12C. The good doorway preserves a beautiful medieval frieze in relief.

In the disappointing INTERIOR the nave and aisles are divided by Roman columns built up into piers. The dome was painted by *Pomarancio*. The precious *MOSAIC in the apse, the earliest of its kind in Rome, dates from 390. It was damaged by a 16C restoration, which removed the two outermost Apostles at each end and cut the others in half. It shows Christ enthroned holding an open book between the Apostles and two female figures representing the Church of the Jews and the Church of the Heathen crowning St Peter and St Paul. The Roman character of the figures is marked; the magisterial air of Christ recalls the representations of Jupiter, and the Apostles, in their togas, resemble senators. Above is a jewelled Cross and the symbols of the Evangelists, and buildings (including houses, thermae, and a basilica) representing Jerusalem and Golgotha.—In the chapel at the end of the left aisle an altar, presented by Card. Wiseman, encloses part of the legendary communion-table of St Peter; the rest of it is in St John Lateran. The marble group of Christ entrusting the keys to St Peter is by *G.B. della Porta*. The Cappella Caetani, opening off the aisle is a rich Baroque work, by *Franc. da Volterra*, finished by *Carlo Maderno*. The altar relief is by *P.P. Olivieri*. Behind the apse are fragments of frescoes and a statuette of the Good Shepherd.

Through a door in the left aisle (apply to sacristan, but usually closed) is a courtyard, showing part of 2C baths, and, up some stairs, the *Oratorium Marianum*, containing 11C frescoes and brick stamps of Hadrian's time, discovered during excavations. The building incorporates part of the baths said to have been erected by Novatian and Timotheus, the brothers of Pudentiana and Praxedes, above the so-called house of Pudens. The baths extend on to the pavement in Via Balbo; the frescoes are also visible from here. Excavations under the church in 1933 revealed Republican mosaics and walls, with a 2C house; these, however, have been closed since 1970 when they were badly flooded.

Via Urbana continues to the undulating Via Panisperna in which is the church of **San Lorenzo in Panisperna** (Pl. 5; 5), the traditional site of the martyrdom of the saint, in a delightful court of old houses, and a villa to the left (part of the Ministry of the Interior, see below). The church contains a vast fresco of the martyrdom by Pasq. Cati. The huge *Palazzo del Viminale* (1920), now the Ministry of the Interior fronts Piazza del Viminale on Via Agostino Depretis. On the parallel Via Napoli, off Via Nazionale, is the American episcopal church of **St Paul's**, a neo-Gothic structure by G.E. Street (1879), containing a mosaic by Burne-Jones. In Via Viminale is the *Teatro dell'Opera*, built in 1880 by Achille Sfondrini for Domenico Costanzi. The Roman première of Verdi's 'Falstaff' was performed here in 1893. It was acquired by the Comune of Rome in 1926, and restored and enlarged by Marcello Piacentini in 1959–60. It is the most important lyric theatre in Rome.

12 St John Lateran and Santa Croce

On the edge of the Celian hill, around the busy PIAZZA DI SAN GIOVANNI IN LATERANO (Pl. 10; 3) are assembled some of the most important monuments in Christian history, including the first church of Rome. Here in 1588, on a line with Via di San Giovanni and Via Merulana, Domenico Fontana set up a red granite *Obelisk*, the oldest in the city.

The Obelisk was erected by Thothmes IV in front of the Temple of Ammon at Thebes (15C BC), and brought to Rome by Constantius II (357) to enhance the Circus Maximus, where it was discovered in three pieces in 1587. It is the tallest obelisk in existence (31m high, 47m with the pedestal), though 1m had to be sawn off during its reconstruction.—On the W side of the square is the *Ospedale di San Giovanni*, the main hospital in Rome for emergencies ('pronto soccorso'; car accidents, etc.). Excavations in 1959–64 beneath the hospital revealed remains of a villa, thought to be that of Domizia Lucilla, mother of Marcus Aurelius.

The church of ***St John Lateran** (*San Giovanni in Laterano*; Pl. 10; 3; open 7–18; summer 7–19) is the cathedral of Rome and of the world ('Omnium urbis et orbis Ecclesiarum Mater et Caput'). Founded by Constantine, it was the first Christian basilica to be constructed in Rome. It is significant that it was built on a basilican plan: it served as a model for the churches that followed it. Until 1870 the popes were crowned here.

The basilica derives its name from the rich patrician family of Plautius Lateranus, who, having been implicated in the conspiracy of the Pisoni, was deprived of his property and put to death by Nero. Recent excavations in the neighbouring Via Aradam have revealed a large Roman building thought to be the house of the Pisoni and Laterani expropriated by Nero. The property afterwards passed to Constantine as the dowry of his wife Fausta. In this 'Domus Faustae' church meetings were probably held as early as 313. The Emperor presented it, together with the land occupied by the barracks (excavated in 1934–38 beneath the nave of the present basilica) built in the 2C for his private horseguards, 'the Equites Singulares', to St Melchiades (pope 311–314), for the purpose of building a church for the see of Rome. The original five-aisled church with an apse, probably built between 314 and 318, was dedicated to the Redeemer and later to Saints John the Baptist and John the Evangelist. Partly ruined by the Vandals, it was restored by St Leo the Great (440–461) and Hadrian I (772–795) and, after the earthquake of 896, by Sergius III (904–911). Nicholas IV (1288–1292) enlarged and embellished the building to such an extent that it was considered the wonder of the age; it was this church that Dante described with admiration on the occasion of the first Jubilee, or Holy Year, proclaimed on 22 February 1300 by Boniface VIII from the central loggia of the E façade.

The church was destroyed by fire in 1308 and rebuilt by Clement V (1305–14) soon afterwards; it was decorated by Giotto. In 1360 it was burnt down again and its ruin was lamented by Petrarch. Under Urban V (1362–70) and Gregory XI (1370–78) it was entirely rebuilt by the Sienese Giovanni di Stefano. Martin V (1417–31), Eugenius IV (1431–47) and their successors added to its splendour (Sixtus V employing Dom. Fontana, and Clement VIII, Giac. della Porta). In 1646–49 Innocent X commissioned Borromini to rebuild the church yet again, and in 1734 Clement XII added the E façade. The ancient apse was entirely reconstructed in 1875–85 and the mosaics reset after the original designs.—The basilica has been the seat of five General Councils: in 1123, 1139, 1179, 1215, and 1512.

Under the Lateran Treaty of 11 February 1929, this basilica, with those of San Paolo fuori le Mura and Santa Maria Maggiore, was accorded the privilege of extraterritoriality. After the ratification of the treaty the pope, for the first time since 1870, left the seclusion of the Vatican. On 24 June 1929, Pius XI officiated at St John Lateran, and the annual ceremony of blessing the people from the loggia was later resumed. The Pope traditionally attends the Maundy Thursday celebrations in the Basilica.

Exterior. The principal or EAST FRONT, overlooking Piazza di Porta San Giovanni, is a theatrical composition by *Aless. Galilei* (1734–36). It consists of a two-storied portico surmounted by an attic with 16 colossal statues of Christ with the Apostles and saints. On Maundy Thursday the pope gives his benediction from the central loggia. Beneath the PORTICO, the bronze central doors were first used for the Curia, and later the church of Sant' Adriano in the Forum. On the left (A) is a statue of Constantine, from his Baths on the Quirinal.—The NORTH FRONT, on Piazza di San Giovanni in Laterano, is also a

The cloister of St John Lateran by Iacopo and Pietro Vassalletto (c 1220–36)

portico of two tiers; it was built by *Dom. Fontana* in 1586. Beneath it, on the left, is a statue of Henry IV of France, by *Nicolas Cordier* (c 1610), erected in gratitude for his gifts to the chapter. The two towers behind date from the time of Pius IV (1560).

The **Interior**, 130m long, with two aisles on either side of the nave, preserves in part its original 4C proportions, although it was entirely remodelled by *Borromini* in 1646–49. In the niches of the massive piers which encase the verde antico pillars are colossal statues of Apostles made in the early 18C by *Lor. Ottoni, Camillo Rusconi, Gius. Mazzuoli, Pierre Legros, Pierre Monnot, Angelo de̓ Rossi*, and *Fr. Moratti*. Above them are stuccoes designed by *Algardi* with scenes from the Old and New Testaments. Higher still are paintings of Prophets (1718) by *Dom. Maria Muratori, Marco Benefial, Gius. Nicola Nasini, Giov. Odazzi, G. Paolo Melchiorri, Seb. Conca, Bened. Luti, Fr. Trevisani, And. Procaccini, Luigi Garzi, Gius. Chiari*, and *Pierleone Ghezzi*. The rich ceiling is by *F. Boulanger* and *Vico di Raffaele*, and the marble pavement is of Cosmatesque design.

The outer aisles were also decorated by *Borromini*, and the funerary monuments reconstructed and enclosed in elegant Baroque frames. RIGHT AISLES. On the nave piers: Boniface VIII proclaiming the Jubilee of 1300 (B), a fragment of a fresco from the exterior loggia recently restored and now considered to be by the hand of *Giotto*; cenotaph of Sylvester II (died 1003; C), by the Hungarian sculptor *William Fraknoi* (1909); beneath is a curious medieval memorial slab to the pope; tomb of Alexander III (D), the pope of the Lombard League; tomb of Sergius IV, with a medieval figure of a Pope (E); tomb of Card. Ranuccio Farnese (F), by *Vignola*. In the outer aisle: tomb of Paolo Mellini (1527), in the embrasure of the Porta Santa (G; opened only in Holy Years), with a damaged fresco; between 1st and 2nd chapels, tomb of Giulio Acquaviva (1574), made cardinal at the age of 20 by Pius V. The CAPPELLA TORLONIA (H), richly decorated by *Raimondi* (1850), is closed by a fine iron balustrade, and has a

sculptured altarpiece (Descent from the Cross) by *Pietro Tenerani*.
Over the window-screen outside the adjoining Cappella Massimo is
a fragment of the original altar with a statuette of St James, attrib. to
And. Bregno; towards the end of the aisle, enclosed in Borromini's
Baroque frames, tombs of Card. Casati (1290), by the *Cosmati*, and of
Card. Ant. de Chaves (1447) attrib. to *Isaia da Pisa*.—LEFT AISLES. At
the beginning of the outer aisle (K) is a sarcophagus with the cast of a
recumbent figure of Card. Riccardo degli Annibaldi (1276) by
Arnolfo di Cambio (the original is now exhibited in the Cloisters, see
below). The CAPPELLA CORSINI (L), a graceful early 18C structure by
Aless. Galilei, contains above its altar a mosaic copy of Guido Reni's
painting of St Andrea Corsini; on the left, tomb of Clement XII
(Lorenzo Corsini; died 1740), a porphyry sarcophagus from the
Pantheon, and in the vault below (apply to sacristan) a Pietà by *Ant.
Montauti*. In the aisle, tombs of the Archpriest Gerardo da Parma
(1061; U) and of Card. Bern. Caracciolo (died 1255; V); at the end,
beyond the pretty CAPPELLA LANCELLOTTI (W), by *Fr. da Volterra*
(1585–90, rebuilt 1675 by *G.A. de Rossi*), is the tomb of Card.
Casanate (1707; X), founder of the library that bears his name.

The TRANSEPTS were built under Clement VIII (1592–1605) by
Giac. della Porta, and the large frescoes of the conversion of Constantine, his gift to the pope, and the building of the Basilica,
completed in 1600 under the direction of *Cav. d'Arpino* (by *G.B.
Ricci, Paris Nogari, Crist. Roncalli, Orazio Gentileschi, Cesare Nebbia, G. Baglione*, and *Bern. Cesari*). In the central space is the *Papal
Altar*, reconstructed by Pius IX, containing many relics, including the
heads of Saints Peter and Paul, and part of St Peter's wooden altar-
table. Above is the Gothic *Baldacchino by *Giov. di Stefano* (1367),
frescoed by *Barna da Siena*. In the enclosure in front of the confessio
is the *Tomb-slab of Martin V (died 1431), by *Sim. Ghini* (M).—In the
right transept is the great organ (1598; by *Luca Blasi*), supported by
two columns of giallo antico, and the tomb (N) of Innocent III (died
1216), by *Gius. Lucchetti* (1891), erected when Leo XIII brought the
ashes of his great predecessor from Perugia. In the corner, to the right
in the little Cappella del Crocifisso (O), is a kneeling statue of
Boniface IX (Cosmatesque; late 14C).—In the left transept is the
tomb of Leo XIII (P), by *Giulio Tadolini* (1907). At the end is the Altar
of the Holy Sacrament (Q), by *Pietro Paolo Olivieri* (from the time of
Clement VIII), flanked by four antique bronze columns. On the right
is the CAPPELLA DEL CORO (R), with fine stalls of c 1625.

The APSE was reconstructed, at the expense of Leo XIII, by *Virginio* and *Fr.
Vespignani* in 1885 when the fine apse mosaics were destroyed and substituted
by a copy. The original mosaics were designed by *Iac. Torriti* and *Iac. da
Camerino* (1288–94) from an antique model. Beneath the Head of Christ (the
copy of a mosaic fabled to have appeared miraculously at the consecration of
the church) the Dove descends upon the bejewelled Cross. From the hill on
which it stands four rivers flow to quench the thirst of the faithful. On either side
are (left) the Virgin with Nicholas IV and Saints Peter and Paul, and (right)
Saints John the Baptist, John the Evangelist, and Andrew; the figures of St
Francis of Assisi (left) and St Anthony of Padua (right) were added by Nicholas
IV. At their feet flows the Jordan. Kneeling at the feet of the Apostles (in the
frieze below) are the tiny figures of Torriti and Camerino.

The doorway beneath Leo XIII's tomb admits to the SACRISTY, reached by a
corridor containing the tombs of And. Sacchi and the Cavalier d'Arpino, and
(behind the apse) two fine statues of St Peter and St Paul by *Deodato di Cosma*.
On the left is the OLD SACRISTY, with a beautiful Annunciation by *Marcello
Venusti*, after Michelangelo.

In the left aisle (beyond T) is the entrance to the *CLOISTER (open when the
church is open), the masterpiece of *Iac.* and *Pietro Vassalletto* (c 1220–36), a

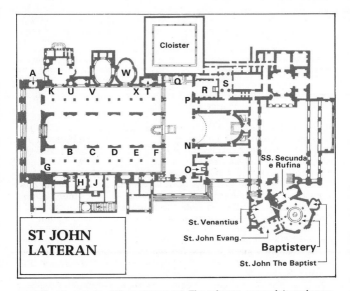

**ST JOHN
LATERAN**

magnificent example of Cosmatesque art. The columns, some plain and some twisted, are adorned with mosaics and have fine capitals. The frieze is exquisite. Many interesting fragments from the ancient basilica are displayed around the cloister walls. From the left: Various pieces of Cosmati work, including Papal throne, an antique marble chair with Cosmati decorations; (behind glass) *Tomb of Card. Riccardo Annibaldi, the first important work of *Arnolfo di Cambio* in Rome (c 1276). It has been reconstructed from fragments, which include reliefs and the recumbent statue; Roman sarcophagus, with four portraits; various pavement tomb slabs, carved in relief; Saints in niches (late-15C).—A room off the cloisters displays church vestments, Florentine tapestries (1595–1608), etc.

In the SW corner of the piazza is the *Baptistery of St John, or *San Giovanni in Fonte*, built by Constantine c 315–24, though not, as legend states, the scene of his baptism as the first Christian emperor (337). It is a centrally planned octagonal building, although the original baptistery, designed for total immersion, and derived from classical models, may have been circular. It was remodelled by Sixtus III (432–40), and its design was copied in many subsequent baptisteries. It was restored again by Hadrian III in 884.

In the INTERIOR (adm 8–12, 16–18; winter 8–12, 15–17; the chapels are unlocked by the sacristan) are eight columns of porphyry erected by Sixtus III; they support an architrave which bears eight smaller white marble columns. In the centre is the green basalt font. The 17C decorations were added by Urban VIII, and the harsh frescoes of scenes from the life of St John the Baptist on the drum of the cupola are modern copies of works by And. Sacchi.—The CHAPEL OF ST JOHN THE BAPTIST was founded by the martyred pope, St Hilary (461–68). It preserves its original doors (once thought to come from the Baths of Caracalla), which resound musically when opened. The CHAPEL OF SAINTS CYRIAN AND JUSTINA (or SAINTS SECUNDA AND RUFINA) occupied the narthex of Sixtus III, altered to its present form in 1154. Over the door is a relief of the Crucifixion after And. Bregno (1492). In one of the apses is a beautiful 5C *Mosaic with vine tendrils on a brilliant blue ground. High up on the wall can be seen a fragment of the original marble intarsia decoration of the baptistery. A door leads out into a courtyard from where can be seen the outer face of the narthex with two beautiful huge antique columns supporting a fine Roman architrave.—The

CHAPEL OF ST VENANTIUS, added by Pope John IV in 640 contains mosaics
commissioned by Pope Theodore I (642–649): in the apse, the head of Christ
flanked by angels and the Madonna with Saints and Pope Theodore, and on the
triumphal arch the martyrs whose relics Pope John brought from Dalmatia and
(high up) views of Jerusalem and Bethlehem. Remains of 2C Roman baths built
above a 1C villa, with a mosaic pavement, may also be seen here. The structure
of the original baptistery can be seen in the walls and beneath the apse.—The
CHAPEL OF ST JOHN THE EVANGELIST, dedicated by St Hilary, with bronze doors
of 1196, is decorated with a vault *Mosaic (5C) of the Lamb surrounded by
symbolic birds and flowers. The altar is adorned with alabaster columns. On the
left, *L. Capponi*, St Leo praying to St John.

Adjoining the basilica on the right, and facing Piazza di Porta San
Giovanni, is the **Lateran Palace** (Pl. 10; 3; no adm), used by the popes
before the move to Avignon in 1309. The old palace, which is traced
back to the time of Constantine, was almost destroyed in the fire of
1308 which devastated St John Lateran. On the return from Avignon
in 1377 the Holy See was transferred to the Vatican. In 1586 Sixtus V
demolished or displaced what the fire had left and ordered *Dom.
Fontana* to carry out a complete reconstruction. It was intended to
make the new Lateran the summer palace of the popes, but the
Quirinal was preferred. The interior was restored in 1838. Under the
Lateran Treaty of 1929, the palace was recognized as an integral part
of the Vatican City. It is now the seat of the Rome Vicariate, the
offices of the Rome diocese. The Lateran museums were moved to
the Vatican in 1963.

In Piazza di Porta San Giovanni are three survivals of the old
Lateran Palace—the Scala Santa, the Chapel of St Laurence, and the
Triclinium. A building (1589) by *Dom. Fontana*, architect of the new
Lateran, opposite that palace, on the E side of the piazza, houses the
first two. The **Scala Santa** is supposed to be the staircase of Pilate's
house which Christ descended after his condemnation. It is said to
have been brought from Jerusalem to Rome by St Helena, mother of
Constantine.

The 28 Tyrian marble steps are protected by boards and may be ascended only
by worshippers on their knees. In the vestibule are 19C sculptures by *Ignazio
Iacometti* (Kiss of Judas) and *G. Meli* (Ecce Homo). The Scala Santa and the side
staircases, by which pilgrims descend, were decorated at the end of the 16C
under the direction of *Giov. Guerra* and *Cesare Nebbia*. At the top is the *Chapel
of St Laurence*, or **Sancta Sanctorum**, the private chapel of the pope in the old
palace, built in 1278 (never open, but visible through the grating). The mosaic of
Christ may be the work of the *Cosmati* or *Rusuti*, or an early work by *Pietro
Cavallini*; the murals could be by Cavallini although they have also been attrib.
to *Cimabue*. Protected by a silver tabernacle presented by Innocent III is the
relic which gives the chapel its particular sanctity. This is an ancient painting on
wood of Christ which could date from as early as the 5C (many times repainted
and restored). It is said to have been begun by St Luke and an angel: hence its
name 'Acheiropoeton', or the picture made without hands. The precious relics
and their reliquaries are exhibited in the Vatican (p 331).

To the E of the Scala Santa is the **Tribune** erected by Fuga for Benedict XIV in
1743 and decorated with good copies of the mosaics from the *Triclinium of Leo
III*, the banqueting hall of the old Lateran Palace. In the centre, Christ sending
forth the Apostles to preach the Gospel; on the left, Christ giving the keys to St
Sylvester and the labarum, or standard of the Cross, to Constantine; on the
right, St Peter giving the papal stole to Leo III and the banner of Christianity to
Charlemagne.—A fragment of the original mosaic is in the Museum of Christian
Art in the Vatican.

Porta San Giovanni (Pl. 10; 3), built in 1574 by Giac. del Duca,
superseded the ancient *Porta Asinaria*, on the site of the *Porta
Coelimontana* of the Servian Wall. To the W of the modern gateway,
between two fine towers, may be seen the old gate with its vantage-

court, excavated in 1954. Here the festival of San Giovanni is celebrated with a traditional fair on the night of 23–24 June. Outside the gate the busy Via Appia Nuova leads out of the city through the extensive southern suburbs towards the Alban Hills.

From Piazza di Porta San Giovanni Viale Carlo Felice leads E. The first turning on the left is Via Conte Rosso, which runs N to the *Villa Wolkonsky*, formerly the German Embassy, and now the residence of the British ambassador. The Embassy has been transferred to its old site in Via Venti Settembre. Viale Carlo Felice ends in Piazza Santa Croce in Gerusalemme, a busy traffic centre. Here is the church of **Santa Croce in Gerusalemme** (Pl. 10; 2), one of the 'Seven Churches' of Rome, occupied by Cistercians since 1561. According to tradition, this church was founded by Constantine's mother, St Helena. It was in fact probably built some time after 326 within part of the large imperial palace erected for St Helena in the early 3C on the SW extremity of the city. The principal edifice was known as the *Sessorium*, and the church took the name of *Basilica Sessoriana*. Here was enshrined a relic of the true cross salved in Jerusalem by St Helena. It was rebuilt in 1144 by Lucius II, who added the campanile, and completely modernized by Benedict XIV in 1743–44.

The impressive theatrical *FAÇADE and oval *VESTIBULE were built to a very original design by *Dom. Gregorini* and *Pietro Passalacqua* in 1744. The 18C INTERIOR has the nave and aisles separated by granite columns, some of them boxed in pilasters. The Cosmatesque pavement was restored in 1933. Near the door is the epitaph of Benedict VII (died 983), who is buried here. In the right aisle, at the second altar, St Bernard introducing Vittore IV to Innocent II, by *Carlo Maratta*. The vault painting of St Helena in Glory is by *Corrado Giaquinto* (1744). An 18C baldacchino covers the high altar over the basalt tomb which encloses the remains of Saints Caesarius and Anastasius. The fresco in the vault of the apse of the Apparition of the Cross is by *Corrado Giaquinto*. In the centre of the tribune, seen through a graceful 17C baldacchino, probably built to a design of *Carlo Maderno*, is the tomb of Cardinal Quiñones (died 1540), by *Iac. Sansovino*. On the apse wall is a fresco of the Invention of the Cross which has been attrib. to *Antoniazzo Romano* or the Umbrian school.

A stairway at the end of the right aisle leads down to the CHAPEL OF ST HELENA. It contains a statue of the saint, originally a figure of Juno found at Ostia, copied from the Barberini statue in the Vatican. The altar is reserved for the pope and the titular cardinal of the basilica. The vault *Mosaic, the original design of which is probably by *Melozzo* (c 1480), was restored by *Bald. Peruzzi* and later by *Fr. Zucchi*. It represents Christ and the Evangelists, Saints Peter and Paul, St Sylvester (who died here at Mass), St Helena, and Cardinal Carvajal. The fragments of 12C frescoes found here were detached in 1968. On the left is the GREGORIAN CHAPEL, built by Cardinal Carvajal in 1523, with an early 17C Roman bas-relief of the Pietà.—At the end of the left aisle in the CHAPEL OF THE RELICS, by *Florestano Di Fausto* (1930), are preserved the pieces of the True Cross, together with other greatly venerated relics.—In a small MUSEUM are to be exhibited fragments of 12C frescoes detached from the roof of the nave, a 14C fresco of the Crucifixion from the Chapel of the Crucifix, and French 14C statues of Saints Peter and Paul formerly in the Gregorian Chapel.

On the right of the basilica are remains of the *Amphitheatrum Castrense* (no adm), a graceful edifice, built of brick by Heliogabalus or Alexander Severus for amusements of the imperial court, incorporated with the Aurelian Wall by Honorius. To the left of the basilica, in the gardens of the *ex-Caserma dei Granatieri* rises a large ruined apsidal hall known since the Renaissance as the '*Temple of Venus and Cupid*'. It was built in the early 4C by Maxentius or Constantine. In the barracks here are two military museums, and a fine **Museum of Musical Instruments** (adm see p 49), inaugurated in 1974, with a remarkably representative display dating from earliest times to the

19C, including the notable collection of the tenor Evangelista Gorga (1865–1957).

The museum is housed in barracks, an attractive building of c 1903 in the Art Nouveau style, looking N to a section of the Aurelian Wall. On the other side of the building, near the basilica, are more Roman ruins. The collection is beautifully displayed in rooms on the first floor. ROOM I. Archaeological material, including works in terracotta and bronze from the Egyptian, Greek, and Roman periods. R. 2. Exotic instruments from the Far East, America, Africa, and Oceania. R. 3. Instruments used for folk-dances and folk-songs made in Naples, Russia, Spain, etc. R. 4. Mechanical instruments (musical boxes, etc.). R. 5. Instruments used in procession, by street musicians, for serenades, etc. R. 6. Military instruments. R. 7. Church music (bells, organs, etc.). R. 8. Pianos, harps, etc. R. 9. 15C and 16C flutes, organs, spinets, and lutes. RR. 10–16 display instruments from the 17C and 18C, including the elaborate Barberini harp (R. 11), and a pianoforte built by Bartolomeo Cristofori in 1722 (R. 15), harpsichords, and clavichords.

To the E of the barracks, across Viale Castrense and outside the Aurelian Wall, excavations in 1959 revealed remains of the extensive *Circus Varianus*, well-preserved, and dating from the reign of Heliogabalus (218–22).

From Piazza Santa Croce Via Santa Croce leads NW to Via Conte Verde and Piazza Vittorio Emanuele. On the left it passes the end of the Villa Wolkonsky (see above). Via Statilia, skirting the N side of the villa, runs parallel to a fine series of arches of the *Aqueduct of Nero*, an extension of the Aqua Claudia (see below), and built by Nero to provide water for his various constructions on the Palatine and Oppian hills.

Via Eleniana leads N from Piazza Santa Croce to the large and busy Piazza di Porta Maggiore. On the W side of this square is the beginning of Via Statilia, with some arches of the Aqua Claudia, restored to carry the Aqua Marcia (1923). On the E side is the **Porta Maggiore**, or *Porta Prenestina* (Pl. 10; 2), built by Claudius in AD 52, formed by the archways carrying the Aqua Claudia and the Anio Novus over the Via Prenestina and the Via Casilina (see below). The Porta Prenestina was a gate in Aurelian's Wall; it was restored by Honorius in 405.

The ancient Via Prenestina and Via Labicana (see below) can still be seen passing under the arches. Also here are foundations of a guard-house added by Honorius. On the outside of the gate, is the curious **Tomb of the Baker** (M. Virgilius Eurysaces, a public contractor, and his wife Atistia), discovered in 1838. This pretentious monument, entirely of travertine, dates from c 30 BC. The circular openings represent the mouths of a baker's oven; above is a frieze illustrating the stages of bread-making.

The **Aqua Claudia** and the **Anio Novus**, or *Acqua Aniene Nuova*, were two of the finest Roman aqueducts. Both were begun by Caligula in AD 38 and completed in 52. They were restored by Vespasian in 71 and by Titus in 81. The water of the Aqua Claudia was derived from two copious springs near Sublaqueum (Subiaco); its length was 68 kilometres. The Anio Novus was the longest of all the aqueducts (86km) and the highest; some of its arches were 33m high. Outside the Porta Maggiore are two main roads.—VIA PRENESTINA on the left, leading to Palestrina (Praeneste), and, on the right, VIA CASILINA, anciently Via Labicana. Via Casilina passes through Labico (Labicum), which gave it its original name.

At No. 17 Via Prenestina, about 130m from the gate, is the entrance to the *Basilica di Porta Maggiore (adm, see p 49), unearthed in 1916. A modern staircase beneath the railway admits to this remarkable building of the 1C AD, in near perfect preservation. It has the rudimentary form of a cult building, with a central porch, an apse at the east end, a nave and two arched aisles with no clerestory. This became the basic plan of the Christian church. The ceiling and walls are covered with exquisite stuccoes representing landscapes, mythological subjects, scenes of child life, etc.; the principal design of the apse is thought to depict the Death of Sappho. The purpose for which the building was built is still under discussion: it may have been a type of funerary hall, or have been used by a mystical sect, perhaps the Pythagoreans.

From Piazza di Porta Maggiore Via Giovanni Giolitti, leading past the Stazione Termini to Piazza dei Cinquecento, passes on the right the so-called **Temple of Minerva Medica** (Pl. 6; 7), now surrounded by ugly buildings. This is the conspicuous ruin of a large ten-sided domed hall dating from the 4C, probably the nymphaeum of the *Gardens of Licinius*. The building owes its name to the discovery inside it of a statue of Minerva with a serpent, which probably occupied one of the nine niches round its walls. The cupola, which collapsed in 1828, served as a model for many classical buildings.

Beyond the temple Viale Manzoni leads left past the end of Via di Porta Maggiore. Near Via Luzzatti is the entrance to the **Hypogeum of the Aureli**, a series of tomb-chambers discovered in 1919. For admission, apply to the Pontificia Çommissione di Archeologia Sacra, 1 Via Napoleone III. On the floor of the first room is a mosaic dedication showing that the vault belonged to freedmen of the Gens Aurelia. The well-preserved wall paintings (AD 200–250), include the Good Shepherd, the Christian symbol of the peacock, and some landscapes of obscure significance, suggesting a mixture of Christian and gnostic beliefs.

Via Giov. Giolitti continues to (right) **Santa Bibiana** (Pl. 6; 5), a 5C church rebuilt by *Bernini* in 1625, interesting as his first architectural work. It contains eight columns from pagan temples, including (left of entrance) that at which St Bibiana was supposed to have been flogged to death. On the architrave are frescoes by (right) *Agost. Ciampelli* and (left) *Pietro da Cortona*. The *Statue of the saint, set in an aedicula above the altar, is a fine early work by *Bernini*.

Just beyond on the left is Piazza Guglielmo Pepe, in which are six arches of an ancient aqueduct.—Archi di Santa Bibiana, leading under the railway to *Porta San Lorenzo* (Pl. 6; 5). Immediately N, in the Aurelian Wall, is *Porta Tiburtina*, built by Augustus and restored by Honorius in 403. The triple attic carried the waters of the Aquae Marcia, Tepula, and Julia. Farther N, in Piazzale Sisto V, is an arch formed out of a section of the Aurelian Wall by Pius V and Sixtus V at the end of the 16C to carry the waters of the Acqua Felice.

13 The Oppian and Celian Hills

The **Oppian Hill** (Pl. 4; 8), just NE of the Colosseum, is one of the four summits of the Esquiline and one of the seven hills of the primitive Septimontium of Rome. On its slopes is the PARCO OPPIO, with its main entrance in Via Labicana. Near the entrance of the park are traces of the *Baths of Titus* and the extensive ruins of a wing of the *Domus Aurea** (Pl. 4; 8) of Nero (Pl. 4; 8; *Nero's Golden House*), overlaid by those of the *Baths of Trajan*. This has been closed since 1984; for admission, see p 48. Excavations have unearthed the vast ramifications of the palace buildings which were buried by the construction of the baths. These subterranean rooms were known to and visited by artists of the Renaissance, who examined the murals and scratched their names on the walls. The type of decoration known as 'grottesques' takes its name from the Domus Aurea, and clearly inspired Raphael when decorating his Logge in the Vatican.

Nero already had one palace, the Domus Transitoria on the Palatine, which was destroyed in the fire of AD 64. Even before its destruction he had planned to build another palace (the Domus Aurea) which, with its outbuildings and gardens, was to extend over part, or all of the Palatine, much of the Celian and part of the Esquiline hills, an area of about 50 hectares. He is reputed to have commented when it was completed that at last he was beginning to be housed like a human being. He employed Severus as architect, and Fabullus as painter, and produced what has been called the first expression of the Roman revolution in architecture. The understanding and use of vaulted spaces in the palace was quite new. It is thought that nearly all the rooms were vaulted, although some of the ceilings in the wing that survives are no longer intact. The atrium or vestibule, with the colossal statue of the emperor (see p 112), was on the summit of the Velia; a Cryptoporticus (p 97) may have united the various palaces of the Palatine; the gardens, with their lake, were in the valley now occupied by the Colosseum.

This grandiose edifice did not long survive the tyrant's death in 68, as succeeding emperors demolished or covered up his buildings. In 72 Vespasian obliterated the lake to build the Colosseum; Domitian (81–96) buried the constructions on the Palatine (except the Cryptoporticus) to make room for the Flavian palaces. Trajan (98–117) destroyed the houses on the Oppian to build his baths; and Hadrian (117–78) built his Temple of Venus and Rome on the site of the atrium, and moved the statue.

Of the *Baths of Titus*, which occupied the SW corner of the Oppian Hill, hardly anything remains. The much larger *Baths of Trajan* are better preserved. There survive some remains of the central hall towards the SE, with exedrae and parts of the wall that surrounded the establishment. A well-preserved feature was formerly part of the Domus Aurea, adapted by Trajan; this is a reservoir called *Le Sette Sale* (p 192). The architect of the baths was Apollodorus of Damascus, whose designs were a model for later builders of imperial baths.

A VISIT TO THE DOMUS AUREA is necessarily confusing, and it is difficult to obtain a clear idea of the layout from the buildings uncovered, which formed only a small part of the vast palace complex. A further difficulty is created by the intrusion of the baths of Trajan at many points. However, it may help the visitor to consider that the rooms which remain probably formed four main areas, and that the design of each of these groups of rooms appears to have been more important to the architect than the way they were joined together. The areas suggested are: I. The rooms around the large room (8) and the five-sided court to the south. II. The complex of rooms around the octagonal hall (13). III. The rooms around the Imperial bedrooms (24 and 25). IV. The internal courtyard (27), which would have included in its design the nymphaeum (5). The other rooms tend to have less intricate design and are often connecting corridors or subsidiary service rooms.

In the small garden (1) is the semicircular wall of the great exedra of the Baths of Trajan. The present entrance passes through the wall (2). A passage leads right past remains of Republican houses recently excavated. At the end of a corridor (4; left) is a Nymphaeum (5). This has an interesting vault mosaic (the only one surviving in the rooms of the palace so far excavated) depicting Ulysses and Polyphemus. On the walls are the remains of a shell decoration, and an opening in the east wall provided for a cascade of water. This formed part of the interior court design to the west (see below, 27). From here there is access into an irregularly-shaped room (6) with traces of red decoration on the walls and vault, and (7) a room with paintings of birds. From here is the entrance to the first designed complex of rooms (see above), centred around the large room (8), and the open courtyard to the South. Beyond is a small room (9) with a painted false window, and the long Cryptoporticus (10) decorated with grotesques, with signatures of 16C artists on the vault (usually difficult to see because of the damp). At the end (right) is a room (11) which has well-preserved frescoes of complicated perspective design, with scenes of Rome, and a mosaic floor.

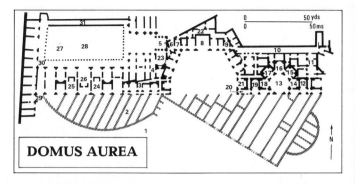

DOMUS AUREA

The most important group of rooms (12–19) are designed around an octagonal atrium (13). The southern prospect of the rooms would have opened on to an extensive garden, looking across the valley where the Colosseum now stands. The openings from the southernmost rooms were blocked up by Trajan, but their outline can still be seen clearly. The Laocoön (now in the Vatican) was found in the apsidal hall (12) in 1506. The atrium has an entirely original design and structure. The light effect is masterly both from the wide central opening in the dome, and from the side rooms. There is an opening for a cascade (16), and good painted stucco decoration (17). Beyond the second apsidal hall (19; compare 12), a corridor (right; 20) has a double-vaulted ceiling, and to the left (21) a room has a well-preserved mosaic floor. Beyond several more rooms is one (22) with more artists' signatures, and (23), an apsidal hall partly open to the sky, which was perhaps a temple. From here the entrance may be regained.

The west wing is reached to the left of the entrance (2). It contains the rooms, called the Imperial bedrooms (24 and 25) and the triclinium (26) which opened on to an interior garden (27), but which was later enclosed by walls of Trajan's baths. Here was found (28) the great porphyry vase now in the Circular Hall of the Vatican. The different building methods and materials used by Nero and Trajan can here be seen clearly. The southern prospect of these rooms (as in rooms 12–19) opened on to the valley, probably beyond a Colonnade. The bases of two columns which could have formed part of the colonnade can be seen in a room beyond (29). A long corridor (30) leads N to another cryptoporticus (31; compare 10).

At the bottom of the hill, on the E side of the Colosseum and between Via Labicana and Via San Giovanni in Laterano (Pl. 9; 1) are remains of the *Ludus Magnus*, the principal training school for gladiators constructed by Domitian, and excavated in 1960–61. Part of the curved wall of a miniature amphitheatre used for training can be seen. Via San Giovanni in Laterano continues past a new office block (beneath which were found remains of houses built before AD 64 with fine mosaics) to *San Clemente* (Pl. 9; 2; open 9–12, 15.30–18.30; fest. 10–12, 15.30–18.30), one of the best preserved of the medieval basilicas in Rome. It is dedicated to St Clement, the fourth pope. It consists of two churches superimposed, raised above a large early Imperial building owned possibly by the family of T. Flavius Clemens.

The *Lower Church*, mentioned by St Jerome in 392, was the scene of papal councils under St Zosimus in 417 and under St Symmachus in 499. Restored in

the 8C and 9C, it was destroyed in 1084 during the sack of Rome by the soldiers
of Robert Guiscard. Eight centuries later—in 1857—it was rediscovered by
Father Mullooly, prior of the adjoining convent of Irish Dominicans, and was
excavated in 1861.—The *Upper Church* was begun in 1108 by Paschal II, who
used the decorative marbles from the ruins of the old church. In the 18C it was
restored by Carlo Stefano Fontana for Clement XI.

The **Upper Church** has its façade turned towards the E. A gabled
porch (being restored in 1988) of four 12C columns leads into the
atrium with Ionic columns surrounding a courtyard with a little
fountain. At the end is the main door of the church (A; usually
closed); there is another entrance by the side door in Via San
Giovanni in Laterano (B).

The typically basilican interior has a nave with a large apse, and aisles
separated by two rows of seven columns, and a pre-Cosmatesque pavement.
The walls of the nave were decorated with a cycle of paintings in 1713–19 under
the direction of *Gius. Chiari*, who also executed the Triumph of St Clement on
the ceiling. The Schola Cantorum (C), from the lower church, contains two
ambones, candelabrum, and a reading-desk, all characteristic elements in the
arrangement of a basilican interior. The *Screen of the choir and sanctuary,
with its transennae, marked with the monogram of John II (533–35), the choir
raised above the confessio, the high altar with its tabernacle, the stalls of the
clergy, and the bishop's throne, are also well preserved. In the PRESBYTERY is
the delicate baldacchino (D) borne by columns of pavonazzetto. The early 12C
mosaics in the apse are especially fine; on the triumphal arch, Christ and the
symbols of the Evangelists; on the right, Saints Peter and Clement, with the
boat and oars, Jeremiah, and Jerusalem; on the left, Saints Paul and Laurence,
Isaiah, and Bethlehem. In the apse-vault, Crucifixion with the Hand of God

*Detail of a fresco by Masolino, probably with the help of
Masaccio (c 1430), in San Clemente*

above and the dome of Heaven, twelve doves (the Apostles), St Mary, and St John; from the foot of the Cross springs a vine with acanthus leaves, encircling figures of St John the Baptist, the Doctors of the Church, and other saints, while the rivers of Paradise flow forth from the Cross, quenching the thirst of the faithful (represented by stags) and watering the pastures of the Christian flock. Below are the Lamb of God and twelve companions. On the apse-wall, impressive large figures of Christ, the Virgin, and the Apostles, a 14C fresco; to the right, is a beautiful wall-tabernacle, probably by *Arnolfo di Cambio*.

In the RIGHT AISLE (E), tombs of Archbishop Giov. Fr. Brusati, by *Luigi Capponi* (1485), and of *Cardinal Bart. Roverella, by *And. Bregno* and *Giov. Dalmata* (1476). In the Baptistery (F), late-16C frescoes attrib. to *Iac. Zucchi*, and a 16C statue of St John the Baptist; in the chapel of St Cyril (K), Madonna, attrib. to *Sassoferrato* (one of several versions). In the chapel by the W door (L) are three paintings of scenes from the life of St Dominic, attrib. to *Seb. Conca*.— LEFT AISLE, Chapel to left of presbytery (G), Our Lady of the Rosary, by *Seb. Conca*; tomb of Cardinal Ant. Venier (died 1479), incorporating columns from a 6C tabernacle. The chapel of St Catherine (H) contains *Frescoes by *Masolino da Panicale*, probably with the help of his pupil, *Masaccio* (before 1430; totally covered for restoration in 1988): on the left entrance pier, St Christopher; on the face of the arch, Annunciation; in the archivolt, the Apostles; in the vault, the Evangelists and Fathers of the Church; behind the altar, Crucifixion; right wall, Life of St Ambrose; left wall, Life of St Catherine of Alexandria. To the right above, outside the chapel, is a sinopia for the beheading of St Catherine (found during restoration) and, on the aisle wall, the sinopia for the Crucifixion.

Off the Right Aisle is the entrance to the **Lower Church** (open at the same time as the upper church, see above) the apse of which was built above a Mithraeum (3C). This formed part of a late-1C apartment house. Below this again are foundations of the Republican period. The staircase, which has miscellaneous fragments of sculpture, descends to the frescoed NARTHEX.

At the foot of the steps a catacomb (see below) may be seen through a grate in the floor. On the right wall is a *Mural (late 11C) of the Legend of St Clement (A), who was banished to the Crimea and there executed by drowning in the Black Sea. The scenes include the Miracle of a Child found alive in a church at the bottom of the sea (full of fish). Below· are St Clement and the donor of the fresco. Farther on, to the right, Translation of St Cyril's body (B) from the Vatican to San Clemente (11C). An archway leads into the aisled church which has a wide NAVE obstructed by the foundation piers of the upper church, and is unequally divided by a supporting wall. Immediately to the left is a 9C fresco (C) of the Ascension, with the Virgin in the centre surrounded by the Apostles, St Vitus, and St Leo IV (with square nimbus). In the adjacent angle (D) the Crucifixion, the Marys at the Tomb, the Descent into Hell, and the Marriage at Cana. Farther along, on the left wall of the nave is the Story of St Alexis (E; 11C): the saint returns home unrecognized and lives for 17 years beneath a staircase; before dying he sends the story of his life to the Pope, and is thus recognized by his wife and father. Above, lower part of a fresco of Christ amid angels and saints. Farther on, Story of Sisinius (F): the heathen Sisinius follows his Christian wife in secret, hoping thereby to capture the Pope, but he is smitten with a sudden blindness; below, Sisinius orders his servants to seize the Pope, but they, also struck blind, carry off a column instead (this fresco more probably depicts the building of the church, as is explained by the painted inscriptions, which are among the oldest examples of Italian writing). Above, St Clement enthroned by Saints Peter, Linus, and Anacletus, his predecessors on the pontifical throne (only the lower part of the fresco survives).—RIGHT AISLE. In a niche, Byzantine Madonna (G; 5C or 6C), which may have been originally a portrait of the Empress Theodora; female saints with the crown of

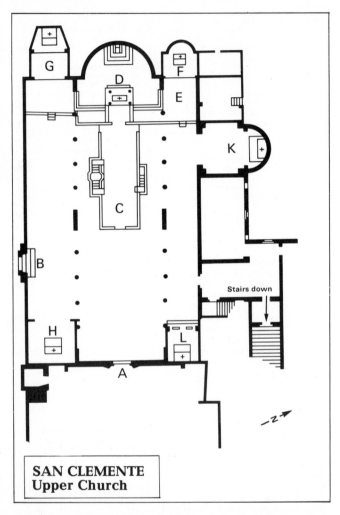

**SAN CLEMENTE
Upper Church**

martyrdom; and a beardless Christ. The frescoes, much damaged, probably depict the Council of Zosimus, the Story of Tobias, and the Martyrdom of St Catherine. At the end, a sarcophagus of the 1C AD with the story of Phaedra and Hippolytus, and a Byzantine figure of Christ (7C or 8C; almost totally obliterated).—LEFT AISLE. Faded frescoes (H) of uncertain subjects. In the floor (I) is a circular recess, perhaps an early baptismal piscina. At the end, remains of a tomb perhaps that of St Cyril (869), the apostle of the Slavs.

From the end of the left aisle a 4C staircase descends to the 1C level with a 'palazzo', and a Mithraic temple of the late 2C or early 3C. Around the corner at the bottom (right) is the pronaos of the temple (J), with stucco ceiling ornaments (very damaged); opposite is

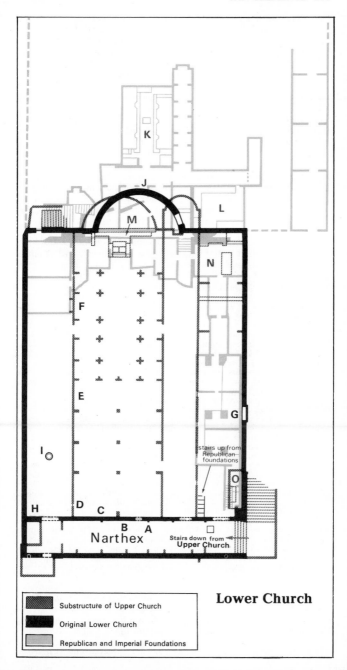

Lower Church

Substructure of Upper Church
Original Lower Church
Republican and Imperial Foundations

the Triclinium (K) with benches on either side and an altar in the centre showing Mithras, in his Phrygian cap, sacrificing a bull to Apollo, and in the niche behind is a statue of Mithras; the vault imitates the roof of a cavern. At the far end of the corridor, to the right, is the presumed Mithraic School (L), where catechumens were instructed, with a mosaic floor and stuccoed vault.

From the pronaos, a door (left) leads to the 1C 'palazzo', probably belonging to Flavius Clemens, which lies beneath the lower basilica. A long narrow passage (M) divides the temple area from the thick tufa wall of the building constructed after Nero's fire on Republican foundations. Only two sides of this building have been excavated. Immediately to the right at the bottom of a short flight of steps, is a series of rooms; the last two are the best-preserved rooms of the Palazzo, showing the original brickwork. The 2nd side of the building is reached by returning to the opening from the corridor; beyond a room (N) with spring water which has been channelled away by tunnels, are seven more rooms, the last of which (O) has a small catacomb (probably 5C or 6C, as it is within the city walls). A staircase (right) leads up to the Lower Church and exit.

Opposite San Clemente is Via dei Querceti at the foot of the high wall of the fortified 12C monastery and church of **Santi Quattro Coronati** (Pl. 9; 2; open 9.30–12, 16.30–18; Sunday 10.30–12), which is reached from here by the steep Via dei Santi Quattro (left). It is a remarkable castellated building of the Middle Ages.

The original 4C or 5C foundation, on a huge scale, was destroyed by the Norman soldiery in 1084, and the present church was erected on a smaller scale in 1110 by Paschal II. It was well restored in 1914 by Muñoz. Its dedication recalls the tradition of five Pannonian sculptors who refused to make a statue of Aesculapius, and of four soldiers (the Coronati; Saints Severus, Severinus, Carpophorus, and Victorinus) who refused to worship it when finished by other hands. The church is specially venerated by sculptors and marble masons.

The entrance gate passes beneath the unusual Campanile, dating from the 9C, a squat fortified tower. The small court which succeeds the 5C atrium has a portico with 16C frescoes, and beyond is a second court, once part of the nave, whose columns have survived. On the right of the portico is the CHAPEL OF ST SYLVESTER (visitors ring for the key at the monastery of the closed order of Augustinian nuns; 1st door on right). It was restored in 1248, and contains a delightful tiny *Fresco cycle of the same date (and particularly well preserved), illustrating the story of the life of Constantine. Two of the scenes show Constantine presenting the imperial headgear to pope Sylvester, and the pope riding off wearing it, led by Constantine. The floor is Cosmatesque.

The church proper lies at the back of the second court. The aisled INTERIOR has a disproportionately wide apse, and a 12C matroneum, or women's gallery. The 12C pavement is in opus alexandrinum. On the W wall and that of the S aisle are remains of 14C frescoes; and against the left pillar of the apse is a beautiful 15C tabernacle attrib. to *And. Bregno* or *Luigi Capponi*. The Baroque apse is effectively decorated with frescoes by *Giov. da San Giovanni* (1630), depicting the history of the Quattro Coronati and the glory of all saints. The tomb of the four martyrs is in the 9C crypt.—From the N aisle is the entrance to the delightful tiny *CLOISTER (ring for adm) of the early 13C, with a 12C fountain and lovely garden. It is one of the most secluded spots in Rome. On the left is the 9C chapel of Santa Barbara interesting for its architecture and fine corbels made from Roman capitals, and with remains of medieval frescoes in the vault.

The monastery of the Santi Quattro Coronati is on the edge of the **Celian Hill** (51m), which extends to the S and W towards the Palatine. Next to the Aventine, it is the southernmost of the Seven Hills of Rome and the most extensive after the Esquiline.

It is supposed originally to have been called *Mons Querquetulanus* from the

oak forests that clothed its slopes. It received its name of Mons *Coelius* from
Caelius (or Coelius) Vibenna, an Etruscan who is said to have helped Romulus
in his war against the Sabine king Tatius, and to have settled here afterwards.
Tullus Hostilius lived on the hill and transferred to it the Latin population.of
Alba Longa. It became an aristocratic district in Imperial times. Devastated by
Robert Guiscard in 1084, it remained almost uninhabited for centuries. Even
today it is sparsely populated, but its ruins and churches are of the highest
interest.

Via dei Querceti leads up to Via Annia and (right) Piazza Celimontana in front of the huge *Ospedale del Celio*. Just S of the military
hospital, near a conspicuous survival of the Claudian aqueduct, Via
Santo Stefano leads left to **Santo Stefano Rotondo** (Pl. 9; 4; entrance
at No. 7), one of the largest and oldest circular churches in existence.
It has been closed for many years for restoration; at present it is only
possible to see the interior from the vestibule through a closed iron
gate (ring at the convent on the right of the portico).

It dates from the time of Pope St Simplicius (468–83). A Mithraeum (2–3C AD)
was found beneath the floor in 1973. The original plan included three concentric rings, the largest 65m in diameter, intersected by the four arms of a
Greek Cross. This complex design was almost certainly taken from eastern
models, perhaps the church of the Holy Sepulchre in Jerusalem, as well as
ancient Roman buildings. The outer ring and three of the arms were pulled
down by Nicholas V in 1450, so that the diameter was reduced to 40m. The
vestibule is formed by the one remaining arm of the Greek Cross. The antique
Roman throne to the left is said to be that of St Gregory the Great. The circular
nave has a double ring of antique granite and marble columns, 34 in the outer
and 22 in the inner series, while 2 Corinthian columns in the centre and 2 pillars
support three arches. The walls were covered with frescoes by order of Gregory
XIII by *Ant. Tempesta* and *Niccolò Circignani* with vivid scenes of martyrdom in
chronological order, in the spirit of the Counter Reformation. In the first chapel
on the left is a small 7C mosaic showing Christ *above* the jewelled Cross, with
Saints Primus and Felician, showing Greek influence. In the second chapel is a
fine 16C tomb.

On the summit of the hill, across Via della Navicella is the church of
Santa Maria in Domnica (Pl. 9; 3, 4), or *della Navicella*, an ancient
foundation and the senior diaconate of Rome; its title is a corruption
of Dominica, i.e. Chief. The alternative name is derived from the
Roman stone *°BOAT, which Leo X had made into a fountain in front
of the church. The boat was probably a votive offering from the
Castra Peregrina, a camp for non-Italian soldiers, situated between
Via Santo Stefano and Via Navicella.

The present church, restored by St Paschal I (pope, 817–24), and practically
rebuilt by Cardinal Giov. de' Medici (Leo X) in the 16C from the designs of And.
Sansovino, has a graceful portico. In the interior (if closed, ring at the door on
the right) the nave contains 18 granite columns; over the windows is a frieze by
Perino del Vaga from designs by *Giulio Romano*. On the triumphal arch, flanked
by two porphyry columns, is a beautifully coloured 9C *°Mosaic of Christ with
two angels and the Apostles, and Moses and Elijah below; in the semi-dome, St
Paschal kisses the foot of the Madonna and Child surrounded by a throng of
angels. In the nave are some interesting Roman sarcophagi.

On the left of the church is the main entrance of the **Villa Celimontana** or *Villa Mattei* (Pl. 9; 3), built for Ciriaco Mattei in 1582 and
celebrated for its splendid gardens (now a public park, adm 7–dusk).
It houses the *Società Geografica Italiana*. In the grounds are ancient
marbles found on the spot, and a granite Roman obelisk, probably
from the Temple of Isis Capitolina, presented by the Senate to Mattei
in 1582. It formed a pair with that in Piazza della Rotonda. The
terrace of the casino and the belvedere at the end of an avenue

provide fine views. There is an exit from the park opposite the church of Santi Giovanni e Paolo (see below).

To the N of Santa Maria in Domnica is the entrance to the former Trinitarian hospice of the church of *San Tomaso in Formis*. The doorway is surmounted by a mosaic (c 1218) of Christ between two Christian slaves, one white, the other a Negro. In the hospice St John of Matha, founder of the Trinitarians, died in 1213.

On the left of Via Claudia, which descends from Santa Maria in Domnica to the Colosseum, are remains of the *Temple of Claudius*, built by Nero's mother Agrippina, fourth wife of Claudius, to whom she dedicated the temple (AD 54). Nero converted it into a nymphaeum for his Domus Aurea, and Vespasian rebuilt it in 69.

The *Arch of Dolabella and Silanus* (AD 10; restored in 1986), a single archway that Nero afterwards used for his aqueduct to the Palatine, leads into the picturesque Via di San Paolo della Croce, which runs between two garden walls (above which can be seen orange trees) to Piazza dei Santi Giovanni e Paolo. Here is the church of **Santi Giovanni e Paolo** (Pl. 9; 3; open 8.30–11.30, 15.30–18; closed Sunday morning), beside the 12C convent built above remains of the Temple of Claudius (see above). The travertine blocks of the temple are clearly visible in the base of the beautiful tall *CAMPANILE (45m), the first two stories of which were begun in 1099–1118, and the five upper stories completed by the middle of the 12C.

The church occupies a site traditionally connected with the house of John and Paul, two court dignitaries under Constantine II, who were martyred by Julian the Apostate. Two Roman apartment houses (2–3C AD) were incorporated in the original sanctuary, founded before 410 by the senator Byzantius and his son Pammachius, a friend of St Jerome. This was demolished by Robert Guiscard in 1084, and rebuilding was begun by Paschal II (1099–1118) and continued by Hadrian IV (Nicholas Breakspeare, the only English pope; 1154–59), who was responsible for the apse and the campanile. Excavations carried out in 1949 on the initiative of Cardinal Spellman revealed the paleochristian façade and some of the ancient constructions beneath the convent.

The 12C Ionic PORTICO has eight antique columns and is closed by an iron grille (1704). Above is a 13C gallery and the paleochristian façade with five arches. The 13C Cosmatesque doorway is flanked by two lions. The INTERIOR, hung with chandeliers, with granite piers and columns, was restored in 1718 for Card. Paolucci by *Ant. Canevari*; Card. Cusani was responsible for the ceiling (1598); the floor, in opus alexandrinum, was restored in 1911. A tomb slab in the nave (protected by a railing) commemorates the burial-place of the three martyrs. Their relics are preserved in a porphyry urn under the high altar.—In the 3rd S chapel (by *Fil. Martinucci*, 1857–80) is the altar-tomb of St Paul of the Cross (1694–1775), founder of the Passionists, whose convent adjoins the church.—The apse has frescoes by *Pomarancio*. In a store-room (unlocked by the sacristan) on the left of the high altar can be seen a remarkable 12C fresco originally over the altar of the church.

From the end of the right aisle (apply to the Sacristan) steps lead down to the **House of Saints John and Paul** (temporarily closed in 1988, but normally open at the same time as the church, see above), an interesting two storied construction, with 20 rooms, originally part of three buildings: a Roman palace, a Christian house, and an oratory, decorated with frescoes of the 2C or the 3–4C. Near the foot of the stairs is a well-shaft. Behind it to the right is a *Nymphaeum* with a striking fresco of Peleus and Thetis (or Proserpine) and a Nereid, and boats manned by Cupids. Beyond a foundation wall of the basilica are two rooms. Off the first (left) is the *Triclinium* with pagan frescoes of peacocks and other birds and youths bearing garlands. A small adjoining room (reached by a flight of steps) has architectural frescoes.—The series of rooms to the left of the entrance have more frescoes, some with Christian subjects, including a large standing figure praying in the early Christian manner, with arms extended and eyes raised. The *Medieval Oratory* (near the road) has been closed during excavation work (and a fresco of the Passion has been removed for restoration). An iron staircase leads up to the *Confessio*, decorated with 4C frescoes the significance of which is not entirely clear. On the end wall is a praying figure, perhaps one of the martyrs, between drawn curtains, and at whose feet are two other figures. On the right, Saints Priscus, Priscillian, and Benedicta (who tried to find the remains of the martyrs and were themselves killed) awaiting execution with eyes bound—probably the oldest painting of a martyrdom.—Stairs lead down from a room N of the Confessio to another series of rooms which were part of the *Baths* in a private house.

Remains of the 'Claudianum', two stories of a huge Roman portico, connected with the Temple of Claudius (see above), can be seen beside the convent (ring for admission at the convent on the right of the portico).

In the piazza outside the church are some arches of Roman shops dating from the 3C. The pretty CLIVO DI SCAURO (the ancient *Clivus Scauri* probably opened in the 1C BC) descends beneath the medieval buttresses of the church spanning the road. Here can be seen the tall façade of a Roman house incorporated in the left wall of Santi Giovanni e Paolo, and the fine *Apse, a rare example of Lombard work in Rome, dating from 1216. Farther down on the left are remains of the 6C basilican hall of the library erected by Agapitus I, and, beneath the Chapels of Sant'Andrea and Santa Barbara (see below), a Roman edifice of the 3C AD. A short road on the left leads up to the church of **San Gregorio Magno** (Pl. 9; 3), a medieval church altered and restored in the 17C and 18C.

A monastery was founded here by St Gregory the Great (590–604) on the site of his father's house, and dedicated to St Andrew. This was demolished in 1573 except for the two chapels of Santa Barbara and Sant'Andrea (see below).

The *EXTERIOR (staircase, façade, and atrium) is by *G.B. Soria* (1633) and is considered his masterpiece. In the ATRIUM are several fine tombs (being restored in 1988), including those of Sir Robert Peckham (died 1659), a self-exiled English Catholic, and Sir Edward Carne (died 1561), an envoy of Henry VIII and Mary I; and, beyond the gate leading to the chapels (see below), those of Canon Guidiccioni (1643) and (on the right, beside the convent door) the Brothers Bonsi (1481), the latter by *Luigi Capponi*.—The INTERIOR (if closed ring at the convent on right of atrium) has 16 antique columns and a restored mosaic pavement; it was rebuilt in 1725–34 by *Fr. Ferrari*. At the end of the right aisle is the CHAPEL OF ST GREGORY, with a fine altar-frontal sculptured by *L. Capponi*. The predella is an early 16C painting, depicting St Michael overcoming Lucifer, the Apostles with St Anthony Abbot, and St Sebastian. A small room on the right contains a chair of the 1C BC known as the throne of St Gregory. In the left aisle is the SALVIATI CHAPEL, by *Fr. da Volterra* and *Carlo Maderno*; on the right is an ancient fresco of the Madonna (repainted in the 14C or 15C) which is supposed to have spoken to St Gregory; on the left, a fine tabernacle, of the school of *And. Bregno* (1469). On either side of the apse are 15–16C statues of Saints Andrew and Gregory.

On the left of the church (reached through a gate in the atrium) is a pretty group of three chapels (still closed for restoration in 1988) surrounded by ancient cypresses. The frescoes inside have deteriorated and are in need of urgent repair. The chapel on the right was built in 1603 and dedicated to **Santa Silvia**, mother of Gregory. It contains her statue by *Nicolas Cordier*, and an *Angel Choir by *Guido Reni*. The other two chapels belonged to the medieval monastery and were built above a Roman edifice (visible from the Clivus Scauri, see above); they were restored in 1602.—In the centre is the chapel of **Sant'Andrea**, preceded by a portico with four antique cipollino columns. Inside is a *Flagellation of the saint (right) by *Domenichino*, and the saint on the road to his Cross, by *Guido Reni*; the peasant-woman on the left repeats the well-known type of Beatrice Cenci. On the entrance wall, Saints Silvia and Gregory by *Giov. Lanfranco*, and on the back wall (beneath the roof) an 11C mural which has recently been discovered.—The third chapel, of **Santa Barbara**, contains a statue of St Gregory by *Nic. Cordier*. The 3C table is supposed to be the one at which he served twelve paupers daily with his own hands, among whom an angel once appeared as a thirteenth; this legend gave the alternative name to the chapel, the *Triclinium Pauperum*. It was in this convent in 596 that St Augustine received St Gregory's blessing before setting out, with forty other monks, on his mission to convert the English to Christianity. A fresco on the left, by *Ant. Viviani* (1602) commemorates the famous incident of the fair-haired English children—'non Angli sed Angeli'—which culminated in St Augustine's mission.

From Piazza di San Gregorio a flight of steps descends to the tree-lined VIA DI SAN GREGORIO, now a busy road with fast traffic. On the line of the ancient *Via Triumphalis* it follows the declivity between the Celian and Palatine hills to the Colosseum. The area to the S, with the Baths of Caracalla, is described in Rte 14.

14   The Baths of Caracalla to Porta San Sebastiano

Bus No. 118 from the Colosseum; request stops outside the Tomb of the Scipios and at Porta San Sebastiano.

PIAZZA DI PORTA CAPENA (Pl. 9; 3) is a busy road junction at the beginning of Via di San Gregorio (which leads to the Colosseum) and adjoining the rounded end of the Circus Maximus. It occupies the site of the *Porta Capena*, a gate in the Servian wall, and the original starting point of the Appian Way. After Aurelian had built his much more extensive walls, the stretch of the road between Porta Capena and Porta Appia (now Porta San Sebastiano; see below) became known as the 'Urban Section' of the Appian Way. This section has now become Via delle Terme di Caracalla as far as Piazzale Numa Pompilio, and, beyond that square, Via di Porta San Sebastiano. On the NE side of Piazza di Porta Capena is *La Vignola*, a reconstruction (1911), with the original stones, of a charming little palace that stood near Via Santa Balbina. The 4C *Stele of Axum*, brought from the ancient capital of Ethiopia in 1937, rises in front of the F.A.O. building (United Nations Food and Agriculture Organization) opened in 1951 on the modern Viale Aventino.

Viale Guido Baccelli leads through the *Parco di Porta Capena*, formerly the *'Passeggiata Archeologica'* opened in 1910. There is now an open-air sports stadium here. In Via Santa Balbina is the church of **Santa Balbina** (Pl. 9; 5; open 9–12, 15–17), entered through the ex-convent on the right of the portico. Founded in the 5C, the church has been rebuilt, and was restored in 1930. The pleasant interior has a wood ceiling bearing the name of Cardinal Marco Barbo (1489). The transennae in the pretty windows, and the schola cantorum were installed in 1931. In the floor are set numerous good Roman black-and-white mosaics (1C AD) found in Rome in 1939. The 13C Cosmatesque episcopal chair in the apse is in excellent condition. The apse fresco of the Glory of Christ is by *Anastasio Fontebuoni* (1523). The fresco fragments include a good Madonna enthroned with four Saints and the Redeemer above, attributed to the school of *Pietro Cavallini*. The bas-relief of the Crucifixion (1460) is attributed to *Mino da Fiesole* and *Giovanni Dalmata*, and the *Tomb of Stefanus de Surdis (1303) is by *Giovanni Cosmati*.

In Via delle Terme di Caracalla is the entrance to the huge ***Baths of Caracalla** (*Terme di Caracalla*), or *Thermae Antoninianae* (Pl. 9; 5; adm see p 48), the best preserved and most splendid of the Imperial

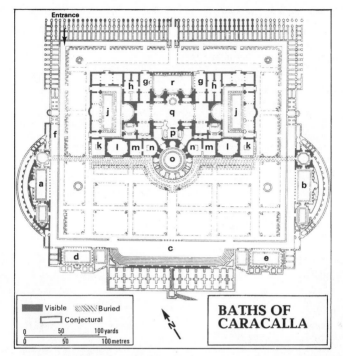

BATHS OF CARACALLA

Entrance

Visible
Buried
Conjectural

0   50   100 yards
0   50   100 metres

N

жoman baths in the city. They could accommodate some 1600
bathers. The romantic sun-baked ruins are on a vast scale.

Begun by Antoninus Caracalla in 212, the Baths were opened in 217 and
finished under Heliogabalus and Alexander Severus. After a restoration by
Aurelian they remained in use until the 6C, when the invading Goths damaged
the aqueducts. The baths, built on an artificial platform, have always been
above ground, but excavations in this century greatly enlarged the area
accessible to the public. In the 16–17C, the Belvedere Torso, the Farnese
Hercules, the Farnese Flora, and many other statues were found among the
ruins, and the mosaic of the athletes, now in the Vatican, also came from here.
Shelley composed a large part of his 'Prometheus Unbound' in this romantic
setting.—Opera performances are given here in summer; during the season the
baths are transformed by the trappings of the set.

The massive brick-built baths are an architectural masterpiece. Their remarkably complex design (comp. the Plan) included huge vaulted rooms, domed
octagons, exedrae, porticoes, etc. as well as an intricate heating system and
hydraulic plant. Of the elaborate decoration only a few architectural fragments
and some floor-mosaic remain, revealing the baroque taste of the 3C in the
introduction of divinities on the fine Composite capitals.

An enclosed garden, now planted with pines, laurel, and cypresses,
surrounds the main buildings of the Baths (see below). Along the
boundary wall were two huge exedrae with an apsidal central hall (a
and b), and in the middle of the S side a shallow exedra in the form of
a *Stadium* (c) with tiers of seats concealing the huge water cisterns.
On either side were two halls (d and e), probably libraries. The
present entrance skirts the boundary wall on the W side past remains
of one of the exedrae (a), and older buildings below ground level,

including a *Mithreum* (f), the largest discovered in Rome (admission only with special permission). Excavations and restorations (including conspicuous reconstructions) have been carried out in the area of the stadium (c) and one of the libraries (d), and on the E side of the garden where a house and triclinium of the time of Hadrian have recently been discovered. This area is still fenced off.

The main buildings of the Baths (220 × 114m) are symmetrically arranged around the huge central hall (q) and the piscina (r; see below). The bathers normally entered through a *vestibule* (g) to reach the *Apodyteria* (h) or dressing rooms. The two *Palestrae* (j), for sports and exercises before bathing, consisted of an open courtyard with porticoes on three sides and a huge hemicycle opposite five smaller rooms. The pavement here has remains of fine polychrome geometric mosaics. The series of rooms (k, l, m, and n) to the S, which may have included a Turkish bath (*Laconicum*; l) led to the circular *Calidarium* (o), 34m across, only part of one side of which remains. It had high windows on two levels designed to admit the sun's rays for many hours of the day, and was formerly covered with a dome. From here the bathers passed into the *Tepidarium* (p) and the large vaulted central hall (q). Beyond is the *Natatio* (r) with an open-air piscina. This has niches on two levels for statues and two hemicycles.

The Baths of Caracalla (AD 212–217)

Opposite the Baths, in Piazzale Numa Pompilio, is the church of **Santi Nereo ed Achilleo** (Pl. 9; 5; open daily except Friday, 10–12, 16–18, ring for custodian), on the site of the Oratory of the Fasciola, named from the bandage which is supposed to have fallen from the wounds of St Peter after his escape from the Mamertine prison.

In 524 the oratory was enlarged into a church by John I, when he brought here the bodies of Nereus and Achilleus, the Christian servants of Flavia Domitilla, who had been martyred at Terracina. The church was enlarged by Leo III c 800, and again by Sixtus IV (1471–84), and was rebuilt by Cardinal Baronius in 1597.

The aisled INTERIOR has frescoes by *Pomarancio*. The ancient ambo and the 15C candelabrum come from other churches; the fine plutei and the high altar, which covers the body of St Domitilla, are of 13C Cosmati work. The mosaic on the choir-arch, of the time of Leo III (815–816), shows the Transfiguration, with a Madonna and an Annunciation at the sides. On the bishop's throne in the apse is carved a fragment of St Gregory's 28th homily, which he delivered from this throne when it stood in the first church dedicated to Saints Nereus and Achilleus in Via Ardeatina.

On the other side of the piazza is the rebuilt church of *San Sisto Vecchio*, with its convent, historically interesting as the residence in Rome of St Dominic (1170–1221). The campanile dates from the 13C.

From Piazzale Numa Pompilio roads lead to four of the gates in the Aurelian Wall: Via Druso NNE to Porta Metronia, Via di Porta Latina SE to Porta Latina ('one way' from the gate), Via di Porta San Sebastiano SSE to Porta San Sebastiano ('one way' to the gate), and the continuation of Via delle Terme di Caracalla S to Porta Ardeatina, adjoining the Bastione del Sangallo.

Via di Porta San Sebastiano, on the line of the urban section of the Appian Way, is a beautiful road (disturbed by fast traffic) running between high walls behind which are fine trees and gardens. On the right, beyond a walled public garden, is the ancient church of **San Cesareo** (Pl. 9; 6; closed for restoration in 1988) rebuilt at the end of the 16C with a façade attributed to *Giacomo della Porta*. Inside is some fine *Cosmati work, including the high altar, the bishop's throne, the transennae, the candelabrum, the ambo, and the fronts of the side-altars. The two angels beneath the high altar are probably from a 15C tomb by *Paolo Romano*. The beautiful wooden ceiling, gilded on a blue ground bears the arms of the Aldobrandini Pope, Clement VIII. The apse mosaic of the Eternal Father was designed by the *Cavalier d'Arpino*. The baldacchino dates from the time of Clement VIII.

Below the church (reached by a stair to the left of the entrance; apply to sacristan), is a large black-and-white *Mosaic of the 2C AD (suffering from humidity). The fantastic sea-monsters, animals, and figures may have decorated the floor of Roman baths. Two apses and the base of a large column, dividing the excavated area, suggest that the first part was later adapted as a church.

Beyond the church, on the right, at No. 8 is the **House of Cardinal Bessarion** (closed for restoration since 1984, but see p 48), the famous scholar (1389–1472), whose tomb is in the church of the Santi Apostoli. The delightful house and garden are a good example of a 15C home. The loggia and several of the rooms are decorated with contemporary frescoes, which have been restored and the false additions removed. From the loggia with landscape scenes, is the entrance to the first large room which has wall-paintings of garlands and ribbons which cast painted shadows, and a fragment (in a niche) of a 15C fresco of the Coronation of the Virgin and two saints. The walls of the room on the right have an over-all pattern of acanthus leaves and pomegranates. The house is furnished in the Renaissance style. The rooms downstairs are used as reception rooms by the Commune of Rome.

About 500 metres farther along the road is (left; No. 9) the **Tomb of the Scipios** (adm see p 50; the ticket includes adm to the Columbarium of Pomponius Hylas, see below). The charming entrance beside two old columns and a little fountain leads into a beautifully kept garden. The tomb, one of the first to be built on the Appian Way, was discovered in 1780. The excavated area is dominated by a three-storied house of the 3C which retains traces of paintings and mosaics and was built above the tomb of the Scipios. In front, is a Columbarium reached by a staircase below ground level, containing numerous niches with funerary urns. To the right of the house, a short passage leads to a small Christian catacomb, with a chapel attached. Store-rooms containing archaeological material found during excavations, can be visited with special permission from the Commune. The Tomb itself is reached from the left of the house.

It was built for L. Cornelius Scipio Barbatus, consul in 298 BC, and great-grandfather of Scipio Africanus. Many other members of the gens Cornelia

San Giovanni a Porta Latina (12C campanile)

were buried here also, up to the middle of the 2C BC, although Scipio Africanus was buried at Liternum (Patria, near Naples), where he died. The sarcophagus of Scipio Barbatus and the funerary inscriptions found here were replaced by copies when they were removed to the Vatican. The other tombs include those of his son, Lucius Scipio (consul 259 BC), the conqueror of Corsica, of Cornelius Scipio Asiaticus, of Cn. Scipio Hispanus (praetor 139 BC) and Aula Cornelia his wife; also an inscription to Publius, possibly the son of Scipio Africanus.

The caretaker conducts visitors through an attractive little public park to the •**Columbarium of Pomponius Hylas**, which is one of the best preserved in existence. The steep original staircase, with a small mosaic inscription, with the name of the founder and his wife Pomponia Vitalis, leads down to the 1C chamber with niches and funerary urns, and decorated with stucco and paintings.

A gate leads out of the park into the pretty rural Via di Porta Latina, in which to the left is the picturesque church of •**San Giovanni a Porta Latina**, in a quiet cul-de-sac, with a large cedar and ancient well. It has a narthex of four ancient columns, and a beautiful 12C campanile. The church, founded c 550, was rebuilt by Hadrian I in 772, and several times restored, but the interior retains its beautiful 11C basilican form. The apse has three lovely windows of selenite, and 12C frescoes (restored in 1940).

In the other direction Via di Porta Latina leads to the Gate, past the little octagonal chapel of **San Giovanni in Oleo** (restored in 1970), traditionally marking the spot where St John the Evangelist stepped out unharmed from a cauldron of boiling oil. Rebuilt during the reign of Julius II, it has an interesting design, usually attributed to *Bramante* (or to Sangallo and his school). It was restored in 1658 by *Borromini*, who added the frieze.

Porta Latina is an opening in the Aurelian Wall (see below) with two towers built by Belisarius. Outside the gate Viale delle Mura Latine skirts the wall to Porta San Sebastiano, and Via di Porta Latina runs SE to Via Appia Nuova.

In Via di Porta San Sebastiano (see above), at No. 13 are other interesting columbaria discovered in the last century in the *Vigna Codini*, now private property (no adm). The largest had room for some 500 urns, another in the form of a horse-shoe has vaulted galleries decorated with stuccoes and paintings.

Near the end of the road is the so-called triumphal *Arch of Drusus*, in fact the arch that carried the aqueduct for the Baths of Caracalla over the Appian Way. Only the central of three openings survives; it is decorated with Composite columns of giallo antico.

Porta San Sebastiano (Pl. 9; 8), the *Porta Appia* of ancient Rome, is the largest and best preserved gateway in the Aurelian Wall. It was rebuilt in the 5C by Honorius and restored in the 6C by Belisarius. The two medieval towers at the sides rest on basements of marble blocks. The Interior has recently been restored as a MUSEUM OF THE WALLS (*Museo delle Mura*; adm see p 49).

For the history and description of the Aurelian Walls, see p 19. It was at the Porta San Sebastiano that the senate and people of Rome received in state the last triumphal procession to enter the city by the Appian Way—that of Marcantonio Colonna II after the victory of Lepanto in 1571. The Museum is arranged in the rooms on two levels above the gate, and in the two towers. It contains prints, models, etc. illustrating the history of the walls. The ramparts along the inner face of the walls, traversing nine defensive towers, are open as far as Via Cristoforo Colombo (see Pl. 9; 8). They provide a very unusual view of rural Rome, skirting overgrown fields and woods, beyond which (towards the end of the walkway) can just be seen, above the trees, the tops of the Victor

Porta San Sebastiano in the Aurelian Wall

Emmanuel Monument, the Baths of Caracalla, and the dome of St Peter's. The
Bastione del Sangallo, a formidable structure built for Paul III in 1537 by
Antonio da Sangallo the Younger, which is beyond Via Cristoforo Colombo,
was still closed for restoration in 1988.

The next stretch of the Appian Way outside the gate is described in Rte 17.

15   The Theatre of Marcellus and Piazza Bocca della Verità

The broad and traffic-ridden VIA DEL TEATRO DI MARCELLO (Pl. 3; 8),
skirting the W base of the Capitoline Hill, was opened in 1933. It
descends past (right) the severe façade of the *Monastero di Tor de'
Specchi* (open to visitors on 9 March every year), founded in 1425 by
St Francesca Romana. The Oratory is decorated by Antoniazzo
Romano. Beyond rises the Theatre of Marcellus (described below). In
Via Montanara is the pretty deconsecrated church of *Santa Rita* by

Carlo Fontana, moved here in 1937 from the foot of the Capitol Hill, below Santa Maria in Aracoeli. The interesting oval interior is used for exhibitions. Beyond opens out the handsome PIAZZA CAMPITELLI, with a fountain (1589) designed by Giac. della Porta. Facing the church are three fine palaces: the 16C *Pal. Cavalletti* (No. 1), and *Pal. Albertoni* and *Pal. Capizucchi* (Nos 2 and 3), both dating from the late 16C and attrib. to Giac. della Porta. The charming façade (blackened by the polluted air) of **Santa Maria in Campitelli** (Pl. 3; 8) was erected by *Carlo Rainaldi* when the church was rebuilt (1662–67) in honour of a miraculous Madonna, which was believed to have halted an outbreak of pestilence.

The fine INTERIOR (closed 12–17) has an intricate perspective effect using numerous arches, columns, and a heavy cornice. In the 2nd chapel on the right is St Anne, St Joachim, and the Virgin by *Luca Giordano* (light on the right); the ornate high altar surrounds the Miraculous Virgin, an image in pietra dura perhaps dating from the 11C. In the 1st chapel on the left are two tombs of the Altieri family, inscribed respectively 'Nihil' and 'Umbra'; in the left transept, *Baciccia*, Birth of St John the Baptist.

Via de' Delfini leads E out of the piazza to the picturesque Piazza Margana, where several houses are hung with old vines.
  Via de' Funari leads out of the N side of the piazza through an area of charming old streets to **Santa Caterina dei Funari** (Pl. 3; 6), a church with a fine façade (restored in 1978) by Guidetto Guidetti (1564) and an original campanile. The interior (which has been closed for restoration for many years) contains 16C paintings by Girol. Muziano, Scipione Pulzone, Livio Agresti, Fed. Zuccari, and Marcello Venusti, and a fine stuccoed and painted *Chapel by Vignola. Across Via Caetani (described on p 119) is the huge **Palazzo Mattei**, which comprised five palaces of the 16C and 17C. The fine façades in Via dei Funari and Via Michelangelo are by Carlo Maderno. In the little Piazza Mattei, Nos 19 and 17 open onto courts, and a third door gives access to a staircase (left) finely decorated with 17C stuccoes surrounding antique reliefs. Inside are frescoes by Domenichino, Lanfranco, and Albani. Part of the buildings, now owned by the State, are used by the Centro Italiano di Studi Americani.—The charming *Fontana delle Tartarughe (in Piazza Mattei) by Taddeo Landini (1584), on a design by Giac. della Porta, was restored in 1658 perhaps by Bernini, when the tortoises were added. At the SW angle of the piazza is *Palazzo Costaguti* (no adm) with ceilings on the first floor painted by Albani, Domenichino, Guercino, Lanfranco, and others.

On the right of the church of Santa Maria in Campitelli the narrow old Via della Tribuna di Campitelli leads past an old house (recently harshly restored) with Ionic columns set into its façade to Via Sant'Angelo in Pescheria which continues to the remains of the **Porticus of Octavia** (Pl. 3; 8). This was reconstructed by Augustus in honour of his sister, and restored by Septimius Severus (AD 203).

The Porticus of Octavia was rectangular, with about 300 columns, which enclosed the temples of Jupiter and Juno. The entrances consisted of two propylaea with 8 columns and 4 piers. The southern extremities of the porticus area have been exposed, and one monumental entrance (an arch was added, and the pediment repaired in the Middle Ages). Remains of columns to the W, and the stylobate to the E can also be seen. Inside the porticus a church was installed in 755 called **Sant'Angelo in Pescheria** from Rome's fish market established in the porch in the 12C (and which survived here until the last century). The church (usually closed) was rebuilt in the 16C and contains a fresco of the Madonna enthroned with angels, attrib. to Benozzo Gozzoli or his school, and an early 12C Madonna and Child. From this church Cola di Rienzo and his followers set out to seize the Capitol on the night of Pentecost, 1347. Here from 1584 until the rule of Pius IX the Jews were forced to listen to a Christian sermon every Saturday.
  The **Ghetto** occupied the district to the W, where from 1556 onwards the Jews were segregated and subject to various restrictions on their personal freedom, although to a lesser degree than in other European countries. The walls were torn down in 1848, and the houses demolished in 1888 before the area S of Via

del Portico d'Ottavia was reconstructed around the new Synagogue.—In Via del Portico d'Ottavia are several medieval houses, and a shop with an ancient Roman architrave framing the door. No. 13 (in very poor repair) has a fine court with loggie. At the end (No. 1) is the *Casa di Lorenzo Manilio*, dating from 1468 (2221 years after the foundation of Rome), decorated with ancient Roman sculptural fragments. The inscription carved in bold stone lettering was set up by Manilio, and includes (on the side facing Piazza Costaguti) the patriotic invocation 'Have Roma'. Via della Reginella here is a survival from the old Ghetto. On the left opens Piazza delle Cinque Scole (laid out in the last century when the Ghetto was demolished) with a fountain from Piazza Giudea by Giac. della Porta. Here is the interesting *Palazzo Cenci*, which belonged to the family of Beatrice Cenci, and was renewed in the 16C. A short narrow road on the right leads up to MONTECENCI, an artificial mound (probably on Roman remains) with a pretty little piazza between Pal. Cenci and the church of *San Tommaso dei Cenci* (usually closed). An antique altar is incorporated into its façade. It contains a chapel frescoed by Sermoneta (1575) and two carved Roman brackets supporting a side altar.—Piazza delle Cinque Scole continues to the river; on the left, on Lungotevere Cenci, rises the monumental **Synagogue** (Pl. 3; 8) built in 1874, with a JEWISH MUSEUM (adm see p 49), illustrating the history of the community in the city.

The area roughly occupied by the old Ghetto, between Piazza Cairoli and the Theatre of Marcellus, and Via del Portico d'Ottavio and the Tiber is now recognized as the site of the *Circus of Flaminius* (221 BC).

To the S of the Porticus of Octavia are the imposing remains of the *Theatre of Marcellus* (Pl. 8; 1; no adm), begun by Julius Caesar. The theatre was dedicated in 13 or 11 BC by Augustus to the memory of his nephew and son-in-law who had died in 23 BC. The exterior was restored in 1932, and it is again being restored. It originally had at least two tiers of 41 arches, the first with Doric and the second with Ionic engaged columns probably crowned by an attic of the Corinthian order. Only 12 arches in each of the two tiers survive; the upper stage has disappeared in the course of various alterations. The building was pillaged in the 4C for the restoration of Ponte Cestio. It was fortified in the early Middle Ages and made into a stronghold by the Fabi. In the 16C it was converted into a palace by Baldass. Peruzzi for the Savelli, and later passed in turn to the Orsini and the Sérmoneta families. The palace garden is the site of the cavea, which held c 15,000 spectators.

In front of the theatre are three Corinthian columns of the *Temple of Apollo Medico*, built in 433 BC and restored by the consul C. Sosius, in 33 BC.

The debris from the demolitions of the Theatre of Marcellus became known as Monte Savello which gave its name to the traffic-ridden piazza to the S. This faces the *Isola Tiberina* (Pl. 3; 8), a pretty little island in the Tiber, reached from here by *Ponte Fabricio*, the oldest Roman bridge to have survived in the city, and still in use for pedestrians. The inscription over the fine arches records the name of the builder, L. Fabricius and the date, 62 BC. The bridge is also known as the Ponte 'dei Quattro Capi' from the two herms of the four-headed Janus on the parapet. Remains of the 'Ponte Rotto' (see below) can be seen upstream.

The island, which provides an easy crossing place on the Tiber, is thought to have been settled early in the history of Rome. A temple of Aesculapius was dedicated here in 293 BC and ever since the island has been associated with the work of healing. It is now largely occupied by the hospital of the Fatebenefratelli, founded in 1548. On the right is the church of *San Giovanni Calibita* founded in the 11C and reconstructed in 1640. In the 18C interior is a ceiling painting by Corrado Giaquinto.—On the left is a tall medieval tower, formerly part of an 11C fortress, and Piazza San Bartolomeo. The island was formerly encircled with a facing of travertine, a portion of which still remains at

Ponte Fabricio (62 BC)

the extremity, which can sometimes be reached through the archway on the left of San Bartolomeo. It is in the form of a ship with the serpent of Aesculapius carved upon it in relief. There are plans to open a Museum illustrating the history of the island in the interesting medieval building here, now owned by the Comune. The church of *San Bartolomeo*, on the site of the temple of Aesculapius, was built in the 10C in honour of St Adalbert, Bishop of Prague, and several times restored, notably by Orazio Torriani in 1624; the tower is Romanesque. The interior contains 14 antique columns, and an interesting sculptured well-head on the chancel steps, probably from the original church. There is a hall crypt beneath the transept.—The S side of the island is joined to Trastevere (Rte 21) by the **Ponte Cestio**, probably built by L. Cestius in 46 BC, restored in AD 370, and rebuilt in 1892 (the centre arch to its original design and measurements).

In Piazza di Monte Savello is the apse of the church of **San Nicola in Carcere** (Pl. 8; 1; open 7.30–12, 16.30–19; fest. 10.30–13), the side door of which can usually be reached from here by a walkway. This 11C church, probably on the site of an older sanctuary, was reconstructed and consecrated in 1128. It was remodelled in 1599 by Giac. della Porta and detached from the surrounding buildings in 1932. It occupies the site of three Republican Temples in the FORUM HOLITORIUM, the vegetable and oil market which extended from the Capitoline Hill to the Tiber. The temples are thought to have been dedicated to *Janus*, *Juno Sospita* and *Spes*. The first, to the right of the church, was Ionic hexastyle, with columns on three sides only, the remains of which can be seen incorporated in the S wall of the church; the second, now incorporated in the church, was Ionic hexastyle peripteral; the third, on the left of the church was Doric hexastyle peripteral. The INTERIOR of the church has fine antique columns from the temples with diverse capitals. At the end of the left aisle is an altarpiece of the Ascension, by Lor. Costa.

The main door of the church faces the wide and busy Via del Teatro di Marcello, across which is a medieval fortified mansion (over-restored). A path with steps (called Via di Monte Caprino) leads up from here to the Capitol hill. Vico Jugario, a road on the site of the Roman road which connected the Forum Holitorium with the Roman Forum skirts the foot of the Capitol to Piazza della Consolazione past Sant'Omobono.

At the beginning of Vico Jugario on the left can be seen the arcades of a portico built of peperino in the Republican era. On the right, around the church of *Sant'Omobono* (usually locked), is the **Area Sacra di Sant'Omobono** (Pl. 8; 1; closed, but partly visible through the railings). Excavations begun in 1937 and continued in the 1960s (and still not completed) have revealed interesting remains on seven different levels, the oldest dating from the 9C–8C BC where traces of hut dwellings similar to those on the Palatine were found. The archaeological evidence has provided new light on the origins of Rome and the presence of the Etruscans here. Two archaic temples (mid 6C BC) dedicated to Fortuna and Mater Matuta and traditionally founded by Servius Tullius rest on an artificial mound c 6 metres high in which were found Bronze Age and Iron Age sherds and imported Greek pottery of the 8C BC. In front of the temples are two archaic altars, possibly dedicated to Carmenta. The most conspicuous remains mostly date from after 213 BC when the temples were reconstructed. The material found on the site, including a terracotta group of Hercules and Minerva from one of the temples is kept in the Antiquarium Comunale.

In Piazza della Consolazione beyond, is the church of SANTA MARIA DELLA CONSOLAZIONE (usually closed). The façade is by *Longhi the Elder* (1583–1606); the upper part was added in the same style in the 19C. In the 1st chapel to the right are frescoes by *Taddeo Zuccari* (1556) of the life of Christ (including the *Flagellation) and the Crucifixion (much damaged). In the apse, Birth of Mary and the Assumption by *Pomarancio*, and over the altar, the Madonna della Consolazione, a 14C fresco repainted by *Antoniazzo Romano*. In the 1st chapel on the left, is a marble relief of the Marriage of St Catherine by *Raffaello da Montelupo* (1530).

The cliff above, on the Capitoline Hill, is thought to be the Tarpeian Rock (see Rte 1).

Via del Teatro di Marcello continues between ugly municipal public offices set up by the Fascist regime to PIAZZA DELLA BOCCA DELLA VERITÀ (Pl. 8; 3), an open space with a picturesque group of buildings now sadly disturbed on all sides by busy traffic. This occupies part of the site of the *Forum Boarium*, or cattle-market, the oldest market of ancient Rome, and here in a little garden stand two ancient Roman temples and a fine Baroque fountain by Carlo Bizzaccheri (1717), opposite the medieval church of Santa Maria in Cosmedin.

On the right of the temples is the eccentric **Casa dei Crescenzi** (no adm), a unique example of a mansion built by a wealthy Roman in the Middle Ages. Formerly a tower guarding the river, it dates from c 1100 and the inscription over the door states that it was erected by one Nicolaus, son or descendant of Crescentius and Theodora, probably members of the Alberic family, the most powerful clan in Rome at the end of the 10C. It is constructed mainly from fragments of classical buildings (or medieval copies of Roman works). The bricks of the lower story are formed into half-columns, with rudimentary capitals. A fragment of the upper story and its arcaded loggia survives. It is now used by the 'Centro di Studi per la Storia di Architettura', and concerts are occasionally held here.

The *Temple of Portunus (no adm), dedicated to the god of harbours, was formerly called the *Temple of Fortuna Virilis*. It dates from the end of the 2C BC. In 872 it was consecrated as the church of *Santa Maria Egiziaca*. This pseudoperipteral temple, with four fluted Ionic columns in front of the portico and two at the sides, escaped alteration in the Imperial epoch and survives as a precious example of the Greco-Italian temples of the Republican age. It has been disengaged, without undue restoration, from the buildings which formerly surrounded it.

The little round *Temple of Hercules Victor was for long known as the *Temple of Vesta*. It also dates from the end of the 2C BC (restored under Tiberius) and is the oldest marble edifice to survive in Rome. An inscription from the base of a cult statue found here confirmed its dedication to Hercules Victor.

This charming little building consists of a circular cella of solid marble, surrounded by 20 fluted columns; one of these is missing on the N side but the base is left. In the Middle Ages the temple became the church of *Santo Stefano delle Carrozze* and later *Santa Maria del Sole*. The original roof and ancient entablature have not survived.—The entrance to a side conduit of the Cloaca Maxima (see below) can be seen under a travertine lid beside the fountain.

Santa Maria in Cosmedin (Pl. 8; 3; open 9–12, 15–17) is a fine example of a Roman medieval church, preceded by a little gabled porch and arcaded narthex.

The building incorporates two earlier structures, the arcaded colonnade of the Imperial Roman *Statio Annonae*, or market inspector's office, and the side walls of a porticoed hall, part of an early Christian welfare centre, or *diaconia* (c 600). Near by was a monumental altar and a temple, both dedicated to Hercules, the latter restored by Pompey. The oratory was enlarged into a basilican church by Hadrian I (772–95), and assigned to Greek refugees driven from Constantinople by the iconoclastic persecutions, and became known as the *Schola Graeca*. Its other name, 'in Cosmedin', probably comes from a Greek word meaning decoration, referring to the embellishments of Hadrian. At that period it had a matroneum and three apses. Cardinal Alfano, chamberlain of Calixtus II, rebuilt the church c 1123, closed the galleries, and added the schola cantorum. The fine tall campanile of seven stories also dates from this time, although it has recently been unfeelingly restored. The church was over-restored and the pretty 18C façade torn down in 1894–99.

Beneath the portico, to the left, is the **Bocca della Verità** proper, a large cracked marble disk representing a human face, the open mouth of which was believed to close upon the hand of any perjurer who faced the ordeal of placing it there. It is in fact a slab that once closed an ancient drain. To the right is the tomb of Cardinal Alfano (see above). The principal doorway is the work of Johannes de Venetia (11C).

The fine INTERIOR with a nave and two aisles each ending in an apse closely reproduces the 8C basilica with some 12C additions. The arcades are supported on antique columns with good capitals grouped in threes between piers. In the first part of the nave remains of the Statio Annonae and diaconia (see above) can be seen. High up on the walls are the remains of frescoes of the 11C. The schola cantorum, rood-loft, paschal candelabrum, episcopal throne, and pavement (1123) are the *Work of the Cosmati. The baldacchino over the high altar (an antique porphyry bath) is by Deodatus, third son of the younger Cosmas (1294). The paintings in the apses are restored. In the sacristy, to the right of the entrance, are some fragments of a mosaic of 706 on a gold ground, representing the Adoration of the Magi, formerly in the oratory of John VII at St Peter's. In the chapel to the left of the sacristy, over the altar, is a Madonna and Child attributed to the late 15C Roman school. The tiny crypt, reached from either aisle, was built into part of the altar dedicated to Hercules, the columns of which remain.

From the Lungotevere Aventino, W of Piazza della Bocca della Verità, the iron *Ponte Palatino* crosses the Tiber to Trastevere (Rte 21). In the bed of the Tiber, upstream, is a single arch of the *Pons Aemilius*, the first stone bridge over the Tiber (the piers were built in 179 BC, and were connected by arches in 142 BC). From the 13C onwards it was repaired numerous times, and has been known as the *Ponte Rotto* since its final collapse in 1598. From the parapet of the Ponte Palatino the mouth of the Cloaca Maxima (see below), may be seen under the quay of the left bank, when the river is low.

The interior of Santa Maria in Cosmedin

On the E side of Piazza della Bocca della Verità is Via del Velabro, which perpetuates the name of this ancient district of Rome. The *Velabrum*, once a stagnant marsh left by the inundations of the Tiber, extended between the river and the Palatine, and included the Forum Boarium (see above). The derivation of the name is uncertain. The Velabrum is famous in legend as the spot where the shepherd Faustulus found the twins Romulus and Remus.

It was drained by the **Cloaca Maxima**, which was an extensive system serving the valleys between the Esquiline, Viminal, and Quirinal hills, as well as the Roman Forum. At first a natural watercourse to the Tiber, it was later canalized, and arched over in c 200 BC; it is still in use.

In Via del Velabro (Pl. 8; 3) is the massive four-sided **Arch of Janus**, which formed a covered passage at a cross-roads (quadrivium) and provided shelter for the cattle-dealers. Poorly proportioned, it is a work of decadence, dating perhaps from the reign of Constantine, and is built partly of ancient fragments, with numerous niches for statues. It has recently been restored. To the left is *San Giorgio in Velabro (Pl. 8; 1) an ancient church of uncertain date, now in a peaceful corner of the city. It was built over a diaconia established here c 600 perhaps in the 9C or earlier. The 9C portico was restored in the 12C when the campanile was added. The church was further restored in 1926.

The Ionic portico has square pillars of the 7C. The beautiful plain grey interior is basilican, with nave and aisles separated by sixteen ancient columns. The pretty windows were restored in this century. The irregularity of the plan which can be seen from the wood ceiling suggests an earlier construction was incorporated in the 9C building. In the apse is a fresco attrib. to Pietro Cavallini

The interior of San Giorgio in Velabro

(c 1296; repainted) of Christ with the Madonna and Saints Peter, Sebastian, and George. The altar, with some Cosmatesque decoration, and the canopy, date from the 13C.

To the left of the church is the ornate little *Arcus Argentariorum* (AD 204; restored in 1986), which was erected by the money-changers (argentarii) and cattle-dealers in honour of the emperor Septimius Severus, Julia Domna, and their children. The portrait and name of Geta were effaced as a mark of his disgrace.

To the left of the arch, a street leads to the church of **San Giovanni Decollato** (ring at No. 22). The interior has fine stucco and fresco decoration dating from 1580–90. The altarpiece of the decapitation of St John is by *Vasari*. In front of the W door is the entrance to the Oratory with remarkable *Frescoes by the 16C Roman Mannerists, *Jacopino del Conte, Fr. Salviati, Pirro Ligorio*, and others. There is also a 16C Cloister. On the other side of the road, reached by a raised pavement, is *Sant'Eligio dei Ferrari* (open for services on Sunday) with an interesting Baroque interior.

Via San Teodoro to the NE corresponds to the ancient *Vicus Tuscus*, skirting the Palatine on the W. On the right, well below the level of the road, is the small round domed church of **San Teodoro** (Pl. 8; 2; open for services on fest. at 11.30), beside which was found the she-wolf of the Capitol (now in Palazzo dei Conservatori). The church (recently restored) was built on the site of the great granary warehouse known as the *Horrea Agrippiana*, later turned into an early Christian diaconia. It is preceded by a delightful courtyard. The present church dates from c 1453 and it contains an early mosaic in the apse of the old oratory (Christ and saints, c 600), much restored. Remains of earlier buildings, including the Roman structures, have been found beneath the foundations.

From Piazza della Bocca della Verità Via dei Cerchi runs SE. On the left, in Piazza di Sant'Anastasia (reached also from Via di San Teodoro; see above) is the church of *Sant'Anastasia*, dating from 492 and several times restored. The classical façade is by L. Arrigucci. Inside, under the high altar, is a recumbent statue of St Anastasia, begun by Fr. Aprile and finished by Ercole Ferrata. Beneath the church are remains of an Imperial building. Via dei Cerchi skirts the NE side of the **Circus Maximus** (Pl. 8; 4) and ends in Piazza di Porta Capena. From the street there is a good view from below of the ancient buildings on the S of the Palatine (Rte 3). Via del Circo Massimo borders the Circus Maximus on the SW. Half-way along its course the street broadens into the Piazzale Romolo e Remo, in which is a seated bronze statue, by Ettore Ferrari, of Giuseppe Mazzini, unveiled at the centenary (1949) of the Roman Republic. Steps lead down to the floor of the circus, now planted with grass.

The **Circus Maximus** lies in the Valle Murcia, between the Palatine and the Aventine, and was the first and largest circus in Rome. According to Livy, it dates from the time of Tarquinius Priscus (c 600 BC), who is said to have here inaugurated a display of races and boxing-matches after a victory over the Latins; but the first factual reference to the circus is in 329 BC. The circus was altered and enlarged on several occasions. In the time of Julius Caesar its length was three stadia (1875 Roman feet), its width one stadium, and the depth of the surrounding buildings half a stadium. The resultant oblong was rounded at one end and straight at the other. Tiers of seats were provided all round except at the straight end; here were the *carceres*, or stalls for horses and chariots. In the centre, running lengthwise, was the *spina*, a low wall terminating at either end with a *meta* or conical pillar denoting the turnings of the course. The length of a race was 7 circuits of the *spina*. Though primarily adapted for chariot races, the circus was used also for athletic contests, wild-beast fights, and (by flooding the arena) sea battles. The accommodation varied with the successive reconstructions from 150,000 to 385,000. The circus was destroyed by fire under Nero (AD 64) and again in the time of Domitian. A new circus was built by Trajan; Caracalla enlarged it and Constantine restored it after a partial collapse. The last games were held under the Ostrogothic king Totila in AD 549.—The extant remains belong to the Imperial period. Some seats and part of the substructure of the stairways may be seen at the curved E end, around the medieval tower near Piazza di Porta Capena, as well as some shops. In the centre of this curve can be seen fragmentary decorative columns of a triumphal arch commemorating Titus's conquest of Jerusalem in AD 80–85, which formed the entrance gate. Excavations have been in progress here since 1984. The obelisks now in Piazza del Popolo and outside the Lateran once stood in the circus.—At the W end of the Circus, on Via dell'Ara Massima are remains of a large Roman public building (2C AD) with a 3C *Mithreum* beneath (adm only with special permission from the Comune).

16 The Aventine Hill

The **Aventine Hill** (Pl. 8; 3, 5) rises on the SW side of the Circus Maximus (see Rte 15). A secluded residential area with beautiful trees and gardens, it is one of the most peaceful spots in the centre of Rome.

The **Aventine** (40m), the southernmost of the Seven Hills of Rome, was at first not included within the precincts of the city and remained outside the *pomoerium*, or line of the walls, throughout the republican era. For centuries it was sparsely populated. This hill has two summits: the Aventine of ancient Rome, which extends SW of Via del Circo Massimo in the direction of the Tiber, and the so-called Little Aventine, to the S. These are divided by Viale Aventino, which runs SW from the Porta Capena towards the Testaccio.—It was to the Aventine that C. Gracchus, after failing to obtain his re-election as tribune, withdrew with his colleague Fulvius Flaccus for their last stand against the Senate. In the Imperial era the Aventine became an aristocratic district, and in the early Middle Ages it was already covered with elegant mansions.

From Via del Circo Massimo, Clivio dei Publici or Via di Valle Murcia (bordered by a rose garden) mount the hill to Via di Santa Sabina. At the top of the rise the road passes (right) the Clivio di Rocca Savelli, a pedestrian lane which leads back down the hill past the wall of the

12C Savelli castle. Beyond is the delightful walled garden (open to the public) known as the *Parco Savello*, planted with orange trees, and beautifully kept. It has a good view of Rome to the N and NW (steps in the far corner lead down to the Clivio di Rocca Savelli, see above). A door in the wall leads into Piazza Pietro d'Illiria, with a splendid wall fountain. Here is the church of *Santa Sabina (Pl. 8; 3; open 6.30–12.30, 15.30–19), perhaps the most beautiful basilica in Rome which survives from the Early Christian period. It was built by Peter of Illyria (422–32), a priest from Dalmatia, on the legendary site of the house of the sainted Roman matron Sabina, near a temple of Juno. It was restored in 824 and in 1216. In 1219 Honorius III gave it to St Dominic for his new Order. It was disfigured in 1587 by Dom. Fontana and skilfully restored by A. Muñoz in 1919, and by Berthier in 1936–39.

The interior of Santa Sabina

The church has a small 15C portico, and a door on the left leads into a vestibule with sculptural and architectural fragments. On the far left is a remarkable wooden *Door of the early 5C, with 18 panels carved with Scriptural scenes, probably not in the original order. These include one of the oldest representations of the Crucifixion in existence.

The beautifully proportioned classical INTERIOR is modelled on the basilicas of Ravenna. Of its mosaic decoration which formerly covered the nave walls and apse, only one section remains, above the doorway, showing seven hexameters in classical gold lettering on a blue ground, with the founder's name (430), and, at the sides, figures of the Church of the Jews (ex circumcisione), and the Church of the Gentiles (ex gentibus). The wide and tall nave is divided from the aisles by 24 fluted Corinthian *Columns from a neighbouring 2C building. The spandrels of the arcades are decorated with a splendid 5C marble inlay in 'opus sectile', and the beautiful large windows, 34 in all, have their transennae of varied design based on original fragments. In the centre of the NAVE is the unusual mosaic tombstone of Muñoz de Zamora (died 1300), perhaps by *Iac. Torriti*. The schola cantorum, ambones, and bishop's throne (in the choir) have been reconstructed from ancient fragments. The unattractive apse fresco by Taddeo Zuccari has been repainted.—The RIGHT AISLE contains an ancient column, older than the church. Adjacent to it, the Chapel of St Hyacinth, is frescoed by the *Zuccari*; and at the end of the aisle is the tomb of Card. Auxias de Podio (1485), of the school of *And. Bregno*. Beneath the nave excavations have revealed remains of a small temple and an edifice of the early Imperial period with a fine marble pavement.—The Baroque Elci Chapel, in the LEFT AISLE, contains, over its altar, the *Madonna of the Rosary with Saints Dominic and Catherine, by *Sassoferrato*.

In the convent is St Dominic's room, now a chapel. The beautiful *Cloister (1216–25), with 103 columns, is open on request.

Beyond the convent is another little public park with orange trees, pine trees, a palm tree, and bougainvillea. From the parapet the view over Rome includes: in the foreground, the long orange façade of the restoration centre in the Istituto di San Michele, St Peter's with the Janiculum hill to the left, and to the right the dome of Sant'Andrea della Valle, the little spiral tower of Sant'Ivo, the dome of the Pantheon, the Synagogue, the French Academy (on the skyline surrounded by trees), the Victor Emmanuel Monument, the Capitol hill, and the Torre Milizie (just behind the tree on the extreme right). The church of **Sant'Alessio** (Pl. 8; 3; until 1217, *San Bonifacio*), near which the Crescentii built a convent in the 10C, is preceded by an attractive courtyard, and retains its fine Romanesque campanile. The interior of the church (if closed, ring at the door on the left) was modernised by *Tom. de Marchis* in 1750, but two tiny mosaic columns remain on either side of the wooden bishop's throne in the apse. At the W end of the left aisle, set in an altar of 1700 by Andrea Bergondi is a portion of the wooden staircase beneath which St Alexis lived and died.

The street ends at the delightful Piazza dei Cavalieri di Malta, with elaborate decorations by G.B. Piranesi, seen against a background of cypresses and palms. He also designed the monumental entrance in the square to the **Priorato di Malta**, or *Maltese Villa* (Pl. 8; 5), the residence of the Grand Master of the Knights of Malta. A remarkable view of the dome of St Peter's at the end of an avenue may be seen through a keyhole in the doorway. The villa (adm rarely granted; see p 49), contains a Chapter Hall with portraits of the Grand Masters, from Gerard (1113) onwards, and an altarpiece from the church by And. Sacchi. The beautiful garden, planted with palm trees and bay hedges, has a superb view from a terrace looking over the Tiber towards Monte Mario.

On the left, a drive leads to the back of the villa and the church of **Santa Maria del Priorato**, or *Aventinense* (adm see Villa), a Benedictine foundation once incorporated in the residence of the patrician senator Alberic, who was the virtual ruler of Rome in 932–54. It passed into the hands of the Templars, and from them to the Knights of Malta. It was rebuilt in 1765 by Piranesi. The fine façade of a single order crowned with a tympanum, has rich decorative details.

The harmonious INTERIOR is striking, with fine stucco decoration; the Rococo high altar by *Tom. Righi* is cleverly lit. On the right is the 15C tomb of Baldassorre Spinelli, an ancient Roman sarcophagus with reliefs of the Muses, beyond which is a statue of Piranesi by *Gius. Angelini*. In the left aisle is the tomb of Bart. Carafa (died 1405) by *Paolo Salviati*, and a medieval marble reliquary, in the form of a pagan cinerary urn (?10–12C).

On the W side of the Priorato, facing Via della Marmorata, is the ancient brick *Arco di San Lazzaro*, which may have had some connection with the store-houses (*Emporia*) in this neighbourhood.

In Piazza di Sant' Anselmo, just S of the Priorato, is the large *Benedictine Seminary* (1892–96), with the church of Sant' Anselmo, built in 1900 in the Lombard Romanesque style, and noted for its Gregorian chant (9.30 on Sunday).

From Piazza Sant' Anselmo, Via di Sant'Anselmo and Via Icilio (left) lead towards Santa Prisca (beyond Piazza Albinia; comp. the Plan), on the other side of the hill. The church of **Santa Prisca** (Pl. 8; 5; open 8–12, 16–19), possibly dating from the 4C, is said to occupy the site of the house of Aquila and Prisca, who entertained St Peter.

INTERIOR. Pretty frescoes in the nave, by *Fontebuoni*, follower of the Zuccari brothers. Right aisle: Baptismal font made from a large Doric capital, with a bronze cover and the Baptism of Christ, by *Ant. Biggi*. Left aisle (near entrance door): Fragment of a 15C Tuscan fresco (Annunciation). In the sacristy are three detached 17C fresco fragments by the school of Maratta.—Beneath the church (entered from the beginning of the right aisle, but closed indefinitely), besides a Nymphaeum (with a small museum) and the Crypt, is a MITHRAEUM, found in 1958. The interesting remains include frescoes and a statue of Mithras slaying the Bull and the lying figure of Saturn.

Via di Santa Prisca continues down to the wide and busy Viale Aventino. In Piazza Albania (right) are extensive remains of the Servian wall (c 87 BC). Across the square Via San Saba leads up to the 'Piccolo Aventino' and the steps up to the church of **San Saba** (Pl. 8; 6; open 7–12, 16–18.30), with a little porch and walled forecourt. Beneath the church were found fragments of frescoes (now exhibited in the sacristy corridor), belonging to the first church founded in the 7C by Palestinian monks escaping from the Eastern invasions. The present church may date from c 900, although it has been rebuilt several times and was restored in 1943. In 1463, under Cardinal Piccolomini, the loggia was added above the portico and the four original windows bricked in.

In the portico are sculptural fragments, some Oriental in character (rider and falcon), also a large Roman sarcophagus with figures of a bridegroom and Juno Pronuba. The fine doorway is by Giacomo, the father of Cosma, who also probably executed the floor. In the right aisle are the remains of a schola cantorum, a patchwork of Cosmatesque ornament. On the left-hand side of the church is a short fourth aisle, formed by wide decorated arches, within which are remains of 13C frescoes of St Nicholas of Bari. High up on the arch over the apse is an Annunciation, also added for Card. Piccolomini. In the apse, above the Bishop's throne is a fine Cosmatesque marble disk and a 14C fresco of the Crucifixion.

Porta San Paolo and the area farther S are described in Rte 25.

17   The Appian Way and the Catacombs

The Appian Way may be reached from the Colosseum by Bus No. 118. This runs by Via San Gregorio, Via delle Terme di Caracalla, Via di Porta San Sebastiano, Porta San Sebastiano and Via Appia Antica as far as the Osteria Belvedere. The service is infrequent (every 20–40 mins).—Bus No. 218, starting from St John Lateran joins Via Appia Antica outside Porta San Sebastiano and then branches off beyond the church of Domine Quo Vadis to the Fosse Ardeatine.

The **Appian Way** is narrow and traffic ridden for the first few kilometres which makes this section of the road unpleasant to explore on foot. A recommended way of seeing it to best advantage is to walk from Piazzale Numa Pompilio (see Rte 14) along Via di Porta San Sebastiano as far as Porta San Sebastiano. From the gate Bus 118 may be picked up as far as the Catacombs of San Callisto or San Sebastiano. From San Sebastiano it is little more than a kilometre to the Osteria Belvedere where the bus diverges from the Appian

Way. The remaining four kilometres as far as the Casal Rotondo (see below) take in the most beautiful and characteristic section of the road. It now becomes one-way for cars leaving Rome. It is possible to diverge at the Casal Rotondo by a road to the left which leads to Via Appia Nuova where Bus No. 664 can be taken back towards the centre of the city. At the bus terminus is the 'Colli Albani' station of the underground railway (Line A) for the Station and Piazza di Spagna. The Appian Way is crossed by the Rome Circular Road (Grande Raccordo Annulare) near the 7th Roman mile (see p 245).

The ***Appian Way** (*Via Appia Antica*, Pl. 9; 8) begins outside Porta San Sebastiano, in the Aurelian Wall, continuing the line of its urban section (see Rte 14). Called by Statius the queen of roads (regina viarum), it was the most important of the consular Roman roads, and is still remarkably well preserved. It was built by the censor Appius Claudius in 312 BC as far as Capua, and later extended to Beneventum (Benevento) and Brundusium (Brindisi). The most interesting section of the road is the first 8km between Porta San Sebastiano and Casal Rotondo.

Paved throughout, the Appian Way served for the first part of its course as a patrician cemetery, and was lined on either side by a series of family graves. At some points the ancient paving, of massive polygonal blocks of basaltic lava from the Alban Hills, is in good preservation, and at the sides are the *crepidines*, or sidewalks. In places the road is raised above the surrounding country, and provides good views; in other parts it is sunk below ground level. Few of the ruins have been identified with certainty and in many instances nothing is left but a concrete core, while only one milestone survives. The tombs vary greatly in form and size, but the predominating types are the tower and the tumulus. In the Middle Ages watch-towers and fortalices were often built on the solid bases of the tombs. There is a long-standing plan to make part of the area bordering the Appian Way into a National Park.

The initial section of the Appian Way, the ancient *Clivus Martis* is now a busy but rather inconspicuous road. It gently descends from Porta San Sebastiano, and about 120m from the gate is the site of the *First Milestone* (marked by a column and an inscription; see the Plan on pp 238–9). The road passes under a fly-over bearing a new fast road (where excavations have revealed Roman remains), and then under the main Rome-Civitavecchia railway. It then crosses the brook *Almone* (or *Marrana della Caffarella*), where the priests of Cybele, the Magna Mater, used to perform the annual ceremony of washing the image of the goddess. Tombs appear here and there. On the left nearly 1km from the gate, is a conical Roman mound with a house on the top, and the little church of **Domine Quo Vadis**.

This stands on the spot where, according to tradition, St Peter on his way from the city met an apparition of Jesus and so returned to Rome and martyrdom (the legend was the subject of a novel by Sienkiewicz).

By the church Via Ardeatina branches off to the right to (1km) the Fosse Ardeatine (see below). At this fork is the entrance for cars to the catacombs of St Calixtus (see below). The drive, along a beautiful cypress avenue, passes the fields and farm of the monastery.

About 100 metres from the church of Domine Quo Vadis is a turning on the left, called Via della Caffarella. Less than a kilometre along this lane is a path (left), leading to the so-called *Temple of the Deus Rediculus*, by a mill near the Almone brook. The 'temple' is really a sumptuous tomb of the 2C, once identified as that of Annia Regilla, wife of Herodes Atticus (see below).

After making a short ascent (retrospective views of the walls of Rome; the Alban Hills to the left), the Appian Way passes a trattoria (No. 87; left) which incorporates remains of the so-called *Columbarium of the Freedmen of Augustus*, where some 3000 inscriptions were found. At No. 101 is the little *Hypogeum of Vibia* (no adm), with interesting pagan paintings of the 3C AD. Beyond (No. 103) is the site of the *Second Milestone*. At No. 110, on the right, is the entrance to the ***Catacombs of St Calixtus**, the first official cemetery of the early Christian community, and usually considered the most important of the Roman Catacombs.

THE CATACOMBS

For **Admission Times**, see p 48. The Catacombs most often visited (St Calixtus and San Sebastiano on the Via Appia, and St Domitilla on Via delle Sette Chiese) all have guided tours in several languages, and tend to be crowded with large tour groups which can impair the visit for those on their own. In some catacombs explanatory films are shown before the visit. Routes often vary and are shortened at the height of the tourist season. The catacombs have some steep stairs and unlevel narrow corridors (often poorly illuminated) and the visit is therefore not normally advisable for those who have difficulty in walking. The catacombs of St Agnes on Via Nomentana, and of Priscilla on Via Salaria, of no less interest, are usually less crowded. For permission to visit the catacombs not regularly open to the public (see the Index), apply to the Pontificia Commissione di Archeologia Sacra.

The Catacombs were used by the early Christians as underground cemeteries outside the walls of Rome. They were often situated on property donated by wealthy Romans, after whom the cemetery was named (i.e. Domitilla, Agnese, Priscilla, and Commodilla). They were easily quarried in the soft tufa, and provided space for the tombs of thousands of Christians since burial within the walls was forbidden (pagan Romans were cremated). They were in use from the 1C up until the early 5C. Many martyrs were buried here and the early Christians chose to be buried close to them. Later they became places of pilgrimage until the martyrs' relics were transferred to various churches in Rome. They were pillaged by the Goths (537) and the Lombards (755), and by the 9C they were abandoned. They received their name from the stone quarries ('ad catacumbas') on the site of the cemetery of San Sebastiano. In the 16C Antonio Bosio visited the catacombs, but they were not systematically explored until 1852 when the famous archaeologist G.B. De Rossi carried out excavations (first at St Calixtus), and the Pontificia Commissione di Archeologia Sacra was set up. They were opened to the public and became one of the most famous sights of Rome, when visits by candle-light fired the romantic imagination of 19C travellers. The popular belief that they were used as hiding places by the early Christians has been totally disproved.

The Catacombs are a system of galleries of different sizes, often arranged on as many as five levels, and sometimes extending for several kilometres. In the walls simple rectangular niches (*loculi*) were cut in tiers where the bodies were placed wrapped in a sheet. The openings were closed with slabs of marble or terracotta on which the names were inscribed (at first in Greek, later in Latin), sometimes with the date or the words 'in pace' added (almost all of these have now disappeared). Terracotta lamps were hung above the tombs to provide illumination in the galleries. A more elaborate type of tomb was the *arcosolium*, which was a niche surmounted by an arch and often decorated. Small rooms or *cubicula* served as family vaults. The shallowest of the galleries are 7–8m beneath the surface, while the deepest are some 22m below ground level. Openings in the vaults, some of which survive, were used for the removal of earth during the excavations. Most of the tombs were rifled at some time over the centuries in the search for treasure and relics, but the inscriptions and paintings which survive are of the greatest interest.

The CATACOMBS OF ST CALIXTUS (adm see p 48) were named after St Calixtus (San Callisto) who was appointed to look after the cemetery by Pope Zephyrinus (199–217), and who enlarged it when he himself became pope in 217. It was the official burial place of the bishops of Rome. It was first investigated in 1850 by G.B. De Rossi (see above) and is not yet fully explored. The monastery, in a beautiful open landscape, is surrounded by an extensive farm.

Visitors are conducted by an English-speaking priest to a small basilica with three apses, the *Oratory of Saints Sixtus and Cecilia*, where the dead were brought before burial in the catacombs. Here are inscriptions and sculptural fragments from the tombs, and a bust of De Rossi. Pope St Zephyrinus is generally supposed to have been buried in the central apse.

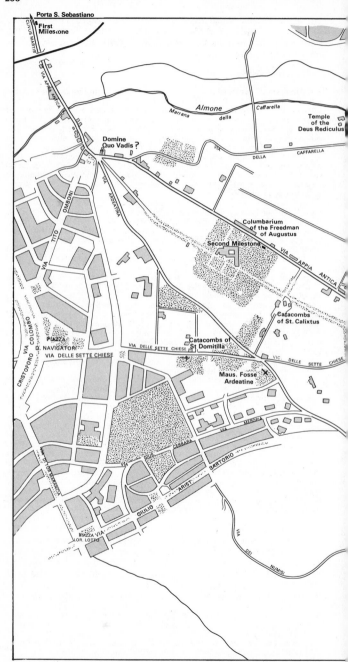

Porta S. Sebastiano
First Milestone
CLIVUS MARTIS
VIA APPIA ANTICA
Almone
Marrana
della
Caffarella
Temple of the Deus Rediculus
Domine Quo Vadis?
VIA
DELLA
CAFFARELLA
VIA ARDEATINA
VIA TITO OMBONI
Columbarium of the Freedman of Augustus
Second Milestone
VIA APPIA ANTICA
VIA CRISTOFORO COLOMBO
VIA D. NAVIGATORI
PIAZZA
VIA DELLE SETTE CHIESE
Catacombs of St. Calixtus
Catacombs of St Domitilla
VIA DELLE SETTE CHIESE
VIC DELLE SETTE CHIESE
Maus. Fosse Ardeatine
VIA MEROPIA
VIA DI TOR MARANCIA
VIA SUS CERBARA
VIA SARTORIO
ARIST
GIULIO
PIAZZA LOR. LOTTO
VIA
VIA DEI NUMISI

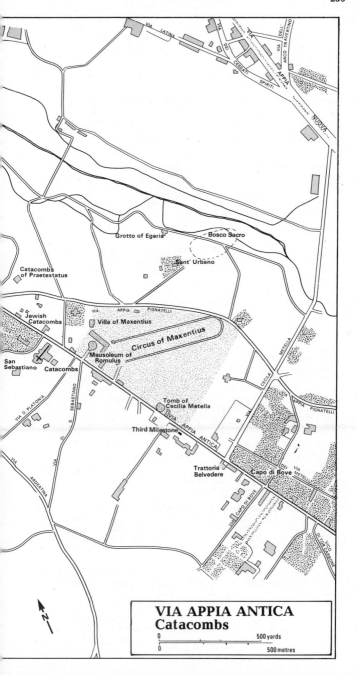

VIA APPIA ANTICA
Catacombs

| 0 | | | | | 500 yards |
| 0 | | | | | 500 metres |

The catacombs excavated on five levels are reached by an ancient staircase. The tour usually remains on the second level, from which several staircases can be seen descending to other levels. The *PAPAL CRYPT preserves the tombs with original Greek inscriptions of the martyred popes, St Pontianus (230–35), St Anterus (236), St Fabian (236–50), St Lucius (253–54), martyred under Valerian's persecution, St Stephen I (254 57), St Dionysius (259–69), and St Felix I (269–75). In honour of the martyred popes, Pope St Damasus (366–84) set up the metrical inscription seen at the end of the crypt.

In the adjoining crypt is the *Cubiculum of St Cecilia*, where the body of the saint is supposed to have been buried after her martyrdom at her house in Trastevere in 230. It is thought that it was moved by Paschal I in 820 to the church built on the site of her house. Here has been placed a copy of Maderno's statue of the saint in the church. On the walls are very worn 7–8C frescoes: Head of Christ, St Urban, and other saints. Beyond the crypt, a 3C passage leads down a short flight of stairs, with Christian symbols carved on stone slabs, to the *Cubicula of the Sacraments*, with symbolic frescoes. In the first cubicle are frescoes of the Raising of Lazarus, and opposite, the Miracle of the Loaves and Fishes. On the end wall, a fine double sarcophagus, with a lid in the form of a roof. The other cubicles have similar frescoes, several depicting the story of Jonah. Farther on is the *Crypt of St Eusebius*, martyred in 310. In the adjoining cubicles are the sepulchral inscriptions of Pope St Gaius (283–96) and two sarcophagi with mummified bodies. Next is the *Tomb of Pope St Cornelius* (251–53), with a contemporary Latin inscription containing the word 'martyr', and fine 6C Byzantine paintings. Adjoining is the *Crypt of Lucina*, the oldest part of the cemetery.

Near the Catacombs of St Calixtus are further burial-places, including the Catacomb of the Holy Cross, discovered in 1953. Here are believed to have been the Tombs of Saints Marcus and Marcellianus and the *Hypogeum of St Damasus*.

Just beyond the Catacombs of St Calixtus, Via Appia Pignatelli branches off to the left, a road opened by Innocent XII (1691–1700) to link the Appian Way with the Via Appia Nuova.

Near the beginning of Via Appia Pignatelli, on the left, are the **Catacombs of Praetextatus** (adm only with special permission; see p 48). Above ground are pagan, below ground Christian sarcophagi. Here were buried several Christian martyrs. In the crypt is the large *Spelunca Magna*, in which were buried the martyred companions of St Cecilia. In a cubicle excavated in 1850 are 2C paintings.—The next turning to the left, Vicolo Sant'Urbano (private road) leads to a villa gate. A path (left) signed '*Per il tempio*', leads to the lonely church of **Sant'Urbano** in a classical landscape. This was originally a temple forming part of the villa of the wealthy Herodes Atticus, patron of arts and man of letters of the time of the Antonines, famous above all for his numerous buildings in Greece. The temple was converted into a church in the 9C or 10C and was restored in 1634, when four fluted columns from the pronaos were incorporated into the wall of the church. Inside (apply at villa for key) are remains of stucco ornamentation and interesting *Frescoes by a certain Bonizzo (1011): over the door, Crucifixion; on the end wall, Christ blessing, with saints and angels; on the other walls, Life of Jesus, and Lives of St Cecilia and her companions, and of St Urban.

Not far away, on a hill looking towards the Alban Hills, is the *Bosco Sacro* (Sacred Wood), once mistakenly identified as the place where Numa Pompilius used to consult the nymph Egeria. On the other side of the hill is the so-called *Grotto of Egeria*, watered by a branch of the Almone. The Fountain of Egeria was near the Porta Capena.

In the Appian Way, at No. 119A, is the entrance to the **Jewish Catacombs** (adm only with special permission; see p 49), excavated in 1857. The tombs, in the form of loculi or niches, are for the most part cut on end and date from the 3C to the 6C. Among the symbols are the cornucopia (Plenty), the palm-leaf (Victory), and the seven-branched candlestick. The epitaphs are mostly in Greek.

The road now descends to a small piazza in which, on the left, is a column of Pius IX (1852), and, on the right, the basilica of San

Sebastiano. **San Sebastiano**, one of the seven pilgrimage churches of Rome, was originally dedicated to Saints Peter and Paul and called the *Basilica Apostolorum*. It was built in the first half of the 4C over the cemetery into which the bodies of the Apostles had been temporarily moved from their tombs in St Peter's and San Paolo fuori le Mura; this is said to have occurred in 258 during the persecution of Valerian. At a later date St Sebastian, who suffered under Diocletian in 288, was buried here. After the 9C the association with the Apostles was forgotten and the church was named after St Sebastian. It originally had a nave and two aisles; the aisles were walled up in the 13C. In 1612 it was rebuilt for Card. Scipio Borghese by Flaminio Ponzio; the façade has a portico with six Ionic columns, taken from the preceding 15C portico.

INTERIOR (usually visited at the end of the tour of the Catacombs, see below). The 17C wood ceiling is by Vasanzio. On the right is an apsidal chapel containing a stone which was once believed to bear the imprint of Christ's feet, and other relics. In a chapel off the left side is a late-14C wooden crucifix (restored). Opposite is the tomb chapel of the Albani family, built by Carlo Fontana for Clement XI. On the high altar, four columns of verde antico.—On the left, St Francis of Assisi, attrib. to *Girol. Muziano*; in a chapel near the entrance, recumbent *Statue of St Sebastian, by *Ant. Giorgetti*, from a design by Bernini. Near the entrance is a stone from the catacombs with an inscription in honour of the martyr Eutychius, by Pope St Damasus.

The *Catacombs of San Sebastiano** (entrance to left of church; adm see p 48) have two special claims to fame: they are the only ones that have always been known, visited, and therefore damaged, and they were originally the only underground burial place to receive the name of Catacombs—*ad catacumbas* (literally, by the caves, since they were built in an abandoned stone quarry here).

A stair with fragments of terracotta lids of sarcophagi lead down to the catacombs excavated on four levels. The order of the guided tour may not necessarily correspond with the description given below. The *Chapel of Symbols* has carved Christian symbols. Beyond is an area below the basilica (the walls of which can be seen) known as the '*Piazzuola*' which has three elaborate pagan *Tombs of the early 2C. They each have a façade with a terracotta tympanum. The first, on the right, has a fresco above the tympanum of a pastoral scene and a banquet. The marble inscription names this as the sepulchre of M. Clodius Hermes. The interior has a vault fresco with a Gorgon's head, and decorative frescoes on the walls, including a beautiful composition with a vase of fruit and flowers flanked by two birds. The floor preserves a mosaic. The centre tomb has a magnificent stucco vault, dating from the early 2C, terminating in a shell design decorated with lotus and acanthus leaves and a peacock. It is believed both pagan and Christian burials took place in this composite tomb on several levels. The Tomb to the left has a well-preserved stucco vault which descends to a lunette finely decorated with a grape and vine design. The cubicles here are also decorated with stucco.—From here ascends a steep staircase to the *Triclia*, a room reserved for the funerary banquets held in honour of the Apostles, Peter and Paul. There is a bench around the wall, and remains of red-painted decorations and fragments of pictures. The walls are inscribed with graffiti invoking the Apostles, including one dating from 260. The *Crypt of St Sebastian* (restored) is reached from the church. Here is a copy of a bust of St Sebastian, attrib. to Bernini.

An ARCHAEOLOGICAL MUSEUM was opened in 1972 in the *Ambulatory* which forms an outer aisle of the church and runs round the apse. Here the construction of the 4C basilica can be seen clearly. The left wall is covered with epitaphs found in the course of excavations. In the centre, cases display objects found in the catacombs, and three models of the church and catacombs. To the left steps descend to the *Platonia*, the tomb of St Quirinus. Also off the left side: the Chapel of Honorius III with 13C paintings, and an apsidal cubiculum with graffiti which indicate that this was the temporary grave of St Peter. Around the apse have been placed sarcophagi and fragments of sarcophagi.—Other parts of the catacombs are not usually shown. In the vicinity of the basilica are numerous tombs and mausolea, some of them still visible. From the 3C to the 9C this was the most venerated area of subterranean Rome.

Just short of San Sebastiano, Via delle Sette Chiese, on the right, leads to Via Ardeatina (600m) and (250m farther) the Catacombs of St Domitilla (see below). In Via Ardeatina (bus, see above), a little to the left of its junction, is the **Mausoleo delle Fosse Ardeatine**, scene of one of the more horrifying occurrences of the Second World War. On 24 March 1944, by way of reprisal for the killing on the previous day of 32 German soldiers by the Resistance Movement in Via Rasella, the Germans, then in occupation of Rome, shot 335 Italians. The victims, who had no connection with the killing of the Germans, included priests, officials, professional men, about a hundred Jews, a dozen foreigners, and a boy of 14. After the incident, the Germans buried the bodies under an avalanche of sand artificially caused by exploding mines. Local inhabitants who had taken note provided a medico-legal commission with the means of exhuming and identifying the bodies after the retreat of the Germans. The scene of the massacre, below a huge tufa cliff, now has cave chapels. The 335, reinterred after identification, are commemorated by a huge single concrete slab placed in 1949 over their mass grave, with a group of standing figures, in stone, by *Francesco Coccia* (1950).

The ***Catacombs of St Domitilla** (adm see p 48), or *Catacombs of Saints Nereus and Achilleus*, farther along Via delle Sette Chiese, are among the most extensive in Rome and may be the most ancient Christian cemetery in existence. Here were buried St Flavia Domitilla (niece of Flavia Domitilla, sister of Domitian) and her two Christian servants, Nereus and Achilleus, as well as St Petronilla, another Christian patrician, perhaps the adopted daughter of St Peter. The catacombs contain more than 900 inscriptions.

At the foot of the entrance stairway is the aisled *Basilica of Saints Nereus and Achilleus*, built in 390–95 over the tombs of the martyred saints. There are traces of a schola cantorum, and ancient columns probably from a pagan temple. The area below the floor level has sarcophagi and tombs. By the altar is a rare small column, with the scenes of the martyrdom of St Achilleus carved in relief. The adjoining chapel of St Petronilla (shown during the tour of the catacombs) with a fresco of the saint, contained the sarcophagus of the saint until the 8C, when it was removed to St Peter's.—A friar conducts groups from the Basilica to the catacombs, excavated on two levels. The *Cemetery of the Flavians* (the family of Domitilla) had a separate entrance on to the old Via Ardeatina. At this entrance, is a vaulted vestibule probably designed as a meeting-place for the service of Intercession for the Dead, with a bench along the wall, and a well for water. A long gallery slopes down from here, having niches on either side, with 2C frescoes of flowers and genii. From the original entrance a gallery leads to another *Hypogeum*, with four large niches decorated with 2C paintings (Daniel in the lions' den, etc.).—At the foot of a staircase is another ancient section; here is a cubicle with paintings of winged genii and the earliest representation of the Good Shepherd (2C).—On the upper level is the *Cubiculum of Ampliatus*, with paintings in classical style.—Other sections contain more paintings, including the Madonna and Child with four Magi; Christ and the Apostles; and a Cornmarket.

The Appian Way continues, leaving behind the area of the catacombs, and entering upon the finest section of the road. On the left, in a hollow, at No. 153, are the extensive remains of the **Villa of Maxentius** (recently reopened to the public; admission see p 48), built in 309 by the Emperor Maxentius. This includes a palace, a circus, and a mausoleum built in honour of his son Romulus (d 307).

The ***Circus** is the best preserved of the Roman circuses, and one of the most romantic sites of ancient Rome. From it is the best view of the Tomb of Cecilia Metella (see below). The Circus was excavated by Nibby in 1825 for the Torlonia, and restored in the 1960s and 1970s. The stadium (c 513 × 91m) was probably capable of holding some 10,000 spectators. The main entrance was on the W side with the 12 *carceres* or stalls for the chariots and quadrigae, and, on either side, two square towers, with curved façades. Two arches, one of which has been restored, connected the towers to the long sides of the circus and provided side entrances. In the construction of the tiers of seats amphorae were used to lighten the vaults (these can still clearly be seen). In the centre of the left side is the conspicuous emperor's box, which was connected by a portico to his palace on the hill behind (see below). At the far end was a triumphal arch where a fragment of a dedicatory inscription to Romulus, son of Maxentius, was found which identified the circus with Maxentius, previously attributed to Caracalla. In the centre, restored in 1971, is the round *meta* and the *spina*, the low wall which divided the area longitudinally (and where the obelisk of Domitian, now in Piazza Navona, originally stood). The course was seven laps around the *spina*. The spina and the carceres were both somewhat obliquely disposed to equalize as far as possible the chances of all competitors, although it is likely that the circus was never actually used since Maxentius fell from power in 312.—On the hillside to the left, towards Via Appia Pignatelli, are the overgrown remains (fenced off) of the **Palace** which include fragments of baths, a basilica, and a cryptoporticus.—The conspicuous high wall near the W end of the circus belongs to the quadriporticus around the **Mausoleum of Romulus**, which faces the Via Appia. Some of the pilasters of the quadriporticus survive, as well as much of the outer wall. In the centre is the circular tomb preceded by a rectangular pronaos which lie beneath a derelict house. The entrance is in front of a palm tree: beyond the pronaos is the mausoleum with niches in the outside wall for sarcophagi, and a huge pilaster in the centre also decorated with niches. The upper floor, probably covered with a cupola, has been destroyed.— Nearby, beside the Via Appia is the so-called *Tomba dei Sempronii*, probably dating from the Augustan era. It is not open to the public while excavations are still in progress.

The road rises to the famous *Tomb of Cecilia Metella**, a massive circular tower of the Augustan period, 29·5m (100 Roman ft) in diameter, rising from a square base, and extremely well preserved (admission, see p 49; informed custodian).

Much of the marble facing is still intact as is also part of the elegant frieze surrounding the upper part, with garlands of fruit and bucrania (hence the name *Capo di Bove* given to the adjacent ground). A relief represents a soldier with Gallic shields and a prisoner from Gaul kneeling at his feet. Also on the side nearest the road is the inscription to Caecilia, daughter of Quintus Metellus Creticus and wife of M. Licinius Crassus (elder son of the triumvir and one of Caesar's generals in Gaul). In the 13C the Caetani transformed the tomb into a crenellated tower to serve as the keep of their castle which they built across the roadway and included a Gothic church, the ruins of which can be seen on the other side of the road. The interior of the tomb (now inhabited by pigeons), constructed with small flat bricks, is particularly interesting; the roofless room on the right contains a collection of inscriptions and fragments from other tombs. The *Third Milestone* has recently been set up outside the enceinte of the castle, just to the left of the road, beneath the two-light windows.

A short distance farther on is the *Osteria Belvedere*, where the bus coming from the Colosseum diverges left from the Appia Antica along Via Cecilia Metella, which leads to Via Appia Pignatelli and Via Appia Nuova. The road, now mostly asphalted but retaining its ancient tombs, becomes more and more interesting as the view of the Campagna opens out. To the left is seen the imposing aqueduct of the Aqua Marcia and the Aqua Claudia. About 4km from Porta San Sebastiano the **Ancient Section of the Appian Way** is reached, excavated in 1850–59 between the 3rd and 11th milestones, the most picturesque and the least damaged part of the whole road. For ten Roman miles or more it was formerly bordered with tombs on both sides, and remains of these have been in many cases recovered while others have been reconstructed as far as possible. Some of the original sculptures have recently been removed to the Museo Nazionale Romano and replaced here by casts (easily identified by their yellow tint).—On a brick pilaster, on the left, opposite the site of the *Fourth Milestone*, are fragments of a tomb of a member of the Servilian gens. An inscription records that this was a gift made by Canova in 1808, who, contrary to the general practice of his time, felt that objects found during excavations should be left in situ. Beyond is the so-called *Tomb of Seneca* (left; replaced by casts), immediately followed by the *Sepolcro Rotondo* (round tomb), a cella with four 'loculi', and the *Tomb of the Children of Sextus Pompeius Justus* (partly replaced by casts). Beyond this, set back from the road, is a so-called *Temple of Jupiter*, square with apsidal niches. On the right, in the Proprietà Lugari (near a clump of huge umbrella pines), is a superb monument in the form of a shrine (supposed to be that of St Urban), surrounded by the ruins of what was probably a villa. Then come, in the next 550 metres, the *Tombs of the Licinii*, of *Hilarius Fuscus* (the five busts replaced by casts), of the *Freedmen of the Claudian Gens*, and of *Q. Apuleius Pamphilius*. Beyond a sepulchre in the form of a temple is the *Tomb of the Rabirii* (the three busts replaced by casts). Beyond more tombs, one in peperino (decorated with festoons), and another with four busts (casts) the road crosses Via Erode Attico.—At a point marked by a group of gigantic pines, near the *Fifth Milestone*, the road makes a bend, probably to avoid some earlier tumuli, one of which (now surmounted by a tower) passes for the burial-place of one of the legendary *Curiatii*, while two others, surrounded by pines, about 350m farther on (right), represent those of the *Horatii*. In the field to the right of the first are the remains of an *Ustrinum* (cremation place). A gate on the left opens on a by-road leading to the estate of *Santa Maria Nuova*, built over ruins (see below), and, farther on, on the same side, is a great pyramidal tomb. Then, opposite the second of the graves of the Horatii, an inscription of the 1C BC marks the tomb of M. Caecilius, in whose family grave (according to Eutropius) was buried Pomponius Atticus, the friend of Cicero. Just beyond are the magnificent and picturesque ruins of the *Villa of the Quintilii**, now part of the property of Santa Maria Nuova (see above). The ruins sprawl across fields through which sheep are grazed.

These are so extensive as to suggest a town rather than a villa and in fact they used to be called *Roma Vecchia*. The villa, of which the principal mass dates from the time of Hadrian, belonged under Commodus to the wealthy brothers Quintilii, Maximus, and Condianus, consuls under Antoninus Pius (AD 151) and writers on agriculture, who were put to death by Commodus for the sake of their possessions, including the villa. This was kept in repair till the 4C. Near the road are the remains of a nymphaeum (converted in the 15C into a castle), a hippodrome, and an aqueduct, and, a little in front of them, a cryptoporticus. But the greater portion of these ruins lies nearer the Via Appia Nuova, where there are high walls with windows and boldly-executed arcades, also the floor of a small amphitheatre of later date and traces of thermae. Beyond the Via Appia Nuova is a fine monument, converted into a tower by the Saracens.

The road now becomes more peaceful, and the monuments more widely scattered.—8km The **Casal Rotondo**, a large round tomb on a square base, with an incongruous modern house and an olive garden on the summit.

This huge tomb, the largest on the Appian Way, dates from the Republic but was enlarged in early Imperial times. It is said to have been erected to the memory of the poet Messala Corvinus by his son Valerius Maximus Cotta. The stylobate is 120 Roman ft (c 36m) in diameter.—Attached to a wall close by are to be seen fragments of the tomb. Facing this monument is a smaller one attributed to the Aurelian gens.

Just beyond the Casal Rotondo are cross-roads, on the far side of which was the *Sixth Milestone*. Here also the Rome–Naples railway passes diagonally below in a short tunnel. The road to the right is Via di Torricola, leading to Torricola and Via Ardeatina.

4·5km from the intersection with the latter road is the **Santuario del Divino Amore**, at Castel di Leva. The sanctuary, crowded with pilgrims on Whit Monday, was inaugurated in 1745 to enshrine a picture of the Virgin painted by an unknown 14C artist in the surviving tower of the *Castel di Leva*, a castle of the Orsini which passed to the Savelli before its destruction in the 15C. The painting, credited with miraculous powers of protection, is said to have saved the life of a pilgrim attacked here by mad dogs.

On the left Via di Casal Rotondo, bearing left after a short distance slopes down to the Via Appia Nuova. This is a convenient point at which to leave the Appian Way; otherwise it may be followed as far as Frattocchie.

Beyond the Casal Rotondo is a tomb with reliefs of griffons and a columbarium. Opposite another columbarium on the right of the road, is a tomb with four busts (casts). Some way farther on (about 1km from the Casal Rotondo) is the *Torre in Selce*, a pyramidal tumulus with a medieval tower, 107m above sea-level. The remainder of the road is less interesting and finally becomes impracticable for wheeled traffic.

Beyond inscriptions of M. Julius Pietas Epelides and C. Atilius Eudos, a jeweller, the road swerves a little and begins to descend, and the arches of an aqueduct by which the water of a sulphur spring near Ciampino was formerly conveyed to the villa of the Quintilii, are prominent. Near this point the Appian Way is intersected dangerously by the Circular Road (*Grande Raccordo Anulare*; radius 11–16km), linking all the consular highways that lead out of Rome. The first section was opened in 1951 and it has only recently been completed. Its total length is 68km. It is already too narrow to carry the volume of traffic passing round Rome, and is always very busy.—The Appian Way then returns to its original direction and it passes in succession (left) the stump of an apsidal monument; the *Torre Rossa* (a 12–13C structure on a Roman base); a restored tomb; another core of concrete; a tall square monument; and, at about the end of the 8th Roman mile, a sepuchral chamber (or possibly a sanctuary of the mysteries), known as the 'Pillars of Hercules'.

Farther along Via Appia, beyond the *Torraccio del Palombaro* (a monument preserved through having been turned into a church in the 10C), is a path that leads on the right to *La Giostra*, a little hill upon which are ruins, once identified with the ancient Latin city of *Tellene*, but now thought to be a 4C Roman fortified outpost. Then come other tombs, more or less ruined (including one called the *Ruzzica d'Orlando*); and at the *Ninth Milestone* is what is left of the *Villa of Gallienus*, with a fine circular ruin that is regarded as the mausoleum of that emperor. Still passing traces of the past, the road crosses the Rome–Terracina railway and, a little beyond the *Twelfth Milestone*, the old road joins the Via Appia Nuova.

18 San Lorenzo fuori le Mura

The **Basilica of San Lorenzo** in Piazzale del Verano is reached by numerous buses and trams from the centre of the city (i.e. No. 71 from Piazza San Silvestro, 11 from the Colosseum, etc.).

The basilica of *San Lorenzo fuori le Mura (Pl. 6; 4) is one of the seven pilgrimage churches of Rome and consists of two churches placed end to end. Beside the 4C covered cemetery basilica of *San Lorenzo* (to the E) Pelagius II built a new church in 579. The church of the *Madonna* dates from the time of Sixtus III (pope, 432–440). These churches were united in 1216, when Honorius III demolished their apses; they were skilfully restored in 1864–70. San Lorenzo was the only church in Rome to suffer serious damage during the Second World War, having been partly destroyed in an air raid on 19 July 1943. The façade and the S wall of the church of the Madonna were rebuilt after the war, and the basilica was reopened for worship in the summer of 1949.

The simple Romanesque CAMPANILE dates from the 12C.—The façade of the church was formerly decorated with paintings of its builders and restorers; the reconstructed 13C NARTHEX of six antique Ionic columns has a carved cornice and a mosaic frieze. Inside are two curious tombs, a tablet (1948) commemorating repairs ordered by Pius XII after war damage, and a monument to the statesman Alcide De Gasperi (died 1954) by Manzù; the 13C frescoes depict the lives of Saints Laurence and Stephen.

The basilican 13C INTERIOR has a chancel and no transept. Twenty-two Ionic columns of granite support an architrave, and the floor is paved with a 12C Cosmatesque mosaic. On the right of the entrance is the tomb of Cardinal Fieschi, a large Roman sarcophagus converted to its present use in 1256; it was rebuilt from the original fragments after the bombardment. Near the end of the nave on the right is a cosmatesque ambone and the twisted stem of a paschal candlestick.—The baldacchino in the CHOIR is by *Augusto* and *Sassone*, sons of the mastermason Paolo (1147; upper part modern). The episcopal throne dates from the 13C. Inside the triumphal arch is a 6C mosaic of Christ with saints, and Pelagius offering the Church, reset during the Byzantine revival. The raised *CHANCEL incorporates Pelagius', 6C church (except for its apse). The Corinthian columns support an entablature of antique fragments, and above, an arcaded gallery.

The 6C chancel of San Lorenzo fuori le Mura

Stairs lead down to the level of the earliest basilica, with some of the original pillars. In its former choir, now beneath the high altar, are preserved the remains of Saints Laurence, Stephen, and Justin. The original narthex, at the end, is now the Mausoleum of Pius IX (died 1878), rebuilt by *Cattaneo* in 1881 and decorated by *Lod. Seitz*. The lunette mosaics are good; the coats of arms commemorate the families that subscribed to the tomb.—In the Sacristy, off the right aisle, is the entrance to the beautiful *CLOISTER built in 1187–91, with varied columns, and inscriptions and fragments on the walls, and pagan sarcophagi. Off the cloister are the extensive *Catacombs of St Cyriaca* (usually closed) where the body of St Laurence is said to have been placed after his death in 258.

To the right of the church is the entrance to the huge municipal

cemetery called **Campo Verano** (Pl. 6; 4), on the site of the estate of
the emperor Lucius Verus.

At the entrance to the cemetery are four large allegorical figures. Among the
tombs is that of Goffredo Mameli (died 1849), the soldier-poet (first avenue to
the left). On the high ground beside Via Tiburtina is a memorial of the battle of
Mentana (1867). In the zone of the new plots is a First World War memorial, by
Raff. De Vico.

PIAZZALE SAN LORENZO, a busy traffic centre and bus and tram
terminus, is traversed by Via Tiburtina, on the site of the ancient
Roman road to Tibur (now Tivoli). Viale Regina Elena leads NW
between the *Istituto Superiore di Sanità* with a research centre for
chemical microbiology, and (left) the **Città Universitaria** (Pl. 6; 3, 4),
built by Marcello Piacentini, and others.

This extensive series of buildings, formed into a 'city', was completed in 1935, in
which year the seat of the University of Rome was transferred from its cramped
quarters in Palazzo della Sapienza. The main entrance is in Viale delle Scienze.
From the monumental entrance a broad road leads to the *Foro Universitario*, in
which is a water tank, with a statue of Minerva, by Arturo Martini. Behind the
statue rises the Rectorial Palace, with various faculties and the University
Library. In the Faculty of Letters is the *Museo dei Gessi*, with reproductions of
Greek and Hellenistic statuary. The road passes (right) the faculties of
Orthopaedy and Chemistry, and (left) those of Hygiene, Physics, Mineralogy,
and Geology. A side turning to the left leads to the church of *Divina Sapienza*
(1947). To the right of the Rectorial Palace is the School of Mathematics and,
behind it, the faculties of Botany, General Physiology, Anthropology, and
Psychology.—To the S, at the junction of Viale delle Scienze with Via dei
Marrucini, is the building of the *National Council of Research*, by Ortensi.

Across Viale delle Science is the *Air Ministry* by Roberto Marino
(1931), and beyond Viale dell'Università is the **Policlinico** (Pl. 6; 1, 3),
a large teaching hospital, designed by Giulio Podesti (1893). To the
W are the buildings (entrance on Viale Castro Pretorio), opened in
1975, of the **Biblioteca Nazionale Centrale Vittorio Emanuele II** (Pl.
6; 1) on the site of the **Castro Pretorio**, the huge Roman barracks of
the Praetorian Guard.

The **National Library**, the largest in Italy (open weekdays 9–18.30, Saturday 9–
13.30) was founded in 1877 with the contents of the library of the Jesuit Collegio
Romano (its former seat), and later enriched with the books of 70 monastic
libraries. It now has about 2,300,000 volumes (nearly 1900 incunabula) and
6200 manuscripts.
　　The *Praetoriae Cohortes*, or emperor's bodyguard, originally nine or ten
cohorts (9000–10,000 men), were instituted by Augustus and concentrated into
a permanent camp at this spot by Sejanus, minister of Tiberius in AD 23; some
portions of his building survive. In later Imperial times the Praetorian Guard
acquired undue influence in the conduct of affairs of state. As Gibbon pointed
out, emperor after emperor had to bribe them on his accession with a 'donative';
on one occasion, after the death of Pertinax in 193, they put up the Roman
Empire for sale by auction; it was bought by Didius Julianus, who enjoyed his
purchase for 66 days. Centuries later the Castro Pretorio passed into the hands
of the Jesuits, who renamed it *Macao*, after their most successful foreign
mission. It was again used as barracks in this century.

Via San Martino della Battaglia leads SW to PIAZZA DELL' INDIPENDENZA, on the
site of the *Campus Sceleratus*, where vestals who had forgotten their vows of
chastity were buried alive. Via Solferino continues to Piazza dei Cinquecento in
front of the Railway Station (Rte 10).

19 Porta Pia and Via Nomentana (Sant'Agnese fuori le Mura)

The important church of **Sant'Agnese fuori le Mura**, a long way from the centre of the city along a relatively uninteresting road, may be reached from Piazza Venezia by Bus No. 60.

Porta Pia (Pl. 5; 2), a high isolated arch, was Michelangelo's last architectural work, commissioned by Pius IV in 1561. The exterior face is by Vespignani (1868). It stands at the beginning of Via Nomentana.

The ancient *Porta Nomentana*, walled up by Pius IV, is in Piazza della Croce Rossa to the right. The N tower has been preserved. The Castro Pretorio here and the area to the S are described in Rte 18. It was by the Porta Pia that the Italian troops under General Raffaele Cadorna entered Rome on 20 September 1870 and so ended the temporal power of the popes. The actual breach was, however, a few steps to the left of the gate, in Corso d'Italia (commemorative stones). In the small courtyard of the gateway is the *Museo Storico dei Bersaglieri*); a monument (1932) is outside the gate.

Inside the gate, on the left, is *Villa Bonaparte*, seat of the French Embassy to the Vatican. It was the home of Pauline Bonaparte from 1816–24, and was once famous for its garden. On the other side of Via XX Settembre is the *British Embassy*, a conspicuous building surrounded by water, by Sir Basil Spence opened in 1971, on the site of the *Villa Torlonia* damaged by a terrorist's bomb in 1946.

The wide **Via Nomentana** (Pl. 12; 8) runs NE from Porta Pia, traversing a residential district of the city, with palaces and villas, many with beautiful gardens. It follows the line of the ancient Roman consular road to Nomentum, now Mentana, c 20km NE of Rome. Any of the buses here pass the church of Sant'Agnese fuori le Mura (see below). On the right, in Via dei Villini, at No. 32 are the *Catacombs of Nicomedes*, named after a martyr of the reign of Domitian (adm only with special permission). Beyond Viale Regina Margherita on the left is Villa Paganini (a public garden), and on the right is the garden of **Villa Torlonia** (Pl. 12; just beyond 8), which became the private residence of Mussolini after 1929. It is now a municipal public park (13·5 hectares; adm 9–dusk; poorly maintained). By the entrance gate, near a grove of palm trees is a neoclassical villa built by Valadier in 1806. Several neo-Gothic garden buildings here built in 1840 by Giuseppe Japelli are in need of restoration. Beneath the house and grounds are *Jewish Catacombs* (2C or 3C), originally extending for over 9km, but now mostly caved in (and closed indefinitely). For the other Villa Torlonia, see Rte 20.

About 2km from Porta Pia, opposite a fountain of the Acqua Marcia, stands the church of *Sant'Agnese fuori le Mura, in an important group of paleochristian buildings. These consist of the ruins of a large cemetery basilica built probably after Constantine's death by his elder daughter Constantia in 337–350 on her estate next to the tomb of the martyred St Agnes (304). Above the crypt sanctuary and catacombs Honorius I (625–38) built a second church, when the Constantinian basilica was already in ruins. Next to the basilica (and with an entrance from its S aisle) Constantia built her mausoleum in which she and her sister Helena were buried.

According to a Christian tradition, St Agnes, having refused the advances of a praetor's son, was exposed in the Stadium of Domitian, where her nakedness was covered by the miraculous growth of her hair. She was then condemned to be burned at the stake, but the flames did not touch her, so that she was finally beheaded by Diocletian. The 'Pallium' worn by the Pope is made of the wool of lambs blessed annually on the day of her festival, 21 January.

The most direct entrance is on Via Sant'Agnese, but visitors can also enter through the gate of the convent of the Canonici Lateranensi on Via Nomentana, from which the campanile of the basilica of Honorius and the small colonnaded front can be seen. On the right of the court is a hall (originally a cellar) into which Pius IX and his entourage were precipitated, though without injury, by the collapse of the floor of the room above in 1855. Beyond a fine tower is the entrance to the 7C **Basilica of Sant'Agnese fuori le Mura** (open 9–12, 16–18; Sunday 16–18), restored in 1479 by Giul. Della Rovere (Julius II), by Cardinal Varallo after the sack of 1527, and by Pius IX in 1856. It is reached by a staircase of forty-five white marble steps (1590), the walls of which are covered with inscriptions from the catacombs, including St Damasus's record of the martyrdom of St Agnes (on the right near the bottom).

In the INTERIOR of the church (best light in the afternoon) the nave and aisles are separated by fourteen ancient Roman columns of breccia and pavonazzetto. There is a narthex for the catechumens, and a matroneum was built over the aisles and the W end in 620. The carved and gilded wood ceiling dates from 1606 (restored in 1855). In the 2nd chapel on the right, over a Cosmati altar, is a fine relief of St Stephen and St Laurence, by *And. Bregno* (1490), and a bust of Christ once attributed to Michelangelo and probably the work of Nic. Cordier. On the high altar, in which are preserved the relics of St Agnes and St Emerentiana, her foster-sister, is an antique torso of Oriental alabaster restored in 1600 as a statue of St Agnes, beneath a baldacchino (1614) supported on four porphyry columns. On the left of the altar is a fine candlestick, thought to be a neo-Attic work of the 2C. In the apse is the original plain marble decoration and an ancient episcopal throne. Above, a *Mosaic (625–38), representing St Agnes between Popes Symmachus and Honorius I, two restorers of the basilica, a model of which is held by Honorius. The simplicity of the composition, against a dull gold background is striking.

In the left aisle is the entrance to the *Catacombs of St Agnes, the best-preserved and among the most interesting Roman catacombs (open at the same time as the church, see above). They were discovered in 1865–66. Visitors are conducted. The atmosphere in these catacombs, not normally visited by travellers in large groups offers a striking contrast to that in the more famous catacombs on the Appian Way (see Rte 17) which are always crowded with tours. These contain no paintings but there are numerous inscriptions and many of the loculi are intact. They may date from before 258 but not later than 305; the oldest zone extends to the left of the basilica. A chapel was built where the body of St Agnes was found, and a silver coffer provided in 1615 by Pope Paul V.

On the other side of the entrance court a path leads to the round *Mausoleum of Constantia*, called the church of ***Santa Costanza** (open at the same time as Sant'Agnese, see above; if closed apply at the sacristy in Sant'Agnese; it is often in use for weddings). This was built probably before 354 by Constantia as a mausoleum for herself and her sister Helena.

The charming INTERIOR is annular in plan—twenty-four granite columns in pairs with beautiful Corinthian capitals and pulvinated imposts supporting the dome—which is 22·5m in diameter. Sixteen clerestory windows provide light. On the barrel-vaulting of the encircling ambulatory are remarkable paleochristian *Mosaics (4C), pagan in character. They are designed in pairs on a white ground. Those flanking the entrance have a geometric design, and the next, a circular motif with animals and figures. Vintage scenes and vine tendrils with grapes follow, and the 4th pair have roundels with a leaf design, busts, and figures. On either side of the sarcophagus are leaves, branches, amphorae and exotic birds. Over the sarcophagus only a fragment remains of a mosaic with a star design. The two side niches also have fine mosaics (5C or 7C).—

Constantia's magnificent porphyry sarcophagus was replaced here by a cast when it was removed to the Vatican.

Two small gates on the right of the mausoleum lead into an overgrown garden and orchard with the remains of the huge **Constantinian basilica** (see above), identified in 1954. They include the outer walls with a round window in the apse, sustained on the outside by huge buttresses. In plan it was typical of the early cemetery basilicas of Rome, such as San Lorenzo fuori le Mura, San Sebastiano, etc.

4C mosaic of vintage scenes in the barrel vault of Santa Costanza

Beyond the church of Sant'Agnese Via Nomentana continues NE towards the river Aniene. On the right, incorporated in the garden wall of the *Villa Blanc*, is a 2C circular tomb looking like a small copy of the Mausoleum of Cecilia Metella. The gardens of the Villa were designated a public park in 1974, but are still not open to the public and are in a state of abandon. Farther on, to the left, in Via Asmara (No. 6), is the entrance to the *Catacombs of the Cimitero Maggiore* (adm only with special permission), with interesting frescoes. The road crosses the river Aniene by the modern *Ponte Tazio*. The Aniene, the ancient *Anio*, rises near Tivoli, where it falls in cascades on its way to the Campagna. Here the river is quiescent. On the right of the new bridge is the Roman *Ponte Nomentano, rebuilt by Narses in 552 and guarded by a medieval watch-tower. Beyond the river is the dismal modern QUARTIERE DI MONTE SACRO, named after the *Mons Sacer* (37m), which rises to the right. This was the scene in 494 BC of the first secession of the plebs, who were induced to return to Rome by the fable of the belly and its members recited to them by Menenius Agrippa. From the top of the hill there is a good view.

20 Via Salaria (Villa Torlonia and the Catacombs of Priscilla)

The **Catacombs of Priscilla**, a long way from the centre of the city, can be reached from the Station by Bus No. 319 (nearest stop, Via di Priscilla).

PIAZZA FIUME (Pl. 12; 7) is on the site of the Roman *Porta Salaria*. The gate no longer exists but the bases of two tombs in the square define its width. Here begins **Via Salaria** (Pl. 12; 7, 5, 4, 2), one of the oldest Roman roads, which takes its name from its association with the salt trade between the Romans and the Sabines. It runs (now the modern N4) via Rieti and Antrodoco to Ascoli Piceno and the Adriatic near San Benedetto del Tronto. Some 300 metres outside the gate it passes the large park (right) of *Villa Torlonia (Pl. 12; 5, 6), formerly *Albani*, built in 1760 by Carlo Marchionni for Card. Aless. Albani, whose valuable collection of classical sculpture was here arranged by Winckelmann in 1765. By order of Napoleon 294 pieces of this collection were removed to Paris; after Waterloo nearly all of them were sold at Munich instead of being returned. The original collection, however, continued to increase. In 1852 it passed into the possession of the Chigi and in 1866 it was bought, with the villa, by Princess Aless. Torlonia.—Visitors are sometimes admitted, but only after previous written application to the Amministrazione Torlonia, 30 Via della Conciliazione.

There are two villas of the same name, the one described here, and the former residence of Mussolini, in Via Nomentana (Rte 19).

From the entrance gate a magnificent avenue leads to a rotunda surrounded by umbrella pines, on which converge several other avenues; all of them are lined with boxwood hedges. One leads on the left direct to the **Casino**. This comprises a main building with a portico, and two re-entrant wings, also with porticoes, defining an elegant garden. In front is a *Hemicycle*, with 40 Doric columns; in its centre is a hall called *Sala del Canopo* or *Caffè*. In the garden are busts and Roman fragments; small fountains play in front of the wings.

Ground Floor. PORTICO. In the niches are busts of Roman emperors. From the left, 52. Herm of Mercury; 54. Tiberius; 55, 60. Colossal masks; 58. Ptolemaeus, last king of Numidia; 64. Trajan; 65. Altar with Hecate and the Four Seasons; 69. Bowl of Karystian marble; 74. Altar with Eleusinian divinities; 87. Statue of a man in armour (head of Augustus added).—From the Portico is access (left) into the ATRIUM OF THE CARYATIDS. 16, 24. Kanephoroi (baskets modern); 19. Bacchante in the style of the 5C with a caryatid head from another statue by Kriton and Nikolaos of Athens; below (20) a relief, the so-called Kapaneus struck dead by Zeus (5C).—In the adjoining FIRST GALLERY, Collection of herms. The following ascriptions are mostly conjectural: 27. Themistocles; 29. Epicurus; 30. Hamilcar; 31. Leonidas; 32. Xenophon; 40. Hannibal; 43. Agrippa; 45. Scipio Africanus.—Beyond an antechamber on the left is the STAIRCASE. In front, on the left, 9. Rome, a relief dating from the reign of Trajan; 11. Sepulchral relief of Tiberius Julius Vitalis, sausage vendor. On the landings: 885. Frieze of Diana slaying the Niobids, possibly reproduced from the composition of Pheidias for the throne of Zeus Olympios; 889. The robber Sinis; 891. Thanatos; 898, 899. Bacchantes.

First Floor. OVAL HALL. Ceiling painting of Aurora, by *Ant. Bicchierari*. 905. Apollo with the tripod, the omphalos, and a crouching lion; *906. Statue of athlete, signed by Stephanos, pupil of Pasiteles (1C BC); 915. Cupid bending his bow; above the door, 921. Mithraic relief.—GREAT HALL, on the right, with a ceiling painting of *Parnassos by *Raphael Mengs*. Numerous low reliefs. 1014. Apollo, Artemis, and Leto before the Temple at Delphi, archaistic votive offering of a victor in the Pythian games; 1007. Bacchante; 1008. Hercules in the garden of the Hesperides; 1009. Daedalus and Icarus; 1011. Ganymede; 1018. Antoninus Pius, Faustina, and Rome; *1012. Albani Pallas, wearing the diplax or folded mantle with a clasp (the head, from another statue, has a wolf's head headdress), Attic School; 1015, 1016. Sphinxes, Roman copies; 1017. Alabaster tripod; 1019. Jupiter; 1026. Messalina; 1029, 1030. Silenus; antique mosaic frieze.

RIGHT WING. ROOM 1. On the ceiling, *Ant. Bicchierari*, Venus and Cupid; *Paolo Anesi*, Landscapes. 1033. So-called Sappho, a Pheidian head of Aphrodite; *1031. Orpheus and Eurydice at the moment when Orpheus turns round, and Hermes, replica of a 5C original in the Pheidian style; 1034. Theophrastos; 1036. Hippocrates.—R. 2. Paintings. 35. *Luca Signorelli* (attrib.), Madonna with saints and donor; 36. *Nic. da Foligno*, Madonna and saints (signed and dated 1475); 37. *Perugino*, Polyptych: Adoration of the Shepherds, Crucifixion, Annunciation and Saints; 46, 47. *Giov. Paolo Pannini*, Arch of Constantine.—R. 3. 51. *Honthorst*, Decapitation of John the Baptist; 52. *Pompeo Batoni*, Madonna and Child; 55. *Van Dyck*, Crucifixion; 56. *Taddeo Zuccari*, Deposition of Christ; 60. *Tintoretto*, Crucifixion; 64. *Ribera*, Head of an old man ('The thinker'); 73. *Guercino*, St Luke.

LEFT WING. ROOM 1. On the ceiling, *Bicchierari*, Saturn devouring his children; low reliefs by *Thorvaldsen*; *994. Antinöus, a celebrated relief from Hadrian's Villa, the only piece brought back from Paris in 1815; 995, 996. Herms in Oriental alabaster; 997. Female satyr playing the flute; 100. Bowl of green porphyry.—R. 2. 967. Dancing girls, relief possibly after an original by Kallimachos; 970. Minerva, archaistic; *980. So-called Leucothea, relief of the beginning of the 5C BC; *985. Battle-scene, fine 5C relief, characteristic of Pheidias; 998. Fragment of frieze in the archaic style of the Dii Consentes; 991. Relief made up of two fragments found at Tivoli.—R. 3. Paintings. 17, 18. Sketches by *Giulio Romano* of the story of Psyche in Palazzo del Te at Mantua; 21. *Holbein* (attrib.), Sir Thomas More; 23, 24. *Philip Roos*, Landscapes; 28. *Borgognone*, Battle-scene.—R. 4. Ceiling by *Bicchierari* and *Lapiccola*. 931. Diana; 933. Herakles, bronze copy of an original by Lysippos; 942. Diogenes; 944. Hecuba; *952. Apollo Sauroktonos, ancient copy after Praxiteles; *953. Bust of Quintus Hortensius; *957. Apotheosis of Hercules, in the style of the Tabula Iliaca in the Capitoline Museum; 960. Persius (?); *964. Aesop (so called), a naturalistic nude statue of a hunchback, possibly a portrait of a court dwarf of the time of Hadrian.—Paintings. *Luca Giordano*, Caritas Romana, in the Flemish style; 5. *Marco David*, Portrait of Innocent XII; 6, 7. *Gaspare Vanvitelli*, Landscapes.—From the Oval Hall stairs lead down to the ground floor.

Ground Floor (continued). Beyond the portico is the ATRIO DELLA GIUNONE. 90. Pertinax; 91, 97. Kanephoroi; 93. Juno(?); 96. Marcus Aurelius.—GALLERY. *103. Bacchante with nereids; 106. Faun and the youthful Bacchus; 110. Faun; 112. Numa, 115. Pindar, 122. Persius (attributions of these three conjectural); 120. Gaius Caesar.—The STANZA DELLA COLONNA is a room with 12 fine columns (one fluted, in alabaster). *131. Sarcophagus, marriage of Peleus and Thetis, considered by Winckelmann to be one of the finest in existence; 132. Lucius Verus; 135. Hippolytus leaving for the chase; 137, 138. Alabaster lion masks; 139, 140. Sarcophagus, Rape of Proserpine.—R. 1. 146. Aesculapius and Hygieia, votive relief; 157. Polyphemus and Cupid; 161. Alexander visiting Diogenes; 164. Daedalus and Icarus, relief in rosso antico; terracottas.—R. 2. 185. Leda and the swan.—R. 3. 204. Theseus and the Minotaur; 212. Recumbent statue of a man; 213. Bacchic procession.—R. 4. 216. Sleep, low relief.

An ilex avenue leads from the Casino to the BIGLIARDO (billiard pavilion). Beyond is the HEMICYCLE. 594. Alcibiades (?), after the original in the Museo Torlonia; 596. Mercury; 604. Mars; 607. Antisthenes; 610. Chrysippos; 612. Apollo in repose; 617. Hadrian; 628. Caryatid; 633, 634. Caligula; 636, 647. Actors removing their masks after applause.—Beyond the door into the Hall: 721. Homer; 725. Caryatid; 737. Bust, of Jupiter or Neptune; *749. Proserpine, a beautiful copy of a bronze by Pheidias; 754. Commodus; 757. Bacchus; 753. Venus, of the type of the Capuan Venus; 741. Herakles, copied from a bronze original perhaps by Praxiteles; 744. So-called Peisistratos, in the style of Myron.—From the middle of the Hemicycle is the entrance to a VESTIBULE. 711. Iris; 706. Theseus and Aethra; 641. Marsyas bound to the tree; 639. Venus and Cupid; statues of comic actors.—SALA DEL CANOPO or CAFFÉ. Elegant low reliefs reproducing famous antiques; paintings by *Lapiccola* and *Paolo Anesi*. In the pavement Roman mosaic. 659. Diana of the Ephesians; 662. Artemis (5C BC); 663. Mosaic of seven philosophers; 676. Colossal head of Jupiter Serapis, in black basalt; 678. Boy with comic mask; 682. Ibis, in rosso antico; 684. Atlas supporting the heavens; 691. Canopus, rare sculpture in green basalt, with reliefs of Egyptian gods; 696. Hercules freeing Hesione, fine mosaic; 700. Diana of the Ephesians; 702. Caracalla; 704. Silenus; 706. Theseus, low relief.

Opposite Villa Torlonia is the circular *Mausoleum of Lucilius Peto*, dating from the time of Augustus. Behind the mausoleum, on the corner of Via Po and Via Livenza a 4C *Hypogeum* was discovered in 1923, 9m below ground level. It contains frescoes and mosaics, and may have been a cult sanctuary or possibly a monumental fountain (it is not normally open to the public).—Via Salaria continues to the road junction with Viale Regina Margherita (right) and Viale Liegi (left) which leads to the PARIOLI, a fashionable residential district of the city.

In this area are a number of catacombs not normally open to the public, but sometimes open to visitors with special permission (see Rte 17). In Piazza Verdi is the *Istituto Poligrafico dello Stato* (Government Printing Works, 1930), and, beside a church of the same name, the *Catacombs of Panfilo* (Pl. 12; 5), visited in 1594 by Ant. Bosio and further excavated in this century. They contain frescoes, and tombs decorated with lamps and statuettes. At 13 Via Bertoloni are the *Catacombs of Sant'Ermete* (Pl. 11; 4), with a large underground basilica, containing an 8C fresco of the Madonna and angels with Saints Hermes and Benedict, the earliest known painting of the last.—On the other side of Via Salaria, at No. 2 Via Simeto, is the entrance to the *Catacombs of Santa Felicità* or *Massimo* (Pl. 12; 5), with a small underground basilica.

Via Salaria continues past St George's English School (left), and now widens with a line of pines down the centre. Via Panama skirts the wall of the vast expanse of *Villa Ada* (formerly Savoia; Pl. 12; 1, 2), the garden wall of which extends for a long way along Via Salaria. This was once the private residence of Victor Emmanuel III, and is now the embassy of the United Arab Republic. Part of the grounds are open as a public park.

On the other side of Via Salaria, on the corner with Via Taro, is the entrance to the *Catacombs of the Giordani* (Pl. 12; 4; adm only with special permission), believed to be the *Catacombs of Trasone* before excavations were carried out in 1966–69. These are the deepest catacombs in Rome, with five tiers of galleries, and contain a fine 4C mural of a woman in prayer. Farther on, between Nos 2 and 4 *Via Anapo* (Pl. 12; 4) is the entrance to another *Catacomb*, formerly thought to be the cemetery of the Giordani. This contains interesting frescoes of Old and New Testament scenes, dating from the 3C and 4C. Adm only with special permission.

At No. 430 Via Salaria is the entrance to the **Catacombs of Priscilla** (Pl. 12; 2; adm see p 48), the most important catacombs on Via Salaria, and among the most interesting in Rome. Visitors are taken in groups by an English-speaking nun. The tour is on the road level, although there are further catacombs (unlit) below. The exit is usually on the other side of Via Salaria.

The dating and significance of the various areas of the catacombs are still under discussion. Several parts were found to have a layer of lime, formed after centuries of earth had been packed against the walls, and this was removed in some places, and the frescoes beneath saved. It is now thought a villa of the Roman family of Acilii existed above the cemetery, to which the cryptoporticus (with cross-vaulting and remains of Pompeian-style frescoes) and a nymphaeum probably belonged. Many popes were buried here between 309 and 555. The so-called *Greek Chapel* (from the Greek inscriptions found here) is an interesting funerary chapel with frescoes of Biblical scenes and good stucco decoration. A banquet scene on the apse arch includes the figure of a woman. These paintings, once thought to date from the 2C, were probably not in fact executed before the end of the 3C. In the area of the 'arenario' (probably a pozzolana stone quarry) is the *Cubiculum of the Velati* with late-3C scenes from the life of the deceased woman including a woman and child, once taken to be the Madonna and Child and so erroneously thought to be one of the earliest known representations of this familiar subject.

Nearly 4km from Piazza Fiume Via Salaria crosses the Aniene, near its confluence with the Tiber, by the Roman *Ponte Salario*. This was rebuilt in 565 by Narses, and then reconstructed after it was blown up by papal troops in 1867. Only the two side arches are original.

Close by is the traditional spot where, in 360 BC, Titus Manlius Torquatus killed the gigantic Gaul in single combat and robbed him of his torque or collar. Just short of the bridge a by-road leads left to a hill (62m; military zone) commanding a view of the confluence of the Tiber and Aniene. This was the site of the ancient Sabine town of *Antemnae*, said to have been founded by the Siculi. It had probably already disappeared by the time of the kings, leaving as its chief memorial the story of the rape of the Sabines.—At the foot of Monte Antenne the foundation stone was laid in 1984 of Rome's first *Mosque*, with an approach road from the Parioli hill.

21   Trastevere

Trastevere (Pl. 7; 2, 4), the area 'across the Tiber' (*trans Tiberim*), has been, since the Middle Ages, essentially the popular district of Rome, and its inhabitants seem to retain the characteristics of the ancient Romans, who are said to have been proud and independent. This area of the city has been distinguished by its numerous artisans' houses and workshops since Roman times. In the last decade or so it has become a fashionable place to live, and it now has a cosmopolitan atmosphere.

In earliest Republican days this bank of the Tiber was occupied by Lars Porsena in his attempt to replace the Tarquins on the Roman throne; and here was the scene of the exploits of Horatius, Mutius Scaevola, and Cloelia. Under the Empire, though it was still called the 'Ripe Veientana' it became densely populated by artisans and dock workers. On the higher ground, and along the water-front suburban villas were built by the aristocracy. These included the houses of Agrippa and of Clodia, both of which have been identified with the late-Republican villa excavated in 1880 next to the Farnesina (and then destroyed), the magnificent wall paintings of which are preserved in the Museo Nazionale Romano. Trastevere was the stronghold of independence during the Risorgimento; here Mazzini found support for his Republic of 1849, and here Giuditta Tavani Arquati, with her family made an attempt to incite the city on Garibaldi's behalf in 1867. In July, the lively festival of *'Noi Antri'* ('we others') takes place here.

The **Tiber**, or *Tevere* (418km long), is the most famous though not the longest of the rivers of Italy. It is said originally to have been called *Albula* and to have received the name of *Tiberis* from Tiberinus, king of Alba Longa, who was drowned in its waters.

It rises in the Tuscan Apennines, NE of Arezzo, and fed by numerous mountain streams, is liable to sudden flooding. Its swift waters are discoloured with yellow mud, even far from its source: hence the epithet *flavus* given to it by the Roman poets. The deposits brought down by the river have appreciably advanced the coastline; long ago the port of Ostia was rendered useless by silting up. The salt marshes near the river-mouth have been drained in a reclamation scheme. There are long-term plans to clean its polluted waters.

Ponte Garibaldi (Pl. 7; 2), a modern bridge, with small obelisks, leads to the busy Piazza Gioacchino Belli, named after the Roman dialect poet and containing a monument (1913) to him. Here begins the wide and traffic-ridden VIALE TRASTEVERE. On the left is the over-restored 13C PALAZZO ANGUILLARA, with its corner tower, the last of many which once guarded Trastevere.

The picturesque courtyard is virtually a modern reconstruction of ancient material. The building is now the *Casa di Dante* (tablet), where readings from the 'Divine Comedy' have been given by leading Italian men of letters since 1914 (now on Sunday from November–mid March, 10.30–12). The Library (open Monday, Wednesday, and Friday 17–20) has the best collection in Italy of works relating to Dante.

On the other side of the Viale is the church of **San Crisogono** (Pl. 7; 4), founded in the 5C and rebuilt by John of Crema between 1123 and 1130. It was reconstructed by G.B. Soria in 1623 and restored in 1866. The campanile dates from the 12C. Inside are 22 ancient Roman Ionic columns separating the nave from the aisles; the triumphal arch is supported by two huge monolithic porphyry columns. The baldacchino rests on four columns of yellow alabaster. The 13C opus sectile pavement has been restored. A mosaic in the apse, attrib. to the school of Pietro Cavallini, depicts the Madonna and Child betwen Saints James and Chrysogonus.—Beneath the church (entered through the sacristy in left aisle, down a spiral staircase unlocked by the sacristan on request) is an interesting 5C subterranean church, on the site of a late-Imperial Roman edifice later adapted for Christian use. The annular crypt was added by Gregory III (731–741); its mural decoration survives, as well as later frescoes and a number of fine sarcophagi.

Behind the church is the huge hospital of *San Gallicano*, a remarkable and utilitarian building by Fil. Raguzzini (1724). The handsome long low façade, with the two floors divided by a balcony, incorporates a church in the centre.
    The description below follows a somewhat circuitous route through old Trastevere to the church of Santa Cecilia (Pl. 8; 3); the direct approach to this church is via Via dei Genovesi which runs left from Viale Trastevere.

Across Viale Trastevere the old Via della Lungaretta leads E on the line of the last stretch of the ancient Roman Via Aurelia. The first turning on the right, in Piazza del Drago (Via di Monte Fiore), leads to the *Guardroom of the Seventh Cohort of Vigiles* (Roman firemen).

Remains can be seen from the street: the interior (entrance at No. 9, Via della VII Coorte) can only be seen with special permission. It contains interesting graffiti referring to reigning emperors, from Severus to Giordian III, and a bath or nymphaeum. The barracks were built on the site of a 2C private house.

Via della Lungaretta continues to Piazza in Piscinula (Pl. 8; 3). In the far corner on the right is the small church of *San Benedetto*, with a charming 11C roofed campanile. (If closed, ring at the door to the right of the façade.)

On the left of the vestibule, a fine doorway leads into an ancient cross-vaulted cell, in which St Benedict is said to have lived. To the left of the entrance door is a detached 13C fresco of St Benedict (restored). Inside, eight antique columns with diverse capitals divide the nave from the aisles. The fine pavement is Cosmatesque. Above the altar is a 15C painting of St Benedict, and a damaged fresco of the Madonna and Child (14C).

Opposite is the medieval *Casa dei Mattei* (restored), with a 15C loggia, and 14C cross-mullioned windows.
    Via dell'Arco dei Tolomei leads out of the other side of the piazza through an arch, and Via dei Salumi diverges left. A short way along on the right is Vicolo dell'Atleta (interesting house at No. 14 where the bronze horse now in the Capitoline Museum, and the statue of the Apoxyomenos now in the Vatican, were found), which leads to Via dei Genovesi, and its extension (left), Via Augusto Jandolio. Immediately opposite is a house (Nos 9, 10) with wooden eaves (characteristic of this area). To the left, at the end of the street, can be

seen the restored church of Santa Maria in Cappella (No. 6), dating
from 1090, with a contemporary campanile. From the charming
garden courtyard (right; now an old people's home) is a fine view of
the Aventine hill. The lovely old Vicolo di Santa Maria in Cappella
leads to Piazza dei Mercanti (with fine 15C houses, including one on
the right recently over-restored). The piazza now has several restaurants (not cheap).

In the piazza to the right is the church of **Santa Cecilia in
Trastevere** (Pl. 8; 3; usually open 10–12, 16–17.30), on the site of the
house of St Cecilia and her husband St Valerian, whom she converted to Christianity. This mansion was adapted to Christian use,
but the first basilica was probably that of Paschal I (817–24). The
church, radically altered from the 16C onwards, was partly restored
to its original form in 1899–1901. The slightly leaning campanile
dates from 1120.

St Cecilia, a patrician lady of the Gens Cornelia, was martyred in 230, during
the reign of Alexander Severus. She was shut up in the calidarium of her own
baths (see below), to be scalded to death. Emerging unscathed, she was
beheaded in her own house, but the executioner was so maladroit that she lived
for three days afterwards. She was buried in the Catacombs of St Calixtus,
where her body remained until its reinterment in her church in 820. As the
inventor of the organ, she is the patron saint of music. On her day, 22
November, the churches hold musical services in her honour.

An atrium, with a fountain made from a large antique marble basin for
ceremonial ablutions in a lovely garden, and a portico with four antique Ionic
columns bearing a frieze of 12C mosaic medallions precede the Baroque façade.
The INTERIOR, an aisled 18C hall whose piers (1823) enclose the original
columns, contains a ceiling fresco of the Coronation of St Cecilia by *Seb. Conca*.
On the left of the door, *Monument of Cardinal·Nic. Forteguerri (died 1473), the
assistant of Pius II and Paul II in their suppression of the great feudal clans. The
parts of this splendid work by *Mino da Fiesole* were dispersed about the church
until the restoration of 1891, as were those of the tomb on the other side of the
door, by *Paolo Romano*. This tomb, adorned with the arms of England, is that of
Cardinal Adam Easton (died 1398), a distinguished English churchman who
was appointed cardinal in 1381, deposed by Urban VI (c 1386), and reappointed
by Boniface IX in 1389. In the 1st chapel on right, fresco of the Crucifixion
(?14C), and to the left, 15C Madonna enthroned.

The corridor on the right, with landscapes (very ruined) by *Paul Brill* and a
marble figure of St Sebastian attrib. to *Lorenzetto*, leads to the ancient
CALIDARIUM (closed indefinitely), where St Cecilia was to be scalded to death
by steam but was miraculously preserved. The steam conduits are still visible.
On the altar is the Beheading of St Cecilia, and opposite, Saints Cecilia and
Valerian, by *Guido Reni*. Next to the corridor opens the CAPPELLA DEI PONZIANI,
with ceiling-frescoes and, on the walls, Saints George, Catherine of Alexandria,
Sebastian, and James, all by *Ant. da Viterbo*. The CAPPELLA DELLE RELIQUE is by
Luigi Vanvitelli. The last chapel on the right contains the theatrical tomb (1929)
of Card. Rampolla, who was responsible for the excavations beneath the
church. In a small room preceeding it is a tondo of the Madonna, by *Perugino*.—
In the chapel at the end of the aisle, Discovery of the Body of St Cecilia, 12–13C
fresco (much damaged), detached from the portico.

In the SANCTUARY is a fine *Tabernacle (1293), signed by *Arnolfo di Cambio*.
Beneath the altar is the famous *Statue of St Cecilia, by *Stef. Maderno*. The
body of the saint is represented lying as it was found when her tomb was
opened in 1599, on which occasion the sculptor was present.—The 9C mosaic in
the APSE shows Christ blessing by the Greek rite, between (right) Saints Peter,
Valerian, and Cecilia, and (left) Saints Paul, Agatha, and Paschal (the last with
the square nimbus); below are the flock of the Faithful and the Holy Cities.—
The ROMAN EDIFICES BENEATH THE CHURCH AND THE CRYPT are entered from
the W end of the N aisle. The excavations have not yet been fully explained, but
are generally thought to consist of two Roman houses (possibly including the
house of St Cecilia), probably united in the 4C for Christian use. Some scholars
also believe there are remains here of a paleochristian basilica. In the various
rooms are mosaic pavements and a number of Christian sarcophagi. A 2C room
with eight huge basins in the floor was probably used as a tannery. A Lararium

*Detail of the Last Judgement, a fresco by Pietro Cavallini
(c 1293) in the convent of Santa Cecilia in Trastevere*

with Republican columns contains a niche with a relief of Minerva in front of an altar.—The CRYPT is decorated in the Byzantine style by *G.B. Giovenale* (1899–1901), with luminous mosaics by *Gius. Bravi*. Behind a grille are the sarcophagi of St Cecilia, St Valerian and his brother St Tiburtius, St Maximus, and the Popes Lucius I and Urban I. The statue of St Cecilia is by *Cesare Aureli*.

Inside the CONVENT (adm to left of portico), in the Nun's choir can be seen the splendid *Fresco of the Last Judgement (restored in 1980) by *Pietro Cavallini*, a masterpiece of medieval Roman fresco painting (c 1293). This used to be on the inside façade of the old church. It can normally be seen on Sundays (11.30–12.30).

From the piazza Via di Santa Cecilia leads left to reach Via dei Genovesi, which leads left again to the church of *San Giovanni Battista dei Genovesi* (1481; restored). The remarkable 15C *Cloister is entered along Via Anicia on the left (ring at No. 12). It has an arcaded lower gallery and a trabeated upper story, with a beautiful garden of orange trees. Via Anicia continues past (right), the church of *Santa Maria dell'Orto*, with an unusual façade attrib. to Vignola crowned with obelisks, and an ornate interior.

Opposite the church, the road of the same name leads to the immense buildings, formerly occupied by the *Istituto Romano di San Michele*, founded in 1683 by Tommaso Odescalchi, nephew of Innocent XI, as a refuge and training centre for vagabond children. It is now owned by the State and is used as a restoration centre by the *Istituto Centrale del Restauro*. Exhibitions are sometimes held here. The equestrian statue of Marcus Aurelius from the Capitol Hill has been undergoing a lengthy restoration here since 1981. Beyond is the Tiber, crossed by *Ponte Aventino*. The original bridge at this point, the *Pons Sublicius*, was the first bridge across the Tiber; it is said to have been built by Ancus Marcius, fourth king of Rome, to connect the Janiculum with the city. On the right, the *Porta Portese*, built by Urban VIII (1623–44) replaces the former *Porta Portuensis*, dating from the time of Honorius. The Porta Portese 'flea' market is farther S, near Stazione Trastevere. Open only on Sunday mornings, it is the largest general open market in Rome, noted for clothes.

Via Anicia ends in Piazza San Francesco d'Assisi, in which is the church of **San Francesco a Ripa** (Pl. 7; 4), built in 1231 to replace the old hospice of San Biagio, where St Francis stayed in 1219. The last chapel on the left has the famous *Statue of Beata Lodovica Albertoni, showing her in a state of mystical ecstasy. It is a late work by *Bernini*, displayed effectively by concealed lighting. Above is an altarpiece by *Baciccio*. The CELL OF ST FRANCIS (apply at the sacristy), contains relics (displayed in an ingenious reliquary), and a 13C painting of the saint, in the style of Margaritone d'Arezzo.

Via Tavolacci rejoins Viale Trastevere, across which Via Morosini leads past the right side of the Ministero di Pubblica Istruzione. Via Roma Libera is the first road to the right, and here, at No. 76 is the old people's *Hospice of Regina Margherita* (formerly the convent of San Cosimato).

Visitors are admitted to see the beautiful 12C cloister with twin columns, and in a garden on the left, the church of SAN COSIMATO dating from the 10C, rebuilt in 1475. It has a good doorway, and contains (on the left of the altar) a 15C fresco of the Virgin with Saints, and the tomb of Cardinal Alderano Cybo (died 1550), ascribed to Iac. Sansovino (this is now a second altar in a chapel to the left). The second cloister has 15C octagonal columns.

From Via Roma Libera the original narthex can be seen, and beyond is Piazza San Cosimato with a large market. Via di San Cosimato leads N via Piazza San Calisto to **Piazza di Santa Maria in Trastevere** (Pl. 7; 4), the characteristic centre of Trastevere. The handsome

The mosaics on the triumphal arch and apse (1140) of Santa Maria in Trastevere

*Fountain, of Roman origin, was restored by Carlo Fontana (1692). *Palazzo di San Calisto* on the left of the church, was rebuilt in the 17C by Orazio Torriani. The large basilica of **Santa Maria in Trastevere** (Pl. 7; 4) was constructed by Julius II (337–352), and was probably the first church in Rome dedicated to the Virgin.

According to legend a 'taberna meritoria' or hostel for veteran soldiers existed near the site, and some sort of Christian foundation is known to have existed here under St Calixtus (pope, 217–22). The great basilica of Julius II was rebuilt by Innocent II in 1140, and slightly modified later. The campanile is Romanesque.

The FAÇADE bears a 12–13C mosaic of the Madonna surrounded by ten female figures with lamps (two of which are extinguished), of uncertain significance. In the Portico added by *Carlo Fontana* in 1702 are a small lapidary collection, and 15C frescoes of the Annunciation (very worn). In the aisled INTERIOR are 21 vast ancient columns from various Roman buildings, some with fine bases and (damaged) capitals. The opus sectile pavement is made up of old material; the ceiling was designed by *Domenichino* (1617), who painted the central Assumption. The decoration on the walls of the nave and triumphal arch was carried out when the church was remodelled by Pius IX in the 19C. The charming tabernacle at the beginning of the S aisle is by *Mino del Reame*. In the N aisle is the tomb of Innocent II (died 1143), erected by Pius IX in 1869; and beyond that is the domed *Avila chapel, with charming Baroque decorations by *Ant. Gherardi* (1680–86).

The CHOIR is preceded by a marble screen made up of transennae and plutei, many of them remade in the 19C. Near a Paschal candlestick here is the spot on which a miraculous fountain of oil is supposed to have flowed throughout a whole day in the year of Christ's Nativity in the 'taberna meritoria'. The tabernacle of the high altar is by *Vespignani*.—The *MOSAICS of the triumphal arch and apse (1140) are particularly fine; on the arch, the Cross with the symbolic Alpha and Omega between the seven candlesticks and the evangelical emblems; at the sides, Isaiah and Jeremiah, with the rare and touching symbol of the caged bird (Christus Dominus captus est in peccatis nostris). In the semi-dome, Christ and the Virgin enthroned beneath the hand of God bearing a wreath and the monogram of Constantine. On the right, Saints Peter, Cornelius, Julius, and Calepodius; on the left Saints Calixtus and Laurence, and Pope Innocent II with a model of the church.—Lower are six *Mosaics of the Life of Mary, by *Pietro Cavallini* (c 1291), and, in the drum of the apse, Saints Peter and Paul presenting the donor, Bertoldo Stefaneschi, to the Madonna (1290).

To the right of the choir are the Armellini monument (1524) with sculptures by *Michelangelo Senese*, and the WINTER CHOIR, with decorations after *Domenichino*'s designs. The chapel was restored by Henry of York in the 18C.—To the left of the choir is the ALTEMPS CHAPEL, frescoed by *Pasquale Cati* (1588), with a scene of the Council of Trent. On the altar was a Madonna flanked by angels, traditionally attrib. to the 8C, though possibly earlier. Since its restoration it has been kept at the Istituto Centrale del Restauro. On the left wall outside the chapel is the tomb of Cardinal Stefaneschi (died 1417) by 'Magister Paulus', beside the monument to Cardinal Filippo d'Alencon (died 1397) which includes his effigy and the relief of the Dormition of the Virgin, also attrib. to 'Magister Paulus' or a follower of Orcagna.—The SACRISTY, approached by a passage with two exquisite tiny Roman mosaics, one of marsh birds and the other a port scene, contains a Madonna with Saints Sebastian and Roch of the Umbrian School (very worn).

Via della Paglia skirts the N side of the church. To the right opens Piazza Sant'Egidio, where, at No. 1B a *Folklore Museum* was opened in 1978 (adm see p 49). On the first floor are exhibits relating to G.G. Belli, the popular romagnole poet, and a series of life-size tableaux of Roman scenes by Orazio Amato (1884–1952) based on paintings by Pinelli. On the floor above is material related to another poet 'Trilussa' (Carlo Alberto Salustri, 1871–1950), and his studio has been charmingly reconstructed here. The building is used as a cultural centre.—Via della Scala leads out of the piazza past the ornate church of SANTA MARIA DELLA SCALA (1592), containing (over the 1st altar on the right), St John the Baptist by Honthorst, and a ciborium over the high altar by Carlo Rainaldi (1647). If closed, the church can be entered through the Carmelite Monastery (right) which adjoins the *Pharmacy of Santa Maria della Scala*, administered by the monks. The old 17C pharmacy may be seen upstairs. Via della Scala ends at PORTA SETTIMIANA (Pl. 7; 2), incorporated in the Aurelian Wall and rebuilt by Alexander VI (1492–1503).

The street to the right, just before the gate, is Via Santa Dorotea. At No. 20 is the medieval *Casa della Fornarina*, the supposed house of Raphael's mistress. Other houses of this type may be seen in Vicolo dei Moroni. Via di Ponte Sisto leads to **Ponte Sisto** (open for pedestrians), erected for Sixtus IV (1471–84), probably by Baccio Pontelli, to replace the ancient *Pons Janiculensis* (or the *Pons Antoninus*).

The unusual and attractive VIA GARIBALDI leads uphill from the gate towards the Janiculum (Rte 22). At the end of the first straight section of the road (before a sharp turn to the left) is the entrance at No. 27 to the convent of **Santa Maria dei Sette Dolori**. The church was begun by Borromini in 1643, and its unfinished façade (1646) can be seen through the gate. The vestibule and interior of the church are entered through the convent; door to the right of the façade. The church is oblong with rounded ends, with two apses in the middle of the long sides, and a continuous series of pillars connected by a heavy cornice. The disappointing interior decoration was added later in the 17C.

Porta Settimiana marks the beginning of VIA DELLA LUNGARA (Pl. 7; 2, 1), the longest of the 'rettifili', or straight-drawn streets built by the Renaissance popes. It was laid out c 1507 by Julius II to connect Trastevere with the Borgo. On the left is the building which housed the **Museo Torlonia**, considered to be the most important private collection of ancient sculpture in existence. For years closed 'for restoration' the interior was converted into flats in the 1970s and the works put in store. In 1977 the palace and collection were officially sequestered, but interminable bureaucratic procedures are still under way in an attempt by the State to acquire the collection (with the long-term project to rehouse it in Palazzo Altemps, near Piazza Navona). For further information apply to the Amministrazione Torlonia, 30 Via della Conciliazione.

The museum was founded by Gian Raimondo Torlonia (1754–1829) with sculptures from Roman collections, to which were added later the yields of excavations on the family estates at Cerveteri, Vulci, Porto, etc. There are 620 pieces of sculpture, some over-restored, including a few Greek originals. The most important works include the *Giustiniani Hestia*, attributed to Kalamis (5C BC), and a bas-relief of *Herakles liberating Theseus and Peirithöos* (school of Pheidias; 4C BC). There are numerous Roman copies of works by Greek sculptors, notably Kephisodotos, Polykleitos, Praxiteles, and Lysippos. Of the Roman originals perhaps the most striking is a portrait statue of *Lucilla*, daughter of Marcus Aurelius, the Roman iconographic collection contains over one hundred busts of the Imperial era. The valuable Etruscan paintings (4C BC) are from Vulci.

At the end of Via Corsini (No. 24) is the *Orto Botanico* (adm 9–13 exc Sun) occupying the former Corsini garden on the slopes of the Janiculum. It has good palms and yuccas.

In Via della Lungara, just beyond Via Corsini, on the left, is **Palazzo Corsini** (Pl. 7; 1, 2), built by Cardinal Domenico Riario in the 15C, and rebuilt by Ferd. Fuga for Cardinal Neri Maria Corsini, nephew of Clement XII in 1732–36. Cardinal Corsini's fine collection of paintings was acquired by the State in 1883 and became part of the **Galleria Nazionale d'Arte Antica** (which is now divided between this palace and Palazzo Barberini). Both galleries are in the course of rearrangement, and the original Corsini collection is being returned here (these pictures carry the Inventory No. 1–606), The present arrangement is extremely crowded, but more rooms may eventually be opened to the public. The pictures are all labelled. Admission, see p 48.

The palace was the residence of Queen Christina of Sweden, who died here in 1689. In 1797 Gen. Duphot was killed near here in a skirmish between the French democratic party and the papal dragoons, and in 1800 Madame Letizia, mother of Napoleon, came to live in the palace.

On the first floor is a Vestibule with neo-classical sculptures by *John Gibson, Antonio Solà, Pietro Tenerani*, etc. ROOM I. Portraits of the Corsini, and a bust of Clement XII Corsini by *Pietro Bracci. Pompeo Batoni*, Nativity; *Sebastiano Conca*, Adoration of the Magi; *Francesco Trevisani*, Nymphs and Satyrs; two 18C bronze statuettes. ROOM II. 558. *Giovanni da Milano*, Madonna and Child and scenes from the Life of Christ; *464. *Murillo*, Madonna and Child, one of the finest versions by the painter of this familiar subject; works by *David Teniers the Younger*, and *Marten van Cleve*; 111. *Van Dyck*, Madonna and Child, probably painted during his stay in Italy; 388. *Rubens*, St Sebastian tended by angels; 350. *Pourbus the Younger*, Portrait of a man; 347. *Joos van Cleve*, Portrait of Bernardo Clesio; 354. *Perino del Vaga*, Portrait of Cardinal Alessandro Farnese; 318. *Federico Barocci*, Self-portrait; 140. *Titian*, Philip II; 193. *Jacopo Bassano*, Adoration of the Shepherds; 99. *Andrea del Sarto*, Madonna and Child; 488. *Franciabigio*, Portrait of a man; 221. *16C Roman School*, La Fornarina; 116. *Fra Bartolomeo*, Holy Family; 397, 396, 395. *Fra Angelico*, Triptych; 436. *Francesco Francia*, St George and the dragon; 686. *Alessandro Algardi*, Baptism of Christ (small bronze).

ROOM III (ahead). Works by *Michelangelo Cerquozzi* and *Simon Vouet*; 441. *Gerard Seghers*, Judith with the head of Holofernes; *107. *Orazio Gentileschi*, Madonna and Child; *433. *Caravaggio*, St John the Baptist.—ROOM IV. Works by *Callot, Van Bloemen, Luca Carlevaris, Gaspard Dughet* (386. Landscape), and *Jan de Momper* (73, 75. Landscapes).—ROOM V survives from the old Palazzo Riario. It is decorated by a follower of the Zuccari. Queen Christina of Sweden is supposed to have died in this room in 1689. A terracotta bust of Alessandro VII Chigi attributed to *Bernini* is exhibited here, as well as works by *Jan Miel* and *Michael Sweerts*.—ROOM VI. In the centre is the Corsini throne, dating from the 2C or 1C BC and present in the palace since 1700. 1696. *Sarzana*, Hagar and the angel; 186. *Francesco Furini*, Andromeda; 371. *Baciccio*, Portrait of Cardinal Corsini.—ROOM VII. 276. *Guercino*, Adoration of the Shepherds; 273. *Sassoferrato*, Madonna and Child; 279, 287. *Guercino*, Madonna and Angel, and Annunciation; 79. *Donato Creti*, Jacob's Dream; works by *Giovanni Lanfranco*; 191. *Guido Reni*, Salome with the head of the Baptist.—ROOM VIII. Works by *Luca Giordano*, including (394.) Jesus in the Temple; works by *Salvator Rosa*, including (484.) Prometheus; *Mattia Preti*, 117. Tribute Money, 1154. Eneas and Anchises.

The Accademia Nazionale dei Lincei, founded by 'Prince' Federico Cesi in 1603 for the promotion of learning, is said to be the oldest surviving institution of its kind. Galileo was a Lincean. The administrative offices are in the Villa Farnesina (see below). With it are incorporated the *Biblioteca dell'Accademia* (1848), with 100,000 volumes and other publications, the *Biblioteca Corsiniana*, founded in 1754 by Mgr Lorenzo Corsini, with a valuable collection of incunabula, manuscripts, and autographs, and the *Fondazione Caetani*, whose object is to promote scientific knowledge in the Muslim world. The library may be visited (9–13; also 15–18.30 on Friday; entered from the ground floor to the right, up a spiral staircase). A series of rooms lead to a terrace overlooking the garden.

Opposite Palazzo Corsini is the entrance to the graceful Renaissance *Villa Farnesina (Pl. 7; 2), built by *Baldassare Peruzzi* (1508–11), as the suburban residence of Agostino Chigi, 'the Magnificent', the banker who controlled the markets of the East. It is surrounded by a lovely garden, once much larger. Admission, see p 50.

The Galatea by Raphael in the Villa Farnesina

Here Agostino Chigi entertained in grandeur Pope Leo X, cardinals, ambassadors, artists, and men of letters, and here he died on 10 April 1520, four days after Raphael. At a celebrated banquet in a loggia overlooking the Tiber (demolished in the 19C) silver plates and dishes were thrown into the river after every course (although it was later learned that a net had been in position to recover them). In 1590 the villa passed to Card. Alessandro Farnese, and received its present name, and through the Farnese it was inherited by the Bourbons of Naples in 1731. Since 1927 it has been the property of the State, and houses the administrative offices of the Accademia dei Lincei (see above).

The painted decoration in the Villa was carried out between 1510 and 1519, and was beautifully restored in the 1970s and 1980s. On the ground floor is the festive *LOGGIA OF CUPID AND PSYCHE, which formerly opened directly on to the garden. The ceiling has famous frescoes illustrating the legend of Apuleus in a beautiful painted pergola with festoons of fruit and flowers. The decorative programme was provided by *Raphael* (who probably also made the preparatory cartoons), and the paintings executed by his pupils, *Giulio Romano, Fr. Penni, Giov. da Udine,* and *Raffaellino del Colle.*—To the right is the LOGGIA OF THE GALATEA. The ceiling is frescoed with the constellations forming the horoscope of Agostino Chigi, by *Peruzzi.* The lunettes, with scenes from Ovid's 'Metamorphoses' are by *Seb. del Piombo,* although the colossal monochrome charcoal head here, a striking work, is now ascribed to *Peruzzi.* On the walls: the giant Polyphemus by *Seb. del Piombo,* and the celebrated *Galatea by *Raphael,* a superb composition. This interrupts the decorative sequence and seems to have been painted just after the works by Sebastiano. The other scenes were added in the 17C by *Gaspard Dughet.*—A little room off the Loggia (door unlocked), known as the SALA DEL FREGIO, contains a beautifully painted frieze with mythological scenes by *Peruzzi.*

On the upper floor is the *SALA DELLE PROSPETTIVE, the drawing room, with charming trompe l'oeil views of Rome and mythological subjects by *Peruzzi.* The Bedroom, known as the SALA DELLE NOZZE DI ALESSANDRO E ROSSANA, contains *Frescoes by *Sodoma.*

Wall-paintings and stuccoes found in a Roman house in the grounds of the Villa are exhibited in the Museo Nazionale Romano.

On the second floor of the Villa Farnesina is the **Gabinetto Nazionale delle Stampe** (open 9–13), with an exceptionally fine collection of prints and drawings housed in a series of beautiful rooms. Exhibitions are held here periodically.

Via della Lungara continues along the right bank of the Tiber past the *Regina Coeli* prison and the 16C *Palazzo Salviati* to Piazza della Rovere (Pl. 2; 5). The Borgo beyond is described in Rte 23.

22 The Janiculum Hill

The Janiculum is traversed by Bus No. 41 from Corso Vittorio Emanuele (Via Paola), near the Tiber (Pl. 2; 5). By foot the prettiest approach is from Trastevere (Via Garibaldi, or Vicolo del Cedro behind Piazza Sant'Egidio; see Rte 21).

The **Janiculum** (82m; Pl. 7; 1, and 1; 8; in Italian, *Gianicolo*), not counted as one of the Seven Hills of Rome, is a ridge rising steeply from the Tiber and approximately parallel to its course for the whole of its length. It is now mostly covered with parks and gardens, and has two important churches, San Pietro in Montorio and Sant'Onofrio at its southernmost and northernmost end.

On the W side it slopes gently away towards the Campagna. Its highest point, at Porta San Pancrazio, is near the S end; to the N it reaches almost as far as Piazza San Pietro. Its upper surface is formed of yellow sand which gave the hill its ancient alternative name of *Mons Aureus*; this name is preserved in the title of the church of San Pietro in Montorio. The name of Janiculum (*Mons Janiculus*; in Italian, *Monte Gianicolo*) is derived from the old Italian deity Janus, who is said to have founded a city on the hill; his temple was in the Roman Forum. Numa Pompilius, the Sabine successor of Romulus, was buried on the Janiculum, and Ancus Marcius, the fourth king, is said to have built the Pons Sublicius over the Tiber to connect the Janiculum with the city of Rome.

The hill was the natural bulwark against the Etruscan invaders, but it does not appear to have been fortified until the time of the Republic. Part of it was included within the Aurelian Wall, and it was completely surrounded by Urban VIII when he built his wall in 1642. It was the scene of Garibaldi's stand against the French troops of Marshal Oudinot in 1849.—The *Views from the ridge are famous.

VIA GARIBALDI (Pl. 7; 1, 2) mounts the hill from Trastevere. Above the church of Santa Maria dei Sette Dolori (described in Rte 21), on the right, is the former entrance gate to the *Bosco Parrasio*, where in 1725 was established the academy of **Arcadia**, founded in 1690 to carry on the work of the academy inaugurated by Queen Christina of Sweden ten years before for the discussion of literary and political topics.

The garden can sometimes be seen on request at No. 32 Via di Porta San Pancrazio. Beyond a lovely circular dining-room with a dome (1725) is an amphitheatre, beyond which stairs wind down through a small wood, circling a giant Roman pine.

The object of Arcadia was to eliminate bad literary taste and to purify the Italian language. Although its members indulged in the fantasies often associated with the name of Arcadia, especially in the matter of nomenclature, it exercised a profound influence on Italian literature during the 18C. In 1786 Goethe was admitted as a 'distinguished shepherd'. Later its importance waned and in 1926 it was absorbed into the Accademia Letteraria Italiana. The paintings which belong to the academy are at present kept at the Museo di Roma.

Via Garibaldi continues to mount, in sweeping curves (pedestrians can take a short cut via steps to the right of the road), until it reaches a terrace. Here is the church of *San Pietro in Montorio (Pl. 7; 3, 4), built on a site wrongly presumed to have been the scene of St Peter's crucifixion. Mentioned in the 9C, the church was rebuilt in the late 15C at the expense of Ferdinand of Aragon and Isabella of Castile. The apse and campanile, damaged in the siege of 1849, were restored in 1851. Raphael's Transfiguration (now in the Vatican) adorned the apse from 1523 to 1809. In front of the fine simple façade (attributed to the school of Andrea Bregno) is a group of palm trees and a terrace with a view towards the Victor Emmanuel Monument, and, in the distance among the trees of its garden, the Villa Medici.

INTERIOR (lights in each chapel). RIGHT SIDE: 1st chapel, *Scourging of Christ, a superb work by *Seb. del Piombo* (1518) from designs by Michelangelo, and other frescoes by the same artist; 2nd chapel, Madonna della Lettera, by *Pomarancio* (detached fresco fragment), and above, *Coronation of the Virgin, and four Virtues, attrib. to *Peruzzi*; 4th chapel, Ceiling fresco, St Paul, by *Vasari*, and two tombs, with statues, by *Ammannati*. In front of the high altar are the tombstones of Hugh O'Neill of Tyrone and Roderick O'Donnell of Tyrconnel (1608), leaders in the Irish revolt against James I. Here also was buried the body of Beatrice Cenci, beheaded as a parricide at St Angelo in 1599.—LEFT SIDE: 5th chapel, Baptism of Jesus, by *Dan. da Volterra*; 4th chapel (perhaps by Carlo Maderno with stucco work by Giulio Mazzoni), Descent from the Cross and other frescoes, by *Dirk Baburen* (1617), a pupil of Caravaggio; 3rd chapel, Saints Mary and Anne, after *Antoniazzo Romano*. The 2nd chapel (Raimondi; being restored) is an early work by *Bernini*, with an unusual relief of the Ecstasy of St Francis, executed by his pupils *Fr. Baratta* and *And. Bolgi*.—1st chapel, St

Francis receiving the Stigmata, by *Giov. de Vecchi*; near the door, tomb of Giul. da Volterra; (died 1510), by a follower of And. Bregno.

On the right of the church is the court of the famous **Tempietto by *Bramante* (1499–1502), erected on the supposed exact site of St Peter's martyrdom. This jewel of the Renaissance, a small circular building with 16 Doric columns of granite, combines all the grace of the 15C, with the full splendour of the 16C. The Interior (including a crypt with pretty stuccoes by G.F. Rossi) may also be seen (ring at the convent, 8–12, 16–19).—To the right of the court is the *Spanish Academy*.

The Tempietto by Bramante (1499–1502) in the courtyard of San Pietro in Montorio

Via Garibaldi continues to the neo-classical *Monumento ai Caduti di 1849–70* (left), by Giov. Iacobucci (1941), which commemorates the defenders and deliverers of Rome, incorporating the tomb of Goffredo Mameli. Farther on is the fountain of the **Acqua Paola**, constructed for Paul V (as the handsome inscription states), by Giov. Fontana and Flaminio Ponzio (1612), using marble from the Roman Forum. The water, which flows abundantly from the subterranean Aqueduct of Trajan (from Lake Bracciano), falls into a large granite basin added by Carlo Fontana in 1690, beneath six columns (four of which are from the façade of Old St Peter's). On the right of the road is a subsidiary entrance to the Passeggiata del Gianicolo (see below).—At the top of the hill is the **Porta San Pancrazio** (Pl. 7; 3), built by Urban VIII, breached by Oudinot in 1849, and rebuilt by Vespignani in 1857.

This gate, once known as the *Porta Aurelia*, was the starting-point of the **Via Aurelia**. It followed the line of a still older road which linked Rome with the Etruscan towns on the Tyrrhenian coast. It reached the shore at Alsium (Palo Laziale), a port of the Etruscan city of Caere (Cerveteri), and then followed the coastline to Pisa and Genoa. It ended in Gaul at *Forum Julii* (Fréjus, on the French Riviera). Today the *Via Aurelia Antica* branches to the right just W of the gate, and skirts the N side of the Villa Doria Pamphilj (see below). About 8km W of Rome it joins the modern Via Aurelia, which starts from Largo di Porta Cavalleggeri, to the S of St Peter's.

From the gate Viale delle Mura Gianicolensi leads S to the *Villa Sciarra*, an attractive public park (open 9–dusk). Beyond is the residential district of *Monteverde*.

In front of Porta San Pancrazio Via di San Pancrazio leads SW to the ruins of the *Vascello*, a Baroque villa where Goffredo Mameli and Luciano Manara were killed in a last sally in 1849. Farther on is the entrance to the *Villa Doria Pamphilj* or *Belrespiro*, by far the largest park in Rome (9km round). It was laid out for Prince Camillo Pamphilj, nephew of Innocent X, by Algardi in 1650. The park, also created in the 17C, is owned partly by the State and partly by the Commune of Rome and is open to the public (daily, sunrise to sunset). The views take in the Campagna as well as the city, and the umbrella pines are a feature of the park. The grounds are crossed by Via Olimpica.

Via di San Pancrazio passes the **Basilica of San Pancrazio**, on the site of the tomb of St Pancrazio, who according to Christian tradition, was martyred under Diocletian in 304. A Christian cemetery and 5C oratory existed here, and the present large basilica was built by Honorius I in 630, and remodelled in the 17C. The Baroque interior incorporates the apse, part of the transept and the annular crypt of the 7C church. The 4C *Catacombs of San Pancrazio* (adm from the church) contain oriental inscriptions.

Beyond Porta San Pancrazio is the beginning of the *Passeggiata del Gianicolo* (Pl. 7; 1), a promenade laid out in 1884 across the Villa Corsini. At Piazzale del Gianicolo the road is joined by that from the Acqua Paola (see above). Here stands the conspicuous equestrian **Statue of Garibaldi**, by Emilio Gallori, erected in 1895 on the site of the hero's exploits of 1849. Around the base are four bronze groups (in poor condition): in front, Charge of Manara's Bersaglieri (Rome, 1849); behind, Battle of Calatafimi (1860); at the sides, Europe and America. The statue itself is 7m high.

The Passeggiata now goes downhill. On the right is the former *Casino Lante* (16C); on the left, the bronze equestrian *Statue of Anita Garibaldi*, by Mario Rutelli, presented by the Brazilian Government in 1935 to honour her Brazilian origin. At the foot of the statue (in need of restoration) lies the body of Anita, transferred to this place from her grave at Nice. Farther on is a *Beacon*, presented by Italians in Argentina.

From this point there is an especially fine *View of Rome. On the extreme left is the dome of St Peter's, then Castel Sant'Angelo, San Giovanni dei Fiorentini, Palazzo di Giustizia and the modern Prati district, with the green slopes of the Villa Borghese, the Pincio, and the Villa Medici behind, among which the French Academy and the Trinità dei Monti stand out. To the right is the façade of Montecitorio with its clock, behind which rise the Pinciano and Salario districts. Below the hill is the prison of Regina Coeli, and beyond the river the spiral campanile of the Sapienza, the dome of the Pantheon, and the Quirinal. Farther to the right is Sant'Andrea, and, more distant, the tower and domes of Santa Maria Maggiore. Then come the Torre delle Milizie, the triple-arched loggia of the Palazzo Farnese, the Victor Emmanuel Monument, the Torre Capitolina, and the dome of the Synagogue. Behind them are the white palazzo on the Viminal and the statues of St John Lateran. Among the trees of the Janiculum, on the extreme right, is the Acqua Paola. The Alban, Tiburtine, and Praenestine hills fall away gradually on the right.

The Passeggiata continues downhill. A stairway on the right ('Rampa della Quercia'), avoiding a sweep of the road, leads direct to *Tasso's Oak*, the dead battered trunk (now supported by iron girders) of the tree beneath which Tasso used to sit (tablet; 1898), and around which St Philip Neri played 'sapiently' with the Roman children ('si faceva co' fanciulli fanciullo sapientemente').

Near the end of the promenade a short flight of steps leads up to the little Piazzale di Sant'Onofrio, with ilex trees and a fountain. Here is the church of **Sant'Onofrio** (Pl. 1; 8; open 8–12 only), founded by Blessed Nicolò da Forca Palena in 1419 and restored by Pius IX in 1857.

A graceful L-shaped Renaissance portico connects the church and monastery. In the lunettes beneath the portico are three scenes from the life of St Jerome (Baptism, Chastisement for reading Cicero, Temptation) all frescoes by *Domenichino*, and over the door, a Madonna also attributed to *Domenichino*. By the convent entrance is the tomb of the founder.
    The dark INTERIOR (if closed, ring bell to the right) is paved with numerous tombstones. On the left, 1st chapel, monument to Tasso, by *Gius. de Fabris* (1857); 3rd chapel, tombstone of Card. Mezzofanti (died 1849), who could speak 50 or 60 languages. In the pretty apse over the main altar are repainted frescoes by the school of Pinturicchio; above them, Scenes from the life of the Virgin. The fresco of St Anne teaching the Virgin to read, on the right, above the monument of Giovanni Sacco (died 1505), is by a pupil of Andrea Bregno. In the 2nd chapel on the right, Madonna di Loreto, by *Annibale Carracci* (or his school); in the vault pendentives above the altar in the 1st chapel, *Annuncia-tion, by *Antoniazzo Romano* (light).
    The **Monastery** has a charming 15C cloister, with frescoes of the life of St Onophrius, by *Giuseppe Cesari, Sebastiano Strada,* and *Claudio Ridolfi*. It is now occupied by American Friars of the Atonement. Torquato Tasso (1544–95), the epic poet, spent his last days and died here. In the atrium is a monument to the 'Arcadian' poet, Alessandro Guidi (died 1712). In the upper corridor, above a Della Robbia frieze, is a fresco of the Virgin with a donor, much repainted, attributed to *Boltraffio*. The MUSEO TASSIANO (adm only by appointment with the Cavalieri del Santo Sepolcro, 33 Via della Conciliazione) occupies two rooms, containing the poet's death-mask, his armchair, crucifix, inkstand, mirror, etc.; and MSS., editions, and translations of his works.

The steep Salita di Sant'Onofrio leads down to Piazza della Rovere (Pl. 1; 6), the end also of Via della Lungara. A gentler descent is by the road to the left, which passes the buildings of the pontifical *North American College*, transferred from Via dell'Umiltà in 1953. *Ponte Principe Amedeo* (1942) crosses the Tiber, and on the left is the road tunnel known as the *Traforo Principe Amedeo*, which leads under the Janiculum to Largo di Porta Cavalleggeri. In front is *Porta Santo*

Spirito, an unfinished gateway begun in 1540 by Ant. da Sangallo. It leads by Via dei Penitenzieri into the *Città Leonina*, or Rione of the Borgo (see Rte 23).

23   The Borgo and Castel Sant'Angelo

The **Borgo** (Pl. 1; 4, 6 and Pl. 2; 5), the district on the right bank of the Tiber between the Janiculum in the S and Monte Mario in the N, was known in ancient Rome as *Ager Vaticanus*. It was the stronghold of the papacy from 850, when Leo IV surrounded it with a line of walls, until 1586, when it was formally incorporated in the city of Rome.

The **Ager Vaticanus** was chosen by Caligula (AD 37–41) for his circus, which was enlarged by Nero (54–68). It then became known as the *Circus of Nero*. Its site has been verified by excavations begun in 1940 under St Peter's and it has been located just S of the basilica. In the adjoining gardens many Christians were martyred under Nero in AD 65. St Peter suffered here and he was buried in a pagan cemetery near by. Over his grave the first church was built (c AD 90) to commemorate his martyrdom (St Peter's). In 135 Hadrian built in the Ager Vaticanus his mausoleum, now the Castel Sant'Angelo.

Paganism retained its hold with great tenacity in this district until the late 4C, as is evinced by inscriptions on the temples of Cybele and Mithras. Despite this tendency, churches, chapels and convents were built round the first church of St Peter and the district, attracting Saxon, Frank, and Lombard pilgrims, came to be called the *Borgo* (borough), a name of Germanic origin from 'borgus' meaning small fortified settlement. In 850 Leo IV (847–55) surrounded the Borgo with walls 12m high, fortified with circular towers, to protect it from the incursions of the Saracens: hence the name *Civitas Leonina* or *Città Leonina*. Remnants of Leo IV's wall survive to the W of St Peter's. The Leonine city became the papal citadel: within its walls John VIII (872–82) was besieged in 878 by the Duke of Spoleto; in 896 Arnulph of Carinthia attacked it and Formosus crowned him emperor. Gregory VII (1073–85), having taken refuge in the Castel Sant'Angelo from the Emperor Henry IV, was rescued by Robert Guiscard in 1084. After the coronation in 1167 of Barbarossa in St Peter's, the Romans attacked the Leonine City, and it was again assailed by them twelve years later.

During the 'Babylonian captivity' (1309–78) the Borgo fell into ruin, but when the popes returned from Avignon to Rome and chose the Vatican as their residence in place of the Lateran, a new era of prosperity began. In the 15C Eugenius IV (1431–47) and Sixtus IV (1471–84), and early in the 16C Julius II (1503–13) and Leo X (1513–21) were active in developing and beautifying the Borgo as well as the Vatican. The original area of the Borgo was enlarged by the addition, on the N of the Borgo Angelico, a name which survived in the Porta Angelica now demolished, and still survives in the name of a street.

After the sack of Rome in 1527 the district, deserted by the richer citizens, became one of the poorest and least populated districts of Rome, and the papal court, neglecting the Borgo, confined its activity to the embellishment of the buildings and gardens of the Vatican. In 1586 Sixtus V (1585–90) relinquished the papal claim to the Borgo, which was thereupon united to the city of Rome. In 1870, when Rome was united to the kingdom of Italy, the Borgo remained unaffected by the extraterritoriality conceded to the Vatican and St Peter's.

Five (originally seven) streets in the Leonine City have the prefix Borgo. Borgo Sant'Angelo and Borgo Santo Spirito run respectively N and S of Via della Conciliazione. In the construction of that street, the central Borgo Nuovo and Borgo Vecchio were eliminated. The remaining streets—the Borghi Angelico, Vittorio, and Pio—survive between the Castel Sant'Angelo and the Vatican.

The celebrated ***Ponte Sant'Angelo** (Pl. 2; 5; pedestrians only), the ancient *Pons Aelius* or *Pons Adrianus*, was built by Hadrian (P. Aelius Hadrianus) in 134 as a fitting approach to his mausoleum—the Castel Sant'Angelo, as it has been called since the Middle Ages.

In 1530 Clement VII erected the statues of St Peter (school of *Lorenzetto*) and of St Paul (school of *Paolo Taccone*, 1464) at the end towards the Castel Sant'Angelo. Ten statues of angels, by pupils of *Bernini* (1688; to his design) completed the decoration; two of the angels are copies of originals in the church of Sant'Andrea delle Fratte. The central three arches are part of the original structure; the end arches were restored and enlarged in 1892–94 during the construction of the Lungotevere embankments. The Tiber in flood may rise to the top of the arches.—Upstream is *Ponte Vittorio Emanuele* (1911), decorated with monumental groups.

Facing the bridge is ***Castel Sant'Angelo** (Pl. 2; 5), originally the *Mausoleum of Hadrian*, an enormous circular structure begun by Hadrian c AD 130 as a sepulchre for himself and his family. It was completed in 139, a year after his death, by his successor Antoninus Pius. It now contains the Museo Nazionale di Castel Sant'Angelo. Adm see p 48.

The mausoleum consisted of a base 89m square, supporting a round tower 64m in diameter, of peperino and travertine overlaid with marble. Above this was an earthen tumulus planted with cypress trees. At the top was an altar bearing a bronze quadriga driven by a charioteer representing Hadrian, as the Sun, ruler of the world. Inside the building was a spiral ramp (still in existence), which led to a straight passageway ending in the cella, in which was the imperial tomb. Hadrian and Sabina (his wife), and his adopted son L. Aelius Caesar, were buried in the mausoleum; and succeeding emperors until Septimius Severus.

When Aurelian built his wall round Rome, he carried it on the left bank of the Tiber above the Porta Settimiana. He built the Porta Aurelia Nova on the city side of the Pons Aelius and made Hadrian's mausoleum into a bridgehead on the other side of the river. He surrounded his bridgehead with a wall strengthened with towers. In this wall a gate, later known as the Porta San Pietro, gave access in the Middle Ages to the Vatican by means of the *Covered Way* (see below), used as an escape route by Alexander VI in 1494 and by Clement VII in 1527.

In the early Middle Ages the tomb was surrounded with ramparts and became the citadel of Rome. Theodoric (474–526) used it as a prison and for a time it became known as the *Carceri Theodorici*. According to legend, St Gregory the Great, while crossing the Pons Aelius at the head of a procession to pray for the cessation of the plague of 590, saw on the top of the fortress an angel sheathing his sword. The vision accurately presaged the end of the plague and from then onwards the castle bore its present name.

For centuries the possession of Castel Sant'Angelo was contested between popes and antipopes, the imperial forces and the Roman barons (Alberic, Crescentii, etc.). In 1084 Gregory VII was rescued from Henry IV's siege by Robert Guiscard. By the late 12C it was established as papal property. It was from here that Rienzo, at the end of his first period of dictatorship, fled to Bohemia on 15 December 1347. In 1378 the castle was severely damaged by the citizens of Rome, resentful of foreign domination. Shortly afterwards, in the reign of Boniface IX (1389–1404), it began to be rebuilt. The antipope John XXIII (1410–15) began the Covered Way to the Vatican; Alexander VI (1492–1503) completed it. He also had Ant. da Sangallo il Vecchio complete the building of the four bastions of the square Inner Ward (see below) which had been begun by Nicholas V (1447–55). Julius II (1503–13) built the South Loggia, facing the river. When Clement VII and some 1000 followers (including 13 cardinals and 18 bishops) took refuge here in 1527 from the troops of Charles V, the defence was materially assisted by Benvenuto Cellini, who tells in a famous passage of his 'Autobiography' about his gifts of valour and marksmanship. Paul III (1534–49) built the North Loggia, to counterbalance the South Loggia of Julius II (see above). Under Paul III the interior was decorated with frescoes and a marble angel, by *Raffaello da Montelupo*, was placed on the summit of the castle. The Outer Ward, with its defensive ditch, was the work of Pius IV (1559–65). Urban VIII (1623–44) provided the castle with cannon made of bronze taken from the ceiling of the Pantheon portico, and he employed *Bernini* to remodel the outworks. Benedict XIV (1740–58) replaced the marble angel with the bronze statue by *Verschaffelt* that is there today.—From 1849 to 1870 the castle was occupied by French troops. Under the Italian Government it was used as barracks and as a prison until 1901 when, thanks to the initiative of Gen. Mariano Borgatti, the work of restoration was begun. This was intensified in 1933–34, when the castle was adapted for use as a museum and the surrounding area was cleared of obstructions.

As it is today, the Castel Sant'Angelo rises from a square INNER WARD, with bastions named after the four Evangelists at each corner: NW St Mark, NE St Luke, SW St Matthew, SE St John.

Outside this enceinte is the pentagonal OUTER WARD. This had five bastions: from left to right, Santo Spirito (demolished by Pius IV to make room for Piazza Pia), San Pietro, San Paolo, Santa Maria, San Salvatore (eliminated during the construction of the Lungotevere). Between the two enceintes is the ditch, revealed during the excavations of 1933–34 after having been filled in for centuries. The area between the two enceintes has been laid out as a public garden, known as *Piazzale Pio IV*. The garden may be entered from the N and W sides. The *Covered Way* leads from the Bastion of St Mark across the garden on its way to the Vatican.

The *Museo Nazionale di Castel Sant'Angelo** was inaugurated in 1925. It is arranged in 58 rooms of the castle, which have been decorated over the centuries and are of the highest interest. The views of Rome and the Tiber are superb. The military collections give a comprehensive review of arms from the Stone Age to the present day, and the art collections include paintings, antique furniture, tapestries, etc.

In its general plan, the castle follows the design of Hadrian's mausoleum. The curtain walls of the inner ward, between the medieval bastions, are original; so is the entrance, except that the Roman threshold was lower. The round tower is Hadrian's, without its marble facing and its statues. Above it are the Renaissance and later additions, such as the arcaded galleries. The place of the earthen tumulus is taken by the papal apartments. The central tower is the base of Hadrian's quadriga, now replaced by the bronze angel.

The various features of the interior are all numbered with arabic numerals, which correspond to the numbers given in the description below. Rooms are often closed for rearrangement. Refreshments available on the Gallery of Pius IV (60). There is a lift reserved for the staff, and the disabled.

The entrance to the castle is by the bronze doors in the S side between the bastions of St Matthew (left) and of St John (right). To the left of the *Cortile del Salvatore* is the *Antiquarium* (74–76), containing architectural and sculptural fragments found in the castle, many from Hadrian's original Mausoleum; vaults show the original construction of the base of the tomb. From the court steps descend to a spacious *Vestibule* (1), with models of the castle, which leads into the interior. On the left is the shaft (2) of a lift built for the infirm Leo X and, in front, a niche for a statue of Hadrian.

On the right begins the *SPIRAL RAMP (3), 125·5m long, which rises gently to the sepulchral cella (see below). The ramp is in a wonderful state of preservation; the floor has remains of mosaic decoration. Along it are four ventilators, the last but one of which was converted into a prison, mentioned by Benvenuto Cellini.

At the end of the ramp the *Staircase of Alexander VI* (5), which cuts diametrically across the circular building, mounts to the left. By means of a bridge (6) built in 1822 by Valadier in place of a drawbridge the staircase passes above the SEPULCHRAL CELLA (7), of which only the travertine wall blocks survive, with some fragments of marble decoration. Here were kept the urns containing the imperial ashes. Hadrian's porphyry sarcophagus was annexed by Innocent II (1130–43) for use as his own tomb in the Lateran, where it was destroyed by the fire of 1360.

At a landing lit by a round window (9) the Staircase of Alexander VI originally turned to the right. Paul III closed this section and opened one to the left (10; by *Ant. da Sangallo the Younger*), to give access to the COURT OF THE ANGEL (11), named from the *Angel* (13) of Raffaello da Montelupo, moved here from the top of the castle to make room for the bronze angel. The courtyard is decorated with marble and stone cannon balls collected here in piles; they formed part of the castle's ammunition store. Here also are four 15C bombards.

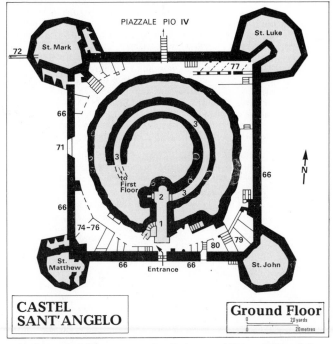

At the end of the court are the *Staircase of Urban VIII* and the façade (attrib. to Michelangelo; being restored) of the *Medici Chapel*, built for Leo X (12). On the right is a series of rooms (14, 15, II–VII, on two levels) which house a *Collection of Arms and Armour*, from the Stone Age to the 18C. The first (14) contains 17C arms, and 14C–17C swords. R. II. Weapons from prehistoric times to the Middle Ages. R. III. 14–17C defensive arms. R. IV. Swords and pikes. R. V. Firearms from 15–18C. Stairs lead up to three rooms (usually closed) containing 19–20C arms from Western countries, and a last room (VII) with exotic arms from Africa, China, and other countries.

From the Court of the Angel there is access to the ROOMS OF CLEMENT VIII (16, 17) and the Hall of Justice (18) all of which are usually open only for exhibitions. The HALL OF JUSTICE (18) is so called because it was the seat of the tribunal of the 16–17C, and because of its fresco, Giustizia, by *Perino del Vaga*. It was built in Roman times above the sepulchral cella.

The HALL OF APOLLO (19), is so called from the subject of the mythological grotesque decoration attributed to *Luzio Luzzi*. On the right is a trap-door covering a cellar 9m deep; adjacent is the top of the lift-shaft seen from the spiral ramp (see above). Leading out of this room (right) is the CHAPEL OF LEO X (20). It contains a 17C relief of St Philip Neri praying, a charming polychrome wood group of the Deposition, and a wooden model of the Archangel Michael attributed to *Pietro Bracci* since its restoration in 1986. In a glass case are antique vestments.

ROOMS OF CLEMENT VII (21, 22). In the first room is a frieze by *Giulio Romano*, and a coffered ceiling. The paintings include: two detached frescoes of the 15C Lombard School; *Fiorenzo di Lorenzo*, St Sebastian (fresco); *Tuscan 15C School*, Madonna enthroned; *Niccolò l'Alunno*, St Sebastian and St John the Baptist; *Zavattari* brothers, Polyptych; *Carlo Crivelli*, Christ blessing, St John the Baptist.—Room 22: *Martino Spanzotti*, Pietà; *Bart. Montagna*, *Madonna and Child; *Luca Signorelli*, Madonna and Saints.

A passage (23) leads right out of R. 19 into the large COURTYARD OF ALEXANDER VI (24), with a fine marble well. Theatrical performances were given here under Leo X and Pius IV.—A small staircase (26) leads to the charming BATHROOM OF CLEMENT VII (27) decorated with stuccoes and frescoes by *Giulio Romano*. This room communicates with a small dressing-room on the next floor (closed).

On the right side of the courtyard is a semicircular two-storied building, the rooms of which (25) were formerly used as prison cells. In the second room from the right Benvenuto Cellini was imprisoned during the first period of his captivity.

Adjacent is the *Court of Leo X* (28) with a loggia; below it is a 15C casemate. Adjacent is a small triangular courtyard from which stairs lead to a chamber

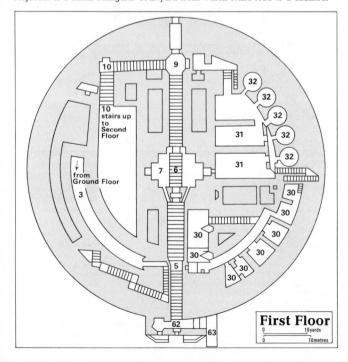

First Floor

which had a stove for heating the bath water and the air which circulated between the hollow walls.

A small doorway (30; or, if closed, a door on the opposite side of the courtyard) in the Courtyard of Alexander VI leads to the HISTORICAL PRISONS (also 30). A sloping passage descends to a large underground room, at the end of which is a winding vestibule leading to a corridor on which open the doors of some small cells. The numerous bones found under the floors indicate that the prisoners were buried where they had died. Despite tradition, there is no proof of identity of any of those incarcerated here, though Benvenuto Cellini is said to have passed the second period of his captivity in the last cell.—Beyond the prison cells are two large underground *Oil Stores* (31), containing 84 jars, with a capacity of c 22,000 litres. The object of the stores was twofold: to feed the garrison and to discourage assailants by pouring boiling oil on them.—On the right of the oil stores are the *Grain Silos* (five chambers; 32), later used as prison cells.

Stairs lead back up to the Courtyard of Alexander VI, and from there a staircase (33) continues to the LOGGIA OF PAUL III (34; left), built by *Ant. Sangallo the Younger* and decorated with stuccoes and Mannerist grotesques in 1543–48. From here and from the adjacent semicircular galleries there is a comprehensive *View of the pentagonal Outer Ward.—To the right of the Loggia of Paul III extends the semicircular GALLERY OF PIUS IV (35), on the inner side of which

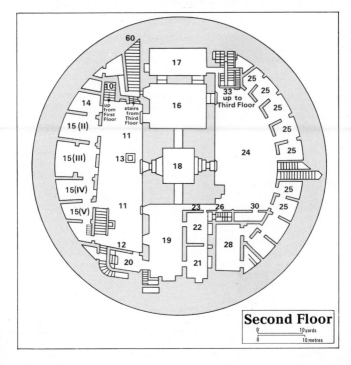

is a series of small rooms used originally as quarters for the household of the papal court and later as political and military prison cells. The first (36: closed) is a reconstruction of a political prison in the first half of the 19C. In the rest (37; often closed) is an interesting muster of uniforms, decorations, and medals of the various Italian states before the Unification.

From the vestibule at the end there is access to a terrace overlooking the Courtyard of Leo X. Beyond is the LOGGIA OF JULIUS II (38), built by *Bramante*; it faces S and the Ponte Sant'Angelo.—A staircase leads from here to the **Papal Apartments** (39–49).

SALA PAOLINA or DEL CONSIGLIO (39), adorned with *Stuccoes by *Girol. da Sermoneta* and *Baccio da Montelupo*. Walls decorated by *Pellegrino Tibaldi, Dom. Zoga, Perino del Vaga, Polidoro da Caravaggio, Giov. da Udine*, and others. On the right is an amusing trompe-l'oeil fresco of a courtier entering the room through a painted door. In the floor, coat-of-arms of Innocent XIII, who restored the room.—CAMERA DEL PERSEO (40), so called from the subject of the beautiful frieze by *Perino del Vaga* and his bottega (restored in 1982). The wooden ceiling is intaglio work of the 16C. The tapestries come from State collections and the room is appropriately furnished. The contents are mainly from the Contini donation, as are those of RR. 44–49; the paintings are frequently changed around.—Christ carrying the Cross, by *Paris Bordone*; tapestry with an episode in the life of Julius Caesar.— CAMERA DI AMORE E PSICHE (41; seen beyond a railing), is called after another frieze recently restored by *Perino del Vaga* and his bottega, illustrating the story of Cupid and Psyche in 17 episodes. Fine carved gilt 15C ceiling. Large 16C canopied bed, clavichord, and other furniture; Girl with a unicorn, by an unknown 16C artist; statuette attrib. to *Iac. della Quercia*; *Sebastiano del Piombo*, Christ carrying the Cross.

From the Sala Paolina a corridor (43) frescoed in the Pompeian style by *Perino del Vaga* and his bottega (restored in 1982) leads to the HALL OF THE LIBRARY (44), with ceiling frescoes by *Luzio Romano* and stuccoes by *Sicciolante da Sermoneta* (16C). Marble chimney-piece by *Raff. da Montelupo*. The furniture includes four cassoni, a 15C wardrobe, chairs and candelabra.—ROOM OF THE MAUSOLEUM OF HADRIAN (45), so called from the frieze by *Luzio Romano* and his school. The paintings include: three works representing Bacchanals by *Dosso Dossi* (removed for restoration), *Jacob Jordaens*, and *Nic. Poussin* (a copy of a work by Giov. Bellini); and *Lor. Lotto* (attrib.), *Madonna between Saints Roch and Sebastian. R. 46 contains a small painting of *St Jerome by Lor. Lotto (recently restored).—A short flight of stairs leads up to the APPARTAMENTO CAGLIOSTRA (47–49), three 16C rooms decorated with grotteschi by *Luzio Romano* and containing a collection of majolica (15C 'alberelli', floor tiles, Deruta and Faenza ware).

A small vestibule leads out of the Hall of the Library into the central ROOM OF THE SECRET ARCHIVES or of the TREASURE (50). The walnut cupboards in this room were used for the archives inaugurated by Paul III. In the middle are some large chests in which Julius II, Leo X, and Sixtus V kept the sacred treasure.

A Roman staircase ascends to the ROUND HALL (51), situated beneath the statue of the angel and above the last room. Formerly used as a political prison, it now contains the original armature of Verschaffelt's angel (see below), a cast of the head, and the original sword.—A short staircase leads to the HALL OF THE COLUMNS which, with the two adjoining rooms (52–53), is only open for exhibitions.

At the top of the staircase the TERRACE (54) is reached, familiar to play and opera-goers from the last act of 'Tosca'. *Peter Anton Verschaffelt*'s huge bronze *Angel (4m high), in the act of sheathing his sword, stands on a small higher terrace (inaccessible to the public). Finished in 1752, this replaced a marble angel of 1544 by Raffaello da Montelupo. It was restored in 1982–6. Nearby is the *Campana della Misericordia*, the bell which used to announce the execution of capital sentences.

The *View from the terrace is superb. On the left, in front, is the Palace of Justice, with the Trinità dei Monti behind. Farther to the left, the Prati district; at the back the green park of the Villa Borghese and of the Pincio. Across the Tiber, the Ministry of Finance, with the Quirinal in front; then Palazzo della Consulta, with Santa Maria Maggiore behind it. To the right, on the skyline, the Torre delle Milizie, with the cupola of the Pantheon in front. Next comes the Victor Emmanuel Monument, with St John Lateran behind it. In the background, the Castelli Romani. Continuing to the right, the Capitol; in front, the two cupolas of Sant'Andrea della Valle and San Carlo ai Catinari. Then is seen the Aventine, with San Paolo fuori le Mura in the background. Farther right, is Trastevere and the Janiculum; St Peter's and the Vatican; Monte Mario. Immediately below, Ponte Sant'Angelo and Ponte Vittorio Emanuele, with the Lungotevere.

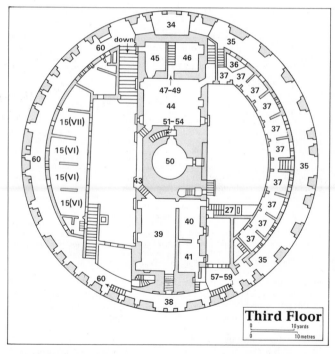

Third Floor

From the terrace visitors are asked to descend by a modern staircase which passes three rooms of the APPARTAMENTO DEL CASTELLANO with remains of frescoes and some paintings of the Castle. The stairs continue down to emerge on the Gallery of Pius IV beside the Staircase of Urban VIII which continues down to the Court of the Angel. Otherwise visitors may return from the terrace down the same staircase to the Hall of the Library (44), which should be crossed diagonally, passing through a door on the left of the fireplace. Stairs lead to the Loggia of Paul III, from which another flight of stairs continues down to the Courtyard of Alexander VI.

After this the route follows Paul III's staircase (10), and Alexander VI's staircase (5), at the foot of which is a small guard-room (62). From here a gateway leads on to a drawbridge (63). An external staircase on the left from this point leads to the castle entrance.—To the right the *Bastion of St Matthew* may be reached by means of a walkway (66) between the Roman structure and the square inner ward, completely encircling the cylindrical centre, with several radial cells opening out of it. At the next corner steps lead down into the *Bastion of St Mark* (70). Here is the beginning of the *Passetto Vaticano*, or Covered Way (72). On the left are the *Mills* (Mole; 71), used from the time of Pius IV to grind the castle flour. Between the bastions of St Mark and St Luke is a passageway leading into the public garden (Piazzale Pio IV). By the *Bastion of St Luke* is the *Chapel of the Crucifix* or of *Clement XII* (77), in which condemned criminals had to attend mass before execution. The circuit continues past a reconstruction of the entrance gate to the castle which, built in 1556 by *Giov. Sallustio Peruzzi* for Paul IV, was adapted in 1628 for the use of barracks built by Urban VIII. It was demolished in 1892 when the Lungotevere was built. On the inner side of the *Bastion of St John* are further oil stores (79). Finally, beyond a radial cell (80) containing Byzantine and Roman marbles, the entrance gate is reached.

Beside Castel Sant'Angelo, on the river front, is the huge **Palazzo di Giustizia** (Pl. 2; 3), the Palace of Justice, known as the 'Palazzaccio'. A colossal ornate building in solid travertine, decorated with sculptures by Enrico Quattrini and Ettore Ximenes, it was built between 1889 and 1910. It has been closed since 1970 when it was evacuated because it was in danger of collapse, and it is not known whether the foundations can be strengthened. New Judiciary offices and law courts have been built by Gius. Perugini, and others in the CITTÀ GIUDIZIARIA (Pl. 15; 7), in Piazzale Clodio.

To the N, beyond Piazza Cavour, an important traffic centre and terminus for buses, are the PRATI and TRIONFALE districts. In Via Pompeo Magno is the church of *San Gioacchino* (Pl. 2; 3), erected by Raffaele Inganni in 1890 to commemorate the sacerdotal jubilee of Leo XIII (Gioacchino Pecci). The church has bronze capitals and an aluminium cupola painted inside to represent a star-strewn sky.—Farther on, at No. 11 Via Andreoli, is the well-arranged **Museo Storico delle Poste e delle Telecommunicazioni** (Pl. 1; 2; adm see p 49). The postal display begins with a casket of 1300 used by the Pontifical Post Office of Urbino and 17C letter boxes, including a 'bocca di leone', and there is a fine copy of the Peutinger Table on tile. Later postal history (pioneer air-mail flights; Ethiopian military cancellers, etc.) is well chosen. The history of telegraph and telephone is copiously illustrated by original appliances, including apparatus used by Marconi in his 1901 experiments between Cornwall and Newfoundland.—In Viale Gius. Mazzini to the left is the church of *Cristo Re* by Marcello Piacentini next to the headquarters of the *R.A.I.* (the Italian state-owned radio and television network).—Farther N is the **Museo dell' Arma del Genio** (Pl. 15; 6; adm see p 49), illustrating Italian military transport, bridge building, and communications. It includes a military aircraft of 1909, and models of historical fortifications, and armoury from Roman times to the present day.—**Monte Mario** which rises to the NW is described in Rte 24.

From Castel Sant'Angelo the unattractive cold **Via della Conciliazione** (Pl. 1; 6) leads towards St Peter's. The approach to the great basilica was transformed by this broad straight thoroughfare, typical of Fascist urban planning, which was completed in 1937. In its construction two characteristic streets of the Città Leonina—the Borgo Nuovo (opened in 1499) and Borgo Vecchio (known as the Spina di Borgo)—and the buildings between them were erased, and one ancient palace suffered transplantation (see below). The colon-naded piazza in front of St Peter's was not originally designed to be seen from a distance; its impact is therefore lessened by this monumental approach.

Via della Conciliazione first passes (right) the Carmelite church of *Santa Maria in Traspontina* (1566–87). Beyond is *PALAZZO

TORLONIA (formerly *Giraud*), a delightful reproduction of the Palazzo della Cancelleria, built by *And. Bregno* in 1495–1504 for Card. Adriano da Corneto. Then comes *Palazzo dei Convertendi*, built in the second half of the 17C, and re-erected in its present position in 1937. It originally occupied the site of a house built by Bramante for Raphael, who died in it in 1520.—On the S side of the street is PALAZZO DEI PENITENZIERI built (probably) by *Baccio Pontelli* for Card. Dom. della Rovere in 1480. it is now occupied by the Penitentiaries, whose office it is to hear confessions in St Peter's. Via della Conciliazione ends in *Piazza Pio XII*, in front of Piazza San Pietro (described in Rte 27).

Borgo Santo Spirito runs parallel to Via della Conciliazione to the S. Here a flight of steps leads up to the little church of SAN MICHELE E MAGNO (open on Sunday morning), founded in the 8C and retaining a 13C campanile. Inside is the tomb of Raphael Mengs (died 1779). On the corner of Via dei Penitenzieri is **Santo Spirito in Sassia** (Pl. 1; 6), a church founded in 726 for Saxon pilgrims by Ine, king of Wessex, who died in Rome in the same year.

The church was rebuilt in 1540 by *Antonio da Sangallo the Younger*: the design of the façade was probably his, but the work itself was done in 1585 by *Ottavio Mascherino*. The campanile, entirely Tuscan in character is one of the most graceful in Rome. It is ascribed to *Baccio Pontelli*.—It was from the ramparts of the Leonine City near here that Benvenuto Cellini, according to his own statement, shot the Constable de Bourbon in 1527; a tablet on the outer wall of the church, however, attributes the deed to Bern. Passeri, another goldsmith.— Adjoining are the buildings of the huge **Arcispedale di Santo Spirito**, founded by Innocent III c 1198 as a hospital and hostel, and rebuilt for Sixtus IV by various architects (c 1473–78). The first building, the Palazzo del Commendatore (i.e. the house of the director of the hospital), with a spacious courtyard, dates from c 1567. The harmony of the proportions of the main building was spoilt by Alexander VIII, who added a story, and by Benedict XIV, who blocked up the arches of the portico. The portal is an effective example of the early Renaissance style. The chapel (adm by special permission only) contains an altar with a baldacchino of the time of Clement VIII (1592–1605) and an altarpiece (Job) by *Carlo Maratta*. The river front, the Lungotevere in Sassia, was rebuilt and extended in 1926 in harmony with the old style.

The hospital contains several institutions devoted to the history of medicine: the *Lancisiana Library* (founded 1711; in the Palazzo del Commendatore), the *Historical Medical Academy*, and the *National Museum of the History of Medicine*, unique in Italy. Adm see p 49.

24 Monte Mario and Ponte Milvio

The foot of *Monte Mario* (Piazza Maresciallo Giardino) is reached by Bus No. 90 from the Corso. Bus No. 911 runs from the Mausoleum of Augustus to the *Foro Italico*. *Ponte Milvio* may be reached from Piazzale Flaminio by Bus Nos 1, 202, 203, etc.

Monte Mario (139m; Pl. 15; 5) is the ancient *Clivus Cinnae* and the medieval *Monte Malo*. Its present name is taken from the Villa Mario Mellini built on the summit. Via di Villa Madama climbs the E slope of the hill to *Villa Madama (Pl. 15; 3; no adm). This suburban villa, begun for Cardinal Giuliano de' Medici (Clement VII) by *Giulio Romano* was designed by *Raphael*. It was altered by *Ant. da Sangallo the Younger*. Later it came into the possession of 'Madama' Margaret of Parma and was afterwards owned by the kings of Naples. Today it is used by the Italian Government for the accommodation of prominent visitors.—For permit to view, apply to the Foreign Office, Viale della Macchia della Farnesina.

The beautiful loggia, decorated with stucco reliefs by *Giov. da Udine* and paintings by *Giulio Romano* (1520–25) after Raphael's designs, rivals and even excels the famous Logge of the Vatican. In one of the rooms is a frieze of Cupids by Giulio Romano. A lovely *View of Rome is obtained from the balcony of the main façade. The attractive *Garden served as a model for many Italian gardens.

On the S slope of the hill is the round *Church of the Rosary* (Pl. 15; 7, 5; 109m; *View). Beyond the ditches of the Fort of Monte Mario, a road leads right to the summit at the *Villa Mario Mellini*, now incorporated in the **Astronomical and Meteorological Observatory** (Pl. 15; 5), with the Copernicus Museum.

At the foot of Monte Mario, extending along the river front is the **Foro Italico** (Pl. 15; 4, 2), an ambitious sports centre built in 1931 by the former Accademia Fascista della Farnesina. Facing the entrance is *Ponte Duca d'Aosta* (1939).

A marble monolith, 17m high, inscribed 'Mussolini Dux', rises at the entrance in front of an imposing avenue paved with marble inlaid with mosaics, and ending in a piazza decorated with a fountain and with a huge marble sphere. On either side of the avenue are marble cubes, with inscriptions recording events in the history of Italy. At the end, beyond the piazza, is the *Stadio Olimpico*, finished for the Olympic Games in 1960, with accommodation for 100,000. To the right is the *Stadio dei Marmi*, capable of seating 20,000 spectators, with 60 colossal statues of athletes. There are open-air and enclosed swimming-baths, the latter with good mosaics, lawn-tennis and basketball courts, running tracks, gymnasium and fencing halls, reading rooms and other facilities.

Lungotevere Maresciallo Diaz continues along the Tiber passing the *Casa Internazionale dello Studente*, and, behind it, the *Italian Foreign Office* (1956), known as the 'Farnesina' from the name of the road here. Farther back is the *French Military Cemetery*, with the graves of 1500 French who died in the Second World War. The Lungotevere ends at Piazzale Milvio (Pl. 15, just beyond 2), where several roads converge.

To the right, between Via Cassia (N 2 to Viterbo, Siena, and Florence) and Via Orti della Farnesina, is the church of *Madre di Dio*, rebuilt by Cesare Bazzani in 1933. Ahead Viale di Tor di Quinto continues along the river to *Ponte Flaminio*, opened in 1951, a seven-arched entrance to the city from the north. Along it runs Corso di Francia, which passes above the *Villaggio Olimpico*, built to accommodate athletes in 1960, and now a residential district.

Ponte Milvio or **Ponte Molle** (*Pons Milvius*), over the Tiber, was built by the censor M. Aemilius Scaurus in 109 BC. Remodelled in the 15C, by Nicholas V, who added the watch-towers, it was restored in 1805 by Pius VII, who commissioned Valadier to erect the triumphal arch at the entrance. Blown up in 1849 by Garibaldi to arrest the advance of the French, it was again restored in 1850 by Pius IX. The bridge was reopened to pedestrians after its restoration in 1985.

It was at the Pons Milvius that Cicero captured the emissaries of the Allobroges in 63 BC on the occasion of the conspiracy of Catiline; and it was from the bridge that the Emperor Maxentius was thrown into the Tiber and drowned after his defeat by his co-emperor Constantine on October 28, 312 (see below).

Across Ponte Milvio is Piazza Cardinal Consalvi, with a shrine containing a statue by Paolo Taccone, erected by Pius II in 1462 on the spot where he had met Card. Bessarion returning from the Morea (Peloponnese) with the head of St Andrew. The straight Via Flaminia returns from here to Piazza del Popolo and the centre of the city.

A short way along Via Flaminia which runs parallel with Viale

Tiziano ('one way' going out of the city) is Piazza Apollodoro. To the left is the *Palazzetto dello Sport*, an adventurous and striking construction by Pier Luigi Nervi and Annibale Vitellozzi, designed for the Olympic Games in 1960. Beyond is the Villaggio Olimpico (see above). A little to the S is the *Stadio Flaminio*, designed in reinforced concrete by Pier Luigi and Antonio Nervi in 1959 on the site of the old Stadio Nazionale. In addition to the football ground, which can accommodate 45,000 spectators, there are gymnastic halls, a fencing school, and a swimming-pool.

On the right of Piazza Apollodoro in Via Guido Reni, is the church of *Santa Croce*, built by Pius X in 1913 to commemorate the 16th centenary of the Edict of Milan (March 313), which conceded civil rights and toleration to Christians throughout the Roman Empire.

Further S, on the left Viale Tiziano widens to form Piazzale Manila, from which Viale Maresciallo Pilsudski leads NE and then E towards the Parioli district (Pl. 11; 2, 3).

On the right are the remains of the *Basilica of St Valentine*, built by St Julius I (pope 337–52) over the tomb of the saint; adjoining are the *Catacombs of St Valentine* (adm only with special permission).—Farther on (left) is the Corso di Francia (see above), and still farther the entrance to the *Parco di Villa Glori* (Pl. 11; 1). This park was converted in 1923–24 by Raff. De Vico into the **Parco della Rimembranza**, to commemorate the heroism of the Brothers Cairoli, who were killed in 1867. The park, planted with cypresses, oaks, elms, maples, horse-chestnuts and other trees, has a column to the dead of 1867 and preserves the trunk of the almond tree beneath which Enrico Cairoli died. A clump of oak trees commemorates heroes of the First World War. There is a fine *View of the Tiber valley.—Beyond is the mineral spring called *Acqua Acetosa*; the well-head was built by Bernini in 1661.

Via Flaminia continues to the graceful little circular church of *Sant'Andrea in Via Flaminia* by Vignola (1550–55), erected by Julius III to commemorate his deliverance from Charles V's soldiers while he was a cardinal. It is now between Via Flaminia and Viale Tiziano. Further S, on the left, is the beginning of Viale delle Belle Arti, which passes Villa Giulia (Rte 9). On the right, beyond Piazzale delle Belle Arti, is *Ponte del Risorgimento*, a reinforced-concrete bridge with a single span of 100m.

At the corner of Viale delle Belle Arti is the Palazzina of Pius IV (see Rte 9), and where Via di Villa Giulia leads left, is a fountain of Julius III, beneath an imposing façade, originally of only one story, by Bart. Ammannati (1553); the second part was added by Pirro Ligorio in 1562. In Piazza della Marina is the vast *Ministry of Marine*, by Giulio Magni (1928), which has another façade on the Tiber. Via Domenico Alberto Azuni leads to Ponte Matteotti. Beyond the wooded grounds on the left of Villa Strohl Fern is Piazzale Flaminio (Pl. 2; 2), the starting-point of the Via Flaminia. On the E side are the main entrance to the Villa Borghese (Rte 9), and the beginning of Viale del Muro Torto, which runs outside the Aurelian Wall to Porta Pinciana.

Porta del Popolo opens into Piazza del Popolo (Rte 7).

25 Porta San Paolo and San Paolo fuori le Mura

The UNDERGROUND (line B) from the Station and Colosseum runs to *Porta San Paolo* ('Piramide') and the basilica of *San Paolo fuori le Mura* ('San Paolo').—BUS 673 from the Colosseum via Porta San Paolo, or No. 170 from the Station, Piazza Venezia, and Largo Argentina, both terminate at San Paolo fuori le Mura.

The well preserved **Porta San Paolo** (Pl. 8; 7), the *Porta Ostiensis* of ancient Rome, preserves its inner side, with two arches from the time of Aurelian. The outer face, rebuilt by Honorius in 402, has been restored. The gate houses the *Museo della Via Ostiense* (closed indefinitely), which illustrates the history of the road to Ostia. It includes milestones and reliefs (some only casts), together with models of Ostia and its port in Imperial times. Among the tomb paintings are three frescoed lunettes from a tomb of the Servian period. On the S side of the gate the square is called Piazzale Ostiense, an important traffic centre, with a station of the underground, and the railway station for the branch line to Ostia and Lido di Roma.

On the W side of the square, across the line of the city wall, is the *****Pyramid of Gaius Cestius** (died 12 BC), praetor, tribune of the plebs, and member of the college of the Septemviri Epulones, who had charge of solemn banquets. This is a tomb in the form of a tall pyramid of brick faced with marble, 27m high with a base 22m square. An inscription records that it was built in less than 330 days. It was included in the Aurelian walls in the 3C, and remains one of the most idiosyncratic and best preserved monuments of ancient Rome. Adm only by special permission.

Beyond the pyramid to the left extends the so-called **Protestant Cemetery** (Pl. 8; 7; open 7 till dusk; visitors ring at No. 6, Via Caio Cestio), romantically set with dark green cypresses. The earliest recorded grave dates from 1738.

It was of the *Old Cemetery* (left of the entrance), that Shelley wrote 'it might make one in love with death to think that one should be buried in so sweet a place'. The tomb in the far corner is that of John Keats (1796–1821; 'Here lies one whose name was writ in water'); close by lies his friend Joseph Severn (1793–1879); behind, John Bell (1763–1820), the surgeon. In the *New Cemetery* lie the ashes of P.B. Shelley (1792–1822; 'cor cordium'), with a monument by Onslow Ford (1891). Close by lies his friend Edward Trelawny (1792–1881). Here are buried also J. Addington Symonds (1840–93), the historian of the Renaissance; John Gibson (1790–1886), the sculptor; William Howitt (1792–1879) and his wife Mary (1799–1888), R.M. Ballantyne (1825–94), and Julius Goethe (died 1830), the only son of the poet.

Just beyond the Protestant Cemetery, at the end of Via Caio Cestio, and across Via Nicola Zabaglia is the **Rome British Military Cemetery**, where 429 members of the three Services are buried. The cemetery is beautifully situated along the line of the city wall. If the gates are locked, telephone the Area Office (address and telephone number are given on a notice).

To the N of the British Military Cemetery and W of Via Nicola Zabaglia rises the curious **Monte Testaccio** (Pl. 8; 7), an isolated mound 54m high and some 1000m round, entirely composed of potsherds (testae) dumped here from the neighbouring EMPORIA, or storehouses, which anciently lined the Tiber between Ponte Testaccio and Ponte Sublicio. The storehouses were served by the landing-stage of the Marmorata, long since vanished. Among the finds here was a hoard of amphorae, used to import oil from Spain, with official marks scratched on them, which are of fundamental importance to our knowledge of the economic history of the late Republic and early Empire. The top of Monte Testaccio (entered from the corner facing Via Galvani and Via Zabaglia) commands a fine view. The neighbourhood was the scene of jousts and tournaments in the Middle Ages.

From Piazzale Ostiense the broad uninteresting VIA OSTIENSE leads almost due S through a depressing part of the town. It is not recommended to walkers; bus No. 23 follows it to (2km) the basilica of San Paolo. It crosses under the Pisa railway; beyond, to the left, are the Mercati Generali and, to the right, the headquarters of the Gas Works. Some distance farther, on the left, is the site of an oratory marking the spot where, according to tradition, St Peter and St Paul greeted each other on the way to martyrdom. To the E extends the modern *Quartiere della Garbatella*. In the middle of the road just before San Paolo is a small necropolis known as the *Sepolcreto Ostiense*, which contained pagan and perhaps Christian tombs. The site, seen through railings (adm only by special permission) extended over a wide area; another part is visible left of the road.

Here the narrow and long Via delle Sette Chiese, passing the *Catacombs of Commodilla*, (adm by special permit), branches off to join, eventually Via Ardeatina and the Appian Way (Rte 17).

*San Paolo fuori le Mura (2km from Porta San Paolo; Pl. 8; 7; open 7–18.30) is the largest church in Rome after St Peter's. The present building, third on the site, is a cold 19C reconstruction, replacing the ancient basilica virtually destroyed by fire in 1823. In plan and dimensions, if not in spirit, the new basilica follows the old one almost exactly. One of the four great patriarchal basilicas, it commemorates the martyrdom of St Paul and is believed to contain the Apostle's tomb.

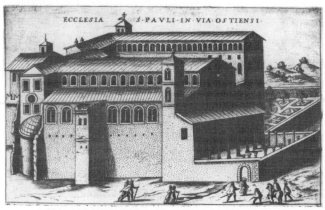

The old basilica of San Paolo fuori le Mura, an early 17C engraving

According to Christian tradition the Roman matron Lucina buried the body of Paul in a vineyard on this spot. A small shrine existed here when in 384 a large basilica was begun by Valentinian II and Theodosius the Great at the request of Pope Damasus. It was enlarged by Theodosius' son Honorius and decorated with mosaics by Galla Placidia, sister of Honorius. The basilica was further embellished by Leo III (Pope, 795–816) and it became the largest and most beautiful church in Rome. In the 9C it was pillaged by the Saracens and John VIII (872–82) enclosed it in a fortified village known as *Giovannipolis*. It was restored c 1070 by Abbot Hildebrand, later Gregory VII. The façade, overlooking the Tiber, was preceded by a colonnaded quadriporticus. Before the

Reformation the King of England was *ex officio* a canon of San Paolo and the abbot, in return, was decorated with the Order of the Garter. This great basilica was almost entirely destroyed by fire on the night of 15–16 July 1823.

Leo XII (1823–29) ordered the reconstruction, which was directed by Pasquale Belli, Bosio, and Camporese, and afterwards by Luigi Poletti. In their enthusiasm for the work of rebuilding the architects pressed on with new materials and disregarded much of the old work that could have been preserved after repair. The transept was consecrated by Gregory XVI in 1840 and the complete church by Pius IX in 1854. In 1891 an explosion in a neighbouring fort broke most of the stained glass; its place has been taken by slabs of alabaster. Here in March 1966 took place a service performed by Pope Paul VI and Dr Ramsey, Abp. of Canterbury, when they issued a joint declaration of amity. It is one of the three basilicas of Rome which has the privilege of extraterritoriality.

EXTERIOR. The Romanesque campanile was pulled down to make way for the unattractive CAMPANILE by *Luigi Poletti* on Via Ostiense. *Poletti* was also responsible for the NORTH PORTICO which incorporates 12 Hymettan marble columns from the old basilica. On one of the nearest columns, close under the frieze, is a 4C inscription of Pope Siricius (384–99). The façade (right) is preceded by a great QUADRIPORTICUS with 146 enormous monolithic granite columns, added by *Gugl. Calderini* (1892–1928) in keeping with the frigid 'air of conscious bravado' with which the rebuilt church seems to be endowed. The elaborate frescoes on the façade date from 1885. The central bronze doors (1) are by *Ant. Maraini* (1928–30). The PORTA SANTA (2) has the bronze *Doors (recently restored; seen from the inside of the basilica) which belonged to the old basilica. They were made at Constantinople by Staurakios in 1070, inlaid with silver in 54 panels of scenes from the Old and New Testament.

INTERIOR. The nave and transept form in plan a tau or Egyptian cross, 132m by 65; the height is 30 metres. The highly polished marble, alabaster, malachite, lapis, and porphyry give an impression of neo-classical splendour. The Nave, with double aisles separated from one another by eighty columns of Montórfano granite, is the new part of the basilica. In the centre of the ceiling, which is richly decorated with stuccoes in white and gold, are the arms of Pius IX. The paintings executed in the mid-19C between the windows depict scenes in the life of St Paul (by *Pietro Gagliardi, Fr. Podesti, Gugl. De Sanctis, Fr. Coghetti*, and *Ces. Mariani*); under these (and in the aisles), forming a frieze, are the portraits in mosaic of all the 263 popes from St Peter to Paul VI. In the outermost aisles are niches with statues of the Apostles. The six huge alabaster columns beside the doors were presented by Mohammed Ali of Egypt. The statue of St Peter (3) is by *Giacometti* and of St Paul (4) by *Revelli*.

The *TRIUMPHAL ARCH, a relic of the old basilica, is supported by two colossal granite columns. Its mosaics (much restored) are due to Galla Placidia. They represent Christ blessing in the Greek manner, with angels; Symbols of the Evangelists; the Elders of the Apocalypse; Saints Peter and Paul. On the other face of the arch are the remains of mosaics by *Pietro Cavallini*.—Over the high altar, supported by four porphyry columns, is the famous *Tabernacle (5), by *Arnolfo di Cambio* and his companion *Pietro (Oderisi?*, 1285). The old tradition which places the tomb of St Paul beneath the altar is well-founded. Excavations before the rebuilding in 1823, revealed a 1C tomb, surrounded by Christian and some pagan burials. When the grating of the Confessio is opened, the inscription 'Paolo Apostolo Mart', dating from the time of Constantine, may be seen. The huge 12C paschal *Candlestick (6) is by *Nicolò di Angelo* and *Pietro Vassalletto*.

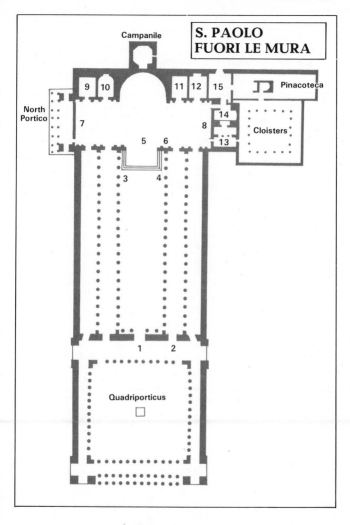

The magnificent ceiling of the transept is decorated with the arms of Pius VII, Leo XII, Pius VIII, and Gregory XVI, as well as with those of the basilica (an arm holding a sword). The walls are covered with rare marbles.—The Corinthian pilasters are made up of fragments of the old columns.—The great *Mosaic of the APSE was executed c 1220 by Venetian craftsmen sent by Doge Pietro Ziani at the request of Pope Honorius III. It was heavily restored in the 19C after damage in the fire. The subjects are Christ blessing in the Greek manner, with Saints Peter, Andrew, Paul, and Luke; at the feet of Christ, Pope Honorius III; below this, a gem-studded Cross on the altar, angels and apostles. On the inner face of the arch, Virgin and

Child with St John blessing Pope John XXII.

At either end of the transept is an altar of malachite and lapis lazuli, presented by Nicholas I of Russia: the Conversion of St Paul (7) is by *Vinc. Camuccini*, and the mosaic (8), a copy from the Coronation of the Virgin, by *Giulio Romano*. The Chapel of St Stephen (9) has a statue of the saint by *Rinaldi*, and paintings of his expulsion from the Sanhedrin, by *Coghetti*, and of his stoning, by *Podesti*. The Chapel of the Crucifix (10), by *Carlo Maderno* was the only chapel salved in the fire; on the altar, Crucifix attrib. to *Tino da Camaino*. In a niche to the right of the door, statue of St Bridget by *Stef. Maderno*; to the left, statue of a Saint in wood. In this chapel, in 1541, St Ignatius de Loyola and the first Jesuits took the corporate oaths formally establishing their society as a religious order.—The Chapel of the Choir or of St Laurence (11), is by *Gugl. Calderini*; 15C marble triptych, frescoes by *Viligiardi*. Chapel of St Benedict (12), a sumptuous work of *Poletti*, who has reproduced in it the cella of an ancient temple; the 12 fluted columns are from Veii.

The SALA DEL MARTIROLOGIO (13), has badly damaged 13C frescoes, and a bust of Poletti. The Baptistery (14; designed by Arnaldo Foschini in a Greek cross in 1930) leads into the Vestibule (15) preceding the S door of the church, which contains a colossal statue of Gregory XVI by Rinaldi, and 13C mosaics from the old basilica. A door to the right off the vestibule leads to the *Cloisters (open daily 9–13, 15–18) belonging to the old Benedictine convent. They have coupled colonnettes of different forms decorated with mosaics, with tiny couchant animals (most of which have now disappeared) between the columns. In the centre is a rose garden. The cloisters were begun under Abbot Pietro da Capua (1193–1208) and finished after 1228, and are the work, at least in part, of the Vassalletti. Along the walls are placed inscriptions and sculptured fragments: XIV. Statue of Boniface IX; XVII. Sarcophagus with the story of Apollo and Marsyas; XIX. An inscription recording the suicide of Nero (probably a 17C forgery); XX. Statue of a prophet. The painted wood roof is noteworthy.—Off the Cloister is the *Chapel of Reliquaries*, with a gilded silver cross, and the *Pinacoteca*, with works by Antoniazzo Romano (Madonna and four Saints) and Bramantino (Flagellation), as well as old prints showing the damage caused by the fire.

From San Paolo the road continues S. After a short distance, a road to the right leads via Viale Marconi to Via del Mare (for Ostia and Lido di Roma; Rte 28).— For E.U.R. and the Monastery of Tre Fontane (Rte 26) Via Laurentina forks left from Via Ostiense under the railway, and soon joins Via Cristoforo Colombo.

26 E.U.R. (Esposizione Universale di Roma)

Approaches. E.U.R. is easily reached in 12 minutes from the Stazione Termini by the Metropolitana, on which it is the penultimate station. The line ends at Tre Fontane (Laurentino). It is also reached by the following buses: No. 93 from Stazione Termini, No. 97 from Piazza Sonnino, or No. 223 from San Paolo fuori le Mura.

For motorists the quickest route is by Via Cristoforo Colombo (c 6km), which starts at Porta Ardeatina (reached from the Colosseum by Via di San Gregorio and Viale di Caracalla). It passes through the arches of the Aurelian wall with its gallery, and a sepulchre to the left. It continues as a ten-lane highway, and passes straight through the middle of E.U.R.

Another route is via San Paolo. From Piazza Venezia to San Paolo, see Rte 25. From the front of the basilica Viale San Paolo and Via Levi Civita lead to Via Guglielmo Marconi, which continues left for 1·5km before joining Via Cristoforo Colombo (see above).

Motorists returning towards the N part of the city can take *Via Olimpica*, a road, 15km long, built for the Olympic Games of 1960. This links the two important sporting centres of E.U.R. and Foro Italico (Rte 24), avoiding the centre of the city. Crossing the Tiber by *Ponte Marconi* it runs by way of the Circonvallazione Gianicolense, and passing across the Villa Doria Pamphilj reaches the Piazzale degli Eroi. Beyond the Foro Italico it turns E to recross the Tiber by the new *Ponte Tor di Quinto*. From here it passes the Centro Sportivo dell'Acqua Acetosa and joins the Via Salaria (Rte 20).

Esposizione Universale di Roma (now always abbreviated to **E.U.R.**; Plans 13 & 14) was begun in 1938 to the designs of *Marcello Piacentini*. An ambitious project to symbolize the achievements of Fascism, it was to have been opened in 1942. Its buildings were only partly completed, however, and the site suffered some war damage. After 1952 the original buildings were restored, new ones were added, and Government offices and public institutions were moved to the site, which has also developed as a residential quarter but not as a social centre. The huge buildings are spaciously set out with wide avenues and parks. The roads are comparatively deserted.

Via Cristoforo Colombo passes over the Centro Sportivo delle Tre Fontane, before reaching Piazza delle Nazioni (Pl. 14; 1), with twin palaces whose façades form two hemicycles. Viale della Civiltà del Lavoro leads right to the *Palazzo E.U.R.* and, at the end, the *Palazzo della Civiltà del Lavoro* (Pl. 13; 2), popularly known as the 'square Colosseum', with statues symbolizing the arts beneath the lowest arches. At the opposite end of Viale della Civiltà is the *Palazzo dei Congressi*.

Beyond is the vast Piazza Marconi (Pl. 14; 3), in the centre of which is a Stele of Carrara marble (45m) by *Arturo Dazzi* (1938–59), dedicated to Marconi. On the right are two edifices with symmetrical fronts (*Palazzi dell'Esposizioni*), while between them, farther back, is the *Grattacielo Italia*, with a cinema and hotel. On the left, joined by a huge colonnade, are two palazzi of similar design. The one to the left facing the colonnade contains the **Museo delle Arti e delle Tradizioni Popolari** (Pl. 14; 3; adm, see p 48).

This museum, divided into ten sections, occupies the first floor of the building. It contains material collected by Lamberto Loria (1855–1913) for the Museo di Etnografia Italiana, founded in Florence in 1906, and illustrates with models, reconstructions, etc. the various aspects of Italian life. The sections are: 1. The cycle of the year; 2. The cycle of human life; 3. The home; 4. Agricultural and pastoral life; 5. Seafaring; 6. Town life; 7. Popular Art; 8. Song, music, and dancing; 9. Costume; 10. Religion.

To the right of the colonnade is the *Palazzo delle Scienze* which contains the **Museo Preistorico ed Etnografico Luigi Pigorini** (Pl. 14; 3). For adm, see p 49.

The museum, one of the most important of its kind in the world, is derived from the collection formed in the late 17C by Father Anastasius Kircher in the Collegio dei Gesuiti. From 1871 onwards it was greatly enlarged by Luigi Pigorini and in 1876 it became the Museo Preistorico del Nuovo Regno d'Italia. Later it grew to such an extent that in 1913 some dispersal became necessary; protohistoric objects went to Villa Giulia, classical and Christian antiquities to the Museo Nazionale Romano, and medieval exhibits to Palazzo di Venezia.

The MUSEO PREISTORICO is arranged geographically to indicate the way civilization developed regionally through the Stone, Bronze and Iron Ages. Most of the exhibits are Italian, of the prehistoric period. They include specimens from all parts of the peninsula, so that a complete idea may be obtained of the growth of its civilization and of the commercial and artistic influences of the East and of the countries bordering on the Aegean. The descriptive labels, maps and diagrams are very informative.

Noteworthy in the collection are: material from cemeteries in the Lazio area; finds of the Italian School in Crete; curious Sardinian statuettes of priests and warriors in bronze; Tomb from Golasecca, representative of the western civilization of Northern Italy. The objects found in the cemeteries of Western and Southern Etruria (Vetulonia, Tarquinii, Vulci, Veii, etc.) are particularly interesting; among them are well-tombs (10–8C BC), with ossuaries resembling those of Villanova, closed with a flat lid or shaped like a house, and trench-tombs (8–7C BC) showing the influence of Greek commerce, especially on pottery.

The ETHNOGRAPHICAL COLLECTION includes material from Brazil, Argentina, and the Amazon region; Polynesia; Arctic circle, American Indian material from North America, Central and South America; New Guinea; Borneo; Oceanic islands; Solomon islands; Fiji; New Caledonia; Australia; Indonesia; North Africa, Ethiopia; Sudan, Nigeria, Uganda, Zaire, Tanzania, East Africa; Zimbabwe, South Africa; India, Burma, and Syria.

Farther along the colonnade, on the right, at Viale Lincoln, is the entrance to the **Museo dell'Alto Medioevo**, which is on the first floor of the Palazzo delle Scienze. A disappointing collection made in 1967, it contains seven rooms of Italian material from the fall of the Roman Empire to the 10C AD. Adm see p 48.

R. I. Head of a Byzantine Emperor and Empress, gold fibula, all of the late 5C found on the Palatine.—R. II. Pottery, glass and gold work (including beautiful jewellery) found in a 7C tomb at Nocera Umbra.—R. III. Contents of a 7C tomb at Castel Trosino, including more very fine jewellery (B, 115, 16), a blue glass rhyton (119), a gold dagger case (F), glass containers (37–45), and fragments of a shield (T).—RR. IV–V. Collection of 7–10C church reliefs and friezes (some of them formerly in the Museo Nazionale Romano).—R. V. Finds from the site of S Cornelia, near Formello, excavated by the British School in 1963–65. Three distinct constructions were found: an early Roman house, a cult building of c 780, and a monastic complex of 1100.—R. VI. 8–9C pottery from the Roman Forum.—R. VII. Fabrics (5–8C), etc.

Beyond the colonnade Viale della Civiltà Romana, leads to the piazza flanked by two symmetrical buildings again joined by a colonnade, the building of which was financed by the Fìat organization. Here is the **Museo della Civiltà Romana** (Pl. 14; 4). Adm, see p 48, but often closed.

The museum was formed from exhibits from the Archaeological Exhibition of 1911 and from the Mostra Augustea della Romanità of 1937. They consist entirely of plaster-casts of famous statues and monuments, and reconstructions of buildings which illustrate the history of Rome and the influence of Roman civilization throughout the world. They are displayed in 59 rooms of monumental proportions. Among the most interesting are a reproduction of the pronaos of the temple of Augustus at Ancyra (R. IX; a model of Roman Bath in England, R. XXIX); a complete collection of casts from Trajan's Column (R. LI), and a reconstruction of part of the Column of M. Aurelius (R. LIX). In R. XXXVII is the celebrated *Plastico di Roma*, a model of Rome as it was in the 4C.

Viale dell'Arte leads left; the second turning to the right is Viale Europa. Here are the ministries of Foreign Trade and Finance, built after the war. Viale Europa ends in steps which lead up to the massive church of *SS. Peter and Paul* (Pl. 13; 3), with a cupola almost as large as that of St Peter's. The first turning right at the foot of the steps leads to the *Piscina delle Rose* in Viale America and a large open-air theatre. Parallel to this road is the *Lake*, divided into three basins, the sides of which are planted with cherry-trees from Japan. This area is perhaps the most successfully planned within the E.U.R. complex. Bridges lead to the *PALAZZO DELLO SPORT* (Pl. 13; 6), designed by Pier Luigi Nervi and Marcello Piacentini for the Olympic Games of 1960, and an outstanding work of modern architecture. Constructed of prefabricated concrete, it is covered by a fine rib-vaulted dome 100 metres in diameter, and seats 15,000 spectators. The *Velodromo Olimpico*, for cycling events, is about 500m E.

About 1km E of the point where Via Cristoforo Colombo crosses Via delle Tre Fontane, and reached by the latter and Via Laurentina, is the **Abbazia delle Tre Fontane** (Pl. 14; 2). This was built on the traditional site of the martyrdom of St Paul, whose severed head, rebounding three times, is supposed to have caused three fountains to spring up. A monastic community from Asia Minor was established here by 641. St Bernard is believed to have stayed here on his visit to Rome in 1138–40. Three churches were built, but the locality was afterwards abandoned as malarial. In 1868 it was acquired by the Trappists, who drained the ground and planted large groves of eucalyptus. A eucalyptus liqueur is distilled in the community. This and chocolate made by the monks are on sale.

An ilex avenue leads to a medieval fortified gate, with a frescoed vault. A small garden contains classical fragments, and is filled with the sound of doves and a fountain. Ahead is the porch of *Santi Vincenzo ed Anastasio. It was founded by Honorius I (625), rebuilt by Honorius III (1221), and has been restored by the Trappists. The spacious plain interior preserves its marble windows. In the nave are poorly restored frescoes of the Apostles (16C).

On the right on high ground, is **Santa Maria Scala Coeli**, an old church with an octagonal interior, rebuilt by *Giac. della Porta* (1582). The design can best be appreciated from the outside. It owes its name to the legend that St Bernard, while celebrating mass, saw in a vision the soul for which he was praying ascend by a ladder from purgatory to heaven. The Cosmatesque altar which was the scene of this miracle is still preserved in the crypt. The mosaics in the left-hand apse (Saints with Clement VIII and his nephew Aldobrandini) are by *Fr. Zucchi* from designs by *Giov. de' Vecchi*.

From the left of this church an avenue leads to **San Paolo alle Tre Fontane**, a 5C church, rebuilt by *Della Porta* in 1599, with a good façade. Inside to the right, is the pillar to which St Paul is supposed to have been bound; on the floor are two Roman mosaic pavements from Ostia.

27 The Vatican City. St Peter's and the Vatican Museums

The **Vatican City** (*Città del Vaticano*; Pl. 1; 5, 6) lies on the right bank of the Tiber. Through the Lateran Treaty (*Il Concordato*) signed at the Lateran Palace on 11 February 1929, the Vatican City has the status of an independent sovereign state. It has no frontier formalities, since it is entirely surrounded by Italian territory. With an area of 43 hectares (less than half a square kilometer) and a population of about 500, it is, in size, the smallest independent state in existence. The States of the Church before the unification of Italy in 1870 extended for 44,547 square kilometres. As the residence of the Pope and the site of St Peter's, the most important Roman Catholic church, it attracts pilgrims from all over the world. The decorations in the Vatican Palace include frescoes in the Sistine Chapel and the 'Stanze' which are the masterpieces of Michelangelo and Raphael. The famous art collections are unique in their scope, quality, and abundance.

The Concordat defined the limits of the Vatican State. They are (counterclockwise) St Peter's Colonnade, Via Porta Angelica, Piazza del Risorgimento, Via Leone IV, Viale Vaticano (which almost encircles the area), Via della Sagrestia, St Peter's Colonnade. The city is surrounded by a high wall, skirted by Viale Vaticano for the whole of its length. A walk round the confines takes about half an hour. On the N side, Viale Vaticano rises fairly steeply, past (left) the entrance to the Vatican Museums, to the top of the hill, known as *Monte Vaticano*. The city wall towers above the street the whole way. At the top Viale

Vaticano bears left and after another left incline, still accompanied by the wall, descends towards St Peter's Colonnade.

The Lateran Treaty also accorded the privilege of extraterritoriality to the basilicas of St John Lateran (with the Lateran Palace), Santa Maria Maggiore and San Paolo fuori le Mura, and to certain other buildings, including the Palazzi della Cancelleria, di Propaganda Fide, del Sant'Uffizio, and dei Convertendi, and to the Pope's villa at Castel Gandolfo. Special clauses in the treaty provide for access to the basilica of St Peter and the art collections of the Vatican Palace. Under the treaty, Italy accepted canon law on marriage and divorce and made religious teaching compulsory in secondary as well as primary schools (clauses which have since been modified). She also agreed to pay 750 million lire in cash and the income from 1000 million lire in Italian State 5 per cent bonds, in final settlement of the claims by the Holy See for the loss of papal property taken over by the Italian Government. After the execution of the Lateran Treaty the Pope, for the first time since 1870, emerged from the Vatican. On 24 June 1929, Pius XI visited St John Lateran. A new Concordat was signed between the Italian Government and the Vatican on 18 February 1984 in Villa Madama. This made religious instruction in schools optional, and contained modifications to the Lateran Treaty regarding marriage, etc.

By the Vatican City law of Pius XI, dated 7 June 1921, the Pope is head of the legislature, executive, and judiciary. He delegates the Cardinal Secretary of State to represent the Vatican in international relations, and nominates the General Council and the Governor of the Vatican. The State has its own postage-stamps, and its own currency. Its newspaper, the *Osservatore Romano*, has a world-wide circulation. It owns a radio transmitting station (prominent in the Second World War) and has its own railway-station, now used only for merchandise.

Security. Within the Vatican City and in the buildings enjoying extraterritoriality, police duties are discharged by the *Swiss Guard*, a corps founded in 1506, which retains the picturesque uniform said to have been designed by Michelangelo. The Noble Guards and Palatine Guards established in the 19C, were disbanded by Pope Paul VI in 1970, and the Pontifical Gendarmes transformed into a private corps.

The Hierarchy. The Sovereign Pontiff is Bishop of Rome, successor to St Peter, and, as such, the head of the Roman Catholic Church and the Vicar of Christ. He enjoys the *primatus jurisdictionis*, that is, the supreme jurisdictional power over the whole Church. He is assisted by the Sacred College of Cardinals and by the Roman Curia. The SACRED COLLEGE OF CARDINALS was limited by Sixtus V to 70, but after the consistory of March 1962 the number was increased to 87. John XXIII created 46 new cardinals, and laid down that they should all enjoy the episcopal dignity. At present there is no limit to the number of cardinals who can be appointed. The College consists of six Cardinal Bishops (whose dioceses are the suburbicarian sees of Ostia, Velletri, Porto and Santa Rufina, Albano, Frascati, and Palestrina), nearly 70 Cardinal Priests, and 14 Cardinal Deacons. The ROMAN CURIA comprises the 12 *Sacred Congregations*, which deal with the central administration of the Church, the three *Tribunals*, and the six *Offices*: among these last is that of the Segretario di Stato.

Conclave (Latin, a room that may be locked). On the death of a pope, the cardinals (only those under the age of 80) confine themselves in a chosen locality—usually the Sistine Chapel—to elect a new pope. The place chosen is locked both inside and outside and it includes rooms for the cardinals and their attendants. The internal guardian is the Camerlengo; the external guardian the Commander of the Swiss Guard. The cardinals meet twice daily and, having sworn to elect the individual who, under God, shall deserve the honour, proceed to the voting and the scrutiny of the votes. The result of their deliberation is indicated to the waiting world by the colour of the smoke which issues from a vent above the Sistine Chapel. If the smoke is black the election is still in doubt; if white, the new pope has been elected. The old practice of burning the voting papers (mixed with damp straw for the black) to produce the smoke, was discontinued after the conclave of 1958. The final result is proclaimed from the central balcony of the façade of St Peter's, from where also the newly elected pope blesses the city and the world. Since the proceedings must take some time, there is always an interregnum (of 15–20 days) between the death of a pope and the election of his successor. So that Paul VI died on 6 August and John Paul I was elected on 26 August 1978; John Paul I died on 29 September and John Paul II was elected on 16 October 1978.

Holy Year. In adapting the Jewish idea of the jubilee, which was secular in content, the Roman Catholic Church gave it an exclusively religious meaning, and for the remission of debts substituted the remission of the temporal punishment due to sin. The first Holy Year was proclaimed from the balcony of St John Lateran on 22 February 1300, by Boniface VIII. The pope gave a plenary indulgence to those confessed communicants who, on the occasion of every centenary of the birth of Christ, should visit the four major basilicas—St Peter, St Paul, St John Lateran, and Santa Maria Maggiore—within a specified time. In 1343 Clement VI reduced the interval from 100 to 33 years and Paul II (1464–71) to 25 years. This quarter-century interval has been maintained, with few exceptions, ever since: i.e. in 1900, 1925, 1950, and 1975. In addition to the regular celebrations, a Jubilee may occasionally be proclaimed for a special reason, as in 1933, when Pius XI commemorated the 19th centenary of the Crucifixion, or in 1983/4 when John Paul II commemorated the 1950 years since the death and resurrection of Christ.

The Holy Year is usually inaugurated on the preceding Christmas Eve with the opening of the *Holy Doors* of the four major basilicas. The Holy Door of St Peter's (Porta Santa) is opened by the Pope; the other three are opened by their respective archpriests. In the past the Pope used a silver hammer and the wall in front of the door, having been previously cut round the edges, fell inwards. In 1983 the Pope instead used a bronze hammer and the Porta Santa was unlocked for him. The Pope, bareheaded and bearing a torch, crosses the threshold, followed by his cardinals and attendants. At the end of the Holy Year the Holy Doors are reclosed by the Pope.

Access to the Vatican City. For adm to St Peter's and to the Vatican Museums and Sistine Chapel (see pp 294, 303). A ticket must be purchased in advance (see p 341) to join the organized tours of the Vatican City and gardens. The entrances to the Vatican City are three. The famous BRONZE DOOR (*Portone di Bronzo*), to the right and in front of St Peter's, is the main entrance; it is reserved for ecclesiastical and civil dignitaries; it was kept closed from 1870 to 1929. The *Arco delle Campane* (Arch of the Bells), to the left of St Peter's is used by the organized tours of the gardens and City; it is also the means of access to the Necropolis below St Peter's. The *Cancello di Sant' Anna* (Gate of St Anne), in Via di Porta Angelica, to the right of St Peter's, is used for the Polyglot Printing Press and the offices of the *Osservatore Romano*.—The *Entrance to the Vatican Museums*, in the Viale Vaticano, gives access to the museums only, and not to the gardens outside them.

An **Information Office** is open every day except Sunday (8.30–18.30) in St Peter's Square to the left of the façade of the basilica. In St Peter's and the Vatican city visitors are not allowed to wear shorts, and ladies must have their shoulders covered.

Audience of the Pope. Application to attend can be made in writing to the Prefetto della Casa Pontificia (Prefect of the Pontifical Household), Città del Vaticano, 00120 Rome, or in person, preferably 1–2 days before the Audience. Applicants enter by the Bronze Door (open 9–13.30) on the right of the Piazza. At the far end of the entrance hall (Corridore del Bernini) is the Scala Regia, the staircase leading to the Sala Regia. At a table just within the entrance a form must be completed and taken to the office of the Prefettura, on the first floor of the Staircase of Pius IX (Scala Pia). Applicants are asked to state the period within which the audience is requested, their nationality, and address in Rome, with telephone number. Written permission is then received from the Prefettura.

General Audiences normally take place at 10 or 11 o'clock on Wednesday mornings in the New Audience Hall (see p 342), reached under the colonnade to the left of the façade of St Peter's. A special section is set aside for newly-married couples. Audiences are now also sometimes held in St Peter's, or in the Piazza (when the Pope is transported by jeep).

A. St Peter's

*Piazza San Pietro (Pl. 1; 6), the masterpiece of *Bernini* (1656–67), is one of the most superb conceptions of its kind in civic architecture, and is a fitting approach to the world's greatest basilica. Partly enclosed by two semicircular colonnades, it has the form of an ellipse adjoining an almost rectangular quadrilateral. At the end, above a triple flight of steps, rises the basilica, with the buildings of the

Vatican towering on the right. Each of the two colonnades has a quadruple row of Doric columns, forming three parallel covered walks. There are in all 284 columns and 88 pilasters. On the Ionic entablature are 96 statues of saints and martyrs. In the middle of the piazza is the *Obelisk of the Vatican* and on either side a fountain. Traffic is now excluded from the Piazza.

The **Obelisk**, devoid of hieroglyphics, is 25·5m high; on a high plinth, it is surmounted by a cross. It was brought from Alexandria (where it had been set up by Augustus) in AD 37 and placed by Caligula possibly on the spina of his circus, later called the Circus of Nero. In 1586 Sixtus V ordered its removal from the S of the basilica to its present site and put Dom. Fontana in charge of operations. No fewer than 900 men, 150 horses, and 47 cranes were required. The task was completed on 18 September 1586. It is said that Sixtus V forbade the spectators, under pain of death, to speak while the obelisk was being raised into position. A sailor, Bresca, seeing that the tension on the ropes had not been correctly assessed and that they were giving way under the strain, transgressed the order, shouted 'Acqua alle funi' ('Wet the ropes') and so averted catastrophe. The Pope rewarded him by granting his family the privilege of supplying St Peter's with palms for Palm Sunday. The incident, now discredited as an 18C fabrication, is said to have been the origin of the industry, still flourishing at Bordighera, of exporting palm. Round the foot of the obelisk is a plan of the mariner's compass, giving the names of the winds. The globe which surmounted the obelisk until 1586, when it was replaced by a cross, is now in Palazzo dei Conservatori.

The two *Fountains* are beautifully designed. The one on the right is by Carlo Maderno (1614), although a similar fountain had existed in the piazza since 1490. It was moved to its present site and slightly modified by Bernini in 1667, when the second fountain was begun. The two are remarkable for their abundance of water, supplied by the Acqua Paola. Between the obelisk and each fountain is a round porphyry slab from which the spectator obtains the illusion that each of the colonnades has only a single row of columns.

Panorama from the dome of St Peter's showing the Borgo
before the construction of Via della Conciliazione in 1937

In the Piazza on 13 May 1981 a Turk, Mehmet Ali Agca made an attempt on the life of John Paul II.

Covered galleries, also decorated with statues, unite the colonnades with the portico of St Peter's. The gallery on the right, known as the *Corridore del Bernini* and leading to the Scala Regia, is closed by the BRONZE DOOR (*Portone di Bronzo*), the main entrance to the Vatican. That on the left is skirted outside by Via della Sagrestia, one of the frontier streets of the Vatican city. The centre of the square is largely taken up by the great staircase, of three flights, leading up to the portico of the basilica. At the foot are colossal statues of St Peter, by *Gius. de Fabris*, and of St Paul, by *Adamo Tadolini*, set up here by Pius IX in place of two older statues now in the Vatican radio building.

To the S of St Peter's Colonnade, outside the Vatican City, but enjoying the privilege of extraterritoriality is **Palazzo del Sant'Uffizio**. The Holy Office, commonly known as the Inquisition, was established here in 1536 by Paul III to inquire into charges of heresy, unbelief, and other offences against religion. In Rome and the Papal States the Holy Office exercised a severe control over heresy and the suspicion of heresy but never, so far as is known, ordered the death of anyone found guilty, and the excessive rigours of the Spanish Inquisition were condemned by the Renaissance popes. The preparation of the Index of Prohibited Books was originally entrusted to the Congregation of the Holy Office. In 1571 Pius V established a special Congregation of the Index, which survived until its suppression by Benedict XV in 1917, when the duties were resumed by the Holy Office. The tribunal was formally abolished by the Roman Assembly in February 1849, but it was re-established by Pius IX a few months later. To the right the former *Palazzo del Museo Petriano* has been taken over by Vatican Radio.

To the S of the Palazzo del Sant'Uffizio, at the W end of the Traforo Principe Amedeo, is the site of the *Porta Cavalleggeri*, named after a cavalry barracks in the vicinity. Close by is Largo di Porta Cavalleggeri, starting-point of the Via Aurelia.

St Peter's, or the **Basilica di San Pietro in Vaticano (Pl. 1; 5, 6), is perhaps the most imposing church of Christendom. Though neither a cathedral nor the mother church of the Catholic faith, it is the composite work of some of the greatest artists of the 16C, and a masterpiece of the late Italian Renaissance. Orientated towards the west and approached through the monumental piazza, the church has its fitting culmination in Michelangelo's dome.

History. According to the Liber Pontificalis, Pope St Anacletus built an oratory (c AD 90) over the tomb of St Peter, close to the Circus of Nero, near which he had been martyred. Modern research, however, points to a confusion of names and the likelihood that Pope St Aniceths (155–66) was responsible. On the site of this oratory Constantine, at the request of Pope St Sylvester I, began to build a basilica c 319–22; it was consecrated on 18 November 326. The basilica was 120m long and 65m wide, about half the size of the present edifice. It was preceded by a great quadrangular colonnaded portico. The nave and double aisles were divided by 86 marble columns, some of which were said to have been taken from the Septizonium on the Palatine (if so, this was long before the demolition of that building by Sixtus V). Adorned with numerous monuments of popes, emperors, and others, and enlivened with frescoes and mosaics, it attracted pilgrims from all over Europe. Charlemagne was crowned here by Leo III in 800. Some of its relics are preserved (see below). Its façade is shown in the painting 'Incendio di Borgo' in Raphael's Stanza dell'Incendio in the Vatican.

In the middle of the 15C the old basilica showed signs of collapse, and Nicholas V (1447–55) resolved to rebuild it, realizing its importance to the prestige of the Roman Catholic faith. He entrusted the work to *Bern. Rossellino, Leon Batt. Alberti*, and *Giuliano da Sangallo*, but on the death of Nicholas in 1455 it was virtually suspended for half a century. Julius II (1503–13) decided on a complete reconstruction. He employed *Bramante*, who started work in 1506. Bramante began by dismantling the greater part of the old church and destroying much that might have been preserved: so much so that he gained the nickname of 'Bramante Ruinante'. His plan for the new basilica was a Greek cross surmounted by a gigantic central dome and flanked by four smaller

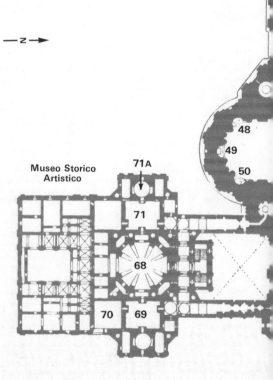

ST PETER'S

| 0 | 10 | 20 | 30 yds |
| 0 | 10 | 20 | 30 ms |

N →

Museo Storico Artistico

71A

71

68

70 69

48

49

50

1

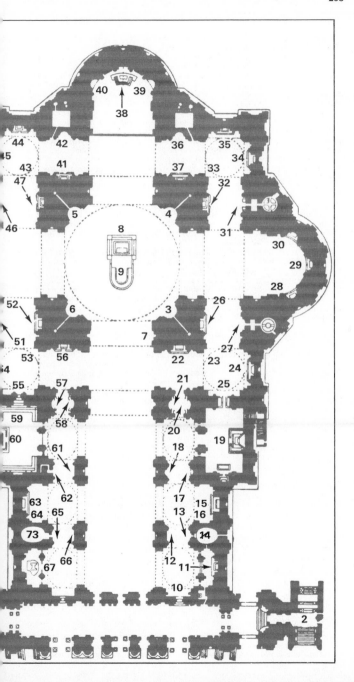

cupolas. When he died in 1514, the four central piers and the arches of the dome had been completed.

From now on the history of St Peter's is one of conflicting plans, each architect (with few exceptions) reversing the policy of his predecessor. Bramante's Greek cross did not find favour with his successor, who planned a Latin cross. After that Greek and Latin alternated four times, Latin finally prevailing.

Leo X (1513–21), who succeeded Julius II, summoned *Raphael* to direct the work in collaboration with *Fra Giocondo* (died 1515) and *Giul. da Sangallo* (died 1516). Raphael's plan envisaged a Latin cross, but on his death in 1520 *Bald. Peruzzi* reverted to Bramante's design. Neither Adrian VI (1522–23), the austere theologian who regarded art as hostile to the Church, nor the hapless Clement VII (1523–34), overwhelmed by political disturbances brought about by the Reformation, and culminating in the sack of Rome (1527), were interested in the progress of the basilica. However, under Paul III (1534–49) the work received fresh impetus from *Ant. da Sangallo the Younger*, who adopted the Latin cross plan. At his death in 1546, *Michelangelo*, then seventy-two years old, was summoned by Paul III. He decided on the Greek cross originally planned by Bramante, and developed Bramante's idea with even greater audacity. Regarding the Pantheon as unambitious, he took Brunelleschi's Florentine cupola for his model, and substituted piers of tremendous strength for those of Bramante, though deriving from the Pantheon his plan for the façade. Confirmed in his appointment by Paul III's successors, he continued to direct the work until his death in 1564. His successors *Vignola* and *Pirro Ligorio* were followed by *Giac. della Porta* (assisted by *Carlo Fontana*), who completed the dome in 1590, and added the two smaller domes.

In 1605 Paul V demolished what had been left of the old basilica, pulled down the incomplete façade and directed *Carlo Maderno* to lengthen the nave towards the old Piazza San Pietro. The present façade and portico are Maderno's work. Thus, after many vicissitudes, the plan of the Latin cross has triumphed. On 18 Nov. 1626, the 1300th anniversary of the original consecration, Urban VIII consecrated the new church. *Bernini*, who succeeded Maderno in 1629, and was charged with the decoration of the interior, wished to erect two campanili by the façade, but the one that he completed began to crack on its sinking foundations and was pulled down, much to Borromini's satisfaction. Alexander VII kept Bernini as architect of St Peter's, and under him the piazza was begun in 1656. The Sacristy was built in the 18C.

In 1940 systematic excavations were begun beneath St Peter's. Beneath the Vatican Grottoes the excavators discovered the ancient cemetery in which St Peter was buried after his crucifixion. On 23 Dec. 1950, the Pope announced that the tomb of St Peter had been identified (see p 302).

Dimensions. The exterior length of the church, including the portico is 211·5m; the cross on the dome is 136·5m above the ground. The façade is 115m long, and 45·5m high. Within, the church is 186m long and 137m wide across the transepts. The nave is 60m across (including the aisles) and 44m high; the diameter of the dome is 42m or 1·5m less than that of the Pantheon. The total area is 49,737 sq. m (St Paul's in London is 26,639 sq. m).

Admission. The basilica is open daily from 7–19 (18 in winter). Visitors are not allowed to enter the Basilica wearing shorts, and ladies must not have bare shoulders. Mass is held on Sunday at 7, 8, 9, and 10 (Sung Mass at 10.30), and frequently during the week. Holy Communion may be taken in the Cappella del Santissimo Sacramento throughout the day on Sunday.

Exterior. At the top of the triple flight of steps rises the long FAÇADE. Its great size impairs the view of the dome from the piazza. Eight columns and four pilasters support the entablature. A dedicatory inscription on the frieze records its erection in 1612, during the pontificate of Paul V. The attic, almost without ornament, is surmounted by a balustrade on which are statues of Christ, St John the Baptist, and eleven of the Apostles (St Peter's statue is inside), and two clocks, by *Valadier* (near the ends). Under the left-hand clock are the six bells of the basilica, electrically operated since 1931. The oldest bell dates from 1288; the largest (1786) is 7·5m round and weighs 9·75 tons.

Above the doors and extending beyond them on either side is a row of nine large windows with balconies. The central balcony is that from which the senior cardinal-deacon proclaims the newly-elected pope and from which the Pope blesses the city and the world. The ceremony, discontinued in 1870, was revived by Pius XI after the concordat. Below the balcony is a relief, by *Ambr. Bonvicino*, of Christ handing the keys to St Peter.

The PORTICO is prolonged by vestibules at both ends connecting with the covered galleries of the piazza.

The pavement was designed by *Bernini*. The vault is magnificently decorated in stucco, by *Martino Ferrabosco*; in the lunettes below it are 32 statues of canonized popes. Of the five entrances to the church, that on the extreme right is the HOLY DOOR (*Porta Santa*), opened only in Holy Years. The central *Bronze Doors, from Old St Peter's, were decorated by *Filarete* in 1439–45 with reliefs of Christ, the Virgin, SS. Peter and Paul and their martyrdom, and events in the life of Pope Eugenius IV; the whole is enclosed in a frieze of classical and mythological subjects, animals, fruits, and portraits of emperors. Between the doors are three inscriptions. From the left, Commemorating the donation by Gregory II of certain olive trees to provide oil for the lamps over the tomb of St Peter; Latin epitaph of Adrian (772–95), attributed to Charlemagne; Bull of Boniface VIII proclaiming the first jubilee or Holy Year (1300). The other doors are modern: the one on the extreme right (the Porta Santa) is by *Vico Consorti* (1950), and the one to the right of the main door, is by *Venanzio Crocetti* (1968); the door on the extreme left is by *Luciano Minguzzi* (1977), and the one to the left of the main door by *Giacomo Manzù* (1963), with sculptures depicting the death of religious figures and abstract themes of death.—In the tympanum, above the central entrance (that is, looking backwards, against the light) is the famous *NAVICELLA, a mosaic representing Christ walking upon the waters, executed by *Giotto* for the old basilica. Because of frequent removals it has suffered from resetting and restoration, and is now virtually a copy of the original.

The equestrian statue of Charlemagne (1), at the left end of the portico, is by *Cornacchini*; that on the right, of *Constantine (2) by *Bernini*, is beyond a door which gives access to the corridor leading to the Scala Regia. This is often open for visitors leaving the Sistine Chapel.

The immensity of the vast **Interior** is disguised by the symmetry of its proportions. The work of *Bernini* for this majestic church, which had begun with the Ponte Sant'Angelo and was continued in the piazza, culminates in the magnificent baldacchino and exedra in the tribune. As the shrine of St Peter, the whole has a ceremonial air, with temporary pews beneath the gilded coffered ceiling designed by *Bramante*. The coloured marble of the walls and pavement is the work of *Giac. della Porta* and *Bernini*.

NAVE. The first part of the nave, with its aisles and three side chapels, is Maderno's extension, which transformed the plan of the church from a Greek to a Latin cross. The round slab of porphyry let into the pavement in front of the central door is that on which the emperors used to kneel for their coronation in front of the altar of the old basilica. Farther on are metal lines indicating the lengths of the principal churches of Europe. The nave is separated from the aisles by colossal piers, each decorated with two fluted Corinthian pilasters, supporting great arches. In the niches between the pilasters of the nave and transepts are statues of the founders of the religious orders. The aisles have sumptuous decorations by Bernini. Over the spaces between the piers are elliptical cupolas—three on either side—elaborate with mosaics. In addition to these six minor cupolas there are four circular domes over the corner chapels in the main body of the church, where the sessions of the second Vatican Council took place in 1962–65.

The *DOME is an architectural masterpiece. Simple and dignified, and flooded with light, it rises immediately above the site of St Peter's tomb. Four pentagonal PIERS support the arches on which rests the drum of the cupola. The piers are decorated with balconies and niches designed by Bernini. Each balcony has two spiral columns taken from the saint's shrine in the old basilica (another of these columns is the Colonna Santa; see below). The niches are filled with colossal statues, which give each of the piers its name. Beginning from the right (NE) and going counter-clockwise, they are: *St Longinus (3), by *Bernini*; St Helena (4), by *And. Bolgi*; St Veronica (5), by *Fr. Mochi*; St Andrew (6), by *Fr. Duquesnoy*. On the balconies are reliefs referring to the 'Reliquie Maggiori'; these relics, which are displayed in Holy Week, are preserved in the podium of the pier of St Veronica. They are the lance of St Longinus, the soldier who pierced the side of Christ on the Cross, presented to Innocent VIII; a piece of the True Cross, collected by St Helena; and the napkin of St Veronica, with the miraculous image of the Saviour. The head of St Andrew, presented to Pius II in 1462 by Thomas Paleologos, despot of the Morea, was recently returned to the Greek Orthodox Church at Patras.

The Latin inscription on the frieze of the dome is a continuation of the Greek inscription in the tribune. In the pendentives of the dome are mosaics of the Evangelists; the scale of the decorations will be appreciated when it is realized that the pen of St Mark is 1·5m long. On the frieze below the drum is inscribed in letters nearly 2m high: 'Tu es Petrus et super hanc petram aedificabo ecclesiam meam et tibi dabo claves regni caelorum.' The dome is divided into sixteen compartments, corresponding to the windows of the drum, by ribs ornamented with stucco; in these compartments are six bands of mosaic by the *Cav. d'Arpino*, representing saints, angels, and the company of Heaven; in the lantern above is the Almighty.

Under a canopy against the pier of St Longinus, facing inwards, is the famous bronze *STATUE OF ST PETER (7), seated on a marble throne. It was once believed to date from the 5C or 6C, but is now considered to be the work of *Arnolfo di Cambio* (c 1296). The extended foot of the statue has been worn away by the kisses of the faithful. The statue is robed on high festivals. Above is a portrait in mosaic of Pius IX (1871).

Over the high altar rises the great *BALDACCHINO (8), designed by *Bernini* and unveiled on 28 June 1633, by Urban VIII. This colossal Baroque structure, a combination of architecture and decorative sculpture, is cast of bronze taken from the Pantheon. Four gilt bronze solomonic columns rise from their marble plinths, which are decorated with the Barberini bees. The columns resemble in design the Colonna Santa (see below) but are decorated with figures of genii and laurel branches. They support a canopy from which hang festoons and tassels and on which angels (by *Duquesnoy*) alternate with children. From the four corners of the canopy ascend ornamental scrolls, which support the globe and cross. Inside the top of the canopy is the Dove in an aureole.

The HIGH ALTAR, at which only the Pope may celebrate, is formed of a block of Greek marble found in the Forum of Nerva and consecrated by Clement VIII on 26 June 1594. It covers the altar of Calixtus II (d 1123) which in turn encloses an altar of Gregory the Great (d 604). It stands over the space which is recognized as the tomb of St Peter.

In front (9) is the CONFESSIONE, built by *Maderno* and encircled by perpetually burning lamps. When excavations began in 1940, it was discovered that the foundations of the Confessione were hollow. When they were opened, they led into the ancient Roman necropolis below the Vatican Grottoes. Here was found the Tropaion of Gaius.

RIGHT AISLE. Above the Porta Santa is a mosaic of St Peter (10), designed by *Ciro Ferri* (1675). The CAPPELLA DELLA PIETÀ (11) is named after *Michelangelo*'s exquisite *Pietà (1499; restored and protected by glass since its damage in 1972), executed in the artist's 25th year for the French ambassador, Card. Villiers de la Groslay. This is perhaps the most moving of all Michelangelo's sculptures and is the only one inscribed with his name (on the ribbon falling from the left shoulder of the Virgin). The mosaic decorations of the cupola, by *Pietro da Cortona* and *Ciro Ferri*, depict the Passion. The triumph of the Cross is by *Lanfranco*.—Under the first arch of the aisle are a monument to Queen Christina of Sweden (12), by *Carlo Fontana* (1689), and opposite, a statue of Leo XII (13), by *De Fabris* (1836). Beneath it is the entrance to the small CAPPELLA DEL CROCIFISSO (14; usually closed), with a Crucifixion ascribed to *Pietro Cavallini*.

The CAPPELLA DI SAN SEBASTIANO (15) has an altar mosaic of the saint's martyrdom, after *Domenichino*. The monument to Pius XI (d 1939; 16) is by *Fr. Nagni*. Opposite, a monument to Pius XII (d 1958) by *Francesco Messina*. Under the next arch are the fine Baroque monument to Innocent XII (d 1700; 17), by *Filippo Valle*, and one by *Bernini* (18) of the Countess Matilda of Tuscany (d 1115), whose remains were moved from Mantua in 1635.—The iron grille of the *CAPPELLA DEL SANTISSIMO SACRAMENTO (19) was designed by *Borromini*. Over the altar is a gilt bronze ciborium by *Bernini*, modelled on Bramante's 'tempietto' at San Pietro in Montorio. The two angels also form part of this unfinished composition. Behind is the Trinity, by *Pietro da Cortona*. Over the altar on the right is a mosaic, Ecstasy of St Francis, after *Domenichino*.—Under the next arch are the interesting monument (20) to Gregory XIII (d 1585), the reformer of the calendar (by *Rusconi*; 1723), and the unfinished tomb (21) of Gregory XIV (d 1591). Opposite, on the pier of St Longinus, is a *Mosaic of the Communion of St Jerome (22), after *Domenichino*.

The CAPPELLA GREGORIANA (23) was built by Gregory XIII from designs by *Michelangelo*, with a cupola 42m above the floor. The chapel is dedicated to the Madonna del Soccorso, an ancient painting on part of a marble column from the old basilica, placed here in 1578 (24). Beneath the altar is the tomb of St Gregory Nazianzen, and on the right is that of Gregory XVI (d 1846), by *Luigi Amici* (1855; 25).— Under the next arch is the Altar of St Basil (26); over it is the Mass of St Basil, a mosaic after *Subleyras*. Opposite is the tomb of Benedict XIV (27), by *Bracci*; the statue of the Pope (d 1758) shows him proclaiming the Holy Year of 1750. Here is the present entrance to the cupola (see below).

The RIGHT TRANSEPT was used for the sessions of the council in 1869–70. Its three altars are decorated with mosaics; St Wenceslas (28), after *Angelo Caroselli*; the Martyrdom of SS. Processus and Martinian, St Peter's gaolers, after *Valentin* (29); the Martyrdom of St Erasmus (30), after *Nic. Poussin* (1629).—In the arch beyond are the celebrated *Monument of Clement XIII (31), by *Canova*, and, against the pier of St Helena, the Altar of the Navicella (32), with a mosaic of Christ walking on the waters, after *Lanfranco*; the subject is the same as that of Giotto's mosaics in the portico.

The CAPPELLA DI SAN MICHELE (33) contains mosaics of St Michael (34), after *Guido Reni*, and of *St Petronilla (35), by *Cristofari* after *Guercino*. This chapel, in the NW corner of the basilica, has a round cupola, decorated with mosaics of angels, and pendentives with mosaics of the Doctors of the Church, after *Romanelli* and *Sacchi*.— To the left (36) is the monument of Clement X (d 1676), by *De Rossi* and others; opposite, on the pier of St Helena, is a mosaic of St Peter raising Tabitha, after *Placido Costanzi* (37).

Two porphyry steps from the old basilica lead to the TRIBUNE, the most conspicuous object in which is the *CHAIR OF ST PETER (38), an ambitious and theatrical composition by *Bernini* (1665). This enormous gilt bronze throne is supported by statues of four Fathers of the Church: SS. Augustine and Ambrose, of the Latin Church (in mitres), and SS. Athanasius and John Chrysostom, of the Greek Church (bareheaded). It encloses an ancient wooden chair inlaid with ivory, said to have been the episcopal chair of St Peter. A great halo of gilt stucco surrounds the Dove set in the window above the throne; outside the halo is a circle of flying angels.—On the right of St Peter's Chair is the fine *Monument to Urban VIII (died 1644), also by *Bernini*, with statues of the pope and allegorical figures of Charity and Justice (39). The design of the tomb is clearly influenced by the Medici tombs in Florence by Michelangelo. The use of different materials in the sculpture give an effective colour to the monument. On the left is the Monument to Paul III (died 1549; 40), by *Gugl. della Porta*, a less successful attempt at the same type of tomb sculpture and design.—Beyond the tribune, on the pier of St Veronica, is a mosaic of St Peter healing the paralytic, after *Fr. Mancini* (41); opposite is the monument to Alexander VIII (died 1691; 42), by *Arrigo di San Martino*; the bronze statue of the pope is by *Gius. Bertosi*, and the other sculptures are by *Angelo De Rossi*.

LEFT AISLE. The CAPPELLA DELLA COLONNA (43), one of the corner chapels with round cupolas, was decorated in 1757 with figures of angels carrying garlands and with symbols of the Virgin. The lunettes have mosaics after *Fr. Romanelli*. In this chapel is the tomb of St Leo the Great (died 461; 44); above is a *Relief by *Aless. Algardi* (1650), representing St Leo arresting the progress of Attila with the aid of SS. Peter and Paul. On the altar (left, 45) is an ancient and greatly venerated representation of the Virgin painted on a column from the old basilica. In the middle of the chapel is the tombstone of Leo XII (died 1829).—Under the next arch is the monument of Alexander VII (died 1667; 46), *Bernini*'s last work in St Peter's. Although the design is original, the execution is not very careful. Opposite is a mosaic (47), Apparition of the Sacred Heart, after *Carlo Muccioli*, set here in 1922 by Benedict XV in place of an oil-painting on slate (Punishment of Simon Magus, by Fr. Vanni).

The LEFT TRANSEPT contains confessionals for foreigners, served by the Penitentiaries, who hear confessions in ten languages. The three altars are decorated with mosaics; St Thomas (48), after *Vinc. Camuccini*; Crucifixion of St Peter (40), after *Guido Reni*; and St Joseph (50). In front of the central altar is the tomb of Palestrina (1594) by Achille Funi.

Over the door to the Sacristy (see below) is the neo-classical monument to Pius VIII (died 1830), by *Pietro Tenerani* (51); opposite, against the pier of St Andrew, Ananias, and Sapphira (52), a mosaic after *Pomarancio*.—The CAPPELLA CLEMENTINA (53) is the fourth of the corner chapels with round cupolas; the cupola is decorated with mosaics after *Pomarancio*; in the pendentives are four Doctors of the Church. The chapel is named after Clement VIII (died 1605), who ordered *Giac. della Porta* to decorate it for the jubilee of 1600. It contains the tomb of St Gregory the Great (died 604; 54), beneath the altar. Above it is a mosaic of a miracle of St Gregory, after *And. Sacchi*.—To the left of the altar is the monument to Pius VII (died 1823), by *Thorvaldsen*, a classical work showing the influence of Canova (55).

On the E side of the pier of St Andrew is a Mosaic of the Transfiguration (56), after *Raphael*, four times as large as the original in the Vatican. Opposite, beneath the aisle arch, are the monuments of *Leo XI, who reigned for only 27 days (died 1605; 57), by *Algardi*, and of Innocent XI (died 1689; 58), by *Pierre Monnot* (the urn decorated with a relief of the liberation of Vienna by John Sobieski).—The CAPPELLA DEL CORO (59) is richly decorated in stucco by *G.B. Ricci* after designs by *Giac. della Porta*. It is closed by a fine gate with the arms of Clement XIII. It is furnished with elegant classical stalls by *Bernini*, and two large organs. The altarpiece (60), after a painting by *Pietro Bianchi*, represents the Immaculate Conception. In the pavement is the simple tombstone of Clement XI (died 1721).—Under the next arch is the bronze *Monument to Innocent VIII (died 1492; 61), by *Antonio Pollaiuolo*, the only monument from the old basilica to be recreated in the new. The Pope is represented by two bronze statues; one recumbent on the urn, the other seated and holding in the left hand a spearhead, in allusion to his reception from the sultan Bajazet II of the spear that pierced the side of Christ. Opposite (62) is the monument to St Pius X (died 1914), by *Pier Enrico Astorri*. The ceremony of the canonization of Pius X took place on 26 May 1954.

The CAPPELLA DELLA PRESENTAZIONE (63) is named after its altar-mosaic of the Presentation of the Virgin, after *Fr. Romanelli*; beneath the altar is the tomb of St Pius X. The cupola is decorated with a mosaic, after *Carlo Maratta*, exalting the glory of the Virgin. On the right is a monument to Pope John XXIII, by Emilio Greco. On the left is the monument to Benedict XV (died 1922; 64), by *Pietro Canonica*.—Under the next arch are the Stuart monuments: above the door on the right (now used as an exit from the cupola, see below) is the monument (65) to Clementina Sobieska (died 1735), wife of James Stuart, the Old Pretender (she is here called Queen of Great Britain, France, and Ireland), by *Barigioni*; on the left is the *Monument to the last Stuarts (66), by *Canova*, with busts of the Old and Young Pretenders (died 1766 and 1788) and of Henry, Cardinal York (died 1807). George IV contributed to the expense of this monument.

In the BAPTISTERY (67) the cover of a porphyry sarcophagus, placed upside-down, is used as the font. It formerly covered the tomb of the Emperor Otho II (973–83; in the Grottoes). According to a tradition (now discredited), the sarcophagus came from the sepulchral cella of Hadrian's mausoleum (Castel Sant'Angelo) and was the emperor's own. The present metal cover is by *Carlo Fontana*. The mosaics reproduce paintings of the Baptism of Christ, by *C. Maratta*; of St Peter baptizing the centurion Cornelius, by *And. Procaccini*; and of St Peter baptizing his gaolers SS. Processus and Martinian, by *Gius. Passeri*.—At the end of the nave can be seen the back of the doors by *Giac. Manzù*, with a dedicatory inscription.

The **Treasury** is entered by the door under the monument to Pius VIII (51). It was transformed in 1975 into modern exhibition rooms and arranged as a museum (adm 9–18.30; in winter 9–12.30 and 15–16.30). The harsh illumination in the dark rooms has been justly criticized.—In the VESTIBULE is a large stone slab with the names of the popes buried in the basilica, from St Peter to Pius XII. A corridor leads to the entrance of the Museum.

The Treasury was plundered in 846 by the Saracens, and again during the sack of Rome in 1527 by Imperial troops, and was impoverished by the provisions of the Treaty of Tolentino (1797), which Pius VI was constrained to conclude with Napoleon. It still, however, contains objects of great value and interest. The exhibits include vestments, missals, reliquaries, pyxes, patens, chalices, monstrances, crucifixes, and other sacred relics, as well as candelabra and ornaments.

ROOM I. The *Colonna Santa, a 4C Byzantine spiral column, one of twelve from the old basilica (eight decorate the balconies of the great piers of the dome in St Peter's; the remaining three are lost). The column was once thought to be that against which Christ leaned when speaking with the doctors in the Temple. The gilt bronze Cock (9C) used to decorate the top of the campanile of the old basilica.—R. II SAGRESTIA DEI BENEFICIATI; 71). *Crux Vaticana, the most ancient possession of the Treasury, dating from the 6C, the gift of the emperor Justinian II. It is made of bronze and set with jewels. So-called *Dalmatic of Charlemagne, now usually considered to date from the 11C or the early 15C; Byzantine case with an enamelled Cross; fragment of a Byzantine diptych in ivory; copy (1974) of the ancient Chair of St Peter, now incorporated in Bernini's decoration in the Tribune of St Peter's.—CAPPELLA DELLA SAGRESTIA DEI BENEFICIATI (71A). Here is the beautiful *Ciborium of Donatello (c 1432), from the old basilica. Inside is preserved a painting of the Madonna della Febbre (the protectress of malaria) attrib. to Lippo Memmi. Over the chapel altar is St Peter receiving the keys, by Girol. Muziano. A plaster-cast of Michelangelo's Pietà in St Peter's is also displayed here.—ROOM IV. *Monument of Sixtus IV, a masterpiece in bronze by Ant. Pollaiuolo (1493). It can be seen to advantage from the raised platform.—ROOM V. Ceremonial ring of Sixtus IV (1471–84); Reliquary Bust of St Luke the Evangelist (13C–14C), and a wood Crucifix probably dating from the 14C.

A passage containing illuminated manuscripts, including one from the Giulia choir (1543) and a 17C ivory Crucifix leads to ROOM VI. Here are displayed a Cross and Candelabra by Seb. Torrigiani; a Crucifix and six candelabra (1581; removed for restoration in 1984) made by Ant. Gentili for Card. Aless. Farnese and presented by him to the basilica in 1582; and two huge *Candelabra of the 16C, traditionally attrib. to Cellini.—R. VII. Model of an Angel in clay by Bernini (1673) used for one of the angels flanking the ciborium in the Cappella del Sacramento; 13C Slavonic icon in a jewelled silver frame, and reliquaries.—R. VIII. Gilt bronze tiara (early 18C) for the statue of St Peter; on high festivals this statue is attired in full pontificals. Gold Chalice set with diamonds (18C), bequeathed to the Vatican by Henry Stuart, Cardinal York; Platinum Chalice, presented by Charles III of Spain to Pius VI, interesting as the first recorded use of platinum for such a purpose—R. IX. *Sarcophagus of Junius Bassus, prefect of Rome in 359. This was found near the Basilica in the 16C, and is superbly carved.

From the entrance, to the museum a second corridor leads right, off which is the Sacristy (68; open only 7–12). Known as the Sagrestia Comune its construction was ordered by Pius VI in 1776; he gave the work to Carlo Marchionni, who completed it in 1784. It is an octagonal hall with a cupola supported by pilasters of yellow Siena marble and grey marble columns from Hadrian's Villa near Tivoli.

To the left is the SAGRESTIA DEI CANONICI (69; special permit required, but sometimes open in the morning), with a chapel containing a Madonna and Saints by Fr. Penni, and an early Madonna with St John by Giulio Romano.— The adjoining Chapter House (70) contains paintings of saints by And. Sacchi.

Ascent of the Dome. Admission daily 8–one hour before the basilica closes, except Christmas Day and Easter Day, and when the Pope is in the basilica (often on Wednesday morning). The entrance is at present at the end of the right aisle beneath the tomb of Benedict XIV (27). The dome was completed as far as the drum by Michelangelo (d 1564); the vault and the lantern were added by Giac. della Porta in 1588–90. Clement VII (1592–1605) covered the vault with strips of lead reinforced with bronze ribs.

To reach the roof there is a lift (Lire 3000) or a staircase (Lire 2000). On reaching the Roof there is a close view of the spring of the dome, whose cross is 92m above. The two side cupolas by Giacomo della Porta are purely decorative and have no opening into the interior of the church. On the roof are buildings used by the 'sampietrini', masons and others employed on the maintenance of the fabric. Two stairways lead to a curving corridor from which is the entrance into the first circular gallery around the interior of the drum of the dome (53m above the ground and 67m below the top of the dome). From here there is an impressive view of the pavement far below and of the interior of the dome; its immensity may be gauged by the coarseness of the mosaic and the vast scale of the decorative details. The higher circular gallery is closed to the public.—Signs indicate the way on up via a spiral staircase with lancet windows, and a curving narrow stair between the two shells of the dome. The first big window has a view S, with the roof of the huge Audience Hall (1971) directly below. Iron stairs continue up to the tiny marble stairs which emerge on the loggia around the pretty Lantern, 537 steps above the pavement of the basilica. There is a close

*View of the Vatican city and gardens, and beyond, on a clear day, of the whole of Rome and of the Campagna from the Apennines and the Alban hills to the sea. The cross surmounting the copper Ball (2·5m in diameter, just large enough to hold 16 people) is 132·5m above the ground.—Another staircase leads down and out onto the roof with a view from the parapet, beside the huge statues on the façade, of Piazza San Pietro. The exit is at present under the Sobieska monument, next to the baptistery (65).

The **Vatican Grottoes** *(Grotte Vaticane)* are open on weekdays 8–17 or 18, except when the Pope is in the basilica. The entrance is at present by the pier of St Andrew (6) although one of the other three entrances at the piers can sometimes be in use (see the Plan below, and the exit on the outside of the church, to the right of the main door. In the space between the level of the existing basilica (30m above sea-level) and that of the old one (27m) the Renaissance architects formed the so-called *Sacred Grottoes* and placed in them various monuments and architectural fragments from the former church. They were used for the burial of numerous popes and other illustrious personages. In 1940 excavations were begun at the instance of Pius XII, below the level of the old basilica; they continued until 1957.

The Grottoes, which follow the outline of the basilica above them (except for their annexes), are in two adjoining sections. The OLD GROTTOES have the form of a nave with aisles (corresponding to Maderno's nave but extending beyond it); on either side are the annexes discovered during the excavations. The NEW GROTTOES are in the form of a horse-shoe, with extensions. The centre is immediately below the high altar of St Peter's. Four of the extensions reach to points below the four piers of St Longinus, St Helena, St Veronica, and St Andrew.

Stairs lead down from the church (6) to the **New Grottoes**. To the left is a horse-shoe corridor, lined with fine reliefs attributed to Matteo del Pollaiuolo of the life of St Peter which decorated the tabernacle over the high altar of the old basilica. Beyond a modern chapel is the 14C chapel of the Madonna della Bocciata (2) and the 15C chapel of the Madonna delle Febbri (3). The Clementine Chapel (4) is immediately beneath the centre of the church above. Here the rear wall was breached during the excavations for St Peter's tomb. Behind is the foundation of the altar of Calixtus II enclosing that of Gregory I. The Tropaion of Gaius (see below) is therefore beneath (5). Openings to the left and right show the structure of the foundations more clearly (visible only when the grille is opened on a guided tour of the Necropolis—see below). Opposite the chapel is (6) the tomb of Pius XII (died 1958). Another chapel (7) has the unfinished tomb of Paul II (died 1471) by Mino da Fiesole, Giovanni Dalmata, and others.

The area of the **Old Grottoes** lies at the W end of the right aisle. Immediately to the right is a chapel (8) with a 15C altar of the Virgin, and the tomb (9) of Pius VI (died 1799) in an early Christian sarcophagus. At the W end of the nave (seen across the barrier) is the 15C *Altar of Christ in majesty with the Evangelists (10), by *Giovanni Dalmata*. Continuing down the aisle, the route passes the tomb of Pope John XXIII (died 1963; 11). Beyond on the left (12) is the tomb of Christina of Sweden (died 1689), and opposite (13), the tomb of Queen Charlotte of Cyprus (died 1487). After a short flight of steps are more tombs: on the left (14) Innocent IX (died 1591), and right (15) Benedict XV (died 1922), followed by (16) Marcellus II (died 1555), and (28) John Paul I (died 1978). The chapel (17) beyond has a relief of the Madonna attributed to Isaia da Pisa. Here is the plain tomb slab of Paul VI (died 1978).—A turning left leads away from the Old Grottoes, passing left (18) the tomb of Julius III (died 1555) into the N ANNEXE, a series of four rooms (19–22; sometimes closed) containing interesting inscriptions and fragments from the old basilica. In the two rooms to the left (19 and 20; sometimes unlit) is the sarcophagus of Anicius Probus, Prefect of Rome in 395.—At the W end of the Grottoes (23) has been placed the kneeling *Statue of Pius VI by *Canova*, removed from the Confessione of the Basilica in 1980. The present exit is through a corridor where some column bases from Constantine's basilica can be seen, and the cenotaph of Calixtus III with good reliefs. The corridor leads out to the portico of the church beside the equestrian statue of Constantine I by Bernini (keyed 2 on the plan of St Peter's).

*Necropolis and St Peter's Tomb**. Application may be made in writing or in person to the Ufficio Scavi (beneath the Arco della Campana, left of the Basilica) for permission to join the groups of 15 which are conducted on most days (9–12, 14–17; the visit takes c 1½ hrs). Details of name, number of people, and language should be sent together with length of stay, address and tel. no. in Rome. A double row of mausoleums, dating from the 1C AD, running from E to W were discovered below the level of the old basilica. The extreme W series of these is on higher ground and adjoins a graveyard which is immediately beneath the high altar of the present church. Constantine significantly chose to erect his basilica above this necropolis, a most difficult undertaking because of the slope of the hill. He had to level the terrain and make use of supporting foundation walls. A baldacchino in the presbytery covered the *Tropaion of Gaius*, a funerary monument in the form of a small aedicule or niche, referred to c 200, and probably built by Pope Anicetus.

Excavations have discovered this monument, which backs on to a supporting wall plastered with red, dating from the same period. An empty space beneath it is believed to be St Peter's Tomb—what was probably a mound of earth covered by brick slabs, and showing signs of the interference which history records. That this was a most revered grave is evident from the number of other graves which crowd in upon one another, without cutting across or lying upon it, seemingly in an effort to be near it. In front of the red wall, on which a Greek inscription is taken to name the saint, is a later wall, scratched with the names of pilgrims invoking the aid of Peter. Bones, obviously displaced, of an elderly and powerfully built man, were found beneath this second graffiti wall and declared by Paul VI to be those of St Peter.

The site of the Circus of Nero, the most likely place of St Peter's martyrdom, lay along the S flank of the basilica, and extended as far as Via Sant'Uffizio.

Visitors meet inside the Vatican City, entered through the Arco delle Campane, which is protected by a member of the Swiss Guard, and cross Piazza dei Protomartiri Romani. The visit usually commences at the S ANNEXE (24) of the Old Grottoes, through two rooms (25 and 26) with 14–15C tomb slabs and sarcophagi. A third room (27) has transennae and architectural fragments of the

4–9C, and part of the nave foundation wall of the old basilica; from here stairs lead down to the Necropolis. (If, however, work on the excavations prevents this route being used, visitors are conducted into St Peter's and through the new Grottoes (5), from which these stairs can also be reached.)

The necropolis is well-preserved and was in use until Constantine's reign. Among the 18 loculi cleared the one purely Christian mausoleum provides the most ancient mosaics yet discovered on a Christian subject. Here, on the vault richly decorated with a vine pattern, Christ is depicted as Helios, the sun-god. On the walls the sinopie remain of mosaics which have become detached from the surface (on the left, Jonah, and ahead, Fishermen). In the other mausoleums Oriental cults and those of Greece and Rome are combined. Christians were also buried in the mausoleum of the Caetenii, where is the grave of Aemilia Gorgonia; in the magnificent stuccoed mausoleum of the Valerii, with reliefs in niches, where the inscription of Valerinus Vastulus, despite the pagan sarcophagus (3C), specifies his Christian burial; and in the so-called Egyptian chamber. The paintings of peacocks in the mausoleum of the family of P. Aelius Tyrannus, the marble bust of the woman in that of the Valerii, and the remarkable sarcophagus of Q. Marcius Hermes and his wife mirror the tastes and wealth of the families of freedmen to whom the loculi belonged. Among the many sarcophagi is one for a child, with figures of the mourning parents.

B.　The Vatican Palace

Admission. The Vatican Museums and Galleries are open Monday–Saturday from 9 to 14; in July, August, and September, and during the Easter period they are open from 9–17 (the ticket office closes one hour before closing time). They are also open free on the last Sunday of the month, unless it is a feast day. The museums and galleries covered by the ticket (8000 lire, 5000 lire for students)—for one single visit—are the Gregorian Museum of Pagan Antiquities and the Pio Christian Museum (both formerly in the Lateran), the Picture Gallery, the Museo Pio-Clementino (sculpture), the Museo Chiaramonti (sculpture), the Egyptian Museum, the Etruscan Museum, the Museum of Pagan Antiquities, the Exhibition Rooms of the Library, the Museum of Christian Art, the Borgia Rooms and the Gallery of Modern Religious Art, the Raphael Rooms, the Sistine Chapel, the Chapels of Nicholas V and of Urban VIII, the Room of the Chiaroscuri, the Hall of the Immaculate Conception, the Gallery of Maps, the Gallery of Tapestries, and the Ethnological Missionary Museum. The last museum is only open on Wednesday and Saturday.

The Vatican collections are closed on Sundays (except the last in the month) and on the following days: New Year's Day, 6 January, 11 February (Anniversary of the founding of the Vatican City State), Easter Monday, 1 May, Ascension Day, Corpus Christi, 29 June, 15 August, 1 November, 8 December, Christmas Day and Boxing Day, and whenever special reasons make it necessary.

A **Bus Service** runs daily, except Sunday and Wednesday, every half hour (between 9 and 12.30, and between 9 and 14 in July–September and the Easter period) from the Arco delle Campane (left of the façade of the basilica) through the Vatican gardens to a side entrance to the Museums, at the Ambulatory (5 minutes; 1000 lire). This is recommended not only as the most convenient way of reaching the museums from St Peter's, but also it provides the opportunity of seeing part of the Vatican city and gardens, which can otherwise be seen only on an organized tour (see p 341). It can also be taken back from the Museums to St Peter's (10.40, 11.10, etc).

Refreshments are available at a self-service restaurant and snack bar below the courtyard outside the *Quattro Cancelli*.

The *** *Vatican Palace** contains some of the world's greatest art treasures. The extensive buildings and interior courts cover an area of 5·5 hectares. Most of the palace is open to the public, as the apartments reserved for the Pope and the papal court are contained in a relatively small area. The gardens and city can only been seen on an organized tour (see p 341). As well as the remarkable Greek and Roman sculpture museums, the gallery of paintings, the library, the

Egyptian and Etruscan collections, ethnological material, etc. the palace contains the famous Sistine Chapel frescoed by Michelangelo and the 'Stanze' decorated by Raphael. Because of the number of different museums it contains and the vast extent of the halls and galleries on two floors, it is not practicable to see them all in a single visit. Visitors are strongly recommended not to attempt to see too much in one visit, and to plan to return at least two or three times.

History. In the days of Pope St Symmachus (498–514) a house was built beside the first basilica of St Peter. This house was not the residence of the popes as, until the migration to Avignon in 1309, they lived in the Lateran Palace; but it was used for state occasions and for the accommodation of foreign sovereigns. In it Charlemagne stayed in 800 and Otho II in 980. By the 12C it had fallen into disrepair. Eugenius III (1145–53) was the first of numerous popes to restore and enlarge it. In 1208 Innocent III built a fortified residence here which was added to by his successors. When Gregory XI returned from Avignon in 1378 he found the Lateran uninhabitable and he transferred his residence to the Vatican. On his death in the same year, the first Conclave was held in the Vatican. To safeguard the security of the occupants, the antipope John XXIII began in 1410 to build the Covered Way to the Castel Sant'Angelo.

Nicholas V (1447–55) transformed the house into a palace, built round a courtyard—the Cortile dei Pappagalli. In 1473 Sixtus IV added the Sistine Chapel. Innocent VIII (1484–92) built on the N summit of the Vatican Hill the Belvedere Pavilion; the architect was Giac. da Pietrasanta. Alexander VI (1492–1503) decorated a suite of rooms on the first floor of the palace of Nicholas V and they became known, after his family name, as the Appartamento Borgia; he also added the Borgia Tower. Julius II (1503–13) began to form the famous collection of classical sculpture, which he placed in the courtyard of the Belvedere Pavilion. He also commissioned Bramante to unite this pavilion with the palace of Nicholas V by means of long corridors, thus creating the great Courtyard of the Belvedere.

Leo X (1513–21) adorned the E side of the palace with open galleries looking on to the Courtyard of St Damasus, one of which became known as the Loggia of Raphael. Paul III (1534–49) employed Ant. da Sangallo the Younger to build the Cappella Paolina and the Sala Regia. Under Pius IV and Gregory XIII various additions were made by Pirro Ligorio. Sixtus V (1585–90) assigned to Dom. Fontana the construction of the block overlooking Piazza San Pietro and of the great Library, which was formed at right angles to the long corridors and thus divided the Courtyard of the Belvedere in two. The Scala Regia of Bernini was begun under Urban VIII and completed under Alexander VII (1655–67). The Museum of Pagan Antiquities was founded by Clement XIII (1758–69).

Clement XIV (1769–74) converted the Belvedere Pavilion into a museum which Pius VI (1775–99) enlarged; hence its name 'Pio-Clementino'. The architect was M. Simonetti, who altered the courtyard and added several rooms. Pius VI was also the founder of the Picture Gallery. Pius VII (Chiaramonti; 1800–23) founded the Sculpture Gallery which bears his name and added the New Wing (by Raff. Stern), which paralleled the Library. Its construction divided the Courtyard of the Belvedere into three. From now on the sections became known as the Courtyard of the Belvedere (retaining the old name; nearest the pontifical palace), the relatively small Courtyard of the Library and the Courtyard of the Fir Cone (Pigna; after a bronze fir cone placed in it by Paul V; 1605–21; nearest to the Belvedere Pavilion). Gregory XVI (1831–46) was responsible for the Etruscan and Egyptian Museums. Pius IX (1846–78) closed the fourth side of the Courtyard of St Damasus and built the Scala Pia. Leo XIII (1878–1903) restored the Borgia Rooms and reopened them to the public. Under Pius XI (1914–39) were built the new Picture Gallery and the new entrance to the Vatican Museums in the Viale Vaticano, both of them dating from 1932. A new building was opened in 1970 by Paul VI to house the former Lateran museums (the Gregorian Museum of Pagan Antiquities and the Pio Christian Museum); in 1973 the Ethnological Missionary Museum was opened beneath, and a Historical Museum was built under the gardens (the contents have since been transferred to the Lateran Palace). An extensive series of galleries in and around the Borgia apartments were opened in 1973 as a Museum of Modern Religious Art.

The most convenient way of reaching the Vatican Museums from St Peter's is by the Vatican bus service (see above). Otherwise, from St

Peter's it is a long walk along Via di Porta Angelica (Pl. 1; 4) to the right (N) of Bernini's colonnade in Piazza San Pietro. At the beginning of the street is the battlemented Covered Way to Castel Sant'Angelo. The site of Porta Angelica was the modern Piazza del Risorgimento. On the left is the Cancello di Sant'Anna, one of the entrances to Vatican City. The road skirts the city wall, and turns left out of Piazza del Risorgimento. Continuing along the wall Viale Vaticano (p 287), leads left to the **Entrance to the Vatican Museums** (Pl. 1; 3, 4). The ENTRANCE HALL has a ticket office for tour groups, an Information Office, and Lifts for the Museums. Visitors may also use the monumental *DOUBLE STAIRCASE built in 1932 by G. Momo, with independent ascending and descending spirals, carved out of the hill, to connect the street level with that of the museums. The bronze balustrade is by A. Maraini.

The AMBULATORY at the top of the staircase, with mosaics and busts, has the Ticket Office for individual visitors (separate office for students), the bus terminus from St Peter's, a bank, a post office, telephones, bookstalls, cloakrooms, etc. Beyond the TICKET GATES a short flight of steps mounts to the *Vestibule* decorated with three mosaics from Hadrian's Villa. In summer (and on fine days) visitors are directed instead outside to the *Cortile delle Carozze* where the *Base of the Column of Antoninus Pius has been placed since its restoration. A monolithic block of Greek marble it has high reliefs on three sides with the Apotheosis of Antoninus and his wife Faustina, who are being conduted to Heaven by a winged Genius personifying Rome, and delightful scenes of cavalcades (AD 138–161). It was found in 1703 in Via della Missone, near Montecitorio. On the right is the entrance to the new building which houses the Gregorian Museum of Pagan Antiquities and the Pio Christian Museum. Beyond is an open court (below which is a self-service restaurant). On the left is the entrance known as the *Quattro Cancelli* (Four Gates), which gives access to the Sculpture Galleries, to the Sistine Library and, beyond these, to the rest of the Vatican Museums. In front a passageway leads to the Picture Gallery.

The collections are so extensive and their layout is so complicated that it is not practicable to see them all in a single tour. To add to the complication, the exhibits are arranged on different floors, and, in the case of the Sculpture Galleries, on two floors. However the visit is planned a certain amount of duplication cannot be avoided.

Four one-way itineraries have been imposed by the Vatican authorities and visitors are expected to chose one of the four 'tours' depending on the time at their disposal. This is primarily to regulate the flow of people to the Sistine Chapel and tour groups have to take the signposted routes. However, with some persuasion, these may be disregarded to some extent, especially by those on their own. Visitors wishing to see one particular collection only, and especially those who already know the Museums will not be helped by the one-way systems, since, in some cases, access from one part of the museums to another is no longer possible. The number of people and tours in the Vatican can seriously impede the visitor's enjoyment of the museum. Those with time may do well to proceed straight to the Sistine Chapel at opening time in order to enjoy it in comparative peace, and then return to the Quattro Cancelli to begin the detailed tours described below. It should be noted that visitors are now often able to leave the museums through the Sistine Chapel by the Scala Regia which descends directly to the portico of St Peter's.

The four separate tours suggested below can at present be made taking into account the one-way systems, although these may be changed in the future.

I. Quattro Cancelli—Simonetti staircase—Egyptian Museum—Museo Chiaramonti—New Wing—Museo Pio Clementino—upstairs to the Room of the Biga—Etruscan Museum—return to the Quattro Cancelli.

II. A very long and tiring route which should, if time permits, be taken in two stages. Quattro Cancelli—upstairs to the Gallery of the Candelabra—Gallery of Tapestries and Gallery of Maps—Hall of the Immaculate Conception—Raphael Rooms—Room of the Chiaroscuri—Chapel of Nicholas V—Chapel of Urban VIII—Borgia Rooms and Gallery of Modern Religious Art—Sistine Chapel— Museum of Christian Art—Sistine Hall and Library—Quattro Cancelli.

III. Quattro Cancelli—Vatican Picture Gallery—Quattro Cancelli.

IV. Vestibule—Gregorian Museum of Pagan Antiquities—Pio Christian Museum—Ethnological Missionary Museum—Vestibule.

The itineraries described below follow the above scheme.

I.   The Museums of Antiquities: The Egyptian Museum, Museo Chiaramonti, New Wing, Museo Pio Clementino, and Etruscan Museum.

The Vatican Palace houses the largest collections of ancient sculpture in the world. These collections owe their origin to the Renaissance popes, and in particular to Julius II. Many of the pieces were, however, afterwards dispersed, Pius V (1566–72) being largely responsible, with his gifts to the city of Rome and to private individuals. This trend was reversed by the popes of the late 18C and early 19C, who reassembled the old collections and formed new ones.

The contents of the sculpture galleries are mainly Greek originals, Roman originals, or Roman copies of Greek originals executed in the 1C and 2C AD. In some cases the Roman sculptor when copying a Greek model placed a contemporary portrait head on his copy; modern restorers have often made additions in marble, stone, or plaster and have also, on occasion, put heads on statues to which they do not belong. In addition, all the male sculpture has been ludicrously disfigured by prudish plaster additions, and there are few undraped female statues (this does not apply to the Gregorian Museum of Pagan Antiquities, described in Section IV).

The **Vatican Inventory Numbers** given in the following description are inconspicuously marked on the right side or back of the works themselves. The other more prominent numbered labels (some of them missing or difficult to decipher), usually in red, attached below each work should be ignored. The keyed plans in each room of the most important works also carry the Vatican Inventory numbers.

The one-way systems (see above) make it, at present, obligatory to approach the sculpture galleries through the Egyptian Museum.

The Egyptian Museum

The **Egyptian Museum** occupies rooms in the lower floor of the Belvedere Pavilion adjoining the Museo Pio-Clementino. The entrance is at the top of the first flight of the Simonetti Staircase outside the Hall of the Greek Cross (described below). The museum was founded by Gregory XVI in 1839 and was arranged by Father Luigi Maria Ungarelli, one of the first Italian Egyptologists to continue the scientific research of G.G. Champollion. The rooms were decorated in the Egyptian style in the 19C by G. De Fabris. The collection is in the process of rearrangement.

ROOMS I and II were closed in 1988, and their arrangement will probably be altered when they reopen. Room I. Statues in black granite of the lion-headed goddess Sekhmet (XVIIIth Dynasty); two crouching lions, once part of a monument to Nectanebo I (XXXth Dynasty); they were removed by Gregory

XVI from the Fontana dell'Acqua Felice; funerary stelae.—ROOM II reproduces an underground tomb chamber in the Valley of the Kings. Here are displayed three lidless sarcophagi in black basalt, with Hieroglyphic inscriptions, of the Saitic period (6C BC) and mummies and canopic jars. The papyrus of the Book of the Dead, which belonged to a priest of the Saitic period, is being restored; a photocopy is displayed.—R. III contains works by Roman artists of the 2C and 3C in imitation of Egyptian art. Most of them come from Hadrian's Villa at Tivoli, others from the Temple of Isis, in the Campus Martius. Statue of Antinous in white marble; colossal bust of the goddess Isis; Grey marble statue personifying the Nile.—R. IV. Basalt statuette of Psammeteksenb, a priest-physician of the XXVIth Dynasty, depicted as a naophoros, i.e. carrying a small temple; basalt statuette of the naophorus Udjeharresnet who was present when the city of Sais was taken by the Persians under Cambyses in 525 BC.

ROOM V, THE HEMICYCLE, conforms in shape to the Niche of the Bronze Fir Cone. Here are displayed part of the throne of a seated statue of Rameses II (XIX Dyn.); *Colossal statue of Queen Tuaa, mother of Rameses II; *Sandstone Head of Mentuhotep IV (XIth Dynasty), the oldest portrait statue in the museum; Colossal granite statue of Ptolemy Philadelphos (285–247 BC) and his wife Arsinoe, and of a Princess of the Ptolemy family.—R. VI. Statuettes of sacred animals. Objects from the Greek, Roman, and Coptic periods.—R. VII. The Carlo Grassi collection, including glass.—R. VIII. Material from Palestine.—R. IX. Exquisite *Bas-reliefs from Mesopotamia.

The **Niche of the Bronze Fir Cone** (*Nicchione della Pigna*), reached from a door (locked) in the Hemicycle, is the apse at the N end of the extensive COURTYARD OF THE FIR CONE (*Cortile della Pigna*; open if fine), one of the three sections into which Bramante's Courtyard of the Belvedere was eventually divided. Here stands the colossal bronze FIR CONE, placed here by Paul V (1605–21). The cone, over 4m high (recently restored), was found near the Thermae of Agrippa and formed the centrepiece of a fountain beside the Temple of Isis; this is inferred from the holes in the top of the scales. It was made by a certain P. Cincius Salvius, in the 1C AD. In the middle ages it was in the portico of Old St Peter's, together with the two bronze-gilt peacocks on either side of it; these came from Hadrian's Mausoleum and probably stood at one of its entrance gates. The fir cone was seen by Dante ('Inferno', xxxi, 53) and gave its name to a district of the city, the Quartiere della Pigna.

From the landing outside R. IX of the Egyptian Museum stairs lead down to the Chiaramonti Sculpture Gallery, and a door into the Courtyard of the Fir Cone.

The Chiaramonti Gallery

The **Chiaramonti Sculpture Gallery** is reached by stairs leading down from the landing outside the Egyptian Museum and near the Round Vestibule (see below). This gallery is named after its founder Pius VII (Chiaramonti) and it was arranged by Canova who designed the lunette frescoes with scenes from the life of Pius VII as patron of the arts (by Fr Hayez, Philippe Veit, etc.). With it are associated the New Wing and the Gallery of Inscriptions. The Chiaramonti gallery occupies a considerable section of Bramante's E corridor and is 300 metres long. It flanks and overlaps the Courtyard of the Fir Cone. The exhibits are divided into 59 Sections, numbered with roman numerals (odd numbers on left, even numbers on right).

Section I. 1195. Sarcophagus of C. Junius Euhodus and his wife Metilia Acte, sometime a priestess of the Magna Mater at Ostia, with relief of the story of Alcestis; the faces of Alcestis and her husband Admetus are portraits of the Roman couple (2C AD).—*II.* 1211. Herm of Hephaistos (Vulcan); the head may be derived from a statue by Alkamenes; Roman copy of a 5C Greek original.—*IV.* 1246. Statue of Hygieia, part of a group of Hygieia and Asklepios, Roman copy of a 4C original by the sons of Praxiteles in the Asklepieion on the island of Kos.—*V.* 1252. Antoninus Pius, wearing armour.—*IX.* 1314. Herakles with his son Telephos; the statue of Herakles is after a 4C original, that of Telephos after a 3C original; the group is a Roman synthesis.—*X.* 1343. Sepulchral monument of P. Nonnius Zethus and his family (1C AD), a square marble block with eight conical cavities for the various members of the family. The reliefs—of a mill being turned by a donkey and of baking implements—probably indicated the man's trade.—*XI.* 1359. Portrait bust of Cicero; 1365. Sarcophagus lid.—*XII.*

1370. Relief from a 3C sarcophagus, with a mule in blinkers turning a wine-press.—*XIII*. 1373. Hermes, from an original of the 5C BC; 1376. Ganymede and the eagle, copy of a 3C Hellenistic original.—*XV*. Portrait bust of Pompey.

XVI. *1434. Head of Athena, copy of a Greek original of the 5C BC; the eyes are restorations but they indicate the skill with which Greek artists caught the expression of the human eye. The whites of the eyes were probably of ivory, the pupils of semi-precious stone, and the lashes and brows of bronze.—*XVII*. 1441. Silenus with a panther, copy of a 3C Hellenistic original.—*XIX*. 1487. Portrait-head of a priest of Isis (1C BC); 1488. Head of a Roman of the late Republican period.—*XX*. 1507. Athena, from a Greek original of the 5C BC.—*XXI*. 1509. Eros bending his bow, probably a copy of a bronze original by Lysippos; *Statue of a boy.—*XXIII*. *1558. Fragment of a relief of Penelope in her characteristic attitude: sitting on a chair and resting her head on her right hand; from a Greek original of the 5C BC.—*XXVI*. Head of the Discobolos of Myron, Roman copy of the 5C Greek original; *Head from a Palmyran sepulchral relief, in the limestones typical of Palmyran sculpture, which was a fusion of Syrian and Hellenistic-Roman styles; 2C AD.

XXIX. 1639. Colossal head of Augustus; 1641. Statue of Tiberius; 1642. Head of Tiberius.—*XXXI*. 1669. Relief of the Three Graces, Archaic period.—*XXXII*. 1697. Dacian prisoner of high rank, Roman art of the 2C AD.—*XXXV*. 1751. Roman pontiff in the act of sacrifice (1C BC).—*XXXVI*. 1765. Resting athlete, Roman copy of a 4C original.—*XXXVII*. 1771. Statue of Herakles; from a Greek original of the 4C BC.—*XL*. 1839. Statue of the Muse Polyhymnia, Roman copy of a Hellenistic original of the 3C or 2C BC; 1841. Statue of Artemis (Diana), Roman copy of a 4C Greek original.—*XLIII*. *1901. Statuette of Ulysses, part of a group of Ulysses offering wine to Polyphemus, Roman copy of a 3C Greek original.—*XLV*. Colossal head of Trajan.—*XLVII*. 1975. Portrait bust of a lady of the Julio-Claudian gens; the hair is typical of the fashion of the age of Augustus (1C AD); Portrait statue of a Roman thought to be Sulla (1C BC).—*LVIII*. 663. Personification of Winter; the female figure is wrapped in a cloak and holds a pine branch in her left hand; she is reclining near a stream where cupids are catching waterfowl and fishes; a Hellenistic-Roman work of the 2C AD; 664. Sepulchral relief of a Roman family (1C BC).—*LIX*. 2166. Personifica-tion of Autumn, a companion piece to Winter (above); the female figure is surrounded by cupids gathering grapes; 664. Sepulchral relief of a Roman family (1C BC).

At the end of the Chiaramonti Gallery is a gate (closed), beyond which is the **Gallery of Inscriptions** (*Galleria Lapidaria*), open only to scholars with a permit from the Director-General. It occupies the remaining part of Bramante's E corridor. The gallery was founded by Clement XIV and reorganized and classified by the celebrated epigraphist Monsignor Gaetano Marini (1742–1817). It contains over 5000 pagan and Christian inscriptions from cemeteries and catacombs.

On the right a door leads into the **New Wing**, or *Braccio Nuovo*, an extension of the Chiaramonti sculpture gallery constructed by Raffaele Stern (1817–22) for Pius VII. It contains some of the most valuable sculptures in the Vatican. The impressive hall, 70m long and 8m wide, has a vaulted coffered ceiling and an apse in the middle of the S side, facing the Courtyard of the Library. The floor is inlaid with mosaics of the 2C AD from a Roman villa at Tor Marancia.—2296. Caryatid, copy of one of the Caryatids of the Erechtheion on the Acropolis of Athens (5C BC); 2293. Head of a Dacian, from the Forum of Trajan (2C AD); 2292. Silenus carrying the infant Dionysos, copy of an original ascribed to Lysippos; *2290. The AUGUSTUS OF PRIMA PORTA, one of the most famous portraits of the emperor, found in Livia's villa at Prima Porta.

The emperor, who appears to be about 40 years old, is wearing a cuirass over his toga; he holds a sceptre in his left hand; his raised right hand shows that he is about to make a speech. The head is full of character and the majestic pose suggests the influence of Polykleitos. The cuirass, a remarkably delicate piece of work, is decorated with scenes that date the statue. The central scene depicts the restoration by the Parthians in 20 BC of the eagles lost by Crassus at Carrhae in 53 BC. The small cupid riding a dolphin, placed as a support for the right leg, may be a portrait of Gaius Caesar, grandson of Augustus.

*2284. Modesty, so called, probably Mnemosyne, copy of a Greek original of the 3C BC; 2282. Statue of Titus.

In the rectangular recess opposite the apse, 2276. Priestess of Isis. In the centre, *Bust of Julius Caesar; above is an alabaster cinerary urn said to be that of Livilla, daughter of Germanicus. At the sides are six tombstones found near the Mausoleum of Augustus; five of them belong to the Julian family and the sixth to Vespasian's.—2272. Wounded Amazon (see below); 2265. Bust of Trajan; 2268. Selene (the Moon) approaching the sleeping Endymion, copy of a Hellenistic original of the 4C–3C BC; 2266. Statue of a tragic poet (the head of Euripides does not belong), copy of a 4C original (? Aeschylus); *2261. Portrait bust of a Roman (1C AD).

Returning down the other side: *2255. DEMOSTHENES. This is a replica of the original statue by Polyeuctos of Athens, set up in Athens in 280 BC to the memory of Demosthenes, the orator and statesman. The hands were originally joined, with the fingers crossed. The mouth plainly suggests the stutter from which the great Athenian suffered.—Portrait bust of Ptolemy of Numidia (1C AD); *2252. Wounded Amazon, a replica of one of the statues from the Temple of Diana at Ephesos, by Polykleitos. According to the Elder Pliny, this statue won the prize in a competition in which Polykleitos, Pheidias, Kresilas, and Phradmon entered. The arms and feet were restored by Thorvaldsen; 2247. Bust of Hadrian wearing armour; 2246. Statue of Hera, copy of a 5C Greek original (attributed to Alkamenes); 2244. Fortune, copy of a 4C Greek statue (the head, though antique, is from another figure; the oar and globe are Roman additions); Portrait bust of an unknown Roman of the 2C AD; Statue of a man, a Greek portrait of the 4C BC; *2240. Statue of Artemis, from a 4C original.

In the apse. *2236. Bust of a man of the late Republican era, possibly Mark Antony; Bust of Marcus Aurelius as a young man; statuettes of athletes; 2226. Statue of Diana; in the floor, mosaic of Diana of the Ephesians; *2300. THE NILE, a fine Hellenistic work, found, in 1513, with a statue of the Tiber (now in the Louvre), near the Temple of Isis (recently restored).

The river-god, who reclines near a sphinx and holds a horn of plenty, has the calm benevolent expression of a benefactor who enjoys his munificence. The sixteen children who frolic over him are supposed to symbolize the sixteen cubits which the Nile rises when in flood. The plinth is decorated with characteristic scenes of life on the banks of the Nile.

2225. Statue of Julia, daughter of Titus; *2223. The GIUSTINIANI ATHENA, after a Greek original of the 4C BC; this is the best existing copy of an original in bronze attributed to Kephisodotus or to Euphranor; it happily portrays the goddess's twofold function as the divinity of the intellect and of arms. 2222. Portrait bust of an unknown Roman of the 1C AD, possibly Cn. Domitius Ahenobarbus; 2221. Statue of a man wearing a toga, with the head of Claudius; *2219. RESTING SATYR, copy of the famous statue by Praxiteles (replica in the Gallery of Statues; others in the Museo Gregoriano Profano and in the Capitoline Museum); 2218. Bust of Commodus (180–92); 2217. Statue of an athlete with the head of Lucius Verus; the body is a copy of a 5C Greek original; 2216. Bust of the emperor Philip the Arabian (244–49); *2215. DORYPHOROS OF POLYKLEITOS, copy of the famous bronze statue of a young spear-bearer.

Polykleitos, the greatest sculptor of the school of Argos and Sikyon, devoted himself especially to the study of the proportions of the human body.

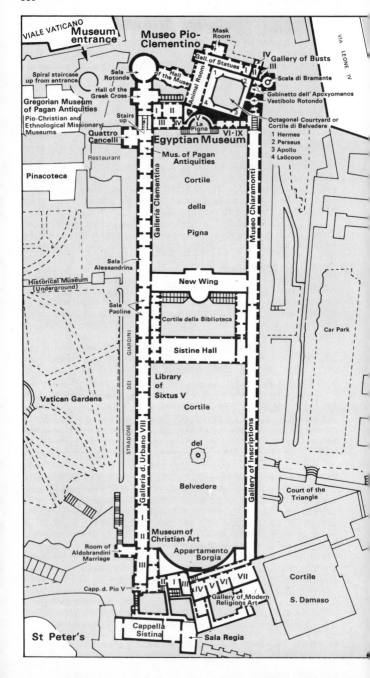

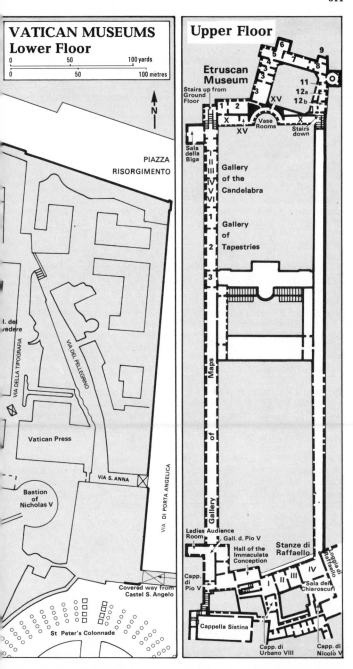

VATICAN MUSEUMS
Lower Floor

0   50   100 yards
0   50   100 metres

N

PIAZZA
RISORGIMENTO

I. del
vedere

VIA DELLA TIPOGRAFIA

VIA DEL PELLEGRINO

Vatican Press

VIA S. ANNA

VIA DI PORTA ANGELICA

Bastion
of
Nicholas V

Covered way from
Castel S. Angelo

St Peter's Colonnade

Upper Floor

Etruscan Museum

Stairs up from
Ground Floor

6
5   7   9
4   8
3
3   11
XV   12a
12b
1   2
X
Vase   XV   X
Rooms   Stairs
down

Sala
della
Biga

II   Gallery
III   of the
IV   Candelabra
V
VI

1   Gallery
of
2   Tapestries

3

Maps

of

Gallery

Ladies Audience
Room   Gall. d. Pio V

Hall of the
Immaculate   Stanze di
Conception   Raffaello

Loggia di
Raffaello

Capp.
di
Pio V   I   II   III   IV   Sala dei
Chiaroscuri

Cappella Sistina

Capp. di   Capp. di
Urbano VIII   Nicolò V

Innumerable copies were made of the Doryphoros, with a head of the dolichocephalic type, and a youthful male form of beautiful proportion.

Head of a Dacian, from Trajan's Forum (see No. 2293 above); *Statue of Domitian, wearing a cuirass.

It is now necessary to return through the Chiaramonti Gallery to the landing outside the exit from the Egyptian Museum. Ahead is the present entrance to the Museo Pio Clementino.

Museo Pio-Clementino

This sculpture gallery occupies two floors of the Belvedere Pavilion, which was adapted by M. Simonetti for the purposes of a museum. The present entrance is from the landing outside the exit from the Egyptian Museum.

In the first vestibule is the *Sarcophagus (1191.), in peperino, of L. Cornelius Scipio Barbatus, from the Tomb of the Scipios; the sarcophagus is in the form of a Doric altar but the general character is Etruscan. The archaic inscription, in Saturnine verse, is said to be by Ennius. Above are two inscriptions, also from the Tomb of the Scipios, to the son of Scipio Barbatus, who conquered Corsica in 259 BC.

Ahead is the **Round Vestibule** (*Vestibolo Rotondo*). Here are a large bowl of pavonazzetto and sculptural fragments.—Beyond is the **Gabinetto dell'Apoxyomenos**. *1185. APOXYOMENOS ('The Scraper'), a finely built athlete scraping the oil from his body with a strigil, from a bronze original by Lysippos; this was the masterpiece of the sculptor's maturity (c 330 BC) and illustrated his canon of proportions. The statue was found in Trastevere (Vicolo dell'Atleta) in 1844.—Above, Archaic Latin inscriptions from the Tomb of the Scipios; to the right, Inscriptions, among them that of L. Mummius Achaicus, the conqueror of Greece (146 BC). 1186. So-called Casali Altar, Roman, 2C AD, with reliefs on all four sides.—Annexe. 31680. Relief of a Roman galley; above, amusing mosaic panels. Through a glass door here can be seen the *STAIRCASE OF BRAMANTE, which ascends to the floor above. The design is masterly; at each revolution the order changes, starting with Tuscan at the bottom and ending with Corinthian at the top.

From the Round Vestibule is the entrance to the **Octagonal Courtyard** of the Belvedere (not to be confused with the larger courtyard of the Belvedere, to the S), where Julius II placed the first classical sculptures to form the nucleus of the great collections now in the Vatican. When Pius VI had the museum enlarged in 1775, Simonetti made the courtyard into an octagon by forming the recesses (gabinetti) in the four corners.

To the left is the **Gabinetto dell'Apollo**. Here is the famous *APOLLO BELVEDERE (1015.), a 2C Roman copy of a bronze original probably by Leochares (4C BC). The slender elegant figure of the young god is stepping forward to see the effect of the arrow that he has just shot. The statue has been greatly admired as one of the masterpieces of classical sculpture since it was brought to the Vatican in 1503. It was beautifully restored in 1982.—Under the adjoining colonnade: *Relief of a procession, from the Ara Pacis Augustae, an original fragment not returned to the altar on its reconstitution in 1937–38; nearly all the heads are restorations.

The **Gabinetto del Laocoönte** contains the famous group of *LAOCOÖN (1059.) and his two sons in the coils of the serpents, a vivid and striking illustration of the story related by Virgil in the Aeneid.

Laocoön, priest of Apollo, warned his fellow Trojans against the trickery of the Greeks and entreated them not to admit the wooden horse into the city. At this the serpents were sent either by Apollo or by Athene to crush him and his young sons to death in their coils. This group, of Greek marble, was found on the Esquiline hill, in 1506, and was at once recognized as that described by Pliny, though it is not carved from a single block, as he states, but from at least three pieces. It was purchased by Julius II after its discovery and brought to the Vatican. It is ascribed to the Rhodian sculptors Agesander, Polydoros, and Athenodoros (c 50 BC). The violent realism of the conception as well as the extreme skill and accurate detail with which the agonized contortions of the bodies are rendered are typical of the sculpture of the late Hellenistic period. One of the best known classical sculptures, it influenced Renaissance and Baroque artists, and was particularly admired in the 19C (Byron, in 'Childe Harold' describes 'Laocoön's torture dignifying pain'). The group acquired its present appearance in a recent reconstitution. Its more familiar appearance as restored by Montorsoli on the opinion of Michelangelo is preserved in a plaster-cast which can be seen from a window of the Gregorian Profane Museum (see below).

Flanking the doorway beyond are two *Molossian Hounds of the school of Pergamon.—**Gabinetto dell'Hermes**. *907. Hermes (formerly thought to be Antinoüs), perhaps Hermes Psychopompos, the conductor of souls to the underworld, copy of an original by Praxiteles. The head is reminiscent of that of his famous Hermes at Olympia. It was restored in 1984.

In the portico beyond (niche), Venus Felix and Cupid: the body is copied from the Venus of Knidos in the Mask Room; the inscription on the plinth states that the group was dedicated to Venus Felix by Sallustia and Helpis. It has stood in the courtyard since Julius II began the collection here.—Small marble funerary urn in the shape of a house or shrine, and beyond, Sarcophagus with a battle of the Amazons, Achilles, and Penthesileia grouped in the centre, 3C AD.
The **Gabinetto del Canova** contains three neo-classical statues by *Antonio Canova* placed here when most of the classical masterpieces were taken to Paris by Napoleon in 1800, after the Treaty of Tolentino. 969. Perseus, inspired by the Apollo Belvedere and the boxers, Creugas and Damoxenes (968., 970.).

Beneath the following portico, Sarcophagus of Sextus Varius Marcellus, father of Heliogabalus; Sarcophagus with curved ends and a relief of a Bacchic procession.—Beneath the porticoes are six granite basins, the four smaller ones from the Baths of Caracalla.

The door flanked by the two Hounds leads out of the Courtyard and into the **Animal Room** (*Sala degli Animali*). Most of the animal statues are by *F.A. Franzoni* (1734–1818), who made them for this room for Pius VI. Some are entirely Franzoni's work; others were made up by him from ancient fragments. The antiques include: (in the room on the left), Sow with litter of twelve, perhaps of the Augustan period; (under the far window) 511. Colossal head of a camel (fountain head), copy of a Hellenistic original of the 2C BC; *490. Meleager with his dog and the head of a boar, copy of a 4C original by Skopas; 464. Triton and nereid, with cupids, perhaps a Hellenistic original of the 2C BC; 461. Head of a minotaur, copy of a 5C Greek original. In the room on the right, 437. Mithras slaying the bull (2C AD); (on the wall behind), *421, 423. Mosaics with animals, from Hadrian's Villa at Tivoli (2C AD).—In the pavement of each room, Mosaics, with animals and plants (2C AD).

The **Gallery of Statues** (right) is part of the original Belvedere Pavilion built by Innocent VIII. Remains of paintings by Pinturicchio may still be seen on the walls.—To the right: *769. EROS OF

CENTOCELLE, replica of a Greek original of the early 4C BC. Also called the 'Genius of the Vatican', it is probably a statue of Thanatos, the god of death, from an original attributed to Kephisodotos. It was found at Centocelle by Gavin Hamilton. 767. Discobolos of Polycletus, replica of the second half of the 5C BC; 762. Seated statue of Paris, possibly a copy of an original by Euphranor (4C BC); 756. Apollo Kitharoidos, restored as Minerva, late 5C; 754. Seated statue of Penelope (so called; with a head from another antique statue); *750. APOLLO SAUROCTONOS, representing the god watching a lizard that he is about to kill, an attractive composition, copy of the famous bronze original by Praxiteles; 748. So-called Mattei Amazon, from an original attributed to Kresilas (head from another statue); 747. Satyr; 745. Muse, restored as Urania, belonging to the series found at Tivoli (see above); 735, 588. Poseidippos and Menander (?), the comic poets, copies of Hellenistic originals, forming a pair; 575. Narcissus, a Roman work of Alexandrian type; 573. Roman, traditionally identified as the emperor Macrinus (AD 217–18); 571. Aesculapius and Hygieia, of Alexandrian type; 567. Two children of Niobe, fragment of the well-known Florentine group; 563. Danaid, or nymph holding a cup; *561. RESTING SATYR, one of several known replicas of the famous statue of Praxiteles; *551, 547. The BARBERINI CANDELABRA, a famous pair, with representations of divinities, from Hadrian's Villa at Tivoli, Roman work in neo-Attic style (2C AD); *548 Sleeping Ariadne, copy of a Hellenistic original of the 3C or 2C BC; below, 549. Sarcophagus with a gigantomachia, 2C AD after a Hellenistic original of the 2C BC; 540. Relief of Bacchus and Ariadne, from Hadrian's Villa; 544. Hermes, copy of a 5C Greek original (school of Myron); 541. Statue of Augustus of the 1C AD with the head of Lucius Verus (AD 161–69). On the bases of several of the statues are inscriptions relating to the gens Julia-Claudia found near the Mausoleum of Augustus.

At the end is the **Gallery of Busts** divided by arches into four little rooms. ROOM I. To the right (above) 711. Caracalla; 704. Marcus Aurelius; 703. Antoninus Pius; (below) 723. Trajan; 718. Nero idealized as Apollo; 716. Old man wearing a crown of vine-leaves, possibly a priest of Dionysos, Hellenistic, 2C BC; 715. Head of Augustus as one of the Fratres Arvales, and as a boy (714); Julius Caesar, Column with three dancing Hours, found near the Ara Pacis; 598. Porphyry bust of a youth perhaps Philip the Arabian, emperor in 244–49; *592. Portrait group, Cato and Porcia, probably from a Roman tomb, 1C BC.—R. II. 702. Apollo; 698. Saturn, after an original of the 5C or 4C BC; (above) 689. Colossal bust of Serapis; 697. Isis; 694. Head of Menelaus, from a group of Menelaus with the body of Patroclus (see Pasquino). In the middle of the room, Base in the form of a rectangular chest standing on legs of winged lions, the lid decorated with flowers and foliage; on the sides, reliefs of uncertain significance.—R. IV (the recess to the left). 641. Mask of Jupiter Ammon, copy of a 4C original; 637. Woman in the attitude of prayer, Augustan after a 5C original *636. Bust of Antinoüs, an exquisite portrait; 626. Head of Juno, after a Greek original of the 5C BC.—R. III. *671. Seated statue of Zeus (Jupiter Verospi), copy of a Hellenistic original (the lower part is a restoration); 784. Celestial globe; 654. Head of one of the Diadochoi wearing the regal fillet; 653. Augur; 651. Mithras in Phrygian cap; 675. Pan.

The so-called **Open Loggia** (*Loggia Scoperta*), not always open to the public, skirts the N side of the Belvedere Pavilion as far as the Mask Room. 858.

Fragment of relief depicting a youth taking part in a Bacchic procession, 3C AD; 862. Frieze, in two sections, with scenes of farm activities and of the sale of bread in a baker's shop, 3C AD; over the door to the Mask Room, Sepulchral relief of Galatea, a priestess of Isis, with her husband, 2C AD.

The **Mask Room** (*Gabinetto delle Maschere*; usually locked, but visible through a glass door), entered also from the Gallery of Statues, derives its name from four *Mosaics of theatrical masks in the pavement. They came from Hadrian's Villa and date from the 2C AD. The border is of the time of Pius VI and bears his coat of arms. Opposite the entrance, *812. VENUS OF KNIDOS, a fine copy of the famous statue of Praxiteles. The head belongs to another copy of the statue; the limbs are mainly restorations. The goddess is about to bathe; she has a towel and, near by, a pitcher (hydria).—On the left, 810. The Graces, from an original perhaps of the 2C BC. In the niche opposite, 801. Satyr, in rosso antico, from a bronze original (Hellenistic, 2C BC). On the wall between the doors, 815. Venus at her bath, copy of a larger original by Doidalsas, a Bithynian sculptor of the 3C BC (being restored).

From the Animal Room (see above) is the entrance to the **Hall of the Muses** (*Sala delle Muse*) with paintings by Tommaso Conca; it comprises an octagon, with a vestibule at either end. FIRST VESTIBULE. Herms (including, 322. Sophocles). Reliefs (above): 321. Pyrrhic dance, a 4C Attic work; Birth of Bacchus.—OCTAGON, a magnificent hall with 16 columns of Carrara marble. Seven of the statues of the Nine Muses in this room were found, together with that of Apollo, in a villa near Tivoli, and are generally held to be copies of originals, apparently of bronze, by Praxiteles or his school, but possibly they do not all belong to the same group. 317. Erato; 312. Calliope; 310. Apollo Kitharoidos, an expressive figure; 308. Terpsichore. Nos. 303 and 293 (Euterpe and Urania) were not found with the rest and were not, in fact, originally intended for muses. 299. Melpomene; 295. Thalia; 291. Clio; 287. Polyhymnia. The statues alternate with hermae: Metrodorus; So-called Alcibiades; 315. Homer; 314. Socrates; Strategos (Alcibiades?); 305. Plato (not Zeno); 302. Euripides; 301. Epicurus; 289. Demosthenes. In the centre, *1192. BELVEDERE TORSO, found in the Campo dei Fiori at the time of Julius II, and bearing the signature of Apollonios, an Athenian sculptor of the 1C BC. The figure is sitting on a hide laid over the ground. Greatly admired by Michelangelo, Raphael, and other Renaissance artists, its subject is uncertain: Hercules, Polyphemus, Prometheus, Sciron, Marsyas, and Philoctetes, are among the guesses.—SECOND VESTIBULE. Herm of Pericles, copy of a 5C original by Kresilas; herms of Bias and Periander.

Circular Hall (*Sala Rotonda*) designed on the model of the Pantheon. In the pavement, Mosaic of Otricoli, representing a battle between Greeks and Centaurs, Tritons, and Nereids; in the centre of the room, a huge monolithic porphyry vase found in the Domus Aurea; *257. Jupiter of Otricoli, a colossal head of majestic beauty, attributed to Bryaxis (4C BC); 256. Antinoüs (died AD 130) as Bacchus, from a Greek prototype of the 4C BC (the drapery, which was originally of bronze, was restored by Thorvaldsen); 255. Faustina the Elder (died 141), wife of Antoninus Pius; *254. Female divinity, perhaps Demeter, wearing the peplos, after a Greek original of the late 5C BC. 253. Head of Hadrian, from his mausoleum; 252. Hercules, colossal statue in gilded bronze, an early Imperial copy of a work of the school of Skopas; 251. Bust of Antinoüs; 249. Juno (the Barberini Hera), a Roman copy of a cult-image in the manner of the late 5C; 248. Marine divinity (from Pozzuoli), believed to personify the Gulf of Baiae, an interesting example of the fusion of marine elements and human features; *246. Nerva (or Galba), after a statue representing Jupiter; 245. Bust of Serapis, after a work by Bryaxis; 243. Claudius as Jupiter; 242. Head of Claudius; 241. Juno Sospita from Lanuvium, dating from the Antonine period; 240. Head of Plotina (died 129), wife of Trajan; 258. Head of Pertinax (?); 259. Genius of Augustus; 260. Head of Julia Domna (died 217), wife of Septimius Severus.

Hall of the Greek Cross (*Sala a Croce Greca*). To the left of the doorway, 199. C. Caesar, nephew of Augustus, sacrificing. *238. Sarcophagus in porphyry, of St Helena, mother of Constantine, decorated with Roman horsemen, barbarian prisoners, and fallen soldiers; *237, Sarcophagus of Constantia, daughter of Constantine, in porphyry, decorated with vine-branches and children bearing grapes, peacocks, and a ram (Christian symbols); this sarcophagus was once in the church of Santa Costanza, in Via Nomentana, built by Constantine as a mausoleum for his daughter. 236, 239. Two granite sphinxes; and, in the pavement, Mosaics: *Basket of flowers, Shield with the head of Minerva and the phases of the moon.

Ahead is the landing of the Simonetti Staircase. It ascends to a second landing outside the Gallery of the Candelabra (p 320) and the Room of the Biga (right).

The **Sala della Biga** (with glass doors, usually locked) is a circular domed hall by *Camporese*. *2368. BIGA, or two-horsed chariot, a reconstruction in 1788 by *F.A. Franzoni* from ancient fragments; only the body of the chariot and part of the offside horse are original. The body was used as an episcopal throne in the church of San Marco during the Middle Ages. The bas-reliefs suggest that the Biga was a votive chariot dedicated to Ceres and that it dates from the 1C AD.— Along the wall, from the left, 2344. Charioteer; with the head from another statue; *2346. Discobolos, a copy of Myron's work with the head wrongly restored; 2347. Hermes (so-called Phokion), from a 5C original (head a copy of a head of a 4C strategos); *2349. Discobolos, from a bronze original by Naucides, nephew and pupil of Polykleitos, a fine example of Peloponnesian sculpture of the 5C BC; *2355. Roman in the act of sacrifice (early Empire), with voluminous draperies; *2363. Bearded Dionysos, called Sardanapalus, a work of the early 4C BC, attributed to Kephisodotos.—2364, 2356, 2348 2341. Sarcophagi of children (3C AD); the first three are adorned with circus scenes, with cupids as competitors; the fourth represents the chariot race between Oinomaos and Pelops.

The Simonetti staircase continues up to the Etruscan Museum.

The Etruscan Museum

The *Etruscan Museum, reached by a staircase from the landing outside the Room of the Biga, was founded in 1837 by Gregory XVI and its official name is *Museo Gregoriano Etrusco*. One of the most important collections of its kind in existence, it has been undergoing a complete reorganization since the time of Pio XII; this has recently been completed. Most of the contents come from Southern Etruria, but there are also outstanding examples of Greek and Roman art, the collection of Greek vases being especially notable.

R. I, OF THE SARCOPHAGI. Sarcophagi from Tuscania, with the slaughter of the Niobids, and from Tarquinia, with mythological scenes (1C BC); Sarcophagi with scene of procession (3C), and a wedding (?) procession from Caere (Cerveteri; 5C); Cippus from Todi, with bilingual inscription in Latin and Celtic.

R. II, OF THE REGOLINI-GALASSI TOMB. The interesting frescoes are by *Fed. Barocci* and *Taddeo Zuccari*. The room contains objects found in 1836 in an Etruscan necropolis S of Caere where a small group of tumulus chamber-tombs have been unearthed; the most important is the *REGOLINI-GALASSI TOMB, named after its discoverers. The funeral equipment of at least two individuals is involved; they were buried around the middle of the 7C. The contents are arranged in a large wall case according to the position in which the objects were found (as illustrated). They include: *Gold clasp, with repoussé decoration; gold necklaces; bracelets. Ivories, cups, plates, and silver ornaments, of Greco-Oriental provenance. Lebes, or libation bowl, with six handles in the forms of animals: reconstructed chair.—Equipment of a man, who was probably a lucumo or priest-king. *Vase, where ashes were found (possibly a cremation urn); series of fictile statuettes; equipment of a buried man, who was doubtless a warrior of high rank. Bronze incense-burner in the shape of a wagon. Bronze stand with repoussé figures; two five-handled lebetes. Silver drinking cup; small dishes of Eastern origin. In the middle of the room, the reconstructed Biga, funeral chariot and bronze bed.—The two cases on the window wall contain the equipment of tombs in the immediate vicinity of the Regolini-Galassi Tomb, including Bucchero Vases in relief, and ceramics from another tomb in the necropolis.

ROOM III, OF THE BRONZES. The frescoes were painted under Pius IV by *Nic. Pomarancio* and *Santi di Tito*. It contains a rich collection of objects in common use.—In glass cases: incense-burner, tripod, buckles, jars, small throne, etc. Two statuettes of children wearing the bulla.—*Mars of Todi, wearing armour, a bronze statue dating from the beginning of the 4C, but inspired by Greek art of the 5C. In glass cases to left, Mirrors and Candelabra; to the right, Mirrors, cistae, paterae, sheet bronze, vases, etc. Among them note the *Mirror engraved with Herakles and Atlas, and another with Chalchas, the soothsayer, transformed into a haruspex, both designs derived from Greek models of 5–4C BC; oval *CISTA, with a battle between Greeks and Amazons, the handle formed by a satyr and a nymph riding on swans (from Vulci). Most of these cistae, which were used to hold toilet implements, came from Praeneste. Patera with the figure of Eos (Aurora) carrying away Kephalos.—R. IV, OF THE URNS. Cinerary urns of marble, travertine, and alabaster. They are of the type from Chiusi and Volterra. Notable is the *Alabaster urn, with relief of the chariot-race between Pelops and Oinomaos (2C BC).

A short flight of stairs leads up to the next series of rooms (temporarily closed in 1988), all with extensive views over Rome, towards Monte Mario.—R. V. THE GUGLIELMI ROOM, named after Benedetto Guglielmi of Vulci, was opened in 1937 to mark the centenary of the museum. All the exhibits are from Vulci. Of particular interest are: Bronze incense-burner supported by the figure of a youth (in the wall-case to the left, with no number); Bucchero jar with incised decoration and a 6C inscription (in the wall-case to the right, on the extreme left with no number); *Red-figured hydria, perhaps by the Athenian Euthymides c 520 (opposite, in Case K). Other glass cases contain bronzes, Greek red- and black-figured vases, Etruscan vases, and gold objects.—R. VI (to the left) contains a collection of jewellery, mostly from Vulci. Interesting are: Necklace with pomegranate drops; coronets and diadems used as funerary wreaths; bulla in gold, on a chain, found at Ostia; silver and bronze clasp in the Daedalic style (7C BC).—R. VII, OF THE TER-RACOTTAS, contains cinerary urns in cases, Bucchero vases, ante-fixes, statues, votive objects, etc. Etruscan portrait heads of both sexes and all ages date from the Archaic period to the 1C AD. They were probably ex-votos, as were the models of legs, feet, etc. The animated expression of the heads is heightened by the colouring. Some of the urns bear traces of their original colour. The fronts are decorated with reliefs of funeral or mythological scenes after Greek models, or scenes of combat, abduction, or the chase. In Case M is a lifelike figure of a young man. There are also lids of sarcophagi in the shape of beds on which the deceased are lying. On the end wall is a group of terracotta statues from a temple in Tivoli, including part of a frieze with male and female heads flanked by figures of children.

R. VIII. ANTIQUARIUM ROMANUM. This room is in three sections. Section 1. On the right wall, cases A and E: Three reliefs showing Hercules fighting the lion, the hydra, and the bull; Roman scales; bronze weight in the shape of a crouching pig, marked C (i.e. 100 Roman pounds); armour in bronze and iron; rings, pins, keys, etc. In the other wall cases (B, C, F, and G) are antefixes and friezes in terracotta, and architectonic fragments. In the centre (D), ivory and bone objects, including a doll with movable limbs (4C AD), also bronze statuettes.—Section 2. To the right, fragmentary bronze male torso.—Cases I and K: Ceramics from Arezzo, finely decorated; Roman lamps. Case M: Roman glass vases, some of which still have their lids. Other cases contain terracotta wall reliefs, alabaster phials of Greek and Eastern origin found in Etruscan tombs, and ivory work.—Section 3. Bronze head of a woman (1–2C AD); portrait of a Roman wearing a laurel crown (3C AD); fragment of a bronze portrait-statue of a Roman (1C BC). From the second section of the Antiquarium there is access to R. IX (the FALCIONI collection), containing bronze, gold, and terracotta objects coming from the neighbourhood of Viterbo.

Just before R. XI, the *STAIRCASE OF BRAMANTE (described above) which descends to the Museo Pio-Clementino, can be seen through a glass door. R. 12a and b. formerly housed the Greek originals now displayed in the Museo Gregoriano Profano (see below).

A corridor, with objects from the Antiquarium Romanum, bends to the left, and ends on a landing at the top of the *Staircase of Assyrian Reliefs* (usually closed), with reliefs and inscriptions of the 9–7C BC; also some Cufic sepulchral inscriptions of the 11–12C AD (some of which are now on display in the Egyptian Museum, see above). The staircase goes down to the landing near the Round Vestibule (p 312).

RR. XIV–XVIII. The **Vase Rooms** include two floors of the hemicycle (RR. XVI, XVII) which looks out on the Cortile della Pigna. They contain a valuable *COLLECTION OF GREEK, ITALIC, AND ETRUSCAN VASES. Most of them come from the Etruscan tombs of Southern Etruria, where they were discovered in the course of the excavations of the first half of last century. At the time of their discovery, when the science of archaeology had scarcely developed, the vases were all indiscriminately called Etruscan. It was only later that the Greek origin of many of them was realized and, with this realization, was appreciated the importance of the commercial relations between Greece and Etruria. From the end of the 7C to the later 5C many

Greek vases were imported. By the middle of the 4C the Greek imports were largely replaced by the products of Magna Graecia, Lucania, and Campania.

R. XVIII. ITALIOT VASES. Here are interesting examples of the products of Magna Graecia. During the 4C the centres of ceramic activity shifted from Attica to the Greek colonies in Southern Italy. Conspicuous among these Italiot vases were the products of the potteries of Tarentum. Among them is a vase with elaborate handles, illustrating the myth of Triptolemos, the inventor of agriculture. Another (4C BC) has a caricature of a classical myth.—R. XVI (hemicycle), with frescoes of the time of Pius VI, depicting Rome, the Vatican, and scenes in the Papal States. There is a view of St Peter's Sacristy, then recently built. (In the courtyard a building 12 metres below ground level was opened in 1981 to house the Secret Archives of the Vatican Library). Here are displayed ATTIC VASES. Among the BLACK-FIGURED type is an *Amphora signed by Exekias, who flourished in the second half of the 6C. One side shows Achilles and Ajax playing with dice; on the other side Castor and Pollux are being welcomed on their return home by their parents, Tyndareus and Leda. Another amphora shows Eos grieving over the dead body of her son Memnon. There are also Panathenaic amphorae, with the figure of Athena Promachos, of the type given to winners at the great Athenian festivals. Until the end of the 6C figures had been painted in black on the red background; colours were often added to the black; white to indicate flesh and red or violet for draperies. Now the process was reversed. The figures were surrounded with black and appeared in the natural red colour of the vase. This technique survived until the Hellenistic period to the exclusion of that of the black figures, except for the Panathenaic vases (see above) which retained the old style. A kylix with a black figure of a running youth inside and red figures outside is an interesting example of the transition. Another kylix with a similar subject has all the figures in red. Both are of the 6C. *Kylix by the famous 5C vase painter Duris, with Oedipus trying to solve the riddle of the Sphinx.—In the upper hemicycle (R. XVII) the display includes: *Hydria, with Apollo flying over the sea; Amphora, with figures of Achilles and Briseis (5C); *Krater with a white background, depicting Hermes carrying the infant Dionysus to the nymphs of Mount Nysa, who are to bring him up; *Oinochoë (wine jug), with two youths about to set on their fighting cocks (5C BC).

R. XV, frescoed by Pomarancio, contains the private collection left to the Museum in 1967 by Astarita of Naples. It includes a large Krater of the late Corinthian period showing Ulysses and Menaleus asking for the return of Helen.—R. XIV contains specimens of EARLIER PERIODS. Among them are examples of the Geometric style, which reached its peak of development in the 8C, and of the orientalizing style, which appeared in the 7C. As its name implies, the Geometric style relied on geometric designs and excluded floral and animal motifs. In the later style representations of animals and mythological figures began to appear. The most important vases in this new style were made in Corinth, and the first examples were called Protocorinthian.

Decorated with geometric designs and made by hand are Cinerary urns of the Villanova period (1st Iron Age; 9–8C), so called after Villanova, near Bologna, where an important necropolis was discovered. There are also Protocorinthian aryballoi (oil jars used by athletes); the human figures show the orientalizing style (7C). Note also Corinthian dinos (wine-cooler); Caeretan hydria, so called because the type came from Caere (Italic, showing the influence of Ionia, 6C); Laconian kylix, from Sparta, with figures of Tityos and Sisyphos (6C).

The Simonetti staircase leads back down to the Quattro Cancelli.

II. Gallery of Tapestries, Raphael Rooms, Borgia Rooms and Gallery of Modern Religious Art, Sistine Chapel, Museum of Christian Art, Sistine Hall and Library

From the Quattro Cancelli the Scala Simonetti leads up two flights of stairs to the landing outside the Room of the Biga. Here is the beginning of Bramante's long West Gallery with the Gallery of the Candelabra, the Gallery of Tapestries, and the Gallery of Maps.

The **Gallery of the Candelabra** (80m long) is named after the pairs of marble candelabra, of the Roman Imperial period, placed on either side of the arches which divide it into six sections. The ceiling has frescoes (restored in 1974) by *D. Torti* and *L. Seitz* illustrating events in the pontificate of Leo XIII. In the pavement are inserted marbles from the Emporia, the warehouses of ancient Rome.

SECTION I. 2422. Sarcophagus of a child, Roman, 3C AD; Pair of candelabra from Otricoli, with reliefs of Bacchic rites and of Apollo and Marsyas, Roman, 2C BC.—SECT. II. Pan extracting a thorn from a satyr's foot, copy of a 2C Hellenistic original; 2505. Diana of the Ephesians, 3C AD; 2513. Sarcophagus with the legend of Orestes, 2C AD; 2487, 2482. Candelabra of the 2C AD from a Roman villa later used in the churches of Sant'Agnese fuori le Mura and Santa Costanza; 2465. Sarcophagus with the story of Protesilaos and Laodamia; 2445. Ganymede carried off by the eagle, after a bronze original by Leochares.

SECT. III. On the walls, Fragments of frescoes from a Roman villa at Tor Marancia (near the Catacombs of Domitilla), with flying figures, 2C AD; 2580. Mosaic of fish, fruit, etc.; Apollo from an archaic Greek type; 2555. Satyr with young Dionysos on his shoulders (1C AD).

SECT. IV. Statuette of Maritime Victory, from a Hellenistic original (the head is from another figure); Portrait statue of a woman (with substituted head), 1C AD; *2698. Sarcophagus with Dionysos and Ariadne and Dionysiac scenes, 2C AD; *2684. Fisherman, a realistic work of the school of Pergamon (3C BC); 2673. *Upper part of a statue of Cronos (Saturn), copy of a 4C original; *2672. Tyche (Fortune) of Antioch, from a bronze by Eutychides, a pupil of Lysippos; *2655. Boy with goose, from a bronze by Boethus of Chalcedon, 3C BC; *2635. Sarcophagus with the slaughter of the Niobids, a fine work of the 2C AD; 2622. Boy of the Julio-Claudian family, 1C AD.

SECT. V. *2784. Girl running in a race during a Peloponnesian religious festival, Roman copy of a Greek bronze original of the 5C BC (being restored); 2760. Young satyr playing the flute.—SECT. VI. 2834. Artemis, from a Prax-itelean original; the head (which does not belong) is a copy of a 5C bronze; 2826. Statuette of a woman wearing a cloak, copy of a Hellenistic original of the 4C or 3C BC; Sarcophagus with Diana and Endymion; 2807. Youth wearing the Phrygian cap, in the manner of Praxiteles; Niobid, copy of a Hellenistic original of the 4C or 3C BC; *2794. Fighting Persian, statuette after an original bronze belonging to the series of statues given by Attalos I of Pergamon to the Athenians which were placed on the Acropolis in Athens; 2796. Sarcophagus with the rape of the daughters of Leukippos.

The **Gallery of Tapestries** is divided into three rooms, and contains the so-called 'New School' series of tapestries executed after Raphael's death from cartoons by his pupils, some of which were copied from drawings he had left. Also displayed here are Roman and Flemish tapestries. ROOM 1. Raphael 'New School' tapestries, woven in Brussels in the 16C: *149. Adoration of the Shepherds; *151. Adoration of the Magi; 148. Presentation at the temple.—209, 210, 211. Tapestries illustrating the life of Urban VIII, the most important product of the Barberini workshop active in Rome, 1627–83.—ROOM 2. Raphael 'New School' tapestries: *152. Resurrection of Christ; 156–154. Massacre of the Innocents (from a cartoon attrib. to *Tomaso Vincidor*); 146. Christ appearing to Mary Magdalene; 147. Supper at Emmaus.—215, 213, and 212. More 17C Roman tapestries illustrating the life of Urban VIII (see above).—ROOM 3. 79. Death of Julius Caesar, Flemish (1594).

The **Gallery of Maps** (*Galleria delle Carte Geografiche*) was decorated in the time of Gregory XIII, the reformer of the calendar. On the walls are maps and plans painted in 1580–83 by the Dominican cosmographer, architect, and painter, *Ignazio Danti* of Perugia. They represent ancient and modern Italy various regions of Italy and the neighbouring islands; and the papal territory of Avignon. There are also several town plans and views of seaports, including one (on the end wall) of *Venice.—The ceiling was decorated with stuccoes and frescoes by a group of painters under the direction of *Girolamo Muziano*. Along the walls are herms of Socrates, Plato, and others.

Beyond the Gallery of Maps is the **Gallery of Pius V** in which are more tapestries of the late 15C: 33. Scenes of the Passion; *34. The Creed. On the right, 157. Religion, Grace, and Charity, woven in 1525 in Brussels; 143. Coronation of the Virgin, woven in Brussels in the 16C from a cartoon of the

New School' of Raphael. To the right is the **Ladies' Audience Room** (*Sala delle Dame*; closed indefinitely), added by Paul V (1605–21). This room was formerly used as a private audience chamber for ladies, who were not admitted into the pontifical apartments. The frescoes, by *Guido Reni*, represent the Transfiguration, Ascension, and Pentecost.—At the end of the gallery is the *Chapel of St Pius V*, one of three superimposed; to the left is the SOBIESKI ROOM, where the floor is inlaid with mosaics from Ostia. The room is named from a painting by *J. Matejko*, Relief of Vienna by John Sobieski on 12 Sept. 1683.

Beyond is the **Hall of the Immaculate Conception**, a room decorated with frescoes by *Fr. Podesti* which illustrate the definition and proclamation of the dogma of the Immaculate Conception pronounced by Pius IX on 8 December 1854. On the ceiling are the arms of Pius IX; the floor has 2C mosaics from Ostia.—Beyond are the Raphael Rooms.

* * Stanze of Raphael

The series of rooms was built by Nicholas V, and the walls were originally painted by Andrea del Castagno, Piero della Francesca, and Bened. Bonfigli. Julius II employed a group of great artists to continue the decoration, including Luca Signorelli, Perugino, Sodoma, Bramantino, Bald. Peruzzi, Lor. Lotto, and the Flemish painter Jan Ruysch. Bramante, the Urbinese architect of St Peter's, recommended his fellow-citizen, Raffaello Sanzio, and the Pope sent for him, and set him to a trial work immediately on his arrival in Rome in 1508. The result proved so satisfactory that Julius dismissed all the other painters, ordered their works to be destroyed, and commissioned Raphael to decorate the whole of this part of the Vatican. The Stanze are the painter's masterpiece; they show the extraordinary development which took place in his art during the years between his coming to Rome and his early death in 1520.

When Raphael arrived, the court of Julius II was an intellectual centre of the first rank; the College of Cardinals and the Curia included among their members many celebrated savants, humanists, and men of letters; and a crowd of artists, led by Bramante and Michelangelo, were at work in the city. In this highly cultured environment Raphael, who had great powers of assimilation, acquired an entirely new manner of painting.—The chronological order of the paintings is as follows: the Astronomy, Apollo, Adam and Eve, and Judgment of Solomon, in the Stanza della Segnatura (II), which were probably his trial works; next come the other frescoes in this room, then successively, the Stanza d'Eliodoro (III), Stanza dell'Incendio (I), and Stanza di Costantino (IV).—The frescoes in the Stanza dell'Incendio are being restored in 1988.

The entrance to the Stanze has been altered. A covered balcony from the Hall of the Immaculate Conception leads direct to the farthest room, the Sala di Costantino (IV), and the rooms then have to be visited in reversed chronological order, as described below.

IV. **Sala di Costantino**, painted almost entirely in the time of Clement VII (1523–34), after Raphael's death, by *Giulio Romano* with the assistance of *Francesco Penni* and *Raff. del Colle*. On the wall facing the window is the VICTORY OF CONSTANTINE OVER MAXENTIUS near the Pons Milvius, for which Raphael had made some sketches.

The reddish tint which suffuses the picture is characteristic of Giulio Romano. To the right are figures of St Urban, Justice, and Charity; to the left, St Sylvester, Faith, and Religion.

On the entrance wall: CONSTANTINE ADDRESSING HIS SOLDIERS AND THE VISION OF THE CROSS, by *Giulio Romano*, perhaps from Raphael's design; to the right of this, St Clement, Temperance, and Meekness; to the left, St Peter, the Church, and Eternity.—On the wall opposite the entrance: The BAPTISM OF CONSTANTINE by St Sylvester (a portrait of Clement VII), by *Fr. Penni*, and at the sides (right) St Leo, Innocence, and Truth, and (left) St Damasus, Prudence, and Peace.—On the window wall: CONSTANTINE'S DONATION OF ROME TO SYLVESTER, by *Raff. del Colle*. At the sides: (right) Gregory VII (?) and Fortitude; (left) St Sylvester and Courage. Below are other scenes from the life of Constantine. On the ceiling, the Triumph of Christianity, by *Tomaso Laureti*. In the floor is a 2C Roman mosaic with the Seasons.

It is now necessary to interrupt the visit to the Stanze in order to see

the Room of the Chiaroscuri and the Chapel of Nicholas V. From the
Sala di Costantino a door leads into the **Room of the Chiaroscuri** or
the *Room of the Grooms* (*Sala dei Palafrenieri*). This room has a
magnificent carved and gilded *Ceiling, with the Medici arms, but
the frescoes by Raphael were obliterated by Pius IV, and the existing
monochrome frescoes were added under Gregory XIII.—The adjoining **Chapel of Nicholas V** has *Frescoes by *Fra Angelico*, painted
between 1448 and 1450. These represent scenes from the lives of the
deacon saints Stephen (upper section) and Laurence (lower section);
especially fine is the painting of St Stephen preaching. On the ceiling
are the four Evangelists and on the pilasters the Doctors of the
Church.

The **Loggia of Raphael** (formerly reached from the Sala di Costantino) has been closed to the public for a number of years (adm to
scholars only with special permission). The long gallery of 13 bays
overlooks the Courtyard of St Damasus with a fine view of Rome
beyond. Situated on the second floor of the palace, it was begun by
Bramante about 1513 and completed after Bramante's death by
Raphael and his pupils. The vault of each bay has four little
paintings, so that there are 52 in all. The grotteschi of the borders are
considered to have been inspired by those in the Domus Aurea of
Nero, which were discovered in 15C and known to Raphael. The
designs were carried out by *Giulio Romano, Giov. da Udine, Fr.
Penni, Perino del Vaga, Polidoro da Caravaggio*, and others. Contro-
versial restoration work was carried out on the paintings in 1978.

The subjects of the paintings in the vaults are (beginning at the other end of the
Loggia): I. Separation of light from darkness; Separation of land and water;
Creation of sun and moon; Creation of the animals.—II. Creation of Eve; the
Fall; Expulsion from Paradise; Adam and Eve labouring.—III. Building the Ark;
the Deluge; Coming out of the Ark; Noah's Sacrifice.—IV. Abraham and
Melchisedek; God's covenant with Abraham; Abraham and the three angels;
Flight of Lot.—V. God appearing to Isaac; Abimelech spying upon Isaac and
Rebecca; Isaac blessing Jacob; Jacob and Esau.—VI. Jacob's dream; Jacob and
Rachel at the well; Jacob reproaching Laban; Jacob's journey.—VII. Joseph
telling his dream to his brethren; Joseph sold by his brethren; Joseph and
Potiphar's wife; Joseph interpreting Pharaoh's dream.—VIII. Moses in the
bulrushes; the Burning Bush; Pharaoh drowned in the Red Sea; Moses striking
the rock.—IX. Moses receiving the Tables of the Law; Worship of the Golden
Calf; Moses and the pillar of fire; Moses showing the Tables of the Law to the
people.—X. Crossing of Jordan; Fall of Jericho; Joshua making the sun stand
still; Joshua and Eleazar dividing Palestine among the twelve tribes.—XI.
Samuel anointing David; David and Goliath; Triumph of David; David and
Bathsheba.—XII. Crowning of Solomon; Judgment of Solomon; Queen of
Sheba; Building of the Temple.—XIII. Nativity; the Magi; Baptism of Christ;
Last Supper.

A door leads back into the Raphael Stanze from the Room of the
Chiaroscuri. ROOM III. **Stanza d'Eliodoro**, painted by *Raphael* in
1512–14; the subjects were nearly all chosen by Julius II. On the
principal wall (right) is the EXPULSION OF HELIODORUS FROM THE
TEMPLE at Jerusalem, alluding to Julius II's success in freeing the
States of the Church from foreign powers. The picture illustrates a
story in the Apocrypha (Macc. II, 3), which tells how King Seleucus
sent his treasurer Heliodorus to Jerusalem to seize the Temple
treasure, and how the crime was avenged by a horseman assisted by
two angels with whips.

In the middle of the crowd on the left appears the figure of Julius II, carried on
the sedia gestatoria, the front bearer being a portrait of the engraver
Marcantonio Raimondi. In the centre of the composition, under the vault of the

temple, the high priest Onias renders thanks to God before the Ark of the Covenant.

On the left is the MASS OF BOLSENA, a representation of a famous miracle which took place in 1263. A priest, who had doubts regarding the doctrine of Transubstantiation, saw blood issue from the Host at the moment of the sacrifice, and became convinced. (The stained corporal is preserved in the cathedral at Orvieto.) The allusion is to the vow made by Julius II when, on his first expedition against Bologna in 1506, he stopped at Orvieto to pay honour to the corporal. He is shown kneeling opposite the priest, in place of Urban IV, the contemporary pope. The warm colouring and, especially, the harmony of reds show the influence of the Venetian painters who had arrived in Rome (Seb. del Piombo, Lor. Lotto, etc.).

On the long wall is LEO I REPULSING ATTILA, a subject originally selected by Julius II and taken up again at the instance of Leo X, considerable changes then being made in the design, and executed partly by Raphael's school. The scene representing the banks of the Mincio, where the event took place, was replaced by the environs of Rome, and the figure of the Pope, on a white mule, was brought from the back of the picture into the foreground in order to accentuate the allusion to the battle of Ravenna (11 April 1512), at which Leo X, then a cardinal, was present, and which resulted in the expulsion of the French from Italy. Attila, mounted on a white horse, and the Huns behind him, are struck with terror by a vision of St Peter and St Paul.

On the fourth wall is the DELIVERANCE OF ST PETER, alluding to the captivity of Leo X after the battle of Ravenna. Three episodes are skilfully shown: in the middle, the interior of the prison is seen through a high barred window, with St Peter awaking as the Angel frees him from his chains; on the left are the guards outside the prison; and on the right St Peter escaping with the Angel. These night scenes have remarkable light effects.

The decoration of the lower part of the walls, with caryatids and four herms is now attrib. to *Perino del Vaga*. The ceiling paintings of God appearing to Noah, Jacob's dream, the Burning Bush, and Abraham's Sacrifice are generally attrib. to *Peruzzi*.

ROOM II. The **Stanza della Segnatura**, where the pope signed bulls and briefs, has the most beautiful and harmonious frescoes in the series. It was painted entirely by *Raphael* in 1508–11. On the long wall opposite the entrance is the famous DISPUTA or DISPUTATION ON THE HOLY SACRAMENT, representing a discussion on the Eucharist but essentially intended as a Glorification of Catholicism. Given an extremely difficult subject, the painter has succeeded in making the relatively limited space occupied by the composition, which is divided into two zones, appear far larger than it is.

In the celestial portion Christ appears between the Virgin and St John the Baptist; above is God the Father surrounded by angels; beneath, the Holy Dove between the four angels holding the book of the Gospels; on the left are St Peter, Adam, St John the Evangelist, David, St Lawrence, and Jeremiah (?); on the right, St Paul, Abraham, St James, Moses, St Stephen and Judas Maccabaeus. In the middle of the terrestrial portion stands an altar on which is a monstrance with the Host; on the right are SS. Augustine and Ambrose, on the left SS. Gregory and Jerome; around, an assembly of doctors of the Church, popes, cardinals, dignitaries, and the faithful. Certain figures are thought to be portraits of Duns Scotus, SS. Dominic, Francis, Thomas Aquinas, and Nicholas of Bari; the man pointing upward with his right hand is said to be Pietro Lombardo; on the right appears the head of Dante crowned with laurel, and, beyond him (in a black hat), Savonarola; on the extreme left is Fra Angelico in the black Dominican habit and, in the foreground, Bramante.

Beneath the picture are three monochrome paintings by *Perino del Vaga*:

Pagan Sacrifice, St Augustine and the child on the seashore, and the Cumaean Sibyl showing the Virgin to Augustus.

On the wall nearest the Courtyard of the Belvedere is the PAR-NASSUS. Apollo is playing the violin in the shade of laurels surrounded by the nine Muses and the great poets.

Calliope is seated on the left, and behind her are Melpomene, Terpsichore, and Polyhymnia; on the right, also seated, is Erato, and behind her are Clio, Thalia, Euterpe, and Urania. In the group of poets on the left appears the figure of the blind Homer, between Dante and Virgil; lower are Alcaeus, Corinna, Petrarch, and Anacreon, with the voluptuous form of Sappho seated beside them. In the group on the right are Ariosto (?), Ovid, Tibullus, and Propertius, and, lower, Sannazaro, Horace, and Pindar, seated.

Below the picture are two monochrome subjects: on the left, Alexander placing Homer's poems in the tomb of Achilles (or, possibly, the discovery of a sarcophagus containing Greek and Latin MSS on the Janiculum in 181 BC); on the right, Augustus preventing Virgil's friends from burning the Aeneid (or else the consuls causing Greek works to be burned as harmful to the Roman religion). Below these again is some very fine painted intarsia-work by Fra Giovanni da Verona.

18C engraving of Raphael's School of Athens in the Vatican

On the wall facing the Disputa is the splendid SCHOOL OF ATHENS, which represents the triumph of Philosophy, forming a pendant to the triumph of Theology opposite. The scene is a portico, at the sides of which are statues of Apollo and Minerva, with steps ascending to the façade of the palace of Science, a magnificent example of Renaissance design for which Raphael was indebted to Bramante. The splendid vaulting, well depicted in light and shade, is clearly inspired by the Baths of Caracalla. In this stately framing the greatest philosophers and scholars of all the ages are gathered round the two supreme masters, Plato and Aristotle. Plato (thought to be intended as a portrait of Leonardo da Vinci) points heavenward, symbolizing his system of speculative philosophy, while Aristotle's calm gesture indicates the vast field of nature as the realm of scientific research.

At the top of the steps, on Plato's side, is the bald head and characteristic profile of Socrates: Aeschines, Alcibiades (represented as a young warrior), Xenophon, and others are conversing near him; the beckoning figure next to Xenophon is evidently Chrysippus. At the foot of the steps on the left is Zeno, an old man with a beard, seen in profile; near him Epicurus, crowned with vine-leaves, is reading a book; in the foreground Pythagoras is writing out his harmonic tables, with Averroes, in a turban, and Empedocles looking over. The young man sitting down is Federico Gonzaga, who was included by order of Julius II; the handsome youth standing up is Francesco Maria della Rovere; beside him, his foot resting on a block of marble, is Anaxagoras or Xenocrates, or, according to some, Aristoxenus. The seated figure of Heracleitus, isolated in the centre foreground, was not part of the original composition; obviously inspired by Michelangelo's work in the Sistine chapel (the first section of the vault was uncovered in 1510), it has also recently been suggested that it was intended as a portrait of him. On the right, around Aristotle, are the students of the exact sciences; at the foot of the steps is Ptolemy, with his back to the spectator, and, because of a confusion with the Egyptian kings of the same name, wearing a crown. Opposite him is Zoroaster, holding a sphere, and near by, in the right-hand corner, Raphael has introduced portraits of himself and Sodoma. To the left is Archimedes or Euclid (with the features of Bramante), surrounded by his disciples and bending over a blackboard on which he is tracing figures with a compass. The solitary figure on the steps is Diogenes, also thought to be a portrait of Michelangelo.

The monochromes beneath the picture are by *Perino del Vaga*, and represent Philosophy, Astrologers in conference, and the Siege of Syracuse with the Death of Archimedes.

On the fourth wall, above the window, are the three CARDINAL VIRTUES, Fortitude, Temperance, and Prudence. On the left of the window, Justinian publishing the Pandects, representing CIVIL LAW, and beneath, Solon haranguing the Athenians, by *Perino del Vaga*. On the right, Gregory IX (in the likeness of Julius II) handing the Decretals to a jurist (1227), to represent CANON LAW. The prelates around the Pope are portraits of Raphael's contemporaries; on the left, in front, is Giov. de' Medici, afterwards Leo X, then Cardinal Antonio Del Monte, Alessandro Farnese (Paul III), etc.

Beneath are Moses bringing the Israelites the Tables of Stone, by *Perino del Vaga*.—The ceiling was also painted by *Raphael*: above the Disputa, Theology; above the Parnassus, Poetry; above the School of Athens, Philosophy; and above the window wall, Justice. In the pendentives, Adam and Eve, Apollo and Marsyas, Astronomy, and the Judgement of Solomon. The small central octagon is attrib. to *Bramantino*.—The floor, in opus alexandrinum, shows the arms of Nicholas V and Leo X, and the name of Julius II.

1. **Stanza dell'Incendio**. On the ceiling is the Glorification of the Holy Trinity by *Perugino*, Raphael's master (the only work not destroyed when Raphael took over the decoration of the Stanze). The walls were painted in 1517 by Raphael's pupils (*Giulio Romano*, *Francesco Penni*, and perhaps *Perino del Vaga*) from his own designs. The subjects chosen were events of the times of Leo III (795–816) and Leo IV (847–55), most of which, however, allude to episodes in the history of Leo X.

Facing the window is the INCENDIO DI BORGO, illustrating the fire that broke out in Rome in 847, and was miraculously extinguished when Leo IV made the sign of the Cross from the loggia of St Peter's.

It was probably intended as an allusion to the achievement of Leo X in restoring peace to Italy. In the background the flames are seen threatening the old church of St Peter, the façade of which is shown; on the right, the Pope is seen coming out of the Vatican. On the left is depicted the Burning of Troy, with naked figures scaling the walls and Aeneas carrying his father Anchises on his back, followed by his wife Creusa and their son Ascanius.

Opposite the entrance wall is the CORONATION OF CHARLEMAGNE BY LEO III in 800, an obvious reference to the meeting of Leo X and Francis I at Bologna in 1516, for Leo and Charlemagne have the features of the later pope and king.—On the opposite wall the subject is the VICTORY OF LEO IV OVER THE SARACENS AT OSTIA (849), in allusion to the Crusade against the Turks proclaimed by Leo X, who is again represented in the figure of Leo IV, the two cardinals behind him being portraits of Cardinal Bibbiena and Giulio de' Medici.—On the window wall is the *Oath of Leo III*, with which that pope cleared himself in St Peter's, on 23 Dec. 800, of charges that had been brought against him. The allusion is to the Lateran Council held by Leo X.

The monochrome figures below the paintings represent Godfrey de Bouillon, Ethelwulf of England (called Astolfo), Charlemagne, Lothair I and Ferdinand of Castile.

From the Stanza dell'Incendio a door leads into the Chapel of Urban VIII, richly decorated with frescoes and stuccoes by *Pietro da Cortona*.

Outside the chapel a stairway leads down (right) to the Borgia Rooms and the new Museum of Modern Religious Art. It is possible at this point to proceed direct (left) to the Sistine chapel instead of approaching it through the Borgia Rooms and the Museum of Modern Religious Art. However the first six frescoed Borgia Rooms should not be missed even if it is not intended to continue through the 50 subsequent galleries of the Museum of Modern Art.

The Borgia Rooms and Gallery of Modern Religious Art

The **Borgia Rooms** (*Appartamento Borgia*) are named after Alexander VI (Borgia; 1492–1503), who adapted for his personal use a suite in the palace of Nicholas V and had it decorated by Pinturicchio. There are six rooms. The first two are under a quadrilateral tower—the Borgia Tower—built by Alexander VI; the last was originally part of the house that preceded the palace of Nicholas V.

After the death of Alexander VI, the Borgia Rooms continued to be occupied as papal apartments until Julius II abandoned them in 1507. Leo XIII had them restored by Lod. Seitz in 1889–97 and opened them to the public. The first two rooms (under the Borgia Tower) are immediately beneath the Hall of the Immaculate Conception; the other rooms are beneath the Raphael Rooms. The *Frescoes were executed by *Pinturicchio* and his school in 1492–95. They have recently been hung with incongruous modern paintings.

R. I, OF THE SIBYLS, is square and has 12 lunettes each with a sibyl accompanied by a prophet. The juxtaposition of sibyls and prophets illustrates an ancient belief that the sibyls foretold the coming of the Messiah to the heathen (comp. Santa Maria in Aracoeli). Here Caesar Borgia was imprisoned by Julius II in 1503, in the very room where he had caused his cousin Alfonso of Aragon to be murdered in 1500.—R. II (left) contains copes designed by *Matisse*.

R. III, OF THE CREED, is named after the scrolls on which are written the sentences of the Creed, held by the twelve Apostles depicted in the lunettes. Each Apostle is accompanied by a prophet holding an appropriate inscription. These frescoes are attributed to *Pier Matteo d'Amelia*, a successor of Pinturicchio.

R. IV, OF THE LIBERAL ARTS, symbolises the seven liberal arts: the *Trivium* (grammar, dialectic, rhetoric) and the *Quadrivium* (geometry, arithmetic, astronomy, music) which were the basis of medieval learning. The paintings are attributed to *Ant. da Viterbo*, a pupil of Pinturicchio. The Arch of Justice, in the middle, is named after its subject: the treatment is of the 16C. The ceiling is decorated with squares and grotesques alternating with the Borgia bull. The fine chimney-piece is by or after Sansovino. In this room was found the hidden treasure of Alexander VI.

R. V, OF THE SAINTS. The walls and the vault are covered with *Frescoes by Pinturicchio*, considered his greatest achievement. The room is divided by an arch into two cross-vaulted areas forming six lunettes. On the ceiling, Legend of Isis; Osiris and the bull Apis (in reference to the Borgia arms; comp. above), with reliefs in gilded stucco. Above the door, Madonna and Child with saints (medallion), not portraying Giulia Farnese. Entrance wall, the Visitation; SS Paul the Hermit and Anthony Abbot in the desert (right); End wall, *Disputation between St Catherine of Alexandria and the emperor Maximian; the saint's head has been wrongly thought to be a portrait of Lucrezia Borgia or Giulia Farnese; Pinturicchio's self-portrait is seen behind the throne; in the background is the Arch of Constantine. Window wall, Martyrdom of St Sebastian, with a view of the Colosseum. On the exit wall, Susanna and the Elders; Legend of St Barbara.

R. VI, OF THE MYSTERIES OF THE FAITH. The frescoes, partly by *Pinturicchio*, represent the Annunciation, Nativity, Adoration of the Magi, *Resurrection (the kneeling pontiff is Alexander VI), Ascension, Pentecost, and Assumption of the Virgin. The last fresco includes a portrait of the donor, perhaps Francesco Borgia. In the ceiling are stuccoes and paintings of prophets.

R. VII, OF THE POPES. The frescoes and stucco ornamentation of the splendid vaulted ceiling are by *Perino del Vaga* and *Giov. da Udine*, who carried out the work at the order of Leo X (1513–21). The room is named after portraits of the popes which have disappeared.

The **Gallery of Modern Religious Art** was arranged in 1973 in the Borgia Apartments, and in 50 or so rooms (previously closed to the public), lavishly renovated. It is an exhibition of works presented to the Pope by invited artists from all over the world. They include: Pietro Annigoni, Francis Bacon, Giac. Balla, Bernard Buffet, Carlo Carrà, Marc Chagall, Salvador Dali, Giorgio De Chirico, Fil. de Pisis, Max Ernst, Paul Gauguin, Renato Guttuso, Wassily Kandinsky, Paul Klee, Oskar Kokoschka, Fernand Leger, Carlo Levi, Giac. Manzù, Marino Marini, Arturo Martini, Henry Matisse, Henry Moore, Giorgio Morandi, Edvard Munch, Ben Nicholson, José Clemente Orozco, Pablo Picasso, Auguste Rodin, Georges Rouault, David Alfaro Siqueiros, Mario Sironi, Ardengo Soffici, Graham Sutherland, Maurice Utrillo, Maurice de Vlaminck, and numerous others. The works are arranged in no particular order, but they are fully labelled, and a hand list is available at the door.

Stairs lead up from the last gallery to the Sistine Chapel.

**The Sistine Chapel

The present entrance to the chapel is in the W wall, to the right of the altar.

The chapel takes its name from Sixtus IV who had it rebuilt by Giov. de' Dolci in 1473–81 as the official private chapel of the popes, and for the conclaves for the election of the popes which are still held here. It is famous for its superb frescoes by *Michelangelo*, perhaps the greatest pictorial decoration in Western art. The great hall is a rectangle 40m long, 13m wide, and nearly 21m high. It is lit on either side by six windows, placed rather high up.

Ceiling Frescoes. The barrel-vaulted ceiling is entirely covered by the celebrated FRESCOES OF MICHELANGELO. He is known to have been reluctant to take up this commission from Julius II, but having accepted, he completed the vault between 1508 and 1512. The complex design, which has received various theological interpretations, combines Old and New Testament figures, as well as themes from pagan prophecy and Church history. The powerful sculpturesque figures are set in an architectural design with an effect of high relief and rich colour on a huge scale. Work on the ceiling was begun at the main entrance, in the area farthest from the altar: the development in the artist's skill and his facility in the technique of fresco painting can be seen in the later figures at the altar end. The scaffolding was taken down and the first half of the ceiling revealed in 1510 to the wonder of all who came to see it.

Late 18C engraving of the Temptation and Expulsion from Paradise by Michelangelo on the vault of the Sistine Chapel

Restoration of the frescoes was begun in 1980 and is expected to continue until about 1992. The chapel is being kept open to the public throughout this remarkable operation, which will end with the restoration of the Last Judgement. The frescoes have been discoloured by dirt and candle smoke, and damaged by poor restorations in the past. The lunettes have been completed and (in 1988) six of the nine central panels of the vault. Their brilliant original colour has been restored. Important details about the way in which Michelangelo worked on this great commission have also been discovered. The holes for the scaffolding have been found beneath the windows which would seem to confirm that the scaffolding bridge from which the whole ceiling was painted was without support on the ground. Each lunette was painted in three days directly onto the fresh plaster, without the help of a preliminary cartoon or the transfer of a preparatory sketch.

Looking from the high altar, on the lower curved part of the vault are the Hebrew Prophets and pagan Sibyls sitting on architectonic thrones with mouldings in warm grisaille. Above the Last Judgement is the splendid figure of Jonah issuing from the whale. Nearest the altar, on the right side: the Libyan Sibyl; Daniel writing; the Cumaean Sibyl; Isaiah, in deep meditation; and the Delphic Sibyl. At the far end above the entrance is Zachariah. On the left side, from the altar end: Jeremiah; the Persian Sibyl; Ezekiel, with a scroll; the Erythrean Sibyl; and Joel.—Along the centre of the vault itself are nine scenes from Genesis, from the Creation to events in the life of Noah. Again looking from the altar, these are: Separation of Light from Darkness; Creation of the Sun, Moon, and Planets; Separation of Land and Sea and the Creation of the fishes and birds; Creation of Adam, perhaps the most beautiful work on the ceiling; Creation of Eve; Temptation and Expulsion from Paradise; Sacrifice of Noah; the Flood; and the Drunkenness of Noah. These are framed by decorative pairs of nudes, Michelangelo's famous 'ignudi', the most idiosyncratic elements in the ceiling and a remarkable celebration of the nude figure.—In the lunettes over the windows are figures representing the forerunners of Christ. In the spandrels on either side of the prophet-sibyl sequence are scenes of Salvation from the Old Testament: over the altar, Moses and the Brazen Serpent (right) and the Death of Haman (left); at the other end, Judith and Holofernese (right) and David and Goliath (left).

More than twenty years later, in 1535–41 *Michelangelo* was commissioned by Paul III to paint his great fresco of the **Last Judgement** on the altar wall. This involved the walling-up of two windows and the destruction of two frescoes (both by Perugino) on the side walls. The huge altarpiece, 20m by 10m, has been blackened by incense and stained with damp, and the surface has deteriorated. The unity of the conception is extraordinarily fine, and the crowded composition, with innumerable nude figures, contains a remarkable sense of movement and high relief. In the upper centre is the enigmatic figure of Christ, beardless, and seemingly derived from classical models. Near him are the Madonna and (probably) Adam, and on the right St Peter with the keys. At Christ's feet are seated St Laurence and St Bartholomew with his flayed skin (the caricature of a face seen in the folds of the skin is a self-portrait of Michelangelo). In the lunettes high up above the figure of Christ are two groups of angels bearing the instruments of the Passion. Beneath, in the central zone, on the left, are the elect ascending to heaven with the help of angels; in the centre is a group of angels with trumpets; on the right the damned are being hauled into hell and their resistance is being overcome by other angels. Especially striking is the figure of the Soul in Despair (Disperato) looking down into the abyss. In the lowest zone, on the left, is represented the Resurrection of the Body; in the centre is a cave full of devils; on the right is the entrance to hell, with the boat of Charon (as in Dante's description) and Minos, the guide to the infernal regions. Minos has the features of Biagio da Cesena (with ass's ears); he was Master of Ceremonies to Paul III and he had objected to the nudity of the figures. On the same ground Pius IV at one time intended to destroy the fresco but he contented himself with ordering Daniele da Volterra to paint garments on some of the figures.

A graceful marble screen by *Mino da Fiesole, Giov. Dalmata,* and *And. Bregno* divides the chapel into two unequal parts, a larger choir and a small nave. The same artists were responsible for the cantoria. The 15C mosaic pavement is a fine example of opus alexandrinum.

The *Frescoes (1481–83) on the long walls depict parallel events in the lives of Moses (left) and of Christ (right). There are six (originally seven) on either side; the two nearest the altar were eliminated to make room for Michelangelo's Last Judgement.

Left (South) Wall, beginning from the altar: *Pinturicchio,* Moses and Zipporah his wife in Egypt and the Circumcision of their son; *Botticelli,* *The Burning Bush, with Moses slaying the Egyptian and driving the Midianites from the well; *School of Ghirlandaio,* Passage of the Red Sea; *Cosimo Rosselli,* Moses on Mount Sinai and the Worship of the Golden Calf; *Botticelli,* *Punishment of Korah, Dathan, and Abiram (in the background are the Arch of Constantine and the Septizonium); *Luca Signorelli* and *Bart. della Gatta,* Moses giving his rod to Joshua and Mourning for the death of Moses.— Right (North) Wall, beginning from the altar: *Perugino* (?) and *Pinturicchio,* Baptism of Christ; *Botticelli,* Cleansing of the Leper and the Temptation in the Wilderness (in the background, the hospital of Santo Spirito); *Dom. Ghirlandaio,* *Calling of Peter and Andrew; Cosimo Rosselli* and *Piero di Cosimo,* Sermon on the Mount and Healing the Leper; *Perugino,* *Christ giving the keys to St Peter; Cosimo Rosselli,* Last Supper.—On the East Wall are two frescoes overpainted at the end of the 16C by Arrigo Fiammingo and Matteo da Lecce; they were *Dom. Ghirlandaio,* Resurrection, and *Salviati,* St Michael defending the body of Moses.—In the niches between the windows are 28 portraits of the first popes, by Fra Diamante, Dom. Ghirlandaio, Botticelli, and Cosimo Rosselli.—The celebrated tapestries of Raphael, now in the Vatican Pinacoteca, were first exhibited here in 1519.

Through the main door of the Sistine Chapel the sumptuous **Sala Regia** (no adm) can sometimes be seen. It was begun by Ant. da Sangallo the Younger in 1540, but not completed until 1573, and originally intended for the reception of ambassadors. The rich stucco decorations of the ceiling are by *Perino del Vaga;* those of the walls by *Dan. da Volterra.* The large frescoes are by *Vasari, Salviati,* and the *Zuccari.* They depict Gregory VII releasing the emperor Henry IV from excommunication; Charles V at the battle of Tunis; Return of Gregory XI from Avignon; Reconciliation of Alexander III and Barbarossa; Battle of Lepanto; Massacre of St Bartholomew. Here the first official meeting since the Reformation took place between the Pope and the Archbishop of Canterbury in 1966.— Adjoining is the vast AULA DELLE BENEDIZIONI, situated above the portico of St Peter's. From the central window of this hall the Pope blesses 'Urbi et Orbi'.

Visitors not wishing to continue the tour of the museums are sometimes able to leave the chapel by the *Scala Regia* (when open), an imposing staircase built by Bernini which descends past a statue of Constantine to the portico of St Peter's.

A special permit must be obtained from the Governor of the Vatican City to visit the Sala Regia, the Aula delle Benedizioni, the **Sala Ducale** of Bernini, and the **Cappella Paolina,** by *Ant. da Sangallo the Younger.* The Sala Ducale is decorated with landscapes by *Paul Brill,* and the Cappella Paolina with two *Frescoes by *Michelangelo* (Conversion of St Paul and Crucifixion of St Peter), painted in 1542–45 and 1546–50.

The Chapel is left by a small door in the N wall of the nave, which leads to the Museum of Christian Art.

Museum of Christian Art

In order to view the rooms of this museum in the correct order, it is necessary to proceed to Room I, through the Chapel of Pius V (left) and two rooms beyond the Room of the Aldobrandini Marriage which is passed on the left.

The Museum (*Museo Sacro*) was founded by Benedict XIV in 1756 and was enlarged in the 19C, partly by the acquisitions of Pius IX but chiefly by the yields of excavations carried out in the catacombs by De Rossi and his successors. In 1934 more rooms were added, and the museum was rearranged to illustrate the historic development of the Christian minor arts.

ROOM I. Early Christian Antiquities from the Catacombs of St Calixtus, St Domitilla, St Sebastian, and other cemeteries. Wall case I. Collection of glass, some of the finer specimens gilded.—Table 1. Monogram of Christ; Christian, gnostic, and pagan objects in bone, ivory, and glass.—Case II. Engraved 4C Christian glass from Ostia; multicoloured glasses known as *millefiori* (2–3C).— Table 2. Christian and pagan lamps (1–4C), some with symbolic representations, such as the Good Shepherd, the fish, the peacock, the monogram of Christ.—Case III. Flagon (7–8C) from a church of St Laurence; Situla with representation of Christ and the Apostles (5C). Inlaid enamel *Reliquary (9C), from the church of the Santi Quattro Coronati; 3C pyx from Africa. Bronze lamps (3–5C).—Table 3. Objects in gold and bronze: Byzantine weights, amulets, and crosses.—Table 4. Objects from the East in soap-stone, semi-precious stones, and metal; 11–12C, Italian triptych; Byzantine mosaic with representation of St Theodore (12C); 12C Byzantine wax cast.—Case IV. 11–13C Church embroideries.—Table 5. Christian and pagan lamps.—Case V. Pottery.—Table 6. Earthenware lamps.

ROOM II, OF THE PAPYRI, was originally intended for the reception of the 6–9C papyri from Ravenna. It dates from 1774, the last year of Clement XIV, and has frescoes by *Raff. Mengs* and his assistant *Christopher Unterberger*. It contains two cases of gilt-engraved glass of the 3–5C from Roman catacombs.

ROOM III, OF THE ADDRESSES (*degli Indirizzi*), was so called because in the time of Pius XI, the address or congratulatory documents sent to Leo XIII and Pius X were kept here. In the cases is a splendid collection of church furniture in metal, ivory, enamel, majolica, etc. Case 1. Italian silver sacramental objects, mainly 18C.—Case 2. 18–20C missals.—Case 3. 14–16C crucifixes in silver and gold.—Case 4. 18C Roman and Neapolitan silver vessels; Gold roses of the type blessed by the pope in Lent and presented to Catholic sovereigns (originally the traditional papal gift to the prefects of Rome).—Case 5. Papal rings, with imitation stones (14–16C).—Case 7 and 8. Limoges and other enamels.—Case 9. Early crucifixes.—Cases 10–14. Carved ivories. Case 12. Diptychs and triptychs (9–15C): *Ramboyna Diptych (c 900), Christian scenes with representation of the Roman wolf in the bottom of the left-hand panel; *Five-panelled wooden tablet with Christ blessing, part of the cover of the New Testament; the other half is in the Victoria and Albert Museum, London; *Book Cover with the Nativity, from the Convent of St Gall, Switzerland. On exit wall, fragment of mosaic of the head of an Apostle from the Lateran Triclinium (c 800); fresco of Charlemagne from the Pincio.—In the table case, glass and precious stone objects.—Cases 16–19. Late 16C silverwork from Germany, Rome, France, and Genoa (early 17C). In the table case, seals, cameos, and crosses.

The **Room of the Aldobrandini Marriage** (right) was built by Paul V in 1611 and restored by Pius VII in 1817. In 1838 Gregory XVI placed the wall-painting here that gives the room its name. The ceiling frescoes are by *Guido Reni*. In the pavement is a 2C geometric mosaic; in the centre, within an octagon, is Achilles dragging the body of Hector. On the upper part of the walls are *Frescoes of the 1C BC, with scenes from the Odyssey, found on the Esquiline in 1848. Lower down are paintings of famous women of antiquity, five of them from Tor Marancia, and paintings of children, from Ostia (1C AD).

On the centre wall is the *ALDOBRANDINI MARRIAGE (*Nozze Aldobrandine*), a masterpiece of Augustan art inspired by a Greek model of the 4C or 3C BC, found on the Esquiline in 1605 and kept in one of the garden pavilions of the Villa Aldobrandini until its removal to this room. The painting of a marriage scene, combines realism and symbolism.

At the end of the corridor is the **Chapel of St Pius V**, decorated by *Giac. Zucchi* after the designs of *Vasari*. The portrait of St Pius V is on the right in the apse. In the wall case is part of the *Treasure of the Sancta Sanctorum, the pope's private chapel in the old Lateran Palace. The relics were contained in precious reliquaries inside a case made of cypress wood at the command of Leo III (795–816). Here can be seen objects from 9C–12C, including a large enamelled *Cross presented by St Paschal I (817–24), containing five pieces of the True Cross; large Greek Cross of gold filigree work containing a small piece of the True Cross, decorated with precious stones and still partly covered with the balsams with which it was anointed every year by the Pope.

From the first room of the Museum of Christian Art there is access to the first of the exhibition rooms of the Vatican Library.

The Vatican Library

The **Vatican Library** (*Biblioteca Apostolica Vaticana*) was founded by Nicholas V with a nucleus of some 350 volumes, which he increased to 1200. Sixtus IV brought the total to 3650. The Library suffered loss in the sack of 1527, but soon afterwards resumed its growth, and the problem of accommodation became increasingly acute. Before the end of the 16C Sixtus V commissioned Dom. Fontana to build the great Sistine Hall. Later popes adapted numerous rooms in Bramante's W corridor to house the ever-increasing gifts, bequests, and purchases. Among the notable acquisitions are the Biblioteca Palatina of Heidelberg (1623), the Biblioteca Urbinas (1657), founded by Federico, Duke of Urbino, Queen Christina of Sweden's library (1690), the Biblioteca Ottoboniana bought in 1748 (formerly the property of Alexander VIII Ottoboni), the Jesuit Library (1922), the Biblioteca Chigiana (1923), and the Biblioteca Ferraioli (1929). There are now about 60,000 MSS, 7000 incunabula, and 1,000,000 other printed books. Leo XIII added a reference library; Pius X reorganized the manuscripts and provided a room for their study; and Pius XI carried out further reorganization. A disastrous collapse in December 1931 of part of the ceiling of the Sistine Hall was repaired two years later. The Library may be visited by students, by introduction, on weekdays between 8 and 13.30. The *Vatican Archives* are available on weekdays 8–13.30 to students who have obtained a permit from the Prefecture.

The exhibition rooms of the Library are the Museum of Pagan Antiquities, the Clementine Gallery, the Alexandrine Room, the Pauline Rooms, the Sistine Hall, the Sistine Rooms, and the Gallery of Urban VIII. All the rooms, except the Sistine Hall, are in Bramante's W corridor. The literary contents are not normally visible, as they are kept in cupboards; but in the Sistine Hall there is usually an exhibition (changed annually) of valuable MSS and printed books.

The first room is the **Gallery of Urban VIII**. By the entrance wall are two statues, left the sophist Aelius Aristides (AD 129–189) dating from the 3C; on right the Greek orator Lysias, dating from the 2C. Here are shown astronomical instruments, sailing directions dating from the early 16C, and the Farnese Planisphere (1725), given to Leo XIII by the Count of Caserta.

Beyond are the two **Sistine Rooms**, part of the Library of Sixtus V (see below). In the first, paintings of St Peter's as planned by Michelangelo, and of the erection of the obelisk in Piazza San Pietro. Over the doors of the second room, Sixtus V proclaiming St Bonaventura Doctor of the Church in the church of the Santi Apostoli (Melozzo's frescoes are seen in their original place on the wall of the apse); Canonization of San Diego in Old St Peter's.

The *Sistine Hall, named after its founder Sixtus V, was built in 1587–89 by *Dom. Fontana* across the great Courtyard of the Belvedere, cutting it into two. It was later paralleled by the New Wing, the construction of which created a small central courtyard, known as the Courtyard of the Library. Beneath this an underground deposit was constructed in 1983 to house the precious collection of Vatican manuscripts, and incunabula. The Sistine Hall is 71m long, 15m wide, and 9m high; it is divided into two vaulted aisles by seven columns. The decorations of the hall embody two main themes—the glorification of literature and of the pontificate of Sixtus V. At the ends of the aisles and in the lunettes over the windows are paintings, most of them views of Rome in the time of the pope and some of them illustrating events of his reign, such as his coronation on the steps of St Peter's, and the papal processions to the Lateran and to Santa Maria Maggiore, the latter for the inauguration of the special Holy

Year of 1585. *Exhibitions here of the precious possessions of the Library are changed annually.

Under the arches of the hall are displayed some of the gifts (vases, etc.) made to the popes by various foreign rulers.

In the VESTIBULE (left), which is divided into two small rooms, is a pair of colossal enamel and gilt candelabra used at Napoleon I's coronation and presented by him to Pius VII. Above the doors are paintings of the Lateran Palace before and after its reconstruction by *Dom. Fontana.* Here are displayed the largest and smallest MSS in the Vatican Library, namely the Hebrew Bible of Urbino (1295) and the Masses of SS. Francis and Anne, decorated with 16C miniatures.

Beyond the two PAULINE ROOMS, added by Paul V, and decorated in the Mannerist style of 1610–11 (with a press designed by Bramante for sealing papal bulls), is the ALEXANDRINE ROOM, adapted in 1690 by Alexander VIII, and decorated with scenes in the life of Pius VII by *De Angelis.* It contains an early embroidered cope and altar cloth (11–12C).

The **Clementine Gallery**, in five sections, was added to the Library by Clement XII in 1732; in 1818, under Pius VII, it was decorated by *De Angelis* with paintings of scenes in the life of that pope. The first two rooms contain a collection of plans of Rome, including one by *Ant. Tempesta* (1606), and valuable 16–17C Italian and German bookbindings, and bozzetti by Bernini. The last room has a 4C Greek relief of a horseman presented to Pius IX by Ferdinand II of the Two Sicilies, a bronze head of a Muse (Roman copy of a Hellenistic original), and two bronze hippogriffs of the Imperial period. On either side of the entrance are two Mithraic divinities.

Beyond is the main hall of the *Museum of Pagan Antiquities of the Library (Museo Profano della Biblioteca),* a museum and coin collection of the 18C, with additions from the excavations of 1809–15. It was begun under Clement XIII in 1767 and completed in the time of Pius VI, when it was furnished by Valadier. The ceiling paintings symbolize Time.

In the cupboards in the right wall; carved Roman ivory, busts in semi-precious stones, a miniature torso, and a mosaic from Hadrian's Villa at Tivoli. Beyond, Roman bronze statuettes (1–3C AD) and Plaques with inscriptions.—In the cupboards on the left wall: head and arm of a chryselephantine statue of Minerva, claimed to be a 5C Greek original; Etruscan bronzes and carved Roman ivory. Beyond, Etruscan and Roman objects found in Rome and the Pontine Marshes. On the end wall in a niche to the left, *Bronze head of Augustus, on right, bronze head of Nero.

Beyond the Museo Profano della Biblioteca is (left) the Quattro Cancelli.

III.   The Vatican Picture Gallery

The ***Vatican Picture Gallery** (Pinacoteca Vaticana)* is reached by the passageway from the open court beyond the Quattro Cancelli.

The gallery owes its origin to Pius VI (1775–99), who formed a collection of pictures from the museums and library. Under the Treaty of Tolentino (1797), which he was forced to conclude with Napoleon, he had to surrender the best works to France. Of these, 77 were recovered in 1815. The gallery has had various homes. The present building, of 15 public rooms, in the Lombardic Renaissance style, by *Luca Beltrami* (1854–1933), was opened in 1932.

ROOM I. BYZANTINE SCHOOL AND ITALIAN PRIMITIVES. *Ant. Veneziano,* 16. St James, 19. Mary Magdalene; 18. *Jacopo da Bologna,* Death of St Francis; 17. *Vitale da Bologna,* Madonna and Child;

20. *12C Roman School*, Christ in judgement; 23. *Giunta Pisano*, St Francis, and panels illustrating his life; *526. *Giovanni* and *Niccolò* (Rome; late 11C), Last Judgement, the oldest picture in the gallery; 2. *Margaritone d'Arezzo*, St Francis of Assisi; (window wall) 14. *Giov. del Biondo*, Madonna and Child with saints; 169. *Taddeo di Bartolo*, Death of the Virgin; 9. *Giov. Bonsi*, Madonna and saints, signed and dated 1371; *146–150, 158–161. *Bern. Daddi*, Legend of St Stephen. Also works by *Niccolò di Pietro Gerini*, and the Florentine School.

ROOM II. In the centre, *120. The STEFANESCHI TRIPTYCH, by *Giotto* and assistants. This altarpiece for the Confessio of Old St Peter's painted on both sides (recently restored), represents Christ enthroned, the martyrdom of SS. Peter and Paul (at the foot of the throne is the donor, Card. Stefaneschi); on the back, St Peter accepting the triptych from the Pope; at the sides, four Apostles; on the predella, other Apostles.—Around the walls is an exquisite series of small paintings: 168, 166, 163, 170. *Pietro Lorenzetti*, Christ before Pilate, St John the Baptist, St Peter, the Virgin; 165. *Simone Martini*, Redeemer; *174. *Bern. Daddi*, Madonna of the Magnificat; 102, 97, 101. *Mariotto di Nardo*, Nativity, St Nicholas freeing three knights, Annunciation; works (136, 138) by *Sano di Pietro*; 132. *Giovanni di Paolo*, Nativity; 234. *Sassetta*, Vision of St Thomas Aquinas; 193. *Lorenzo Monaco*, Stories from the life of St Benedict; 247–50. *Gentile da Fabriano*, Stories from the life of St Nicholas of Bari; 2139. *Sassetta*, Madonna and Child; (window wall) 263. *Fr. di Gentile*, Madonna and Child.

R. III. FRA ANGELICO AND OTHERS. *Masolino da Panicale*, 260. Crucifixion, 245. Transition of the Virgin; *Fra Angelico*, *251, 252. Scenes from the life of St Nicholas of Bari, 253. Madonna and Child with saints; 243. *Filippo Lippi*, Coronation of the Virgin, a triptych; 262. *Benozzo Gozzoli*, St Thomas receiving the Virgin's girdle.

R. IV. MELOZZO AND PALMEZZANO. 269. Remaining fragments (restored in 1982) of the *Fresco by *Melozzo da Forlì* formerly in the church of the Santi Apostoli; another portion is in the Quirinal. The fragments in this room represent the Ascension; note the eight *Angel Musicians. *270. *Melozzo*, Sixtus IV conferring on the humanist Platina the librarianship of the Vatican in the presence of Giuliano Della Rovere (afterwards Julius II), his brother Giovanni, and Girolamo and Raffaele Riario, a fine fresco transferred to canvas.—On the right wall, *80. Tapestry of the Last Supper (16C Flemish, from Leonardo's fresco in Milan); *Marco Palmezzano*, 619, 273. Madonna and saints.

R. V. 15C ARTISTS. 286. *Fr. del Cossa*, Predella with Miracles of St Vincent Ferrer; 275. *Lucas Cranach*, Pietà; 294. *Giov. Battista Utili*, Madonna and Child.

R. VI. POLYPTYCHS. *Carlo Crivelli*, 297. Madonna (dated 1482), 300. Pietà. *Vitt. Crivelli*, Madonna with saints (dated 1481); *Niccolò l'Alunno*, 299. Crucifixion, 307. Polyptych of Montelparo; *Ant. Viviani*, St Anthony Abbot (in relief) and other saints (signed and dated 1469).

R. VII. UMBRIAN SCHOOL. 312. *Pinturicchio*, Coronation of the Virgin; 313. *Umbrian 15C school*, Madonna with St John; 316. *Lo Spagna*, Adoration of the Magi ('Madonna della Spineta'); *Perugino*, *317. Madonna enthroned with saints (318. Resurrection), 319–321. Part of predella with SS Benedict, Flavia, and Placidus; 326. *Giov. Santi* (father of Raphael), St Jerome.

R. VIII, the largest room in the gallery, is devoted to the works of

RAPHAEL. It contains three of his most famous paintings, two pre-dellas, and 10 tapestries executed after his original cartoons. *334. Coronation of the Virgin, belonging to Raphael's first Perugian period and his first large composition, painted in 1503, when he was 20 years old; (in a table case) 335. Predella to the above, The Mysteries, i.e. Annunciation, Adoration of the Magi, and Presentation in the Temple. *329. The MADONNA OF FOLIGNO, a mature work painted about 1511. It was a votive offering by Sigismondo Conti in gratitude for his escape when a cannon-ball fell on his house during the siege of Foligno. He is shown with St Jerome, and in the background is Foligno during the battle. From 1565 until carried off by Napoleon in 1797, it was in the Convent of Sant'Anna in that city.

*333. The TRANSFIGURATION, *Raphael*'s last work, commissioned in 1517 by Card. Giul. de' Medici for the cathedral of Narbonne. From 1523 to 1809 it was in the church of San Pietro in Montorio. It was restored in 1972–77. The superb scene of the transfiguration of Christ is shown above the dramatic episode of the healing of the young man possessed of a devil. It is not known how much of the painting was finished at Raphael's death in 1520, and it seems likely that, although the composition is Raphael's, it was completed in the lower part by his pupils *Giulio Romano* and *Fr. Penni*.

In the cases are the ten celebrated *TAPESTRIES representing scenes from the Acts of the Apostles. Intended for the Sistine Chapel, they were ordered by Leo X and woven in Brussels by *Pieter van Aelst* from cartoons drawn by Raphael in 1515–16. They have recently been restored.

Seven of the cartoons (three of them having been lost) are in the Victoria and Albert Museum, London, though some scholars believe that these seven, which were bought in 1630 by Charles I of England, are 17C copies and that all the originals have been lost. Other tapestries from the same cartoons, but of inferior quality, are in Hampton Court Palace near London, in the Palazzo Ducale at Mantua, and in the Palazzo Apostolico at Loreto. The tapestries were first exhibited in 1519, in the Sistine Chapel. They have borders of grotesque ornamentation and broad bases decorated with bronze-coloured designs; most of this work is by *Giov. da Udine*. The subjects are: A. Blinding of Elymas (this tapestry was cut in halves during the sack of Rome in 1527), B. Conversion of St Paul, C. Stoning of St Stephen, D. St Peter healing the paralytic, E. Death of Ananias, F. St Peter receiving the keys, G. The miraculous draught of fishes, H. St Paul preaching in Athens, I. Inhabitants of Lystra desiring to sacrifice to SS Paul and Barnabas, L. St Paul in prison at Philippi.—These tapestries belong to the so-called 'Old School' series. Ten of the 'New School' series are in the Gallery of Tapestries (p 320).

R. IX. LEONARDO DA VINCI AND OTHER 15–16C MASTERS. *337. *Leonardo da Vinci*, St Jerome; 340. *Lor. di Credi*, Madonna; 339. *16C Lombard School*, Christ at the Column, Portrait of Bramante (?); *290. *Giov. Bellini*, Pietà (removed for restoration).

R. X. TITIAN, VERONESE, FRA BARTOLOMEO. 347. *Girol. Genga*, Madonna and saints; 346. *Veronese*, Allegory; 349. *Moretto*, Madonna and Child enthroned with saints; 351. *Titian*, Madonna of San Niccolò de' Frari; *445. Doge Niccolò Marcello (being restored); 352. *Veronese*, St Helena; 354. *Paris Bordone*, St George and the Dragon; 355. *Garofalo*, Apparition of the Virgin to Augustus and the Sibyl; *359. *Giulio Romano* and *Fr. Penni*, 'Madonna of Monteluce'; 336. *Lombard 16C School*, 'Madonna della Cintura'.

R. XI. BAROCCI and others. 363. *Vasari*, Stoning of St Stephen; 365. *Cav. d'Arpino*, Annunciation; 368. *Muziano*, Raising of Lazarus; 372. *Cola dell'Amatrice*, Assumption of the Virgin; *Barocci*, 375. Head of the Virgin; 376.

Annunciation, *377. Rest on the Flight into Egypt (recently restored), 378. The Blessed Michaelina, 380. St Francis receiving the stigmata.

R. XII. 17C MASTERS. There is a fine view of the cupola of St Peter's from the window. 381. *Valentin*, Martyrdom of SS Processus and Martinian (mosaic in St Peter's); *382. *Sacchi*, Vision of St Romauld; 383. *Guercino*, Incredulity of St Thomas; *384. *Domenichino*, Communion of St Jerome (signed and dated 1614, his first important work; mosaic in St Peter's), 385. after *Caravaggio*, Denial of St Peter; *386. *Caravaggio*, Descent from the Cross, 1602 (copy in St Peter's Sacristy); *Guido Reni*, 387. Crucifixion of St Peter (mosaic in St Peter's), *389. The Virgin in glory with saints; 388. *G.M. Crespi*, Holy Family; *Guercino*, 391. Mary Magdalene, 392. St Margaret of Cortona; 394. *Nic. Poussin*, Martyrdom of St Erasmus (signed); 381.*Valentin de Boulogne*, Martyrdom of Saints Processo and Martiniano (recently restored); *395. *Guido Reni*, St Matthew.

R. XIII. MARATTA, RIBERA, VAN DYCK, and others. *396. *Sassoferrato*, Madonna and Child; 1059. *Orazio Gentileschi*, Judith; *775. *Van Dyck*, St Francis Xavier; 1931. *P.F. Mola*, Vision of St Bruno; 405. *Pietro da Cortona*, Appearance of the Virgin to St Francis; 408. *Ribera* (or his pupil *Henry Somer*), Martyrdom of St Laurence; 410. *Pietro da Cortona*, David and a lion; 415. *Pompeo Batoni*, Appearance of the Virgin to St John Nepomuc.

R. XIV. FLEMISH, DUTCH, GERMAN, FRENCH, and ITALIAN PAINTERS (17–18C). *Daniel Seghers*, 416, 418. Small religious pictures with flower borders; 421. *Rosa da Tivoli*, Hunter; 419. *Matthias Stomer*, Orpheus, Pluto, and Proserpina; 784. *Rubens*, Triumph of Mars, mainly executed by his pupils; 432–439. *Donato Creti*, Astronomical Observations; 815. *Nic. Poussin*, Gideon; 423. *Van Bloeman*, Horses.

R. XV. PORTRAITS. 446. *Bernardino Conti*, Fr. Sforza, 447. *P. Meert*, Philosopher; 448. *Sir Thomas Lawrence*, George IV of England; 451. *David Teniers the Younger*, Old man; 1210. *Muziano*, Idealized portrait of Gregory XII, who abdicated in 1415; 455. *Pompeo Batoni*, Pius VI; 457. *Scipione Pulzone*, Card. Guglielmo Sirleto; 458. *G.M. Crespi*, Benedict XIV, painted while still a cardinal (papal robes added afterwards); *460. *Carlo Maratta*, Clement IX.

IV.   The Gregorian Museum of Pagan Antiquities, Pio Christian Museum, and Ethnological Missionary Museum

The Gregorian Museum of Pagan Antiquities is reached from the vestibule by the entrance to the Museums. This striking building was designed by a group of Italian architects headed by the Passarelli brothers, and opened in 1970. Using the latest methods of display, it contains the collections that were in the Lateran, comprising the ***Museo Gregoriano Profano** (*Gregorian Museum of Pagan Antiquities*), consisting entirely of Roman and neo-Attic sculpture, a section which includes some Greek originals, the **Pio Christian Museum**, and the **Ethnological Missionary Museum**, as well as additional material.

The arrangement is still not complete, and the section containing the Pagan Inscriptions has not yet opened to the general public. The exhibits are not fully labelled. The design of the building precludes divisions between the various sections, but the visitor is directed by arrows.

The Museo Profano was founded by Gregory XVI (1831–46) to house the overflow of the Vatican Museums and the yields of excavations during his pontificate at Rome, Ostia, Veii, and Caere (Cerveteri). It was enriched by further excavations up to 1870, and at the end of the 19C by a collection of pagan inscriptions. John XXIII was responsible for its removal to the Vatican.

Near the entrance (left) are Roman copies of original Greek sculpture (torsoes, statuettes, and heads), and (ahead) MARSYAS (1), a marble copy of a bronze by Myron which formed part of a group placed at the entrance to the Acropolis in Athens in the mid-5C BC. Marsyas is attracted by the sound of the double flute, which Athena had invented and just thrown away. He tries to pick up the instrument, but is foiled by Athena's commanding gesture (the statue of Athena is a cast).

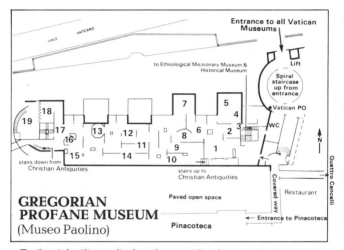

GREGORIAN PROFANE MUSEUM
(Museo Paolino)

To the right (2) are displayed some *Greek originals (formerly in part of the Etruscan Museum). These include: a superb sepulchral stele, showing a young man with his small slave handing him a strigil and a flask of oil (5C BC); two heads, fragments from one of the metopes and from the N frieze of the Parthenon, and fragment of a horse's head from the W pediment of the Parthenon, probably one of Athena's horses; Head of Athena, a 5C original from an acrolith; on the head was a helmet, probably of bronze; the eyes are made of polished grey stone in which were set glass pupils; the eyebrows and eyelashes were made of thin strips of bronze, and the ears had gold earrings. Two relief fragments of horsemen, perhaps part of a frieze, resemble in style the Parthenon frieze. The relief of dancing nymphs is an Attic work of the 4C. Stairs (3) lead up to an area which contains the Lateran collection of PAGAN INSCRIPTIONS (open only to scholars with special permission).—There follow a series of HERMS (4), and, on the floor, the *HERACLITUS MOSAIC (5) of an unswept floor from the triclinium of a house on the Aventine, showing the remains of a banquet. It is signed 'Heraclitus', and may be a copy of a celebrated work by Sosus of Pergamon. Other works in this section include: Round altar, with a faun playing for two dancing women; Triangular tripod base, with reliefs of dancing figures taking part in Dionysiac rites, a neo-Attic work in Pentelic marble of the 1C BC, after a 4C original; Copy of the Resting Satyr of Praxiteles (others in the Museo Pio-Clementino and the Capitoline Museum); Colossal statue of Poseidon (Neptune), after a bronze original by Lysippos (with several restorations).

Beyond is a relief of Medea and the daughters of Pelias whom she is inducing to kill their father, neo-Attic copy of a late 5C BC original. It is one of a series of four relating to the dramatic competitions in

Athens. The best copy of the second (Orpheus and Eurydice) is in the
Naples Museum, a third (Herakles, Theseus, and Peirithöos) is in the
Museo Torlonia.

Beyond a colossal statue of Zeus are the remains of the large
circular VICOVARO MONUMENT (6), dating from the early 1C AD. The
marble statue of Sophocles from Terracina, with fine drapery, is a
copy of a 4C work.—In the next recess is the CHIARAMONTI NIOBID
(7; being restored), a fine Roman copy of an original by Leochares of
the 4C BC; head of a Muse, crowned with ivy, in the manner of
Praxiteles (good copy of a 4C BC original); Torso of a statue of Diana;
the motion expressed in the drapery is particularly fine in this Roman
copy of a Greek original of the 4C BC; two Roman orators in togas
(1C AD); fine Roman portrait heads (the last two perhaps portraits of
Virgil).

The following sections contain Roman sculpture in chronological
order, beginning with the late Republican era:

Opposite two statues of the sleeping Silenus (copies of Hellenistic
works), found in the Roman Theatre at Caere (see below), are a series
of funerary reliefs: the first with portraits of parents and a young son,
and the second with five busts of members of the Furia family. In the
centre, circular altar dedicated to Piety, from Veio, decorated with
garlands, citharae, and the attributes of Vulcan (1C AD).

Around to the left are a group of STATUES FROM THE ROMAN
THEATRE AT CAERE (8), mainly of the Julio-Claudian family: Agrippina, mother of Nero and wife of Claudius, as a goddess; Colossal
seated statue of Claudius as Jupiter; Relief with figures symbolizing
three Etruscan cities—Vetulonia, Vulci, and Tarquinia—found with
the statue and believed to have been part of his throne; Colossal
head, probably of Augustus; Colossal seated statue of Tiberius
idealized as Jupiter; Series of inscriptions found with the statues,
explaining their identity; Drusus and elder, with a cuirass decorated
with bas-reliefs of two griffins and above, a gorgon; Altar dedicated
to C. Manlius, a censor of Caere, by his clients (1C AD); Statue of an
Emperor in a cuirass, decorated with reliefs.

Next comes the so-called ALTAR OF VICOMAGISTRI (9), 1C AD,
found near the Cancelleria. The relief is of a sacrificial procession,
followed by four figures carrying statuettes of lares and by priestly
officials known as Vicomagistri.—Two Statues of young boys wearing togas, belonging to the Julio-Claudian family (one with a 3C
head); more Roman portrait busts and heads.

To the left is an area with CINERARY URNS (10), among which are:
Urn with finely carved reliefs, with the head of Medusa in the centre,
and below a cock-fight. At the sides festoons, with eagles and genii;
Covered urn with good reliefs and an inscription relating to Quinto
Volusio Antigono.—The next section has architectural fragments,
and some exquisite decorative reliefs with small Bacchic scenes and
vine-leaves (1C AD).—The area is dominated by two large CAN-
CELLERIA RELIEFS (11), dating from the Flavian period (AD 70–96).

The frieze on the left (damaged) represents the return to Rome of Vespasian
(who appears on the extreme right of the 3rd panel). Surrounding the Emperor,
are Vestals, the Roman Senate and people, and the seated figure of Rome. The
frieze on the right represents the departure from Rome of Domitian who
appears (restored as Nerva), in the second panel from the left, surrounded by
(left) Minerva, Mars, and Victory, and (right) Rome with soldiers.

Beyond more portrait busts is the sculpture from the TOMB OF THE
HATERII (12), near Centocelle: Two similar niches with well-

modelled portrait busts of a man and woman; three Reliefs of ceremonies of a woman's funeral: Body lying in state, surrounded by relatives and mourners in the atrium of a house; Funeral procession, passing buildings on the Via Sacra; Sepulchral monument of the Haterii, with a view of the inside and the apparatus used in its construction. Above, High relief with three busts of gods of the underworld; triangular pillar, beautifully carved, with candelabrum, rose branches, and birds.—Relief of a procession of Roman magistrates before a temple (1C AD). A head was restored (erroneously) by Thorvaldsen to represent Trajan.

Towards the windows, large Funerary relief of a woman (the head is a portrait) lying on a bed with a small dog; Sepulchral relief of a chariot race, a side view of the circus seen from above. The organizers of the games in whose memory the relief was made appear on the left (early 2C AD); two Columns, carved with a papyrus motif and lotus leaves around the base.

To the right, colossal STATUE OF A DACIAN (13), of the time of Trajan, found in 1841 in Via dei Coronari, on the site of a sculptor's studio of the Imperial era.

A series of capitals and antifixes follow, with two fragments of an architectural frieze from the forum of Trajan, with cupids and griffins and a neo-Attic amphora.

The next sections contain *PAGAN SARCOPHAGI (14), with mythological scenes. Among them, several depicting the story of Adonis, of Hippolytus and Phaedra (with scenes of the wild boar hunt), of Orestes, and of the slaughter of the family of Niobe. Farther on, the triumph of Dionysos (Bacchus). He is represented as a victor on his return from India in a triumphal car drawn by two elephants, and being crowned by Nike (Victory)—fine workmanship of the 3C AD.

Beyond is a colossal statue of Antinöus as the god Vertumnus (with finely modelled drapery; the head is modern); fragment of a relief with two boxers, presumably part of a large monument (2C AD).

Fragment of the large oval PLOTINUS SARCOPHAGUS (15), with figures in relief in philosophical discussion (?), and part of a lion hunt; on the wall behind, Sepulchral relief with the deceased man reading from a large scroll, surrounded by his family and pupils (3C AD); on the right, Funerary monument in high relief of a warrior saluting his wife who is seated; a horse stands ready, and a snake is depicted in the tree above. Fragments of draped IMPERIAL PORPHYRY STATUES (16).—Towards the windows, Relief of a nymph feeding an infant satyr from a large horn-shaped vessel, while in a grotto near by a young Pan plays the syrinx. Known as the Amaltheia relief, this was originally part of a fountain.—To the right is the STATUE OF DOG-MAZIO (17). Another area (18) contains Roman religious sculpture, including statues of Mithras and the bull (3C AD), Diana of the Ephesians, and Asklepios.

To the right of the stairs are fragments of a group with a boy riding a horse, and a naiad on a sea centaur. Upstairs a walkway passes above a MOSAIC OF ATHLETES FROM THE BATHS OF CARACALLA (19) and a black marble statue of a stag (Roman copy of a 4C Greek original). Beyond a double row of laughing silene busts and some exquisite bas-reliefs (including one of Hercules and the Lion), a balcony overlooks a second fine mosaic from the Baths of Caracalla (and there is a view of the dome of St Peter's from here).

The rest of the upper floor is occupied by the **Pio Christian Museum of Antiquities**, founded by Pius IX in 1854 with objects found mainly in the catacombs, and displayed by subject matter. The display begins at the other end of the mezzanine floor, at the entrance to the building. The first section is devoted to the valuable collection of Christian sarcophagi of the 2–5C, of the highest importance to students of early Christian iconography; some famous sarcophagi owned by the Vatican but not on view here are represented by casts (numbered with Roman numerals). At the beginning on the left wall, are fragments of sarcophagi representing the Nativity and Epiphany (124, 190.) of the 4C AD. Farther on (right) is a sarcophagus showing the Crossing of the Red Sea.—Three steps lead up to the next section: in the middle, cast of the Sarcophagus of Junius Bassus (the original is in the Treasury of St Peter's). Round the corner to the left is a sarcophagus (164.) with five niches showing Christ triumphant over death, Cain and Abel, Peter taken prisoner, the Martyrdom of Paul, and Job.—Another short flight of steps ascends past (right) 152. Sarcophagus of the husband and wife Crescentianus and Agapene, found in the Vatican necropolis. At the top of the stairs (left) is a large sarcophagus (104.) with episodes from the Bible. To the right: panels (184, 189, 178, 175, 183A.) with scenes from the Old and New Testaments; cast of the Sarcophagus from Sant'Ambrogio in Milan.—The next part of the gallery contains more sarcophagi (including one from St Calixtus) and some mosaic fragments.—Three steps lead up to the last section of the Museum. On the left is a well-preserved sarcophagus (150.) with traces of the original polychrome decoration. At the end, 191A. Sarcophagus illustrating the Good Shepherd. On the right wall begins the collection of tablets from the MUSEUM OF CHRISTIAN INSCRIPTIONS, the largest and most important collection of Christian inscriptions in existence. The whole collection was arranged and classified by G.B. De Rossi (1822–94) in four series.

FIRST SERIES. Inscriptions from public monuments connected with Christian worship. The exhibits include a fragment of the sepulchral inscription of Publius Sulpicius Quirinus (Cyrenius), Governor of Syria, who took the census at the time of the birth of Christ; inscriptions of Pope St Damasus (366–84).—SECOND SERIES. Dated sepulchral inscriptions. Dogmatic inscriptions, including the (fish) acrostic.—Inscriptions relating to the ecclesiastical hierarchy, virgins, catechumens, senators, soldiers, officials, and workers, etc.

THIRD SERIES. Chi-Rho and other symbols and representations of Christian dogma.—FOURTH SERIES. Topographical. Inscriptions from the cemetery of Priscilla, the cemetery of Praetextatus on the Appian Way, Sant'Agnese fuori le Mura, Ostia, tombs near the Vatican, San Lorenzo fuori le Mura, San Pancrazio, Monte Mario. These inscriptions range from 2C–6C.

The statue of the Good Shepherd is a fine work dating from the late 3C. A passage continues past (177.) a sarcophagus from San Lorenzo fuori le Mura, and the cast of a seated statue of the martyred doctor St Hippolytus. On the left of his chair is a list in Greek of the saint's works, and on the right a paschal calendar for the years 222–334. The original was moved by Pope John XXIII to the entrance of the Biblioteca Vaticana, in the Belvedere Court (see below).—On the balcony overlooking a mosaic from the Baths of Caracalla (see above) is a fragment of the tombstone of Abercius, bishop of Hierapolis (Phrygia), who lived in the reign of Marcus Aurelius (161–180), discovered by Sir William Ramsay and presented to Leo XIII. The Greek text is in three parts: in the first part Abercius says that he is a disciple of Christ the Good Shepherd, in the second he mentions his journey to Rome and the East, in the third he asks the faithful to pray for him and threatens defilers of his grave.

ETHNOLOGICAL MISSIONARY MUSEUM
(Museo Paolino)

The *Ethnological Missionary Museum** (adm see p 303) occupies the whole of the area below ground level. It was established by Pius XI in 1927 as a development of the Vatican Missionary Exhibition of 1924–26. The primitive and more recent cultures of each country have been arranged according to subject matter; labelling is kept to a minimum. The countries are indicated by a letter (see the plan), and the visitor is directed by arrows. The exhibits illustrate the ways of life and religious customs in: *China* (A), with fine Buddhist sculpture and religious figures of the Ming and T'ang dynasties; *Japan* (B), with ceremonial masks and paintings of martyrs; *Korea* (C); *Tibet, Mongolia* (D); *Indochina* (E), where examples of local art and manufacture show the adaptation of European sacred art to the local genius; **Indian sub-continent* (F), illustrating Shivaism and Vishnuism; *Indonesia, Philippines* (G); *Polynesia* (H); **Melanesia* (I), with protective spirits, ceremonial masks and costumes, and the reconstruction of a hut of the spirits from New Guinea; *Australia* (J); *North Africa* (K); *Ethiopia* (L); *Madagascar* (M); *West Africa* (N), with statuettes of tribal gods; *Central Africa* (O); *East Africa* (P); *Southern Africa* (Q); *Christian Africa* (R); *South America* (S), including ancient wood sculpture from Columbia; *Central America* (T); *North America* (U); *Persia* (V); *Middle East* (W); and Christian art from countries penetrated by the missions. A mezzanine floor contains study collections open to students.

The **Historical Museum** has been transferred to the Lateran Palace.

V.   Visit to the Vatican City and Gardens

Tours of part of the Vatican city and gardens are organized at the Information Office to the left of St Peter's façade. Tickets should be obtained at least one day in advance. The tours, partly by bus and partly on foot (c 2 hrs) depart at 10 on Tuesday, Friday and Saturday (Lire 9000); the tours on Monday and Thursday include the Sistine Chapel (3 hrs; Lire 18,000). From November to February there are tours only on Tuesday, Thursday and Saturday of the gardens and city (Lire 9000). Individual visitors are not admitted to the city or gardens (except with a special permit).

The **Vatican Gardens** cover the N and W slopes of the Vatican Hill. Although somewhat diminished in extent by intrusive constructions such as the new building of the Museo Gregoriano Profano, the Seminario Etiopico, and the Vatican Radio Station, they retain the charm and elegance of the 16C.

The *Arco delle Campane* is protected by a sentry of the Swiss Guard, armed with a rifle instead of the halberd carried by the guard at the Bronze Door. The square beyond is Piazza dei Protomartiri Romani, the site of the martyrdom of the early Christians near the Circus of Nero. On the left is the *Camposanto Teutonico*, dating from 779, and probably the oldest of medieval cemeteries; it is still reserved for Germans and Dutch. In the adjacent *Collegio Teutonico* are a small museum and a library. Beyond, against the wall of the city, is the new *Audience Hall* (1971), by Pier Luigi Nervi. Designed in the shape of a shell it has seating for 8000 people.

In the pavement in front of the first arch of the passage beneath the Sacristy of St Peter's a slab marks the former site of the obelisk in Piazza San Pietro. A road leads beneath the Sacristy to emerge into Piazza Santa Marta. Here, on the right, is a fine view of the left transept of St Peter's in all its grandeur; on the left is the *Palazzo dell'Arciprete di San Pietro*. At the W end of the square is the *Palazzo di Giustizia*.

Opposite the majestic W end of St Peter's is the little church of *Santo Stefano degli Abissini*, built by Leo III as Santo Stefano Maggiore. In 1479 Sixtus IV conveyed it to Coptic monks; it was rebuilt by Clement XI.

A road ascends past the *Studio del Mosaico*, with an exhibition room, and (right) the modern Governor's Palace (*Palazzo del Governatorato*), seat of the civic administration of the Vatican City. To the S is the little-used *Vatican Railway Station*. Viale dell'Osservatorio continues through the gardens past the *Seminario Etiopico*. At the W extremity of the city are a reproduction of the Grotto of Lourdes, presented by the French Catholics to Leo XIII, and a stretch of the wall built by Nicholas V on the site of the ancient walls put up by Leo IV. Here the *Tower of St John*, once an observatory, is now used as a guest-house. Below is the first building used by the Vatican Radio Station, designed by Marconi and inaugurated in 1931. On the westernmost bastion of the city walls is the *Heliport*.

The descent is through exotic vegetation past the *Vatican Radio Station* and the *Fontana dell'Aquilone* (1612; by Jan van Santen), with a triton by Stefano Maderno. Nearer the huge Museum buildings is the *Casina of Pius IV*. The two little buildings by *Pirro Ligorio* (1558–62) form a masterpiece of Mannerist architecture. In the villa, now the seat of the *Pontifical Academy of Sciences*, Pius IV held the meetings which received the name of *Notti Vaticane*; at them were held learned discussions on poetry, philosophy, and sacred subjects. Pius VIII and Gregory XVI used to give their audiences here.

Towards St Peter's a group of buildings include the *Floreria*, formerly the *Mint* (Zecca), founded by Eugenius IV. The *Stradone dei Giardini*, an avenue which skirts Bramante's W corridor, ends at the Quattro Cancelli; it is necessary to return through Piazza del Forno (overlooked by the Sistine Chapel) around St Peter's to leave the city by the Arco delle Campane.

The northern part of the city, normally closed to visitors, is entered through the *Arco della Sentinella*. On the left is the Borgia Tower. Beyond this are two more courtyards, in the heart of the Vatican Palace. The first is the *Cortile Borgia*, the second the *Cortile dei Pappagalli*, so called from its frieze of parrots, now almost obliterated. A subway leads to a fourth courtyard, *Cortile di San Damaso*, overlooked by the Loggia of Raphael.

From the Cortile della Sentinella there is access via the *Grottone* into the vast *Courtyard of the Belvedere* which, before the construction of the Sala Sistina was far more extensive. It acquired its present dimensions when the New Wing was built. In the middle of the courtyard is a fountain with a large basin.—A subway leads out into Via del Belvedere. In this street are the *Pontifical Polyglot Printing Press* and the *Vatican Post Office*. On the right are the barracks of the Swiss Guard.

In 1956 a Pagan Necropolis (tombs of 1–4C) was discovered beneath the car park. The cemetery was alongside Via Triumphalis, the line of which is now followed by Via del Pellegrino. It may be visited with special permission.

Beyond the Post Office the animated Via del Pellegrino leads to the left. On the left of this street is the building of the *Annona* (victualling board); on the right are the *Casa Parrochiale*; the workshop where Vatican tapestries are repaired; the restored church of *San Pellegrino*; the offices of the *Osservatore Romano*; and other offices.

From Via del Belvedere, on the left can be seen the church of *Sant' Anna dei Palafrenieri*, the parish church of the Vatican City, built in 1573 by the Papal Grooms (Palafrenieri della Corte Papale) to the designs of *Vignola*. The exterior is later. Immediately beyond the church is the *Cancello di Sant' Anna*, which leads out into Via di Porta Angelica.

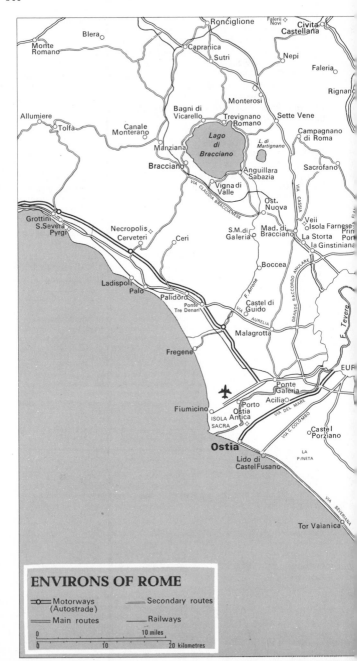

ENVIRONS OF ROME

- =o= Motorways (Autostrade)
- Main routes
- Secondary routes
- Railways

0		10 miles
0	10	20 kilometres

Ronciglione — Falerii Novi — Civita Castellana
Blera — Capranica — Sutri — Nepi — Faleria — Rignano
Monte Romano — Monterosi — Sette Vene — Campagnano di Roma
Allumiere — Tolfa — Canale Monterano — Bagni di Vicarello — Trevignano Romano
Manziana — Lago di Bracciano — L. di Martignano — Anguillara Sabazia — Sacrofano
Bracciano — Vigna di Valle
VIA CLAUDIA BRACCIANESE
Ost. Nuova — Veii — Isola Farnese — Prin Por
Grottini — S.Severa — Pyrgi — Necropolis Cerveteri — Ceri — S.M.di Galeria — Mad. di Bracciano — La Storta — la Ginstiniana
VIA CASSIA
F. Arrone
Boccea
GRANDE RACCORDO ANULARE
Ladispoli — Palo — Palidoro — Ponte Tre Denari — Castel di Guido — Malagrotta
VIA AURELIA
Fregene — Ponte Galeria — EUR
Fiumicino — Porto — Ostia Antica — Acilia
ISOLA SACRA — VIA DEL MARE
Ostia — Castel Porziano
VIA C.COLOMBO
Lido di Castel Fusano — LA PINETA
F. Tevere
VIA SEVERIANA
Tor Vaianica

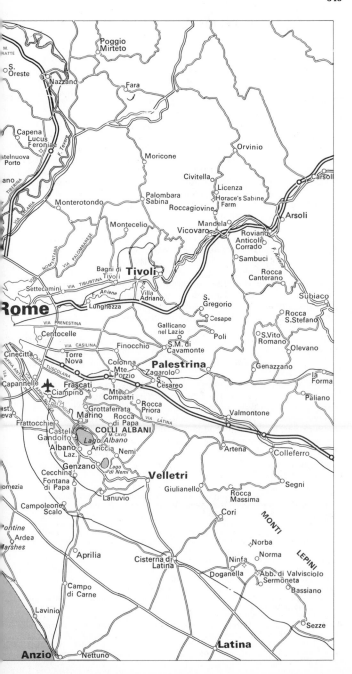

ENVIRONS OF ROME

The **Roman Campagna** (40–70m), the country surrounding Rome, is an undulating plain, with indeterminate limits, extending from the Tyrrhenian Sea to a semicircle of hills some distance inland. These are the Monti della Tolfa and Monti Sabatini, to the NW of Rome, the Monti Tiburtini and Monti Prenestini, to the E, and the Monti Lepini and Monti Ausoni, to the SE. The area is traversed by the Tiber, into which flow the Aniene and other tributaries. In the Tertiary Age the plain was occupied by a gulf of the sea, which went even beyond its limits. In this gulf volcanic eruptions formed numerous islands. In the centre the islands became the Alban Hills. In the NW they formed a series of ranges, one behind the other, having craters now filled up by lakes, namely the Monti Sabatini, with the Lago di Bracciano, the Monti Cimini, with the Lago di Vico, and the Monti Volsini, with the Lago di Bolsena. The lava from the eruptions spread as far as the hills where Rome later was built.

The name of *Campania Romana*, dating from the time of Constantine and replacing that of *Latium*, was used to distinguish the area from that of the Campania Felix, which surrounds Naples. In the widest sense of the term, the Roman Campagna includes the *Agro Pontino*, formerly the Pontine Marshes. In a more restricted connotation it is taken to comprise the area between the sea, the Monti Sabatini, and the Alban Hills, thus corresponding roughly to that of the *Agro Romano*, or administrative division of the Commune of Rome, with an area of 2074 sq. kilometres and forming a considerable part of the Province of Rome.

The *Province of Rome* (8438 sq. km) is one of four that make up the modern region of *Lazio*; the others are Frosinone (3064 sq. km), Rieti (2737 sq. km), and Viterbo (2934 sq. km). The area of Lazio is thus 17,174 sq. km.

The Campagna was the focus of almost all the people who were to form the Italic race. Here, in prehistoric times, originated the legends of the earliest struggles of the Romans, and here was displayed the nascent power of the city that was to dominate the world. The land was fertile in Roman times, although even then malaria was prevalent in certain districts. Later, when the work of drainage was abandoned and the waters were allowed to stagnate, the disease impoverished and sterilized the whole region. Nowadays the ancient fertility has returned.

RECLAMATION. In the early days of Rome the growing of corn was the main activity of the Campagna. After their Mediterranean conquests the Romans were able to import cereals and they gave their attention to the planting of gardens and orchards, which they sustained by irrigation. The ruins of the villas, aqueducts and cisterns found in every part of the Agro Romano testify to the productivity of the farms that once surrounded the city. In the early days of the Empire the farms began to be displaced by the large landed estates (*latifundia*), fertility declined, and the population dwindled. The decadence was accelerated by invasions and by malaria. As time went on, some of the popes tried without success to help the area with schemes of repopulation and the setting up of agricultural centres for the feeding of the city.

United Italy found the Agro Romano one vast malarial desert. The first efforts of the Government (1878) were directed to the drainage of the marshes and stagnant waters and to the reclamation of a belt extending to 10 kilometres from the centre of the city. At the same time the Government divided up the estates of the suppressed religious organizations. In 1883 it established the principle of compulsory cultivation on pain of expropriation. Further measures culminated in the law of 23 January 1921, which extended the principle of compulsion to the whole of the Agro Romano. The first effect of these laws was the recuperation of the unhealthy marshy districts, involving the construction of watercourses, drainage canals, and other works, with a view to the re-establishment of agriculture. In the years following the First World War, farms, orchards, and gardens made their appearance and scientific methods were applied to agriculture. New villages were built, replacing the characteristic *capanna*, or hovel, in which, for centuries, the nomadic shepherd had found shelter. The Agro Romano is now covered with cornfields, pasture-land, gardens, orchards, vineyards, and olive groves. Parts of the territory have been left in their natural state.

The environs of Rome are still reached on the line of the ancient Roman roads, with comparative ease and speed from the centre of the capital. They are well served by public transport (all services are run by A.CO.TRA.L, Telephone number: 57531), but are most conveniently reached by car. The routes given are each intended as a day's excursion from Rome; the more hurried visitor may sometimes combine two routes in a day. The country looks its best in the spring, when the Campagna is in flower, and in autumn, when the hills are ablaze with colour.

28 Ostia

The extensive ruins of the Roman city of **Ostia Antica**, in a beautiful park of umbrella pines and cypresses, should not be left unvisited. The excavations give a remarkable idea of the domestic and commercial architecture prevalent in the Empire in the late 1C and 2C AD (hardly any of which has survived in Rome itself). The remains are as important for the study of Roman urban life as those of the older cities of Pompeii and Herculaneum.

The **Lido di Ostia**, now often more appropriately called the Lido di Roma, is the over-crowded seaside resort of Rome. There are more pleasant bathing beaches to the S (Tor Vaianica) or N towards Fregene.

A.   Ostia Antica and the Isola Sacra

ROAD to Ostia Antica, 23km. VIA DEL MARE (N. 8) from Viale Marconi (beyond San Paolo fuori le Mura). This fast two-lane road reaching the coast (28km) at the W end of the Lido di Ostia (see Rte 28B), was opened in 1928. It runs parallel to the old Via Ostiense for the whole of its length. The *Via Ostiensis*, one of the earliest consular roads, dates from the victorious campaign of the Romans against the inhabitants of Veio to secure their salt supply (5C BC). It ran to Ostia from where, under the name of *Via Severiana*, it followed the coast to Laurentum (near Castel Fusano), Antium (Anzio), and Terracina, where it joined the Via Appia.

RAILWAY. *Metropolitana* trains from Termini run c every 20 minutes for Ostia Antica and Ostia Lido. Limited stop trains from Porta San Paolo call at Tor di Valle—Vitinia—Acilia—Ostia Antica—Lido Centro—Stella Polare—Castel Fusano—Lido Cristoforo Colombo.

Outside Porta San Paolo (Pl. 8; 7) Via Ostiense leads S. After 1·5km, just before the Basilica of San Paolo, Lungotevere San Paolo branches right. This joins Viale Marconi, and off this (right) begins Via del Mare proper.

The road runs parallel to Via Ostiense, which is on the left. Farther to the left many prominent buildings of E.U.R. (Rte 26) are conspicuous. To the right is a road to the racecourse of Tor di Valle.—12km Crossing of the Grande Raccordo Anulare (Rome Circular Road).—13km *Mezzocammino*; on a hill are the remains of a Roman villa and between the two roads is the tomb of a Roman knight. The road runs close to the Tiber for a very short period.—18km *Acilia*. Here excavations were begun in 1976 of *Ficana*. From here three parallel roads continue to the sea.—23km Ostia excavations (turning right; *Scavi di Ostia Antica*).

From the railway station of Ostia Antica Via Ostiense and Via del Mare are crossed by a footbridge; straight ahead is the entrance of the excavations.

At least half a day should be devoted to the *Excavations of Ostia which are open every day from 9 to one hour before sunset. The Museum is closed between 13 and 14. Cars may be left at the ticket entrance or (more conveniently) in the car park near the Museum. Refreshments, see below.

Ostia, or *Ostia Antica*, is named after the ostium, or mouth of the Tiber. In antiquity the river flowed past the city on the N in a channel, the *Fiume Morto*, dry since a great flood in 1557. According to legend, Ostia was founded by Ancus Marcius, fourth king of Rome, to guard the mouth of the river Tiber. The surviving remains are not, however, older than the 4C BC, and the city, which was probably the first colony of Rome, may have been founded about 335 BC. It was originally a fortified city (*Castrum*), whose walls survive in part; later it became a much larger commercial city (*Urbs*), also surrounded with walls. Its first industry was the extraction of salt from the surrounding marshes, but it soon developed into the commercial port of Rome and, shortly before the outbreak of the First Punic War (264 BC), it became also a naval base. The link between the port and the capital was the *Via Ostiensis*, which, carrying as it did all Rome's overseas imports and exports until the construction of the Via Portuensis, must have been one of the busiest roads in the ancient world.

The commerce passing through Ostia was vital to the prosperity and even the existence of Rome. One of its most important functions was the organization of the *Annona*, for the supply of produce, mainly corn, to the capital. At the head of the Annona was originally the *Quoestor Ostiensis*, who had to live at Ostia. He was appointed by lot and his office, according to Cicero, was burdensome and unpopular. By 44 BC the Quoestor was replaced by the *Procuratores Annonoe*, answerable to the Praefectus Annonae in Rome. The organization involved the creation of a large number of commercial associations or guilds covering every aspect of trade and industry. Numerous inscriptions referring to these associations have been found in the Piazzale delle Corporazioni. Ostia suffered a temporary setback in 87 BC, when it was sacked by Marius, but Sulla rebuilt it soon afterwards and gave it new walls.

As the city continued to thrive, it outgrew its harbour and the construction of another port became, by the 1C AD, an imperative necessity. Augustus planned, Claudius and Nero built, to the NW of Ostia, the new Portus Augusti, which Trajan enlarged (Porto; see Rte 28C). For a time Ostia remained the centre of the vast organization for the supply of food to the capital. It added to its temples, public buildings, shops and houses, and it received especial marks of favour from the emperors.

The decadence of Ostia began in the time of Constantine, who favoured Porto. The titles conferred by the emperor on the newer seaport must have been particularly galling to the inhabitants of Ostia. But even in the 4C, though it had become a residential town instead of a commercial port, it was still used by notable people travelling abroad. In 387 St Augustine was about to embark for Africa with his mother, St Monica, when she was taken ill and died in a hotel in the city. In the following centuries Ostia's decay was accelerated by loss of trade and by the scourge of malaria. Its streets and temples were neglected and looted. Columns, sarcophagi and statues stolen from the ruins have been found as far afield as Pisa, Amalfi, Orvieto, and Salerno. An attempt to revive the city was made by Gregory IV, when he founded the present village of Ostia. In 1756 the city, which at the height of its prosperity had had a population of some 80,000 had 156 inhabitants; half a century later there were only a few convicts of the papal Government; Augustus Hare, writing in 1878, speaks of one·human habitation breaking the utter solitude.

Excavations of the site began on a small scale at the beginning of the 19C, under Pius VII. Further work was instituted in 1854 under Pius IX, but systematic excavations did not begin till 1907. They have been continued with few interruptions, until the present day. The work carried out in 1938–42 by Guido Calza and others brought to light many monuments of great interest. The excavated area has been doubled and is now c 33 hectares, or half the area of the city at its greatest extent.

DWELLING HOUSES. One result of research has been the great increase in knowledge of the various types of house occupied by Romans of the middle and lower classes. Since it is not likely that the domestic architecture of Ostia differed radically from that of the capital, the examples that have been unearthed of the lower-grade house at Ostia may be taken as typical of such dwellings in Rome itself. The middle- and lower-class house at Ostia (*Insula*) was in sharp contrast to the typical Pompeian residence (*Domus*), with its atrium and peristyle, its few windows and its low elevation. This occurs only rarely at Ostia.

The ordinary Ostia house usually had four stories and reached a height of 15 metres—the maximum permitted by Roman law. It was built of brick, probably not covered with stucco, and has little in the way of adornment. Sometimes bricks of contrasting colours were used. The entrance doors had pilasters or engaged columns supporting a simple pediment. There were numerous rooms, each with its own window. The arches over the windows were often painted in vermilion. Mica or selenite was used instead of glass for the windows. The façades were of three types: living-rooms with windows on all floors; arcaded ground floor with shops, living-rooms above; and ground floor with shops opening on the street, living-rooms above. Many of the houses had balconies, which were of varying designs. The apartment houses contained numerous flats or sets of rooms designated by numbers on the stairs leading to them. They too, were of different types; some were of simple design and others were built round a courtyard.—The rare *Domus*, built for the richer inhabitants, were usually on one floor only and date mostly from the 3C and 4C. They were decorated with apses, nymphaea, and mosaic floors. The rooms often had columns and loggias.

RELIGION. In Ostia, as elsewhere in the Roman world, different religious cults flourished without disharmony. As well as temples dedicated to the traditional deities such as Vulcan, Venus, Ceres, and Fortuna, there was a vigorous cult of the emperors and a surprisingly large number of eastern cults, such as the Magna Mater, Egyptian and Syrian deities, and especially Mithras. Singularly few Christian places of worship have been found.

The city of Ostia appears to have been divided into at least five *Regiones*, the precise limits of which are not yet determined. It has, however, been found convenient to classify the various monuments according to the region to which they are believed to belong. The streets and buildings are thus marked with signs indicating (*a*) the number of the region, (*b*) the number of the block (*c*) the type of construction, such as temple, warehouse, dwelling-house (insula), residence (domus), etc., (*d*) the traditional name of the street or building.—Some of the *Mosaics discovered in the ruins are occasionally covered with wind-blown sand.

The entrance to the excavations (at the ticket office) leads into *Via Ostiense*, outside the walls (since the description of the site begins here, those using the car park near the Museum, see above, should return to the ticket office entrance, see the plan). Parallel on the S is Via delle Tombe. This street is also outside the walls, in conformity with Roman law, which prohibited intramural burials. In it are a few terracotta sarcophagi and sealed graves, as well as columbaria for the urns holding the ashes from cremations.

The entrance to the city is by the *Porta Romana*, with remains of the gate of the Republican period; some fragments of a marble facing of the Imperial era have been found and placed on the inner walls of

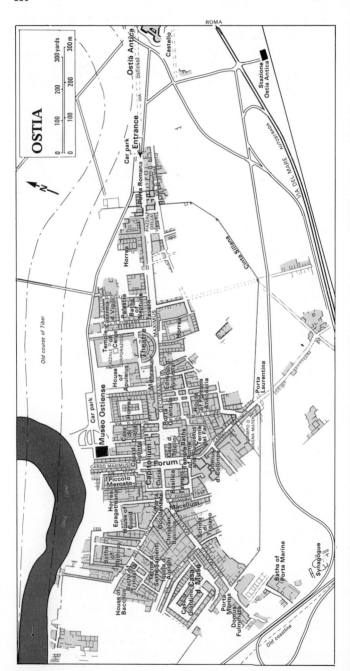

the gate.—The PIAZZALE DELLA VITTORIA is dominated by a colossal **Statue of Minerva Victoria**, dating from the reign of Domitian and inspired by a Hellenistic original. The statue may once have adorned the gate.—On the right of the square are the remains of *Horrea* (warehouses), later converted into baths. In the *Thermae of the Cisiarii* on the far side of the warehouses are several mosaics, one with scenes of life in Ostia.

Here begins the **Decumanus Maximus**, the main street of Ostia. It runs right through the city and is c 1200 metres long. A little way along this street, on the right, is a flight of steps leading to a platform, on the second story of the BATHS OF NEPTUNE. From the platform can be seen the tepidarium and calidarium, remains of columns, and the floor of the large entrance hall with a *Mosaic of Neptune driving four sea-horses and surrounded by tritons, nereids, dolphins, etc. In an adjoining room is another mosaic: Amphitrite escorted by Hymen. The platform provides a fine view of the excavations and of the country from the Alban Hills to the mouth of the Tiber.—Adjoining is the *Palaestra* (Gymnasium) a large colonnaded courtyard surrounded by rooms.

Just short of the Baths of Neptune is *Via dei Vigili* (Street of the Firemen), the construction of which involved the demolition of some earlier buildings, to which belonged a mosaic (displayed nearby) representing the Four Winds and Four Provinces (Sicily, Egypt, Africa, Spain). The street leads to the *Caserma dei Vigili* (Firemen's Barracks), built in the 2C AD. It has an arcaded courtyard, a shrine dedicated to Fortuna Santa, and an *Augusteum*, or shrine for the cult of the emperors.

An archway leads into *Via della Fontana*, one of the best-preserved streets in Ostia. Here is a typical apartment house, with shops and living-rooms over them.

To the right the street joins *Via della Fullonica*, named from its well-equipped fullers' establishment, complete with courtyard for cloth-drying.

The street rejoins the Decumanus Maximus at the *Tavern of Fortunatus* in which is a mosaic pavement with the broken inscription: 'Dicit Fortunatus: vinum cratera quod sitis bibe' ('Fortunatus says: drink wine from the bowl to quench your thirst'). The next street to the right (W) is *Via delle Corporazioni*; in it is a well-preserved apartment house, with paintings on the walls and ceilings. On the other side of the street is the *Theatre*, built by Agrippa, enlarged by Septimius Severus in the 2C.

The theatre is a semicircular building of the usual Roman type. It has two tiers of seats (originally three), divided by stairways into five sections or *Cunei*. It could accommodate 2700 people. Of the *Stage* there survive a tufa wall with some marble fragments and three marble masks. Behind the stage have been set up some cipollino columns that once decorated the third tier of the auditorium. In the main façade, towards the Decumanus Maximus, is a series of covered arcades with shops, one appropriately used as a **Refreshment Bar**. Between the arcades and the street are areas paved with travertine and adorned at either end with a fountain. Into the fountain on the E side was built a *Christian Oratory* in honour of St Cyriacus and his fellow-martyrs of Ostia.

Behind the theatre extends the spacious *PIAZZALE DELLE CORPORAZIONI* (Square of the Guilds). In this square were 70 offices of commercial associations ranging from worker's guilds to corporations of foreign representatives from all over the ancient world. Their trade-marks are preserved in the mosaic floors of the brick-built arcade running round the square. The trade-marks of the foreign representatives are historically valuable, as they tell from where the merchants came (e.g. Carthage, Alexandria, Narbonne, etc.) and what was their trade. Equally informative are the inscriptions relating to the citizens, some of whom were employed in ship repair and construction, in the maintenance of docks, warehouses, and embankments, as dockers, salvage crews, and customs and excise officials.—In the middle of the square are the stylobate and two columns of a small temple in antis known as the *Temple of Ceres*, and the bases of statues erected to the leading citizens of Ostia.

Beyond the square is a handsome house of the Pompeian type, rare at Ostia, with an atrium and rooms decorated with mosaics. It is called the *House of Apuleius*. Beside it is a *Mithraeum*, one of the best-preserved of the many temples dedicated to Mithras in the city. It has two galleries for the initiated, on the walls of which are mosaics illustrating the cult of the god. There are also casts of the marble relief of Mithras which was found here, with several inscriptions.

In front are four small tetrastyle *Temples*, erected in the 2C BC upon a single foundation of tufa. They are supposed to have been dedicated to Venus, Fortuna, Ceres, and Hope. In the square in front of the temples are the remains of a *Nymphaeum* and of a *Sanctuary of Jupiter*.

From the Decumanus Maximus can be seen, on the right, large *Warehouses (Horrea)* for the storage of corn. They have over 60 small rooms, some of them arranged round a central colonnaded courtyard. At the corner of the next street on the right—*Via dei Molini*, so called after a building in it containing millstones—are the remains of a *Republican Temple*. Here is the *Porta Orientale*, the East Gate of the original fortified city, or Castrum; to the left are the original tufa walls. At this point the Decumanus Maximus has been excavated down to the level of the ancient city and is liable to flooding in bad weather.

A street on the W side of Via dei Molini—*Via di Diana*—takes its name from a house called the *CASA DI DIANA. The façade is characteristic: shops on the ground floor, rooms with windows on the first floor, and a projecting balcony on the second floor. The house is entered through a vaulted corridor. On the ground floor is a room (left) whose ceiling and walls have been restored with fragments of frescoes. The small interior courtyard has a fountain and a relief of Diana. At the back of the premises are two rooms converted into a Mithraeum. Opposite the entrance to the Casa di Diana Via dei Lari opens into *Piazzetta de Lari*, with a round marble altar dedicated to the Lares of the Quarter.

In Via di Diana beyond the Casa di Diana, is (left) the *Thermopolium*, which bears a striking resemblance to a modern Italian bar. Just outside the entrance, under the balcony, are two small seats. On the threshold is a marble counter, on which is a small stone basin. Inside the shop is another counter for the display of food dishes; above are wall-paintings of fruit and vegetables. On the rear wall is a marble slab with hooks for hats and coats. Beyond is a delightful court and fountain.

At the end of Via di Diana (right) is an apartment house, originally of four stories, called the CASA DEI DIPINTI. A staircase leads up to the top floor from which there is a fine view of the excavations. The ground floor (entered around the corner from Via dei Dipinti) has been closed for many years: the corner room has a mosaic floor and 'architectural' wall-paintings; beyond is a fine *Hall painted with mythological scenes, human figures, and landscapes. In the garden of the house are numerous *Dolii*, large terracotta jars for the storage of corn and oil.—At the end of the street is the Museum, which contains the principal finds from the excavations.

The ***Museo Ostiense** is housed in a building dating from 1500 and originally used by the authorities concerned with the extraction of salt; it was given its neo-classical façade in 1864. The exhibits are well arranged.

ROOM I (left). *Bas reliefs showing scenes of everyday life (including various arts and crafts, the scene of a birth, a surgical operation, etc.); by the window, two bas-reliefs with the plan of a temple and the topographical plan of a city.— ROOM II. Architectural and decorative terracotta fragments; Statue of Fortune (2C AD).—Off the Atrium (with a statue of Apollo Kitharoidos of 2C AD) are (left) RR. III and IV with works relating to Eastern cults. R. III. In the niche at the end, *Mithras slaying the bull, from the Baths of Mithras, signed by Kritios of Athens (first half of the 2C BC); in the niche to the right, group of 18 cult statues found in the Sanctuary of Attis (AD 140–170); circular *Altar with reliefs of the Twelve Gods, a neo-Attic work of the 1C BC.—R. IV. Recumbent figure of a priest of Cybele (second half of 3C AD); Egyptian-Roman relief in black basalt of Asklepios; Stele with a boy initiated in the cult of Isis (early 4C AD).

Steps descend from the Atrium into ROOM VI. To the left is R. V with sculpture inspired from Greek art of 5C BC: inscribed Bases testifying to the presence of Greek artists; Head of Hermes; Votive relief (an original Greek-Italiot work of the first half of 5C BC); three heads of Athena, from originals of the Phidias type, the Kressilas type, and the Kephisodotos type (first half of 4C BC); upper part of a herm of Themistocles, copy of an original of the 5C; Omphalos Apollo, from the 5C original; Head of an unknown man.—R. VI contains sculpture inspired by Greek art of the 4C and 3C BC: two copies of Eros drawing his bow (one a replica of an original by Lysippos); cult statue of Asklepios (?); two herms of Hermes (of the Alcamene type); Dionysos (with elements inspired by Praxiteles). In the centre, fragment of a group of Wrestlers dating from the Trajan era on a Hellenistic model.—R. VII. Sculpture inspired by Hellenistic works. Head of a satyr and of a barbarian of the Pergamene type (2C BC); two heads of Korai; Head of Victory (Giulio-Claudian era); Perseus with the head of Medusa; Cupid and Psyche from the House of Cupid and Psyche; replica of the crouching Venus of Doidalsas (3C BC); Statue of the Three Graces.

The glass cases between R. VI and R. VIII contain Attic pottery (including a fragment of a red-figure cup showing Orpheus dating from the second half of 5C BC), Aretine vases, and 'terra sigillata' ware.—R. VIII (SALA GUIDO CALZA). Roman sculpture from the 1C BC to the mid-2C AD. *Headless male statue, nude except for the drapery over the left arm, signed with the name of the donor C. Cartilius Poplicola, whose sarcophagus is near Porta Marina. This statue is regarded as the best extant copy of the type known as the Hero in Repose; Portraits of Augustus, Trajan (including a statue of him wearing a cuirass), Hadrian, Sabina, wife of Hadrian, and a group of portraits of members of the family of Marcus Aurelius. Herm of Hippocrates (from an original of 3C BC); funerary statue of Giulia Procula; relief (fragment of an architectural frieze) showing the sacred geese in front of the Temple of Juno Moneta on the Capitoline.—The small cases between R. VIII and R. X contain kitchen pottery, terracotta statuettes, and oil lamps.

ROOM IX (left of R. X). Roman sarcophagi of the 2–3C AD, including the *Sarcophagus of a boy, from the Isola Sacra Necropolis, a magnificent example of the Attic type, dating from the 2C AD; on the lid is the figure of a boy lying on a couch decorated with bas-reliefs; while three sides have reliefs of Dionysiac rites with a charming frieze of putti (illustrating the direct influence sarcophagi of this type had on artists of the Renaissance). On the back is the scene of a wrestling match which was left in a rough, unfinished state. Also displayed here, Sarcophagus with a scene of Lapiths and Centaurs.—R. X. Roman sculpture (end of 2C to 4C AD). Maxentius (?) as Pontifex Maximus, found in the Edificio degli Augustali; Statue of Fausta, sister of Maxentius (AD 310–312); Giulia Domna, in the semblance of Ceres, and a bust of Septimius Severus, her husband.—R. XI. Roman art of the 4–5C AD. Magnificent *Opus sectile panels found in an edifice near Porta Marina. The design includes various portraits, and a head thought to be that of Christ (with a halo), and two scenes of a lion attacking a horse. Relief showing scribes recording an orator's speech (thought to have a Christian significance).—Between R. IX and R. XII cases display

Roman glass (including a cup engraved with the figure of Christ, the Cross, and the Monogram, 4–5C), and objects in bone, ivory, bronze, and lead.—R. XII. Imperial wall paintings and mosaic fragments.

Parallel with Via dei Dipinti, on the W is the wide CARDO MAXIMUS with arcaded shops, which runs from the Tiber to the Forum and from there to the Porta Laurentina. To the W of this street and also parallel is the narrow *Via Tecta*, on the brick walls of which have been affixed many of the best preserved inscriptions found in the ruins. Via Tecta runs beside a grain warehouse called the *Piccolo Mercato*; some of its rooms form the Antiquarium Ostiense housing archaelogical material (no adm). In the S wall have been incorporated several layers of the tufa blocks of the primitive city walls.—The Cardo Maximus runs S to the **Forum**, which is traversed from E to W by the Decumanus Maximus. At the N end of the Forum is the *Capitolium, the city's most important temple, dedicated to Jupiter, Juno, and Minerva. This prostyle hexastyle building, dating from the first half of the 2C had six fluted white marble columns. The pronaos is reached by a wide flight of steps, before which is an altar (reconstituted). In the cella are niches and a plinth for statues of the deities.

During the invasion of the barbarians the temple was stripped of nearly all its marble facing, but a magnificent slab of African marble is still in place on the threshold and a few surviving marble fragments have been placed to the E of the building under a colonnade, which defined the sacred area.

Opposite the Capitolium, on the S side of the Forum, are the remains of the 1C TEMPLE OF ROME AND AUGUSTUS. Like the Capitolium it had six fluted marble columns across the front, but with two side staircases. Fragments of the pediment have been placed on a modern wall to the E; the cult statue of Rome as Victory, dressed as an Amazon, has been placed inside the temple on a plinth, and a headless statue of Victory near the rearranged pediment fragments.

On the E side of the Forum are the BATHS OF THE FORUM, built in the 2C and restored in the 4C. When restored the baths were adorned with mosaics and cipollino columns; some of the columns have been re-erected. The *Frigidarium* survives, together with a series of rooms warmed by hot air. Off the N side is the town *Forica*, with its 20 seats all but completely preserved.—Also on the E side, at the corner where the Decumanus Maximus enters the Forum, is the *Casa dei Triclini*, so called from the couches to be found in each of the three rooms on the right wing of the central courtyard. Behind the courtyard is a room with a high podium decorated with coloured marbles.

Opposite, on the W side of the Forum, is the BASILICA, or law courts and place of assembly. The façade towards the Forum had a portico of marble arches with a decorated frieze. Fragments of this decoration and of the columns have been preserved. To the S of the Basilica is the *Tempio Rotondo*, dating from the 3C and probably an *Augusteum*, or temple erected to the worship of the emperors. The peristyle was paved with mosaics and surrounded by marble-faced niches. It was reached by a flight of steps (preserved), which led to the pronaos; this comprised a portico with brick piers faced with marble and with cipollino columns. In the cella are seven niches, three rectangular and four circular. Between the niches are column bases; to the right are the remains of a spiral staircase that led to the dome.

Also on the W side, N of the Decumanus Maximus, is the *Curia*, or senate house. The inscriptions on the walls are lists of *Augustales*, citizens of Ostia belonging to the cult of the emperors.—Beside the Curia is the *Casa del Larario*, or House of the Shrine of the Lares, a combination of a house and shopping centre.

Leaving the Forum the Decumanus Maximus continues to the *Porta Occidentale*, the West Gate of the original Castrum; the ancient walls are well seen in Via degli Horrea Epagathiana, a turning on the right. In this street are the *HORREA EPAGATHIANA ET EPAPHRODI-TIANA, warehouses in a remarkable state of preservation, and used as a sherd store (no adm).

These warehouses were built by two Eastern freedmen, Epagathus and Epaphroditus, whose names are preserved on a marble plaque above the entrance; this is a brick portal with two engaged columns supporting a pediment. The inner courtyard was surrounded by an arcade of brick piers, repeated on the upper floor. On the walls of the vestibule and courtyard are four intact aediculae. In a large vaulted room at the rear of the Horrea are further remains of the primitive town wall.

The region to the W of the Decumanus Maximus is that excavated in 1938–42. The Decumanus Maximus now forks. The right fork is *Via della Foce* (Street of the River Mouth); it has been excavated for c 270m. The left fork is the continuation of the Decumanus Maximus (see above) and runs SW to the Porta Marina, or Sea Gate.

In Via della Foce, on the left, a long passageway leads to the *Mitreo delle Pareti Dipinte*, built in the 2C into a house of the Republican period. The Mithraeum is divided into two sections by partly projecting walls with ritual niches. The two stucco-faced galleries of the inner section also have niches. In the rear wall is the brick-built altar, with a marble cippus on which is a bust of Mithras. On the N wall are paintings of initiation rites.

A short street to the right leads to the *Sacred Area of Three Republican Temples*. The central and largest is the prostyle hexastyle *Temple of Hercules Invictus*. The pronaos, paved with mosaics, is reached by a flight of nine steps as wide as the façade. Inside the cella was a small marble column carved to represent the club of Hercules with the lion skin thrown over it. The temple, which may date from the time of Sulla, was given an altar in the 4C AD by Hostilius Antipater, Praefectus Annonae.—On the N side of the Sacred Area is a *Tetrastyle Temple* (dedication unknown) of the same date as the first.— Between the Temple of Hercules and Via della Foce is the *Temple of the Amorini*, named after a round marble altar with winged cupids found there. It was built in the early republican and rebuilt in the Imperial period. Its final form was distyle in antis.

Behind the temple is a street leading to the *House of Cupid and Psyche*, a Domus dating from the end of the 3C. It is named after a marble group found in it and now in the Museum. On the W side of the central atrium are four rooms, one with a pavement of coloured marbles (and a copy of the statue); on the E is an attractive nymphaeum in a courtyard with columns and brick arches. At the N end of the Atrium is a large room paved with opus sectile, and preserving some marble mural facing.—Farther along Via della Foce, is *Via delle Terme di Mitra* (right). The BATHS OF MITHRAS date from Trajan and were rebuilt in the 2C. They had elaborate arrangements of heating and for pumping the water. In the basement is a Mithraeum, in which was found the group of Mithras and the Bull, now in the Museum.

On the left side of the main street are three blocks of small apartment houses; then follows a complex of two apartment blocks with baths between them. The *Insula di Serapide* is named after a

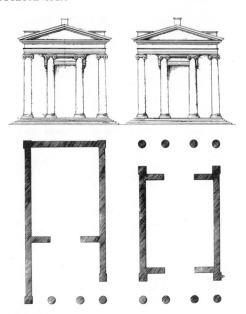

Roman temples 'in antis', after Vitruvius, architect and surveyor to Augustus ('De architectura', before AD 27), published by Carlo Amati in 1829

figure of Serapis in an aedicula which adorns the courtyard.—The *Terme dei Sette Sapienti* were so called from a satirical painting of the Seven Sages found in one of the rooms. The Sages are distinguished by name (in Greek); to each of them is attached a frank inscription on the subject of rude health. The baths have a round central hall (once domed), paved with a beautiful *Mosaic with five concentric rows of hunting scenes, including what appears to be a tiger. In a room next to a marble plunge pool is a painting of Venus Anadyomene.—A passage leads to the extensive *Insula degli Aurighi*, an apartment block with a large central courtyard. Two small paintings of charioteers belonging to opposing factions in the E wall of the arcade give the house its name. Off the N walk is a flat of six rooms with interesting paintings. Beyond the E side of the courtyard is a shrine presumably of Mithras.

Farther along Via della Foce, on the left, is a group of buildings of Hadrian's time. The *Baths of Trinacria* preserve good mosaics, and interesting installations for heating and conducting the water. On the other side of Via Serapeo is the *House of Bacchus and Ariadne*, with rich floral mosaics. The *Serapeum*, behind, was dedicated in AD 127, and included a temple, with courtyard flanked by porticoes and cult rooms. To the W, originally connected with the Serapeum, is an admirable domus, with more mosaics.

Beyond the Insula degli Aurighi is *Via degli Aurighi*, which runs E to join the extension of the Decumanus Maximus. In this street are the *Insula delle Celle* (left), a type of warehouse with small rooms, and, opposite, a modest hotel with a stable called *Albergo con Stalla*. This inn also faces a street named after the *Insula delle Volte Dipinte* (no adm), with painted ceilings. Across the street is the *Casa delle Muse (closed in 1988), dating from the time of Hadrian. This house has a central courtyard with a covered arcade. The restored wooden roof of the arcade rests on the ancient brick cornice. In a room to the E are paintings of Apollo and the Muses; in one to the N are panel paintings of divinities and satyrs. On a wall of the arcade are some graffiti, one of them representing the lighthouse of Ostia.

To the right is the *Casa a Pareti Gialle*, or House with the Yellow Walls. This looks on to a vast square of four large apartment houses built round a garden and known as the *Case a Giardino*. The scale of construction, the provision of a private garden, and the absence of shops all indicate that the flats in these buildings were intended for the wealthier inhabitants of Ostia.

The Decumanus Maximus and its extension from the fork outside the West Gate, continues SW and runs for 350m to the Porta Marina and, beyond it, to the sea-coast. The *Porta Marina*, or Sea Gate, was an opening in the walls built by Sulla, remains of which may be seen. Just inside the gate is a wine-shop, the *Caupona di Alexander*, and, outside, a large square. The extension of the Decumanus Maximus beyond the gate, built in the time of Augustus, ran through an earlier cemetery (see below). On this section is the *Santuario della Bona Dea*, a small prostyle tetrastyle temple, whose four column bases survive. Farther towards the sea is the *Domus Fulminata*, with a small monument recording the fact that the house had been struck by lightning.—Opposite, Via di Cartilio Poplicola leads to the *Baths of Porta Marina* past the *Tomb of L. Cartilius Poplicola*, a prominent citizen. The surviving fragment of its decorative frieze shows a trireme adorned with the helmeted head of a goddess. This and another tomb close by attest to the existence of a cemetery in the Republican era.

On the outskirts of the town towards the shore, between the sea and the ancient Via Severiana (on the SW side of this street) has been excavated (1961–63) the most ancient Jewish *Synagogue* known from monumental remains. It was in continuous use from the 1C to the 5C AD. Ritual carvings and poorly preserved mosaics have been found; several Ionic columns have been re-erected. It was discovered while the new road to Fiumicino airport was being constructed.

The Decumanus Maximus returns past the charming *Fontana a Lucerna*. In a street to the S beyond the junction with Via degli Aurighi is a block of shops with windows beside their doors. Close by is the SCHOLA DI TRAIANO, seat of an Ostian corporation named after a statue of Trajan found in it. In the courtyard, which has stuccoed brick columns, is a long basin provided with niches. The central room has a headless statue of Fortuna and a mosaic pavement. The school overlay earlier constructions, among them a 1C Domus; its nymphaeum has been partly restored.—On the opposite side of the main street is the *School of the Naval Smiths*, with a temple. The arcade of the courtyard in front of the temple was evidently a marble store: unused and partly finished columns, bases and capitals have been found in it. The store appears to have belonged to Volusianus, a senator of the 4C, as his name is carved on some of the column shafts. Adjoining is the *Christian Basilica*, an unpretentious structure with two aisles divided by columns and ending in apses.

Vico del Dionisio leads S to the *Cortile di Dionisio*, surrounded by several houses, and to the *Mitreo delle Sette Porte*, a Mithraeum which displays in seven arches the seven grades of the Mithraic cult.

The Decumanus Maximus continues to (right) the *Macellum*, or Market, which occupies the area between the Decumanus and a street running S, *Via Occidentale del Pomerio*. The market has numerous shops; two fish-shops open on to the Decumanus. Behind them is the market-place.—Via Occidentale del Pomerio and Via del Tempio Rotondo behind the Tempio Rotondo at the S end of the Forum lead to the S continuation of the Cardo Maximus. On the right here is the *Domus di Giove Fulminatore*, a house of the Republican period remodelled in the 4C, with a striking phallic 'doormat' mosaic. Beside it is the *Domus della Nicchia a Mosaico*, another Republican house, twice rebuilt. It is named after a semicircular niche faced with polychrome mosaic in the tablinum. Adjoining is the *Ninfeo degli Eroti*, with well-preserved marble floor and walls and niches in which were found two copies of the Eros of Lysippos. The next building is the DOMUS DELLE COLONNE, a large corner house, with façades on the Cardo Maximus and on Via della Caupona del Pavone (right). In the centre of the courtyard is a stone basin with a double apse and short white marble columns; beyond is the large tablinum with its entrance between two columns.

In the side street is an ancient wine-shop, the 3C *Caupone del Pavone*. One of its rooms is decorated with paintings of flying bacchanals and muses; beyond is the bar, with a counter and small basins.—On the opposite side of the street is the *Domus dei Pesci*, evidently a Christian house. A vestibule has a mosaic with a chalice and fishes. A large room on the S side, with two marble columns, has a fine *Mosaic Floor.

The Cardo Maximus passes on the right the *Portico dell'Ercole*; opposite is a fulling mill. Adjoining are the TERME DEL FARO. In a floor of the Frigidarium of the baths is a mosaic with fishes, sea monsters, and a lighthouse (pharos), after which the baths were named. One of the rooms has a white marble pool and frescoed walls in the 3C style.—A ramp leads from the Cardo to the triangular CAMPO DELLA MAGNA MATER, one of the best preserved sacred areas of the Roman world. At the W corner is the prostyle hexastyle *Temple of Cybele*. At the E corner the *Sanctuary of Attis* has an apse flanked by telamones in the shape of fauns. On the same side is the *Temple of Bellona*, dating from the time of Marcus Aurelius, and, opposite, the *Schola degli Hastiferes*, seat of an association connected with the cult of Bellona.—The sanctuary is close to the *Porta Laurentina*, which retains the tufa blocks of Sulla's circumvallation (c 80 BC).

To the S of the Porta Laurentina, along the line of the ancient Via Laurentina, is (500m) the *Cemetery of the Porta Laurentina*, first excavated in 1865 and systematically explored in 1934–35. Many of the inscriptions relate to freedmen. Beyond the motorway, in the locality called Pianabella, excavations are in progress of a necropolis and Christian church.

A short distance back along the Cardo Maximus, the *Semita dei Cippi* leads to the right (N). This street is flanked by two cippi and contains a 3C Domus (*Casa del Protiro*), its reconstituted portal prettily flanked by cypresses. To the N a right turn leads into a street named after the *House of Fortuna Annonaria*, which has a garden in its peristyle. On the W side of the peristyle is a large room with three arches, columns, and a nymphaeum.

At the end of the street, on the right, is another temple of Bona Dea, with a mithraeum next door, notable for its mosaic pavement.

Also in the street is the *Domus Republicana*, with four Doric columns;

it is adjoined by the *Edificio degli Augustali*, the headquarters of the Augustales. This building has another entrance in Via degli Augustali, which leads to the Decumanus Maximus, and the main entrance.

Near the entrance to the excavations lies **Ostia**, a fortified village whose walls are still standing, founded by Gregory IV in 830 and given the name of *Gregoriopolis*. Today Ostia (3000 inhab.) is a collection of picturesque old houses, most of them restored, within the walls, and some modern houses outside. Its dominant feature is the *CASTELLO (closed for restoration in 1988), built in 1483–86 by Baccio Pontelli for Julius II while still a cardinal. It contains archaeological collections of minor importance from the excavations, medieval material and frescoes attrib. to Baldass. Peruzzi. The church of *Santa Aurea*, by Baccio Pontelli or Meo del Caprina, contains the body of the martyred St Aurea (died 268), and, in a side chapel, a fragment of a gravestone which is most probably that of St Monica (died 387), mother of St Augustine. The Episcopal Palace is the residence of the Bishop of Ostia, holder of one of the six suburbicarian sees allotted to the cardinal bishops.

Via del Mare continues to the coast and (4km) *Lido di Ostia* (Rte 28B). A branch road skirts the excavations, curving right (signposted to Fiumicino) on a spur from Via del Mare. It crosses the Tiber to the **Isola Sacra**, a tract of land made into an island by the cutting of Trajan's canal, the Fossa Traiana, from Porto to the sea (see Rte 28B). It derives its name from the necropolis of the ancient seaport. Its area has been considerably increased by silt deposits.

The region, once a flourishing horticultural centre, was abandoned after the fall of the Western Empire and degenerated into an uninhabited malarial marsh. So it remained until 1920 when it was reclaimed, and swamps were drained, roads ballasted, canals dug, and houses, schools, farms, and silos built.

About 1km farther on is a small signpost (right) for the **Necropolis of Isola Sacra** or the *Necropolis of Portus Romae* (closed in 1988). A track leads to the delightfully planted site. This was the cemetery of Trajan's seaport, later known as Portus Romae and still later as Porto. It was not used for burials from the earlier Portus Augusti (see below). It was in use for c 250 years, from the 2C to the 4C. Only part has been excavated as much of it is under cultivation.

Since the necropolis was the burial-place of the middle- and lower-class inhabitants of Porto such as merchants, artisans, craftsmen, sailors, and the like, there are no elaborate mausolea. The tombs, which have been preserved by the sand that covered them for centuries, are arranged in groups. They have or had barrel vaults of brick and masonry faced with stucco; some of them had gable roofs. Internally they are decorated with stuccoes, paintings, and mosaics. Sarcophagi and urns in columbaria have been found, often in the same tomb—evidence of the simultaneous practice of burial and cremation. Many of the sarcophagi are adorned with mythological reliefs; terracotta reliefs are found with representations of arts and crafts, indicating the trade of the deceased. Nearly every tomb has a name inscribed over the door. The tombs of the wealthier citizens have sepulchral chambers, with fanlights. Outside, by the door, are couches for funeral feasts.

Some of the tombs are like old-fashioned round-topped travelling trunks, and recall similar examples in North Africa. The poorest citizens, who could not afford the cost of a monument buried their dead in the ground and marked the place with amphorae through which they poured libations; or they set up large tiles to form a peaked roof over the remains.

The road through the cemetery—the Via Flavia—is a section of the ancient road from Ostia to Porto. Of particular interest are a *Chamber Tomb* (11), with a marble sarcophagus with a scene of a funeral feast, and two other sarcophagi; the *Tomb of the Children* (16), with mosaics, an entrance adorned with Nile, and a beautiful sarcophagus now in the Museo Ostiense; the *Tomb of the Smith* (29), with a façade divided by three pilasters and terracotta reliefs indicating the man's trade; the *Tomb of Telesphorus and Julia Eunia* (39), with the Christian symbols of the lamb, dove, and anchor, apparently unique in this cemetery; a two-storied tomb (41); a tomb with a ship mosaic with the Pharos of Porto (43). In the row behind are two tombs (55 and 56), the first pedimental, the second with a square-corniced façade, both preserving their inscriptions. Close by are a series of *Four Chamber Tombs* (77–80), with pedimental façades with reliefs (the paintings from these tombs are in the Ostia Antiquarium).—Near the necropolis is the church of *Sant'Ippolito* where excavations have revealed interesting paleochristian remains and a large medieval basilica.

B.   Lido di Ostia

ROAD. The fastest route is by the motorway, VIA CRISTOFORO COLOMBO (27km).

RAILWAY. Trains from Porta San Paolo and the Metropolitana from Termini run c every 20 minutes to Lido Centro—Stella Polare—Castel Fusano—Lido Cristoforo Colombo, via Ostia Antica.

BUSES The sea-front from Castel Fusano to Fiumicino is served by frequent bus services.

Via Cristoforo Colombo is a straight four-lane motorway, which is a continuation of the road running through the centre of E.U.R. (Rte 26). It reaches the coast at **Castel Fusano** and the beautiful pine forest of Rome (*La Pineta*). This spreads over 4km and has convenient interior roads.

The first pines were planted c 1710. In 1755 the property was acquired by the Chigi family and was afterwards let as a royal chase. In 1932 it was bought by the Commune of Rome and in 1933 part of it was opened as a public park. There are plans to connect it, as one huge nature reserve, to the forests of Castel Porziano and Capocotta to the S (see Rte 29).

Lido di Ostia itself extends for several kilometres to the W. It has been the capital's seaside resort since the First World War. New hotels, villas and blocks of flats continue to be built in this over-crowded summer town, all but deserted in winter. On the E, Via del Mare from Rome (Rte 28A) terminates, and farther along the esplanade a road leads to the *Idroscalo*, the former seaplane station near the mouth of the Tiber. On 2 November 1975 the writer and film director Pier Paolo Pasolini was found murdered here (monument).

C.   Porto and Fiumicino

MOTORWAY. Air passengers for Fiumicino (the main airport of Rome) take Autostrada N 201 from Stazione Trastevere. At 21km A12 diverges to the right for Civitavecchia, but an extension continues to the airport.

BUSES for the Airport from Via Giolitti; from Piazzale Ostiense to the resort of Fiumicino.

VIA PORTUENSE runs via Porto to Fiumicino. Beyond Stazione Trastevere, at the end of the broad Viale Trastevere, Via Portuense diverges right. This follows the ancient *Via Portuensis* which ran on the right bank of the Tiber to Portus Augusti, later Portus Traiani, and now the modern village of Porto.

24km **Porto**, now 5km inland, was once a seaport of greater significance than Ostia. To the W of the village, on the right of the road, is the hexagonal basin of the *Port of Trajan* (see below). To the right are the graceful cantilevered buildings of *Leonardo da Vinci Airport*, still usually called 'Fiumicino', officially brought into operation early in 1961. The important Roman remains in this area of the Port of Claudius and Port of Trajan (now partly occupied by a safari park, and by a villa of the Torlonia) are to be expropriated, and it is hoped that the archaeological site will then be opened to the public. So far a *Museo delle Navi Romane* has been opened in a pavilion (signposted from the airport; adm 9–13, 14–17; Sunday 9–13; in summer every day 9–13, 14–17). Here are displayed seven Roman cargo boats found at the entrance to the Port of Claudius, which were used to carry goods upstream to Rome. They include flat-bottomed barges, and a fishing boat. Various objects found in the excavations are also displayed here.

When the harbour of Ostia, already inadequate for its trade, began to silt up with the action of the Tiber, Augustus planned the creation of a larger port in the vicinity. In AD 42 Claudius began operations. His harbour was sited about 1km W of the basin which Trajan built later. It was connected to the Tiber by a canal. The work was completed in 54 by Nero, who issued commemorative coins stamped *Portus Augusti*. Of the *Port of Claudius* (now within the airport enclosure) there survives part of the quay in which was incorporated the form of Caligula's ship (104m × 20) which brought the obelisk, now in Piazza San Pietro, from Egypt, and the base of a lighthouse. Even this harbour proved insufficient and in 103 Trajan constructed a new basin, the *Portus Traiani* to the S, farther inland and better protected. Hexagonal in shape (650m across), it was surrounded by a wall and warehouses, and formed the nucleus of a city. It is now merely a picturesque little lake (Lago Traiano), but shows up excellently from the air when landing at Fiumicino. Excavations have unearthed the remains of granaries, a wall, a high arch in red brick, an underground passageway, porticoes, etc. To the W are more ruins, at present still overgrown and abandoned. Trajan as well as Claudius, dug canals in connection with the seaport. The *Fossa Traiana* survives as a navigable canal between the Tiber and the sea, forming the Isola Sacra (see Rte 28A). In this island was the city's cemetery.—Porto was favoured by Constantine at the expense of Ostia; in 314 it had its own bishop and became known as *Portus Romoe* or *Civitas Constantina*. In the village are the church of *Santa Rufina* (10C, rebuilt), an old episcopal palace, and the Villa Torlonia. The suburbicarian see of Porto and Santa Rufina is one of the six held by the cardinal bishops.

28km **Fiumicino** is a small seaside resort, which was heavily bombed in the Second World War.—From Fiumicino by road to Ostia and Lido di Ostia across the Isola Sacra, see Rte 28A and 28B.

29 Anzio and Nettuno

ROAD (Via Pontina), 60km. Buses from Rome (E.U.R. 'Fermi' station on the underground) to *Anzio* and *Nettuno*.

RAILWAY. From Rome (Termini) to *Anzio* (57km) in c 1 hr; to *Nettuno*, (60km) in 3 minutes more.

Both road and railway cross the AGRO PONTINO, a tract of land with an area of c 750 square kilometres formerly known as the *Pontine Marshes* or *Pomptine Marshes* and regarded as a part of the Roman campagna in the widest sense of that term. The Agro Pontino is a plain extending SW to the coast of Latium from the Via Appia (N 7) between Cisterna di Latina and Terracina. As its former name implies, the plain, even in Roman times, was marshy, though, when the Appian Way was built in 213 BC, the marshes must have covered a relatively small part of the whole, which is said to have supported 23 towns. One of these towns was the long-vanished *Pontia*, which gave its name to the district. The marshes were mainly formed by numerous small streams which could not find their way to the sea and therefore stagnated. When the marshes spread the inhabitants, attacked by malaria, died off or moved elsewhere if they could. Until recent years it was sparsely populated and it had a sinister reputation.

Julius Caesar planned to drain the marshes but his assassination wrecked the project. In the time of Augustus a navigable canal, which partly drained off the waters, ran alongside the Appian Way. Horace used this canal in the course of his journey from Rome to Brundusium in 37 BC (*Satires*, I, 5); he embarked on the canal barge at Appii Forum (at the 43rd milestone on the Appian Way) and left it at Anxur (Terracina). No further work of importance was undertaken until the 16C, when Leo X (1513–21) cut the *Canale Portatore* to run from the Appian Way into the sea at Porto Badino, W of Terracina. Sixtus V (1585–90) built a more ambitious canal, the *Fossa Sisto*, which runs parallel to the Appian Way on its SW side and reaches the sea to W of Leo X's canal. Pius VI (1775–99) enlarged the Canale Portatore and built the *Canale Linea Pio*, which accompanies the Appian Way for 30 kilometres.

Not until 1928 did reclamation of the marshes begin in earnest. The Agro Pontino was divided into two reclamation areas, the Bonifica di Piscinara and the Bonifica Pontina, one on each side of the Fossa Sisto. More canals were built, as well as roads and other works. In 1932 Littoria, now Latina, was founded in the centre of the Agro Pontino. There followed in 1934 Sabaudia, on the coast near Monte Circeo; in 1935 Pontinia, SE of Latina; in 1937 Aprilia, to the NW; and in 1939 Pomezia, NW of Aprilia. The Agro Pontino was completely reclaimed, as well as a considerable area outside its confines. There were five main canals, including a deep collecting-canal which became the right flank of the Anzio bridge-head, and a network of secondary canals, 1300km of roads and some 4000 settlers' houses. Many of these houses were grouped in villages called Borghi.

The Second World War caused immense damage, due largely to the repercussions of the bridge-head landings at Anzio (see below). Nearly 800 houses were destroyed or damaged. Livestock decreased from 30,000 to 4000; 80 sq. kilometres were mined and an almost equally large area flooded. The work of reconstruction was begun immediately after the end of the War.

Via Cristoforo Colombo leaves Rome and passes through E.U.R., see Rte 26.

Via Laurentina, diverging to the left and skirting E.U.R., runs S to join N 148 at (32km) *Santa Prócula Maggiore* (see below).

The road passes under the Rome Circular Road. At (16km) *Osteria del Malpasso* is an entrance to *Castel Porziano*, once a royal chase and now a holding of the President of the Republic. There are plans to protect the coastal forests of Castel Porziano, Castelfusano, and Capocotta as one huge nature reserve. Among interesting Roman remains here are a villa of the early Imperial period at Tor Paterno and an aqueduct. The Via Severiana, built by Septimius Severus to link Fiumicino with Terracina can still be seen in many parts of the forest.—28·5km *Pomezia*, the westernmost and latest (1939) of the new towns of the Agro Pontino (see above), stands at cross-roads. A road (right) leads to (2km) *Prática di Mare*, on the site of LAVINIUM, which, according to an ancient legend, was the town founded by Aeneas, after his escape from Troy, and named after his wife.

Numerous ancient Roman historians, as well as Virgil, upheld this myth, and as early as 300 BC a tradition existed at Lavinium itself which attributed its foundation to the Trojan hero. Thirteen archaic altars (6C BC) have been found here, as well as a tomb sanctuary of Aeneas, in the form of a tumulus burial chamber, which was restored in the 4C. An Iron Age necropolis with some 70 tombs has been identified. To the E, across the modern road to Rome, another sanctuary, dedicated to Minerva, has been excavated. Here the votive deposit included more than 70 remarkable statues (some more than 2m high) made by local Italic craftsmen in the 5C to 2C BC. The terracotta sculptures, many of which have been carefully restored, include some beautiful female portraits, and striking representations of Minerva as the warrior goddess with unusual attributes. The excavation of the city on the hill occupied by the village and Borghese castle continues: so far fragments of 6C walls and the E gate, and Baths from the time of Constantine have been found.

Farther along N 148, to the right, is a German military cemetery, and beyond (33·5km) *Santa Prócula Maggiore*, the cross-roads where Via Laurentina comes in.—*Ardea*, 4·5km to the right, the capital of Turnus, king of the Rutuli, is now a village with some antique remains (temples, a basilica, and fortifications). It is the birthplace of the Italian sculptor Giacomo Manzù, and there is a museum (open 9–18; Saturday and Sunday 9–13.30; closed Monday) of his work just outside the village.—A crossing is soon made into the province of Latina, and Via Pontina runs through the middle of the area of land reclamation (see above).—44km **Aprilia** (28,300 inhab.), the fourth of the new towns of the Agro Pontino, was founded in 1937. It lies to the left of the road on a spur of the Alban Hills, 80m above sea-level.

After the Allied landings at Anzio and Nettuno on 22 January 1944, Aprília was fought over, bombed, and shelled, and the town destroyed in 4 months of fighting. It has been completely rebuilt. The main buildings are grouped round Piazza Roma, with the church of *San Michele Arcangelo*.

Via Nettuense (N 207) leads S. Beyond (48km) *Campo di Carne* the road traverses an extensive oak wood called the Bosco di Padiglione.—59·5km *Anzio (Beach Head) Cemetery*, with the graves of 2312 members of the British forces who lost their lives in the beach-head operations.

Farther on, the trees of the Villa Aldobrandini are seen on the left. A few metres N of the railway, which is recrossed, is the smaller *Anzio Military Cemetery*, with 1056 British graves. On rising ground near by is the Carmelite *Santuario di Santa Teresa del Bambino Gesù* (1939), in the Romanesque style. Beyond the railway the road descends.

60km **ANZIO** (22,900 inhab.), the *Antium* of antiquity, has been known to history from the 5C BC. It became prominent again in the landings of January 1944, and suffered great damage in the ensuing fighting. Now largely rebuilt, it is a popular seaside resort of the Romans.

History. Antium was one of the chief cities of the Volsci, an ancient people constantly at war with the growing might of Rome. The city was a centre of commerce and its ship captains were notorious pirates. When Coriolanus was banished from Rome in 491 BC he went over to the enemy against whom he had won fame in battle, and sought protection at Antium, and it was to Antium two years later, in response to the entreaties of his wife and mother, that he withdrew from the gates of Rome. In 468 BC Antium was captured by the Romans, who planted a colony there. In a subsequent revolt it established its independence, but was finally subdued in 338 BC when all its ships were seized and their beaks sent to adorn the Rostra in the Roman Forum. In the late Republic and early Empire it was a summer resort of the wealthier Romans. Cicero describes his villa at Antium in his letters to Atticus, and Horace, in his Ode to Fortune, refers to her temple at 'loved Antium'. Caligula and Nero, both natives of the town, embellished it. Nero built a magnificent villa, traces of which survive, and the original harbour. The ancient city was situated some-what to the NE of present-day Anzio on high ground above the Villa Aldobran-dini and the Villa Borghese. In the middle ages it declined. The Saracens destroyed the harbour. A new harbour was built in 1698 by Innocent XII, to the E of the old one, and round it grew the modern town.

The landings during the Second World War, far in advance of the main battle line, and timed to follow an Allied attack on it, were devised to cut the German line of communications, to link up with the main Allied forces advancing from the S, and to seize the Alban Hills. The principal objective was to draw off and contain German forces from NW Europe, with the subsidiary hope of capturing Rome. Though the landing operations were completely successful, the initial surprise was not exploited. The reactions of the Germans was violent and four months of bitter fighting ensued.

The tree-lined Piazza Pia is the centre of Anzio. From the railway station it is reached by the wide Viale Mencacci, Via Claudio Paolini, Piazza Cesare Battisti, in which is the *Municipio*, and Via dei Fabbri. In Piazza Pia is the church of *San Pio*, with a neo-classical portico. The bus terminus for Nettuno is near by. From the square Via Venti Settembre leads to the Riviera Mallozzi, a broad thoroughfare follow-ing the coastline to the W, with villas and bathing establishments. It passes the ancient harbour built by Nero. At the end of the avenue, high up, are the so-called *Grottoes of Nero*, a complex of rectangular chambers. A little farther, near the promontory of *Arco Muto*, are the ruins of an **Imperial Villa**, known as 'Nero's Villa', built of opus reticulatum. It dates from 2C BC–3C AD.

Here were found the Apollo Belvedere, now in the Vatican, during the pontificate of Julius II (1503–13), the Borghese Gladiator, now in the Louvre in Paris, and (in 1878) the Maiden of Anzio, now in the Museo Nazionale Romano. Arco Muto is the probable site of the Temple of Fortune once visited by countless pilgrims and mentioned by Horace in his Ode to Fortune. A Republi-can villa is being excavated here. Near the lighthouse some ancient sculptures have been discovered.

On the way back along the shore, the harbour built by Innocent XII is passed on the right. On the right is the breakwater, with a splendid view towards the E: it takes in Villa Aldobrandini and part of Villa Borghese on the left of the town and the wooded coast-line as far as Torre Astura, with Monte Circeo in the distance. Via Porto Inno-cenziano runs along the harbour.—From the station Viale Mencacci to the right leads to the railway bridge. *Villa Spigarelli* (adm on request), reached by Viale Oleandri (left), incorporates remains of a Republican Villa, and has some well-preserved ancient tombs. On the high ground above is the site of the ancient city of *Antium*; the remains include a small theatre of the Imperial era.

From Piazza Pia, Riviera di Levante, close to the shore, or the parallel Via Gramsci lead out of the town. On the latter road is the *Villa Borghese* (left; adm on application to the owner) with its fine *Park. The coast-line between Anzio and (63·5km) Nettuno is almost completely built up.

Nettuno (24,800 inhab.), comprises a medieval walled town and a modern district in process of rapid development.

The well-preserved CASTLE (*Forte*) was built for Alexander VI by Ant. Sangallo the Elder or Baccio Pontelli. Rectangular in plan, with corner bastions and a portcullis, it is surrounded by a moat.—Piazza Mazzini is the centre of the modern town. To the right is the medieval Borgo, with its narrow winding alleys and its partly-surviving walls. Near Piazza Vittorio Emanuele is the medieval *Palazzo Colonna*.— Beyond Piazza Mazzini the *Belvedere* commands an extensive view of the bay.

About 1km N of the town, off Via Santa Maria, is the *American Military Cemetery*, the larger of the two remaining in Italy, with 7862 graves of Americans who lost their lives in the beach-head operations.—For *Torre Astura*, 13km S, see 'Blue Guide Southern Italy'.

The return to Rome (71·5km) may be made via Ostia on the coast road, Via Severiana. This passes through an almost continuous line of unattractive resorts, and can be very crowded in summer. Beyond *Tor Vaianica* (28·5km), building is restricted and the President's game reserve stretches on either side of the road.—44·5km. *Ostia* (Lido di Castel Fusano), and from there to Rome, see Rte 28B.

30 The Alban Hills

The *Alban Hills *(Colli Albani) are an isolated volcanic group over 60km in circumference rising from the Roman Campagna, with foothills reaching to within twelve kilometres of Rome. They comprise a vast crater in the form of a horseshoe, with its open end on the Via Appia. The numerous summits on the rim of the crater include Monte Salomone (773m), Monte Ceraso (766m), Maschio di Lariano (891m), Monte Peschio (939m) and Maschio d'Artemisio (812m), highest peak of the Artemisio range. Near the open end of the horseshoe are smaller craters, two of them filled with water and forming the lakes of Albano and Nemi, and a third, now dry, comprising the Valle Aríccia. In the centre of the complex is a secondary crater, from which rise the peaks of Monte Cavo (949m) overshadowing Rocca di Papa, and Maschio di Faete, the highest of all (956m) as well as others, including Colle Iano (938m) and La Forcella (807m).

The outer slopes of the Alban Hills are planted with vineyards producing the well known *Vini dei Castelli*, and with olive groves; the interior is pasture and woodland, with chestnut trees predominating. Distributed over the area are the picturesque towns known as the **Castelli Romani**, some of them of great antiquity but most of them owing their origin to the initiative of the popes and the patrician Roman families. There are in all thirteen Castelli, properly so called, some of them widely known, others scarcely known outside Lazio. In the N are Frascati, Monte Porzio Catone, Monte Cómpatri, Rocca Priora, and Colonna; in the centre Rocca di Papa; in the W and SW Grottaferrata, Marino, Castel Gandolfo, Albano Laziale, Aríccia, Genzano, and Nemi.

All the Castelli suffered in the Second World War, particularly during the period between the end of January 1944, after the landings at Anzio, and the beginning of June in the same year, when the Allies, having overrun the German Alban Hills defences, entered the city of Rome. Many works of art were lost.

The Alban Hills, with their attractively sited little towns and their varied scenery are a pleasant excursion from Rome. To those who can spare only one day the following rather strenuous itinerary is recommended. Morning: Frascati; from there via Grottaferrata, and Castel Gandolfo to Albano. Afternoon: Lake Albano, Aríccia, and Genzano, with a visit to Lake Nemi.

ROAD. **A**. VIA TUSCOLANA. 21km *Frascati.*—24km *Grottaferrata.*—**B**. VIA DEI LAGHI, skirting Lake Albano and Lake Nemi, beautifully landscaped and well provided with parking places and viewpoints. 22km *Marino* (left).—27km By-road left for *Rocca di Papa.*—31km By-road right for *Nemi* (1km).—**C**. VIA APPIA NUOVA. 21km *Castel Gandolfo.*—24km *Albano Laziale.*—26·5km *Aríccia.*—29·5km *Genzano.*—39km *Velletri.*

RAILWAY. Routes from Rome (*Termini*) diverge at Ciampino Station for Frascati, Velletri, and Albano Laziale (via Marino and Castel Gandolfo).

BUSES from the 'Anagnina' station of the underground (line A) to Frascati, Rocca di Papa, Grottaferrata, Marino, Castel Gandolfo, Albano, Aríccia, Genzano, Nemi, and Velletri.

CIRCULAR COACH TOURS are arranged by various tourist agencies. A typical half-day excursion includes Frascati, Grottaferrata, Via dei Laghi, and Castel Gandolfo.

A.   Rome to Frascati and Grottaferrata

The direct road to Frascati (21km) is the VIA TUSCOLANA. Rome is left by Porta San Giovanni (Pl. 10; 3); Via Appia Nuova continues for a short distance to Piazza Sulmona where (left) Via Tuscolana (N 215) begins.

The *Via Tuscolana* was a short branch of the Via Latina and ran to Tusculum, to the E of present-day Frascati. The VIA LATINA, issuing from the Porta Capena (Rte 14) passed through Ferentinum (Ferentino), Frusino (Frosinone), Aquinum (Aquino), Casinum (Cassino), and Venafrum (Venafro) to Beneventum (Benevento) where it joined the Appian Way. At *Ad Bivium*, c 145km ESE of Rome, it was joined by the *Via Labicana*, now Via Casilina or N 6 (see Rte 31).

7·5km *Porta Furba* incorporates an arch of the Acqua Felice, with a fountain built by Clement XII (1730–40); near by are picturesque remains of the Aqua Claudia. Farther on, beyond the railway, to the right is seen *Monte del Grano*, where a sarcophagus formerly thought to be that of Alexander Severus was found (now in the Capitoline Museum).—10km *Cinecittà*, centre of the Italian film industry, built in 1937, was damaged in the Second World War but rebuilt. Now increasingly used by foreign companies, it preserves some of the largest sets ever constructed. On the right, beyond an avenue of pine-trees, are seen the scattered ruins of the Villa of the Quintilii (see Rte 17). On the left is the 13C *Tor Fiscale*.—At (11·5km) *Cantoniera* Via Anagnina forks to the right (see below); while this road crosses the Ring Road.

On the right is the medieval *Torre di Mezzavia* (76m), marking the half-way point between Rome and Frascati. A little farther is (left) the battlemented *Torre dei Santi Quattro*.—17km *Osteria del Vermicino*, with a fountain dating from the time of Clement XII. The road crosses over the old Rome-Naples railway and the Frascati railway (retrospective views of Rome), and soon passes on the right the *Villa Sora*, once a residence of Gregory XIII (1572–85) and now the College of the Salesians.—21km *Frascati*.

Frascati (18,000 inhab.) delightfully situated on the NW slopes of the Alban Hills, was, until its partial destruction in 1943–44, when it was the Army Headquarters of Field-Marshal Kesselring, the most elegant and prosperous of the Castelli Romani. It has again become a holiday resort in spring, summer, and autumn. It is noted for its oncesumptuous villas and for its white wine. The suburbicarian see of Frascati is one of the six held by cardinal bishops.

History. Frascati was overshadowed by Tusculum in Roman days. A small village in the middle ages, it expanded in 1191, when the inhabitants of Tusculum, after the destruction of their city, sought protection there around the ancient churches of Santa Maria and San Sebastiano in Frascata. Later it was a feudal holding and at the beginning of the 16C, it passed into the possession of the Holy See. Henry, Cardinal York, was Bishop of Frascati and died there in 1807; the body of his brother, the Young Pretender (died 1788) was at first buried in the Duomo at Frascati; it is now in the Vatican Grottoes. As German Army Headquarters in 1943–44, Frascati suffered a severe attack from Allied bombers early in September 1943, just before the landings at Salerno. Between then and the following June over 80 per cent of the buildings were destroyed or damaged, including all the churches to a greater or less extent and the principal villas. The churches and other public buildings were restored wherever possible, as well as some of the villas.

Information about visits to the villas should be obtained from the Azienda Autonoma di Soggiorno e Turismo, Piazza G. Marconi.

The vast tree-planted Piazza G. Marconi is the town centre and bus terminus. In the middle is a Monument to the Dead of the First World War, by *Cesare Bazzani*. The balustrade on the NW side of the square overlooks the railway station, to which it is connected by a long flight of steps. On the opposite (SE) side is the monumental entrance with a magnificent hedge forming an avenue to *Villa Aldobrandini, or Belvedere*, the finest of the villas at Frascati. Visitors enter from Via Cardinal Massaia, a continuation of Corso Italia from Piazza San Pietro. Concerts are held here in summer.

Villa Aldobrandini (no admission) was built by Giac. della Porta in 1598–1603 for Card. Pietro Aldobrandini. The rooms are decorated with paintings by the Zuccari, the Cavalier d'Arpino, and of the school of Domenichino. The superb *Park (open 9–13 except Saturday and Sunday; permission to visit it must be obtained from the Azienda Autonoma del Turismo, see above), with its statuary, grottoes, and fountains was badly damaged in the war, but it was repaired. There is a magnificent view from the front, extending to Rome and, in clear weather, to the hills behind the city.

Via Massaia continues to the *Capuchin Church* (300m; left). It contains a replica of an altarpiece by Giulio Romano, and other paintings by Girol. Muziano, and Paul Brill, and the tomb of Card. Massaia (died 1889), missionary to Abyssinia. There is also an Ethiopian Museum.

The *Municipio*, on the NE side of Piazza Marconi, escaped serious damage; it contains a collection of local antiquities and a statue of Canova, by Giov. Ceccarini.—On the SW side of the square is the beautiful park (open to the public) of *Villa Torlonia*, which formerly belonged to Annibale Caro (1563–66). It is remarkable also for its fountains (Teatro delle Acque, by Carlo Maderno), and for its views. There is a swimming-pool open in summer.

To the N of Piazza Marconi, beyond Piazza Roma and Via Battisti, lies Piazza San Pietro, rebuilt after tragic devastation. The fountain, by Girol. Fontana was restored. The *Duomo*, on the right, has preserved most of its façade, also by Girol. Fontana, as well as the unattractive campanili of later date.

The INTERIOR has an interesting plan by Mascherino (1598). It contains a Madonna of the Rosary after Domenichino (3rd chapel on right) and a relief by Pompeo Ferrucci over the high altar. To the left of the main door is the cenotaph of Prince Charles Edward (see above).

In Piazza del Gesù, beyond the fountain, is the church of *Gesù*, attributed to Pietro da Cortona, restored after war damage. It contains remarkable perspective paintings by Andrea dal Pozzo. Via Cairoli, to the left of the church, leads to Piazza Paolo III, in which is the *Castle*, built with three towers; it is now the bishop's palace. Beyond it is the rebuilt church of *Santa Maria del Vicario*, or *San Rocco*, with a fine Romanesque campanile.

From Piazza Marconi, to the left of Villa Aldobrandini, the curving road for Tusculum (see below) leads to *Villa Lancellotti* (formerly Villa Piccolomini; no adm) with a graceful nymphaeum and an ancient mosaic found at Tusculum in 1863. The road continues between park walls (passing a splendid gate-way by Borromini, with a tree growing through it) to *Villa Falconieri*, built in 1545–48 for Bp

Aless. Ruffini and enlarged by Borromini. It was occupied before 1914 by Wilhelm II of Germany, was presented by the State to Gabriele d'Annunzio in 1925, and is now a European Centre for Education where courses are held by the Italian Ministry of Education (no adm).—About 2km E is the Camaldoli Convent (see below).

About 1·5km E of Frascati is *Villa Mondragone*, formerly a Jesuit seminary. It is reached by Via Matteotti, to the right of the fountain in Piazza San Pietro, and then Via di Villa Borghese to the right. This road leads to *Villa Parisi* (formerly Villa Borghese) and, just beyond this villa, to the gates of Villa Mondragone. This was built in 1573–75 for Card. Altemps mainly by Martino Longhi the Elder. In 1613 it was bought by Card. Scipio Borghese, who enlarged it. The so-called *Portico of Vignola is by Vasanzio. The terrace commands a good view of Rome.

Below it two roads unite in a cypress avenue which ascends to the monumental entrance of the villa on the San Cesareo road. On 24 February 1582, Gregory XIII here issued his famous bull for the reform of the calendar.

ENVIRONS OF FRASCATI

1. TO TUSCULUM. ROAD 5km. The road to the left of Villa Aldobrandini leads out of Frascati through wooded country, near the beautiful 16C *Villa Rufinella*, or *Villa Tuscolana*, with its expanse of gardens, fountains and woods (adm on request). The villa, damaged by bombing, has had several owners, including Lucien Bonaparte, Queen Maria Christina of Sardinia, and Victor Emmanuel II, passing c 1874 to the princely family of Lancellotti. From the villa a steep path leads up to the ancient paved road leading to the amphitheatre and city of Tusculum.

Tusculum (610m) said to have been founded by Telegonus, son of Ulysses and Circe, is certainly Etruscan in origin. It was the birthplace of Cato the Censor (234–149 BC). On the surrounding hills were villas, of which no fewer than 43 are mentioned in classical literature. The most famous of these was the *Tusculanum*, or Cicero's Villa, where the Tusculan Disputations were supposed to have been held. The exact site of the villa has for long been disputed. In 1191 the Romans destroyed Tusculum in revenge for their defeat at Monte Porzio Catone in 1167 (see below), and the inhabitants escaped to Frascati.

The ascent passes the overgrown remains of the *Amphitheatre* (80 by 53m; arena 48 by 29m), with room for 3000 spectators. It has been given the name of *School of Cicero*.—After ¼ hr more uphill is the so-called *Villa of Cicero*. Continuing to the left are the ruins of the *Forum*, more probably a quadrilateral annexe to the *Theatre*, which is just beyond. This elegant little building, excavated in 1839, is well preserved. Its cavea was hewn out of the hillside. On the summit of the hill, marked with a cross (760m), are traces of the citadel or *Arx*. The *View is splendid: it takes in the Castelli, with the Monti Sabatini, Soratte, and Cimini on the right, the mountains of Lazio on the left, and the city of Rome in the distance.—On the way back a fork right leads to the *Convent of Camaldoli*, on a hill and dating from 1611, often visited by James Stuart, the Old Pretender.

2. TO MONTE PORZIO CATONE, MONTE COMPATRI, AND SAN CESAREO. ROAD, 16km; bus in 45 minutes. The road leaves Frascati to the NE, and at a road fork bears right (the left fork is Via Colonna, leading to Via Casilina at Colonna; Rte 31).—It passes on the right the entrance to Villa Borghese and the monumental entrance to Villa Mondragone.—Near (2km) *Le Cappellette* are the ruins of a Roman villa said without justification to be that of Cato.—3·5km **Monte Porzio Catone** (451m), is one of the 13 Castelli, with 4000 inhabitants. It takes its name from the family of the Catos. Both Cato the Censor and Cato of Utica (95–46 BC) may have had villas here, though the place is first mentioned in history in the 11C. Here the Tusculans, helped by Frederick Barbarossa, gained a victory over the Romans in 1167; for the sequel, see above.—6·5km **Monte Compatri** (583m), is another of the Castelli, with 5400 inhabitants. It is charmingly situated on a rise. Successor to the ancient *Labicum*, it was owned by the Annibaldi, the Colonna, and other families in turn. Its 17C parish church was enlarged in the 19C.—A short distance SW of the town is the ancient *Convento di San Silvestro*, with a fine view.

Outside the town the road forks; the right branch leads in 3·5km to Rocca

Priora (see below). This route follows the left branch and, traversing the Piano
della Faeta and the Campo Gillaro, reaches Via Casilina 1km before the village
of San Cesareo.—16km *San Cesareo*, see Rte 31.

3. TO ROCCA PRIORA. TWO ROADS: (*a*) via Monte Compatri, 11km; bus in ½ hr,
(*b*) by the Via Anagnina, 9·5km; bus c 5 times daily.

For the route via (6·5km) *Monte Compatri*, see above.—The alternatiye route
(*b*) is followed by the main Marino–Albano road to the S, and after 3km turns
left into Via Anagnina. The road climbs past two wooded hills on the right; on
the first is the little church of the *Madonna della Molara*; on the second the ruins
of the Greek monastery of *Sant'Agata*. On the left are the ruins of Tusculum; a
by-road on the right leads to Rocca di Papa. The road passed through a cutting
and then emerges in a spacious upland valley, with meadows and cornfields,
corresponding to the *Albana Vallis* of Livy.—Farther on this road bends sharply
to the left and ascends; the ancient Via Latina keeps straight on. On the right a
short cut leads to the *Oratory of St Sebastian*, which the road passes later on,
shortly before joining the road from Monte Compatri.

9·5km **Rocca Priora** (768m), another of the Castelli, with 4400 inhab. is
situated on the N side of the great crater of the Alban Hills, overlooking the
ancient Valle Latina. It is said to have been built over the ancient town of
Corbio, long in dispute between the Romans and the Aequi, and is believed to
have been the first town built in the neighbourhood after the destruction of
Tusculum. In the 14C it belonged to the Savelli, after which it passed into the
possession of the Holy See.

From Piazza Marconi Viale Vittorio Veneto runs below Villa
Torlonia, and branches left for Grottaferrata (3km).

   Grottaferrata (329m; 11,300 inhab.), is situated amid vineyards
producing some of the finest Castelli wines. The lively little town,
which escaped major war damage, is famous for its monastery. From
the bus station Corso del Popolo leads right to reach the *Abbazia di
Grottaferrata**, which has the appearance of a castle, with its walls,
bastions, and defensive ditches.

The Abbazia is a monastery of Basilian monks, who celebrate according to the
Greek office. Founded by St Nilus, a Calabrian abbot, who died there in 1004,
and built by his disciple St Bartholomew of Rossano (died 1064), it enjoyed the
favour of Gregory IX (1227–41) and other pontiffs, and it was enclosed in a
defensible enceinte by Card. Giul. della Rovere, afterwards Julius II (1503–13).

Across the defensive ditch is the entrance to the CASTLE COURT-
YARD, with a statue of St Nilus, by Raff. Zaccagni (1904). Beyond an
anteroom (ring if closed) is the FIRST COURT, at the back of which is
the **Monastery** (adm 8.30–12, 16.30–18 except Monday).

Visitors ring at the door of the monastery and are accompanied by a monk
(offering expected). It contains a rich library with precious codices, and a
museum of classical and medieval sculptures, including a fine Attic *Stele of the
5C BC. There are also icons, vestments, and detached frescoes from the church.

From the castle courtyard there is access to the SECOND COURT, a
smaller enclosure on the right of the anteroom. Here is the church of
Santa Maria, consecrated by John XIX in 1025, redesigned internally
in 1754 and restored in 1902–30. The pronaos is ancient, and the fine
campanile dates from the 12C. In the beautifully carved Romanesque
portal of marble is a door of carved wood (11C), surmounted by a
*Mosaic of Christ between the Virgin and John the Baptist. The font
is an antique marble urn, decorated with swimming cupids.

INTERIOR. Nearly all the inscriptions are in Greek. The roof of the nave dates
from 1595; the Byzantine mosaic of the Apostles on the triumphal arch and the
damaged fresco above date from the 13C. Frescoes from the clerestory walls
have been detached and are now in the Museum (see above). Off the right aisle
opens the **Chapel of St Nilus**, the frescoes in which, depicting the lives of St
Nilus and St Bartholomew, are masterpieces by *Domenichino* (restored by
Camuccini in 1819). To the right of the entrance, St Nilus before the Crucifix,

and St Nilus averting a tempest by his prayers. Inside the chapel, to the left: St Nilus and the Emperor Otho III (the page holding the emperor's horse is Domenichino, and the figures on the right of the horse are Guido Reni and Guercino). On the right, St Bartholomew averting the fall of a pillar during the building of the convent; on the end wall (left of the altar), Exorcism of a devil and (right) the Virgin presenting a golden apple to Saints Nilus and Bartholomew; in the lunette, Death of St Nilus; in the triumphal arch, Annunciation. At the altar is a Virgin, by *Ann. Carracci.*—A door from here leads into the sacristy, off which are two small rooms, dating from Roman times with iron grille windows. Known as the 'crypta ferrata', these were transformed in medieval times into a Christian chapel. It is thought that here the name of the monastery, and later the town, originated.

The return to Rome may be made by Via Anagnina (21km). The road partly follows the line of the ancient Via Latina.—3km The *Borghetto*, or *Castel Savelli* (325m), a ruined 13C castle with 13 towers, built on Roman foundations, passed from the counts of Tusculum to the Savelli, and later to Julius II, who converted it into an outwork of the Abbey of Grottaferrata.—The road passes over the old Rome–Naples railway, near (5km) *Villa Senni*, where some 4C catacombs have been discovered, and the Frascati railway.—At (11km) *Cantoniera*, this route rejoins Via Tuscolana to return to (21km) Rome.

B.   Via dei Laghi

VIA APPIA NUOVA (N 7) starts from Porta San Giovanni (Pl. 10; 3, 6).— 7·5km Intersection of the Via Latina, issuing from the Porta Latina. Via Latina is no longer a continuous street.

Via Latina leads to the left (signed 'Tombe della Via Latina'), crosses the Albano railway and reaches in 5 minutes a group of *Tombs dating from the 1C and 2C. Most of them are square and brick-built, with recesses on the outside and interior chambers with interesting stucco ornamentation. Two of the best-preserved may be visited (caretaker near the railway line). On the right is the *Tomb of the Valerii* (AD 160), a subterranean chamber decorated with fine reliefs, in stucco on a white ground, of nymphs, sea-monsters, and nereids. On the left is the 2C *Tomb of the Pancratii*, with landscape paintings, coloured stuccoes, and four bas-reliefs: Judgment of Paris, Admetus and Alcestis, Priam and Achilles, and Hercules playing a lyre with Bacchus and Minerva.—Behind the tomb are the ruins of the 5C *Basilica of St Stephen.*

Farther on the ancient Appian Way, with its tombs and other buildings, becomes conspicuous on the right. On the left is the long line of arches of the Aqua Claudia.—The road crosses the Rome–Naples railway near (11·5km) *Capannelle*, noted for its racecourse. On the right can be seen the road to the Casal Rotondo on the Appian Way.—The road passes under the Rome Circular road near (13·5km) *Barbula*, and soon passes (15km) the entrance (left) to Ciampino Airport. Just beyond the airport, **Via dei Laghi** (N 217) diverges to the left. The road leads E and SE towards the Alban Hills climbing steadily as it nears (22km) Marino.

Marino, situated at the N end of Lake Albano, can be seen from the road which by-passes it to the S. The town, with 23,800 inhab., is less of a tourist centre than some of the other Castelli, but is celebrated for its wines. It suffered much damage during the Second World War. A colourful market is held here on Sunday mornings.

Marino lies near the ancient *Castrimoenium*, colonized under Sulla and long since vanished. The modern name appears in the 11C. In the 13C Marino was a stronghold of the Orsini; in 1347 Giordano Orsini, who had been driven out of Rome by Rienzo, was here besieged unsuccessfully by the tribune. In 1419 the town passed to the Colonna. Many of its inhabitants took part in the battle of Lepanto (1571). Vittoria Colonna (1490–1548) and the musician Giacomo Carissimi (1604–74) were born at Marino. Annually on the first Sunday in October the town celebrates the *Sagra dell'Uva* when the fountains of the central piazza flow with wine.

In Piazza San Barnaba is the restored 17C church of *San Barnaba*. It contains a Martyrdom of St Barnabas by Benedetto Gennari, and a Turkish shield taken at the battle of Lepanto. In the neighbouring Piazza Lepanto is the bomb-damaged *Fountain of the Four Moors*, by Pompeo Castiglia da Marino (1642), commemorating the battle of Lepanto. The 16C **Palazzo Colonna** is now the Town Hall, and contains an antiquarium.

In the church of the *Trinità* is a painting attributed to Guido Reni, and in the church of *Santa Maria delle Grazie* a St Roch, of the Emilian school. Attached to the Dominican convent is the church of *Madonna del Rosario*, with an elegant Rococo interior.—Near the station is a *Mithraeum*, with interesting frescoes discovered in 1963.

Via dei Laghi continues to climb, with magnificent views, skirting *Lake Albano*.

This charmingly situated sheet of water, elliptical in shape, occupies one of the smaller craters of the volcanic Alban Hills. It is 10km round and has an area of c 518 hectares; its extreme depth is 170m. It is fed by underground sources and by the drainage of the surrounding crater. Teeming with trout and other fish, it is much visited by anglers. It is the *Lacus Albanus* of antiquity, and in the Imperial era its banks were adorned with villas and its waters used for mock sea-fights (naumachiae). Regattas are held on them today. In 1985 Middle Bronze Age finds were made in the lake.—It is possible to walk round the lake in 2 hrs by a track.

27km *Ponte di Nemi*. Road left for Rocca di Papa (3km), with good views of the country from Lake Albano to Grottaferrata.
    Rocca di Papa (681m; 7800 inhab.), built up in picturesque terraces on the flank of Monte Cavo, is the highest of the Castelli Romani. The lower part of the town is modern, the upper part medieval. Charmingly situated amid chestnut woods, it is a summer resort.

History. Rocca di Papa, originally *Rocca di Monte Cavo*, is said to occupy the site of the ancient Latin town of *Cabum*. It appears under its present name for the first time in the 12C, the name being derived from a castle built here by the popes. From them it passed in turn to several owners, among them the Annibaldi and the Colonna. The artist and statesman Massimo d'Azeglio lived here in 1821.

From Piazza della Repubblica there is an excellent view of the medieval town, with the observatory at its top, and of Monte Cavo. Relics of the *Castle* are still to be seen at the highest point of the town, from which there are views of the Campagna and of the lakes of Albano and Nemi.

SHORT EXCURSIONS may be made SE to (½ hr) *Campi d'Annibale* and SW to (1½ hrs) the *Sanctuary of the Madonna del Tufo* (see below).

ASCENT OF MONTE CAVO. BY ROAD, 5·5km. The road runs S from Rocca di Papa (leading back to Via dei Laghi).—1km *Sanctuary of the Madonna del Tufo*, built over a block of tufa whose fall on to a passer-by was miraculously arrested by the Virgin. Just beyond, a good private road (toll) diverges left to wind up to the summit. A short way up, a sign indicates the ancient *VIA SACRA*, called *Via Triumphalis* which climbs up the hill-side to the left. Perfectly preserved, it can be followed on foot for a considerable way, through beautiful woods. It was built to reach the Temple of Jupiter Latiaris on the summit of Monte Cavo (see below), and for triumphal processions by generals whose feats of arms were not considered important enough for a triumphal procession along the Via Sacra in Rome.

BY PATH. Steep and narrow streets lead up through the town, past the remains of its castle at the top, to the edge of the Monte Cavo crater, where a path leads to the right. On the left, in the crater, is a flat floor called the *Campi d'Annibale*, the traditional halting-place of Hannibal in his march on Tusculum and Rome in 211 BC, though it is more probable that it was the Romans who had a force here to command the Appian Way and the Latin Way. The ascent, which commands splendid views, follows for some time along the Via Triumphalis (see above).

Monte Cavo (949m), the second highest summit of the Alban Hills (*Maschio di Faete*, 956m), is the *Mons Albanus* of antiquity, the sacred mountain of the Latins. On its slopes was Alba Longa, the most ancient town in Latium. The name Monte Cavo is supposed by some to be derived from the ancient town of Cabum (see above), and by others from the word 'caput'. On its summit stood the *Temple of Jupiter Latiaris*, the sanctuary of the Latin League, said to have been built by Tarquinius Superbus. Here the league's religious festivals, the *Ferioe Latinoe*, were celebrated in spring and autumn by the 47 towns of the confederation. Excavations have failed to find any trace of the temple and it may be that no building existed, but merely a sacred area with an altar. On the presumed site of the temple Henry, Cardinal York, built a Passionist Convent in 1783; this later became an observatory, founded by Father Angelo Secchi in 1876; today it is a hotel-restaurant. The walls of the convent garden are built partly with blocks from ancient buildings. Here is also a television station.

The splendid *View, takes in the full circle: the coast from Monte Circeo to Civitavecchia, the Tolfa and Cimini ranges, the Sabine, Tiburtine and Praenestine Hills, and the Monte Lepini.—The descent may be made through the woods to Nemi (about 4km) and the walk continued from there to Genzano (Rte 30C).

Via dei Laghi continues to (31km) the turning (right) for Nemi and its lake. The road skirts the E and S sides of the lake, while a turning to the right after 1km leads to the village of **Nemi** (521m; 1300 inhab.) picturesquely situated above the NE side of the lake. It has an impressive castle which belonged in the 9C to the counts of Tusculum, later to Cistercian monks, and in 1428 to the Colonna. It later passed into the hands of the Orsini, and is now the property of the Ruspoli. It is well-preserved, and the road out of the village passes under the entrance bridge.

A festival of wild strawberries (*Sagra delle Fragole*) is held here every June. A narrow, poorly surfaced road descends to the lake-side and the ship Museum (better reached from the other side of the lake, see below), passing the so-called Giardino, in which are the ruins of the *Temple of Diana Nemorensis*, excavated in 1885; some of the finds are in the Museo di Villa Giulia in Rome. Further excavations in 1924–28, revealed a theatre.

The lake road continues above the E and S side through delightful stretches of ilex and manna-ash woods (branch roads lead down to the lake-side).

*Lake Nemi (*Lago di Nemi*; 316m) is the pearl of the Alban Hills. Almost circular in shape, it is 5·5km round, with an area of 189 hectares and a maximum depth of 34m. Its vivid blue waters are encircled by solitary wooded hills. There is a well-known painting by Turner of the lake. The lake is the ancient *Lacus Nemorensis*, called also the Mirror of Diana, to whom were consecrated the grove and the temple on its NE side. Both lake and grove were sometimes called the lake and grove of Aricia. The waters are now gravely polluted.

Diana was worshipped here with savage rites: her priest, called *Rex Nemorensis*, was a killer and became a victim. The office could be held only by a run-away slave who had qualified by breaking off a branch (the golden bough) from a certain tree in the grove. Success in the attempt entitled him to fight the reigning priest in single combat; if he killed him he became the next Rex Nemorensis. The new priest-king, in his turn, was liable at any time to be challenged by a further aspirant. It was the investigation of this sinister rule of succession to the priesthood of Diana that led Sir James Frazer to write 'The Golden Bough'.

Before the approach to Genzano (see below), the road bears right round the lake-side to reach the **Nemi Museum of Roman Ships** (closed for many years, but due to be reopened) replacing the one which, in 1932–44, housed the two ancient ships built by Caligula (AD 37–41) to convey visitors across the lake for the festival of Diana. The ships were sunk at the time of Claudius, and they were located at the bottom of the lake in 1446 by Leon Battista Alberti, but nothing important was done for 400 years. In 1895 Eliseo Borghi recovered some fine bronzes; in 1928–31 the lake was partly drained and in 1932 the ships, of remarkable size, were taken out and placed in the museum. The larger was 71m long and had a beam of 20m; the other was 73m by 24m. On 1 June 1944 they were burned, with the museum, by German soldiers.

In the *Salone* are models of the ships, on a scale of one-fifth. The *BRONZES escaped the fate of the ships. Among them are: Head of Medusa; Open hands—charms against the evil eye—found in the sterns; four Heads of a wolf, three of a lion, and one of a panther which covered the beams at the ships' side; ring from a rudder with a lion's head; small double-sided Herm with heads of Silenus and a satyr; another with two maenads (fragments of a balustrade).—In the *Galleria Centrale* is an iron anchor resembling in design the Admiralty anchor badge adopted by Great Britain in 1852. Glass cases contain gilded bronze plates, bronze and iron nails, cups, lamps, and other fittings from the ships.—The upper floor displays casts of monuments connected with naval engineering.

From here it is possible to return to Via dei Laghi (turning right for *Velletri*, 7·5km, described in Rte 30C, or left to return to Rome) or take the road which climbs the hill-side to Genzano, passing a path (left) which leads to the *Outlet* of the lake, comprising two superimposed tunnels 1650m long, used when necessary to drain the lake (see above). *Genzano* (Rte 30C) is entered at Piazza Dante; from the centre Via Appia Nuova leads back to Rome (29km).

C. Castel Gandolfo, Albano, Genzano, and Velletri

Via Appia Nuova leads out of Rome. To (15·5km) the junction with Via dei Laghi, see Rte 30B. The road continues, crossing the Terracina railway 1km before (20km) *Frattócchie*, where this route is joined by Via Appia Antica. Here was the 12th (Roman) milestone. N 7 is now known simply as Via Appia. Via Nettunense branches off to the right for Anzio and Nettuno (Rte 29); on the left is the *Palazzetto della Sirene*, built by Card. Girol. Colonna and now a Trappist monastery. The road passes the ruins of tombs and other buildings that lined the Appian Way. Four imposing stumps of towers make their appearance, the first of them cylindrical and called the *Torraccio* (left), the others square. A track to the right leads to the ruins of the ancient Latin town of *Bovilloe*; these include a circus, a cistern, and numerous tombs.

21km Turning left for **Castel Gandolfo**. A good road climbs to this

gay little town in 3km. With 4700 inhab. it is situated on the lip of the
Lake Albano crater at a height of 426m above the sea. Here the Pope
spends the summer.

The town occupies the site of the citadel of *Alba Longa*, founded, according to
legend, by Ascanius, son of Aeneas. It was so called because it extended in a
long line up the slopes of Mons Albanus. Head of the Latin League, Alba was
the mother city of many of the Latin towns, and of Rome itself. Its war with Rome
in the time of Tullus Hostilius, decided by the single combats of the three
Roman Horatii and the three Latin Curiatii, the treachery of its dictator Mettius
Fufetius, and its destruction by the Romans are famous episodes in the
legendary history of Rome. The town was never rebuilt though its temples were
respected and were still standing in the days of Augustus. Domitian built a villa
here, ruins of which are visible (see below). Of the ancient town there is not a
trace, but to the W of Castel Gandolfo there is an extensive necropolis of the
early Iron Age (9–7C BC), discoveries from which are in the Prehistoric Museum
at E.U.R.

Castel Gandolfo derives its name from a castle of the Gandolfi, a Genoese
family of the 12C. The castle passed to the Savelli and, in 1596, to the Camera
Apostolica. In 1604 it was declared an inalienable domain of the Holy See. After
the papal palace was built (see below), it became the summer residence of the
popes and it has been used as such ever since, except for the period from 1870
to 1929. Many distinguished people have lived at Castel Gandolfo: among them
Goethe, Winckelmann, Angelica Kauffmann, and Massimo d'Azeglio. The town
was little damaged in the Second World War.

A bus service connects Castel Gandolfo with *Lake Albano*.

At the N entrance of the town, 133m above the lake, extends the vast
Papal Palace, built on the ruins of the castle and retaining some of its
towers and walls. It was erected in 1624 by Carlo Maderno at the
instance of Urban VIII and enlarged by Alexander VII, Clement XIII,
and Pius IX. The palace, with its gardens and the former Villa
Barberini, enjoys the privilege of extraterritoriality.

A special permit is necessary from the Director to visit the palace. The chapel
has frescoes of the school of the Zuccari.

Since 1936 the villa has housed the **Vatican Observatory**, one of the most
important in Europe. It was founded by Gregory XIII and from 1908 to 1936
occupied the Casina of Leo XIII in the Vatican Gardens. The observatory
specializes in the study of variable stars; it contains a laboratory of astrophysics.

A short alley to the right of the palace leads to a terrace with a fine view. In
the piazza are an elegant fountain and the church of *San Tomaso da Villanova*
(1661, with a good cupola), both by Bernini. Inside are a painting of St Thomas
of Villanova, by Pietro da Cortona, and an Assumption by Maratta.

At the S end of the town is the *Villa Barberini* (now Vatican property;
no adm). With its fine gardens, now added to those of the palace, it
occupies the greater part of a site once covered by the Villa of
Domitian. Traces of nymphaea, cisterns, of a small theatre, and of the
royal mansion are still visible.—At the beginning of the road to
Ercolano is the *Villa Torlonia*, with sculptures by Thorvaldsen and
modern paintings, and a fine park.

The **Emissarium** or outlet of Lake Albano is reached in ½ hr from Castel
Gandolfo. It is reached by the road to the railway station, and, beyond the line,
by a track going downhill. At a gate a path leads right, at the end of which is
another gate. It is necessary to descend toward the lake as far as a cave,
occupied by the custodian (tip). The Emissarium, which maintains the water of
the lake at a constant level, is a tunnel cut through the solid rock by the Romans
in 397 BC (according to legend, though probably later) because an oracle had
declared that Veio would not fall until the lake was drained. The tunnel is
1425m long, 1m wide, and 1·5m high; it pierces the rim of the crater and
emerges at *Le Mole*, to the SW.

The two celebrated ilex-bordered roads which lead from Castel Gandolfo to
Albano Laziale were both opened by Urban VIII. They are known as the
Galleria di Sopra and the *Galleria di Sotto* because the branches of the trees

interlace above the roadways, forming arboreal tunnels. The less attractive lower road is used by the buses.—The Galleria di Sopra, that to the left of the exit of Castel Gandolfo, follows the lip of the crater and affords magnificent *Views of Lake Albano, the Campagna, and the neighbouring towns. Half-way along it is the summer convent of the *Collegio di Propaganda Fide*. Close to the Capuchin Convent, the road forks. The left fork leads to Arìccia; the right fork to Albano Laziale, past the church of San Paolo. A path to the left of the convent leads to Palazzolo.

The lower road reaches Albano in under 3km, passing on the right near the junction with the Appian Way, a Republican Tower sepulchre, once some 45m high. This is thought to have been the Tomb of Pompey.

Albano (378m; 24,400 inhab.), officially *Albano Laziale*, is an important town of the Castelli, and a good centre for excursions. The town rises in the form of a triangle from the Via Appia towards the top of the crater of Lake Albano; the crater cuts off the view of the lake from the town. Albano was badly damaged in the Second World War, nearly two-thirds of its buildings having been destroyed or damaged.

History. The name of Albano is derived from Alba Longa, but the town owes its origin to Septimius Severus, who established here (c AD 195) the *Castra Albana* for the 2nd Legion (Parthica), with a view to the protection (among other duties) of the Appian Way. The camp occupied virtually the whole of what is now the town of Albano. Adjoining the camp was a small settlement that gradually developed and eventually overran the military area. Albano became a bishopric in 460; the see was held by Nicholas Breakspeare before he became the only English pope as Adrian IV (1154–59). Albano is one of the six suburbicarian sees held by cardinal bishops. Devastated by the barbarian invasions and in the struggles of the papacy and empire, the town passed in the 13C to the Savelli, whose castle survives (to the W of Albano). In 1697 it was acquired by the Camera Apostolica. The eccentric Earl of Bristol, bishop of Derry, died here in 1803.

The town centre is the spacious PIAZZA GIUSEPPE MAZZINI, a widening of the Via Appia and a busy traffic centre. On the right, coming from Rome, are the *Belvedere* and the *Villa Comunale*, a public park shaded by tall pines and occupying the site of a Roman villa formerly identified with a villa of Pompey. Some ruins of this villa are visible. There is a good view from the Belvedere, extending to Rome.

From Piazza Mazzini Via Cairoli leads to Piazza Sabatini, in which is the *Duomo* (*San Pancrazio*), built and rebuilt on a temple dating from the time of Constantine. The temple columns may be seen incorporated in the walls.

Corso Matteotti leads out of Piazza Mazzini. Here is *Palazzo del Comune*, formerly Palazzo Savelli. In the square opposite is the church of SAN PIETRO, built in the 6C over the remains of the thermae of the Roman camp. The right flank of the church incorporates masonry blocks from the baths; the jambs of a door on the left side are made up of fragments of an ancient architrave. There is an attractive Romanesque campanile. The spacious interior is refreshingly plain. An acanthus cornice supports the modern altar rails. The altar furniture and Stations of the Cross are modern.

Via Aurelio Saffi climbs to the upper part of the town. A turning to the left—Via Don Minzoni—leads to the ruins of the PORTA PRAETORIA OF THE CASTRA ALBANA, revealed by bombing in February 1944. This front gate of the camp, opening from its short S side and facing the Appian Way, had three openings and was flanked by two towers. It was constructed of blocks of peperino. Its frontage was 36m and its height 13m. Only the E opening survived the bombing; of the main central entrance only the lower part is extant.

Via della Rotonda leads left out of Via Saffi to *Santa Maria della Rotonda*, restored in 1937. This medieval circular church, once a nymphaeum belonging to the Villa of Domitian, has a Cosmatesque pulpit supported on a Roman capital. In the sacristy is a small Antiquarium with fragments of sarcophagi, inscriptions, brick stamps, and a funerary stele of 3C AD. Nearby are remains of the walls of the Roman camp. Continuing its ascent, Via Aurelio Saffi leads into the charming Piazza San Paolo, in which is the church of *San Paolo*, built in 1282 and remodelled in 1769. It stands at the apex of the triangle formed by the town. In the wall of the neighbouring *College of the Most Precious Blood* are incorporated further remains of the camp walls. At the top of the hill, beyond the cemetery, Lake Albano can be seen far below on the other side. At No. 100 Via Aurelio Saffi is the entrance to the *Cisternone*, a reservoir hewn out of rock for the use (probably) of the legionaries of the camp. It is still in use today.

The Cisternone (no adm) is a quadrangular underground construction 46m by 30m, reached by 31 steps. It is divided into five compartments, each furnished with rows of columns. The ceilings, 12m high, are perfectly preserved. The floor slopes gently towards the W corner, where there is an underground outlet.

Near the civil hospital, off Via San Francesco, are a rectangular tower and the *Porta Principalis Sinistra*, or E gate of the camp, now walled up.

Via San Francesco leads to the ruins of the AMPHITHEATRE, situated between the church of San Paolo and the Capuchin Convent; it dates from the second half of the 3C and could accommodate 15,000 spectators. On the hill above is the *Capuchin Convent* (1619), surrounded by a turreted wall (only men admitted). On the hill-side extends the *Bosco dei Cappuccini*, a public walk with fine views.— The parallel street to the SE, in which are long tracts of wall returns to the centre of the town.

Just outside Albano, on the right of the road to Ariccia, is a majestic tomb in the Etruscan style, known as the **Tomb of the Horatii and Curiatii**, perhaps modelled on the Tomb of Aruns, son of Porsenna. It has a base, 15m square made of peperino blocks, surmounted by two (originally five) truncated cones. The tomb in fact dates from the late Republican era.

WALKS may be taken from Albano, N to (³/₄ hr) *Castel Gandolfo* by the Galleria di Sopra (reached from the church of San Paolo); NE to (1¹/₂ hr) *Palazzolo*; and W to (¹/₂ hr) *Castel Savelli*. The castle (325m) is reached by a road under the railway and by a path to the right at a road fork. This 13C stronghold of the Savelli was last restored in 1660. For the other Castel Savelli, see above.

Beyond Albano the line of the Via Appia follows a course laid out during the pontificates of Gregory XVI (1831–46) and Pius IX (1846–78); the rectification involved the building of four viaducts over the Valle Ariccia, one of the smaller craters of the Alban Hills.

As the road leaves Albano, the so-called Tomb of the Horatii and Curiatii (see above) can be seen below on the right. This route bears to the left off the ancient Appian Way.

The ancient road descends to the right, passing near the church of *Santa Maria della Stella* (below which are the Catacombs of San Senatore, probably reserved for Christian soldiers of the 2nd Legion), and then crosses the valley by an imposing Roman viaduct (c AD 19) still partly surviving. It rejoins the modern road near the Sanctuary of Santa Maria di Galloro, only to part again soon afterwards before reuniting near Velletri.

The modern road crosses the valley higher up by the viaduct known as the PONTE DI ARICCIA, built by Ireneo Aleandri in 1847–54, partly blown up by the Germans in 1944 and rebuilt in 1947. The viaduct is 312m long 9m wide, and 59m above the valley floor. It is made up of a series of three superimposed arches (six below, twelve in the middle, and eighteen above). Three people were killed in 1967 when two central arches collapsed without warning.

Just short of the viaduct, on the right in a square, is a monument to Menotti Garibaldi, by Ernesto Biondi. Beyond the bridge, on the left, extends the luxurian park of the Palazzo Chigi (see below); on the right there is an extensive view over the valley.

26·5km **Ariccia** (412m; 10,700 inhab.) is charmingly situated in wooded country, with numerous villas. It was also damaged in 1943–44.

The ancient Latin city of *Ariccia*, mentioned in the legends of the kings, took a leading part in the wars with Rome until the dissolution of the Latin League in 338 BC. With three other Latin towns it then lost its independence and received full Roman citizenship. In Cicero's time it was a flourishing municipium. It was the first stage in Horace's journey to Brundusium. In the Middle Ages the town was owned by the counts of Tusculum and later passed to the Savelli; in 1661 it was sold to the Chigi.—Henrik Ibsen 'disillusioned with the theatre' settled at Aríccia with wife and child in 1864 and here wrote 'Brand'. Here in 1826 Massimo d'Azeglio, statesman and artist, entertained Severn, the artist and friend of Keats.

On the N (left) side of the town is the *Palazzo Chigi*, in the form of a medieval castle with four towers, restored by Bernini and later enlarged. It has a delightful and extensive *Park. It has recently been acquired by the Comune and is to be opened as a Museum. On the right is the round church of *Santa Maria dell'Assunzione*, built by Bernini in 1664; it has a large dome and two campanili; inside is a fresco of the Assumption, by Borgognone.—In the centre of the town are remains of a small Republican temple.

On leaving Ariccia the road crosses over a second viaduct; then bends round the head of the valley over a third viaduct. Here the road is lined with ilex and manna-ash trees. On the right, on the NE edge of the Valle Ariccia, is the pilgrim *Sanctuary of Santa Maria di Galloro* (429m) by Bernini, with a venerated painting of the Madonna.—The road ascends gradually amid woods and crosses yet a fourth viaduct. From the top of the rise there is a gentle descent.

29·5km **Genzano**, officially *Genzano di Roma* (435m), famous for its *Infiorata*, a festival held on the Sunday after Corpus Domini, when the main street is carpeted with flowers, is a place of 15,300 inhabitants built in terraces on the outer slope of the crater of Lake Nemi. The town grew up round a castle built in 1235 facing the lake, rebuilt in 1621 by Prince Giuliano Cesarini to face the Via Appia.

The town centre is Piazza Tommaso Frasconi, with a terrace on the right. On the left, beyond an interesting fountain, are three streets— Via Garibaldi, Bruno Buozzi, and Italo Belardi—all going uphill fanwise from the square. The last-named street, scene of the Infiorata, climbs past the Municipio to the church of *Santa Maria della Cima*. Via Bruno Buozzi leads to the modern *Palazzo Cesarini*, which overlooks the lake, 90m below. Via Garibaldi leads to Piazza Dante, where there is a road down to the lake (see above).

Beyond Genzano the road passes between (left) Lake Nemi, glimpses of which may be obtained, and (right) the *Monte Due Torri* (415m), with its remaining şquat medieval tower.—32·5km Turning (right) for *Lanuvio* (3km). The ancient city was famous for its sanctuary of Juno Sospita parts of which are incorporated in the seminary and the Villa Sforza.—The main road turns E and the scenery becomes more and more attractive. The hill-sides are covered with vineyards and chestnut woods. On the left are the wooded slopes and crest of the Maschio d'Artemisio (812m).—Approaching Velletri, the road curves round the head of a valley.—38·5km. At the beginning of the tree-lined Viale Roma this route is joined by Via dei Laghi from Marino (Rte 30B).—(39km) Velletri is entered by *Porta Romana*.

Velletri (332m; 37,900 inhabitants) is picturesquely situated on a spur of the Artemisio range. It was reconstructed after serious war damage.

Velletri is the Volscian *Velester*, subjugated by Rome in 338 BC and called Velitrae. It was the home of the Gens Octavia, of which Augustus was a member. It was an independent commune from c 1000 to 1549, when it was absorbed in the States of the Church. From a window in the Palazzo Ginnetti Charles of Bourbon escaped in August 1744 from the Irish General U.M. Brown's Austrian troops, later decisively defeating the Austrians in the same engagement. Velletri is one of the six suburbicarian sees; its bishop is Dean of the Sacred College of Cardinals.

VIA VITTORIO EMANUELE runs through the town from N to S following the contour of the hill from Piazza Garibaldi, site of the Porta Romana, to Porta Napoli. About one-third of the way along opens Piazza Cairoli, the town centre, almost completely rebuilt except for the *Torre del Trivio* (c 50m), a striking Romanesque campanile, dating from 1353, of alternate black-and-white courses, with single and double window-arches; it was cleverly restored after bomb damage.

To the right Via del Comune leads up to the piazza of the same name, the highest part of the town. Here is *Palazzo di Giustizia* (1835); in front are the little church of *San Michele* (1837) and the octagonal oratory of *Santa Maria del Sangue*, by Aless. da Parma (1523–79). To the left is the 16C *Palazzo Comunale*, reconstructed since 1945 almost from the foundations. The *Museo Comunale* (entrance at the back) contains a collection of antiquities.

Via Vittorio Emanuele continues S to the 18C church of *San Martino* (left) with a Madonna of 1308 behind a high-altar tabernacle. After a bend to the right and Piazza Mazzini a road continues S to Piazza Umberto I. In a small square to the left is the entrance to the CATHEDRAL (*San Clemente*), a 13C church built on the remains of a Roman basilica many times altered, and rebuilt in 1660. It was patched up after the war and its remaining points of interest have to be sought for amid the conflicting styles.

The basilican INTERIOR has a rebuilt 13C apse and a restored ceiling, with a huge painting (1954) by Angelo Canevari. The windows have been filled with stained glass in a strong modern style at variance with the remainder of the present decoration. The Baldacchino is surmounted by a Cosmatesque tabernacle. On the right of the 17C high altar is a candelabrum attrib. to *Iac. Sansovino*. In the second chapel on the right is a Madonna and Child by *Antoniazzo Romano*. At the end of the left aisle a Renaissance doorway (1483) leads past a fine wall lavabo into the *Sacristy*, in which is a Byzantine painting of the Saviour.—The entrance to the MUSEO CAPITOLARE is beneath the portico. Among the paintings are versions of the Madonna by *Gentile da Fabriano* (recently restored) and *Antoniazzo Romano*. 13. Fragments of an *Exultet* (School of Montecassino; 12C); 14. Story of the Passion (late 13C; English); *16. Jewelled 12C Byzantine cross-reliquary; *42. Ornamental parts of the chasuble of Benedict XI (1303–4).

Just beyond the Cathedral the road leaves the town by the Porta

Napoli, flanked by cylindrical towers; the railway station lies to the left.

Via dei Laghi (Rte 30B) leads back to Rome.

31   Palestrina

ROAD. VIA CASILINA, 38km (return by VIA PRENESTINA, 37km). Frequent buses from Piazza dei Cinquecento along Via Prenestina.

AUTOSTRADA DEL SOLE, 27km to San Cesareo, then 10·5km E to Palestrina.

RAILWAY from *Rome* (Termini) to *Palestrina*, 37km in 1 hr.

Rome is left by Porta Maggiore (Pl. 6; 8). The right-hand road of the two main roads beyond the gate is Via Casilina. For the first 18·5km the road passes through perhaps the most unpleasant suburbs of Rome.—5km *Tor Pignattara* (45m; somewhat hidden to left, behind a school, but no adm), all that remains of the tomb of St Helena (died c 330), mother of Constantine. It is circular outside and octagonal, with niches, in the interior. The modern name is taken from the terracotta amphorae (*pignatte*) introduced into the vaulting to diminish the load. St Helen's sarcophagus is in the Vatican. No. 643, next door, is the entrance to the *Catacombs of Saints Pietro and Marcellino* (3–4C), the most pictorially decorated in Rome (adm only with special permission).—7·5km *Centocelle*; on the right is the military air station of that name and beyond can be seen the arches of the Aqua Claudia; on the left are the Tiburtine and Prenestine Hills; to the N the Monti Sabini and to the NW Monte Soratte.—This route crosses the Rome Circular road before (11·5km) *Torrenova*, adjoining the old Borghese Palace.—At (18·5km) *Finocchio* by-roads leads S to Frascati (Rte 30A) and N to the Via Prenestina (see below).—Beyond (20km) *Pantano Borghese* station, the road ascends and becomes more attractive. It passes on the left the *Tenuta di Pantano*, which comprises two dried-up lakes: *Lago Regillo*, drained in the 17C, and the *Lago di Castiglione*, reclaimed in the 19C.

The BATTLE OF LAKE REGILLUS, in 496 BC, was a victory for the Romans over the Latins led by the Tarquins and ended the last attempt of the Tarquin dynasty to recover the kingship of Rome. The Romans are said to have been miraculously assisted by the Dioscuri, Castor and Pollux, in whose honour a temple was accordingly built in the Roman Forum. Between the two lakes is the ancient line of the Via Prenestina, with the ruins of Gabii (see below).

26km Road right to (1km) *Colonna*, the northernmost of the Castelli Romani. This little town is situated on a park-like hill (343m), with numerous vineyards; a road, the Via Colonna, leads SW to Frascati.—At 30km, a road from Monte Compatri and Frascati comes in from the right (see Rte 30A).—31km *San Cesareo*. This route leaves Via Casilina 2km farther on, and Via Prenestina Nuova continues (left).—33·5km Road left for **Zagarolo** (2·5km; 303m), a town of 10,000 inhabitants, recorded in the 12C under the name of Gazzarolo and a fief of the Rospigliosi from the 17C. The wines from its vineyards are renowned.

The medieval part of the town is entered through a gateway erected by the Rospigliosi (and including Imperial Roman fragments). The Piazzetta delle Tre Cannelle has a pretty group of houses and a fountain made up from a Roman sarcophagus. Beyond lies Piazza Indipendenza with the imposing *Palazzo*

Colonna (Palavicini) with two red granite columns supporting two sarcophagi. Via Fabricci continues past the church of *San Pietro*, a fine Baroque building, to Piazza Marconi. Here the church of *San Lorenzo* (containing a triptych in the manner of Antoniazzo Romano) faces two scenographic palazzi, fine works attrib. to Maderno.

The road ascends. At 36·5km it is joined on the right by the Olmata di Palestrina a road leading to the Via Casilina near Palestrina station (6·5km). The hill of Palestrina suddenly comes into view, with Castel San Pietro Romano near the top.

38km **PALESTRINA** (11,500 inhab.), the ancient *Praeneste*, occupies the S slope of Monte Ginestro, a spur of the Monti Prenestini. Its steep narrow streets are often stepped. It is renowned for its Sanctuary of Fortune, a masterpiece of Roman architecture, important elements of which were revealed by the clearance of buildings destroyed by bombing in 1944. Palestrina is one of the six suburbicarian sees.

Praeneste, one of the oldest towns of Latium, is said to have been founded by Telegonus, son of Ulysses and Circe. It was a thriving place as early as the 7C BC Strongly fortified, it long resisted the attacks of the Romans, but in 499 BC it joined its traditional enemy. Later it revolted and took a prominent part in the Latin War of 340–338, after which it became subject to Rome. Refuge of the younger Marius, it was besieged in 82 BC by the troops of Sulla, and destroyed. The Sanctuary of Fortune, whose oracle delivered the 'Praenestinae sortes', became famous, and its influence survived until the 4C AD. In the golden age of Rome 'cool Praeneste', as Horace calls it, became a retreat of the patricians from the heat of summer.

In the Middle Ages a town called *Città Prenestina* was built over the abandoned sanctuary. In 752 this town was occupied by Astaulph, king of the Lombards. Later it passed to the counts of Tusculum and in 1043 to the Colonna; it thus became involved in the feuds of the Guelphs and Ghibellines, being several times destroyed and rebuilt. In 1630 Francesco Colonna sold it to Carlo Barberini, brother of Urban VII. The most famous native was Giov. Pierluigi da Palestrina (1524?–94), the father of polyphonic music.—In the history of art Palestrina is noted for its cistae or bronze caskets (used as 'beauty cases') of a type seldom made elsewhere.

Via degli Arcioni passes large blocks of tufa which supported the first terrace of the city. Beyond is the battlemented 17C *Porta del Sole*. Viale Duca d'Aosta swings round to the entrance to the town (left) by Viale della Vittoria which ends in Piazzale Santa Maria degli Angeli, with a stretch of the ancient polygonal walls. From here Via Anicia continues to the central Piazza Regina Margherita, which occupies the site of the **Forum** on another terrace. In the middle of the square is the monument to Palestrina, by Arn. Zocchi (1921); the composer was born in a little house in the neighbouring Vicolo Pierluigi. The **Cathedral**, dating from the 5C, was rebuilt in the Romanesque style in the 12C and altered again later. The façade presents an interesting ensemble of ancient fragments (many of them Roman). Remains of part of a pagan Roman edifice in tufa have been excavated beneath the church. This may be a Temple of Imperial Jupiter dating from the 4C BC. There is also a stretch of Roman road visible through a grille at the end of the right aisle (opened by the sacristan). In the left aisle is a copy of the Pietà of Palestrina formerly attrib. to Michelangelo (see below).—Outside, on the right of the Cathedral (below ground level) are further remains of the Roman road and the steps of the Roman building known as the Iunonarium. Behind rises the high wall of the *ex-Seminario* which incorporates four Corinthian half-columns from the façade of the Apsidal Hall (see below).

The other public buildings connected with the Forum are at present closed to the public. They are in an area formerly known as the *Santuario Inferiore* since they were mistakenly thought to be part of the Sanctuary of Fortune. They are reached through the ex-Seminary. The various buildings, dating from the 2C BC, were skilfully constructed on several levels, with columns one above the other, to make use of the uneven ground. The *Aerarium*, or treasury, a small barrel vaulted room with a contemporary inscription, contains busts, votive offerings, architectural fragments, and two pieces of an Egyptian granite obelisk. Beyond the courtyard, known as the *Area Sacra*, carved out of the hillside, is the so-called *Antro delle Sorti*, a small cave sanctuary with three deep niches and preceded by an arch. Remains of an extensive polychrome *Mosaic depict an Egyptian seascape, possibly the port of Alexandria, a remarkable Hellenistic work by craftsmen from Alexandria. The cave may have been used as a Serapeum. On the other side of the court is an *Apsidal Hall* (formerly part of the Seminary). This is a rectangular room in opus incertum, with an apse and a frieze of metopes and triglyphs, and niches framed in half columns and a white mosaic. Here was found the Barberini mosaic now in the Museum (see below). It has recently been suggested that the hall was used as a sanctuary of Isis.

From the piazza Corso Pier Luigi da Palestrina leads to Piazza Liberazione. Below the gardens of the Villa Comunale can be seen a long stretch of the wall of the first terrace and part of a Roman road.

The ***Sanctuary of Fortuna Primigenia**, mentioned by Cicero, is a colossal monumental edifice laid out in a series of terraces conforming to the slope of the hill and connected by ramps and staircases converging towards a temple on the summit. Much of the medieval town was built over it. The most grandiose Hellenistic edifice in Italy, it has an important place in the history of architecture since it is one of the earliest instances in which concrete was used by the Romans as a building material in vaulting. Its baroque concept and intricate design, perhaps derived from the smaller sanctuaries in Cos and Rhodes, did not, however, have a direct influence on later Roman buildings. The date of its construction has for long been under discussion. Although some scholars have dated it around 80 BC, after the destruction of the city by Sulla, it now seems more likely that it was built in 130–100 BC.

The plan is a quadrangle 118m square. The sanctuary was dedicated jointly to Fortuna and Juno. The cult of Fortuna was connected with an oracle which claimed to foretell the future by delivering to enquirers *sortes* or lots, which were pieces of wood with letters carved in them. When the town was bombed in 1944 the houses on Via del Borgo were destroyed and clearance of this part of the sanctuary was carried out.

Most of the sanctuary is normally closed to the public (adm only with special permission), except for the remains of the theatre and temple at the top in Palazzo Barberini. Above the level of the Forum (see above) are two terraces beneath the great polygonal wall which supports the double ramp at the foot of the sanctuary. The two great ramps, constructed on rubble, converge on the TERRAZZA DEGLI EMICICLI, which is supported by a massive wall and divided into halves by a central staircase. Along the back of each half ran a Doric colonnade, the line of which was broken by a monumental hemicycle, also colonnaded. Over the hemicycles was a coffered vault carried on Ionic columns, part of which is still in place. A fragment of the high attic and some Ionic columns of the right hemicycle survive. This was the shrine of the oracle of Fortune, the most important part of the sanctuary. A colossal head of Fortune, now in the Museum, was found in the well here from which the *sortes* (see above) were extracted. The view from the terrace is splendid: to the W is Rome, with Soracte in the far distance; to the N the Monte Tiburtini; to the E the Monti Ernici; to the S the Monte Lepini; and to the SW the Campagna as far as the Tyrrhenian Sea.

The central staircase ascends to the next level, the TERRAZZA DEI FORNICI A SEMICOLONNE, also with a colonnade. Above is the highest level, the TERRAZZA DELLA CORTINA, originally the courtyard with side porticoes in front of the cavea of the theatre. This upper sanctuary was probably damaged in the siege of 82 BC and restored by Sulla. The scena of the theatre would have been a temporary construction erected for each performance. The seats of the cavea, destroyed in the 14C were restored when the **Palazzo Colonna Barberini** was built in 1640 by Taddeo Barberini on the site of an 11C Colonna palace. The modernized interior incorporates the foundations of the round (reconstructed) temple at the highest point of the sanctuary, and is the seat of the *Museo Nazionale Archeologico Prenestino* (open every day 9–one hour before sunset). Although many antiquities from Praeneste have been dispersed to Rome (particularly to Villa Giulia) and elsewhere, the museum offers as complete a picture as possible of local civilization from the 8C BC to the 4C AD.

GROUND FLOOR. R. 1. Sculpture fragments from the Roman town.—R. II. Cippus of two praetors (2C BC?); small sculpture with two representations of Fortune (the heads are missing), dating from the late 2C BC.—R. III. *27. Large fragment of a statue of Fortune in grey Oriental marble (Hellenistic Rhodian school) found at the bottom of the well in front of the E hemicycle of the sanctuary.—R. IV. Among the funerary altars: 40. Votive altar to the Di Manes (Flavian period); relief of a she-wolf suckling her young in a wood, a fine work of the Augustan period found in the lower city.—R. V. 44–45. Marble plinths dedicated to Security and Peace by the emperor, and consecrated by the council and people of Praeneste (first half of 1C AD); 52. Base of a candelabrum, with Dionysos, a maenad, and a satyr (neo-Attic.)—R. VI. Portrait busts, fragments of sarcophagus reliefs.—Stairs lead up past remains of part of the portico of the Sanctuary in Piazza della Cortina (see above); the roof has been reconstructed.

FIRST FLOOR. R. VII, 62, 63. Two painted Archaic metopes in terracotta (6C BC), with scenes of horses and chariots.—RR. VIII and IX contain mirrors, cistae, and other toilet articles coming from tombs of the 4C BC. R. VIII. Case III. 64, 65. Mirrors with Silenus on horseback and Silenus and panther; Case IV, 72. *Cylindrical cista with fine graffiti; Case V. 81. Cista with battle between Hercules and the Amazon Hippolyta, and on the lid, two warriors carrying a wounded man; 82. Oval cista with battle scenes, and a female acrobat on the cover; also, 85–87. Three strigili (used by athletes).—R. IX. Case VI. 83. Cista with two figures (a third lacking) forming a circle on the cover; Case VII. Case VIII. 89. Bronze statuette of an ephebe (in the style of an Archaic kouros); Case VIII. Bronze mirrors decorated with mythological scenes; Case X. *Cista with Dionysos supported by Pan on the cover.—R. X. 110. Lid of a sarcophagus in peperino, with a frieze of animals; floor mosaics. Model of the Sanctuary of Fortune. The curved wall here in opus incertum is only part to have survived of the temple which crowned the sanctuary.—R. XI contains decorative fragments and votive objects from the temple.—R. XII. Architectural fragments in terracotta.

From R. XI a staircase ascends to R. XIV with the celebrated *Barberini Mosaic, found in the Apsidal Hall in the Forum of the Roman city. Measuring 5·85 × 4·31m it is one of the largest Hellenistic mosaics to have survived. It probably dates from the 2C BC, although it has been extensively restored. It depicts an Egyptian scene during the flooding of the Nile, from its source in the mountains of Ethiopia to the Delta. At the bottom is a banqueting scene on a canal overshaded with vines. Here is the Canopus of Alexandria, with the Serapeum to the right, before which are warriors and a priestess. Higher, to the right, is a sacred precinct, with pillars, towers and statues; to the left, near a building with obelisks, is a well, perhaps that of Aswan which helped Eratosthenes to calculate the meridian. The highest section shows regions of cataracts and deserts, inhabited by tropical animals.

The left-hand staircase descends; here can be seen the circular *Shrine (reconstructed using many original fragments), which sheltered the well beside the E hemicycle at the back of the Terrazza degli Emicicli of the Sanctuary of Fortune (see above).

To the W of the palace is the charming little church of *Santa Rosalia* (1660) which once contained the Pietà attrib. to Michelangelo, now in the Galleria dell'Accademia in Florence.

FROM PALESTRINA TO CAPRANICA PRENESTINA, 12km; bus in ¹/₂ hr. This road, a continuation of Via Pedemontana, climbs in spirals to (3·5km) *Castel San Pietro Romano* (752m), a hamlet on the site of the citadel of Praeneste. Its church of San Pietro has an altarpiece by Pietro da Cortona. On the top of the hill is the ruined *Castle of the Colonna*. The *View is magnificent, reaching all the way to Rome and beyond.—The road continues to climb. 12km *Capranica Prenestina* (914m).—Beyond this point the road gradually descends in a huge curve round the E side of the Monti Prenestini and across the Monti Tiburtini to (29·5km) *Tivoli* (Rte 32).

FROM PALESTRINA TO TIVOLI (41·5km). Via Prenestina leads out of Palestrina and at 8km a turn (right) leads to *Gallicano nel Lazio*, situated on a high tufa rock between two valleys, probably on the site of the Latin city of *Pedum* conquered by Rome in 338 BC. The present village dates from the 10C, and has picturesque roads leading off the central street.—18·5km *Poli*, a pretty town with a Conti palace (frescoes by Giulio Romano).—25·5km *Casape*, in the wooded folds of the Prenestine Hills.—28·5km *San Gregorio da Sassola*, a charming hill town with a 15C castle, later converted into a baronial palace. From here the road, clinging to the hill-side, passes through olive groves with views to the plain towards Rome on the left.—41·5km Tivoli (Rte 32).

The return to Rome may be made by Via Prenestina (37km).—8km Turning right for *Gallicano nel Lazio*, and other attractive hill towns on a road to Tivoli (see above).—At (8·5km) *Santa Maria di Cavamonte* there is a cross-roads. To the left is Zagarolo (see above); to the right, Tivoli (18·5km). From here the narrow straight Via

Prenestina leads back to Rome, through gently rolling country. The
road passes a long stretch of Roman pavement on the approach
(16·5km) to the ruins of *Gabii* (right), which gave the road its original
name, the *Via Gabina*. It passed through Gabii and Praeneste
(Palestrina) and joined the Via Latina at Anagnina (Anagni). A
legend relates that Romulus and Remus were sent to Gabii to study
Greek, and the ancient Latin town was supposed to have been
captured by Tarquinius Superbus. The ruins (conspicuous to the right
of the road near a tower) include those of a Temple with its altar. This
is known as the Temple of Juno, but may instead have been
dedicated to Fortune. In a sanctuary here a vast number of bronze
statuettes were found in 1976. To the W, at Osteria dell'Osa, recent
excavations have revealed an Iron Age necropolis. In the neighbourhood are the stone quarries from which parts of Rome were built.—
22km *Ponte di Nona*, at the 9th (Roman) milestone, a fine Roman
bridge of the Republican era, in excellent preservation; it has seven
arches and is 72m long.—30km *Tor de' Schiavi* (left; Tower of the
Slaves) is a circular mausoleum, which, with the ruins of an octagonal
hall, and a funerary basilica, formed part of the 3C *Villa dei Giordani*,
one of the largest suburban Roman villas.—37km This route rejoins
Via Casilina, just outside Porta Maggiore to return to the centre of
Rome.

32   Tivoli. Hadrian's Villa. Subiaco

Tivoli is the most famous place near Rome, and is included in numerous tours
from the city. Hadrian's Villa, one of the most important and beautiful classical
sites in Italy, lies in the plain below the little hill town. Subiaco, of particular
significance in ecclesiastical history, is normally reached from Rome by the
road—Via Tiburtina—running through Tivoli and following the valley of the
Aniene.

A.   From Rome to Tivoli

ROAD (VIA TIBURTINA), 31·5km. Buses from Castro Pretorio for
Tivoli; from Via Gaeta (NE corner of Piazza dei Cinquecento) every
half hour 'Via Prenestina' for *Hadrian's Villa*.There is also a bus
service between Tivoli and Hadrian's Villa.—The Motorway (A 24,
for l'Aquila) passes well S of Tivoli, and has little advantage over
the Via Tiburtina.

RAILWAY. A somewhat roundabout route from *Rome* (Termini) to
Tivoli via *Guidonia*, on the Rome–Pescara line (40km in c 1 hr).

VIA TIBURTINA (N 5), on the line of the old Roman road to Tibur
(Tivoli), starts from Porta San Lorenzo (Pl. 6; 5, 4). The road passes
the huge Campo Verano Cemetery on the right, and then crosses the
railway (Rome Tiburtina station, left). The next 10km traverse a
dreary factory area, and the Aniene is crossed by (8km) the *Ponte
Mammolo*, successor (1857) to the ancient *Pons Mammeus*, dating
from the Republican era and rebuilt by Julia Mammaea, mother of
Alexander Severus. On the left is a road leading to Via Nomentana.

The river **Aniene**, the classical *Anio*, rises in the Monti Simbruini, to the E of
Subiaco. It flows past Subiaco and Tivoli, where it forms impressive cascades,

and joins the Tiber N of Rome, near the Ponte Salario. In Roman times its waters
were carried to Rome by two aqueducts—the *Anio Vetus* (70km), begun in 273
BC, and the *Anio Novus* (95km) begun in AD 36.

The Rome Circular Road is crossed just before (13km) *Settecamini*
(48m). Farther on, a road leads S to *Lunghezza*, with a 13C castle.
Here is the site of *Collatia*, where archaeological material dating
from the Iron Age has come to light.—19·5km *Le Tavernucole*; on the
left is the crenellated *Castell' Arcione*, probably erected in the 12C
on ruins dating from the Imperial era, and restored in 1931. Beyond it
are the three summits of the Monti Cornicolani with Monte Gennaro
rising behind them; ahead are Tivoli and the Monti Tiburtini; to the
right the Monti Prenestini and the Alban Hills.—21·5km Turning
(left) for Guidonia.

22·5km **Bagni di Tivoli** (80m), with the *Stabilimento delle Acque
Albule*, which uses the waters of two lakes. There is a strong smell of
sulphuretted hydrogen in the locality.

The hot springs, the Roman *Aquae Albulae*, are charged with sulphuretted
hydrogen, and are beneficial in skin, throat, and urinary affections, etc. The
establishment can accommodate 1000 bathers in four baths, the largest of which
is called the Spiaggia di Tivoli. The two lakes that feed the baths are c 2km N.
The *Lago della Regina*, or *Solfatara*, is the larger. From its depths the water
bubbles up at a temperature of 24°C. At times the water takes on a vivid blue
colour. To the S are remains of Roman thermae. To the E is the smaller *Lago
delle Colonnelle*, also bright blue in colour. To the N is the Lago di San
Giovanni.

Having crossed the railway the road passes through a region of
travertine quarries that provided stone for the Colosseum, St Peter's,
and many other buildings in ancient and modern Rome. The stone is
the 'lapis tiburtinus' which hardens after cutting. The Aniene is
crossed near (26km) the five-arched *Ponte Lucano*, a Roman bridge
named after Lucanus Plautius and rebuilt at various times from the
15C to the 19C. Immediately beyond the bridge is (right) the tower-
like *Tomb of the Plautii*, of the Augustan period and resembling the
Tomb of Cecilia Metella on the Appian Way.

At (28km) *Bivio Villa Adriana* (41m) the road to (1·5km) Hadrian's
Villa branches off to the right. Via Tiburtina now begins its long
serpentine climb to Tivoli, passing through a beautiful olive grove.
The town is entered by Via Nazionale.—31·5km **Tivoli** (230m).

TIVOLI (41,700 inhab.), the classical *Tibur*, stands on the lower
slopes of the Sabine Hills at the end of the valley of the Aniene,
which here narrows into a gorge between Monte Catillo (348m) on
the N and the Colle Ripoli (484m) on the S and discharges the famous
cascades. The river makes a wide loop round the town and borders it
on three sides. Surrounded by olive groves and overlooking the
Roman Campagna, Tivoli stands in a delightful position. In recent
years the Villa d'Este has become the most popular excursion from
Rome.

History. *Tibur* is supposed to have been founded, four centuries before the birth
of Rome, by the Siculi, who were later expelled by Tiburtus and his brothers,
grandsons of Amphiarus. It was captured by Camillus in 380 BC, and by the end
of the 1C BC it had become a holiday resort for the wealthier Romans, who
erected their famous temples to Vesta, Hercules, and other deities. Marius,
Sallust, Cassius, Catullus, Maecenas. Quintilius Varus, and, later, Trajan and
Hadrian all had sumptuous villas at or near Tibur. It was a spot sacred to the cult
of the Sybil Albunea, a favourite haunt of Augustus and the poets Horace,
Catullus, and Propertius, and later on a place of confinement for state prisoners
such as Syphax and Zenobia. In Hadrian's time its splendour was at its height,

and in the 6C Totila, the Ostrogoth, after sacking the place rebuilt it as his capital. By the 10C it had recovered its prosperity. It stood a siege by Otho III, became independent as an imperial free city, was occupied by the Caraffa in the 16C and did not lose its autonomous character till 1816. Among its natives were Munatius Plancus (consul 42 BC), the founder of Lyons, and Popes Simplicius (468–83) and John IX (898–900).

Via Tiburtina enters the town from the SW as Via Nazionale and ends at Largo Garibaldi, a busy traffic centre. On the left is the Giardino Garibaldi, which provides a splendid *View of the open country below. To the NW is the air station of Guidonia, with the Monti Cornicolani villages above it; almost due W is Rome; to the SW the Campagna extends to the sea.

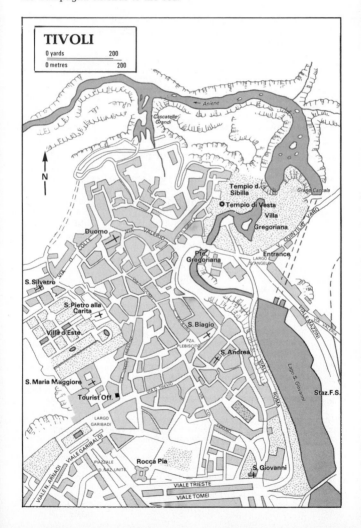

Viale Nazioni Uniti leads out of the right side of the square up past the bus station to the imposing **Rocca Pia** (adm 9–12.30, 15–18.30), a castle built by Pius II (1458–64) to overawe the natives of Tivoli. Exhibitions are held here. It is rectangular in shape and has four crenellated cylindrical towers, two large and two smaller. The castle was built over the ruins of a Roman amphitheatre, best seen from Vicolo Barchetto to the N. Viale Trieste continues to Porta San Giovanni, now the entrance to a hospital. Here is the little church of *San Giovanni Evangelista*, containing good frescoes by Antoniazzo Romano.

From the other side of Largo Garibaldi (see above) Via Boselli leads to Piazza Trento outside the church of *Santa Maria Maggiore*, a Romanesque structure with a fine rose-window attributed to Angelo da Tivoli above the later Gothic narthex (which contains a 13C fresco of the Madonna and Child, in a fine tabernacle).

The interior contains remains of the original floor at the E end. In the presbytery are two triptychs, the one on the right dates from the 16C, and the one on the left is signed by Bart. Bulgarini of Siena (14C). Above the latter, Madonna and Child, by Iac. Torriti. Over the high altar is a Byzantine Madonna (12C?). In the right aisle, Crucifix attrib. to Baccio da Montelupo.

Adjoining the church, on the right, is the entrance to the celebrated **·Villa d'Este** with an ornate garden, famous for its many elaborate fountains. The garden is open every day 9 to dusk; the water pressure diminishes between 12 and 14.30 when the fountains are less impressive. The gardens have also been open and floodlit after dark in summer, but because of damage this may be discontinued.

Originally a Benedictine convent, the property became the Governor's residence after confiscation. In 1550 Card. Ippolito II d'Este was installed here as governor; he commissioned Pirro Ligorio to transform the convent into a sumptuous villa, which his successors embellished. In the course of time it passed by bequest to the House of Austria, but after 1918 the Italian Government resumed possession and undertook a general restoration. The top floor was the Italian headquarters of Franz Liszt (1811–86) from 1865 to the year of his death; from this base he travelled to many parts of Europe and, while here, he composed the third book of his *Années de Pélerinage*, one of the most popular pieces in which is *Les Jeux d'Eau à la Villa d'Este*. A fine Roman mosaic pavement was found beneath the villa in 1983.

Beyond the entrance is a court which was the cloister of the convent, with the entrance to the *Appartamento Vecchio*, ten frescoed rooms containing minor paintings. A staircase at the end descends to a pavilion, fitted with a bar and with a fine view. From here there is access to the walk in front of the villa, below which is the *Fontana del Bicchierone*, by Bernini. A path descends to a lower walk and (left) the *Grotto of Diana*, with stuccoes. Another path leads (right) to the RΟMETTA ('Little Rome'). This has a model of the Tiber with an islet (representing the Isola Tiberina) in the form of a boat, on which is an obelisk. Behind are a seated statue of Rome, with the wolf suckling Romulus and Remus, and miniature reproductions of the principal buildings of ancient Rome. From the Rometta the *Viale delle Cento Fontane* leads right across the garden, parallel to the villa. It is skirted by a long narrow basin with scores of jets and overgrown with maidenhair fern and moss. At the end is the *Fontana dell'Ovato*, by Pirro Ligorio, with the end of a conduit from the Aniene, one of the water supplies for the fountains. In the hemicycle of the fountain are statues of nymphs, by G.B. della Porta. To the right is the *Fontana di Bacco*; to the left is the architectural *Fontana dell'Organo Idraulico*, named after a water-operated organ which was one of the garden's features in the 16C.

Going a little towards the villa, a path turns right into an avenue, half-way along which (left) is the *Fontana dei Draghi*, by Pirro Ligorio, recalling the dragons that formed part of the coat-of-arms of Gregory XIII, a guest of Card. Ippolito d'Este in 1572. At the end of the avenue are the *Fontana di Proserpina* and the bizarre *Fontana della Civetta e degli Uccelli*, once noted for producing alternately by water power the screech of an owl and the song of birds. Leading away from the villa, a path passes (right) the fishponds and (left) the ruined

Fontana di Arianna, and, at the end of the garden, reaches the *Fontana della Natura*, with a statue of Diana of the Ephesians. Opposite the gate, beyond, the central avenue leads back towards the villa; in it is the *Rotonda dei Cipressi*, once a circus with some of the mightiest cypresses in Italy. It is now sadly reduced to a hemicycle since some of the ancient trees, struck by disease, have had to be felled.

From the fishponds there is a superb view (left) of the cascades descending from the Organo (see above). From here paths reascend to the terrace in front of the villa, and a spiral stair beyond the bar (right), emerges into the *Appartamento Nobile*, ten frescoed rooms. The Great Hall has ceiling paintings by the School of Muziano and Fed. Zuccari. From here there is access to the *Loggia dello Scalone*, by Pirro Ligorio, the finest part of the garden façade; the view of the garden is enchanting. A vaulted passageway leads back to the entrance.

The church of *San Pietro alla Carità*, outside the garden to the NE, contains ten cipollino columns, probably from a Roman villa, and an interesting crypt (open Sunday mornings; otherwise ring at the base of the campanile).

From Largo Garibaldi Via Pacifici and Via Trevio lead towards Piazza del Plebiscito (see the Plan), the town centre. On the right is the church of *San Biagio*, dating from the 14C and rebuilt in the neo-Gothic style of 1887 (14–15C paintings and frescoes). To the S, in Via Sant'Andrea, is the church of *Sant'Andrea*, with a Romanesque campanile. From the square Via Palatina and Via Ponte Gregoriano, with interesting medieval houses, lead to Piazza Rivarola, an important traffic centre. From here Via San Valerio leads left to the **Duomo** (San Lorenzo), rebuilt in 1650 but retaining a Romanesque campanile of the 12C.

INTERIOR. RIGHT AISLE, 4th chapel (light on right), *Descent from the Cross, a 13C group of five carved wooden figures, and a copy of the triptych (see below); 3rd chapel (left) so-called *Macchina del Salvatore*, containing a precious 11C or 12C triptych, painted in tempera, with silver and gilt decoration of the 15C and 16C. It is shown only on High religious festivals (copy in the adjoining chapel). Also in the left aisle are two episcopal tombs (late 15C and early 16C).

From Piazza Duomo the medieval Via del Duomo (partly stepped) leads past (No. 78) the entrance to the *Ponderarium*, containing two tables with measures of capacity, used by Roman inspectors of weights and measures.

In Piazza Tani, outside the side entrance to the Cathedral, is a pretty fountain made up from a medieval sarcophagus. From here the narrow Via del Colle (impracticable for cars) descends steeply past medieval houses and remains of ancient buildings through one of the most picturesque parts of the town. It passes the Romanesque church of *San Silvestro* (if closed ring to right of façade at No. 2), recently restored. Inside are interesting 12C or 13C frescoes and a wooden figure of St Valerian of 1138 (right wall). At the end of the street, outside Porta del Colle, is the **Sanctuary of Hercules Victor**, in a large area until recently occupied by a paper-mill. It is now being excavated and studied and there are plans to open it to the public.

This huge Hellenistic sanctuary was mentioned by numerous classical authors as being the most important in the city. There was an oracle here similar to the one in Palestrina. The buildings are thought to date from the end of the 2C BC. The most conspicuous remains are the cyclopean substructures to the NW where the hill descends to the Aniene valley. Above the mighty foundations are arches and vaults which supported a huge Piazzale, with a portico on three sides, a temple, and a theatre. A market was connected to the sanctuary.

From Piazza Rivarola (see above) Via della Sibilla leads NE to the edge of the cliff which dominates the valley, the site of the Roman acropolis. Here is the so-called *Temple of Vesta, a circular Roman temple famous for its picturesque position. It is not known to whom the temple was dedicated; it is circular peripteral and dates from the last years of the Republic. It was converted in the Middle Ages into the church of Santa Maria della Rotonda. Ten of its eighteen fluted Corinthian columns survive, and there is a frieze of bucrania, garlands, rosettes, and paterae. The doors and windows of the well-preserved cella are trapezoidal.—Close by is an earlier temple, known as the **Temple of the Sibyl**, but also of uncertain attribution. It is rectangular with a tetrastyle Ionic façade. Until 1884 it was the church of *San Giorgio.*

From Piazza Rivarola Ponte Gregoriano leads over the Aniene to an open space by the *Porta Sant'Angelo*, a busy traffic centre. Here is the entrance to the *Villa Gregoriana, a natural park enclosing that reach of the Aniene where it plunges down in the cascades (adm daily 9·30–dusk).

The park commemorates Gregory XVI, who took decisive steps to put an end to the periodic local flooding, which in 1826 had seriously damaged the town. On his accession to the papacy in 1831, he instructed the engineer Folchi to build a double tunnel under Monte Catillo, to ease the flow of the river. This tunnel (300m and 270m) became known as the *Traforo Gregoriano*, or *Emissario Gregoriano*, and the water plunged down from it in a new waterfall, from then on known as the Great Cascade.

From the ticket office a path bears a little right, following the direction post ('Grande Cascata') to a terrace, with a view of the temples of Vesta and of the Sibyl across the valley. Farther on the path reaches a parapet overlooking the crest of the *Great Cascade.* Steps lead down to another terrace from which the mouth of the tunnel may be seen. Here the Aniene makes a leap of 108 metres as it emerges from the *Traforo Gregoriano.* The tunnel (no adm) bears inscriptions recording the visits of popes and kings. From the first terrace a path marked 'Ruderi della Villa-Grotte della Sirena, di Nettuno, e Cascata Bernini' descends to another terrace planted with ilexes, at the end of which is a tunnel which passes through remains of a Roman villa. At the exit a path continues to descend with a good view of the *Little Cascades* and of the *Bernini Cascade.* Farther down, a little square is reached marked with two signposts, to the right of which there is a viewpoint about half the height of the Great Cascade, which enables one to appreciate its volume, its noise and the rainbow colours of its spray. From the little square a path follows the signpost marked 'Grotte Nettuno e Sirena, Cascata Bernini', descending for some distance and bearing sharp left at a signpost marked 'Ingresso Grotta della Sirena' to reach the fantastic *Grotto of the Siren*, a limestone cavern in which the water tumbles down a narrow ravine. The other side of the valley may now be climbed. From a fork marked 'Grotta di Nettuno e Tempio di Vesta', a path turns left, passing through two tunnels lit from the side. At another fork a descent (left) leads to the *Grotto of Neptune*, through which the Aniene originally flowed. From the last-named fork the other path (right) leads to the exit-gate close to the temples.

From Porta Sant'Angelo Viale Mazzini leads S to the Station. Here, in a park, the tomb of Vestalia Cossinia has been set up.

VIA DELLE CASCATELLE (3km). From Porta Sant'Angelo Via Quintilio Varo winds between olive plantations, and passes several times beneath the viaducts of the Rome–Tivoli railway. It soon reaches the *Belvedere, with a fine view of the Great Cascade, and, after crossing beneath the railway for the last time, there is an excellent *View of the Great Cascade, the Cascatelle, the town of Tivoli, and the Campagna. The road passes the church of *Sant'Antonio* (left) and the ruined arches of the *Aqua Marcia.* This aqueduct, 58km long and dating from 144 BC, ran from Via Valeria to Rome. Farther on (500m) a by-road (left; unsignposted) diverges from the main road and leads down past a group of houses to the conspicuous *Santuario di Santa Maria di Quintiliolo*, near the ruins of a Roman villa, said to have been that of Quintilius Varus.

The road soon deteriorates and becomes less interesting. Farther on it crosses the *Ponte dell'Acquoria* over the Aniene and, going straight on, begins to climb the *Clivus Tiburtinus*, partly levelled by Constantine. On the right, is the so-called *Tempio del Mondo*, with a large interior chamber and farther on, also on the right, is a Roman building known as the *Tempio della Tosse.* Probably dating from the 4C, this is circular without, octagonal within, and may have been adapted for Christian worship (traces of Byzantine decoration). The road passes round the ruins of the Temple of Hercules Victor (see above).—It re-enters Tivoli by Porta del Colle.

From Tivoli to *Subiaco*, see Rte 32C; to *Palestrina*, see Rte 31.

B.   Hadrian's Villa

ROAD, 28·5km. For buses from Rome, see the begining of Rte 32A.

RAILWAY. The nearest Station is at *Bagni di Tivoli* (see Rte 32A), 7km from the Villa.

From Rome by the Via Tiburtina to (27km) the *Bivio Villa Adriana*, see Rte 32A. At the bus stop the road leads to the right (S; signpost). The entrance to Hadrian's Villa (1·5km) is a good 15 minutes walk from here. The villa is open every day from 9 to dusk; visitors are recommended to bring a picnic.

*Hadrian's Villa, the largest and richest imperial villa in the Roman Empire, was the chosen residence of Hadrian, who became emperor on the death of Trajan in 117. He began to build the villa in 118 and completed it ten years later. It is one of the most evocative classical sites left in Italy.

It is difficult to understand why Hadrian, with all the resources of the Empire at his disposal, should have chosen such an unprepossessing spot for his magnificent estate. Though little more than 5km from the scenic health resort of Tivoli, the low lying surroundings of the villa have no particular attraction. In the emperor's day the flat plain was not even healthy. One reason for the choice of this site is probably the fact that its owner was the Empress Sabina; another reason may have been the emperor's desire to keep himself apart from his courtiers, many of whom owned villas on the hills around Tivoli. Parts of a smaller country house of the 1C BC, overlooking the 'Vale of Tempe', were incorporated into the emperor's villa.

Many of the buildings of the villa take their inspiration from famous classical monuments, many of which impressed Hadrian during his prolonged travels in the Empire. These were the Lyceum, the Academy, the Prytaneum, and the Stoa Poikile in Athens; the Canopus of the Egyptian Delta; and the Vale of Tempe in Thessaly. To these he added even a representation of Hades, as conceived by the poets. His successors enlarged and embellished the villa, but it is said that Constantine rifled it to beautify Byzantium. Barbarian invaders plundered the site, and in course of time it became a quarry for builders and lime-burners. Until the Renaissance the ruins continued to be neglected or abused.

The first excavations were ordered by Alexander VI and Card. Aless. Farnese. Soon after he had begun to live at the Villa d'Este in 1550, Card. Ippolito II d'Este took many of the newly-discovered works of art to decorate his Tivoli villa. Excavations continued in the 17–19C and yielded many valuable discoveries; the engraver G.B. Piranesi (1720–78) left a plan of the ruins and engravings of the buildings and sculptures (now in the Calcografia Nazionale in Rome). A successful attempt to improve the amenities of the site was made in 1730 by Count Fede by the plantations of cypresses and pines. In 1870 the Italian Government acquired most of the site and excavation was systematically planned. It is still, however, far from complete and important discoveries are still being made. The works of art discovered in the villa (more than 260) are scattered in museums and galleries all over Europe. In Rome they are to be found in the Museo Nazionale Romano, the Capitoline Museum, the Egyptian Museum in the Vatican, and elsewhere.

The general plan of the villa, which covers some 120 hectares, is capricious though the buildings individually are quite regular. These are grouped round four principal structures: the Poikile, the Canopus, the Academy, and the Imperial Palace. Guide-posts indicate the names of the buildings and in some instances give a few details about them. The visitor to Hadrian's Villa cannot fail to be impressed by its vast size. A walk round the estate takes some hours; half a day is needed for even a hurried visit.—An extensive system of underground passages (no adm), some corridors and others wide enough for a horse and carriage, exist beneath the villa; these were presumably service areas.

From the ticket entrance, a short drive leads on to the car park (refreshments). A building here displays a model of the villa. In 1985 an 18C villa nearby was opened as a 'didactic centre', with explanations about the site, copies of engravings by Piranesi, photographs of sculptures found here and now in other museums, etc. The entrance to the ruins is through the massive N wall of the **Poikile** (*Pecile*).

The *Stoa Poikile* (painted porch) was a building in Athens famous alike for its varied paintings by Polygnotos and Panainos and for its association with the Stoic philosophers. Hadrian's reproduction is a rectangular peristyle (232 × 97m) with the ends slightly curved. The huge N wall (9m high), running almost due E and W, still exists. On the S side the wall is no longer standing, but there are remains of a pavilion with three exedrae and a fountain. On both sides of it ran roofed colonnades, so that sun or shade could be enjoyed at any hour and warmth or freshness at any season. In the middle of the rectangle the fish-pond has been restored. The free area round it was possibly used as a racecourse. On the SW the Poikile had as a substructure a wall with three rows of small chambers, now called the *Cento Camerelle*, which are supposed to have accommodated the Praetorians.

At the NE angle of the Poikile, a few steps lead up to the *Philosophers' Hall* (17 × 9m), with an apse, seven niches for bookcases, and four side-doors; adjacent is a series of baths. Beyond is a charming circular building, with an Ionic marble peristyle, known as the ***Naval Theatre** (*Teatro Marittimo*), but probably a private retreat for the emperor. A circular moat (3·5m broad), lined with Luni (Carrara) marble, encloses an island on which stand an atrium with fluted Ionic columns in an intricate design, and a series of living-rooms. It could be reached only by a revolving bridge. A reconstruction of one part of the building is displayed on the S side.

On the E side stairs lead up to the first complex of buildings belonging to the **Imperial Palace**, which is disposed parallel to the Vale of Tempe (see below); its elements are grouped round four peristyles. The COURT OF THE LIBRARIES (*Cortile delle Biblioteche*), is now a secluded olive plantation; its NW side is flanked by the so-called *Greek and Latin Libraries*, now identified as summer *Triclinia*, with towers. Behind them new excavations have revealed part of a delightful garden.

To the N of the Cortile are the OSPITALI (*Guest rooms* or a dormitory for the staff), the best preserved part of the Palace complex, with ten small rooms leading off either side of a wide corridor. Rectangular alcoves indicate space for a bed, and the lighting of each room was provided by the high openings. The rooms are decorated with well-preserved mosaics.—Steps lead down to the TRICLINIUM with (left) some capitals with a lotus motif, and a mosaic floor. To the right is a long corridor with oblique openings in the vault, to allow the light of midday to enter. This leads to the PADIGLIONE (*Pavilion*) which overlooks the Vale of Tempe.

From here steps lead up to a path (S) to the GREAT PERISTYLE of the palace, with a private library and other small rooms overlooking the Court of the Libraries. Here also is the *Room of Three Naves*, a delightfully proportioned room with two rows of small columns. Nearby, stairs lead underground to a *Cryptoporticus*, with well-lit corridors. At the other end of this central nucleus of the Palace is the *Room of the Doric Pilasters*, with a fine entablature. The *Barracks of the Vigiles* are beyond the apse of the basilican hall (right). To the left is the *Nymphaeum* which had two round fountain basins, and from here a path leads to the **Piazza d'Oro**, a rectangular area at the SE end of the Palace. It was so named because excavations here yielded such rich finds.

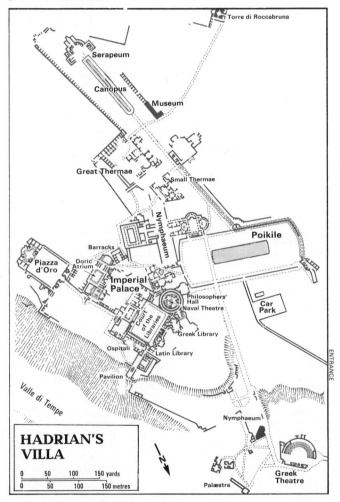

It is entered through the fine octagonal *Vestibule*. The peristyle was formed of alternate columns of cipollino and granite in two rows. On the far side (SE) is an intricate series of rooms, the central one being the most interesting design, a Greek cross with alternate convex and concave sides. A dome used to rest over the four walls nearest the centre.

A path continues W past the back of the Barracks of the Vigiles and a *Quadriporticus* with a pool and a portico of fluted composite columns. Beneath is an extensive Cryptoporticus.

A path descends to a clump of mighty cypresses and the **Small Thermae** and the ***Great Thermae**. The small baths are well-preserved, with a large rectangular hall, perhaps the frigidarium, and an octagonal hall with a domed vault. The large baths contain a circular hall, with cupola and skylight. A huge *Sala Absidata* has a superb cross-vault, mostly collapsed. Opposite is another cross-vaulted room (closed; but well seen from the SE) decorated with exquisite stucco reliefs. On the E is a swimming-bath, bounded on the NW by a *Cryptoporticus* on the ruined walls of which are numerous graffiti of the 16C and 17C. This gives access to the so-called *Praetorium*, a tall edifice which was divided into three stories by wooden floors. It may have been used as a warehouse, or as a service wing.

The celebrated ***Canopus** was designed to imitate the famous sanctuary of Serapis, that stood at the 15th milestone from Alexandria.

Hadrian dug a hollow (185 by 75m), in which he constructed a canal, bordered on one side by a block of 20 rooms and a portico, and on the other by a heavy buttressed wall (238m long), against which were set entertainment booths. The Canopus has for the most part been restored to its old aspect. Around the curved N end of the canal reproductions of statues found on the site have been set up between marble columns surmounted by an epistyle arched over alternate pillars. Along the right side are reproductions of Caryatids and Sileni.

At the S end of the canal is a nymphaeum, commonly called the *Serapeum*, where most of the Egyptian sculptures in the Capitoline and Vatican museums were found. An excellent survey of the greater part of the villa may be obtained from the hill behind.

On the NW side of the hollow is the **Museum**, housing finds from more recent excavations. ROOM 1. Decorative fragments.—R. 2. Bust of Caracalla and other portraits; Venus, copy of a work by Praxiteles.—R. 3. Wounded Amazons, one a mutilated copy of a Polykleitan original, the other a fine replica of the famous original by Pheidias; portrait of Verres, spoiler of Sicily; Athena, from a mid-5C original.—R. 4. Mars also from a mid-5C original; two athletes.—R. 5. Crocodile; tondo of a satyr (bas-relief).—R. 6. Four marble caryatids, copies of the 5C originals on the Erechtheion at Athens; two Sileni.

About 4 minutes W of the entrance to the Canopus is the *Torre di Roccabruna* (view), a belvedere or pharos, rectangular externally and circular within. This is possibly an imitation of the Tower of Timon of Athens, which stood near the Academy. It stands in the Oliveto Roccabruna, which is famous for the size of its olive trees, one of them (the 'albero bello') being reputed the largest in the Tivoli district.

To the SE, within an olive-grove, is the so-called **Accademia**, a complex of buildings which some authorities, however, prefer to identify as a secondary palace. The group includes a round hall, styled the *Temple of Apollo*, a peristyle, and the remains of three rooms with delicate stucco ornamentation. About 300m SE are the remains of an *Odeion or Theatre (45m in diameter) with the imperial box in the centre of the cavea. To the E of the Odeion a path descends to a hollow (150m long), hewn in the tufa and overshadowed by thick vegetation, which leads to a semi-circular vestibule (once perhaps guarded by an image of Cerberus). This was the entrance to **Hades** or the **Inferi**, represented by a quadrangle of four subterranean corridors, 5·5m wide and 91m in total length, with 79 apertures for light. Smaller tunnels connected Hades with various parts of the Villa.

A broad main path returns towards the entrance. To the right, just before the Poikile, is a court with three apses and a long connecting room. The *Nymphaeum* beyond adjoins the *Quadriporticus* (see above). A path leads back across the Poikile to the entrance. From here a fine avenue of cypresses leads N to the Greek Theatre, passing the Casino Fede (now the excavation office), built on part of the ruins of the so-called *Nymphaeum*. Here the *Temple of Venus* was restored in 1959. Beyond, to the right, a walk leads to the modernized *Fontana di Palazzo*, near which are a few traces of the *Palaestra*. Beyond this lies the *Valle Pussiana*, the Emperor's Vale of Tempe, with a streamlet to represent the Peneios. Descending (left) through olives and cypresses, the path passes the **Greek Theatre**, c 36m in diameter; its cavea or auditorium is carved out of the hill-side. Visitors without cars may continue past the theatre back to the ticket entrance; those with cars return up the cypress avenue to the car park.

C.   From Rome to Subiaco

ROAD, via Tivoli, 74·5km. Frequent bus services from Castro Pretorio in c 2 hrs via Castel Madama, and in c 1½ hrs via Vicovaro.

RAILWAY from *Rome* (Termini) via Tivoli to Mandela-Sambuci, 54km in c 1 hour.—Buses connect with the trains from *Rome*, to *Subiaco*, 25km in 40 minutes.

From Rome to (31·5km) *Tivoli*, see Rte 32A. On reaching Tivoli the through buses by-pass the town, taking Viale Trieste, Viale Roma and Viale Giuseppe Mazzini, forking left just before the railway station. The road, still N 5, is now called Via Valeria.

The VIA VALERIA, one of the great Roman roads across the Apennines, passed through Carseoli (Carsoli) and Corfinium (near Sulmona) to Aternum (Pescara), on the Adriatic. From there it followed the coast-line to Castrum Truentium (near San Benedetto del Tronto), where it joined the Via Salaria.

Beyond Tivoli the road accompanies the Rome–Pescara railway as it winds NE between wooded hills up the Aniene valley, followed, farther on, also by an autostrada (A 24; for Aquila).—36km *San Polo* station (*San Polo de' Cavalieri*, with a medieval Rocca, is 7km along a branch road left).—40km Castel Madama station lies 3km below *Castel Madama* whose Orsini castle, on top of a green hill (453m), is prominent to the right.

Remains of arches of the Aqua Marcia are seen here and there. The valley widens and the scenery increases in charm; chestnut trees, olive groves, and vineyards abound.—46km **Vicovaro** (300m; 3600 inhab.) occupies the site of the citadel of *Varia*, a town of the Aequi. The little church of *Sant' Antonio* has antique columns in its portico. The *Orsini Palace* dates from the 13C. The **Tempietto di San Giacomo*, an octagonal Renaissance chapel by Domenico da Capodistria (c 1450), has a rich porch by Giov. Dalmata.—Beyond the little town the *Monastery of San Cosimato* rises to the right.

After several sharp bends in the road, a lovely road diverges left through the valley of the turbulent Licenza (the ancient Digentia). To the right is the beautiful hill-town of Mandela (see below), and on the left *Roccagiovine* with an Orsini castle. Before (8km) Licenza, an unmade road on the left and a footpath lead to the ruin of **Horace's Sabine farm**, given to the poet in 33/32 BC and described in many of his letters. A custodian is usually here; if not, ask at the Comune of Licenza.

From the car park is the entrance to a series of rooms with magnificent mosaic pavements; the first one is the most sumptuous, with an area of different mosaic design for a bed. The rooms are raised above an oblong garden with a swimming-pool in the centre. They are grouped round an open court with a square pool; parts of the original lead piping used to channel the water from it can be seen under the floors of neighbouring rooms. On the W side of the site (most recently excavated) are baths with later Imperial and medieval extensions. Further S is a 2C aquarium, which was later covered by the church of a medieval convent.—The custodian keeps a small collection of fragments of mosaic, glass, and ceramics found during the excavations.

The spring or '*Fonte di Orazio*', presumed to be the Bandusian Spring apostrophized in one of Horace's odes (iii, 13), can still be seen up the rise to the SW of the site (from which its sound can be heard). Farther up is the *Ninfeo* constructed by the Orsini, probably replacing a similar edifice of Horace's time (fragments of which are in the museum in Licenza). The unmade road continues up the valley (although the main road gives easier access) in which stand the two spectacular hill-towns of (8km) **Licenza** and (10km) **Civitella di Licenza**. In the Castle of Licenza a small Antiquarium contains material from the excavations of Horace's villa, including fragments of frescoes, glass, marble decoration, etc.

The route continues along the main road. At 48km another turning left leads to the village of *Mandela* which stands on the spur of a hill to the N. Its position affords magnificent views of the valleys on either side, which are glimpsed down its narrow streets. The castle belonged to the Orsini.—Beyond, a road on the right leads to the village of *Sambuci*, 4km S of the main road. The valley of Subiaco—Valle Santa—soon comes into view.

56km Turning right for **Anticoli Corrado**. The by-road crosses the Aniene and in 2km reaches this small town, beautifully situated on a hill side.

The road climbs up to a spacious main square with a Noah's Ark fountain by Arturo Martini. On the left is the 11C church of *San Pietro*, well-preserved, with early frescoes recently uncovered, the most primitive of which were painted over in several succeeding centuries. From the opposite corner of the piazza, a road leads through the ancient gate of the city up to the *Museum of Modern Art* (damaged by fire in 1974), housed in an old villa, used as a prison in the 16C. The small collection has been donated over the last 50 years by artists of all nationalities who have worked in Anticoli, as well as those who were born here. The story is told of a group of artists in the early 19C travelling to Subiaco, stopping on the way at Anticoli and falling in love with its charm and most of all its beautiful women, using them as models in their work. An artistic community has remained, and the collection is impressive.

At 58km this route leaves Via Valeria and turns right into the beautiful wooded Subiaco road (Via Sublacensis), following the course of the Aniene upstream, with the Monti Simbruini on the left. On the right can be seen the hill town of Marano Equo. In this area are springs, which are the source of the Aqua Marcia, and still supply Rome with water.—64km *Agosta* (left) is a hamlet founded by the monks of Subiaco.—From (68·5km) *Madonna della Pace*, a secondary road, the Via Empolitana, leads W to Tivoli past the conspicuous hill-top village of *Rocca Canterano* (747m).

74km **SUBIACO** (408m; 8400 inhab.) lies near the head of the narrow Aniene valley, on the W slopes of Monte Livata. It is famous as the birthplace of western monasticism under the rule of its founder St Benedict. Modern buildings are fast encroaching on the medieval aspect of the town.

History. Subiaco, anciently *Sublaqueum* ('under the lakes') appears to owe its origin as a town to the necessity of accommodating the workmen employed by Nero to build here a grandiose villa, with an extensive lake in its grounds. There were already in existence three small lakes—the *Simbruina Stagna* mentioned by Tacitus—the level of which was raised by the building of a dam across the Anio. Tacitus relates that at a banquet in the villa the table before Nero was struck by lightning. Nero's lake disappeared after flood waters had breached the dam in February 1305, but traces of his villa survive.

A monastery dedicated to St Clement, was founded at Subiaco early in the history of the church. Towards the end of the 5C Benedetto da Norcia (St Benedict; 480–543?), a rich young man, turning against the dissolute life of his contemporaries, decided to live in a cavern on the slopes of Monte Taleo. Here he stayed, in prayer and contemplation, for three years. The fame of his saintliness spread all over Italy and multitudes journeyed to Subiaco to see him. His cavern was known as the *Sacro Speco* (Holy Grotto). Later, persuaded by his twin sister Scholastica, he built a monastery near the ruins of Nero's villa. This was followed by others, of which only two still exist. After a time, harassed by the persecution of a monk called Fiorenzio (Florentius), St Benedict, guided by three tame ravens, moved to Monte Cassino, where in 529 he founded a new monastery.

Some of his companions stayed behind with the abbot St Honorius, and built the convent of Saints Cosmas and Damian (now St Scholastica) and other retreats. Most of these were destroyed by the Lombards. The golden age of the surviving convents was in the 11–12C, but the ambition of the monks, earthquakes, and the plague of 1348 contributed to their decay. In the 16–18C the monastery was ruled by powerful prince-abbots, first of the Colonna family and later of the Borghese and Barberini, until, in 1753, Benedict XIV abolished the temporal power of the abbots.

Arnold Pannartz and Conrad Sweynheim, pupils of Fust, from Mainz, set up the first printing press in Italy, in the Convent of St Scholastica, in 1464. They soon quarrelled with the scribes in the monastery, and in 1467 transferred their press to Rome (see Palazzetto Massimi).

Outside the town, to the right of the road and reached by a tiny 14C hump-backed bridge (new bridge downstream) is the church of *San Francesco*. Over the high altar is a triptych signed and dated 1467 by Antoniazzo Romano. A wooden altar frames a painting of St Francis receiving the stigmata, attrib. to Seb. del Piombo. In the 3rd chapel on the left are frescoes attrib. to Sodoma, and an altarpiece of the Nativity attrib. to Pinturicchio. The 2nd chapel contains a wooden Crucifix by Piazza (1685).—At the town entrance is the conspicuous *Arch of Pius VI*, erected in 1789 in honour of the Pope, who, as Cardinal Braschi, had been abbot of Subiaco and had done much for its inhabitants.

The 'one-way' main street leads to the *Cathedral* (St Andrew), built by Pius VI, heavily damaged by bombing, and now rebuilt. In the apse is a 16C Crucifix and in the right transept a large painting of the Miracle of the Fishes by Sebastiano Conca. The altars in the transepts incorporate antique marbles from a Roman villa. On the left a road leads up through the medieval part of the town to the *Rocca Abbaziale*, founded in 1073. Pius VI converted the castle, which dominates this part of the town, into a stately residence for high ecclesiastical dignitaries.

The monasteries outside the town are reached by the Ienne road (or on foot by a path which crosses and recrosses the road). The road passes the round chapel of *San Mauro* and continues to ascend. It skirts the ruins of *Nero's Villa*; on the right of the road is the lake (now dried-up) formed by the dam that Nero built across the river.

The road continues to climb to reach (2·5km) the **Convento di Santa Scolastica** (500m; shown by a monk 9–12, 16–18; mass on Sunday 10–11.30), a vast establishment comprising a church and three monasteries. In the middle ages it became a powerful abbey, with feudal privileges. The convent was badly damaged in the war; the rebuilt façade bears the Benedictine motto 'Ora et Labora' over the door. The *First Cloister*, also restored, was built in 1580, and contains fragments from Nero's Villa.

To the right are the *Library* and *Archives* (open to scholars). There are 380 MSS and over 30,000 printed books (among them 90 incunabula), as well as papal bulls, royal and imperial edicts, and other rare documents. It also contains the first two books printed in Italy, Cicero's De Oratore and a Lactantius of 1465.— Between the first and second cloisters is a fresco of James Stuart, the Old Pretender.

The *Second Cloister* is entered through an arch (1450) in the Gothic style with statuettes of German workmanship. The cloister is one of the earliest Gothic works in Italy, and has a crude bas-relief (8C) and a tablet recording the property of the abbey in 1052. There is a fine view of the campanile. In the porch are Cosmatesque fragments.— The *Church of St Scholastica*, built in 975, was reconstructed for the fourth time in 1777 by Giac. Quarenghi. This is the only work in Italy by this architect who lived in Russia and built much of Leningrad. Here are two pillars in cipollino from Nero's villa. Frescoes from the earlier church (1426) are preserved in the vault (visible only with special permission). Beneath the church is the Cappella degli Angeli, with an altar recomposed from Cosmatesque fragments, and an urn containing the ashes of St Scholastica. A corridor from a 9C porch which supports the Campanile, leads to the *Third Cloister* a fine work by the Cosmati (1208–30; signed 'Cosmas et filii'). The walls have over-restored frescoes.

The road continues to the *Convento di San Benedetto, or Sacro Speco* (640m; open daily as for the Convent of Santa Scholastica), consisting of two superimposed churches, chapels, and grottoes, naturally formed in or artificially hewn out of the mountainside. From the car park an easy path leads up through a venerable ilex grove to the entrance gate, above which is an ancient watchtower. A small Gothic door opens into a loggia decorated with 15C Umbrian frescoes. Beyond are two more rooms (the first with frescoes of the school of Perugino) leading into the upper church.

The UPPER CHURCH (c 1350) has an aisleless nave and a chancel, and good cross-vaulting. The nave is decorated with 14C frescoes, mainly of the school of Siena. Outstanding among these are The Kiss of Judas and the Way of the Cross (left wall), the Entry of Christ into Jerusalem (right wall), and the Crucifixion (front wall). The Sacristy has a 15C Crucifixion, two panels of the Sienese School, and a fresco of St Benedict, by Consulus (Consolo) a late-13C master who did much work in the convent. A painting of the Madonna with the prophets on wood by the school of Pinturicchio, has been removed for safety.—Steps before the altar lead down to the LOWER CHURCH, comprising a remarkable series of chapels at different levels. The stairway is decorated with frescoes by Consulus. After a second flight of steps, the level of the **Sacro Speco** is reached, which gave the convent its alternative name. The Holy Grotto is a small dark natural cavern in the rock. Here is a marble statue of St Benedict, by *Ant. Raggi* (1657). The walls of the grotto are lined with cipollino from Nero's villa. Outside it are frescoes by Consulus illustrating the life and death of the saint.

From the landing a little spiral staircase leads up to the *Chapel of St Gregory*, with further frescoes by Consulus, and a *Portrait of St Francis*, without halo or stigmata, painted at the time of his visit to the convent (c 1210) and claimed to be the first example in Italy of a genuine portrait.—From the landing begins the *Scala Santa*, so-called because it is on the line of the path taken by St Benedict on his way to and from his cavern. The stairway is decorated with macabre 15C frescoes depicting Death. It leads to the 14C *Chapel of the Madonna*, covered with contemporary frescoes and, farther down, to the *Grotto dei Pastori*, a small cave where St Benedict is said to have preached to the local shepherds. It contains the oldest fresco in the convent, an 8C or 9C work representing the

Madonna with St Luke and another saint. Outside the cave is a small terrace from which can be seen the great columns and arches supporting the convent buildings. Here is the *Holy Rose Tree*, subject of a miracle performed by St Francis on the occasion of his visit. Centuries before, St Benedict, to mortify his flesh, had lain down on a bramble; St Francis turned the aged bramble into a rose tree. It still blooms today. The *Refectory* (no adm) contains interesting 15C frescoes of the Umbrian school.—Outside, to the right, paths lead through delightful woods with views.

33 Via Flaminia and the Tiber Valley

ROAD (Via Flaminia) to (42km) *Sant'Oreste* (*Civita Castellana*, 57km). Return by Via Tiberina and Via Salaria, 52·5km.

RAILWAY from Rome (Tiburtina), stopping at nearly all stations 3 times a day to Civita Castellana (71km) in 1¼ hr. The railway follows the Via Flaminia as far as Civita Castellana.

Via Flaminia, Via Tiberina, and Via Salaria are taken as central points for this route, but many of the interesting places described are several kilometres to the W or E. Although not well known, or of major importance, this area with its charming medieval villages and often spectacular countryside is typical of the most unspoilt parts of the Roman campagna.

Via Flaminia runs almost due N from Piazzale Flaminio (Pl. 11; 7), just N of Piazza del Popolo. Its initial section is described in Rte 24.

The VIA FLAMINIA, the old great North Road, traverses Umbria and reaches the Adriatic at Fano, from where it continues as N 16 to Rimini. It was named after C. Flaminius, censor and afterwards consul, who was killed at the battle of Lake Trasimene in 217 BC.

At 7·5km the road passes the so-called *Tomb of the Nasoni* (left), discovered in the 17C and now virtually destroyed, and several other tombs. *Grotta Rossa*, with pozzolana quarries.—The road passes under the Rome Circular road which crosses the Tiber and Via Salaria beyond. Here also is the Fosso di Valchetta, which flows past Veio.—At (12km) *Prima Porta* this route leaves the Tiber.

Via Tiberina branches to the right (see below). At the road fork an inscription (1912) commemorates the battle of Saxa Rubra where Constantine defeated Maxentius in 312, after being converted to Christianity by a vision of the flaming Cross with the words 'conquer by this'.

On the hill between the roads are the ruins of the imperial **Villa of Livia** (*ad Gallinas Albas*), the wife of Augustus and mother of Tiberius. The path to the villa leads to the right beyond the houses (guide-post). The fine statue of Augustus of Prima Porta, now in the Vatican, was found here in 1863, as were the frescoes now in the Museo Nazionale Romano.

Beyond the fork, the huge *Cimitero di Prima Porta* extends on the right as far as Via Tiberina.—19·5km *Sacrofano Station*.

A longer but more scenic road leads NW to (7·5km) *Sacrofano*, a picturesque medieval town at the foot of the prominent Monte Musino. The road continues to (15·5km) *Campagnano di Roma*, a larger medieval town. A beautiful road from Campagnano runs E (12km) to rejoin the Via Flaminia 1·5km N of *Morlupo Station* (see below).

The more direct route N along Via Flaminia from Sacrofano Station passes (25·5km) a turning right to *Riano* (2km), with a Ruspoli castle.—At (28km) *Castelnuova di Porta* (right), an ancient fortress remodelled into a palace in the 16C (no adm) dominates the town, which is becoming spoilt by modern buildings.—30·5km *Morlupo Station*. Turning right for *Morlupo* (2·5km), of ancient origins. This road leads in 13·5km via Capena to Via Tiberina (see below).

Via Flaminia, joined by the road from Campagnano di Roma, continues through (39km) *Rignano Flaminio*, which preserves the ruins of a Savelli stronghold. The ancient church of Sant'Abbondio, outside the village to the E, has a campanile and other relics of the 11C.—42km **Sant'Oreste**. The village, 5km E, is the best base for an ascent of *Monte Soratte* (691m) with its long isolated ridge, the Soracte of Horace and Virgil. The view from the summit takes in southern Etruria and the fertile Sabine hills, with the Apennines behind them across the Tiber valley.—The road from here to *Civita Castellana* (10·5km) and the country to the N are described in 'Blue Guide Northern Italy'.

The return to Rome may be made by Via Tiberina and Via Salaria, following the Tiber valley. A somewhat tortuous small road leads from Sant'Oreste Station to **Via Tiberina**, joining it at (15·5km) *Fiano Romano*. This old town, overlooking the Tiber valley, used to have its own river-port and ferry boat in Roman times.—19·5km **Lucas Feroniae**. Here excavations are in progress of the ancient town, famed in antiquity for its Temple of Feronia, founded in the 6C or 5C BC, and sacked by Hannibal in 211 BC. A Museum is being arranged near the entrance to the site. So far the *Forum* and *Amphitheatre* have been unearthed. Some distance away (also approached from the service area on the Autostrada del Sole, prominent to the left) is the *Villa of Gens Vulusia*, one of the most important private villas near Rome, discovered in 1961. Two of the three floors survive and some of the rooms have fine mosaics. Just beyond, a road leads right to *Capena* (5km) on the site of an Etruscan city thought to have been the chief town of the Capenates, an Italic tribe subject to Veio.

At (23km) *Girardi* the road crosses the autostrada and Tiber to (26km) *Torremancina* on **Via Salaria**. It turns S to (28·5km) *Monterotondo-Mentana Station*. Here a road diverges SE via *Monterotondo* (2·5km), with a town hall in a former Orsini palace, to *Mentana* (5·5km), on the approximate site of the ancient *Nomentum*. Piazza San Nicola is picturesque. Near by the Garibaldians were defeated by French and Papal forces in 1867.—Via Salaria returns towards Rome, passing *Marcigliana*, near (36km) *Settebagni*. This was the ancient *Allia*, scene of a disastrous defeat of the Romans by the Gauls in 390 BC. Castel Giubileo, a medieval fortalice, stands above the bank of the Tiber.—40·5km (left) *Villa Spada* on the site of the ancient *Fidenoe*. A colony of Veio, it was taken by Mamercus Aemilius in 440 BC, resettled by the Emperor Tiberius, and destroyed by the Lombards.—42·5km *Urbe Airport* (right) surrounded on three sides by the Tiber. The Aniene is crossed near its confluence with the Tiber at Ponte Salario, and Rome entered at Piazza Fiume, on the site of the vanished Porta Salaria.

34   Veio and Lake Bracciano

ROAD (VIA CASSIA), N 2. 18km Veio.—40km Bracciano.

BUSES from Via Lepanto (corner of Viale Giulio Cesare) for
Bracciano. C.I.T. tours via Bracciano to Cerveteri and Tarquinia.
Bus No. 201 from Piazzale Ponte Milvio for Isola Farnese (Veio).

RAILWAY from *Rome* (Termini), Viterbo line. To *La Storta-Formello*,
for Veio (slow trains only), 27km in c 1 hr; to *Bracciano*, 52km in
1–2 hrs.

From Porta del Popolo (Pl. 11; 7) Via Flaminia and Viale Tiziano lead
to Piazza Apollodoro, from where Corso di Francia turns off to the
right to cross the Tiber by Ponte Flaminio. At the end of the Corso this
route branches left into Via Cassia Nuova.

The VIA CASSIA, originally an unmade road connecting Rome with Etruria, was
paved by C. Cassius Longinus, consul in 107 BC, and was named after him.
Now N 2, it is a beautiful road which runs through Viterbo, Siena, and
Poggibonsi to Florence.

The road undulates between gardens and parks, with lofty pines and
oak-trees, and almost continuous ribbon development. To the left,
soon after the junction with the old Via Cassia, is the *Scots College*
(1962).—9·5km On the left, half-hidden in a clump of cypresses, is the
tomb of P. Vibius Maranus (2C AD), commonly called the *Tomb of
Nero*.

Beyond (13km) *La Giustiniana* the Viterbo railway approaches on
the left.—17km *La Storta* is a former posting stage, dominated by its
large modern church. Near by, a chapel commemorates a vision of
Christ vouchsafed here to St Ignatius in 1537.—17·5km *Madonna di
Bracciano* is a chapel at a road fork.

The left-hand road, the Via Claudia, leads to Bracciano (see
below). To see Veio it is necessary to continue for another 500m on
the Via Cassia. A by-road here leads E (sign-posted 'Isola Farnese e
Veio') to *Isola Farnese* (2km); an alternative route for Veio is 1·5km
farther along the Via Cassia.

Isola Farnese is a tiny hamlet beneath a medieval castle in a pretty position. The
church contains interesting frescoes.

Veio, one of the most famous of the Etruscan cities, was built on a
triangular tufa plateau (124m) bounded by two streams, the Fosso di
Formello-Valca and the Fosso di Valchetta, the ancient Cremera. At
the confluence the sides are precipitous; on the promontory above it
was the citadel, now called the *Piazza d'Armi*. The city was directly
accessible only from the NW angle.

Veio was one of the twelve cities of the Etruscan Confederation and apparently
the largest of them all. Its walls had a circuit of 11km and its territory (*Ager
Veiens*) was extensive, reaching to the right of the Tiber on the S, E, and SW. It controlled
the salt-works at the mouth of the Tiber. On the W its neighbour was Caere.
Veio reached the zenith of its power between the 8C and the 6C BC and its
position brought it into frequent conflict with Rome during the period of the
kings and the early days of the Republic. It took the side of the deposed
Tarquins in their attempt to return to Rome.
  In the year of his third consulship (479 BC) the patrician L. Fabius Vibulanus,
after a disagreement over the treatment of the plebeians, left Rome, and, at the
head of 306 members of his gens, marched towards Veio. The Fabii established
themselves on a hill to the right of the Fosso-Valca, and harassed the
Veientines for two years. In 477 they were trapped in an ambush near the
Cremera and all were killed, except one, from whom all the later Fabii were
descended. In 396, after a historic siege of ten years, M. Furius Camillus

tunnelled through the rock and captured the city. It was destroyed and
remained in ruins until Julius Caesar planted a colony, which Augustus
elevated into a municipium. But the new Veio did not flourish; it was moribund
even in Hadrian's time and soon disappeared from history. Excavations on the
site began in the 18C; the work has now been carried out systematically. Many
of the discoveries are in the Villa Giulia in Rome, among them the celebrated
Apollo of Veio. The splendid bronze coffin of an Etruscan prince was found here
in 1983.

Below Isola Farnese a steep narrow road descends right; it deteriorates as it approaches a barn near the Mola torrent. This can be
forded on foot above the waterfall. A path leads up (right) to the
Portonaccio gate and the ticket entrance (adm normally 9–dusk
except Monday, winter 10–14; but the excavations are often temporarily closed). Beyond, on a terrace, are remains of the *Temple of
Apollo*, a cistern, and a rock-hewn tunnel. Outside the enclosure, and
above it to the east, is the *West Gate* of Veio. Here, besides remains
of walls, are a large cistern and the foundations of a rectangular
building (possibly a temple).
    Other remains are widely dispersed over the site; a whole day is
needed for a complete tour. Since the area is now under cultivation it
is difficult to explore without a guide.

Beyond the ruins of the Roman city (on the S) stands (2·5km) the *Citadel*, which
is separated from the rest by a slight depression. Here the sides of the plateau
are sheer and rise 60m above the torrents, and from the promontory can be seen
Rome and the semicircle of the Alban, Tiburtine, and Sabine hills beyond. Then,
descending to the E into the Cremera valley, a path leads left and comes first to
the ruins of Roman baths, and then (on the right) the *Grotta degli Inglesi* or
Tomba Campana (shown by the custodian). This (discovered in 1843) is a
chamber-tomb of the late 7C cut in the rock, and one of the earliest painted
tombs in existence. It consists of a deep-cut approach flanked by lions (two of
which remain) and two quadrilateral chambers. The arch is of a transitional type
between the beehive and the keystone systems, and on the walls are archaic
paintings representing Mercury conducting the dead, also fantastic animals. A
path continues W up the valley with the city to the left, to reach the *Ponte Sodo*,
a broad gallery cut by the Etruscans to open a passage for the torrent (one of the
most romantic spots in the Campagna). From there a path continues up to the
level of the city and so to Isola; or (easier but longer) the valley may be followed
to the Ponte di Formello, where it is necessary to cross the torrent and bear left
to reach the Fosso di Valca at Ponte di Isola, 1km NW of Isola Farnese, and so
continue back to the main road.

It is necessary to return to the crossroads (see above), and take Via
Claudia (right) for Lake Bracciano. By a tavern, just beyond (24km)
the prominent radio station of the Vatican, a by-road (left) leads to
Santa Maria di Galeria.

Santa Maria di Galeria is a tiny hamlet with a delightful piazza. A fine gateway
leads to a courtyard with old houses and the 15C church of *Santa Maria in
Celsano*, with a good portal. The interior is divided by wide low arches
supported by four columns; the two on the left have fine Corinthian capitals. It
has a painted ceiling, and frescoes on the right wall (probably 16C; restored),
and in the two side apses (much damaged).
    Just before the ascent to the piazza, a road forks below to the right. The first
unmade road to the right leads to the ruins of *Galeria*. Situated above a
beautiful wooded river valley, the castle, with a long history from before the 9C
to the 19C, is a magnificent ruin. It stands on the site of the Etruscan *Careiae*;
more remains can be seen across the river Galera.

Via Claudia continues to (40km) **Bracciano** (280m; 9,400 inhab.), a
small town on the SW shore of the Lago di Bracciano. It was
associated with the Orsini family from the 14C until 1696. From the
station (fine view) a broad road leads direct to the *Castello degli
Orsini* (1470–85), a magnificent and perfectly preserved example of

a Renaissance baronial castle, now belonging to the princely Odescalchi family. It has five crenellated round towers supporting the superb pentagonal structure. It was the first place that Sir Walter Scott wished to visit on his arrival in Rome.

Visitors are conducted every hour, 9–12, and 15–18; winter 10–12, 15–17; on Thursday, Saturday, and Sunday, tours every half hour; the castle is always closed on Mondays.

A steep ramp leads up to the entrance; on the wall to the right are frescoes by Antoniazzo Romano (1491). The vaulted kitchen off an imposing triangular interior courtyard, has huge fireplaces.

FIRST FLOOR. R. I. (*Library*) is decorated with frescoes by the Zuccari.—R. III has a wooden ceiling painted by Antoniazzo Romano and pupils and a 15C bed. In R. IV (*Sala del Trittico*) are the panels of a large triptych (late 15C), with a Crucifixion in the manner of Giotto and an Annunciation.—R. V is frescoed with scenes from the Renaissance legend of the Fountain of Youth.—R. VI. Large fresco by Antoniazzo Romano showing episodes in the life of the Orsini.—R. VII (*degli Orsini*) contains busts (by G.L. Bernini) and portraits of the Orsini and Medici families. The paintings in R. VIII (*Sala del Leone*) are of the 15C. The ceiling of R. IX (*Camera Rossa*) is again painted by Antoniazzo.

SECOND FLOOR. R. XI has a 15C water-clock.—R. XII has a frieze of the Labours of Hercules (15C) and a collection of arms. Interesting in R. XIII (*Sala d'Armi*) are three suits of tournament armour: one Milanese (15C), and two German (16C).—R. XVI contains a collection of finds from the cemeteries at Cerveteri and Palo.—R. XVII gives out on to a loggia from which an enchanting view of the lake can be enjoyed by taking the *Cammino di Ronda*, the rampart walk.

In the town the *Collegiata* (Santo Stefano) has a Baroque façade and a campanile of 1500. Inside are paintings by Trevisani and Domenichino, and a gilded wooden triptych of 1315 by Gregorio and Donato d'Arezzo.

The **Lago di Bracciano** (164m) is the classical *Lacus Sabatinus*, named after the Etruscan town of *Sabate*. A pre-historic village was found here in 1977. It occupies an almost circular crater in the volcanic Monti Sabatini, with a diameter of 9·5km an area of 58 sq. km and a maximum depth of 160m. It teems with trout, tench, eels, and other fish. Its outlet, the Arrone is on the SE side, near Anguillara Sabazia. The *Aqua Traiana*, built by Trajan c 110, from the Lacus Sabatinus to Rome, was reconditioned by Paul V in 1615 to supply some of the fountains in Rome, e.g. the Fontana di Acqua Paola, on the Janiculum.

The waters of the lake, as well as those of the Lago di Vico and the Lago di Bolsena, are harnessed to a great hydro-electric scheme.—To the E of Lake Bracciano is the much smaller *Lago di Martignano* (Alsietinus Lacus), another crater-lake (207m).

The upper road out of Bracciano (the lower one leads only to the lake-side) skirts the entire lake. This beautiful road passes *Bagni di Vicarello*, with springs which were used in Roman times, to (52km) *Trevignano Romano*, a picturesque village reached through the old town gate. Cars should be left in the modern part of the village just outside the gate, or on the lake-side.

A narrow road leads up to the church of the *Assunta*, just below the ruined Orsini castle. Here there is a magnificent view of the lake over the roofs of the village. The interior has a striking fresco (1517) of the death and coronation of the Virgin, by the School of Raphael, beautifully designed to fit the curved apse. On the entrance wall is a stoup of 1541, and over the 1st altar (left), a 13C triptych of Christ enthroned with the Madonna and St John. Over the 2nd altar, a fine 16C fresco of the Madonna with Saints, and on the altar, a marble 16C Pietà.

The road now skirts a small crater lake with a good retrospective view of the village, and passes *Grotta del Pianoro*.—57km Road fork left to join the Via Cassia (see above; an alternative route back to Rome). The lower road to the right leads on to (63·5km) *Anguillara Sabazia* on high ground above the lake. At *Santo Stefano* excavations are in progress of a medieval fortified farm on the site of a

Roman villa. The church of the *Assunta*, with an interesting 18C façade, has a magnificent position above the lake. The growing town can be well seen from the road leading on to Bracciano, now passing through more hilly and wooded country. Soon after *Vigna di Valle* (with a Museum of Military Aeroplanes; open 9–18; winter 9–16; closed Monday) the road recrosses the railway to rejoin (70km) Via Claudia.

The return to Rome may be made by Via Claudia and Via Cassia, or, if time permits, along the sea via *Cerveteri* (Rte 35).

35 Rome to Cerveteri

ROAD. Via Aurelia (N 1), 45km.—The coastal Autostrada, A 16 which follows roughly the same route as the railway, diverging from the Fiumicino motorway (Rte 28C), runs conveniently close to Cerveteri (57km).

BUSES. From Via Lepanto (corner of Viale Giulio Cesare). C.I.T. tours via Bracciano, and including Tarquinia.

RAILWAY (part of the main line from Rome to Pisa, Genoa, etc.). To *Cerveteri-Ladispoli* (51km) in c 1 hr.

The modern Via Aurelia, from its beginning in Largo di Porta Cavalleggeri (Pl. 1; 6), diverges from Viale Vaticano to cross the Vatican and Viterbo railways. Beyond (3·5km) the church of *Madonna del Riposo* (left) the road crosses Piazza Irnerio.—Near (8km) the *Villa Troili* it joins Via Aurelia Antica, from the Porta San Pancrazio.

The road, fringed with pines, planes, oleanders, and cypresses, undulates towards the W crossing the Rome Circular Road.—Before (14·5km) *Malagrotta* it crosses the Fosso la Galeria, where the Anguillara are said to have slain a dragon that once ravaged the countryside.—20·5km *Castel Di Guido* is on the site of *Lorium*, where Antoninus Pius built a magnificent villa, in which he lived and died (in 161); it was a favourite resort of his successor Marcus Aurelius. Interesting prehistoric finds were made here in 1981. Farther on the Arrone is crossed, flowing from Lake Bracciano to the Tiber.

Here a road (left) leads to the attractive little seaside resort of *Fregene* (10km), with a noted pinewood. It occupies the site of the Etruscan *Fregenae*, colonized by the Romans in 245 BC.

Via Aurelia ascends to *Casale Bruciato*, with fine views of the mountains and the sea. On the right is the isolated *Torrimpietra*, followed by a descent, crossing to seaward of the autostrada, to (25km) the *Ponte Tre Denari*. Here the railway comes in from the left.—30km *Palidoro*, on the site of the ancient Baebiana.—Near (32·5km) *Casale di Statua*, a ruined 13C castle, are remains of a Roman bridge.

A little farther, on the right, a by-road leads N to (8km) *Ceri*, a village on a hill (105m), formerly *Caere Novum*, founded in the 13C after the exodus of the inhabitants of Caere Vetus (see below). It has an old castle of the Anguillara.

37km *Palo Laziale* station. On the left is Palo, a fishing village on the site of *Alsium*, a port of Caere, colonized by the Romans in 247 BC. It has a 15C castle, and in the neighbourhood are several chambered tumuli. Remains of a large Roman villa, with good polychrome mosaics were discovered here in 1974. A Museum is being arranged here. A road leads (left) to *Ladispoli* (2km), a popular seaside resort founded by Prince Ladislao Odescalchi in the 19C. The coast to the N is dotted with old defence-towers.

Beyond *Borgo Vaccina* the road crosses (41km) the Fosso di Vaccina, the Amnis Caeritis mentioned by Virgil. A second road leads left for Ladispoli (3km), but this route turns right for Cerveteri (3.5km).

CERVETERI (8400 inhab.), a medieval stronghold on a round tufa hill (81m), derives its name from *Caere Vetus*. The immediate neighbourhood is renowned for its Etruscan tombs.

Caere, called by the Greeks *Agylla*, was a Pelasgic city, capital of Mezentius who was expelled by his subjects for his cruelty. It became one of the most important towns of the Etruscan Confederation and had three seaports—*Pyrgi* (Santa Severa), *Alsium* (Palo Laziale), and *Punicum* (Santa Marinella). Early in its history it was closely allied with Rome. When Rome was taken by the Gauls in 390 BC, Caere gave refuge to the vestal virgins. The city became a dependency of Rome in 351 BC, but without full rights of citizenship. From then onwards it declined. In the early middle ages Caere was the seat of a bishop and a redoubtable fortress. In the 13C its inhabitants abandoned it on account of malaria and founded *Caere Novum* (Ceri). In the later middle ages the town became populated again. It was surrounded with walls, still partly existing, and provided with a castle by the Orsini.

A full tour of the tombs requires 5–6 hours, but the most interesting can be visited in 2–3 hours.

Passing the road up to the Necropolis on the left, the road continues to the medieval city, with appreciable remains, including walls and towers. The old Orsini (later Ruspoli) castle dating from the 16C was donated in 1967 as a *Museo Nazionale di Cerveteri* (adm 9 to one hour before sunset; closed Monday). It stands in an attractive piazza (threatened with 'development').

The Museum is excellently displayed chronologically with groups of objects from individual tombs in two long halls. Below, pots and objects from burials of the 8–6C BC, including protocorinthian ware; continuation upstairs with sarcophagi, sculpture, wall-paintings, terracottas, and two superb groups of black-figured and red-figured *Vases.

From the main square below the castle a road (sign-posted to the Necropolis) leads right; a minor road soon branches right to ascend in 2km to the **Necropolis**. At the car park is the ticket office and the entrance to the MONUMENTAL ENCLOSURE (adm daily except Monday, 9 to one hour before sunset).

This vast cemetery, occupying an area of 270 hectares, not counting isolated groups of tombs, has its nucleus on the tufa hill known as *Banditaccia*, to the NW of Cerveteri. All types of interment are represented: from the earliest *pozzetto* or *fossa* graves to the later tumuli, some of them colossal, with diameters exceeding 40 metres. These contain several hypogea, with chambers modelled in the rock in the form of Etruscan dwellings (which were built in wood). The tombs are especially interesting for their architectural design. From the tombs (dating from the 7th to 1st centuries BC), and their contents it has been found possible to obtain the fullest picture yet available of Etruscan civilization.

The site, which contains hundreds of tombs, is beautifully planted. Only some of the tombs are fully excavated and lit; those which may be entered are described below (and numbered according to the Plan).

On the right of the ticket office VIA SEPOLCRALE PRINCIPALE (right) leads SE between various tombs. The first tomb on the left which is open (and lit) is the *Tomb of the Capitals* (1), dating from the mid-6C

BC, with carved capitals and a roof imitating the wooden roof of a house. Beyond a path which diverges left there follow two huge tumuli (II and I). The first contains four tombs probably all belonging to the same family and constructed over a period of nearly two centuries. Two of these may be visited: the *Tomb of the Thatched Roof* (2; approached by iron steps on the far side of the tumulus) excavated in the tufa to imitate a hut (mid-7C BC), and the *Tomb of the Greek Vases* (3; entered from the side nearest Via Sepolcrale). Beyond the second tumulus, in an opening, steps (guarded by a wood fence) lead down to the TOMB OF THE STUCCOES (4), or of the Bas-Reliefs (often closed), a single chamber with numerous loculi or niches hewn out of the walls; the ceiling is supported by two columns; the walls are decorated with stuccoes and reliefs of arms, utensils, domestic animals, and mythological subjects (end of 4C BC), an important revelation of Etruscan civilization of the period.

Via Sepolcrale continues to a cross-roads where several minor roads meet. In front is the *Tomb of the Little House* (5; no adm); the road on the extreme right (Via della Cornice) leads in a short way to (left) the *Tomb of the Cornice* (6; approached up a short flight of wooden steps) so-called because of a heavy cornice which decorates the rooms. From the Tomb of the Little House, Via Sepolcrale (here with conspicuous cart tracks cut in the tufa rock) diverges left (see below) while VIA DELLE SERPE continues (right) to the NEW AREA OF EXCAVATIONS opened in 1977.

Beyond a short flight of steps the road passes blocks of tombs constructed *a dado* or in cubes, a form of burial which was begun at the end of the 6C BC. The area to the left, traversed by Via dei Monti della Tolfa and the parallel Via dei Monti Ceriti is interesting as an example of 'urban' planning and the symmetrical tombs have fine entrances. The tombs are unlit but may be entered; they have regular plans with small chairs on either side of the entrance. At the end of a long tufa wall a path leads left between a tumulus (left) and a series of cubicle tombs (right) and curves round to end at a flight of tufa steps which lead up to the *Polychrome Tumulus* (7), built of various materials including peperino and tufa. Adjacent is the larger *Maroi Tumulus* (8) which may also be visited. Via delle Serpi continues to the fence which marks the end of the enclosure; some metres before the fence five iron steps lead up past two small tumuli to a path which leads round to the left towards the two largest tumuli in this enclosure (near a group of three cypresses) known as the *Mengarelli Tumulus* (9; approached by a steep flight of steps) and the *Colonel's Tumulus* (10; the path passes beneath an iron bridge which leads into the entrance). Opposite this tumulus a short flight of steps leads up to a path which continues (via another flight of steps) to the Via Sepolcrale (see above). This may now be followed (left) back towards the entrance past the *Tomb of Marce Ursus* (11; with its two entrances facing on to the road) just before the cross-roads (see above) where Via Sepolcrale forms a fork with Via delle Serpe.

Outside the enclosure an unmade-up road (poor surface) continues for c 500 metres to an unenclosed area known as *Bufolareccia*, excavated in the 1960s by the Fondazione Lerici. Here the tufa rock has been uncovered and the tombs left unrestored; the oldest (and simplest) tombs can be seen on the surface (round or oblong sepulchres), while the later tumuli appear on a lower level since they were excavated in the rock when no more surface space was available. The conspicuous track marks are from ploughs which have worked the surface of the earth over the centuries. An impressive

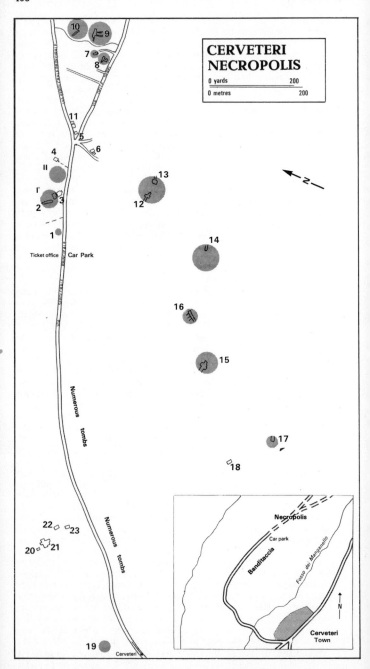

CERVETERI
NECROPOLIS

0 yards   200
0 metres   200

tufa rock face can be seen across the valley, and along to the right, the present town of Cerveteri.

Just beyond, the road ends on an open hill-side from which a good idea of the site of the necropolis surrounded by low hills can be gained. Here VIA DEGLI INFERI curves down to the right between the rocks. This was the first part of the Via Sepolcrale which led from the city to the necropolis. It is practicable on foot for several hundred metres and has conspicuous cart ruts. On the right, at the beginning, is the *Tomb of the Doric Columns* (unlit) with two Doric columns (4C BC).

The other tombs, widely scattered over the Necropolis, can be seen only with a guide (sometimes available at the ticket office) who will unlock them and turn on the light (although most of them are unlit and a torch is needed). Some of these tombs are more or less permanently flooded.

In a tumulus E of the Monumental Enclosure are the *Tomb of the Painted Lions* (12) and the *Tomb of the Chairs and Shields* (13). The former has a fine ceiling decoration and traces of colour on the walls; in the latter the walls are decorated with reliefs of shields and the vestibule has two rock-hewn chairs. Other large tumuli to the SW contain the *Tomb of the Painted Animals* (14), the *Tomb of the Ships* (15), and the *Tomb of Giuseppe Moretti* (16). This is the largest tomb yet known with an atrium with Doric columns and ten rooms (difficult to see as it is normally flooded). Farther S are the *Tomb of the Tablino* (17), and the *Tomb of the Waves* (18), with traces of painted decoration.

Another important group of tombs (all unlit) lies to the NW of the road which leads up to the Monumental Enclosure (see the Plan). These include the *Tomb of the Five Chairs* (19); the *Tomb of the Alcove* (20), with a pillared vestibule and a flight of steps leading up to a rock-hewn alcove with a nuptial bed; the *Tomb of the Tarquins* (21), so called because of the names inscribed in it; the *Tomb of the Sarcophagi* (22); and the *Tomb of the Triclinium* (23), with traces of paintings of a funeral banquet.

On a hill c 2·5km S of Cerveteri is the famous **Regolini-Galassi Tomb** (unlit) the oldest of all (late 7C BC) discovered in 1836. Named after its discoverers, it is a circular tumulus 48m in diameter, surrounded by a double wall and surmounted by the typical conical grass-grown top. Its hypogeum, of two compartments, is divided by a wide corridor with a ceiling of overlapping stone blocks. Its most valuable contents are exhibited in the Etruscan Museum of the Vatican.—In the same area (Ripe Sant'Angelo) rock tombs of the 4C BC have recently been discovered. These can be seen carved in the rock face with 'mock' doors.

About 1·5km NE, on Monte Abetone, is the *Campana Tomb* (unlit) with remarkable carvings imitating household furnishings; 1·5km farther on is the *Tomb of the Round Vestibule*, with a noteworthy fan vault.—To the SE of Monte Padula is another tomb, covered by a kind of pyramid, containing a vestibule, two side chambers, and a central room with two biers and a throne carved in the rock. Close by is the *Torlonia Tomb* (more or less permanently flooded), with a vestibule having columns in the Greek style, and two chambers, of which the first contains 54 locoli.—From this point the Monte Cucco track leads direct to (6·5km) Cerveteri.

Via Aurelia and the autostrada continue N past *Santa Severa*, with the interesting site of *Pyrgi*, a port of Cerveteri, described in 'Blue Guide Northern Italy' to *Civitavecchia* (72km; see 'Blue Guide Northern Italy'), the modern port of Rome and a base of sea communications with Sardinia. If time permits the road inland can be taken for (17·5km) *Bracciano* (Rte 34), and the return to the capital made by Via Claudia.

INDEX OF THE PRINCIPAL ITALIAN ARTISTS

whose works are referred to the text, with their birthplaces or the schools to which they belonged.—Abbreviations: A. = architect, engr. = engraver, G. = goldsmith, illum. = illuminator, min. = miniaturist, mos. = mosaicist, P. = painter, S. = sculptor, stuc. = stuccoist, W. = woodworker.

ABBREVIATIONS OF CHRISTIAN NAMES

Agost.	= Agostino	Gaud.	= Gaudenzio
Aless.	= Alessandro	Giac.	= Giacomo
Alf.	= Alfonso	Giov.	= Giovanni
Ambr.	= Ambrogio	Girol.	= Girolamo
And.	= Andrea	Giul.	= Giuliano
Ang.	= Angelo	Gius.	= Giuseppe
Ann.	= Annibale	Greg.	= Gregorio
Ant.	= Antonio	Gugl.	= Guglielmo
Baldas.	= Baldassare	Iac.	= Iacopo
Bart.	= Bartolomeo	Inn	= Innocenzo
Batt.	= Battista	Ipp.	= Ippolito
Bened.	= Benedetto	Laz.	= Lazzaro
Benv.	= Benvenuto	Leon.	= Leonardo
Bern.	= Bernardino	Lod.	= Lodovico
Cam.	= Camillo	Lor.	= Lorenzo
Ces.	= Cesare	Mart.	= Martino
Crist.	= Cristoforo	Matt.	= Matteo
Dan.	= Daniele	Mich.	= Michele
Dav.	= Davide	Nic.	= Nicola
Def.	= Defendente	Pell.	= Pellegrino
Des.	= Desiderio	Raff.	= Raffaele
Dom.	= Domenico	Rid.	= Ridolfo
Elis.	= Elisabetta	Seb.	= Sebastiano
Fed.	= Federigo	Sim.	= Simone
Fel.	= Felice	Stef.	= Stefano
Ferd.	= Ferdinando	Tim.	= Timoteo
Fil.	= Filippo	Tom.	= Tomaso
Fr.	= Francesco	Vinc.	= Vincenzo
G.B.	= Giambattista	Vitt.	= Vittorio
Gasp.	= Gaspare		

ABBREVIATIONS OF THE NAMES OF TOWNS AND PROVINCES

Anc.	= Ancona	Orv.	= Orvieto
Are.	= Arezzo	Pad.	= Padua
Ass.	= Assisi	Parm.	= Parma
Berg.	= Bergamo	Pav.	= Pavia
Bol.	= Bologna	Per.	= Perugia
Bres.	= Brescia	Piac.	= Piacenza
Crem.	= Cremona	Pied.	= Piedmont
Emil.	= Emilia	Pist.	= Pistoia
Faen.	= Faenza	Rav.	= Ravenna
Ferr.	= Ferrara	Rom.	= Romagna
Fies.	= Fiesole	Sett.	= Settignano
Flor.	= Florence	Trev.	= Treviso
Gen.	= Genoa	Tur.	= Turin
Lig.	= Liguria	Tusc.	= Tuscany
Lomb.	= Lombardy	Umbr.	= Umbria
Mant.	= Mantua	Urb.	= Urbino
Mil.·	= Milan	Ven.	=\Venice
Mod.	= Modena	Ver.	= Verona
Nap.	= Naples	Vic.	= Vicenza

INDEX

Topographical names are printed in **bold type**, names of eminent persons in *italics*, other entries in Roman type. The tombs of popes (given in the list of Popes, p 22), and the building activities of popes and emperors have generally been ignored.

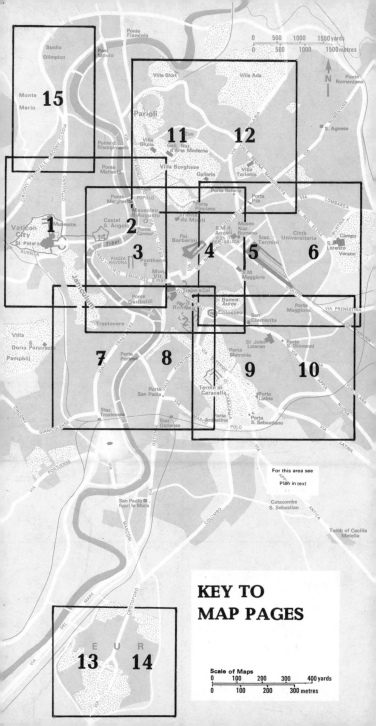

KEY TO MAP PAGES

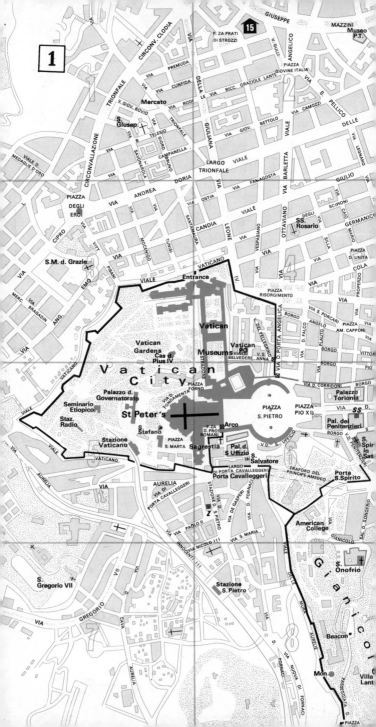

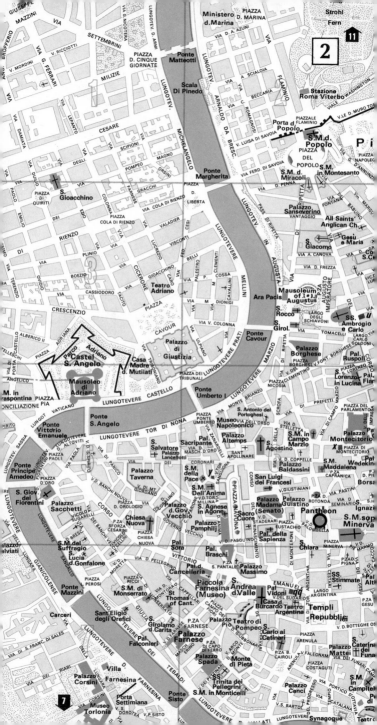

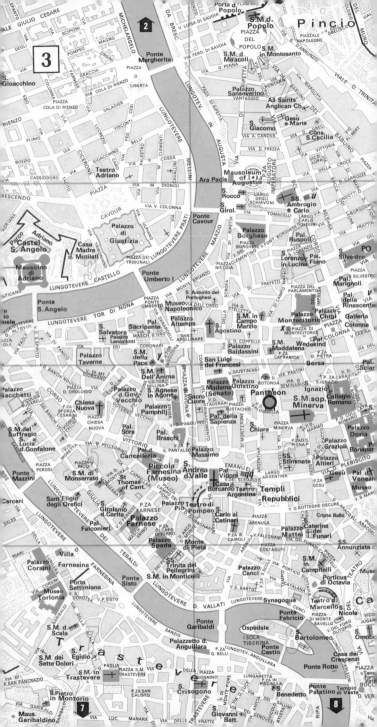

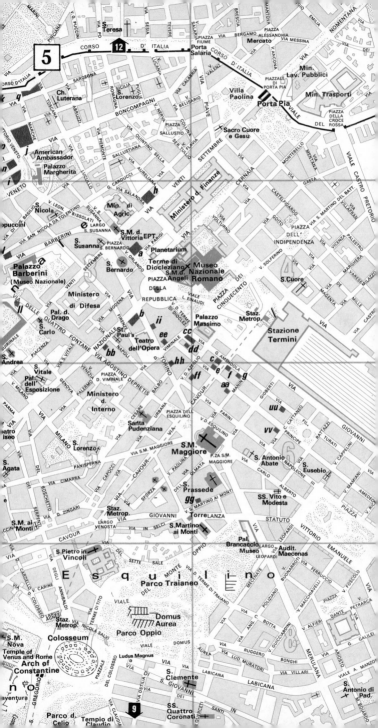

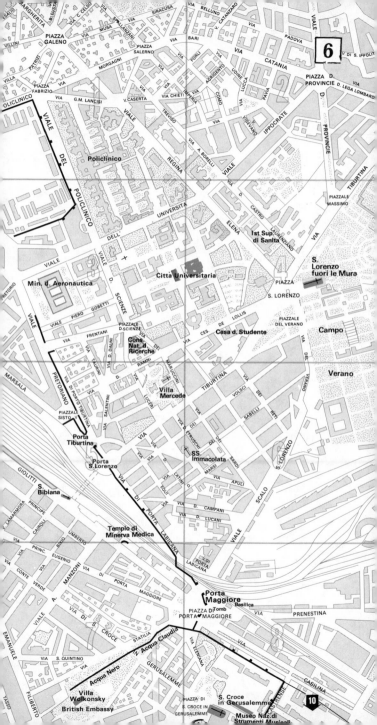

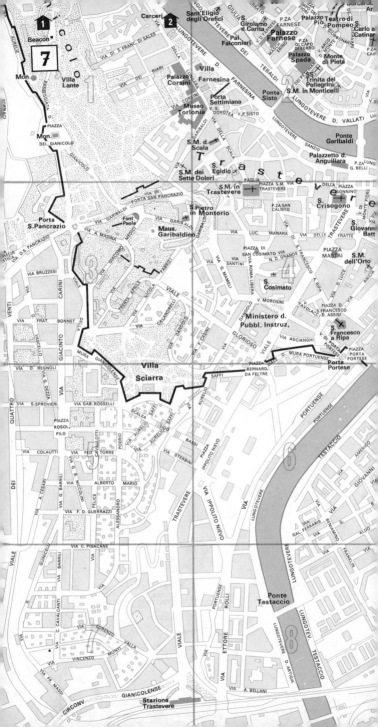

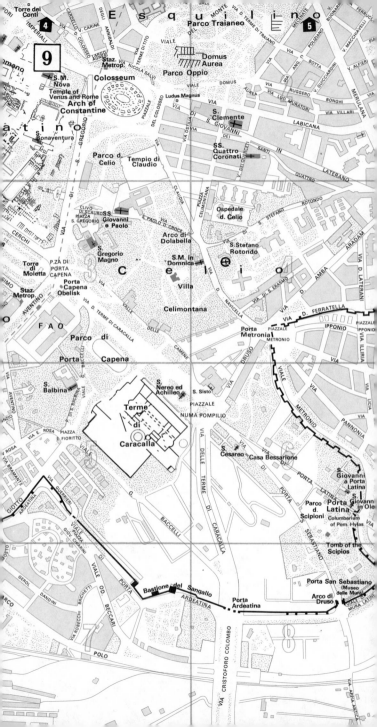

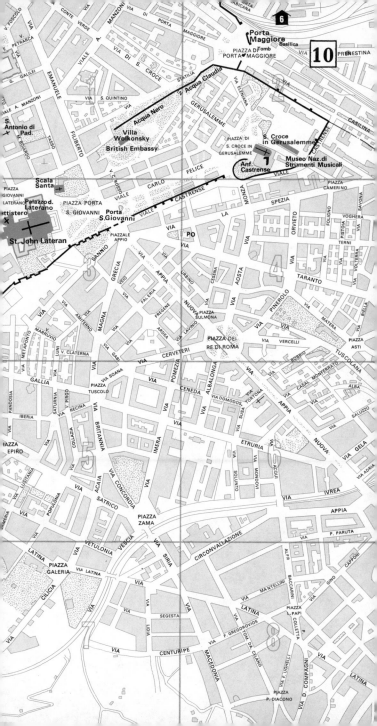

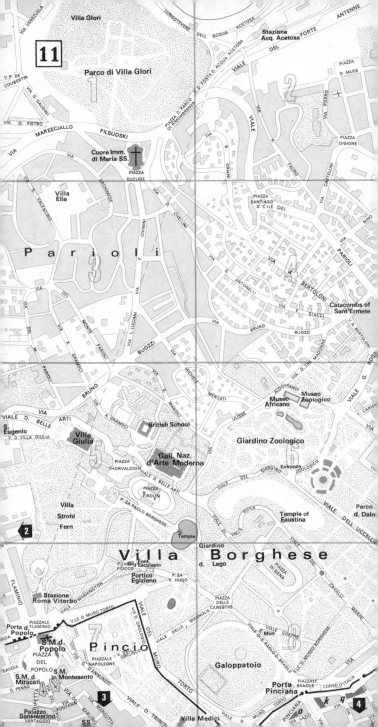

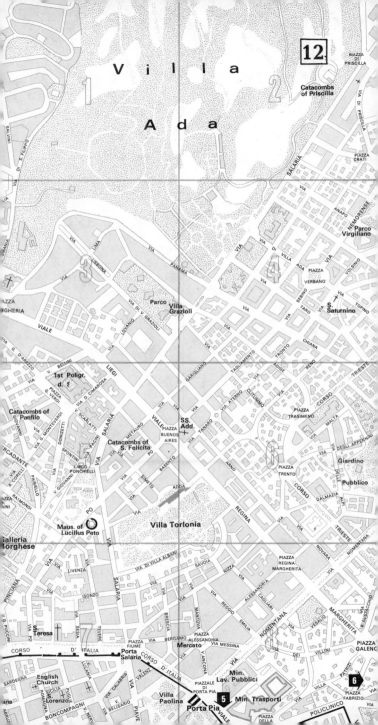

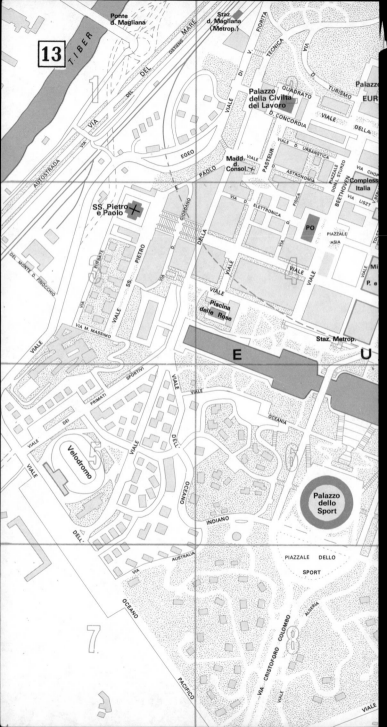

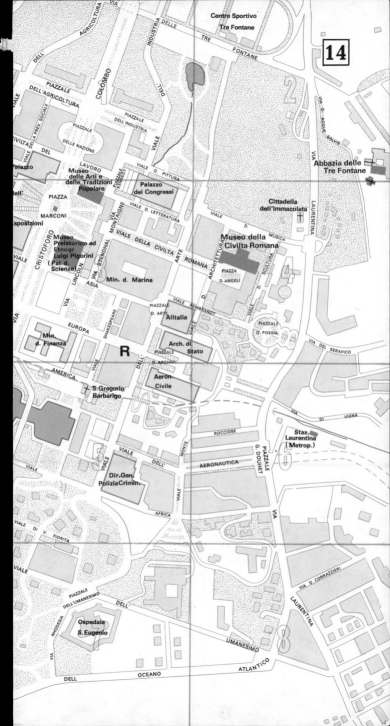

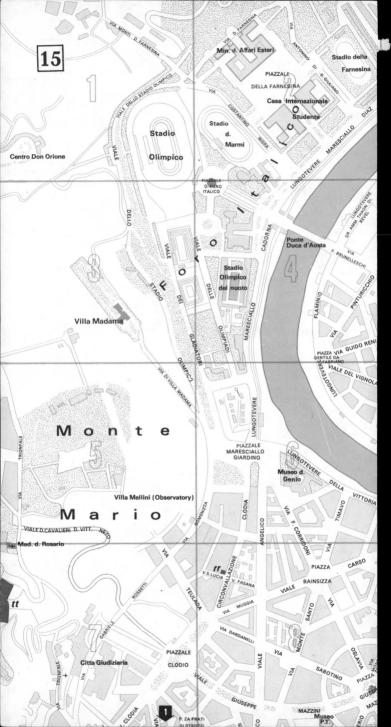